P9-CCZ-951

The Complete

Travel Detective Bible

Presque Isle District Library
Rogers City Branch

181 East Erie Street
Rogers City, MI 49779
Phone: 989.734.2477   Fax: 989.734.4899

DISCARDED

PETER GREENBERG

Travel Editor for NBC's Today Show

The Complete

Travel
Detective
Bible

The *Consummate Insider* Tells You
WHAT YOU NEED TO KNOW
in an INCREASINGLY COMPLEX WORLD

RODALE

Notice

Mention of specific companies, organizations, or authorities in this book does not
imply endorsement by the author or publisher, nor does mention of specific
companies, organizations, or authorities imply that they endorse this book,
its author, or the publisher.

Internet addresses and telephone numbers given in this book were
accurate at the time it went to press.

© 2007 by Peter Greenberg

All rights reserved. No part of this publication may be reproduced or transmitted
in any form or by any means, electronic or mechanical, including photocopying,
recording, or any other information storage and retrieval system, without the
written permission of the publisher.

Rodale books may be purchased for business or promotional use or for special sales.
For information, please write to: Special Markets Department, Rodale Inc.,
733 Third Avenue, New York, NY 10017

Printed in the United States of America

Rodale Inc. makes every effort to use acid-free ♾, recycled paper ♻.

Book design by Tara Long

Illustrations by Dale Mack

Library of Congress Cataloging-in-Publication Data

Greenberg, Peter.
 The complete travel detective bible : the consummate insider tells you what you
need to know in an increasingly complex world / Peter Greenberg.
    p   cm.
 Includes index.
 ISBN-13 978-1-59486-708-8   paperback
 ISBN-10 1-59486-708-9   paperback
 1. Travel. I. Title.
 G151.G737 2007
 910.4—dc22   2007030599

Distributed to the trade by Holtzbrinck Publishers

2 4 6 8 10 9 7 5 3   paperback

We inspire and enable people to improve their lives and the world around them
For more of our products visit **rodalestore.com** or call 800-848-4735

To all the smart travelers who understand it's the experience, not the destination; that it's the process, not the product; and to those who are lucky enough to have both

Contents

Part 1

Basic Facts and Figures

Part 2

Important Facts

Travel by Lifestyle

Active Travel

Travel with a Purpose

Acknowledgments

I've always believed that travel is news. I've also always defined my job with the philosophy that true travelers don't need or want me to tell them that the sun sets nicely in Bermuda, Botswana, or anywhere in between. What people really want is real-time, cutting-edge information; news they can use, so that they can navigate through the travel maze and avoid as much abuse as possible.

We are a world of addicted travelers. And as the word *addict* implies, we take more than our fair share of abuse every time we head out for a trip—and despite all of that, we are still determined to come back for more. That's how much we love to travel. And that may also explain why we are so desperate for good travel information.

This book isn't about pretty destinations. It's not about lovely beaches and rich and famous getaways. And it's definitely not about brochure language and the standard hyperbole that so much of the travel industry still—and inexplicably—continues to embrace.

The Complete Travel Detective Bible is a culmination of a lifetime of travel experiences—good, bad, and yes, sometimes ugly. A guidebook to—and hopefully through—the process of travel. From the inside out.

The logistics of deciphering this ever-changing process is not easy. It's downright difficult. And this book never would have been possible without Sarika Chawla, who tirelessly researched and edited the information. It's always 9 a.m. somewhere in the world, and that meant Sarika never slept as she tracked down Web sites in Dubai and obscure hotels in Peru or checked out lowfare airlines in India and hybrid rental cars in Japan. Not everyone responded quickly—or easily. Not every company or government was ini-

tially forthcoming. But Sarika demanded accurate and timely responses—and she got them. And then, just to make sure, she updated and checked it all over again.

Sarika waded through endless lists, graphs, government reports; seating charts, and flight schedules; she immersed herself in State Department double-speak and arcane airline rules; she researched case law and state attorney general rulings on rental cars. And that was before lunch! And she tracked down information that some folks said was impossible to find—until she found it. Sarika, if anyone deserves a vacation . . . *you* do!

Sarika ran a team that included Sharon Brooke Uy, Matt Calcara, and Monique-Marie DeJong and also had special contributions from Jennifer Gardner.

Huge thank-yous go to my editor, Leigh Haber, who supported this book from the beginning; to my agent, Amy Rennert, who has supported this concept from the beginning; and to the staff and producers of the *Today* show, CNBC, MSNBC, and the rest of the NBC family who allow me to report on travel the way it should be pursued—as news.

And, last but not least, my everlasting thanks to Lyn Benjamin, who supports me and everything I do every day.

Introduction

“I love to travel, but hate to arrive.”

—ALBERT EINSTEIN

This book is the result of more than 18 million miles of lifetime travel—planes, trains, automobiles, and other modes ranging from submarines off the coast of Russia to elephants in Botswana, ziplines in Costa Rica to motorcycles in Jordan and donkeys in the Grand Canyon; from sand surfing in Namibia to bicycles in China. And let's not forget taxis, subways, and yes . . . walking.

When it comes to travel, I firmly believe a plan is only something to depart from and that the serendipity of travel opens my eyes to a world where the arbitrary borders of fear and misunderstanding can be ignored. What follows are my own tried-and-true guidelines for spontaneous journeying—literally—outside the box.

Forget brochures. Brochures lie. They mislead. Almost every word ends in the letters *st* (best, greatest, finest, most). In fact, when someone tells me it's not in the brochure, that's precisely when I get interested in going there.

Be a contrarian. Most travel signs should be disobeyed. Have an early morning flight from an airport with an upstairs departure area? Head for arrivals instead. No one is arriving at 7 a.m., and you'll avoid getting stuck in that traffic. When you land, reverse the order. Don't get picked up at the arrivals area—that will be a zoo and refugee center. Head for the departures area. No one will be departing when you're arriving. And never, never, *never* stand on line. Any line.

Abandon the word *later*. A good friend of mine anguished over accompanying me on a trip to Peru, claiming he could always go another time. Plus, he claimed, he didn't know anyone in Peru. "Does the word *now* ring a bell?" I asked as I pushed him onto the plane. Ten days later, high up in the Andes and quite by chance, I introduced him to the woman who would soon become his wife.

Trust hotel maids. People never talk to hotel maids, but they should. The maids know everything. And they're willing not only to share their knowledge but in many instances to enthusiastically point you in the right direction. In Buenos Aires, one hotel maid took me to the neighborhood where she lived. Better shopping, better history—and dinner with her family! And all I had to do was ask . . .

Listen. Everyone may not be a fascinating storyteller, but everyone does have a fascinating history. Listen for it. I was visiting Shanghai by cruise ship in 1984. As I walked along the pier, heading toward a planned group bus tour of the city, a distinguished-looking, well-dressed man who looked to be in his early forties rode up to me on his bicycle. "You from the ship?" he asked in perfect English. "Yes," I replied. "And do you live here?" He smiled. "All my life!" When I remarked about his mastery of English, he startled me. "Actually," he said, "this is really the first time I've been able to speak it since . . . 1949." I never got on the bus. A few minutes later, 78-year-old Joe Cheng took me on one of the more remarkable journeys of my life—I was with him for the next 2 days—and I got to experience part of the history of Shanghai through his eyes.

If it's cooked, eat it. Some of the more incredible gastronomic experiences happen without printed menus being involved. On my very first trip to Thailand, friends dragged me from the hotel at 10 at night and out to the streets. Their only advice: no raw vegetables, and don't order ice in your drinks; and if the food is hot, it's okay. It was better than okay. I ate some of the best satays and seafood in my life—and as a result, I now always head for street vendors.

Get on the bus. Any bus. It's not where the bus is going but whom you meet along the way. When I was growing up in New York, I watched my mother do this all the time. People thought she was crazy to talk to other people. But, she told me, that's how you meet people. And before long, she even knew the bus drivers. That always helped, because at least *they* knew where the bus was going.

Then . . .

Get off the bus. And create your own guided tour. I was traveling through the Philippine Islands when my bus pulled into a hotel driveway in Legaspi. There, parked along the side, were 10 motorcycles. I asked who owned the bikes. One of the bellmen said he was a medical student and that he and the other medical students in Legaspi had formed a motorcycle club. I asked if I could rent one of the motorcycles. "I've got a better idea," he said. "Would you like for me to round up the other club members and take you for a bike tour?" An hour later, nine motorcyclists, plus me, took off on a 2-day adventure. We were headed to (and through) half a dozen villages and ended up at an active volcano—a tour I'll never forget.

Talk to taxi drivers. Eleven years ago, I exited a Manhattan hotel, terribly late for the airport, and jumped into a yellow cab. "JFK," I ordered, along with specific directions. "No, I'll take you a better way," the driver said in a thick Middle Eastern accent. Better way? "Hey, pal," I shot back. "I'm from New York. Just take me the way that I want to go."

"Let me ask you," he replied. "What terminal do you want?" I told him Terminal 9. "Okay, we take my way, and if you're not at Kennedy in 26 minutes, the ride is free."

Deal. The driver then took me on a route I had never been on in my life. And, shockingly, 22 minutes later I arrived at JFK. The driver smiled. "You owe me," he laughed.

I asked his name. William. Where was he from? Alexandria, Egypt. Was that his own cab? Yes. Then I had an idea. I took down his phone number and his cab number. And for the next 8 years, William Megalla was my driver every time I came to New York. He then drove for other journalist friends. And then he drove for my mother.

One day, driving me into the city from the airport, he said he wanted to tell me some good news. His cousin Billy was getting married, and his family wanted to invite me as an honored guest to the wedding. Would I go? Of course.

Two months later, I was at that wedding—in Alexandria, Egypt! And I learned an important lesson: In New York, William was a cab driver. In Egypt, he was a god. The wedding took place at 10 p.m. inside King Farouk's palace on the Mediterranean. Five hundred celebrating Egyptian Coptics, and a guy from New York having one of the great, and unexpected, travel experiences.

It's been said that you always miss the shots you never take, so take those shots! Once you let common sense and intuition be your guides, you won't just see the world. You'll see it with perspective and understanding, and you'll return not only eager to tell your friends about your experiences—but you'll take them (yes, sometimes kicking and screaming) along with you on your return journeys.

Words for the Travel Industry

Consider this: More people are now traveling than before the year 2000. But have things gotten better? Not even close. I'm convinced that the airline industry is the only one that somehow manages to stay in business by abusing its best customers. And now, much of the hotel industry is following suit. Service and hospitality are being replaced by bottom-line thinking—and the results are awful.

What can we do?

We can start by leaving the moose at home (I'll explain later).

But first, the airlines should:

Abolish the asterisk. Stop insulting us by advertising a flight to Los Angeles at $184—followed by the dreaded asterisk. Read the fine print and you'll see the fare is really a one-way fare requiring a round-trip purchase. That's $368, not $184! Why spend so much money trying to get our attention, only to anger us?

Find an exit strategy. Here's a novel idea that has less to do with bad weather and more to do with airline scheduling and making intelligent decisions that are passenger friendly. When a plane lands at its destination, find a way for us to get off it. From the moment we took off, you've known what time we're landing. So don't make us late by sitting on the concrete, waiting for a jetway. We don't need a jetway. We just need a way out. In the good old days, they had portable stairs. Let's use them. We promise not to complain about the 300-foot walk to the terminal.

Drop the catchy slogans. Delta is not ready when I am. If American truly knows why I fly, then why am I always stuck in the middle seat between two sumo wrestlers? Truth in marketing would require that all airlines substitute this simple catchall phrase: "Sit down. Shut up. We're going."

Establish a Geneva Convention for passengers. Flying may not be torture, but it can be awfully close. Minimum treatment standards for high-altitude, taxiway, and runway captivity would be good for customers—and would help airlines answer this (possibly rhetorical) question: Are they in the passenger service business or the human freight business?

Second, hotel operators should:

Quote the real rates. There are excise taxes, occupancy taxes, sales taxes, and the let's-have-you-build-our-sport-stadium taxes. We need to know what we're getting into before we get our bill.

Abolish forced mood lighting. It puts us in a bad mood. We've got things to do—and see. Give us a 300-watt bulb with a dimmer knob, not a 40-watt bulb with an on/off switch. We don't really change our lifestyles when we change our locations. All hotel room designers must be forced to spend at least 2 nights in the rooms they've configured before a design is approved. I don't want to get injured by my New Age bathroom sink. I just want a sink! And remember, some of us actually like to *read,* maybe even *work,* in our hotel rooms.

Stop nickel-and-diming us. More than $1 for a bottle of water from the minibar should be a prosecutable offense. Period. We'll figure out the specific criminal charges later.

Words for Travelers

But my fellow traveler, you aren't off the hook either. You need to remember:

Just because it has wheels doesn't mean it's a carry-on. There's a big difference between portable and transportable. People have brought automobile driveshafts, dead grandmothers, and a stuffed moose into passenger cabins as roll-aboards. It's just wrong. Do I need to explain further? Leave the moose at home.

Your lunch is everyone's business. Just because airlines stopped serving food doesn't mean you have to bring your own. Nothing smells worse than a half-eaten bag of fried food in the seat-back pocket of the guy sitting next to you on that 5-hour transcon.

Undress before you get to security. The lines are long enough. I don't want to stand behind you while you discover whatever's been in your pockets since 1987. Reverse your conditioning—undress before you get to the airport. Dress after you pass security.

These ideas don't require much capital investment or great physical exertion; they're common sense. Unfortunately, they're also probably too much to ask.

After all, I'm writing this while sitting on a delayed La Guardia–bound flight that pushed back on time but is now stuck on the world's longest, slow-moving taxiway. Assuming we ever leave Miami, and assuming we land in New York, and assuming there's a gate, I'll check in to my hotel in about 5 hours to find a dimly lit "cutting edge" room, a dangerous bathroom sink, and let's not forget that $7 bottle of water on the desk.

And yet, like most of us, I'll take the abuse and keep on traveling. What's the alternative? We still love to travel. And we should.

This book is all about process, not product. It's about the experience, not the destination. Hopefully, it contains the information, the secrets, and the procedures to employ, as well as those to avoid, to make you better travelers. Call me a lone holdout, but I know from experience that when it comes to travel, it's not what the market will bear but what the market will *value*. It's not about price but worth.

And never forget that we're the best arbiters of value and worth. Happy traveling!

PART 1

BASIC FACTS AND FIGURES

CHAPTER 1

Airports

> It can hardly be a coincidence that no language on Earth has ever produced the phrase, 'as pretty as an airport.' Airports are ugly. Some are very ugly. Some attain a degree of ugliness that can only be the result of a special effort.

—DOUGLAS ADAMS

I've spent enough time in airports to almost consider them condominia, and that in itself is scary. But I spend time there more by design than by accident, and that's the key: how and how well you can navigate through—and out of—airports. And when you can't, it's all about how you can make the best of a bad situation. And yes, there is a method to the madness here. Remember, the key here is to look at airports as challenging obstacle courses that can be conquered—by you.

For one-stop-shops on all things airport related, these are the two sites to keep in mind.

The site **www.worldairportguide.com** provides you practically all the information on more than 250 airports around the world "from Aberdeen to Zurich." You can find airport phone numbers, addresses, on-site parking information, which car rental agencies are available, terminal transfers, and nearby hotels.

You're probably familiar with Expedia, but what you may not know is that the booking site **www.expedia.com/daily/airports** has its own roving reporter, Harriet Baskas, who keeps track of the facilities and services at more than 65 airports worldwide. This includes the history of the airport, shops, attractions, and activities close to the airport.

For fun, you can see moving graphics of airplanes that are taking off, landing, and in transit at 18 different airports at **www.passur.com/sites.htm.**

Airport Terminal Maps

When it comes to saving time, it's always a good idea to arm yourself with information in advance. Our friends at www.airportterminalmaps.com offer diagrams of all the major international airports in the United States.

If you're running to catch a connecting flight, it's helpful to know the layout of the airport in advance—it can mean the difference between running a mile with your briefcase and flagging down a cart to take you there. And when driving to the airport, you'll know that if an airport's terminals are set up in a loop, zooming past your terminal can cost you an extra 30 minutes to circle all the way back—just take a look at JFK's layout.

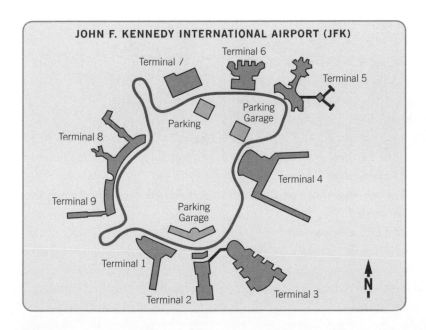

An airport that is more gridlike makes it much easier to maneuver from one terminal to the next. Take a look at LAX.

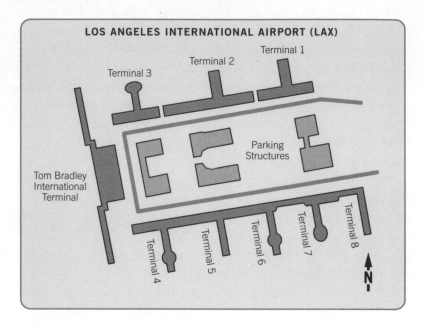

Traveling from one terminal to another at Dallas/Fort Worth is never easy, but, fortunately, the Skylink will get you there a little faster.

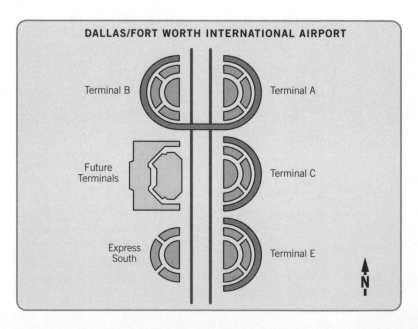

Most Delayed Airports

Now onto the bad news. . .

The Bureau of Transportation Statistics studies the performance of major US carriers—19 carriers reported in 2006, including American Airlines, Continental Airlines, Delta Air Lines, Northwest Airlines, Southwest Airlines, United Airlines, and US Airways.

The reports include both arrival delays and departure delays. Now, one of these is easier to cover up than another—once a flight is closed and departs from the terminal, it is considered to have "departed," even if you sit on the runway for another hour waiting to take off. What's harder to fake, however, is delayed arrival time.

Statistics

In 2004, 78.1 percent of flights arrived on time, 19.9 percent had delayed arrivals, and 1.8 percent were canceled.

In 2005, 77.4 percent of flights arrived on time, 20.5 percent had delayed arrivals, and 1.9 percent were canceled.

In 2006, 75.5 percent of flights arrived on time, 22.6 percent had delayed arrivals, and 1.7 percent were entirely canceled.

Source: *Bureau of Transportation Statistics*

So what is that saying? Basically, that things are only getting worse.

The Bureau of Transportation Statistics puts together monthly reports of on-time performances for departure and arrival times of the top 32 airports in the country. Here's what they have to say.

 Avoiding Crowds

Here's a trick to avoid lines. When you have an airport that's a double level airport, where departures are upstairs and arrivals are downstairs (especially if it's an early morning flight), you're going to be nailed by crowds if you go upstairs. Go downstairs—have somebody drop you off there—then take the elevator upstairs. Just rent a cart for your luggage and you'll save 15 minutes.

RANKING OF MAJOR AIRPORT ON-TIME DEPARTURES
(YEAR TO DATE, JANUARY 1 TO APRIL 30, 2007)

RANK	AIRPORT	ON TIME (PERCENT)
1	Portland, OR (PDX)	83.80
2	San Diego, CA (SAN)	82.93
3	Salt Lake City, UT (SLC)	82.05
4	Oakland, CA (OAK)	80.60
5	Tampa, FL (TPA)	80.36
6	Houston, TX (IAH)	80.14
7	Los Angeles, CA (LAX)	79.90
8	Baltimore, MD (BWI)	78.46
9	Seattle, WA (SEA)	78.13
10	St. Louis, MO (STL)	78.12
11	San Francisco, CA (SFO)	77.56
12	Orlando, FL (MCO)	77.35
13	Minneapolis/St. Paul, MN (MSP)	76.73
14	Phoenix, AZ (PHX)	76.66
15	Las Vegas, NV (LAS)	76.26
16	Fort Lauderdale, FL (FLL)	75.05
17	Cincinnati, OH (CVG)	74.97
18	Denver, CO (DEN)	74.84
19	Miami, FL (MIA)	74.75
20	Washington, DC (DCA)	74.64
21	Atlanta, GA (ATL)	74.39
22	Detroit, MI (DTW)	74.19
23	Chicago, IL (MDW)	72.79
24	Boston, MA (BOS)	72.75
25	Washington, DC (IAD)	72.02
26	Dallas/Fort Worth, TX (DFW)	71.59
27	New York, NY (LGA)	70.62
28	Philadelphia, PA (PHL)	67.33
29	Charlotte, NC (CLT)	66.25
30	Newark, NJ (EWR)	65.30
31	New York, NY (JFK)	64.64
32	Chicago, IL (ORD)	61.16

RANKING OF MAJOR AIRPORT ON-TIME ARRIVAL PERFORMANCE
(YEAR-TO-DATE, JANUARY 1 TO APRIL 30, 2007)

RANK	AIRPORT	ON TIME (PERCENT)
1	Oakland, CA (OAK)	80.60
2	Baltimore, MD (BWI)	78.75
3	Houston, TX (IAH)	78.47

RANK	AIRPORT	ON TIME (PERCENT)
4	Salt Lake City, UT (SLC)	78.41
5	San Diego, CA (SAN)	78.33
6	Atlanta, GA (ATL)	77.82
7	Los Angeles, CA (LAX)	77.05
8	Chicago, IL (MDW)	76.99
9	Phoenix, AZ (PHX)	76.72
10	Las Vegas, NV (LAS)	76.65
11	Portland, OR (PDX)	76.15
12	Tampa, FL (TPA)	75.20
13	St. Louis, MO (STL)	75.03
14	Orlando, FL (MCO)	74.84
15	Cincinnati, OH (CVG)	74.50
16	Denver, CO (DEN)	74.17
17	Minneapolis/St. Paul, MN (MSP)	73.24
18	San Francisco, CA (SFO)	72.80
19	Dallas/Fort Worth, TX (DFW)	72.75
20	Seattle, WA (SEA)	72.46
21	Miami, FL (MIA)	71.58
22	Washington, DC (IAD)	70.90
23	Fort Lauderdale, FL (FLL)	70.88
24	Detroit, MI (DTW)	70.59
25	Washington, DC (DCA)	70.19
26	Boston, MA (BOS)	67.91
27	Charlotte, NC (CLT)	65.99
28	Philadelphia, PA (PHL)	64.85
29	Chicago, IL (ORD)	59.79
30	New York, NY (JFK)	59.68
31	New York, NY (LGA)	58.10
32	Newark, NJ (EWR)	55.04

Source: *Bureau of Transportation Statistics, Airline On-Time Data*

The World's Busiest Airports

According to the 2005 airport passenger statistics, the busiest airports in the world were:

(Atlanta) Hartsfield-Jackson: 85,907,423

Los Angeles International: 61,489,398

(Chicago) O'Hare: 76,510,003

Dallas/Fort Worth: 59,176,265

London Heathrow: 67,915,403

Charles de Gaulle (Paris): 53,798,308

(Tokyo) Narita: 63,282,219

Again, the best way to avoid these airports and flights is to be as informed as possible. You can track real-time flight departure and arrival delays through several different online sources.

The Web site **www.flightstats.com** is one of the handiest resources out there right now. You can track the real-time status of flights departing and arriving by airport, as well as check airport weather conditions, facts and figures of airports (e.g., "LAX is the world's fifth busiest passenger airport, serving over 61 million people in 2005"), reserve parking online, see real-time traffic conditions, *and* see airport security line wait times.

Check **www.flytecomm.com** for real-time on-time rates by flight number, arrival airport, or departure airport.

You can track real-time flights on **www.flightaware.com,** organized by flight number, airport code, or even by aircraft type (such as Boeing 737). You can also see the total number of flights in the air at any given time, graphs that depict a full day of flight activity in the United States, and graphs depicting the total number of flights departing and arriving by airport.

The official Federal Aviation Administration site, **www.fly.faa.gov,** lets you check *general* departure and arrival delays by airport and zoom in by region to get the stats on smaller, alternative airports as well as the major international airports.

Alternate Airports

As a contrarian traveler, I'm a big supporter of choosing alternate airports over the major international airports. It can save you time and money, and, best of all, you can skip the crowds. Think outside of the box. Almost every metropolis has an alternate airport or a nearby city with a smaller airport that can get you close to where you need to go—and the hassle of a one-stop flight or driving an hour or so to get to your destination is far more palatable than being stuck for 6 hours on a runway. Heading to Washington, DC? Think Baltimore. San Francisco? Try Oakland, which is just a few miles away but a million miles from the fog and congestion.

Consider the case of a friend of mine, who was stuck on the nightmarish delay of JetBlue Airways on Valentine's Day in 2007. Here's the e-mail she sent me after getting off the plane . . . 8 *hours* after boarding her flight and going nowhere.

I arrived at the airport at 6:30 a.m.; my flight was to leave at 9:05 a.m. We didn't board the flight until about 5 p.m.; and then they kept us on the plane for 8 hours. The airplane was in riot mode; people were everywhere, screaming, crying—mothers with babies, trapped with all of us on the plane—with no diapers (I even gave one woman a T-shirt from my carry-on bag). We had only Terra Blue chips, water, and soda, but that ran out; toilets overflowed; we could not get off. People were on the phone with their attorneys, people were yelling at each other, babies crying; it was really horrible.

We finally got back to the terminal at 1 a.m.

I then had to search for my luggage downstairs until 2:45 a.m. I managed to book a flight on Continental, traveling the next morning at 8 a.m. I took a taxi over to the Continental terminal, only to sleep on the floor for a few hours before I got in line at 5:45 a.m. to check in for my 8 a.m. that routed me through Houston, and then on to LAX.

I was in a massive line, as you can imagine, and by the time I reached the counter, they told me I was too late for the flight . . . I gave up, grabbed a cab, and went back into Manhattan. Next, I tried calling JetBlue, but their toll-free number just gave out a recording that said they were not taking calls and to call back— and then the connection was cut off.

That's when my friend called me. She was literally trapped in New York with no way to get back home to California.

So I gave her a tip: New York's secret airport, Islip, out on Long Island. She took the Long Island Railroad from Penn Station to the Ronkonkoma Station, then a 5-minute cab ride to Macarthur Airport, where Southwest was operating flights to the West Coast.

A few hours later, I got an e-mail. She had reached the airport easily, and Southwest had booked her on a flight from Long Island to Midway in Chicago, with a quick change of planes back to Los Angeles. And she got home.

Here are just a few of my favorite examples of alternate airports.

Some people actually think that **Newark Liberty International Airport** (EWR) is a great alternate airport to La Guardia or Kennedy International (JFK) in New York. And it does have some redeeming qualities—not the least of which is that it is the second-largest hub for Continental, which translates into nonstop flights at lower prices. For example, a round-trip Continental flight from Los Angeles (LAX) to JFK, booked 6 weeks in advance, requires one stop in Houston and costs $397. Alternatively, a round-trip flight from LAX to Newark on Continental is nonstop and costs less—$355. Now consider the fact that EWR is far more compact than JFK and therefore that much easier to navigate, with an efficient baggage claim area, and is only about 16 miles from midtown Manhattan (JFK is 15 miles away).

To get from Newark Airport to Manhattan, a $14 Olympia Express bus from the airport travels to Port Authority, Grand Central Station, and Penn Station. The AirTrain system is a speedy monorail that takes you to the New Jersey Transit train, which will take you directly to Penn Station for less than $14. A taxi ride costs between $40 and $55.

But the real winners are the secondary airports in other major cities: **Chicago's Midway** instead of Chicago O'Hare. (Other options include Northwest Chicagoland Regional Airport, Central Illinois Regional Airport, *and* Austin Straubel in Green Bay.) And let's not forget the secret third Chicago airport: **Milwaukee.** Think I'm kidding? Check out the parking lot at Mitchell Field—at least a third of the cars have Illinois plates. That should tell you something.

I also love *any* airport that offers free wireless throughout the airport. That includes airports ranging from Orlando to Augusta, Georgia; from Fort Lauderdale to Colorado Springs; from Lexington, Kentucky, to Pellston, Michigan. Want a list of airports that provide free wireless connections? Go to **www.wififreespot.com/airport.html**.

And then, of course, there are price considerations.

A quick online search shows me that a round-trip flight in the spring (booked about 6 weeks in advance) from Dallas/Fort Worth to O'Hare costs $202 on American, $232 on United, and $895 on US Airways. But on Southwest Airlines, you can travel from alternate airport Dallas Love Field to Chicago Midway for $197, and both Dallas Love Field and Midway are located *in* the cities themselves for easy access.

Our friend Johnny Jet (www.johnnyjet.com) operates **www.alternateairports. com,** which offers a comprehensive list of the multiple alternate airports.

You can find the three-letter codes for all US airports, from large hubs to small, at **www.airportcodes.us.** They're categorized by city so you can find the most convenient airport for you.

Airport Amenities

Over and over, travelers point to **Singapore Changi Airport** as being one of the best, if not the best, airports in the world. In 2006 alone, it garnered Best International Airport from *Condé Nast Traveler,* Best International Airport by *Official Airline Guides,* Best Worldwide Airport by Annual Travel Industry Awards, and Best Airport for Duty-Free Shopping by *Business Traveller.* So what makes Changi so special? It's a well-managed airport; it's clean, spacious, and organized. It offers wireless Internet, Ethernet cables, and infrared ports, as well as 300 *free* Internet ports in Terminals 1 and 2. The airport's televisions show more than just the same news loop repeatedly—there is an entertainment lounge, movie "theater," news hub, and "discovery lounge" in Terminals 1 and 2, each with programming to match the theme. If you have time to kill, you can catch a 2½-hour tour of Singapore and even a river tour. Changi is also a great hub airport for the rest of Asia. You can catch a flight from Singapore to just about any major capital in the world. And things also run on time here—it's the Singaporean way.

The good news (sort of) is that depressing airport terminals with nothing but a doughnut shop and magazine store are fast becoming a thing of the past. If you're facing massive delays in an airport, you can kill time by getting a massage, sweating off the stress on a treadmill, playing the slot machines, or even getting dental work! Here's what's going on in the airports these days.

Somebody Call a Doctor

Have you ever thought about going to the airport to get your medication? Well, now you can—more and more airports are offering the services of medical doctors, pharmacists, and even psychiatrists on the premises.

Newark Liberty International recently became the first major US airport to open its doors to an airport pharmacy. Located in Terminal C, near Gate 91, **Harmony Pharmacy** has an on-site nurse practitioner and offers flu shots, vaccinations, and examinations to passengers. Even better, their current slogan is "Check your luggage, then check your cholesterol." You can also find full-service pharmacies in locations like Calgary International Airport,

Melbourne International Airport, and Auckland International Airport.

In Thailand, the country's top hospital, **Samitivej Srinakarin Hospital**, recently opened an office at Bumrungrad International Airport. Located on the third floor of the passenger terminal complex, the center primarily deals with emergency medical treatments for passengers and airport staff, as well as transporting critically ill patients to the hospital.

If you find yourself white-knuckling your lounge chair before you board the plane, rest assured that help is available. In the main terminal of Buenos Aires, Jorge Newbery Airport, there is a private clinic with a psychiatrist, an educational psychologist, and even a retired commercial airline pilot to help you out with your fear of flying (they'll even prescribe medication if necessary!).

Exercising in Airports

The Web site www.airportgyms.com should be your first stop if you're planning to work out during your layover. The site provides a comprehensive list of gyms that are located either inside the airport itself, in an airport hotel, or within a few miles of the airport.

One of the best places to work out is **McCarran International** in Las Vegas. A 24 Hour Fitness center is located on-site, just off the north baggage claim. The fully equipped (no pool) gym is free for gym members, and nonmembers pay just $10 per workout.

At Logan International Airport, the nearby **Hilton Hotel** has a gym and spa that is open to airport passengers. Travelers can join for a day, a week, 2 weeks—whatever is necessary to get you through that layover!

At **Miami International Airport,** the Airport Hotel in Concourse E features a trendy rooftop pool and health club. For $8, you can have access for a full day to the facilities and showers (note that the hotel is renovating this area for about a year, so not everything may be open).

International travelers stopping in **Singapore Changi Airport** can decompress after a long flight as well. A fitness center is located in the Ambassador Transit Hotel in Terminal 1. Use of the gym equipment, including treadmills, bikes, and weight machines, plus a nonalcoholic beverage is under $10, and use of the rooftop pool and Jacuzzi is the same price. Located on the third level of the Departure/Transit Lounge in Terminal 2 is the much more luxurious Plaza Premium Lounge, which is open 24 hours for travelers. Here you'll find not only fitness equipment but also massages, oxygen therapy, a suite designed exclusively for napping, and showers.

The **Fairmont Vancouver Airport Hotel** has a great facility that includes a three-lane lap pool, a whirlpool, two saunas, and a fully equipped fitness center. A day pass to the saunas and showers is $10, and access to the pool and fitness center is $15 a day.

Airport Spas

This is becoming a biggie. Spa services, from full-body massages to quickie manicures, are sprouting up in airports. These are walk-in services, so no booking in advance is necessary. **Xpress Spa** is a full-service spa center that makes sure you're on time for your flight, with 30-minute reflexology foot massages, manicures and pedicures, facials, and waxing. There are several Xpress Spas located in JFK, as well as in the airports in Philadelphia, Pittsburgh, Raleigh-Durham, San Francisco, Cancún, Amsterdam, Frankfurt, and Munich. www.xpresspa.com

The company **10 Minute Manicure** can get you in and out within, yes, 10 minutes—and up to 90 minutes for a full-set gel, plus short massages and reflexology sessions. Locations are in Hartford/Windsor Locks, Cincinnati, Lexington, Ottawa, Toronto, New York-JFK, Miami, Newark, Dulles, and Newark. www.10minutemanicure.com

Luxury spas are also taking hold in airports—the **Oasis Day Spa**, which has locations on Park Avenue and at the Affinia Dumont Hotel in Manhattan, now has a clinic in the JetBlue terminal at JFK. Of course, high-end doesn't come without a price: A "quickie" 30-minute facial starts at $70. www.oasisdayspanyc.com

Technology

With technology seemingly moving at a faster rate than their airplanes, some airports are turning to high-tech tools to make their customers' travels a little easier. The new iPoint information kiosk system is being rolled out to several airports across the country, including **Seattle-Tacoma** and **Detroit Metro.** These information kiosks have screens and ticker tapes, which provide maps, food and attraction directories, local news, traffic, weather, and even conference facility schedules. No one knows more about the impact of travel delays than airports, so some are implementing online services to help travelers deal with the traffic situations . . . before they even get to the airport.

Of course, the bigger the airport, the more confusing it can be, especially for out-of-towners. **Dallas/Fort Worth Airport** just launched its own podcast, which you can download before you even leave for the airport. With both audio and video segments in English and Spanish, there are about 16 packets of information about the airport's layout, its parking structure (including the new 8,000-space terminal), and the new $6 million art display. www. dfwairport.com

Wi-Fi

Whether you're surfing the Web or conducting multimillion-dollar deals, Internet access is one of the most crucial elements for travelers, especially if you're killing time on a long layover. Most airports have those expensive kiosks that move at a snail's pace as your paid minutes tick away. You can also find Wi-Fi in many VIP club lounges, but that's not something that the general public can access. At some point in the future, we can probably expect free Wi-Fi, all the time, but until then, here's what's going on.

There are several Web sites that provide lists of airports with free and paid wireless Internet. Note that as this kind of information changes all the time, it's a good idea to doublecheck with the airport before you pack your laptop.

www.travelpost.com/airport-wireless-internet.aspx

www.wififreespot.com/airport.html

www.jiwire.com

Phoenix Sky Harbor launched its free Wi-Fi in early 2006. Free wireless can be found in all three terminals (Terminals 2, 3, and 4—there is no Terminal 1) and is available in the shop, restaurant, and gate areas, where airport visitors are most likely to be sitting and waiting.

Sacramento International offers free Wi-Fi in all of its public areas.

Portland International has free Wi-Fi in 70 percent of the Oregon airport terminal's main level, which includes most gates, the food court, and lobby areas.

Tampa International offers free Wi-Fi in its main terminal.

Orlando International has free Wi-Fi in all of its public areas.

You can find mostly up-to-date information on Wi-Fi access, both free and paid, in foreign airports at www.travelpost.com/airport-wireless-international. aspx.

Some of the major airports abroad that offer free Wi-Fi (not necessarily airportwide) are located in: Beijing, Hong Kong, Madrid, Moscow, Quebec, San Jose (Costa Rica), São Paulo, Tokyo-Narita, Toronto, Vancouver, and Vienna.

But there are some airports I try to avoid, like Miami (think Saigon,

April 1975). Instead, I use Fort Lauderdale anytime I can. And for another good reason: free wireless!

And, thankfully, a number of airline VIP clubs have finally come to realize that charging for wireless is an insult to their members, who have already paid for the privilege of at least trying to stay connected while traveling. American Airlines, for example, had an ironclad contract with T-Mobile. If you wanted to go wireless inside an American Airlines Admirals Club, you had to sign on and pay $10! On principle alone, I—and many others—refused. And now, the airline has come to its senses; it did not renew its contract and is offering wireless for free. Not only are passengers thrilled but American employees can now stay connected as well.

Gambling Fever

You can take the traveler out of Vegas, but you can't take the Vegas . . . well, you get the point. Airports are more than happy to feed your addiction by supplying hours of entertainment in the form of gambling. **McCarran International Airport** in Las Vegas has a whopping 1,300 slot machines throughout the terminals. Coming in a far second is **Reno-Tahoe Airport**, with 237 slot machines. And in Amsterdam, **Schiphol Airport** ups the ante with roulette and blackjack tables. **Frankfurt International Airport** has a casino in Terminal 1.

City Tours

If you have some time on your hands, why waste it indoors when you could be exploring a whole new city? Travel is all about taking advantage of the opportunities that are offered to you, so here are a few locations where you can exit the airport and get into the city for an unexpected adventure.

At **Chicago O'Hare,** you can hop on the Blue Line for a ride into downtown Chicago. It will take about 45 minutes but costs only $1.75 one way. Dig into some deep-dish pizza or just tour around the Loop and take in the skyscrapers before heading back to the airport and you've spent less than $5.

From **Hartsfield-Jackson Airport,** the MARTA, Atlanta's mass transit system, will get you into the city center in about 15 minutes for only $1.50. You'll have time to take a tour of the Coca-Cola factory before heading back to catch your flight with plenty of time to spare.

A trip to **Reagan National** in Washington, DC, means that you're only a 15-minute metro ride from the Smithsonian. And through April, hundreds of cherry trees are in bloom, which is reason enough to take a stroll in our nation's capital.

San Juan International Airport is a 5-minute cab ride from Isla Verde Beach, Puerto Rico (about $10 each way), where you can rent beach chairs and soak up some tropical sun or make use of nonguest-friendly hotels and their restaurants or pools.

How about a round of desert golf on your layover? That's right—desert golf. The Al Ghazal Airport Golf Course, adjacent to **Abu Dhabi International**, is an 18-hole course of sand. Home to the 2007 World Sand Golf Championships, Al Ghazal rents clubs by the hour for reasonable "browns" fees.

London's **Heathrow** is located where it's easy to take the Express Tube into the city for some quick sightseeing. Their slogan: "15 minutes, every 15 minutes." There are two separate train stations—one for Terminals 1, 2, and 3 and another for Terminal 4 (add an extra 5 to 10 minutes if you're departing from Terminal 4). A return fare to Paddington Station is £29 (about $57). A cheaper alternative is the Heathrow Connect train, which takes about 25 minutes and travels less frequently (about every 30 minutes) but costs only £12.90 (about $25) to Paddington Station.

> The abbreviation ORD for Chicago's O'Hare airport comes from the old name "Orchard Field."

In Zurich, the Swiss railways (SBB) and all the metropolitan rail services (S-Bahn) can take you right into the city in just about 10 minutes from **Zurich Airport**. Trains run between Zurich main station and the airport every 10 minutes during peak periods.

Hong Kong's **Chek Lap Kok** has Airport Express trains that run at 12-minute intervals and can get you downtown in just under 25 minutes. A round-trip ticket to Hong Kong Station is about $23.

Munich Airport International is just about 22 miles outside of the city center by rail, but there are also plans for a high-speed "floating" magnetic levitation train. This train will shorten the 45-minute trip to just 10 minutes—traveling at 310 mph!

Family-Friendly Airports

A 2007 survey of the American Society of Travel Agents (ASTA) asked members which airports they considered to be the most "family friendly." **Orlando** won by a landslide, 41.7 percent, compared with the runner-up, Atlanta's Hartsfield-Jackson at 4.6 percent. Why is Orlando so popular? Airport officials note the open, airy design; indoor trees and foliage; the classical music piped throughout the airport; and the extensive art program. All of these elements do add up, but when it comes down to it, Orlando is simply one of the most kid-friendly cities in the world! Think about it: When you're looking at the only airport that leads to Disney World, incoming and outgoing passengers are saturated with three theme-park stores complete with life-size Disney characters and memorabilia from the Kennedy Space Center. Orlando does come through, however, with large aquariums holding more than 200 fish, whimsical life-size sculptures of sleeping tourists, video games, and intimate seating areas that are designed for families to play board games and cards around the tables. www.orlandoairports.net

Atlanta-Hartsfield's kid-friendly attributes make a little more sense in terms of how other airports can model their own facilities and children's programming. Two kids' play areas, televisions, a children's art gallery that features display cases filled with puppets, and a dinosaur exhibition with a 33-foot-long skeleton have young travelers cheering. www.atlanta-airport.com

London Heathrow also topped ASTA's international list, due to the fact that it has multiple infant feeding and changing rooms, arcades, and kids' play areas. The problem is, navigating Heathrow can be so difficult that finding these amenities can be near impossible. Amsterdam's **Schiphol Airport** came up second, with a large collection of Legos, slides, televisions that show nonstop cartoons, and educational computer games. www.schiphol.nl

Let's take a look at some of the other airports that are making an effort to provide programming for children that make family travel a little less stressful.

Tampa International, which tied for third place on ASTA's list, currently has three kids' play areas with soft foam play sets and is in the process of building two more. One area located in Concourse C has three World War II miniature airplanes; another in Concourse E has a climbing wall and leather airplane seats; and one in Concourse A features trucks, cars, and a control tower. The new areas will have a beach theme, a car and train theme, and an outdoor theme. Local children can even have a birthday party in the airport, complete with a full scavenger hunt arranged by airport officials. www.tampaairport.com

Chicago's O'Hare International Airport has an interactive kids' play area, which was designed by the Chicago Children's Museum. Kids can pretend to be airport employees by weighing baggage and loading the cargo (let's hope they do a better job at not losing bags!), while a child-size air traffic control center puts them in charge. And since we now know that dinosaurs are always a big hit, there's a four-story-tall brachiosaur from the Field Museum towering over United's Terminal 1. www.ohare.com

At **Logan Airport,** designers consulted with the Children's Museum of Boston to create hands-on Kidports in Terminals A and C that relate to traveling and flying. The Kidport in Terminal A even includes a replica of the Logan Control Tower and of the terminal itself. www.massport.com/logan

The **Seattle/Tacoma International Airport** has a 1,400-square-foot play space near the Central Terminal that includes an airplane, a control tower replica, and even a little baggage cart for kids to learn the tricks of the trade. www.portseattle.org/seatac

Mineta San José International Airport in California is home to the Gordon Reynolds KidPort in Terminal C, where kids get to play pilot with video monitors that let them watch the plane traffic and headsets that let them listen in on "tower chatter"—real-time conversations between the pilots and air traffic control. www.sjc.org

In Germany, **Frankfurt International Airport** has three play areas (including one in McDonald's), and kids can climb onto a miniature aircraft to watch the airfield activity. www.frankfurt-airport.de

And in **Kuala Lumpur?** Well, the Malaysian airport may not have designated play areas, but it can brag that it has a rain forest. The futuristic airport itself is set among an astounding tropical rain forest, a portion of which is enclosed to give the sensation that there is a jungle lurking inside the airport. www.klia.com.my

Duty-Free Shopping

Shopping has long been a favorite activity in airports, whether you're looking for a book to read on the plane or Prada sunglasses for your trip. One of the major benefits of traveling internationally is the almighty duty-free shops . . . those brightly lit stores filled with gleaming beauty products, liquor, and candy—the ideal gifts to bring back to your loved ones. But are you really saving anything by shopping duty-free? Let's look at the facts.

If you've ever found yourself carting home a giant box of Toblerone chocolate and your liquor cabinet is filled with funny-shaped bottles from around the world, don't worry, you're not alone. Airport duty-free shops like to catch you at your most vulnerable state: You're about to face a long international flight, your wallet is stuffed with leftover currency, and you can't go into the office tomorrow empty-handed. It's even likely that a diamond-encrusted Dior watch is something you've always wanted—you just didn't know it until now.

Here's a breakdown of how duty-free works: A duty is the customs tax paid to import something into the country, yet airport duty-free shops are exempt. (Since the goods are sold only to people leaving the country from airports, seaports, or borders, goods aren't completely "imported" into the country. Thus, the shop doesn't have to pay a customs tax.) The idea is that these savings get passed on to the buyer.

Just like grocery stores display candy at the checkout line, duty-free shops are located in airports just before you check out of the country for good. They're usually brightly lit and bursting with tempting goods that trigger the impulse buyer in you. In fact, a study commissioned by Halifax Travel Insurance shows that British shoppers have spent £4 billion (about $7.5 billion) in the past 5 years on unplanned purchases at airports—£817 million (about $1 billion) of which was spent to use up leftover local currency. That's why you may find yourself lugging home a 10-pack carton of Marlboros for $15—even if you don't smoke.

The top five cities with the most duty-free sales are London, Singapore, Amsterdam, Paris, and Dubai. Logically speaking, you should find significant savings when you shop duty-free versus places where the items are taxed (i.e., within the cities you're traveling, at home in the United States, or even online). However, keep in mind that these prices aren't standardized; in fact, there is a Web site called **www.thedutyfreepriceguide.com** that now makes it easier by comparing duty-free prices between airports and airlines. For example, a 50-millileter bottle of Calvin Klein Eternity Eau de Toilette spray can cost $32 on Continental Airlines and $51 in the Berlin Airport. Still, that's a far better deal than a bottle of the same stuff in Harrods in London, which will cost you about $61. A liter of Chivas Regal 12-year-old whiskey will cost you about $26 in the Singapore Changi Airport. Compare this with shopping at home, where it costs about $40 in an American liquor store and $41.99 online at Beverages and More. Another instance in which duty-free shops can pay off is that you may have first access to certain products. An increasing number of companies are creating items exclusively for duty-free shops before rolling them out to the general market. Italian celebrity jockey Frankie Dettori did just this with his men's fragrance line, Dettori, which was only available at Heathrow's World Duty Free store in September 2005 before it hit the domestic market.

Cadbury did the same with a particular praline tower pack of 29 individually wrapped chocolates, which was only available on British Airways during the holiday season and became widely available as of January 2006.

In some cases, however, the airport or airline's duty-free shop isn't going to offer you much savings at all . . . because the city doesn't have any sales taxes! Here are just a few cities where you may find better deals before you hit the airport, when you have more flexibility and time for price and brand comparisons.

The best example of the myth of duty-free can be found at the **Hong Kong** airport. Hong Kong doesn't impose sales tax or custom duty on any goods except for tobacco and alcohol. The island claims to be such a shopper's paradise that its tourism board actually began sponsoring an official "Summer Shopping Festival" 3 years ago. Shops offer even deeper discounts and extended store hours to entice visitors during otherwise slow travel months. There's also a slew of entertainment, including the Aqua Fantasia spectacle, featuring a high-tech visual display set against a "water curtain" of Victoria Harbour, plus pyrotechnic shows on Saturdays.

In Hong Kong, you can find almost anything you can imagine, including antiques, furniture, ceramics and porcelain, jewelry, and cosmetics. Just keep in mind that this is also a hot spot for knockoffs and frauds, so if you're looking for the real deal, stick with the name-brand stores or go by personal recommendations. And take note: The government has recently made moves to introduce a goods and sales tax, which would take at least 3 to 5 years to implement but has shoppers and business owners concerned for Hong Kong's future as a major shopping destination. www.discoverhongkong.com/hksf/eng

So when you get to the Hong Kong airport and a store there proudly boasts it's duty-free—think. The prices are *all* duty-free in Hong Kong. But airport rents to concessionaires are steep—and the prices will almost always be higher.

It may be hard to find on a map, but the tiny principality of **Andorra** is a virtual drive-thru duty-free market between France and Spain. It's estimated that about nine million travelers visit Andorra each year, primarily because of the duty-free shopping and its mountain resorts. While Andorra's numerous mini-malls (ambiance is not really a factor here) offer lower-priced electronics, clothing, and cosmetics, one of the more popular purchases here is whiskey. Cava Benito (www.cavabenitowhisky.com), for example, offers about 600 different whiskeys.

Dubai has fast become a mecca for duty-free shopping, where visitors and locals can visit more than 40 malls, boutiques, souks (open-air markets), and street vendors for discounted items, while experiencing concerts, dances, art exhibitions, and promotional raffles (you might actually win a Rolls-Royce). www.mydsf.com

Dubai Duty Free shopping concourse is always worth a mention. Established in 1983, the world-famous center offers 5,400 square meters of shopping, with electronics, cosmetics, liquor, jewelry, clothing, sporting equipment, and nearly anything else you can think of. Think of thousands of passengers a night sprinting to the shopping finish through the aisles of the concourse. It's a wild scene 24 hours a day, and even if you're not shopping, the one thing you can say about Dubai is that duty-free shopping has also become a spectator sport! www.dubaidutyfree.com

Airport Prices

Regardless of what kind of deals (or not) you're getting from the duty-free shop, nothing changes the obscene price of a sandwich in an airport. I've paid up to $12 for a dry turkey sandwich topped with limp lettuce and something resembling a tomato. You would think that we would learn our lesson and simply stop buying food in airports, but what about those $4 bottles of water? Security is going to toss any liquids you bring into the airport, and in some cases, even mayonnaise and mustard packets will be banned. (True story: One passenger reports that she was told if she smeared the mayo and mustard straight onto her sandwich, her "liquids" would be in the clear. Another passenger, who made a peanut butter and jelly sandwich for her kids, was stopped at security. The peanut butter was allowed; the jelly wasn't.) Long story short: They're charging higher prices because they know that we'll pay it. There's no choice!

One of the primary reasons behind the inflated pricing is to make up for the high operating costs. It costs a lot to run a restaurant or fast-food chain inside an airport, and because airports get a cut of their profits (up to 20 percent in some cases), there is no one to look out for the customer. Slowly but surely, things are changing, and airport officials are taking the consumers into consideration and talking about lowering prices to what you would find out in the "real world." The only problem is that many concession contracts last 10 to 15 years, meaning that we just have to wait it out before we see prices fall.

What's even worse is that in some airports, the prices vary between terminals! One study found that in Phoenix Sky Harbor, a meal in Terminal 4 will cost about double that of a comparable meal in other terminals, because of an expiring concession contract with the airport.

Airport Parking

I've found that one of the greatest travel hassles that people forget about is dealing with parking. By the time you get to the airport, find the lot, park your car, and wait for the shuttle to carry you to your terminal, you may have lost 30 to 40 minutes, which you may not have budgeted into your preboarding wait time. Consider elements like ubiquitous airport construction and random security checks and you can expect to add on even more wasted time. One option is to valet your car curbside, but of course that comes with a price tag. The other option is to book your spot in advance: Try Web sites such as **airportparking.com, parknflynetwork.com,** and **airport parkingreservations.com**—you pay about a $5 reservation fee and take a free shuttle to the airport.

Sleeping in Airports

Here's a handy trick for sleeping on the cheap: Try bunking down for the night inside the airport! Between long layovers and delayed flights, sleeping in airports might seem like not only a good idea but a necessary one.

If you're looking for a quick nap, the transit lounges in most airports can do in a pinch. Of course, transit lounges aren't available in every airport—or to every traveler. But some airports, like those in Vancouver, Dubai, and Istanbul, do offer sleeping pods or by-the-hour airport hotels for naps. If you're stranded overnight in an airport due to flight delays, make sure to ask your airline for a hotel or sleeping pod voucher. At the very least, you should obtain access to the lounge facilities.

If a hotel or sleeping pod isn't available and you're thinking about saving some bucks by crashing at the airport, visit **www.sleepinginairports.net.** This site offers the inside scoop from other travelers on the best places to sleep at airports—and hands out the Golden Pillow award to the most sleep-friendly airports around the world. Singapore Changi Airport has swept this category for several years, but a number of others make the list: Amsterdam offers comfortable sleeping chairs in the transit area, plus showers to help you wake up before you finally board. Athens' new airport is clean, quiet, and equipped with padded benches, while Auckland Airport offers movable chairs and benches, sleepworthy couches, a mini-theater with lounge chairs, and few announcements to wake you from your sleep.

At the other end of the scale are the less prestigious Poopy Airport Awards, one of which goes to Bombay for its uncomfortable seating before check-in, mosquitoes, and foul odors. Cairo, which has spent a long time on the worst list, seems to be improving but has notable stories of rats, dogs, less-than-satisfactory bathrooms, and insufficient seating. On the home front, Chicago's O'Hare offers uncomfortably hard plastic seats, frequent overcrowding from stranded passengers, and cold air-conditioning. Further, according to one complainer, it smells like "feet and broccoli."

Airport VIP Lounges

When you fly as often as I do, you have the opportunity to peek behind the frosted doors of VIP lounges. To get past the strict attendants, you need to have in hand a business or first-class ticket, frequent flier status, a premium credit card, or a lounge pass (which I'll get into later).

In the United States, membership in domestic airline VIP lounges isn't based on class—but on your checkbook. If you pay annual fees of about $450, you can become a member of American Airlines' Admirals Club, $500 for United Airlines' Red Carpet Club, and $400 for Delta Air Lines' Crown Room. (At American, a lifetime membership used to run around $6,000 but is no longer offered.) With foreign-based international carriers, the lounges are a little different. Virgin Atlantic, Cathay Pacific, and Lufthansa don't charge a membership fee but are open to first-class and business-class passengers.

What I've noticed in my travels is how much these lounges can vary. Some are nothing more than enclosed seating areas with a few peanuts and soda, while others are sprawling, luxurious spaces with showers, full buffets, sleeping areas, entertainment centers, and WiFi—a business traveler's dream come true.

But then you get into the real issues: Once you've paid your steep annual membership or purchased a pricey ticket, many services at these VIP clubs are à la carte. Want wireless? It'll cost you. A meal? Get out your wallet. And liquor isn't free either. What you're paying for is your own small piece of real estate where you can sit, outside the chaos of the gates, and wait for your flight.

Airline VIP lounges have been around almost as long as commercial flying. But in the last few years, a number of airlines have gone upscale in a big way, figuring that if they can keep their highest-yield first-class passengers happy on the ground, they just might own them in the air as well. Here are a few examples of what's going on in the secret world of airport lounges.

American Airlines has two types of VIP clubs: Admirals Clubs and Flagship Lounges. The former is probably the one you're more familiar with—there are 43 Admirals Clubs worldwide, open to all members, travelers with a business-class or first-class ticket on international flights, and first-class travelers on nonstop transcontinental flights (you still with me?). The latter is open to first-class passengers who are on nonstop transcontinental or international flights. Currently there are Flagship Lounges at Los Angeles, O'Hare, and Heathrow airports and one more opening at Kennedy.

Flagship Lounges have or will offer meals, including continental breakfasts, afternoon tea, and three-course dinners. Inside the lounge, passengers can expect to find amenities like showers, Internet-equipped computers, T-Mobile HotSpot wireless service, and plasma TVs. Signature chocolate and servers in full uniform round out the luxury experience.

The Admirals Clubs vary from location to location, but some notable ones include Concourse D in Miami International, which is actually shaped liked a shell and highlighted by blue glass and a steel accent wall that changes from blue to green for a complete *Miami Vice* feel. A room designed especially for children has computers and a flat-paneled TV with only kid-friendly programming. At JFK's Admirals Club in Concourse C, the three private shower areas have embedded replicas of a New York City manhole cover (okay, not so useful but interesting to look at). Narita International in Tokyo features free Wi-Fi and more than 100 Ethernet cables, and it has more computers than any other Admirals Club in the world. If you're not into working, the lounge also offers spalike shower suites with all the fancy products you need.

In international news, **Air New Zealand** recently opened its "bach" lounge in Melbourne. A bach is the local term for summer home, which is apparent once you see the mock veranda complete with a wooden deck and wicker chairs. You can find Kiwi brands such as 42 Below Vodka, regional wines and cheese, and even New Zealand newspapers. A separate sports area includes a big-screen plasma TV showing games, sports memorabilia, and beer on tap. The airline also recently opened a plush lounge in Los Angeles: A relaxation section has lounge chairs, a library, and panoramic views of the city (if you can see through the smog); a business center offers Internet, fax machines, printers, and photocopiers; a "refresh" zone features six showers; and the entertainment area has a children's play area, a bar, and video game consoles.

Although it's not necessarily a rule of thumb, airlines' VIP lounges tend to be better in their home hubs. For example, **Continental**'s Presidents Club in Terminal E at Houston's Bush Intercontinental is one of the more impressive. It covers 26,000 square feet on three levels. You can have all the amenities such as free Wi-Fi, free beverages and snacks, and showers. A valet will even press your clothes while you shower!

> The world's first duty-free shop was established at Shannon Airport in Ireland in 1946 and contained no liquor or tobacco.

Air France's 300 lounges around the world offer showers and Internet access. The airline's best lounge of all is located in Paris, of course. The first-class and business-class lounges are attached, but in first class, you can linger over a long massage—don't worry about missing your flight, as you'll get limousine service directly to the aircraft!

Air Canada's business-class lounge in Toronto is another standout. Thanks in part to the airline's branding partnerships with companies like Sony, BMW, and Xerox, the lounge offers relaxation rooms, entertainment centers, laptops, and showers.

In Hong Kong, you'll find the Wing, **Cathay Pacific**'s amazing first-class lounge. It comes complete with a full restaurant, lounge, and even a Häagen-Dazs ice cream bar. You'll also find cabanas with resting areas and showers, libraries, state-of-the-art computer workstations, and relaxation areas.

At Heathrow, home airline **British Airways** has a lounge in Terminal 4 with a full buffet and private showers for business-class passengers. In the same airport, the newly renovated **Virgin Atlantic Clubhouse** is nothing short of spectacular: It covers more than 8,000 square feet, but this isn't just any lounge; imagine a place where you get a spa pool, a multiscreen cinema, a game room, and a spa and salon. Want a facial, shoulder massage, manicure/pedicure? Or how about a wet shave for the men? It's all there. And yes, you can even get a haircut. If you've got work to do, the Clubhouse is fully wireless and offers Sony laptops, printers, and recharging stations.

Contrary to this home-base theory, you may have found that **Lufthansa**'s business-class lounges in Frankfurt and Munich were both rather sorry affairs, with just a few selections of beer and snacks to tide you over during your layover. In a recent announcement, Lufthansa stated that it is investing $137 million to revamp its Senator, first-class, and business-class lounges worldwide. In a new first-class lounge in Munich, for example, you can expect to see more than 2,620 square feet housing a gourmet restaurant, separate rooms for working and relaxing, a cigar lounge, and luxury bathroom amenities.

But where Lufthansa shines the most is in its first-class terminal in Frankfurt: It's more than a lounge; it's an entirely dedicated space for first-class passengers. This is such a special facility that some passengers actually arrive 4 to 5 hours early for their flights—and with good reason. The 19,000-square-foot first-class terminal has its own immigration, customs, and security. But that's just the beginning. . .

The restaurant is first class, featuring air-dried ham from Spain, smoked salmon flown in from Scotland, and the finest ingredients from Italy. This place even has its own bakery. And if you're getting in late, not to worry; food is served around the clock. The bar itself may be worth the visit—it stocks more than 80 single malt whiskey brands, and that's just the whiskey. You'll also find a cigar bar, private bathrooms with soaking tubs, private office units, and rest areas with daybeds. And then comes the fun part: getting to the plane.

About 15 minutes prior to takeoff (I'm serious), a person dedicated only to you arrives with your passport, boarding pass, and all of your completed immigration forms (you've already gone through private security when you entered the terminal) and escorts you to an elevator. When the door opens on the ground level, a line of Mercedes S Class sedans or Porsche Cayennes is waiting for you, with drivers. Pick the model you want and head off around runways, tarmacs, and taxiways, as you are driven directly to your plane. Leave it to the Germans to time this perfectly: All the other passengers have boarded, the plane is ready to go, and you are deposited planeside by your driver and escorted up the back stairs to your flight. As you board, they close the aircraft door behind you, and off you go. Now, *that* is first class!

VIP Lounge Passes

Once you've seen what goes on in some of these VIP lounges, you may be tempted to wiggle your way inside without having to pay hefty premiums or purchasing a first-class ticket. Well, the good news is that you can. Something called **Priority Pass** (www.prioritypass.com) offers access to more than 500 airport lounges worldwide. **Lounge Pass** (www.loungepass.com) offers access to more than 130 lounges at 100 airports.

Priority Pass was launched in the United Kingdom about 15 years ago, and today, it boasts about 1.5 million members. Through this service, you can get access to VIP lounges such as Delta Crown Room Clubs, Continental Presidents Clubs, and United Airlines Red Carpet Clubs.

However, this comes with some caveats: For one thing, it's not exactly cheap. Priority Pass's primary plan costs $399 a year for unlimited use; a $249-a-year plan includes 10 free lounge visits for one person, plus $24 per entry after that; a $99-per-year plan costs $24 per person each time you visit a lounge. Lounge Pass starts at about $24 per visit but can go up, depending on where you're traveling.

If you're a frequent traveler, you're mostly likely flying in and out of a select group of airports. So you're probably better off sticking with one or two airlines and buying into their VIP clubs. And if you're *not* a frequent traveler, well then, you're spending a hefty amount of money a year for something you're not using too often.

Also, even with a pass, you won't get into all the VIP lounges, all the time. Lounge Pass is very limited—in fact, in the majority of US airports, the only lounge you'll have access to is Continental's Presidents Club. Priority Pass doesn't work in Tahiti, and at Los Angeles, you can't get into United Airlines' Red Carpet Clubs (but you can get into its first- and business-class lounges).

The other issue relates to what I just described above. If you're going to pay for a service per visit, it should be worth it; but many VIP clubs really are nothing more than slightly quieter, more spacious rooms than waiting by the gate. And if you have to pay extra for every amenity, you're going to be spending a lot more than $24 a visit.

So what are your other options? Well, there is the Canada-based "aviation services company" Servisair Lounge, which has its own private lounges (not affiliated with any airline) with 143 locations in 28 countries (www.executivelounges.com). The company claims that day passes start at $14, although a quick online search shows prices like $22 (Calgary) and $39 (Nice, Hong Kong, Geneva, and Singapore). And again, your options are limited, at least domestically—the only US airport to have a Servisair Lounge is Miami.

Your credit card is another option. If you have an American Express Platinum or Centurion card, you now get Priority Pass access, as well as direct access to some member airlines. A Diners Club card gets you free access to 89 Diners Club Airport Lounges around the world. And once again, these are still limited choices. For example, there are only three Diners Club lounges in the United States, two in Miami, and one in Newark.

CHAPTER 2

Airlines

❝ If Wilbur and Orville were alive today, Wilbur would
have to fire Orville to reduce costs. ❞

—HERB KELLEHER, SOUTHWEST AIRLINES

It's getting tough out there. Airlines are cutting capacity on many routes, which means chances are excellent your plane will push back from the gate 100 percent full, with you in the dreaded center seat, stuck between the two sumo wrestlers. This has resulted in four classes of airline service: first, business, coach, and . . . anger management!

It's no longer a question of whether you will be abused by the airline experience but how, when, and how often. The real advertising motto for most airlines these days is: We're not happy . . . until *you're* not happy.

Having said that, if you understand the rules and can play the game, you can easily minimize the abuse.

Let's first look at some terms and statistics you'll need to know before you get out there in the big bad airline world.

Overbooking and Bumping

It's one of the aspects of flying that travelers hate, and it's not getting any better. Airlines routinely overbook flights to compensate for no-shows: those who reschedule or opt not to fly. Why? Because an empty seat on a plane means a loss of revenue to an airline, but by overbooking by about 20 percent, they're mostly covered.

According to the US Bureau of Transportation Statistics (BTS), in 2006, involuntary bumping was slightly more than 1 per 10,000 passengers, up from 0.9 in 2005. Out of 18 US carriers, the bumping rate during the first quarter of 2007 was 1.5 per 10,000 passengers, up from the 1.3 rate for the first quarter of 2006.

Here's the breakdown of denied boardings (per 10,000 passengers) by airline, as reported by the 2007 Airline Quality Rating report.

AIRLINE	2006	2005
AirTran	0.08	0.37
Alaska	1.26	1.58
American	0.84	0.63
American Eagle	1.31	0.61
ATA	2.19	2.75
Atlantic Southeast	4.47	1.57
Comair	2.47	0.61
Continental	1.74	1.92
Delta	1.70	1.31
Frontier	0.47	NA
Hawaiian	0.13	NA
JetBlue	0.07	0.00
Mesa	1.59	NA
Northwest	0.81	0.96
SkyWest	1.12	0.35
Southwest	0.91	0.69
United	0.51	0.48
US Airways	1.08	0.64

When you are bumped, whether it's voluntary or involuntary, the airline has a legal obligation to rebook you on a later flight and compensate you with up to $400 in cash or its equivalent. This requires some things from the passenger: that you are holding a confirmed reservation and a paid ticket and that you met the check-in time for the flight.

That last one is tricky: It means when you checked in at the departure gate, *not* the ticket counter or baggage check-in. Boarding deadlines vary by airline, and they're getting increasingly strict about shutting the gates for late passengers. For example, in order to qualify for any compensation on an overbooked flight, Alaska Airlines requires that passengers be checked in and at the gate 40 minutes before domestic and international flights. Continental requires you to be there 15 minutes before domestic flights and 30 before international. United requires you to be at the counter 30 minutes before domestic departures and 45 minutes before international flights. US Airways requires you to be there 5 minutes before shuttle flights, 15 minutes before domestic, and 30 minutes before international. My advice? Hedge your bets and get there at least 30 minutes ahead of time; then you're less likely to be bumped than the guy who rolls in 5 minutes before departure time carrying no luggage besides his backpack.

For involuntary bumping, here's what the US Department of Transportation (USDOT) wants you to know.

❗ If you are bumped involuntarily and the airline arranges substitute transportation that is scheduled to get you to your final destination (including later connections) within 1 hour of your original scheduled arrival time, there is no compensation.

❗ If the airline arranges substitute transportation that is scheduled to arrive at your destination between 1 and 2 hours after your original arrival time (between 1 and 4 hours on international flights), the airline must pay you an amount equal to your one-way fare to your final destination, with a $200 maximum.

❗ If the substitute transportation is scheduled to get you to your destination more than 2 hours later (4 hours internationally) or if the airline does not make any substitute travel arrangements for you, the compensation doubles (200 percent of your fare, $400 maximum).

❗ You always get to keep your original ticket and use it on another flight. If you choose to make your own arrangements, you can request an "involuntary refund" of the ticket for the flight you were bumped from. The denied boarding compensation is essentially a payment for your inconvenience.

However, there are always caveats. These include having a confirmed reservation (there should be an okay on your ticket), meeting your airline's deadline for buying your ticket, and checking in on time. Show up late and they'll consider you a no-show. In fact, your best bet is to check in as early as possible. These rules also don't apply to charter flights, planes that carry 60 or fewer passengers, and international flights flying into the United States.

Flights between two foreign cities in the European Union (EU) now have their own set of rules to follow. Passengers traveling on all domestic and international flights that depart from any airport in the EU (that even includes French overseas territories) are covered by these policies, regardless if you're an EU citizen or not. If a passenger is bumped, whether voluntary or involuntary, he can get between €250 ($335) and €600 ($800), depending on the circumstances and the length of the flight. (Before this legislation was passed in 2005, the most an airline had to compensate bumped passengers was between €150 and €300.)

Bumped passengers must be offered the choice of a refund, a flight back to their original point of departure, or an alternative flight to continue their journey. Passengers who are inconvenienced through overbooking are also eligible for vouchers for meals, refreshments, hotel accommodation if necessary, and, in some cases, even free e-mails, faxes, or telephone calls. Now there's a lesson that we can learn from Europe.

Voluntary Bumping

If you're going for the voluntary bumping option, here's something to keep in mind: Airlines are required to offer you compensation. However, instead of cash, many airlines prefer to give vouchers, some of which can actually rise up to the value of $1,000. But what does that mean for you? If you get a restricted voucher, you'll have a free or discounted flight that may be loaded with blackout dates, expiration dates, and other restrictions. I've even heard of travelers who weren't able to redeem their vouchers online, and when they went to an airport counter, they were charged for "issuance of tickets"! In the end, your "free" ticket may be just as useful as your unused frequent flier miles—without the option of trading in the ticket for a toaster. So if and when there's an option, get the cash, *not* the voucher.

And if you want to get involved with what I call the bumping game, it's truly an art form. Savvy bumpees know that the first flights from New York to Detroit, Chicago, and Atlanta are almost always oversold. Simply purchase a full-fare ticket, wait for the overbooking announcement, volunteer to give up your seat, and collect your voucher for later.

According to the Aviation Consumer Protection Division's Fly-Rights site (http://airconsumer.ost.dot.gov/publications/flyrights.htm), there are two important questions that you should consider before you volunteer your seat.

! When is the next flight on which the airline can confirm your seat? The alternate flight may be just as acceptable to you. But if they offer to put you on standby on another flight that's full, you could be stranded.

! Will the airline provide other amenities such as free meals, a hotel room, phone calls, or ground transportation? If not, you might have to spend the money they offer you on food or lodging while you wait for the next flight.

Rule 240 Explained

This was—and remains—my favorite airline rule. Airlines don't want you to know about it. They don't want me to mention it. But it's still on file at the Department of Transportation, and, with few exceptions, it can be your best friend. Rule 240 dates back to the days when the government, in some capacity, controlled and regulated the airlines, and the carriers legally had to be up front about what they offered to passengers whose flights were delayed or canceled. That's no longer the case, but the airlines still have to tell you what they'll provide. It's part of the contract of carriage between you and the airline.

So what is Rule 240? It basically states that the airline has to deliver you to your destination within 2 hours of your scheduled flight time. If that can't happen, then it has to put you on the next departing flight at no additional cost. That's not limited to the same airline you were originally booked on, so it means the *next* departing flight on *any* airline. This has to do with interline agreements among the major carriers.

This little rule can also help you out even before you get to the airport. Check your flight before you leave home (try www.flightstats.com or www. flightarrivals.com). Look up not just your scheduled flight but also the aircraft. If the plane assigned to your flight is in Omaha and you're supposed to be flying out of New York in 4 hours, chances are your flight will be delayed—or canceled, especially if you're flying from an airport where the airline is not based and has no access to an extra airplane. That's when you can enact a preemptive 240.

Find the lead gate agent and explain that you would like to invoke Rule 240. And, with only two exceptions, the agent should get your ticket endorsed over to another airline. The two exceptions? Your originally scheduled flight is the last flight of the day on any airline. And you're dealing with weather-related delays, acts of God, terrorism, or labor disputes. But Rule 240 *does* apply to delays or cancellations that the airline is responsible for, such as mechanical failure or misconnections. Rule 240 also applies only in the United States and doesn't apply to carriers that don't have interline agreements, such as JetBlue and Southwest. (But American, United, Delta, Northwest, US Air, and Continental should abide by 240.)

When you think about it, it makes sense that the airlines have to protect themselves: When they're rebooking you on another airline's flight, they're essentially buying the ticket for you. So if you paid $248 for your host airline's ticket and they have to rebook you for $1,100, they're swallowing the loss.

Each airline's contract of carriage differs in how it deals with rebooking on delayed or canceled flights. American, for example, states that it will reroute you on *their* next available flight. Creative reservation agents will work to send you through alternate airports, rather than sending you to one that is equally congested with rerouted passengers. Northwest will put you on the next available flight of any interlining airline if your flight is canceled or changed by more than 60 minutes (and that may mean an upgrade!). Delta agrees to put you on another carrier if your delay exceeds 2 hours but notes that it's at their "discretion." United will put you on its next flight or on another carrier at the same class of service, and Continental will put you on another carrier, but certain types of tickets are excluded from this.

> A Boeing 747's wingspan is longer than the Wright Brothers' first flight.

These caveats are like the printed disclaimer you get on the back of valet parking tickets, claiming the parking service is not responsible for damage to your car. But any lawyer will tell you—and legal precedent has already been set—that the parking service *is* liable for damage to your car while they are in possession of the vehicle. And the same is said for Rule 240. That said, time and time again, I've heard from travelers who unsuccessfully tried to enact Rule 240. Even when all signs indicate that it should be in full effect, a clueless agent dealing with hundreds of disgruntled passengers at one time may not be on your side. I've heard excuses like "the delay came from air traffic control, so it's not our fault," which is ridiculous. If you find yourself in that situation, that's when you need to go as high up as possible. Get to a manager or supervisor, point out the facts, and show them your contract of carriage.

However, if the airline is unable to rebook you due to weather issues, they are not responsible for putting you up in a hotel or providing meal vouchers. Getting disgruntled and pushy probably isn't going to help you in that situation—but being nice just may. Many airlines have relationships with nearby hotels that can provide distressed passenger rates. American Airlines has a relationship with Hotels.com and can help you out—but they don't have to.

Flight Interruption Manifest

A flight interruption manifest (FIM) is the one thing—other than 240—an airline never wants to give you. It's the document that the airline issues you as a substitute ticket if their failure makes it impossible for you to use your ticket. It's only valid on a new airline, not the one that your original ticket was issued with, and is accepted as a regular ticket on your new, specified flight. And this brings me to why I always suggest getting a paper ticket, not an e-ticket. To produce a FIM, the e-ticket has to be converted into a regular paper ticket, and the data is then sent to the receiving airline. Although airlines are slowly moving into the digital age, they're currently on different Global Distribution Systems. (American uses Sabre, Continental uses SHARES, and others use Apollo, System One, and Worldspan, among others.) These systems can talk to each other, but it's a very slow process, which doesn't bode well when there are lines of delayed passengers who need to be rebooked quickly. So for now, if you can find a ticket/counter agent who won't charge you the premium for issuing them, paper tickets are still the way to go.

Standby

There is no standard definition of the term "standby." In the old days, I used to snag a student standby card, show up at the airport, and, if a seat was available, fly at half price. Nowadays, standby is a status, not a fare. Most airlines define standby as taking a flight other than the one that you hold in your ticket—and an increasing number of airlines are limiting this to a same-day ticket.

But flying standby also means that you're on a waiting list, and this is no first-come, first-served system of democracy. There is a hierarchy of the waiting list, which is dependent on the class of your original ticket, the amount of money you paid for your ticket, and your frequent flier status. Also, your standby status is affected if the city you're flying out of is a major hub—or the headquarters of that airline. And finally, your standby status is often affected by the time you physically check in for your flight at the airport.

Some airlines even want to make standby a revenue generator. In many cases, if you finish business earlier than planned and want to catch an earlier flight back home, many airlines will now charge you (around $25) for a confirmed seat on that return flight.

Other airlines, like US Airways, have now waived that $25 fee for their highest-level frequent fliers.

Code Sharing

"Code sharing" is an airline term that started back in 1990, when Qantas and American combined services from cities in Australia to the United States. The idea is that a flight operated by one airline is marketed as a flight for one or more airlines. These days, you'll notice that you can't get away from code sharing, because almost every flight shares a flight number with another airline. The airline that operates the flight by providing the airplane and crew is called the operating carrier, and the company that sells the tickets but doesn't operate the flight is called the marketing carrier.

The reasons behind code sharing apply to several situations.

- Code sharing can make it clearer for passengers who are on connecting flights. Rather than flying on two different codes, you travel from your originating city to your connecting city to your destination all under one flight number.

- If flights from both participating airlines fly the same route, sharing the same code makes it appear that there is increased service on that route.

- If a carrier does not operate its own aircraft on a certain route, code sharing can provide the illusion that it does.

Delayed and Canceled Flights

Consider it the bane of every traveler's existence: delayed and canceled flights. And with all the miles that I log each year, I'm no exception. I recently had a flight to India that arrived 28 *hours* late! Now, airlines will always tell you that most flight delays arise from weather and congested air traffic. But I'm here to tell you that flight mismanagement, unrealistic scheduling by airlines, and unreasonable connect times between flights were the real culprits in my situation.

And the summer of 2006 was the worst in history for flight delays. There were almost half a million delays of 15 minutes or more. And the summer of 2007 was even worse.

In April 2007, I flew Delta Airlines flight 16, which goes between New York and Mumbai, India. It's scheduled to be a 14-hour nonstop flight, although it can be longer due to wind conditions. I arrived at JFK airport 3 hours ahead of the scheduled 9:55 p.m. departure time and was at the gate 45 minutes before flight time. That's when I discovered that we would be boarding late due to the fact that ground crews still had to finish catering and cleaning the aircraft.

We finally boarded at 10:30 p.m. and were ready for takeoff. But there was a glitch. The in-flight entertainment system in five of the rows didn't work, which meant that the flight attendant call buttons also didn't work. Even though this isn't a required system for a flight to operate, someone decided that it needed to be fixed. I went up to the cockpit and asked the captain whether flight attendant call buttons were on the "no-go" list. "No, they're not," he replied, shrugging. "But that's what Atlanta wants to do."

At 11:20 p.m., they finally figured out that the system couldn't be fixed and got ready to go. Except that now we were number 75 in line for takeoff! Consider the fact that there's about a 3-minute separation between takeoffs and you know you've got yourself a long wait. For some aircrafts, it was even worse, because they waited so long that they actually ran short of fuel. But at 12:40 a.m., what do you think happened to us? Oh, it wasn't a fuel issue. Our crew had "timed out." They were beyond their legal time limits for being on duty and could no longer do the 14-hour flight to India. Now it was 1 a.m. No replacement crew and no other options.

That meant we had to stay in a hotel, and there were only three gate agents to process our hotel vouchers. I didn't get to the hotel until 2:30 a.m. and was told to return to the airport by 1 p.m. the next day for a 3 p.m. departure.

At the hotel, I managed to track down the pilot and chatted with him about the delay. He said it in plain terms: If the plane had been cleaned and catered on time and if Atlanta hadn't decided to fix an electronics item that was not essential to the safe operation of the flight, we would have made it.

There's simply no accounting for mismanagement, poor decision making, and sheer stupidity. Or after-the-fact misleading explanations. About 3 weeks after the incident, Delta sent me a $250 travel voucher, along with a letter explaining the delay as mechanical and safety related, claiming that safety was the airline's primary concern. All well and good, but that was *not* the reason the plane was delayed, delayed again, and then canceled.

You can't protect yourself from cancellations or delays. But you can be ready, anticipate them, and move quickly to recover. Here are some tips you can and should follow.

Insider Tips to Avoiding Delays/Cancellations

! Don't travel at end of the month—that's when most flight and cabin crews have worked their maximum hours for the month, and labor disputes are more likely to happen.

! Travel earlier in the day. If you miss a flight, you'll have more options to fly out. It's also been proven that the odds of a delay increase dramatically in the afternoon and evening—for example, in Boston's Logan Airport, flights between 7 a.m. and 1 p.m. are on time 80 percent of the time, while about half the flights in the evening are late.

! Fly on less busy travel days, Tuesday or Wednesday.

! Pick nonstop flights. Don't confuse this with "direct" flights, in which there is a stop but on the same aircraft. Nonstops go from point to point.

! Pick secondary, alternative airports. The Web site alternateairports. com is a great resource for finding small airports that may get you to your destination without the long lines.

! Don't choose an itinerary based on airport stats; check the individual flight number.

! Look at the departure board to determine your flight number and the gate it is scheduled to leave from. Then, check out the arrivals board for the truth—look for what is arriving at that gate.

Delay and Cancellation Statistics

As mentioned earlier, according to the USDOT, 2006 was quite possibly the most inconvenient year for air travel ever (with 2007 on track to be even worse). On-time performances continued dropping to an all-time low; 75.4 percent of flights were on time in 2006, down from 77.4 percent in 2005 and 78.1 percent in 2004.

According to flightstats.com, between May 25 and June 15, 2006, 22.7 percent of all flights at the 10 biggest airlines were late. This is an improvement over the 25 percent late rate the previous year. The average delay time remained the same at 53 minutes.

There are several resources to figure out which flights are late and, therefore, which ones to avoid. Now here's the trick: Many airlines will boast great on-time departure ratings, but their arrival rates are abysmal. Are the planes making a stop in the Bermuda Triangle? Not exactly. Planes are considered to have "departed" when they pull away from the gate, not when they're airborne! That means you can sit on the runway for 2 hours, but if you're not at the gate, you're not considered to be delayed. So when you're taking into consideration historical flight delays, look at the arrival on-time rankings, not the departure.

The **Federal Aviation Association** provides real-time airport status information, including the average length of flight delays by departure and arrival. For example, Dallas/Fort Worth Airport notes that due to weather and wind conditions, flights destined to Chicago O'Hare are averaging delays of

BUREAU OF TRANSPORTATION STATISTICS DATA FOR 2006

MONTH	ON-TIME ARRIVALS	ON TIME (%)	ARRIVAL DELAYS
January	457,831	78.76%	112,299
February	400,035	75.30%	118,610
March	460,681	76.12%	135,897
April	459,003	78.42%	118,715
May	471,933	78.27%	122,693
June	435,735	72.83%	150,683
July	457,860	73.70%	150,771
August	476,595	75.80%	140,784
September	445,850	76.22%	127,900
October	446,019	72.91%	153,067
November	448,580	76.52%	126,990
December	428,143	70.80%	157,128
2006 (annual)	5,388,265	75.45%	1,615,537

1 hour 13 minutes. General traffic is experiencing departure and arrival delays of 15 minutes. www.fly.faa.gov/flyfaa/usmap.jsp

The **Bureau of Transportation Statistics** (BTS) is a great resource to track historical data on flight arrivals and departures (see table below). The USDOT provides a monthly Air Travel Consumer Report, and the BTS began collecting details on the causes of flight delays back in June 2003. www.transtats.bts.gov

The Web site **www.flightarrivals.com** can give you real-time information on whether a particular flight is delayed. Just plug in the flight number, airline, and/or airport to get the information you need.

The Web site **www.flightstats.com** has both real-time information and historical data on delayed flights.

Avoiddelays.com provides historical data from the USDOT on the "worst offenders" of departure airports, the worst times to fly into delayed airports, and the most delayed flights. According to this, summer travelers should avoid the following "loser flights" (based on data from May 2006).

American Airlines 7:15 p.m. flight from La Guardia to Atlanta

American Eagle 5 p.m. flight from Newark to Raleigh-Durham

Comair 11:55 a.m. flight from La Guardia to Greenville/Spartanburg, SC

Continental 7:35 p.m. flight from Newark to Atlanta

ExpressJet 2:20 p.m. flight from Charlotte to Newark

DELAYED (%)	FLIGHTS CANCELED	CANCELED (%)	DIVERTED
19.32%	9,787	1.68%	1,370
22.33%	11,293	2.13%	1,309
22.45%	7,586	1.25%	1,053
20.28%	6,604	1.13%	1,029
20.35%	7,057	1.17%	1,236
25.18%	10,088	1.69%	1,809
24.27%	10,735	1.73%	1,878
22.39%	9,783	1.56%	1,570
21.87%	9,950	1.70%	1,237
25.02%	11,399	1.86%	1,233
21.66%	9,558	1.63%	1,069
25.98%	18,094	2.99%	1,393
22.62%	121,934	1.71%	16,186

ExpressJet 2:20 p.m. flight from Greenville/Spartanburg, SC, to Covington, KY/Cincinnati

ExpressJet 5:10 p.m. flight from Greenville/Spartanburg, SC, to Newark

ExpressJet 7:05 p.m. flight from Newark to Dayton

ExpressJet 7:30 p.m. flight from Newark to Omaha

ExpressJet 7:45 p.m. flight from Newark to Columbia, SC

Here's the breakdown of on-time performance percentages by airline, according to the Airline Quality Rating 2007.

AIRLINE	2006	2005
AirTran	74.6%	71.3%
Alaska	73.3%	69.7%
American	75.5%	76.9%
American Eagle	71.5%	76.2%
ATA	69.4%	81.3%
Atlantic Southeast	66.0%	70.9%
Comair	73.8%	80.1%
Continental	76.9%	73.4%
Delta	76.3%	76.3%
Frontier	80.7%	NA
Hawaiian	93.8%	NA
JetBlue	72.9%	71.4%
Mesa	73.3%	75.5%
Northwest	75.8%	75%
SkyWest	82.5%	76.8%
Southwest	80.2%	80.7%
United	73.9%	77.6%
US Airways	76.9%	76.2%

Passengers' Bill of Rights (aka the JetBlue Debacle)

According to the USDOT, in 2006, nearly 400,000 (or 5.6 percent) commercial flights had departure delays of 30 minutes or more. Nearly 60,000 flights (less than 1 percent) were held on the runway for up to 2 hours, and more than 1,000 flights were delayed for at least 3 hours. Thirty-six flights were stuck for more than 5 hours.

You probably remember the Valentine's Day JetBlue debacle of February 2007, when passengers were stuck on the runway for up to *10 hours* . . . with no ability to exit the airplane, limited resources of food and water, and increasingly unusable restroom facilities. A heavy snowstorm and a breakdown in the airline's operation system had caused JetBlue to cancel 1,000 flights over the course of 6 days. More than 130,000 passengers were left stranded.

In April 2007, the US Public Interest Research Group and Aviation Consumer Action Project joined to form the Coalition for an Airline Passengers' Bill of Rights. On the same day, the Senate Commerce Committee held a hearing in Washington, DC, to discuss legislation sponsored by senators Barbara Boxer (D-CA) and Olympia J. Snowe (R-ME). The bill would create a federally mandated passengers' bill of rights and allow passengers to deboard the airplane after 3 hours on the ground, unless the pilot believes that this would compromise passengers' safety or that the plane will soon be cleared for departure. Food, water, and adequate restroom facilities must be provided.

The airlines, of course, argued that new arbitrary passenger rights rules would only delay flights more and lobbied hard in Congress to let them make their own rules.

For example, after thunderstorms seriously disrupted American Airlines' operations on December 29, 2006, the carrier announced it was adopting an internal operations rule stating that it would not hold passengers on grounded airplanes for more than 4 hours.

"[B]ecause no similar situation has occurred in the 80-plus years of American's history, it is a rule that may never be used again," American said in statements handed out to Congress and the news media at the time.

Well, guess what? The much-promoted 4-hour rule didn't last very long. On April 24, 2007, another series of storms kept passengers hostage again on American flights.

In the case of JetBlue, after issuing an apology from founder and CEO David Neeleman—who also tried to get out ahead of the story and make that apology to everyone from the US Congress to David Letterman—the airline also issued its own passengers' bill of rights, which stated that travelers could be let off a plane that had been on the ground for 5 hours. And it also provided for compensation to passengers who had been delayed.

The JetBlue response, coupled with intense airline industry lobbying of Congress, was enough to keep various passengers' bills of rights laws locked up in committees—hence, no pro consumer legislation. It wasn't enough to save Neeleman. His own board of directors ousted him a few months later.

In the meantime, you can find the contract of carriage on each airline through individual Web sites or visit www.onetravel.com and click on the "Rules of the Air" link.

Airline Medical Issues

Forget fear of flying. How about fear of getting sick at 37,000 feet? Of course, it doesn't help much when there are headlines in the news like "Dead Man Found in Jet's Bathroom" and "Dead Woman Moved to First Class."

If you're afraid of getting ill or injured while on a plane, rest assured that most major carriers contract with third-party medical care providers that offer consultations from the ground. That means if there's a problem (and no doctor on board), there can still be some effective communication with an expert on the ground to assess the situation properly.

The most common complaints from passengers are fainting while in the air and gastrointestinal problems, followed by respiratory problems and cardiac emergencies. If you get sick or injured while flying Northwest, you're in luck (okay, it's all relative)—the Mayo Clinic offers the airline advice from the ground. A company called MedAire works with more than 80 airlines to provide assistance to those in the air. Flights also have to provide a medical emergency kit, and since 2004, airplanes also have to have an automatic external defibrillator.

One tip is to bring any necessary medications in your carry-on. Don't risk losing them along with your luggage or getting stuck on a delayed flight without them. Even with the new liquid bans in place, you are allowed to bring prescription and over-the-counter medications, and juice or liquid nutrition or gels for a passenger with a disability or medical condition. Life-supporting and life-sustaining equipment is also allowed, except for oxygen tanks.

If you're less worried about catching avian flu on board and more concerned about plane crashes—well, it probably won't help to spout the old adage about your being more likely to die in a car crash than a plane. But it's true. In fact, in 2003, the National Safety Council found that your lifetime odds of dying in an "air or space transport accident" are 1 in 5,051 (http://www.nsc.org/lrs/statinfo/odds.htm). What does that mean? That it's less likely to happen than dying while riding on a three-wheeled motor vehicle; on a bus, train, or streetcar; by drowning; or in an earthquake, to name a few.

If you're still obsessing about airline safety, not to mention crashes, their causes, and frequency, check out the Web site **www.planecrashinfo.com,** which provides up-to-date news on plane accidents around the world. From small jets to major carriers, small fires to devastating midair collisions, it's all here—you can learn the time of the crash, the number of fatalities, and the cause of the crash if known.

AirSafe.com is also a handy resource to learn about accidents and fatal events listed by airline, by model, and by region. Ironically, the site also offers tips on how to deal with the fear of flying and air rage.

Low-Cost Carriers

Budget airlines. They're the new darlings of the airline industry—no-frills airlines that can get you point to point at a fraction of the cost of legacy carriers. These low-cost carriers usually offer one class of service and one type of aircraft (usually the Airbus A320 or Boeing 737), don't offer frequent flier schemes, and tend to fly out of lower-cost secondary or tertiary airports.

An interesting phenomenon has emerged with the arrival of low-cost carriers. It's called the Southwest Effect (named after Southwest Airlines but can refer to any low-cost carriers like JetBlue, Spirit, and Frontier), and it essentially means that when a budget airline enters a new market, other airlines have to compete and lower their prices. Lower prices can mean increased customers, which changes the market drastically. The Southwest Effect took place in Dallas, where the airline is based. It also took place in Baltimore, Denver, Pittsburgh, and Philadelphia, among others.

Budget airlines are often touted as being a great alternative for travelers, particularly when flying within a foreign country or continent. Say, for example, that you want to fly to Rome, but flights from New York are outrageous. (Summer prices can start at $1,300 per person. Ouch!) The idea is that you can fly from New York to London (a slightly more palatable $600 on British Airways), then hop on a low-fare carrier to any point in Europe for a fraction of the price. Ryanair and EasyJet in Europe have been known to tout fares as low as $1! That, of course, is not including taxes and fees, which can push up the price to well over $100, but that's still a savings in the end.

It's certainly not a foolproof plan, for several reasons. For one thing, low-cost carriers tend to fly out of low-cost airports, which means you'll have to get yourself from one airport to the next between your international and domestic flights. Getting from Heathrow to Stansted, where Ryanair flies into, can take up to 2 hours via coach, and it's suggested that you leave at least 3½ hours between landing at one airport and checking in to another. The coach costs about $50 round-trip. And don't forget that you'll be lugging around your suitcases. Then there are the almost (and sometimes totally) hidden fees that you'll be hit with—everything from a can of soda on board to check-in bags. In one case—mine—one low-cost carrier charged more than $1,100 for excess bags that any other carrier would have allowed—on a 40-minute flight from London to Paris! (More on that later . . . much more.)

That said, budget carriers can be a great option, particularly if you're planning on traveling frequently within one destination and can travel light—very light.

Whichbudget.com is a great resource to find out which budget carriers travel where, but here are a few of the low-cost carriers that have been drawing a lot of attention in recent years.

Ryanair is an Irish airline headquartered in Dublin that saw phenomenal growth after the deregulation of the airline industry in 1997. It is currently the largest low-cost carrier in Europe, with its largest base in London's Stansted Airport. Currently, Ryanair has 487 routes across 25 countries in Europe, with 20 bases throughout the continent, including Dublin International, Cork International, Liverpool, Stansted, London Luton, Frankfurt-Hahn, Barcelona Girona, Stockholm Skavsta, Rome Ciampino, and a few others. www.ryanair.com

EasyJet is based out of London's Luton Airport and offers more than 224 routes among 67 European cities. EasyJet's other bases include: Gatwick, Stansted, Edinburgh, Glasgow International, Berlin-Schönefeld, Basel Airport, Geneva-Cointrin, Paris-Orly, Milan Malpensa, Belfast International, and a few smaller ones. www.easyjet.com

Wizz Air is a Polish/Hungarian low-cost airline that can be a great resource for getting you around central and western Europe. There are stops all through Poland, Croatia, Hungary, and Romania, as well as Barcelona, Corfu, London, Glasgow, Brussels, and Paris, among others. www.wizzair.com

Flybe is a British airline based at Exeter Airport in England, with 56 destinations across 12 countries throughout Europe. It has a particularly heavy presence in France, with 13 stops throughout the country, including Avignon, Bordeaux, Nice, Paris, and Toulouse. www.flybe.com

Oasis Hong Kong Airlines was established in 2006 and is based out of Hong Kong International Airport. The small fleet of five aircrafts started out flying between London Gatwick and Hong Kong but quickly added on service between Vancouver and Hong Kong and plans to add on direct service to Oakland, Chicago, Cologne, Berlin, and Milan. www.oasis-air.com

Jetstar is the budget subsidiary of Qantas that was developed to compete with low-cost carrier Virgin Blue. The airline covers much of Australia, from Adelaide to the Whitsunday Coast, and travels internationally to Christchurch and locations throughout Asia, including Hong Kong,

Manila, Phnom Penh, Phuket, and Singapore. www.jetstar.com

IndiGo is one of India's newest low-cost domestic carriers, based out of Indira Gandhi and Chatrapati Shivaji airports. The airline currently serves 14 destinations but hopes to fly to about 30 Indian cities over the next few years. Currently, you can fly between Delhi and Jaipur, Mumbai, Goa, Bangalore, Chennai, and several other major cities in India. book.goindigo.in

Air Arabia was the first low-cost airline in the Middle East, embarking on its first flight in 2003. Based in Sharjah (the third largest emirate in the United Arab Emirates), the airline services a quite a large number of cities in South Asia and the Middle East, including India, Syria, Egypt, Kazakhstan, Jordan, Bahrain, Lebanon, Sri Lanka, Syria, Saudi Arabia, Qatar, Iran, and Oman. www.airarabia.com

Vueling Airlines has been growing rapidly since it started services in 2004, with a fleet that's grown from 2 airplanes to 21. The airline is based out of El Prat International Airport in Barcelona, Spain, and travels to 23 destinations, including Amsterdam, Athens, Brussels, Paris, and Rome, among others. www.vueling.com

Sky Express is a new Russian airline that just began its services in 2006, operating out of Moscow Vnukovo Airport. The airline focuses on domestic routes and can take you to off-the-beaten path destinations such as Sochi, Murmansk, Rostov-on-Don, and Kaliningrad. www.skyexpress.ru/en

Skyway Robbery

There are some drawbacks to discount carriers and plenty of them. How do you think many of these airlines keep their costs so low? By nickel-and-diming their passengers. That means you'll pay for everything from food on board to booking through a live agent rather than online, plus taxes, fees, and surcharges. But the big one? Baggage. And no one knows that better than I do.

In the United States, most airlines enforce a policy of two checked bags per passenger, each not to exceed 50 pounds. And at some airlines, a bag weighing more than 50 but under 70 pounds will cost you an additional $25. It's annoying, and for many passengers, it's an inconvenience, but consider this: At least you're not flying an airline called EasyJet.

When I decided to check out EasyJet, I made an online booking (traveling with one of my staffers) to fly from Luton Airport outside of London to Paris. The fares were certainly cheap enough—about $50 each way. And there was an additional optional box to check on the Internet booking form:

The airline said I was allowed only one check-in bag with a 20-kilogram limit, but if I checked the box and paid an additional fee—5 British pounds per passenger (or about $20 for two people)—I'd be allowed to check two bags. I checked the box. It seemed fair enough.

I arrived 2 hours ahead of time for my flight to Paris, and that's when the airline hit me with a whammy—and a big one.

The counter agent at EasyJet claimed I was 40 kilograms over. How could that be? I had checked the box. I had spent the extra money for the second bag for two people—thus, we were checking in two bags each—and each was 20 kilos or less in weight. I had been careful not to overpack.

But the airline still claimed I was 40 kilos over and they were going to charge me. I wasn't happy, but there was nothing I could do. Was the charge $25? Maybe $50? Hardly. The excess bag charges for one 48-minute flight from the United Kingdom to Paris: a whopping $514.69! I was trapped. I had no choice but to pay. And 2 days later, on another EasyJet flight, they charged me $585.62.

How did this happen? It's all in the fine print. For an additional charge I can check in a second bag on EasyJet, but the airline does not increase the weight allowance—no matter how many additional bags you check!

As a result, I had paid less than $200 for two people to fly on two separate EasyJet flights with baggage that was well within the size and weight limits of any US domestic or international carrier. And the bag charges? $1,100.31!

Now comes the absurd part—I went back and checked the advertised fares for the flights I was on. I could have easily stopped a total of 20 strangers at the airport and offered them a free trip to Paris or London—round-trip—for what it cost two people to check in an additional one bag each!

I checked to see what it would cost me to courier 44 kilos to Paris, not from London but from Los Angeles: $566 on DHL, delivered to my hotel.

I also checked on how much my round-trip fare (plus my companion's) would have been on Air France flying from Heathrow to Charles de Gaulle: $283 each, with two checked bags each allowed, or $566, substantially less than the $1,100 bag charges plus the EasyJet airfare.

EasyJet is by no means the only carrier attempting to get away with sky-way robbery. British Airways has recently instituted the one-bag rule (plus excessive excess-bag charges on the second bag) on their flights from Heathrow to just about everywhere except the United States.

And low-cost carrier Ryanair is even worse. Their weight limit per passenger for checked bags isn't 20 kilos—it's just 15! But as in my case with

EasyJet, most people won't discover this until they're already at the airport, and it's too late to do anything except pay.

On the Ryanair Web site (www.ryanair.com), much like EasyJet, you can quickly book inexpensive flights. For example, with only 2 days' notice, I was able to find a flight from London to Venice for just £29 ($58) one way and about £20 ($40) on the return. But nowhere on the site's main page, or even on the booking page where I had to give my credit card to confirm the reservation and buy the tickets, was there a disclosure about the airline's equally outrageous baggage policies. But after searching, I found it on another "terms and conditions" link, and you've got to see it to believe it. And I quote:

! A Baggage Fee is charged for the carriage of each item of Checked Baggage. The Baggage Fee may be prepaid at the current discounted rate of €6/£5 per item of baggage/per one-way flight when making your reservation. If the Baggage Fee is paid after you have made your booking, either at the airport or through a Ryanair call centre, the full rate per item of baggage/per one-way flight is charged.

! Passenger may purchase up to 5 items of baggage per person. Please Note: That the total Checked Baggage Allowance per person is 15 kilograms irrespective of the number of items of baggage purchased per person. There is no baggage allowance for infants.

! Any passenger checking in baggage exceeding the 15-kilogram checked baggage allowance per person will be charged an excess baggage fee currently at a rate of €8/£5.50 per kilo (or local currency equivalent).

! Passengers may not use the unused checked baggage allowance of other passengers. No pooling/sharing of the checked baggage allowance is permitted, even within a party traveling on the same Confirmation Number.

! One item of hand baggage per person, weighing no more than 10 kilograms and with dimensions of less than 55 × 40 × 20 centimeters, may be carried into the aircraft cabin (restrictions apply from certain countries).

Ouch . . . the fine print says it all. Check anything more than 15 kilograms and mortgage your house. I suspect that pretty soon they'll start weighing *you*.

I e-mailed Sir Stelios Haji-Ioannou, the Greek-born British entrepreneur who founded EasyJet and a man who I've met on numerous occasions at various travel industry conferences (where we've both been speakers), and asked him to

(continued on page 50)

I Don't Hate All Travel Agents . . . Just Bad Ones

I've been approached almost weekly by travel agents who ask me, "Why do you hate travel agents?" I don't. Back in the days before airlines were deregulated, the majority of airline tickets were processed by the airlines, not agents, yet, on any trip my family took, we always went to a travel agent. Why? Because of his expertise, advice, and knowledge of the industry.

Before deregulation, it was a simpler system—there were four classes of airfares: day coach, night coach, day first class, and night first class, and most airlines cost about the same. After deregulation, the system became far more complex, and the last thing the airlines wanted to do was hire more reservation agents. The simple solution was to outsource to travel agents—give them access to the computers without having to pay any salaries, provide health insurance, or cover maternity leave or vacation time.

The result was that travel agents held on to an artificial monopoly on fares and rates for nearly 27 years—until the Internet reared its head. The electronic age meant that anyone could research destinations, compare prices, and reserve their flights, hotels, and car rentals, all from the comfort of their own homes. And yet, people are still using travel agents. In fact, according to the American Society of Travel Agents (ASTA), its members sell 51 percent of airline tickets, 87 percent of cruises, 81 percent of packaged travel, 47 percent of hotels, and 45 percent of car rentals.

Nearly everyone predicted the demise of travel agents, but travel agents persevered—not the lazy ones who were embedded in the airline's computer system but the ones who targeted the right audience (baby boomers and mature travelers) and provided *good* service. That means not just planning your travel itinerary but also negotiating with airlines, hotels, and cruise lines for deeper discounts or scoring space that is sold out. That also means checking on your itinerary frequently to see if better rates come up. If there are any problems on your trip, your travel agent should be your emergency contact and your advocate.

And don't forget, you have a responsibility as well. If you do use a travel agent, it's up to you to find one with whom you can develop a good working relationship. Check with ASTA (www.astanet.com) to see if a particular agent has had any complaints in the past. Compare your agent's quoted fares with ones that you find online to see who comes out the winner. Ask the agent directly if he or she received "override commissions" or a "preferred supplier" with an airline, hotel, or cruise line. If so, remind the agent that he or she is expected to work for you, first and foremost. And if it's not working, go to someone else.

Corporate Travel Agents

Chances are that if you work for a medium to large corporation, your company has a travel policy. And chances are equally good that the company's travel policy requires you to book your travel through an in-house corporate travel agency—and, in many cases, through a "preferred" airline or hotel.

Why does your company elect to use an in-house agency (or, perhaps more appropriately, force you to use one)? For years, the argument has been that it not only allows the corporate bean counters to manage travel budgets, but that the volume of travel the company creates allows the agency to negotiate corporate travel discounts at both airlines and hotels that benefit the corporation's bottom line.

That sounds good until you begin to deconstruct those "discounts." Did you ever wondered who pays full-fare coach or first-class tickets? With the exception of extreme last-minute travelers, the answer is no one.

The reality, one airline CEO recently told me, is that airlines intentionally publish these mostly artificial full fares precisely in order to offer corporate discounts against them. Yes, you're getting a corporate discount—but against a ridiculously high fare that no one pays anyway.

The same is true for hotels. I can cite numerous examples (because I've experienced them myself) where the hotel corporate discount rate for rooms is significantly higher than the rate I can get myself by either calling the hotel directly or going through a third-party Web site.

Here's a no-brainer executive survey: Ask anyone working for a corporation if they—given the choice— would book their own personal travel through the in-house corporate agency, and you'll get an immediate and overwhelming response: no way. They'd rather book it themselves, and for good reason: They've seen the ticket prices on the "negotiated fare" tickets the corporate travel agency has booked or the bills at the hotels where the corporate travel agency reserved the "corporate discount" rooms. And those ticket prices and room rates are disproportionately higher than what the executives could find and confirm on their own.

Example: Recently a friend needed to fly between Los Angeles and San Francisco on a business trip. He had to go through his corporate agency because of the company travel policy. The round-trip fare: a whopping $384 for the 42-minute flight (about the same cost as flying between New York and London!), and that was listed as a corporate discount—in coach.

He then picked up the phone and called the airline's toll-free number

(continued)

and asked for their cheapest available coach fare between the two California cities on the exact flights his company agency had already booked. Are you sitting down? The fare: $54.30 each way, or $108.60 round-trip! That's less than a third of what his company was paying. And yet, when he went to his management, told them about the discrepancy, and offered to save them money by buying the tickets himself, he was told he still had to book the flight through the agency—company policy.

This price disparity is absurd. And it is repeated hundreds—if not thousands—of times a day, thus costing American corporations millions of dollars.

It's also costing them time. A number of years ago, I was working for a company that had a corporate-preferred travel supplier policy; I could only fly one particular airline. I was with four colleagues in Mobile, Alabama, and needed to get to New York. Under company policy, the airline that flew the most-direct route (and with the lowest-fare tickets) was not our "preferred" airline. Instead, we were forced to fly in the opposite direction and connect through Houston, on a much more expensive ticket on a much later flight. We also arrived in New York nearly 6 hours later than if had we taken the flight we wanted.

How did this benefit the corporation? The company spent more money than it ever had to spend. How did this benefit us? We lost valuable, productive time when we were forced to fly an inconvenient route—all because of a corporate travel policy that didn't take into account common sense or long-term financial planning.

I have a simple win-win solution for both companies and executives that will make everyone happy and, in some cases, maybe even mildly ecstatic. It's a corporate travel policy that involves mutual trust but mostly common sense, and, oh yes, let's not forget basic arithmetic.

Here it goes: CFOs should look at individual annual budgets for their

explain these stratospheric charges. His response, in an e-mail back to me:

"Are you saying you believe our people got the weights wrong? Or you are surprised at the per-kilo rate of EasyJet and the dollar-sterling exchange rate?

"I believe our rates are competitive for European economy short haul. . . ."

Competitive? If this is being competitive, okay, I give up. EasyJet might win the short-haul airfare race in Europe. But based on these charges, if we are responsible (and, hopefully, fiscally sane) travelers, they deserve to lose the marathon.

executives who frequently travel. Then they should add 20 percent to those budgets. And then do something revolutionary: Trust the executive to be a better shopper than the corporate travel agency. Each executive would be told that his or her travel budget has a cap of 20 percent above what the company spent the year before. Then the executive would be told to book his or her own company travel, in any class of service, at any fare, through any booking engine or platform, on any airline, and staying at any hotel. And yes, the executive would be allowed to keep any mileage or points earned.

Then, at the end of each year, the total amount the executive spent on travel would be deducted from that travel budget cap, and whatever was left would then be split between the company and the executive as an extra bonus—over and above any other bonus program to which the executive might be entitled.

Talk about an incentive: The motivated executive is rewarded for being smart and for saving the company money. The company is rewarded by the creativity and comparison-shopping techniques of the motivated executive. It is, indeed, a win-win.

I have nothing against in-house corporate travel agencies if they are truly getting great discounts. But preferred supplier relationships at corporate in-house travel agencies hardly benefit the executive, and from a financial perspective, they don't always benefit the company. For the moment, they seem more like expensive conveniences.

All it takes is one large corporation to embrace my idea of trusting the employees to negotiate better deals, and the myth of the so-called corporate discounts will be proven. Instead, we will have an era of financial responsibility, prudent travel thinking, mutual rewards, and happy travelers. And that's a travel policy no company will have problems enforcing.

The moral of this story is simple. If you're a backpacker owning nothing more than T-shirts and flip-flops—and they'd better not be heavy flip-flops—or you're a drifter with no bags, then EasyJet, Ryanair, and, on some flights, British Airways are the airlines for you. But if you're a real traveler, even with modest check-in bags, be prepared for serious—and in my experience, heart attack–inducing—sticker shock. Bottom line: I am no longer flying EasyJet or Ryanair. This isn't just bad passenger service. This is intentional, greedy, and mean-spirited. And in my book, this constitutes nothing less than a declaration of war against all of us. It's time to fight back. I would suggest you avoid these airlines until they change these policies, but if you choose to fly them, remember, you've been warned.

Airline Seats

If you've ever sat in the back of the plane, chances are you've had to fold yourself into a pretzel shape just to fit into the seat. In-flight comfort hasn't been high on the airlines' list of priorities. So how can you score that coveted seat with that precious extra 2 inches of legroom? Well, most airlines won't let you choose the emergency exit row seat when you book online. But there are some options out there.

Our friends at **SeatGuru.com** have put together one of the most helpful travel Web sites, offering airlines' contact information, frequent flier clubs, alliance partners, and, not least of all, seat information. Through SeatGuru.com, you can find out what is the best seat on *each* aircraft on almost every airline! Just click on the airplane that you're flying and you'll get a chart that details which seats are "good," which are "poor," which are the exit-row seats, and which are too close for comfort to the lavatories.

Scroll over the image and you'll even get detailed notes like "Video: Overhead TV" or "Seats 21 D, E, F have extra legroom due to the exit." The proximity of the lavatory can be bothersome. Passengers often congregate in this area as they wait for the lavatory. The tray tables are in the armrests, making the armrests immovable and slightly reducing seat width. You can store baggage under the seats at Row 20. This row is missing a window. It can get very cold by the exits during flight."

Check out the diagram of an American 757 and a United 747, on the opposite page, courtesy of SeatGuru.

There's more. Skytrax's Web site, **www.airlinequality.com,** provides information on the typical recline, pitch, and width of each class of seat on most major airlines ("pitch" refers to how much room is between rows, from seat back to seat back). A United Airlines 747, for example, typically has a pitch of 88 inches in first class, 55 inches in business class, and 31 inches in economy. The site also offers seat tips by airlines: For example, on a US Airways Boeing 767, a reader notes that the economy class seats 12 C, D, and E have more legroom due to the bulkhead positioning. (Remember to do a comparison check on SeatGuru. For example, these particular seats do offer more room, but there are some drawbacks, such as lack of luggage floor storage space and a too-close movie screen.)

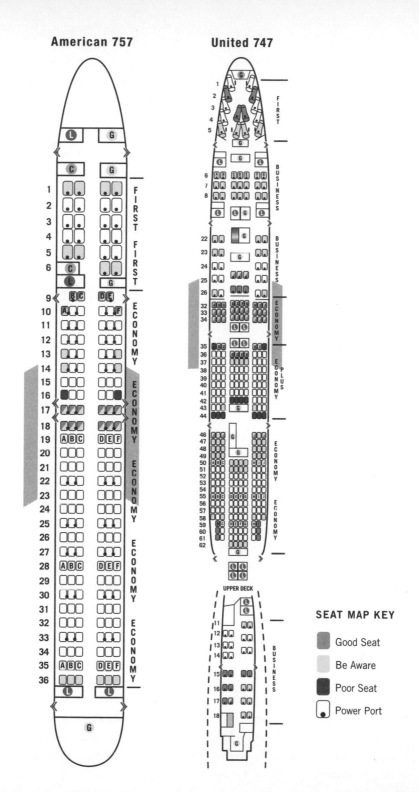

American 757   **United 747**

SEAT MAP KEY

- ■ Good Seat
- ▨ Be Aware
- ■ Poor Seat
- ▢ Power Port

(The site www.airlinequality.com is also a great resource to compare airlines' VIP lounges, get reviews of specific flight routes, and find Skytrax's own World Airline Survey, which measures 35 aspects of customer satisfaction based on more than 13 million responses. See www.worldairlineawards.com.)

The Web site **flatseats.com** also offers useful information on first- and business-class lie-flat and flat-bed seats. You can check out seat ratings for many airlines, ranked from "a great sleep" to "uncomfortable." (Consider skipping your next flight on Biman Bangladesh, Czech Airlines, Egyptair, and Malev Hungarian.)

Here are some of my favorite long-haul business and first-class seats. (Remember that many of these dimensions are not standardized fleetwide, so different aircrafts will have different dimensions.)

AIRLINE	RECLINE (degrees)	WIDTH (inches)	PITCH (inches)
British Airways	180	20	73
South African Airways	180	20.5	78
Virgin Atlantic	180	22	79.5
Air New Zealand	180	22	76
Air Canada	180	21	63
Lufthansa	180	19.7	48
Thai Air	170	20	60
United	150	19	55

Other airlines to keep an eye on: Delta is installing lie-flat seats in 10 of its Boeing 777 aircrafts, reducing its 50-seat business class cabin to 43 seats. The airline plans to have this feature installed in all 77 of its 777 and 767 aircrafts by 2010. American Airlines recently introduced its Next Generation Business Class in its Boeing 777 fleet, with lie-flat seats, on-demand audio and video, and better overhead storage. Now that's called customer service.

Bankruptcy

The airlines have been reeling since September 11 and are only just now starting to work their way out of bankruptcy protection. A business that cannot pay its debts can file with a federal bankruptcy court for bankruptcy protection under either Chapter 7 or Chapter 11. A Chapter 7 filing means that the business is liquidating—that is, selling all of its assets and distributing the money to its creditors. A Chapter 11 filing, which is much more common in the airline industry, means that a bankruptcy court will oversee the business's reorganization to keep the company afloat. This can mean that the business does not have to pay some or all of its debts, can cancel contracts, and can slash benefits, pensions, and the number of employees. And those are just the airlines that filed for Chapter 11 protection and actually recovered.

US Airways filed for Chapter 11 in August 2002 and emerged in September 2005 after merging with America West.

United Airlines filed for Chapter 11 in December 2002 and emerged in February 2006.

Air Canada filed for Chapter 11 in April 2003 and emerged in September 2004.

Northwest Airlines filed for Chapter 11 in September 2005 and emerged in mid 2007.

Delta filed for Chapter 11 in September 2005 and emerged in April 2007 after fighting off a $10 billion hostile takeover by US Airways.

So what should you do if you're flying on a bankrupt airline? Remember, bankrupt doesn't necessarily mean defunct. But you still need to protect yourself.

❗ Buy your tickets with a credit card. The Fair Credit Billing Act guarantees that you'll get your money back from your original ticket if an airline goes under. Keep in mind that you have to submit your airline tickets and receipt to the credit card company within 60 days and explain that the airline went bankrupt before you could use the ticket.

❗ Buy paper tickets. If another airline is even going to consider honoring a bankrupt airline's tickets, it will be easier to make the switch with a paper ticket than an electronic ticket or a receipt.

❗ Buy trip interruption/cancellation travel insurance, but read the fine print: Your insurance should cover "carrier default" or bankruptcy.

❗ Your frequent flier miles aren't necessarily in jeopardy. Your miles are only really at risk when an airline files for Chapter 7 (i.e., liquidation). So you can continue to earn and use your miles. But if the airline does go out of business, you may be out of luck. When National Airlines went under in 2002, members of the National Comps frequent flier program lost their points. MGM Grand Airlines closed in 1992, leaving 33,000 MGM Grand Premiere members empty-handed. However, when Pan Am went under, members' WorldPass miles were transferred to Delta, and TWA's frequent flier miles were incorporated into American's AAdvantage program. Remember that frequent flier miles aren't made of gold; they're not going to gain any value, so why not use them—or redeem them on a more stable partner airline—if you're unsure of an airline's future?

Airline Fares

In spring 2007, it made headline news when Southwest Airlines raised fares systemwide . . . by $2. The airline raised its prices by $1 on flights under 250 miles as well as flights out of its home base in Dallas. Flights between 250 miles and 750 miles were increased by $2 each way. Why would $2 make such waves? This small raise, which was immediately matched by American on routes where it competes with Southwest, represents millions of additional dollars to each carrier's bottom line. It's not going to stop there.

This isn't the first time that low-cost carriers have raised prices. Earlier in 2007, both JetBlue and Southwest announced hikes in airfares, citing jet-fuel prices as their primary motivation.

There's not much we can do about the impact of fuel prices on airfares. Between 1991 and 1999, jet-fuel prices averaged $0.56 per gallon and never went above $0.65. Between 2003 and 2005, the average market price of jet fuel rose from $0.88 to $1.72 per gallon, and after hurricanes Katrina and Rita in 2005, it spiked to $3.13 per gallon.

According to the Air Transportation Association of America, a jet-fuel increase of 1 cent per gallon can cost the industry an additional $195 million. And from 2000 to 2005, the industry's spending on fuel literally doubled, from $16.4 billion to an estimated $33 billion. The price of jet fuel has risen 120 percent since 2001 and 28 percent since 2005.

Fuel Price Monitor

To cover their losses, the airlines employed a clever marketing strategy: A onetime $10 or more fare increase can shift a market away from them. But ten $2 fare increases spread out over 2 months is something the public will tolerate better—or barely notice.

Well, I noticed. And you should, too. The airlines play this game not only with fares but with capacity. If an airline has four flights per day between two locations running at 70 percent of load and can pull one flight out—and allocate that aircraft on a route that can get them a higher fare yield per passenger—it will quietly do so. Result: three flights running at 94 percent full, and then, because seats are tougher to get, the airline also raises the fares. So the end result? We're getting hit with a double whammy—increased fares and decreased capacity.

Bereavement Fares

Bereavement fares are a "courtesy" about which the airlines have been, well, rude. In theory, if a passenger loses a close relative, he presumably needs to fly quickly to a funeral or family gathering. He asks the airline for a bereavement or "compassion" fare. And, again, in theory, the airline offers that passenger a discounted emergency fare to that destination. The tickets are also supposed to be unusually flexible, meaning that the return ticket can be scheduled anytime within a year without any penalty. This isn't something you can do online—you'll have to talk to a ticket agent and be prepared to offer some proof of death.

You should also find out how the airline defines "family"—whether that means parents, grandparents, and children or extends to uncles, nieces, nephews, etc. American Airlines, for example, offers customers bereavement fares when traveling due to a medical emergency or death of a family member but does not limit this to immediate family of the passenger. Domestic partners are also allowed.

United Airlines offers about 50 percent off full-fare coach tickets, which applies to immediate family members (that can include domestic partners). This fare also applies to medical emergencies, which can include hospital, hospice program, urgent care, or treatment. The traveler needs to provide the name of the family member, relationship, funeral home, hospital/hospice, and director's or physician's name and phone number. Travel must occur within 7 days of purchasing the ticket, and your return ticket is open-ended.

Continental recently replaced its half-off bereavement fare with 5 percent off tickets up to $499.99 one way, 5 percent for tickets up to $999.99 round-trip, 10 percent off tickets $500 and higher one way, and 10 percent for tickets $1,000 and above round-trip. US Airways eliminated all of its bereavement fares in January 2006. Alaska Air recently reduced its bereavement discount from 50 percent to 25 percent. As of 2005, Northwest Airlines requires a WorldPerks number for customers to get discounted emergency fares within the United States and Canada.

Even as bereavement fares are slipping away, the real problem is this: Even the most flexible bereavement fares aren't necessarily the lowest prices out there. For years, travelers have complained to me that after jumping through hoops to get a 10 percent discount, they wound up with fares that were even higher than if they had just searched on sites like SideStep and Kayak or on an opaque bidding site like Priceline. While it's good news that discounted and last-minute fares can be available online, it's not exactly fair to ask a grieving traveler to spend hours providing documentation for a 10 percent fare reduction from a full-fare ticket when a substantially discounted ticket is easily accessible online. The only catch: Deeply discounted online tickets don't necessarily have flexible return dates. Back in 2004, there was

Watch Out for Fees

Our friends at Bankrate.com put together this handy chart on what kind of fees you can expect to get nailed with the next time you fly. All rates are accurate as of June 2007.

Air Travel Fee 411
Here are some air travel fees and taxes you'll likely encounter while paying for your next flight.

- **Domestic passenger ticket tax:** 7.5 percent tax on the price of airfare. (This goes into the Airport and Airway Trust Fund to maintain the air transit system.)

- **Segment tax:** $3.40 fee for each takeoff and landing. Change planes and you'll pay twice. (This goes into the trust fund.)

- **Rural airport tax:** 7.5 percent tax on the price of the ticket if you fly into or from a regional airport. You'll pay either this or the domestic passenger ticket tax, depending on whether you're flying through a major or rural airport. (This goes into the trust fund.)

- **Passenger facility charge:** up to $4.50 (varies by airport) each time you use a different airport. Can be charged up to twice one way. (This goes to the airports to offset maintenance and expansion.)

- **Flights to and from Alaska or Hawaii:** $15 for a round-trip flight between the United States or Canada and either Alaska or Hawaii. (This goes into the trust fund.)

- **International departure tax:** $15.10 to leave the United States for a foreign destination, but only if you're not paying the domestic passenger ticket tax. (This goes into the trust fund.)

even a bill introduced in the US Senate to eliminate bereavement fares completely and guarantee that the airlines would provide the lowest possible fare for emergency-case passengers. Again, as with most passenger rights legislation, it was DOA. But the good news is that in many airline markets, you can also get discounted one-way tickets.

One exception: As of April 4, 2003, American Airlines began offering "compassion fares" for relatives and friends of soldiers who are listed as deceased, injured, missing in action, or prisoners of war. American still holds on to one of the better bereavement fare programs out there, as their

! **International arrival tax:** $15.10 to arrive in the United States from a foreign destination, but only if you're not paying the domestic passenger ticket tax. (This goes into the trust fund.)

! **Customs user fee** (if arriving from outside the United States): $5.50. (This is set by the Department of Homeland Security.)

! **Immigration user fee** (if arriving from outside the United States): $7. (This is set by the Department of Homeland Security.)

! **Security fee:** $2.50, up to $5 one-way. (This is set by the Department of Homeland Security.)

! **APHIS (Animal and Plant Health Inspection Service) passenger fee** (if arriving from outside the United States): $5. (This is set by the Department of Homeland Security.)

! **Fuel surcharges:** at the airline's discretion, to offset fuel costs.

! **Paper ticket charge:** Some airlines may charge up to $50 to provide a paper copy of your ticket, rather than an e-copy. Some online vendors will also add a similar fee, in addition to what the airlines charge.

! **Phone reservation charge:** Some airlines and online sellers will charge extra if you book by phone instead of online.

! **Change fee:** Need to change your itinerary after you've bought the ticket? The airline or the online seller may charge you.

© 2007 Bankrate Inc., all rights reserved, used by permission.

policies are not set in stone—you can speak directly with an agent on the phone to negotiate a price, you don't need to book the return portion of your flight, and there is no change fee to book a new flight.

Adoption Fares

Here's a hidden and unpublished discount fare that some airlines are offering to folks who are flying overseas to adopt a child. Delta offers discounted adoption fares, and Northwest Airlines and KLM offer "Special Delivery" fares to families who are adopting children in more than 100 destinations throughout Asia, Africa, Europe, India, and the Middle East. These fares can be discounted as much as 65 percent, but it's the flexibility that makes them worthwhile—no advance purchase is required, penalties are waived for cancellations or changes, and you are able to have open returns and stopovers. And remember, not only is the round-trip fare discounted for the adopting parent, but the airline also sells special discount one-way fares for the child about to be adopted.

Flight Passes

You may not have heard of these—they're a handy little secret that some airlines usually offer to frequent fliers. A flight pass means that you can pay a flat fee for several flights. It can be a great deal if you're traveling for business or embarking on a long trip that requires scheduling several different flights. But if it sounds too good to be true, that means it's time to look at the fine print. Flight pass fees can be compounded by heavy taxes, and the booking process can be complicated—you usually can't just hop on the next available flight but have to schedule in advance. Even if the airline does allow you to change your dates, you'll most likely pay a fee. Add on restrictions, like limited travel periods and limited availability, and it may turn out that you'll be better off booking individual tickets or an around-the-world ticket (more on that later).

Cathay Pacific offers the All Asia Pass, in which you can create an itinerary that includes 23 destinations starting at $1,399 (that's a current promotional rate). The All Asia Pass includes round-trip economy tickets between Los Angeles, New York, or San Francisco and Hong Kong, plus 21 consecutive days of flying to 22 other qualifying Asian cities, including Bali, Ho Chi Minh City, Jakarta, Kuala Lumpur, Manila, and Singapore. The fine print goes like this: If you want to add on any destinations that are not on the list of 23 Asian cities, it will cost you between $300 and $550, one way. If you want to travel on the weekend (Thursday through Sunday), it will cost you an extra $100. Want to travel in the summertime? It will cost you an extra $450. Each city has its own departure tax, ranging from $6 in Mumbai to $65 in Cairns. And anything booked less than 30 days in advance is considered to be a "rush" and will cost you $50. You won't earn any frequent flier miles on these tickets nor can you purchase them with your miles. www.cathayusa.com/offers/AllAsiaPass

Malaysia Airlines offers a similar systemwide pass.

Air Canada now offers a Flight Pass to Canada, which is a fixed monthly payment that allows you to fly as often as you want over the course of a 3- or 6-month period. You can choose your package out of four geographic zones: Canada Commuter (New York, Newark, Boston, or Chicago to Toronto, Hamilton, Ottawa, Montreal); Eastern (extended eastern United States–Canada corridor); Western (extended western United States–Canada corridor); and a North America pass that includes all 120 destinations served by Air Canada in the United States and Canada. Prices range from $1,737 to $3,788 per month (taxes and fees included). Another option on Air Canada is to purchase a fixed number of flight credits that include 10 or 20 prepurchased flights over 12 months. A Small Business pass allows you to buy 30 flight credits for up to eight different travelers in one company, over the course of 6 months. The pass is available only to US residents who are members of the Aeroplan frequent flier program. The good news is that you will accrue miles when using the pass. www.aircanada.com/aco/viewEWallet.do

Qantas offers the Aussie AirPass, which includes an international round-trip ticket to Australia plus three stops within the country. Among types of passes is a Wine and Culture tour, which includes a flight from Los Angeles to Sydney, then to Melbourne, Adelaide, Brisbane, and back to Los Angeles, starting at $1,099 plus taxes and fees. A $1,399 pass can include a flight from Los Angeles to Brisbane, then to Cairns, Ayers Rock, and Sydney before returning to Los Angeles. The fine print states that a minimum stay of 21 days is required (not a bad idea if traveling all the way down under), and locations are broken up by three zones that cannot be combined. www.qantas.com.au/regions/dyn/us/specials/webDeals217

For all things related to flight passes, check out two handy resources: **BestFares.com** and **Airtimetable.com.** You'll find information on air passes on budget carriers worldwide, in Asia, Africa, Europe, South America, and Latin America.

The New Business-Class Jets across the Atlantic

There's a war being fought across the Atlantic—not among low-fare carriers but among all-business-class-configured airlines, which are giving airlines like British Airways, Air France, American, and Alitalia a run for their money. They offer attractive, less expensive (and occasionally two-for-one companion deal) tickets and great service to less-congested secondary airports in England, France, and Italy. Here's the latest breakdown.

Eos

Flies from Kennedy to Stansted, with multiple arrivals/departures on most days. There are four types of fares for round-trip tickets: a "walk-up" unrestricted ticket is currently $7,500, a 7-day advance purchase is $5,800, a 21-day advance is $3,438, and 42-day advance purchase is $3,280.

This is the cream of the crop for transatlantic in terms of space and seating, with planes built for 220 having just 48 passengers. The plane has 78-inch lie-flat beds in 21-square-foot suites, giving you privacy and space to work or eat with another person facing you. Of course, it's also generally the most expensive of these transatlantic contenders. www.eosairlines.com

MAXjet

MAXjet offers several transatlantic routes: You can fly four times a week between Stansted and Washington Dulles or Las Vegas, as well as routes to Kennedy and Los Angeles. All flights start at $700 one way. There are 102 business-class seats with no middle seat and the requisite gourmet meals, wine, and in-flight entertainment.

Critics say that MAXjet's prices are quite competitive, even compared with many transatlantic coach fares, but some complain that this all-business-class airline isn't a whole lot better than coach in terms of roominess and amenities. 888-435-9629, www.maxjet.com

Silverjet

This business-class jet flies from Newark to Luton, starting at $900 one way. The airplane has 100 lie-almost-flat beds on board that are designed to fit passengers up to 6'3" and provides one crew member for every 10 passengers. For the price and the ease of checking in at Silverjet's private terminal, it's a solid deal. 877-359-7458, www.flysilverjet.com

Eurofly

This airline, a former charter arm of Alitalia, is an interesting one because it can get you to six different locations in Italy and to Delhi, India! A trip from New York to Delhi can start at $1,680. It's also a good option for direct flights to Italy, but the business-class fares can be just as expensive as the majors'. Also—and this is a biggie—it only flies between May and November. 800-459-0581, www.euroflyusa.com

L'Avion

You can get from Newark to Paris Orly starting at $797 one way. L'Avion is also known for having great customer service, and a big benefit is that you're flying into a major airport that has easy connections to the city (as compared with Stansted and Luton, which are a distance from London). 866-692-6759, www.lavion.com

Private Air

And then, there's a real (pun intended) sleeper. It's called Private Air. These are generally Airbus 320 jets configured to hold only about 48 passengers, and the company usually operates as a quiet code share with Swiss and Lufthansa on flights between Zurich and New York and Munich/Dusseldorf and Chicago/Newark. Really great service, spacious well-designed seats. Plus you get mileage. You won't see the planes ever designated as Private Air. You just need to ask Lufthansa and/or Swiss if your flight is code shared or operated by Private Air. If the answer is yes, then do not stop, do not pass Go—go directly and jump on that flight!

Alternative Airports

Stansted Airport (STN): This airport rose to prominence in London as the home base for ultra-low-cost carrier Ryanair but now features all sorts of flights from around the world as London's third-busiest.

The airport is about 45 minutes by train from Liverpool Station in London. Bus service also runs between central London and the airport and takes about 90 minutes one way.

Luton Airport: Located about 30 miles north of London, Luton is London's fourth-busiest international airport and a hub for low-cost carriers like EasyJet, Ryanair, Thomsonfly, and Wizz Air.

Luton has no rail connections, only a bus called the Green Line, which links it to central London. There's also the new EasyBus (same company as EasyJet), which is slightly cheaper, with fares cheaper the earlier you book. Both bus lines take about an hour to get into central London, assuming fairly minimal traffic. The EasyBus runs only from 8 a.m. to 11 p.m., while the Green Line is 24 hours.

Bologna Airport: Located about 120 miles east-southeast of Milan, Bologna Airport is a fast-growing, cheap alternative to many of northern Italy's other airports. However, Bologna Airport is not one of Milan's three official airports: Linate, Malpensa, and Orio al Serio.

A high-speed rail line is under construction between Milan and Bologna, which will cut travel time from the current 90 to 120 minutes to an hour or less. Currently, you can get there by train or bus, both options taking about 1½ to 2 hours from Bologna Airport to downtown Milan.

Round-the-World Tickets

This is my all-time favorite airline ticket—the RTW, or round-the-world ticket. Want to fly from Los Angeles to Nairobi? You won't find a discount ticket anywhere. New York to Riyadh? Same problem. In many cases, you're looking at a $1,400 coach ticket. Now comes the fun part. Instead of buying an expensive point-to-point coach ticket, get a round-the-world ticket. For only about $400 more, you could fly Los Angeles to London, then to Paris, take a flight to any number of European destinations, then head to Nairobi, and then continue around the world, stopping in any number of foreign cities—Bangkok, Hong Kong, Tokyo—on to Honolulu and back to Los Angeles. These RTW tickets also come in handy when you're traveling to several different destinations, even if you're not planning to literally go around the globe. It can be a confusing setup, as you have to figure out where you're going, where your ticket will *let* you go, and how long you can be there. The caveats are plentiful; for example, traveling in the summertime will cost you extra. If you want to reroute your tickets, it will most likely cost you, as much as 60 percent. If you don't use all of your tickets, they are not refundable. RTW tickets have been sold since 1978, when Pan American offered a promotion of "Round the World in 80 Days," which cost about half of the regular fare to go around the globe.

There are multiple ticket brokers that can help you arrange your around-the-world itinerary and book your tickets. A company called **Airtreks.com** is one of the more popular ones out there for their price and ease of use—the site has a TripPlanner to help you figure out your own multipoint trip or guide you through existing RTW packages. (Try out one of their Peter Greenberg packages! With the basic package, you can travel from New York to Hong Kong, Dubai, London, and New York, starting at $2,050.)

Airtreks makes things a little simpler because you don't have to travel in one direction for your entire route. You can opt to buy the first part of your trip and then, when you figure out where you want to go, contact the company to purchase your next leg. The company acts like a travel agent, not a consolidator—so rather than buying a bunch of tickets in bulk that they have to get rid of, they have developed contracts with all the major carriers. Their savings get passed on to you.

Airline alliances can be handy when it comes to RTW tickets. The old Pan Am days of one airline flying entirely around the globe are over, but you can certainly make your way from one point to the next through the alliances.

Star Alliance is the largest consortium of airlines that offer around-the-world fares: Air Canada, Air New Zealand, All Nippon Airways, Asiana, Austrian Airlines, British Midland, LOT Polish, Lufthansa, SAS Scandinavian, Singapore Airlines, South African Airways, SpanAir, Swiss International, TAP Air Portugal, Thai Airways, United Airlines, and US Airways. Travel benefits are also available on regional airlines Adria Airways, Blue 1, and Croatia Airlines.

Through these airlines, you can arrange different mileage plans based on three levels of travel: 29,000 miles ($3,800 coach, $7,400 business, and $9,800 first class); 34,000 miles ($4,400, $8,450, $11,200), and 39,000 miles ($5,150, $9,500, $13,200). (Remember that fares may vary depending on where you begin your trip.) This covers almost 850 destinations in more than 150 countries. Therefore, an example of a 29,000-mile sample itinerary would be: Chicago, San Francisco, Honolulu, Auckland, Christchurch, Sydney, Singapore, Bangkok, Delhi, Frankfurt, Rome, Munich, Madrid, London, New York, Chicago. Your journey may last anywhere from 10 days to a year, and you can change the dates of most of your flights—and change your destination for a fee. There is also a fee if you cancel your RTW ticket before you depart, and no refund if you cancel it after departure. You have to stop at a minimum of 3 and a maximum of 15 cities on this ticket, although this may vary by regions.

The **Oneworld alliance** is made up of member airlines American Airlines, British Airways, Cathay Pacific, Finnair, Iberia, Japan Airlines (JAL), LAN, Malév, Qantas, and Royal Jordanian. Affiliate airlines include airlines such as Air Nostrum, American Connection, American Eagle, Binter Canaries, British Mediterranean, Brymon, CityFlier Express, Comair, GB Airways, Lan Express, Lan Peru, Loganair, Maersk Air, Regional Air, and Sun Air. The Oneworld Explorer Fare is based on the number of continents you visit and is not restricted by mileage or the direction you're flying. You can fly to three continents for $3,900 coach, $7,500 business class, and $9,600 first class. The maximum number of continents is six, at the rate of $5,300 for coach, $10,400 for business class, and $13,200 for first class.

Even better, since alliance airlines participate in frequent flier programs, you can accrue miles by flying on an RTW ticket.

You can check the Web site **www.airtimetable.com** for more information on the alliance partnerships, as well as airline timetables, mileage calculator, and airline maps.

Finessing the Upgrade

Though frequent flier perks are growing fewer and farther between these days, there is one perk that remains for some: the upgrade certificate. But what about those of you who aren't interested in playing the often frustrating mileage-redemption game? (Also see Frequent Flier Miles/Loyalty Programs.) Well, there does seem to be a loophole for the anti–frequent flier: You can go online and find that a traveler is auctioning off a certificate that promises you a free upgrade on your next flight. This, too, is an upgrade certificate—but it can also be a lesson of buyer beware.

Traditionally, an upgrade certificate is a perk that's mailed out on occasion to frequent flier program members or is part of an incentive package to sign up for a credit card.

In theory, it sounds like a golden ticket: a free upgrade on your next flight, launching you from the back of the plane to business or first class. So when many of us see the chance to purchase an upgrade certificate on eBay, Craigslist, or even more travel-oriented sites like Hotwire and Priceline, it's certainly a temptation.

But talk to most frequent travelers and you'll find that these certificates often end up in a pile in a drawer collecting dust—for the same reasons that there are 9.7 trillion unredeemed frequent flier miles in the United States.

Just like frequent flier miles, upgrade certificates come with a planeload of restrictions and disclaimers. For example, you can only book the upgrade based on availability within 48 to 72 hours of the flight, the upgrade might apply only to full coach fares, and blackout dates almost always apply. It's also important to note that even if you have an upgrade certificate for one airline, if your flight is actually being operated by another carrier, it may be invalid on any of these code shares.

Keep in mind that there is no one type of upgrade certificate. United, for example, has a traditional paper upgrade certificate that might cover a one-segment upgrade that applies to only one flight number; a one-way upgrade that applies to all distances, legs, and connections; a one-way distance upgrade that is based on how far you're traveling; a standby upgrade. . . you get the point.

How to Contact the Airlines

AirlineTollFree.info: toll-free and international phone numbers for airlines around the world

Your type of ticket can also dictate whether you can even be upgraded at all. For example, a deeply discounted, nonrefundable ticket probably isn't eligible for the upgrade, no matter what kind of certificate you're holding in your hand.

But what about purchasing an upgrade certificate through a third party? The basic rule seems to be this: When it comes to any perks, whether it's an upgrade certificate or free mileage, it officially constitutes a violation of the mileage agreement for anyone to sell it. But while airlines crack down only infrequently, remember, you've been warned. Therein lies the technicality. If you can't buy or sell one, you *can* give or receive one as a gift to or from family and friends.

Finessing the Upgrade, Part Deux

I'm sorry to say that without an upgrade certificate or frequent flier miles to help you along, there is no magic password to score a free upgrade. But there are a few tips that can help you along. With a little luck, you may find yourself transported from the back of the plane into the very front.

! Number one, dress for success. The dormitory days are over, and jeans and a backpack just don't cut it in first class.

! *Don't ask* for an upgrade. Build relationships. Even frequent travelers make a common mistake: They may know the name of the butcher, baker, or candlestick maker, but they don't know the first or last name of a single person who works at the airport or at an airline. They've never taken the time to make/build/nurture those relationships. As a result, and as far as airports and airlines are concerned, without those relationships, every time these travelers go to the airport, they are treated (abused) as if it's their very first flight. The solution is surprisingly simple: Get to know the counter/gate agents. Write your thank you letters—I mean it!

! Is your flight an originating flight and the first flight of the day, or is it a midday flight waiting for other connecting passengers? If it's waiting for connecting passengers, even if the flight is showing full, you stand a better chance of an upgrade because not all the passengers will connect.

I've heard about dying for an upgrade, but this story proves that sometimes it's just not worth it. If you have somewhat of a twisted sense of humor, you'll appreciate the fact that sometimes it takes extreme measures to get bumped up to first class. A British Airways passenger traveling first class had the shock of his life when he woke up to find a dead woman had been placed in the sleeper seat next to him. The woman, who was in her seventies, had died en route from New Delhi to Heathrow, and the cabin staff brought her from economy to first class, where there was more room. When he complained about his "seatmate," an airline flight attendant told him to "get over it." Next time, fly Singapore Airlines—they have a designated "corpse cupboard" on their Airbus 340-500 aircraft.

Airline Food

First they served it to us in unappetizing compartmentalized trays. Then they took it away. Now they're bringing it back with style, but only certain classes get to enjoy it. I'm talking about airplane food. And yes, on some airlines, you can still find it, and it's surprisingly good.

Hawaiian Airlines is taking their in-flight meals to new levels with a tasting menu for first-class passengers. And its cuisine developed by legendary Hawaiian restaurateur Beverly Gannon, who runs the Hali'imaile General Store on Maui. That means you get to create your own meal by pairing three out of five options, such as a Hawaiian crab cake and chicken tandoori with basmati rice pilaf. Add on a pomegranate passion juice and a fruit plate and you've got yourself a pretty high-end meal.

Qantas has also introduced an enviable tasting menu, which features eight courses on its international flights (the plan is starting out in routes from Australia to Bangkok, Singapore, and Los Angeles but is expected to roll out). The food was designed by renowned chef Neil Perry and is matched with wines (Australian and others) that are served throughout the flight.

And Delta has retained Michelle Bernstein, a great chef from Miami, to design its front-of-the-cabin meal choices.

For the rest of you . . .

If you can't deal with the stale sandwich offered on board and aren't willing to pay the sky-high prices at the airport, there is an alternative—at least in Southern California. SkyMeals is a service that delivers prepared meals to travelers on the go. Just order by 3 p.m. the day that you leave and the food will be delivered to you, or you can pick it up at their Santa Monica kitchen. We're talking meals like lox and bagels with orange juice and a blueberry tea loaf, vegetable sushi, giant salads, gourmet sandwiches, and desserts. Meals aren't exactly cheap, ranging between $12 and $25, but you're getting a whole lot more food than an airport meal, with a much nicer presentation. 866-759-6325, www.skymeals.com

But if you're not flying first class, you may as well go into it knowing exactly what's, well, on your plate. Airline food is notoriously packed with more fat, calories, and sodium than you want to know about, and there's not a whole lot you can do about it. However, the Web site www.airlinemeals. net lets you go behind the scenes of airline food. You can see more than 3,300 pictures of airline food served on more than 250 airlines, find out what the crew is eating, and even see what was being served on airplanes back in the 1970s! It won't help your waistline, but at least you can arm yourself with knowledge before you get on board.

Wi-Fi on Airlines

Staying wired while traveling is important to business and pleasure travelers. Why? Because the reality is that we don't really change our lifestyle when we change our location. According to the Travel Industry Association, in 2002, business travelers were well plugged in, as 69 percent of 36.9 million business travelers brought along their cell phones, 25 percent brought their laptops, and 16 percent brought along PDAs on their business trips in the past year. And don't think leisure travelers are unplugging when they unwind—61 percent of them carried cell phones and 9 percent brought laptops . . . on vacation! More recent numbers are even scarier: A poll conducted by the Associated Press in 2007 found that 80 percent of vacationers brought their cell phones on vacation, and 20 percent brought their laptops. So if we're that intent on staying connected on the ground, chances are we want to be connected in the air.

And while a number of European carriers are testing out the use of cell phones on board (and in flight)—something I do not advocate unless these airlines are also constructing special cones of silence on board where cell phone users can gab away incessantly without provoking high-altitude fistfights—the real wave of the future seems to be high-speed wireless high-altitude Internet.

Lufthansa was one of the first carriers to install it, and it worked perfectly. For a nominal fee (about $30), I had unlimited Internet access for the entire flight. Talk about productivity! It was all part of a system called Connexion, developed by Boeing, that the company rolled out in 2004. Other carriers, like Korean Air, Singapore, and Japan Airlines, all installed the system.

But not enough airlines bought in, and Boeing scrapped the system late in 2006. But do not despair. On-board wireless high-speed Internet will be back.

The other big player in the industry was Verizon, which offered wireless telephone service in aircrafts on United, Continental, US Airways, and Delta. (For a fee, your cell phone calls could be rerouted to the Verizon

Airfone in the back of the seats.) However, Verizon shut down that branch of service, taking itself out of the game for any potential wireless Internet service—only United had announced impending plans for installing Wi-Fi on its aircrafts and is currently looking for a new provider.

When the FCC auctioned off air-to-ground broadband frequencies in 2006, JetBlue's subsidiary LiveTV and the technology company AirCell came out the winners. When, and if, these companies will roll out Wi-Fi access on airplanes in our near future remains to be seen.

Airlines are making changes in one area, and that's where you can (literally) plug in. You've seen more and more power outlets and Wi-Fi in airports, but once you're on the airplane, passengers have been stuck running their batteries dry. On an American airplane, you can plug an adapter into the cigarette-lighter outlets that are in most of the first and business-class seats (and a few in coach). Continental is in the process of installing two-pronged outlets on all of its Boeing 757s, and United is working on providing two-pronged outlets on all international flights.

And My Favorite New Web Site

Gethuman.com: Skip the automated system and get directly to a human on the other end of the line. But remember, just getting a real person on the other end of the phone may not always be the answer. So many airlines are outsourcing their reservations staff (and not training them properly) that it can be a frustrating experience. Recently I attempted to make a reservation on Delta on a flight between La Guardia and Birmingham, Alabama. But when I got a real person on the phone at the Delta reservations, my problems were just beginning. "Thank you for calling Delta; my name is Abraham," the agent answered. I told him I wanted to fly between New York and Alabama. I even gave him the desired flight numbers. He claimed Birmingham was in Arkansas and that Delta didn't fly there. After about 2 minutes of trying to help him with basic US geography, I asked him where he was based. Atlanta? Salt Lake City? No . . . India. I then asked him his last name. (And this definitely comes under the category of "you can't make this stuff up.") "Lincoln." It was difficult to suppress my laughter. "That can't be your real name?" I chuckled. "Yes," he admitted, "it is not my real name. But we wanted to pick a name that you would be . . . comfortable with."

With Abraham still convinced Birmingham was in Arkansas, I hung up and waited—on hold for another human being who could actually help me. Moral of . . . the story: We need an emancipation proclamation from outsourcing without proper training.

CHAPTER 3

❝ **Most of American life consists of driving somewhere and then returning home, wondering why the hell you went.** ❞

—JOHN UPDIKE

In the travel industry, the subject of car rentals is one of the least understood. You've got car types, definitions of terms, pricing, fuel, surcharges, and the two most confusing areas: car rental insurance and your rights when/if something goes wrong.

The J. D. Power and Associates 2006 Rental Car Satisfaction Study found that in 2005, Enterprise ranked the highest in customer satisfaction for the third year running, followed by Hertz and National.

The study found that 29 percent of customers waited to pick up their rental cars, which was a 15 percentage-point improvement from 2005. However, the average time it takes to pick up the rental car is $21\frac{1}{2}$ minutes—a detrimental number since overall satisfaction tends to drop when customers have to wait more than 5 minutes.

While the vast majority of vehicles rented are midsize cars (42 percent) or compact cars (14 percent), full-size cars are also growing increasingly popular, jumping from 7 to 12 percent. Even gas-guzzling SUVs have risen from 8 to 11 percent.

There is some bad news on the horizon. For years, car rental companies have used cars that were made in Detroit—usually the generic ones that the regular consumer didn't want to buy. But both Ford and General Motors are downsizing, which means that the more expensive cars are the ones rolling off the assembly line. The result? Higher costs for car rental companies and, therefore, higher prices for us. We're already seeing the effects. Experts are saying that the average base price of a midsize car (excluding extra fees, which I'll talk about later) jumped from $52 to $59 in just 1 year! Avis reported that its fleet costs rose a serious 13 percent in 2006, despite the fact that its fleet size increased only 3 percent.

And the car rental companies are learning from their airline counterparts the business of yield management. Car rental prices can go up and down several times in a day, and I'm talking about huge swings. (This is an opportunity to use some of the opaque Web sites, like Priceline and Hotwire—you bid on a price and discover the identity of the renting company only after you commit your credit card.)

But there's some good news: Hertz has eliminated those costly one-way drop-off charges, mileage fees, and in-state-only rentals, which raise the price of car rentals so drastically. But whether other agencies will follow suit remains to be seen.

Domestic Driving

Which company has the biggest fleet and makes the most money? Check out these statistics.

ESTIMATED CAR RENTAL REVENUE

COMPANY	US CARS IN SERVICE 2006	US LOCATIONS	EST. REVENUE 2006	EST. REVENUE 2005
ACE	11,500	85	$105 million	$101 million
Advantage	17,000	100	$155 million	$150 million
Affordable/Sensible	4,950	250	$36 million	$35.4 million
Avis	190,775	1,199	$2.8 billion	$2.7 billion
Budget	134,225	842	$1.4 billion	$1.4 billion
Dollar Thrifty	85,000	575	$1.5 billion	$1.4 billion
Enterprise	630,066	6,019	$7 billion	$6.4 billion
Fox	6,800	28	$52 million	$40 million
Hertz	290,000	2,875	$3.9 billion	$3.7 billion

COMPANY	US CARS IN SERVICE 2006	US LOCATIONS	EST. REVENUE 2006	EST. REVENUE 2005
Payless	10,000	46	$95 million	$90 million
Rent-A-Wreck	6,700	298	$44 million	$66 million
Triangle	6,000	28	$45 million	$41 million
U-Save	11,500	375	$98 million	$95 million
Vanguard	208,400	623	$2.1 billion	$1.9 billion
Independents (3,000)	70,500	6,800	$696 million	$732.5 million
TOTALS	**1,683,416**	**20,143**	**$20 billion**	**$18.9 billion**

Source: *Auto Rental News*

TOP FIVE RENTAL-VEHICLE MODELS IN 2005

CARS	Ford Taurus 122,561	Chevrolet Impala 96,054	Chevrolet Malibu 84,043	Dodge Stratus 57,724	Dodge Neon 55,457
SUVS	Chevrolet TrailBlazer 59,996	Ford Explorer 45,162	Jeep Grand Cherokee 33,135	Chrysler PT Cruiser 25,877	Ford Escape 22,523
TRUCKS	Ford F-Series 24,935	Chevrolet Silverado 21,437	Dodge Ram 12,471	Dodge Dakota 8,268	Chevrolet Colorado 5,971
VANS	Dodge Caravan 58,972	Chevrolet Town & Country 31,563	Ford Econoline 29,799	Ford Freestar 27,525	Chevrolet Express 19,933

Source: *Auto Rental News*

Merger

The major car rental companies have gotten complacent over the years, as there hasn't been any new competition to speak of. But a recent shake-up occurred in April 2007, when Enterprise Rent-A-Car merged with Vanguard Car Rental Group, the company that controls both Alamo and National. Worth an estimated $7 billion, Enterprise already dominated the market (compared with Vanguard, which was worth $2.1 billion). Although at this point it's too early to say what will happen with all three of the brands, they're likely to keep on running—but at what cost? Without competition, higher prices at the rental counter are practically inevitable.

Taxes and Fees

There is no getting around many taxes and fees when it comes to car rentals. Or is there? The best piece of advice is to make sure that the price you're quoted includes these extra fees, so that you won't be stricken by counter shock when you get the final bill.

More advice? Avoid renting cars at airports. The average car rental rates at airport locations remain significantly higher than at off-airport sites. A 2005 Travelocity study shows airport taxes increased from 24.4 percent to 25.8 percent, while neighborhood taxes average about 14.1 percent of the final cost.

If you're renting a car for more than 1 day, it often makes sense to take a shuttle or cab into town—that $15 cab ride or the tip to the shuttle driver is more than offset by the savings of renting in a neighborhood agency. Fortunately, the trend seems to be shifting this way. In 2004, for the first time, neighborhood rentals actually surpassed airport rentals in terms of revenue: $9.5 billion versus $8.1 billion, respectively.

Our friends at SmarterTravel.com put together this "cheat sheet" on excess fees that you should look out for.

Additional drivers fee: A fee charged for extra drivers other than the renter, this rate can run from $3 to $25 per person. Some companies, such as Avis, Budget, Enterprise, and E-Z, don't charge for a spouse. National doesn't

A Travelocity study found that the 10 airports in 2005 with the largest jump in price between the base rate and the total amount due (including taxes and fees) were as follows:

AIRPORT	JUMP IN PRICE
1. Houston George Bush Intercontinental	66.1%
2. Dallas/Fort Worth International	61.4%
3. Phoenix	52.3%
4. Austin Bergstrom	49.9%
5. Kansas City	45.4%
6. San Antonio	42.4%
7. Baltimore/Washington International	41.0%
8. Tulsa	40.3%
9. Cleveland	39.0%
10. Albuquerque	38.9%

charge for a spouse or domestic partner if you're in the frequent renter club, and Hertz does not charge if you're a frequent renter or if both parties are members of AAA or AARP. In some locations, Fox and Payless don't charge for spouses, but policy varies by location.

Airport concession fees: Also called recoup fees, consolidated facility charges (CFC), facility usage fees, and concession recovery fees, these fees can be as much as 10 percent of the total rental cost. Although base rates may be higher at nonairport locations, you can avoid paying airport taxes and surcharges by renting at a downtown or suburban location.

Convention center/stadium/sports arena tax: The money from this fee goes toward construction of area centers. Charges of this type are calculated as daily fees or as a percent of the rental rate. For example, both Los Angeles and Boston have a $10 charge on rentals in city limits.

Deposit: Rental agencies generally charge your credit card for a deposit on the rental vehicle but do not process the amount unless, upon return, the car has been damaged or misused. The amount varies but may be hundreds of dollars. Make sure to check the car thoroughly before leaving the lot, noting any damage to the interior and exterior of the car.

Drop-off fee: A fee charged for returning the car to a different site than the pick-up location, it includes returning a car to a different location within the same city and a "one-way" fee for dropping it off in a different city altogether. Be careful, as these fees can run into the hundreds of dollars. However, Hertz has abandoned one-way drop-off charges, mileage fees, and fees for in-state rentals. National doesn't charge a drop-off fee, and Enterprise currently allows one-way rentals in Florida, Texas, and California.

Equipment rental fee: This is an extra charge for items such as car seats, ski racks, cellular phones, and GPS devices. Examples of fees for such items include $8 per day for child safety seats from Avis and $6 per day for a cell phone and 10 minutes of use from Budget.

Frequent flier tax: This is a recent—and more often than not hidden—fee. It's a charge that you incur when earning miles for your rental. The fee is usually 7.5 percent of the value of the miles. This charge covers taxes the rental company pays on the frequent flier miles it gives to customers.

Fuel charge: Per-gallon gasoline charges are paid when you return a car without a full tank. Be very wary of this option, as agencies often charge up to double the local price for gasoline.

Late fee: Rates are charged based on the 24-hour clock, meaning that if you pick up your car at 9 a.m., you must drop it off by the same time on the return day. Some agencies, such as Budget, grant drivers a 59-minute grace period; Hertz offers a 30-minute grace period, while others begin charging late fees immediately. Late fees are charged by the hour until the hourly charges exceed the daily rate, at which point most companies charge you for a full extra day.

Mileage fee: For rentals without unlimited mileage, it's a per-mile fee based on the number of miles overall or the number of miles over the per-day allotted usage. Most larger companies offer unlimited mileage at this point, but smaller companies may charge a fee of 15 to 50 cents for mileage above the allotted amount.

Out-of-state fee: This is charged for driving the vehicle outside of the state where you rented it. There is no standard rate, so it is best to call and check with the company before booking.

Parking tax: The agency charges this fee to cover the rental of the parking lot, which is usually just about 30 cents total.

Peak season surcharge: Sometimes car rental companies charge a per-day or flat fee for rentals during popular times. There is no standard rate for this type of fee.

Reimbursement fee/vehicle license fee/vehicle excise tax: The fee that contributes to the cost of registering and titling the car is usually between 3 percent and 8 percent of the base rate.

State and local sales tax: This tax varies by state.

Young drivers fee: This affects all drivers under the age of 25 and can cost anywhere from $10 to $80 per day.

So is there a way around a lot of these taxes and fees? In some cases, the answer is yes—if you know *where* to rent your car. In a report written by senior fellows and researchers of the Brookings Institution and the Urban Institute, appropriately titled "Taken for a Ride: Economic Effects of Car Rental Excise Taxes," an interesting pattern emerged.

The report listed at least 80 car rental taxes in effect in 38 states and Washington, DC. But a great example is in Kansas City, Missouri. In 2004, voters approved a $4-per-day tax on rental car usage, mostly earmarked to finance the construction of a new indoor sports arena. This falls into the category of "arena tax" and raised the cost of an average car rental by more than 14 percent. And what did savvy rental car customers do? They headed right across the river to Kansas, a state where locations weren't taxed. And the number of rentals at taxed branches in Kansas City compared with branches that were not taxed fell by 8.6 percent in 3 years (January 2002 to June 2005). The number of rental days dropped by almost 6 percent, leading to a loss of 3 percent of total revenues. But car renters saved an average of $20 per business week by not renting in Kansas City.

Car Rental Tips

❗ If you possibly can, skip the 800 number. Those go to a national call center, and agents have less leeway when it comes to negotiation. Call the direct number of the agency in the location where you are picking up the car. If the agency won't give you the number, let them know you need to talk to the local manager there and give them *your* number and ask them to call you.

❗ Rent on Saturdays. This is the day when many cars booked for the weekend are not picked up, so the lot may have a surplus.

❗ Book a less expensive car in advance. Chances are they may not have the model you asked for. If you stand your ground, they can upgrade you. Remember that what constitutes a compact car versus a midsize or full-size is different if you rent in Europe—there, a midsize car may in fact be what we call a compact!

❗ Check back. Car rental prices can change 10 to 20 times a day(!), based on demand. Prices can rise as much as 50 percent within a 24-hour period. Check online first, but call the car rental agency (directly, of course) to speak with a human. More often than not, an agent can magically drop the rate for you, but you have to ask.

❗ Take pictures before you drive the car off the rental lot. Turn on the date and time option on your camera and walk around the rental car to take pictures of dings and dents. Show the photos to the car rental agent and get his full name—that way, if you get dinged by repair charges, you'll have proof that the damage was already there.

❗ If you're under 25, you'll usually be hit hard by under-25 fees. We're talking up to $50 *a day*, even if you have a spotless driving record. There's not much you can do about this one, but definitely shop around. These charges are guidelines, not rules, so you may be able to talk an agent down. For example, on average, Dollar charges between $15 and $25 a day, Thrifty varies between $10 and $25 a day, and National ranges from $25 to $50! Tell the agent about your clean driving record and produce a copy of your personal auto insurance, to show you're covered if something goes wrong. Your odds of getting special treatment are exponentially higher if you're a member of the agency's loyalty program.

! **Don't be fuelish.**

- **Make sure you understand the companies' refueling policies.** Some make you pay for a full tank of gas when you rent the car, and you should bring it back as empty as possible. Others give you the option to bring the car back full or they will refuel it themselves. If that's the case, fill it up yourself. Car rental companies often charge up to $7 a gallon!

- **Drive slowly.** The faster you drive, the more fuel you burn, despite the logic that you're getting to your destination more quickly. According to the US Department of Energy, for every 5 miles per hour that you drive over 60 mph, you're actually losing 5.6 percent of fuel efficiency.

- **Shop around to find the lowest price gas.** Airport gas stations are almost always more expensive than neighborhood stations. Visit www.gasbuddy.com, which lists prices by zip code.

Car Rental Amenities

While these items are completely optional, they can be very tempting—and jack up your rental rate by several dollars per day. Find out the price of these extra amenities beforehand and determine if they're something you need.

Electronic payment: Budget and Hertz include the E-Z Pass to pay tolls along the East Coast from Maine to Virginia. Avis and Budget also offer electronic toll collection in Chicago, charging $1.50 a day. Hertz offers it in Houston for $2.50 a day. Dollar and Thrifty have a Pass24 system for tolls in Dallas and Houston and charge $8.50 a day. Note that this charge occurs every day of the rental, not just on the days that you use the pass, and that it doesn't include the tolls themselves.

Navigation systems: National, Enterprise, Dollar, Thrifty, and Alamo offer the Garmin StreetPilot system. Hertz offers the Neverlost system. Avis offers the Where2 system. Each company charges about $8 to $11 per day.

OnStar: Hertz offers OnStar in some vehicles, but it does not subscribe to the service. Instead, you will be connected to a staff member at Hertz. National (GM vehicles), Alamo, and Enterprise offer OnStar. There is no extra fee for this amenity.

Satellite radio: XM Satellite Radio is available in some Avis, National, and Alamo vehicles. Sirius Satellite Radio is available in some Hertz, Dollar, and

Thrifty vehicles. Hertz charges $3 a day for the system, but other companies include it at no extra cost.

Wi-Fi: Avis recently added wireless Internet in 70 locations throughout 10 major markets, at the cost of $10.95 per day. It's a portable system that plugs into the car's power outlet and can be plugged into any electrical outlet in your home or hotel. Hertz offers 40 airport locations for $4.95 per day.

Something different: Hertz recently debuted an hourly car rental service in three Manhattan locations. The idea behind this is to make it easier for people to take care of anything from errands to moving to a quickie day trip. If you've ever had to lug your groceries from the store to your apartment 10 blocks away, you may see the value in this!

Loyalty Programs

Hertz made car history in 1981 when it became a charter member of American Airlines' inaugural frequent flier mile program. Six years later, National Car Rental became the first car rental agency to establish its own loyalty program, designed to attract customers and keep them coming back for more. Many companies offer free express check-in, while others have paid programs that promise more benefits, including earning mileage on your airlines (although figuring out how to redeem them is up to you). Keep in mind that loyalty and frequent renter programs are often targeted toward business travelers, in which case corporations negotiate bulk rates and benefits for their employees. But there are still a few programs out there for individual renters.

COMPARISON OF LOYALTY PROGRAMS

CAR RENTAL COMPANY	LOYALTY PROGRAM	COST	BENEFITS
Alamo	Quicksilver	Free for corporate or business benefit accounts or if you have rented 5 times in the last 12 months.	Expedited counter service and express return. Earn up to 50 mileage points a day on one of 11 airlines.
Avis	Wizard	Free	Keep your profile and preferences on file; express pickup service in 1,400 locations for Avis Preferred members. Frequent renters are eligible for free rental days and other promotional benefits. Earn mileage points on 50 airlines and at 22 hotels.

(continued)

CAR RENTAL COMPANY	LOYALTY PROGRAM	COST	BENEFITS
Hertz	Hertz #1 Club Gold	**Gold:** $50 a year; fee waived for #1 Club members who have 4+ rentals in 1 year. **Five Star:** established to recognize members with 10 to 39 rentals within a calendar year. Membership is earned; joining is not an option. **President's Circle:** established to recognize members with 40+ rentals within a calendar year. Membership is earned; joining is not an option.	Express pickup at more than 40 airports—your car is waiting in a covered section. Express counter service in 1,000 other locations worldwide—your preferences are stored in a database; when you call in advance, your paperwork is at the counter.
Hertz	Hertz #1 Awards Points	Free if you're a member of Hertz #1 Club or Hertz #1 Club Gold.	Earn 1 point per $1 in car rental charges to be redeemed for car rentals, airline tickets, or hotels.
National	Emerald Club	$50 a year	Emerald Club Aisle: Skip the counter and go directly to the "Emerald Aisle" to pick any available intermediate vehicle. If that's not available, you get express check-in. Get an E-receipt for speedy returns and expense reports. No extra driver fee for spouse, business partner, employer, or associate using the car for business. Frequent flier miles are available; note that some airline programs charge 50 cents per rental day. Earn 250 Hilton HHonors partners bonus points per rental.
Thrifty	Blue Chip Express Rental Program	Free	Expedited counter services; 1 free day for every 16 rental days.

Sources: *Fastcompany.com; smartertravel.com*

Car Rental Insurance

If you have personal auto insurance and medical insurance, you may already be covered in the case of an accident in your rental car. But you may not be *fully* covered, so check carefully.

Collision damage waiver/loss damage waiver (about $10 to $20 a day): Keep in mind that this is *not* insurance. It waives the right for a rental car company to recover money if the vehicle is damaged or stolen (this doesn't cover damages you make to someone else's car). Your personal auto insurance will cover this *if* you already have comprehensive and collision coverage. Your comprehensive coverage pays for damage to your auto caused by perils other than a collision. Your collision coverage will pay for damage to your auto regardless of who causes the accident. There are various deductible options, usually $500 or $1,000.

It's important to find out if your comprehensive and collision insurance has a limit. If your car is worth only $5,000 and you total a car worth $20,000, you're out $15,000.

If you don't want to get your personal auto insurance involved with your car rental (and potentially increase your rates), you should consider purchasing the damage waiver. There are different deductibles for this kind of waiver, usually $500 or $1,000, which means that the renter or authorized driver pays for any damages up to that amount. A full-value waiver means that the rental company waives the renter and authorized driver's responsibility up to the full value of the car (including administrative and loss-of-use fees).

Personal accident insurance or coverage (about $3 a day): This provides accidental death and emergency medical expense benefits to the renter and all passengers. This is usually covered by your personal auto or health insurance. For example, Avis offers $175,000 for accidental death, $2,500 for injuries due to an accident, and $250 for ambulance expenses. This may or may not be more than what your personal auto insurance or medical insurance would cover.

Supplemental liability coverage/additional liability insurance (about $10 a day): This protects authorized drivers against claims made by a third party for injury or damages from an accident. It will cover up to $1 million before your personal insurance becomes involved. If your personal auto insurance includes liability insurance, you may not need to purchase this from the rental company.

Personal effects coverage or personal property insurance (about $2 a day): This pays if you have something lost or stolen from your car. According to Avis, the maximum coverage is $600 per claim, with a maximum coverage per individual of $1,800. Personal auto insurance usually doesn't cover this.

Credit card coverage: An increasing number of credit card companies are claiming to offer their own collision insurance. However, there are some issues to keep in mind.

Credit card companies usually offer only secondary coverage. This means that when you decline the damage waiver, your own existing auto policy covers you. That means you're fully liable for any damages. So where does secondary coverage kick in? Only when/if you exhaust all the limits on your primary policy. And the bad news: If you're depending on your credit card coverage to bail you out and you have no existing primary coverage, you're in serious trouble. And even if you do have that coverage, the paperwork on the credit card insurance can be massive. For example, if there is damage or theft to the car, the credit card company would look to your personal auto insurance to cover the claim and then reimburse you for any additional out-of-pocket expenses. And you'll need to submit a police report and a rental company report.

American Express offers secondary coverage. It has no deductible and covers you for up to 30 consecutive days. The fee is $24.95 per car rental. Visa Classic, Visa Secured, Visa Gold, Visa Platinum, and Visa Signature credit card holders receive secondary coverage. It covers you for up to 15 consecutive days domestically and 31 consecutive days internationally. Diners Club members receive automatic *primary* full-value coverage worldwide. That means your personal auto insurance isn't affected. The program pays for covered damages up to the full value of the rental car and includes loss-of-use charges from the rental agency. Corporate card members receive coverage for up to 45 consecutive days, and personal card members receive coverage for up to 31 consecutive days.

In many cases, you may get the hard sell from the car rental company to buy their coverage. How much of a hard sell? J. D. Power might rank Enterprise at the top of their list for car satisfaction, but for pressing renters on insurance, I think that they come in at the bottom of the pack.

In May, 2006, Consumerist.com broke a story when an "enterprising" rental customer lifted a written document of an agent sales memo at one Enterprise location, designed to convince buyers to purchase extra insurance. According to this memo, this is how the Enterprise location instructed its counter agents to talk to renters.

I. Initial Sales Pitches

A. "I assume you want us to protect you bumper to bumper on the car, right?" (Assumption makes the customer feel like everyone takes it.)

B. "You've rented from us before?" If yes: "Then, I'm sure you took our coverage last time, right?" (Customer will feel silly for having not taken it.)

C. "How long do you need the car?"—3 days—"Three days? That's only $60 and protects you the full value of the car!" "It's only $19.99 a day and protects you for the full value of the car!!!" (Make sure the customer feels your excitement.)

II. Handling Objections

A. I have my own insurance—"Yes, but you have exposure. Meaning, if anything happens, we'd have to collect your deductible, place a claim through your insurance, you'd have to worry about surcharges, insurance rates going up, etc. . . ." (*Exposure*, most powerful objection word ever.)

B. No, I'm okay . . . I don't need it—"Well, 80 percent of my customers under 10 days do take it because they would not be responsible for any damage, regardless of fault!" (Customers love to be a part of the majority; it's comforting.)

III. Things You Should Never Say

A. "How do you want to cover the car?" (This gives them the option of their own insurance, and they'll use that option every time.)

B. "Do you want to take our coverage or use your own insurance?" (Are you kidding me?! This is not sales!)

C. "We offer a protection package that can cover you bumper to bumper . . ." (Duh, that is precisely what you'd be doing: offering, not *selling*!)

IV. A True Seller . . .

- Can close the deal within 30 seconds.

- Doesn't even need the "three nos."

- "Persuades" rather than "offers."

- Believes in what he/she is selling.

- Uses one or two powerful words, rather than a novel.

If you work for Enterprise, you are a true seller (you just might not know it yet).

And if you're renting from Enterprise—or any other car rental company—you need to be a true informed consumer. Know your coverage and your rights as outlined throughout this chapter.

Accidents/Stolen Vehicles

As a renter, you are responsible for driving safely, so always use common sense. Even if you purchase insurance, it may be waived if you drive while under the influence of drugs or alcohol, allow an unauthorized person to drive the vehicle, leave the car unlocked or the keys in the ignition, drive off road, or take the car out of the country. You are also liable for all parking and traffic violations.

If you get into an accident, treat it just as you would if it were your own car.

1. Call the local police or appropriate law enforcement agency.

2. Get all relevant information on anyone involved in the accident: full name, mailing address, telephone number, insurance details, and driver's license number. Make note of the vehicle's make, color, brand, and license plate number.

3. Call the nearest office of the rental car company, give them your rental agreement or confirmation number, and explain what has happened.

4. Call your own auto insurance company with information on the incident. You may have to go to an office to fill out paperwork.

However, there are some caveats to consider. Rental cars don't come with a guarantee, and as scary as it sounds, you may end up with a defective car. If your car suffers mechanical damage under your watch, know that there is no standard agreement of what kind of damage for which the renter is liable.

As you may have already experienced, getting emergency assistance from the car rental company if you get into an accident or if your rental car breaks down can be an exercise in futility if you're in a remote location or if it's after hours. Road warrior and rental car safety advocate Frank Whyte found himself in a situation in which his rental car tire went flat due to a faulty repair job. Not only did the car rental agency send him out with a defective tire, but they failed to provide a jack inside the vehicle. Because Whyte was located several hours outside of a major city, the company was unable to help him in a timely fashion. Whyte and automotive expert Pat Goss compiled the following rental car safety checklist. For a complete checklist, visit www.tsod.com/rentalcar/rental_car_checklist.pdf.

- Talk to your road service provider to see if they cover service calls on rental cars.

- Tuck a small flashlight into your carry-on bag. You'll need this to poke around your rental car if you pick it up at night.

- Ask the representative how he knows the car you're renting has completed its prerental maintenance check. If a clerk can't answer a simple question about a car's road readiness, be very suspicious.

- Ask a representative what to do if the car breaks down or you lose the car key. (Better understand up front that lost key charges can be excessive!)

- Look at the tires for inflation, good tread, and uneven tread wear.

- Check the odometer. If it reads more than 25,000 miles, be a bit more thorough in your inspection.

- Check the headlights, turn signals, and interior/dashboard lights.

- Spray the windshield to ensure that the washer system works and the wipers are in good shape. The wiper/washer system is one of the most common sources of safety-related consumer complaints pertaining to rental cars.

- Ensure that there is an owner's manual in the glove box.

- Do an under-hood and under-trunk inspection.

- Check the trunk for a spare tire (push on it to make sure it's actually inflated), jack, and lug wrench. Check the owner's manual for any other tools required to change a tire.

- Open the hood and check the fluids (bring paper towels), including the oil, antifreeze, and washer fluid. Other things to look at are the brake fluid, transmission fluid, and power steering fluid.

There are also some unexpected situations that may or may not be covered under your insurance. Say your car gets flooded by heavy rains, crushed by falling debris, or ripped apart by a twister. If the car is drivable, you'll most likely be asked to take it to the closest rental location to be replaced. If the car can't be driven, the agency should arrange to have the car towed and replaced.

Roadside Assistance

American Automobile Association (AAA) is probably the most well-known roadside assistance service in the country. With your membership, you can get 24-hour assistance, including emergency fuel delivery, towing services, and medical assistance. Membership also makes you eligible for hundreds of discounts, including hotels, restaurants, sporting events, and shops. www.aaa.com

Better World Club is an environmentally friendly auto club, which offers emergency roadside assistance for vehicles and bicycles, insurance options, free maps, and travel tips. Additional benefits include discounts on hybrid and diesel car rentals and gas rebate coupons. Better World Club also donates 1 percent of its annual revenues to environmental cleanup and advocacy. 866-238-1137, www.betterworldclub.com

Auto Club of America offers 24-hour emergency roadside assistance, including towing, flat tire assistance, and gas delivery. 800-411-2007, 405-751-4430, www.autoclubofamerica.com

If you're a member of **Sam's Club,** you can take advantage of its GE Motor Club service, which provides 24-hour emergency roadside assistance. Members pay $58.96 and Sam's Club Plus members pay $34.96 per year for services like towing, jump-starting, and changing flat tires. 866-618-4647, www.sams.gemotorclub.com

Eco-Friendly Car Rentals

A recent survey by Priceline.com found that a huge majority of travelers—72 percent—want car rental companies to add hybrid vehicles to their fleets. Thirty-nine percent of those surveyed even said that they would be willing pay between $1 and $3 more per day to rent a hybrid, and 8 percent said they would be willing to pay up to $7 to $10 a day more (no one was willing to pay more than $10 a day).

Lately, an increasing number of car rental companies have been offering hybrid vehicles in certain locations. In 2006, Hertz launched its Green Collection of fuel-efficient vehicles and recently added 1,000 Toyota Prius hybrids to its fleet. Hertz expects to have 4,300 hybrids in its fleet by mid-2008. Avis immediately followed suit by announcing its addition of 1,000 Priuses to its fleet, mostly in California, Seattle, Portland, and Washington, DC. Both companies guarantee the reservations, which means that if you book a hybrid, they can't substitute it with a nonhybrid vehicle. "Fuel-efficient" is defined as having an EPA highway fuel-efficiency rating of 28 miles or more per gallon, but remember one thing: The EPA often overstates fuel economy, but new 2008 models and beyond will be more likely to reflect the real-world fuel efficiency.

A couple of companies are trying to fill the gap by renting out only eco-friendly vehicles.

EV Rental Cars, which is now partnered with Fox Rent A Car, provides hybrid vehicles at airport sites in Los Angeles, Orange County, San Diego, San Francisco, San Jose, and Phoenix. The fleet is expected to top 500 eco-friendly vehicles, including the Toyota Prius, Honda Civic Hybrid, and the Toyota Highlander. 877-387-3682, www.evrental.com

In Maui and Los Angeles, **Bio-Beetle** rents out cars that operate entirely on biodiesel, including sedans, hatchbacks, and even Jeeps. 877-873-6121, www.bio-beetle.com

Driving Tips

! Watch where you drive. According to AutoVantage, in 2007, the five worst cities for road rage were Miami, New York, Boston, Los Angeles, and Washington, DC. The friendliest cities? Portland (Oregon), Pittsburgh, Seattle-Tacoma, St. Louis, and Dallas–Fort Worth.

! Knowing your freeway systems can reduce your chances of getting lost or confused. East-west freeways are assigned two-digit even numbers, while north-south highways are given two-digit odd numbers. For freeways with three digits, pay attention to the first number. If it's even, you're probably on a looping freeway encircling a major city. Three-digit numbers that begin with an odd number are known as spurs and branch off of a main interstate.

! Obtain a detailed map of your route or consider investing in a navigation system like Garmin or Magellan. Plan alternative routes in case you come across heavy traffic or inclement weather that might affect your driving ability.

▽ Resources

www.aaa.com: Besides roadside assistance, AAA offers detailed driving directions (TripTik), road tripping ideas, airport contact information, and even international travel warnings.

www.fhwa.dot.gov/trafficinfo: Provides information on traffic and road closures nationwide.

www.gasbuddy.com: Find the cheapest gas to get more bang for your buck.

www.rentalcars.com: Compare local and national rates of various car rental agencies.

www.traffic.com: Find up-to-date traffic information and receive local alerts on your cell phone.

Alamo: 800-462-5266, www.alamo.com

Avis: 800-331-1212, www.avis.com

Budget: 800-527-0700, www.budget.com

Dollar: 800-800-3665, www.dollar.com

Enterprise: 800-261-7331, www.enterprise.com

Hertz: 800-654-3131, www.hertz.com

National: 800-227-7368, www.nationalcar.com

International Driving

Although many countries do not recognize US driver's licenses, you may be able to use an international driving permit (IDP). IDPs are accepted in more than 150 countries outside the United States. You can obtain one at a local AAA office and the American Automobile Touring Alliance. You must be at least age 18, and you will need to present two passport-size photographs and your valid US license. There is a fee of about $20 for each permit. travel.state.gov/travel/tips/safety/safety_1179.html

Safety Tips

Safety is a major concern when it comes to driving abroad. According to the US State Department, "an estimated 1.2 million deaths occur each year worldwide due to road accidents." About 70 percent of these occur in developing countries. It is estimated that more than 200 US citizens die each year due to road accidents abroad.

Many major causes of traffic-related injuries are driving under the influence, poorly marked road signs, speeding, unsafe vehicle design, and poor implementation of road safety measures. The United States, Europe, and

Road Signs

Road signs vary wildly throughout the world, so it's important to familiarize yourself with what signs mean. Many countries have bilingual signs, but this may not be the case in more rural or remote areas. Here are some examples of European road signs that you may not be familiar with. How many could you identify without the corresponding tag?

 Double curve

 Uneven road

 Road narrows

 Slippery road

 School crossing

 Pedestrian crossing

 Domestic animal crossing

 Wild animal crossing

 Traffic lights ahead

 Railroad crossing without gates

 Intersection

 Intersection

 Yield

 No vehicular traffic

 No entry

 Passing prohibited

 Customs

 Oncoming vehicles priority

 Sound signals prohibited

 Minimum safety space

 End of all bans (except parking stopping)

 Stopping and parking prohibited

 No parking

 Mandatory right turn ahead

 Snow chains obligatory

 Parking (color indicates zone)

 One-way street

 No through road

 Facilities for handicapped

 Garage

Courtesy of www.europcar.com

other developed countries have implemented preventative measures to help curb the number of traffic-accident fatalities, but developing countries do not strictly enforce traffic safety.

If you're planning on driving abroad, here are a few tips to help ensure your safety.

! Check all spare tires and make sure the car is fully equipped if it breaks down.

! Find out when the car was checked over last in that country.

! It's important that you get as specific directions as possible. When you pick up the rental car, call your first destination and get explicit directions.

! Get familiar with the controls and how the car handles. Start by driving the car in a quiet area that's free of traffic and pedestrians.

! Car manuals will not be in English, so know driving terminology before you start driving.

! If you're in a country that drives on the left side of the road, put a "Keep Left" sign inside the car that is visible to the driver.

Right Side or Left Side?

Road etiquette (or in some cases, the lack of it) can kill you, or, at the very least, put a serious damper on your trip. Turkish drivers pass on the left *and* right. And don't forget the first rule of Italian driving: What's behind you is *not* important (or so they say!).

Start by figuring out if you're on the right or wrong side of the road. Check out Driving Orientation: A World Map at www.strangemaps.word press.com/2007/02/14/203/.

▽ Resources

Auto Europe: Find online auto rentals in more than 4,000 locations worldwide, as well as detailed guides on driving in foreign countries and the region's climate, culture, and embassy and tourist office locations. www.autoeurope.com

Europcar: Book car rentals worldwide and find special rates. www.europcar.com

State Department: The State Department's Web site has links to driving information in foreign countries, including international driving permits, tips on driving abroad, and safety suggestions. http://travel.state.gov/travel/tips/safety/safety_1179.html

CHAPTER 4

Ground Transportation

❝ **It is almost axiomatic that the worst trains take you through magical places.** ❞

—PAUL THEROUX

Although news about buses, trains, and subways tends not to hit the media as often as struggling airlines, the travel and tourism industry is just as dependent on ground transportation as it is on the airline industry. There are more than 6,400 providers of public and community transportation in the United States—including service by buses, subways, trolleys, ferries, and rail (light, heavy, cable car, monorail, and commuter)—and that doesn't include Amtrak or Greyhound.

According to the American Public Transportation Association (APTA), Americans took more than 9.6 billion trips using public transportation last year, and approximately 33 million trips are taken each weekday in the United States. Fifty-four percent of riders use public transit to go to and from work, 15 percent to go to and from school, and 9 percent to go shopping.

In many cases, public transportation is the only option for travelers. This can include those with mobility problems, elderly passengers who are no longer able to drive, those who cannot afford to buy and maintain a personal vehicle, and those living in rural areas. APTA has found that out of the 36 million Americans aged 65 and older, one in five does not drive. It estimates that by the year 2030, the number of Americans in this demographic is going to double! The big problem? Public transportation isn't necessarily convenient or accessible. In fact, more than half of people aged 65 and older who don't drive end up staying at home, partly due to the fact that they don't have easy access to transportation, *but* a 2005 study showed 60 percent of those surveyed would use public transportation more often if it were more readily available. A 2002 APTA study showed that public transportation is available in approximately 60 percent of all rural counties nationwide, for a total of about 1,200 systems.

Even for travelers who do have the option to drive, the tide may be turning toward increased public transportation use: In the summer of 2006, when gas prices rose to more than $3 per gallon, public transportation use reached record numbers, simply due to the money-saving aspect. In 2006, Americans took 10.1 billion trips on public transportation—the highest ridership level in 49 years. The use of public transportation has increased by 30 percent between 1995 and 2006, which beats out the 24 percent growth of highway use in the same period.

Even in the age of hybrid vehicles, environmentalists look to public transportation as a means to drastically reduce pollution. APTA estimates that public transportation use in the United States saves 1.4 billion gallons of gasoline a year—that's almost 4 million gallons of gasoline per day. Compared with private vehicles, public transit produces 95 percent less carbon monoxide, more than 92 percent fewer volatile organic compounds (VOCs), and nearly half as much carbon dioxide and nitrogen oxides (NOx) for every passenger mile. Public transportation reduces annual emissions of VOCs and NOx, which create smog, by more than 70,000 tons and 27,000 tons, respectively. Currently, transit systems are investing in compressed natural gas vehicles, low-sulfur fuel-burning buses, and diesel-electric hybrid buses.

Public Transit Terrorism Concerns

Security issues also plague public transit systems worldwide. Coordinated public transportation attacks took place in Madrid in March 2004, in London in July 2005, and in Mumbai in July 2006. Back in 1995, a religious group released sarin gas in Tokyo's subway system, killing 12 and sickening thousands of others. Bombs exploding on public buses and trains have occurred in Israel, Moscow, Paris, and other cities.

A 2002 report from the Government Accountability Office (GAO) showed that one-third of all the terrorist attacks around the world have occurred on public transportation, and catastrophic attacks on public transportation have already occurred. When it comes to American security, however, the government has fallen behind. While federal funding for aviation security since 2001 has reached nearly $24 billion, public transit has received less than $400 million.

Subways

Travelers who choose not to use public transportation often cite inconvenience as their primary reason. However, in many cities, public transportation is not just the cheapest way to travel but also the easiest. This is particularly true in dense urban areas where traffic can get extremely congested and that are too big to be covered by foot. Below are some of the cities with the best (in terms of convenience, reliability, safety, and cleanliness) public transportation systems.

New York: The Metropolitan Transportation Authority (MTA) operates not just the extensive subway and bus system but also the Long Island Railroad, the Long Island Bus, and bridges and tunnels. The MTA system provides 2.4 billion trips each year—that's a total of about one in every three mass transit users in the entire country and two in every three of the nation's rail riders. Visitors can purchase a 1-day fun pass for $7, which is good for unlimited rides (pay-per-ride tickets are $2 apiece, so make sure you're traveling enough for it to be worth it). For maps and schedules, visit www.mta.info.

San Francisco: In addition to multiple bus and ferry routes, the BART (Bay Area Rapid Transit District) is considered to be one of the best transportation systems in the world. There are 43 BART stations that are located at street level, elevated, and underground.

Find general Bay Area transit information, including transportation, rideshares, and traffic, at www.511.org. BART information is at www.bart.gov.

London: Transport for London includes the famous metro Tube, buses, trams, and even river service. Rates depend on what zone you're traveling to—the further you travel outside of the city center, the more you'll pay. However, the Oyster card is a great resource for travelers that was rolled out only a few years ago. You can choose a pay-as-you-go smartcard or timed passes, which can reduce the price of a ride on public transport by half. www.tfl.gov.uk

Paris: The public transport is operated by RAPT—the subway is commonly referred to as the metro, but the system also includes commuter trains, buses, and Montmartrobus. Nine million passengers take the metro each day. A "Paris Visite" pass gives you unlimited trips on all public transport for one, two, three, or five consecutive days and in three, five, or eight zones. www.parisvisite.com/en/index.php

Prague: You'll find that Prague has one of the best public transit systems in Europe. Between the metro, trams, and buses, two-thirds of Prague's population depends on public transportation, particularly in the congested city center. Tickets have English instructions, so make sure you stamp them every time you get on board, as random inspectors aren't shy about imposing the hefty fines on foreign travelers. www.dp-praha.cz

General visitor information: www.prague-spot.com/transportation, www.myczechrepublic.com/prague/transportation.html

Tokyo: It's probably no surprise that Japan has a very efficient public transit system. Traffic in Tokyo is so busy and congested that traveling by train is the best way to get around. www.kotsu.metro.tokyo.jp/english

Mexico City: Because Mexico City has long been considered one of the most polluted cities in the world, improving its public transportation system is a priority. The metro system, Sistema de Transporte Colectivo, covers practically the entire city with nine routes and carries more than 4.5 million passengers a day. Train cars can get packed, particularly during rush hour, but the first two cars of every train are reserved for women traveling with small children. A new bus system, the Bus Rapid Transit (BRT), covers much of the city, although mass transit is also provided by privately owned microbuses. www.metro.df.gob.mx (Spanish only)

Bangkok: The SkyTrain is a fast, cheap, and efficient way to get around. The elevated monorail goes around the city perimeter, but the relatively new subway system provides more access into the central part of the city. If you're feeling more adventurous, the public bus system is an even cheaper way of traveling throughout the city—the drawbacks are that it's slowed by heavy traffic, can get extremely crowded, and, of course, English instructions are hard to come by. www.bts.co.th/en/index.asp

Unexpected Cities with Good Subway Systems

It's probably no big surprise that major metropolitan areas have the best public transit systems in the world. But in my travels, I've discovered some more offbeat cities boasting mass systems that are efficient, clean, and a lot cheaper than hailing taxis wherever I go.

Sure, the metropolis of Tokyo has an extensive system of mass transit, including subways, buses, and ferries, but the much smaller, historic city of **Kyoto** has a pretty sophisticated mass transit system, too. With a population of around 1.5 million, Kyoto not only has the Kansai Airport Express—a train (or Haruka) that links the city to its main airport—but it also is served by two subway lines. The north-south Karasuma Line has 15 stations, and the east-west Tozai Line presently has 15 as well—they meet at Karasuma Oike station.

Automatic ticket machines predominate, with fares for adults ranging from ¥210 (about $1.82) to ¥340 (about $2.95), and about half that for children, depending on the length of the trip. All-day passes can be purchased for ¥1200, or about $10.40, and include most of the city's buses and subways. www.city.kyoto.jp/koho/eng/access/transport.html

Rennes, France, is the provincial capital of Bretagne (English speakers may know it as Brittany) and one of the smallest cities in the world with a subway system. With just over 200,000 people in the city limits and less than half a million in the entire metropolitan area (similar in size to the Des Moines, Iowa, metro area), Rennes maintains something of a small-town atmosphere. Yet despite the small population, the metro system averages almost 75,000 trips per day—which means that about 15 percent of the entire area's population rides the subway each day. With just a single line, the subway extends about 6 miles and has 15 stations. The Gare de Rennes links the subway lines to the high-speed TGV trains that can transport passengers to Paris in about 2 hours.

The subway makes a walking tour of Rennes a relatively easy proposition, though the city itself is something of a mishmash. Medieval buildings crowd narrow streets in some parts of the city center, while huge neoclassical structures and plazas dominate other parts. Overall, though, the city has a wide range of historic and culturally important structures that belie its longtime importance as a regional capital.

The capital of Georgia, a small ex-Soviet nation on the Black Sea, is **Tbilisi,** with about 1.4 million residents. The Tbilisi Metro, the rapid transit system here, opened in 1966, at the time making it the fourth metro system in the former Soviet Union. With two lines, 22 stations, and about 16 miles of track, the Tbilisi Metro system covers a significant amount of ground.

The Glasgow Subway has run underneath **Glasgow, Scotland,** for more than a century. Opened in 1896, it is considered to be the third oldest subway system in the world, after the London Underground and the Budapest Metro. About 2.1 million people live in the Glasgow area, putting it on a par with such American metro areas as Cincinnati, Sacramento, and Las Vegas. The subway is one circular loop, which is slightly less than 6.5 miles long, and extends both north and south of the River Clyde, with 15 stations. Though residents took to calling it the Clockwork Orange after subway carriages were outfitted with orange during a 1970s renovation, today the orange has been toned down, and most Glaswegians simply call it the subway.

Those interested in participating in a modern Scottish sort of subway ritual can join some University of Glasgow students in a "subcrawl." A take-off of the pubcrawl, the subcrawl involves visiting the pub closest to each subway station for a drink before moving on to the next station—and the next pub. A complete subcrawl, then, would involve 15 drinks.

Daegu is now South Korea's third-largest city, with just over 2.5 million residents, though most travelers will have heard little of it. Two long subway lines, called simply Line 1 and Line 2, have been completed, with long-term plans calling for the eventual construction of six. Line 1 runs for about 16 miles and includes 30 stations, while Line 2 runs for about 17 miles and has 26 stops. Fares range from 800 to 900 won (or about 85 to 95 cents), depending on the distance traveled. www.daegusubway.co.kr/source/eng

▽ Resources

American Public Transportation Association, www.apta.com: You can find statistics, up-to-date news and everything else you need to know about public transportation.

Publictransportation.org: Find news and analyses on the benefits of public transportation.

Subway Navigator, www.subwaynavigator.com: This handy Web site tells you how to get around underground in nearly 150 cities worldwide.

HopStop.com: This is a great navigator for travelers in Boston, Chicago, New York, San Francisco, and Washington, DC. The site can help you get from one point to another via public transport and foot, based on your preferences. For example, to get from my apartment in New York to the *Today* show offices, I have the option of traveling by bus only, by subway only, a combination, or walking only. I can even choose between more walking/fewer transfers or vice versa.

Amtrak

Call it the Great Train Mystery. As our national railway system staggers into another year, it's pretty safe to say that the golden days of the legendary great train rides are mostly a thing of the past. What was once the grand way to travel has been outjetted by faster, cheaper modes of transportation—and these days, our train system is being plagued by all sorts of problems, inside political turmoil, and a severe lack of funding to keep things on track. What travelers are seeing these days are expensive tickets, delayed trains, and diminished routes. So is Amtrak headed for the junkyard, or will it be able to keep chugging along? My hope, of course, as a major train fanatic and supporter of this mode of transportation, is that it can and *must* survive.

First, Let's Talk about the Routes

There are 33 routes available nationwide, serving 46 states in the country (Alaska, Hawaii, South Dakota, and Wyoming are without service). There are also several commuter services in California (Caltrain, Coasters, and Metrolink), Maryland (Maryland Area Regional Commuter), Connecticut (Shore Line East), and Virginia (Virginia Railway Express) operated by Amtrak in conjunction with state and regional authorities.

Amtrak also runs 15 long-distance train services, which typically consist of sleepers, coaches, a diner, and/or a lounge car. Many of these long-distance trains serve small or isolated communities that don't have other transportation options like buses or planes.

The Northeast Corridor, running from Boston to Washington, DC (the Acela Express, Metroliner, and Regional lines), is the busiest passenger rail line, serving more than half of the 25 million Amtrak passengers per year.

What about Those Delayed Trains?

The Bureau of Transportation Statistics reports that in 2004, 71 percent of trains arrived at their final destination on time (within 10 minutes of the expected time). Out of those, 76 percent of short-distance trains like the Northeast Corridor and Empire Service ran on time, while 68 percent of long-distance trains were on time. The worst-performing train in 2005 was the Sunset Limited line between Orlando and Los Angeles, which had only a 7 percent on-time rate.

Part of the problem lies in outdated and aging equipment. In April 2005, the Federal Railroad Administration studied high-speed Acela trains (which run between Washington, DC, New York, and Boston). They found cracks in a train's brake disc rotors and discovered that about half of the discs on any one train might be defective. Acela Express service was suspended from April 15 through July 11, 2005, to accommodate the redesign, manufacture, and replacement of the brake discs.

Another factor in train delays is that Amtrak owns only about 750 out of the 22,000 route miles that it operates (the rest are owned by private freight companies). When you think about it, this is absurd. If you don't control the tracks, you can't control your on-time performance. You can't control your basic scheduling. And this might explain why trains keep getting slower in the United States. Although, legally, passenger trains are supposed to have the right of way, that's not always how it works out. Highly congested areas, or choke points, can cause delays, as do freight train derailments. Amtrak owns most, but not all, of the railway tracks in the Northeast Corridor. Some portions of this area are owned by the Massachusetts Bay Transportation Authority, the Connecticut Department of Transportation, and the Metro-North Railroad. Still, when a freight train needs to pass, in almost all cases Amtrak pulls to a siding and waits.

How Does Amtrak Handle Its Delays?

Usually, a delay of 15 to 20 minutes is not surprising on Amtrak. But if longer delays happen, Amtrak doesn't have any protocol in place. On December 29, 2005, three northbound trains got stuck after a freight train derailed in Savannah, Georgia. Three trains were stuck for 12 to 25 hours. No food or water was provided by Amtrak; some toilets became clogged, and toilet paper ran out; and passengers were not allowed off the train for more than a few minutes at a time. Amtrak didn't implement an alternate plan like busing the passengers to nearby hotels, stating that the delays were longer than anticipated and that due to the holiday season, there weren't enough buses to handle the volume of people on board. Only after the trains began running again and reached Florence, South Carolina, did passengers receive boxed lunches provided by Amtrak.

However, not all delays come without some benefit. In April 2006, Amtrak offered a 10 percent discount on multiride tickets purchased for the Capitol Corridor (which runs between San Francisco and Sacramento) through May 15, 2006. It was an apology for the frequent delays that resulted in a drop in customers. Leaflets were distributed on empty train seats that stated boldly, "Capitol Corridor wants to thank our loyal riders for tolerating our poor on-time performance these past few months. Thanks for sticking with us through the bad times."

So how does this problem get solved? Not easily. Amtrak has no plans (or funds) to acquire more track. In fact, funding is a continuing—and growing—problem for the US passenger train system. And therein lies a painful irony. When America built its interstate highway system, it funded the massive project without regard for tangible return on investment. The interstate system was never set up to make a profit. Why? To paraphrase Dwight Eisenhower, who correctly described it at the time, America didn't build the interstate highway system . . . the interstate highway system built America.

And so it should be with our train system. The way it is currently constructed, it can never make a profit. It will always operate at a loss. (Essentially, that's exactly what the interstate highway system does, except it gets funded!)

Where Does the Funding Come From?

Point-blank, Amtrak is not a moneymaking operation. In its 34-year history, Amtrak has never made a profit, and it is drowning in $3.5 billion of long-term debt.

Although it receives millions from the government and from ticket sales, it still needs more.

The reality is, no national railway system in the world can survive without federal funding. Every year, Amtrak submits a grant proposal to Congress, but the money allocated is less than what can support the entire system. Amtrak needs significant funding for necessary upgrades in order to become a smoother operation, rather than maintaining a failing status quo.

When Amtrak submitted its grant proposal for the fiscal year 2006, President Bush came back with a proposed zero funding for the rail system. Congress balked at this, and the president threatened to enforce his first veto during his presidency. However, on December 3, 2005, Congress passed a bill that appropriated about $1.2 billion to Amtrak for the fiscal year 2006. The bill included caveats requiring Amtrak to start implementing reforms to save money. For the 2007 fiscal year, Amtrak asked for $1.8 billion and was given $1.2 billion. For the 2008 fiscal year, Amtrak estimated its budget would be $3.1 million, and President Bush offered to pay just $800 million, but what the Senate actually appropriates remains to be seen.

Will Amtrak Be Privatized?

Nothing is in place yet. But critics say that some recent developments indicate that Amtrak's board is on its way to dismantling the system for future privatization. In September 2005, the board of directors, appointed by the

Bush administration, voted to create a new subsidiary that would own and operate the Northeast Corridor, thereby separating that network of routes from the rest of the national system. This vote was not made public until a month later, when it was leaked to a Florida newspaper.

Amtrak's board chairperson, David Laney, has publicly explained that this subsidiary only serves as a holding company for the Northeast Corridor's fixed assets to simplify costs and improve financial management.

So What Is the Future of Amtrak and How Does It Affect Me?

To save money, Amtrak is redesigning its first-class dining cars on long-distance trains to the "Simplified Dining Service." So far, this change has been implemented in the Texas Eagle, the City of New Orleans, the Sunset Limited, and the Capitol Limited.

The idea is to decrease the number of dining car employees from five or six per train to three. Portions of the meals come precooked so they need only to be heated in an oven. Amtrak has switched from china to plastic dishes that can be thrown away after use. Reservations for seating are in 15-minute increments, and meal service is available for up to 18 hours a day so that customers can have more flexible eating times.

Amtrak has implemented changes in some of its long-distance carriers to court higher-end travelers who are willing to spend money on a first-class ticket that includes meals and sleeping accommodations. For example, the Empire Builder, which runs from Chicago to Portland, Oregon, began incorporating upgrades in August 2005. First-class passengers receive a glass of sparkling wine or cider upon boarding, followed by a wine-and-cheese tasting on the second day of the trip. Their new menu items include old-school items that are meant to echo the "original recipes of the Great Northern Railway," such as Great Northern baked ham and English beefsteak potpie. If you haven't already fallen into a food coma at that point, you'll get a freshly baked cookie or other treat at bedtime. The upgrades aren't all culinary, though. The sleeping, coach, and dining cars have been refurbished, with new toilets and shower units as well as upgraded cushions, carpets, and drapes.

The Downeaster route from Boston to Portland, Maine, has become one of Amtrak's most successful routes, jumping by 30 percent in 2006, the highest increase across the nation. The route still lost money but is now considered to be a model for expanding passenger rail service on Amtrak.

There has been some discussion on eliminating some travel discounts, but at present there are no specific examples of how this is being implemented.

Amtrak is also reevaluating its 15 remaining long-distance train routes to see what should be added or eliminated. No major restructuring has yet taken place. And if Congress can realize—in time—that these routes are needed beyond just looking at a profit-and-loss statement, there may be a glimmer of hope for Amtrak.

Scenic Train Travel

Even though Amtrak may be struggling, old-world-style train travel is an experience that's still available and shouldn't be missed. Even Amtrak agrees with this philosophy. In the fall of 2007, Amtrak teamed up with Grand-Luxe Rail Journeys to attach seven luxury cars to already scheduled Amtrak trains in cities like Chicago, Los Angeles, Miami, and Denver. The new service, GrandLuxe Limited, offers amenities like five-course meals and butler service, with prices ranging from about $800 to $2,500 for a 2- or 3-day journey, and up to $8,000 for a week to 10-day tour.

Rocky Mountaineer, a train travel company, added two new routes in western Canada. The Whistler Mountaineer train links Vancouver with the mountain resort town of Whistler, British Columbia; the Fraser Discovery route proceeds on a 2-day journey from Whistler to the town of Jasper in Jasper National Park. Both routes wind high through the Canadian Rockies, offering train passengers views that are inaccessible for road-trippers in the area. In fact, a number of rather impressive vistas, including a ride through Fraser River Canyon, are only available on the trains. Roads and sometimes even footpaths can't navigate the challenging terrain in the area.

On longer trips, the trains stop in the evenings, and passengers actually spend the night in local hotels instead of aboard the train. Hotel prices are included in the costs for these Rocky Mountaineer voyages, with "superior" and "deluxe" room upgrades available at an additional cost.

The Whistler Mountaineer offers a fairly straightforward 3-hour journey operating through mid-October, when cold weather tempers demand and makes train travel tougher. Prices start at $85 for one-way trips to Whistler. For the Fraser Discovery route, prices start at $729 for the Red Leaf (basic) level of service, assuming double occupancy. 877-460-3200, www.rocky-mountaineer.com

Taj Hotels operates the **Deccan Odyssey** in India, a 21-coach train that travels on an 8-day journey from Mumbai to Maharashtra. Visit the hopping beach communities in Goa, pass by rural villages, and visit the caves of Ajanta and Ellora. You may mistake yourself for royalty when you get used to this "Palace on Wheels," with five-star cuisine, golden décor, and spacious en suite accommodations. Prices start around $260 a night per person. www. thedeccanodyssey.com

In South Africa, the **Blue Train** claims it's like a five-star hotel on wheels. The blue carriages travel between Cape Town and Pretoria (that's 27 hours) and include gourmet meals paired with South African wines, butler service, and, of course, marbled bathrooms. Prices range from about $1,200 to $2,240 per person. www.bluetrain.co.za

But my favorite South African train experience is **Rovos Rail**, which operates steam-powered locomotives with classic cars between Pretoria and Victoria Falls. The wood-paneled cars feature 36 suites, with prices ranging from about $1,200 to $2,700. www.rovos.co.za

---

Top 5 Languages Officially Spoken in the Most Countries:

English (57)	French (33)
Arabic (23)	Spanish (21)
Portuguese (7)	

The **Mount Ranier Scenic Railroad** is a vintage steam locomotive dating back to the 1920s, taking you on a 90-minute ride through the foothills of Mount Ranier. Prices start at $15. 360-569-2588, www.mrsr.com

The **Xining, Qinghai-Lhasa Tibet** rail line officially opened for passengers on July 1, 2006. A Tibetan railway was first conceived by China's central government to link occupied Tibet with the rest of the country. Stretching for well over 1,000 kilometers over some of the most inhospitable terrain in the world (the Himalayan mountain range), the railway takes travelers through the Chinese countryside all the way from Beijing to Lhasa, the Tibetan capital— for less than $50. The train is something of an architectural marvel; it rises higher than 16,000 feet at the highest point in the journey. By comparison, Colorado's Pikes Peak rises to just over 14,000 feet, while Alaska's Mount McKinley (also known as Denali) soars to 20,320 feet. To prevent passengers from getting altitude sickness at this height, oxygen is added to the train's air supply, and supplemental breathing masks are available if necessary.

You can view Scotland in grand style aboard **The Royal Scotsman**, which offers several excursions throughout the countryside and highlands. A "classic" 4-night journey travels from Edinburgh to Keith, Kyle of Lochalsh, Boat of Garten, and Perth, while the 7-night round-trip includes stops at Spean Bridge, Bridge of Orchy, and Wemyss Bay. www.royalscotsman.com.

Trains versus Planes in Europe

If there is one place where train travel has flourished, it's Europe. Decades of young backpackers and budget travelers have fond memories of traveling from country to country over the course of weeks or even months. The popularity of the European train system was due to prompt schedules, accessible routes, and clean trains, not to mention the backpacker's best friend, the Eurail Pass. By contrast, air travel was expensive, inefficient, and inconvenient. But since the deregulation of European airlines in 1997, the train system may be derailed by a new rival: low-cost air carriers.

While airlines such as Ryanair (www.ryanair.com) and EasyJet (www.easyjet.com) have flourished over the years, that doesn't mean the death of the grand old European trains. Trains have several advantages over planes for some travelers, especially ones under age 26 who qualify for lower student fares. Train stations are usually located closer to the city center than many airports and are linked to other forms of public transit in Europe, like subways and urban trains. Since many low-cost carriers serve newer, more distant airports, getting from the airport to the city center can be problematic.

Eurail Passes can also provide more freedom than point-to-point plane tickets. When riding the rails through France, for example, it's possible to hop off a Bordeaux–Paris train to explore a village in the Loire Valley. Hopping off a plane would mean parachuting into the vineyard.

Eurail is basically a transportation conglomerate whose shareholders are the railways and ferry routes that participate in the network. You can get multicountry passes or single-country passes, both of which offer significant discounts over paying per train trip. Participating countries include Austria, Belgium, Denmark, Finland, France, Germany, Greece, Holland, Hungary, Italy, Luxembourg, Norway, Portugal, Republic of Ireland, Spain, Sweden, and Switzerland. You may even be able to travel to former Eastern Bloc countries such as Bulgaria, Croatia, Montenegro, Romania, and Serbia—even Turkey with some passes. Translation? You can access much of Europe on one pass, and there are several options to choose from.

If you book through Eurail.com, the traditional **Eurail Global Pass** is good for travel within a period of 15 days, 21 days, 1 month, 2 months, or 3 months. You ride in first class, get discounts on high-speed trains and the Chunnel (Eurostar), and receive a few other perks. For 10 days of travel over a 2-month period, it would cost adults $799.

A **Youth Flexi Pass** targets travelers 12 to 26, allowing them to travel among any of the 18 countries over 2 months in second class. For 10 days of travel, it's $519, and for 15 days, it's $681.

A **Eurail Select Pass** allows you to visit three to five adjoining countries during a stay of up to 2 months. For adults, passes start at $429 for 5 days of travel among three countries and rise to $947 for 15 days of travel among five countries over 2 months.

Also available are specific country groupings, single-country passes, and even a **Select Pass 'n Drive**, which includes 3 days of train travel plus 2 days of car rental from Avis or Hertz.

As a general rule on Eurail, overnight trips will often count as 2 days of travel, though it will depend on the routes and tickets you procure. You must begin using the pass within 6 months of purchasing it.

One caution: Just because you have a Eurail Pass doesn't mean that every train operation in Europe will honor it. A number of trains are privately run (this is especially true in Switzerland), so check directly with Eurail Pass to make sure which trains honor the pass.

▽ Resources

Eurail, www.eurail.com: This is the primary Web site for Eurail passes, providing information and booking passes online.

Rail Europe, www.raileurope.com/us: This alternative site provides information on train fares and schedules throughout Europe, including Eurail passes and train services in individual countries.

Seat61.com: You can find times, fares, and explanations of various rail passes, as well as purchase your rail tickets on this independent site.

Budget Buses

The introduction of Megabus seemed to be the culmination of all things budget oriented, as travelers found they could traverse the Midwest for as little as $1.50 round-trip. This is not a typo. That really is one of the published fares on Megabus. The new service launched in April 2006, with nonstop routes between Chicago and Cincinnati, Cleveland, Columbus, Detroit, Indianapolis, Milwaukee, Minneapolis, and St. Louis, Ann Arbor, Pittsburgh, Kansas City, and Louisville. Fares start at $1 (plus a 50-cent booking fee) and can climb up to about $55 round-trip—the price is based on availability, and as seats fill up, prices increase. If you can book your tickets in advance, chances are you may find round-trip rates at just a few dollars apiece—a far better deal than you're going to find with any other bus system, train, or airline. Because the company is Internet-based, there is a very low overhead, which means that savings can be passed on to the customer. 877-GO2-MEGA, www.megabus.com

Unfortunately for non-Midwest travelers, Megabus has no immediate plans to expand into the East or West Coasts. But there's still good news: Intercity buses are still one of the most affordable and safest modes of transportation, serving both major cities and rural towns. And even when fuel costs are at their peak, most companies choose to absorb the costs rather than passing them on to customers. Here are a few companies to get you started.

The Dallas-based **Greyhound** runs the largest intercity bus system in the United States, with a fleet of nearly 1,500 vehicles servicing 1,700 destinations (not to mention Greyhound Australia!). However, as of August 2004, the company has made major cutbacks that have affected about 1,000 locations across the country. Due to an overall drop in bus travel in recent years, the company chose to increase its bottom line by focusing on the more profitable short and medium-length routes. This has directly affected several lower-income and rural neighborhoods, many of which don't have other low-cost options for intercity travel.

The Next French Revolution

On your next trip to Europe, you may find yourself in the midst of a French revolution. No, not that kind. The country has developed a lightning-fast bullet train that travels from Paris to Strasbourg in eastern France, at speeds of nearly 200 mph! This system promises to cut the commuting time from Paris to Strasbourg from 4 hours to about 2 hours 20 minutes and opens up the eastern region that was previously only accessible by air or car. The TGV (Train à Grande Vitesse) system has already been in place for Paris to Marseille, Paris to Bordeaux, Paris to Lille, Paris to Lyon, and Paris to Nantes. So what does this mean for European travel? It may very well provide some serious competition to the airlines. Air France has already cut its service between Paris and the Metz-Nancy-Lorraine Airport and expects to lose about a quarter of its two million passengers in flights between Paris and Strasbourg. You can purchase tickets at the train stations or online at www.sncf.com (in French).

Greyhound is also making some upgrades, most notably in its terminals in Chicago, Milwaukee, Minneapolis, and Texas, and rolling them out in 18 other cities, including Cincinnati, Detroit, Indianapolis, Louisville, Oklahoma City, Pittsburgh, and Wichita. These changes include wireless Internet, plasma televisions, bilingual signs, improved security, and overall renovations to increase seating and space in the terminals. On the coaches themselves, Greyhound regularly refurbishes its buses and has installed more comfortable seats with lumbar support and removable armrests. 800-231-2222, www.greyhound.com

Based in Springfield, Massachusetts, **Peter Pan Bus Lines** is a third-generation family-owned bus line that services only northeastern states. Although it has provided some competition with Greyhound in the past, the two companies actually began coordinating their operations in 1998. For travelers, this means that the two companies' bus schedules are coordinated; you can buy tickets from either line and you may end up on either bus. (*Take note:* Peter Pan shows movies on some of its buses; Greyhound doesn't.) Peter Pan has three different price structures: You'll get the lowest fare if you book online and a discounted rate if you purchase your ticket at the terminal in advance; you'll pay the highest amount if you purchase your ticket in person on the same day of travel. 800-343-9999, www.peterpanbus.com

As many intercity bus riders tend to be students and other budget-minded travelers, Greyhound and Peter Pan have faced some stiff competition with **Fung Wah Bus,** also known as the Chinatown Express. For $30, you get service from a street corner in New York City's Chinatown (138 Canal Street) to Boston's South Station. The Fung Wah bus was founded in 1997 by Pei Lin Liang, a Chinese-born noodle factory deliveryman who emigrated to New York 12 years earlier. Liang borrowed money from his relatives to buy four vans and began transporting Chinese immigrants between Brooklyn and Chinatown in New York; he later began a van service to Boston. Today, the line has 21 buses that operate 18 round-trips a day between Boston and New York, with Liang often at the wheel himself. www.fungwahbus.com

While not exactly in the same league as a traditional bus—and certainly not as low cost—**Limoliner** is fast becoming a popular option for business travelers not wanting to take a plane or train. (Give me the choice: US Airways or Delta shuttle between Boston and New York or Amtrak or Limoliner, and the planes lose each time.) Entrepreneur Fergus McCann launched the Limoliner business in October 2003 after noticing how difficult travel had become after September 11 and also observing the decreasing level of service offered by airlines and

Amtrak. For $79 each way, Limoliner runs five times a day between Boston and New York City and is designed to create a hassle-free travel experience while allowing business professionals to be productive even while they're on the road. The vehicle picks up and drops off at Hilton Hotels in each city and offers free high-speed Wi-Fi, satellite TV, a travel attendant, food and beverage service (but no alcohol), and reclining leather seats. Even their bathroom is nice, with granite countertops and a skylight. 888-546-5469, www.limoliner.com

Which Works for You?

Wherever possible, I'm a big believer in the train alternative—where it works, it really works. Between Los Angeles and San Diego, for example, an airline ticket is more or less prohibitive. But the train between LA and San Diego is a joy—and far less expensive.

A flight between the two cities runs between $300 and $600; Amtrak's Pacific Surfliner is $68, and you get to skip the security, sit in comfortable seats, plug in your laptop and cell phone, and work on adult-size trays. Not to mention that most train stations are far more convenient than airports.

On the East Coast, you have even more options besides airlines. Between New York and Boston, you have the option of Amtrak, a bus such as Peter Pan or Greyhound, or Limoliner. All rates below signify round-trip prices.

AIRLINE (KENNEDY TO LOGAN)	AMTRAK (PENN STATION TO SOUTH STATION)	PETER PAN/ GREYHOUND (PORT AUTHORITY TO SOUTH STATION)	LIMOLINER (HILTON BACK BAY TO HILTON NEW YORK)
From $148 (Delta) to $1,260 (US Airways)	$136	$30 (online booking)	$158

Between New York and Washington, DC, Amtrak wins, hands down. If you did a race between two people—one flying on the La Guardia–DC shuttle and the other taking Amtrak's Acela—it would be a tie, if you factored in time to check bags and go through security, plus waiting time on the runways. And while the bus isn't as comfortable as a train, the price certainly makes it worthwhile. All prices below are round-trip.

US AIRWAYS SHUTTLE (LA GUARDIA TO REAGAN NATIONAL)	AMTRAK (PENN STATION TO UNION STATION)	PETER PAN/ GREYHOUND (PORT AUTHORITY TO WASHINGTON)
$180	$134	$35 (online booking)

CHAPTER 5

❝ The great advantage of a hotel is that it is a refuge from home life. ❞

—GEORGE BERNARD SHAW

First, let's start with the bad news. Hotel rates in the United States are increasing across the board. The reasons? A weak US dollar, making America a bargain for foreign visitors, and in some cities, a bad word for prospective hotel guests: conversion. More and more hotels are closing, and hotel room inventory is shrinking in certain large international gateway cities as developers convert existing properties into condominia or coop apartments. New development is all about "mixed use"—combination hotel room and private residences. New York City is still 5,000 hotel rooms short of where the city needs to be. And while the official report from New York's tourism officials says that the number of rooms has actually increased, in real terms, there have been so many hotels closed for conversions (condos, coops, and simple closures), it helps to explain why Manhattan hotels operate at close to full occupancy and average hotel rates in the city are north of $500 a night. Ouch. Translation: The law of supply and demand has taken over, and demand is winning. The average rate for a hotel room in the United States was $100 per night in 2006, a 6 percent increase over the previous year. But in the bigger cities, that $100 is the average cost of three bottled waters in the minibar! Okay, I exaggerate just a little on the bottled water cost. But here's something that's *not* an exaggeration but, sadly, the truth: A number of hotels in Manhattan have recently boasted average room rates that hovered north of $900 a night!

You may be familiar with many of the major hotel brands, but what you may not know is many of them are owned by a limited number of hotel companies. For a complete list of the top 50 hotel companies, visit the American Hotel and Lodging Association at www.ahla.com/products_info_center_top50.asp.

Inter-Continental Hotel Group has 2,550 properties in the United States and 1,148 properties abroad. Brands include: Candlewood, Centra, Crowne Plaza, Forum Hotel, Holiday Inn, Holiday Inn Express, Holiday Inn Garden Court, Holiday Inn Select, Hotel Indigo, InterContinental, Parkroyal, Posthouse, Staybridge Suites, Sunspree Resorts, and Toby Hotels.

Cendant Corporation has 5,597 properties in the United States and 1,064 properties abroad. Brands include: Amerihost Inn, Days Hotel, Days Inn, Days Serviced Apartments, Howard Johnson, Howard Johnson Express, Knights Inn, Ramada, Ramada International Plaza, Ramada International Hotels & Resorts, Ramada Limited, Ramada Plaza, Super 8, Thriftlodge, and Travelodge.

Marriott International Inc. has 2,286 properties in the United States and 362 properties abroad. Brands include: Courtyard, Fairfield Inn, Marriott Conference Centers, Marriott Executive Apartments, Marriott Hotels and Resorts, Renaissance Hotels & Resorts, Residence Inn, SpringHill Suites, the Ritz-Carlton, and TownPlace Suites.

Choice Hotels International Inc. has 4,032 properties in the United States and 887 properties abroad. Brands include: Clarion, Comfort Inn, Comfort Suites, Econo Lodge, MainStay Suites, Quality, Quality Suites, Rodeway Inn, and Sleep Inn.

Hilton Hotels Corporation has 2,256 properties in the United States and 204 properties abroad. Brands include: Conrad, Doubletree, Doubletree Club, Embassy Suites, Embassy Vacation Resort, Hampton Inn, Hampton Inn Suites, Hilton, Hilton Gaming, Hilton Garden Inn, Homewood Suites, and Scandic Hotel.

Best Western International has 2,201 properties in the United States and

1,754 properties abroad. Its only hotel brand is Best Western.

Starwood Hotels & Resorts Worldwide Inc. has 346 properties in the United States and 374 properties abroad. Brands include: Four Points, Hacienda, Luxury Collection, Sheraton Hotel, St. Regis, W Hotels, and Westin.

Accor International has no properties in the United States and 1,735 properties abroad. Brands include: Century, Coralia, Etap Hotel, Hotel Formule 1, Hotel Novotel, Hotel Sofitel, Jardin, Libertel, Mercure Hotel, Pannonia, Parthenon, and Suitehotel.

Carlson Hospitality Worldwide has 558 properties in the United States and 385 properties abroad. Brands include: Country Inn & Suites, Park Inn, Park Plaza, Radisson, and Regent Hotels.

Accor North America has 1,252 properties in the United States and 27 properties abroad. Brands include: Coralia, Hotel Novotel, Hotel Sofitel, Mercure Hotel, Motel 6, Red Roof Inn, and Studio 6.

Avoiding Brochure Language

Okay, so much for who owns what. Now it's time for substance. Anyone who is familiar with my work knows that I loathe brochures. Glossy hotel brochures are one of the worst culprits of misinformation: Superlatives like "best," "greatest," "luxurious," and "finest" are banned from my lexicon; no hotel has ever fulfilled its brochure promise of only allowing gorgeous couples to check in, who spend all their time parading hand in hand along the beach at sunset.

And let's not forget catchy tourism slogans that often backfire. In 2006, it rained about 40 days straight in Hawaii. Then there was a dam break in Kauai and a sewage spill in Waikiki. As high season approached, tourism officials pumped out an expensive, slick marketing campaign containing the state's newest tourism slogan: "We promise you a vacation unlike any you can imagine."

It was, of course, technically correct.

In brochure language, one of the biggies is the "ocean view" promise. How do you know if it's a sweeping panoramic view or a tiny blue speck from your balcony, viewable only through binoculars? Well, you can always call and ask, but you may not get a very clear answer, as many hotels won't guarantee a specific room, only a specific type of room—and it's always *their* definition. Also keep in mind that there is often a huge difference between "ocean view" and "ocean front." Take the Doubletree Alana Hotel in Waikiki, whose Web site says, "Our standard rooms have great city as well as ocean views." But it also says that it's "less than a 10-minute stroll to the sands of Waikiki Beach." That little detail means that your view is hardly the great blue expanse that you might expect.

If you're hotel hunting in a major city like New York, where space is a precious commodity, be on the lookout for a completely alien definition of terms. For those boutique hotels that brag about being trendy or chic, the end result is often the same: absolutely tiny. For example, the Hudson Hotel offers "Urban adventure, daredevil design, and true affordability . . . the ultimate lifestyle hotel for the 21st century." The reality: A standard room at the Hudson is a whopping 150 square feet. The brochure continues, "Philippe Starck's design includes chartreuse-lit escalators that sweep guests to a 40-foot-high ivy-covered lobby, an enormous indoor/outdoor private park and a ceiling fresco by world-famous painter Francesco Clemente." Here's a clue: Beware of any place that name-drops twice in one paragraph (especially if you've never heard of them before). Then think about whether you want to stay in a place that brags about its escalator lighting on the front page. Enough said.

Brochures and Web sites are also loaded with hard-to-decipher terms, so here's a handy cheat sheet of words to watch for on your next vacation.

Boutique (noun/adj): a small business offering specialized products and services

Translation: a small hotel with rooms the size of a walk-in closet and walls loaded with modern art; most likely has a fountain in the lobby

Gourmet (adj): of or relating to a connoisseur of food and drink

Translation: a restaurant that is not a chain, a diner, or a fast food outlet, but has a liquor license

Guaranteed (adj): assured a particular outcome or condition

Translation: not assured a particular outcome or condition, especially in cases of overbooked hotels, etc.

Unique (adj): being the only one of its kind

Translation: not unique—unless it's made entirely of ice or is located underwater

Run of house (adj): any available room that the staff feels like putting you in

Translation: any bad available room that the staff feels like putting you in

Tropical (adj): of, occurring in, or characteristic of the tropics; hot and humid

Translation: Hot and humid and very rainy.

Hotel Ratings

Once you've deciphered the brochure or Web site language, what about service, cleanliness, and maintenance? In the United States, the two biggest ratings indices are published by the American Automobile Association (AAA) and Mobil—and high ratings are usually proudly worn like a badge of honor by hotels. But what do they really mean?

AAA evaluates more than 60,000 lodging and dining establishments every year, on a scale of one to five diamonds. Anonymous inspectors rate hotels based on 27 requirements covering the lodging's public areas, lobby, grounds, bathrooms, housekeeping, decor, and hospitality. AAA rates only hotels and restaurants that are clean and well maintained, so even a one-diamond hotel can be expected to have the basic amenities.

Mobil star ratings have been in use since 1958, used in rating hotels, spas, and restaurants. Standards are set by hoteliers and restaurateurs and deal only with a certain price point. Every property gets a surprise visit from a facility inspector, who uses a checklist to evaluate cleanliness, physical condition, and location. If a property might qualify for a four- or five-star rating, an anonymous inspector returns for a service evaluation based on more than 500 criteria. http://mobiltravelguide.howstuffworks.com

However, even these two "gold" standards in the hotel industry are highly subjective, which means that I don't necessarily trust them. For one thing, AAA and Mobil ratings don't always synchronize, and the average traveler may not be aware of which criteria are being judged. Mobil's service evaluation for potential four- and five-star hotels includes criteria like staff appearance, behavior, and skill level. Which is all well and good, but I'm more interested in knowing if my room has good water pressure and a functioning fire alarm than whether the bellhop addresses me as "Sir" in the elevator. If a AAA inspector rates a hotel based on the fact that it puts a robe on my bed, I'm more interested in knowing whether my bedspread has been washed in the past month (usually the answer is no).

These days you can also find star ratings on travel Web sites like Travelocity, SideStep, Hotwire, Hotels.com, and Priceline, ranked by the Web site itself and travelers themselves. And more often than not, in many foreign countries a star is actually "awarded" by the local government—not for service but as an indicator of the rates the hotel charges. It's actually a tax designation. How useless is that? Staying in a four-star hotel often means you're paying more than you should.

Then there are the online sites, the bastions of the brave new world of citizen journalism that supposedly offer up-to-the-minute critiques from real guests.

While these sites are certainly entertaining, the underlying problem is how the reviews are vetted. Consider the popular Tripadvisor.com site. After a number of negative reviews of the London NYC Hotel in Manhattan ran on the site, other reviews were posted proclaiming the hotel "the epitome of elegant simplicity" and stating that "the suites offer a distinct refinement." The "review" also gave the hotel a top rating of five in every category, and it was checked off as being a great spot for every demographic from young singles to honeymooners to older travelers and everything in between. One small problem: Unless you were living under a rock, it was easy to decipher that brochure language. Sure enough, the writer was a member of the hotel's own marketing staff.

There are other hotels that actually offer guests a free meal if they write a glowing review of the hotel using the hotel's business center.

Again, these user-generated sites are entertaining, but you must put the information, or misinformation, in proper perspective.

So what do these rating systems mean, if anything? To me . . . not much. If a hotel gets five stars because it has a golf course but I don't golf, how is that hotel a five-star property to me? What's far more important than basing your hotel choices on the number of diamonds, hearts, or stars is to develop your own rating system.

First off, the Hotel and Travel Index covers more than 100,000 properties worldwide, with 10 rankings from Moderate Tourist to Superior Deluxe. You can search individual hotel rankings by location at www.hotelandtravelindex.com.

If you're traveling in Europe, a good first stop is ViaMichelin, which has the prestigious Michelin rankings for hotels, as well as maps and driving directions for visitors; www.viamichelin.com.

I still think Web sites like Tripadvisor are often a good place to *start*, especially when it comes to learning other people's experiences. But again, these are not standardized systems, and in the case of hotels like the London NYC, they're not always trustworthy.

Develop your own rating system. Here are some good questions to keep in mind when you're considering a location.

- Can you check in early, or will you have to kill hours in the lobby before your room is ready?
- What time is checkout, and will they charge you for another day if you check out 1 minute after the hour?
- Is the front desk located near the hotel entrance, or will you have to walk for miles while lugging your suitcases?

! Are there stairs or an elevator close to your room?

! Take note of the tiny details: Are the doorknobs shiny? Are the elevator buttons worn off? Is the ashtray in the hallway overflowing? Are the corridors depressing with bad lighting?

If all else fails, try what I call my Diet Coke test. Several years ago, in a California Ritz-Carlton, the waitress refused to give me a can or bottle of Diet Coke because the hotel bar served their sodas with a gun dispenser. Only after pressing her, pointing out that there *must* be cans of Diet Coke for room service and vending machines, did I get my soda. At a Best Western in Canada, on a freezing cold night, I wandered into the hotel coffee shop. When I requested a Diet Coke, the waitress told me to hold on, put on her coat, and crossed four lanes of highway traffic to a convenience store, where she bought me a six-pack of soda—one for now, five for later. Which of these two hotels do you think had a five-star, five-diamond rating given by AAA or Mobil? And which of these two hotels do you think got *my* five-star rating?

But wait . . . it gets worse.

Hotels are going more over the top than ever and are upping the ante by giving *themselves* six stars and above. Of course, now you know that's not a real rating, but these hotels don't seem to care. They justify it by calling it "marketing."

Take the Hydropolis in Dubai, the under-construction luxury underwater resort that is billing itself a *10-star* hotel. Ten stars? It's not even open yet! The Crown Macau casino on Taipa Island in Macau is billed as the "city's first six-star casino hotel," with 200 VIP guest rooms, including 24 VIP suites and 8 presidential villas, 220 gaming tables, more than 500 slot machines, and a series of private salons. The spa includes eight treatment rooms as well as a private VIP spa room. As for food? Well, you can choose from four fine-dining restaurants and several cafes, or you can hit up one of the trendy bar—all within the hotel. Again, they awarded the six stars to themselves.

Over-the-Top Hotels

Stars and diamonds notwithstanding, we can't really ignore the true over-the-top hotel rooms of the world, with rates starting at $10,000 a night. Here's the latest crop of über rooms for those hedge fund poster children or the petro dollar babies who just have unlimited travel budgets.

At the **Setai in South Beach, Miami,** the penthouse suite takes up the whole 40th floor of the hotel. That's 10,000 square feet of space, a private rooftop pool, two master bedrooms, and your very own 24-hour butler. All this for the price of $25,000 per night.

For $10,500 a day, the **Presidential Suite at the St. Regis** in New York allows guests to hang out in a three-bedroom, four-and-a-half bathroom suite, with a marble foyer, full-sized kitchen, and walnut-paneled library. Meals can be taken in a formal dining room, and a maître d' is available at all times for personal service, plus free clothes pressing when you arrive and daily deliveries of fresh fruit and candy. www.starwoodhotels.com/stregis/index.html

Vegas is all about extravagance, and that comes through clearly in its high-roller rooms, where a continuous war wages on as each hotel tries to outdo the other. At the **Palms Casino Resort**, you can spend $25,000 to party in the Hardwood Suite—the 10,000-square-foot room is two levels and comes with a half basketball court, locker room, pool table, poker table, and 10-person Jacuzzi. And did I mention the "makeout room"? If this room is all booked up, try the Hugh Hefner Sky Villa that's completely decked out *Playboy* style or a two-story bungalow for just $3,000 a night. 866-942-7777, www.palms.com

Of course, you'd expect **The Ritz** to be on this list, and Coco Chanel's suite fits right in. This is where Chanel lived for 37 years, in the center of Paris near the Louvre. The balcony overlooks the Place Vendome, and even the bathroom has a garden view. Unlike some of the over-the-top rooms, this one relies on its elegance and simplicity: Karl Lagerfeld was called upon to restore the suite to reflect Chanel's sensibility. Starting at just $4,300 a night, it's practically a steal—that is, if you can live in a 1,667-square-foot room. In the same hotel are suites named after F. Scott Fitzgerald, Hemingway, and even Elton John. www.ritz.com

The **Westin Excelsior** in Rome is home to the largest suite in Europe. The 11,700-square-foot suite covers two full floors, with six bedrooms, a private fitness room, and a dining table for 10. You can hold your business meetings in the boardroom or the private eight-seat theater, and then relax at night in the sauna, steam bath, or Jacuzzi. For just about $20,000 a night, consider this a steal. www.starwoodhotels.com/westin

African Sapphire Villa at Altamer, Anguilla, British Overseas Territory, is available for $80,000 a week in the high season (mid-December to early January), with a 2-week minimum. You have your pick of three villas, all of

which include your own personal butlers, maids, and private chef. www.
altamer.com

The new Presidential Suite at the **InterContinental** Hong Kong is a modest
7,000 feet. Starting at about $11,000 a night, you can spend a few nights
in the five-bedroom suite with a study, a two-story living room, and a
kitchenette (don't worry if the kitchen is small—you can order room service day or night from celebrity chef Alain Ducasse's restaurant, Spoon.
www.hongkong-ic.intercontinental.com

In the Middle East is the **Emirates Palace in Abu Dhabi,** which currently
claims to be the most expensive hotel ever built and is often unofficially touted
as a seven-star hotel. We're talking about 1,002 Swarovski crystal chandeliers
(which require a full-time staff of 10 to clean them). If you're not in the mood
for a perfume bath, you can pay a little extra to have your tub filled with
champagne. Oh, and each room comes with a butler. About $12,000 per
night, give or take . . . a butler. www.emiratespalace.com/en/main.htm

Dubai is already home to some of the most lavish hotel rooms in the
world, and the **Burj Al Arab** is one of the standouts: Taller than the Eiffel
Tower, it's made up of 202 two-level suites—the largest of the bunch are
the two Royal Suites, which are about 8,000 square feet each, spanning
the entire 25th floor. That includes a living area with private bar, a dining
area, a kitchen with separate butler entrance, a study area and library,
lounge, and two bedrooms each with en suite marble bathrooms. And
hey, you also get a range of full-sized Hermes products for men and
women, a "pillow menu" of 13 pillows and quilts, and a "bath menu" of
music and aromatherapy bath oils prepared by your butler. If you fly in,
you can land your personal helicopter on the hotel's helipad for a fee.
www.burj-al-arab.com

Rent an Island

If an extravagant hotel room isn't enough for you, how about an entire
island? If you thought renting a private island was reserved for billionaires,
think again. You can rent a 3-acre island with a guesthouse in Bora Bora for
just about $4,000 a week. A company called Vladi Private Island offers loca-
tions like Sleepy Cove in Halifax for just about $140 a day. Island Hide-
aways rents out islands in the Caribbean, which, if you go in the low season,
can turn into a better deal than some hotels! Try the Seagrape Cottage on
Little Thatch Island just southwest of West End, Tortola, for $825 a week.
www.islandhideaways.com

Villa Rental

In the travel world, the term "villa" encompasses all kinds of housing: apartments, townhouses, farmhouses, castles, and cottages. Italy, in particular, is a hot spot for villa rentals, where you can live like a local among the vineyards and olive trees. Because they provide more space and privacy than a hotel, they are well suited for large groups and families. As villas are self-catering, they also give you the unique opportunity to get a truly local experience that you won't get from a hotel or tour guide. Daily visits to the village bakery or open-air market encourage you to interact with the town's residents, and it's not unlikely you'll make new friends—your neighbors.

Villas range from $38 to $250 per person per night, though prices vary depending upon size and locale. And if you are looking for a house that has a pool and sleeps more than six, it's a good idea to reserve 9 months to a year in advance to secure the dates and property you want.

Keep in mind, rentals lack hotel services. There's usually no staff to clean your room or make your bed daily and no front desk, concierge, or room service. In fact, the more charmingly rustic your villa is, the more likely it is to have ancient plumbing and a crumbling foundation.

For those of you who aren't do-it-yourself types, some villas provide daily maid service, a gardener, and a butler—but you'll pay for it. These properties can easily run $7,000 to $15,000 per week. For a family of four, that's not a value; but if you're a group of 14, that breaks down to $153 per person per night. As hotels usually begin at $100 per night, that's still a bargain. And you can rent a villa for 1, 2, 3 weeks or more.

Since villas are often located outside the city center, you might need a car, which can run an additional $300 to $600 a week.

Villas are generally fully furnished and include a full kitchen with appliances, towels and bed linens, water, and electricity. But food, cleaning detergents, and heat and air-conditioning—*if* the villa does have air-conditioning—are not included. Heat and air-conditioning costs can be quite high.

While it may seem cheaper to go directly through the homeowner, agencies usually have representatives in Italy who can advocate on your behalf. That can include minor repairs or even moving you to another property if you're not satisfied with your original choice. That's something that the owner can't help you with. Spending $50 to $60 on a broker's fee may help you save on costs and protect you in a foreign company.

Additional fees involved in renting your villa normally include a security deposit to cover damage and charges for utilities not included in the basic rental cost. Both of these are generally paid up front when you are in Italy. The security deposit is given back when you return the key or within a month of your return. Trip insurance is highly recommended and may be available through your agency. This usually runs about 6 to 7 percent of the total rental charge, and you'll be covered for cancellation due to injury, illness, and other unforeseen events.

It's very important to do your homework *before* you go. Read the rental agreement carefully to make sure you understand what's provided as well as all conditions, costs, and penalties.

When should you go? Summer is more expensive because this is when Europeans take their vacations and people look to villas with pools to escape the heat. Renting in April, May, and October is cheaper (rents can often be a third of summer rates), and you'll get the added benefits of mild weather and thinner crowds. Winter offers the lowest prices, but many properties are closed, and those that aren't require you to pay for heat.

If you're looking for more than just a terrace to sip your Chianti on, call the Parker Villas, based in Lynn, Massachusetts, for a free consultation. The company has more than 380 villas throughout Italy available for weekly rental. And they also offer a program called Actividayz—half-day trips (3 to 4 hours long) that run $60 to $100 per person from June to October. These activities include: cultural adventures, wine tours, cooking and art classes, and more. Parker Villas can also arrange maid service at about $20 or a cook for about $40. Through Parker Villas, you can rent a farmhouse in Abruzzo that sleeps four people for $1,000 per week in winter or $1,200 a week in the high season (summer).

▽ Resources

Italian Vacation Villas: 202-333-6247, www.villasitalia.com

Rentvillas: 800-726-6702, www.rentvillas.com

Tuscan House: 800-844-6939, www.tuscanhouse.com

Vacanze in Italia: 413-528-6610, www.homeabroad.com

Parker Villas: 800-280-2811, www.parkervillas.com

Home Away: 0798 938-9815, www.homeaway.com

Celebrity Villas

Okay, so maybe the $12,000 a night accommodations don't fit into every-one's budget. But that doesn't mean you can't live like a star. The term "celebrity villa" has been thrown around in the industry lately, with the intent of adding some glamour to the old tradition of renting a home during your travels. Basically, these are vacation properties owned and often even occupied by celebrities. So while this doesn't mean that you'll be rubbing shoulders with Hollywood's elite when you rent a celebrity villa, you may be sleeping in the bedroom, using the silverware, and living among the collections and clutter of a real celebrity.

For rock fans, **Mick Jagger** has a six-bedroom villa, Stargroves, on Mustique Island, in the Caribbean. The Japanese-inspired beachfront villa comes with a full staff and a Jeep that seats eight. The property includes a koi pond and seven pavilions connected by a raised walkway over a stream. The price tag of $11,000 a week in the off-season and $16,000 during the high season may seem a little steep, but split that among a group of 12 and the price becomes a lot more manageable. You may see next-door neighbor Tommy Hilfiger strolling the beach. And yes, Mick Jagger really does stay here frequently, *and* he has to approve the renters beforehand. www.mustique-island.com

If you're hoping to experience a medieval castle fantasy, actress **Jane Seymour** rents out St. Catherine's Court, a recently restored manor in an English valley near Bath. Since Seymour resides here on occasion, guests are actually sleeping in the star's private master bedroom and utilizing her full staff (even her personal house manager, Beverly Lee). The early Tudor and late Jacobean manor sits on 15 acres of property, with enormous rose beds, a medieval barn and stables, and a tennis court. Bring along 35 of your closest friends, as the house holds 17 bedrooms, nine bathrooms, and two kitchens and costs about $52,000 to $75,000 per week. www.villasoftheworld.com/listing.ihtml?ocref=0102

St. Clerans manor in Galway, Ireland, has the distinction of being passed from one celebrity to another. Director **John Huston** (and daughter Anjelica) possessed the 45-acre estate for 18 years, until **Merv Griffin** visited and fell in love with the property. Griffin renovated the manor to "restore it to its former glory" and reopened it as a 12-room, five-star guest house. Packages include a full Irish breakfast and afternoon tea, and the property features a golf course (Galway Bay Golf and Country Club is also nearby). And of course, there are plenty of pubs in the area. Rates start at $20,000 up to about $55,000 per week. www.villasoftheworld.com/listing.ihtml?ocref=5092

So **David Copperfield**'s resort, the 150-acre Musha Cay at Copperfield Bay in the Bahamas, is a pricey option. At $24,750 per day for a group of up to eight people, you get your very own private resort—the resort actually fits 24 people in five English colonial–style villas, each with its own private beach, and you get to choose who those guests are. www.mushacay.com

Give your trip a little twist of "cuchi, cuchi" by staying in the Kauai estate of **Charo.** Located on Tunnels Beach, the property has seven bedrooms and nine bathrooms, set on 3 acres of property. Starting at about $1,000 a night, this is where you can experience Hawaii, *Love Boat* style. www.villasoftheworld.com/listing.ihtml?ocref=8431

On Necker Island in the British Virgin Islands, **Sir Richard Branson** owns 74 acres of idyllic Caribbean territory. The billionaire loves his property so much that he actually got married here. Guests can rent the entire island for $47,000 a night for up to 28 guests (that's about $1,679 per person, per night) or have individual villas for $22,500 to $24,100 per couple per week. www.necker.com

Named after the airy spirit in Shakespeare's *The Tempest*, **Ariel Sands** on the south shores of Bermuda was the childhood summer home of Michael Douglas. The property has long been owned by the Dill family, and one member, Diana Dill, is Michael Douglas's mother. Now the actor and his wife, Catherine Zeta-Jones, are part owners and frequent visitors of the luxury resort. www.arielsands.com

Snagging Better Deals

If the $1,000 per night rate still doesn't appeal to your wallet, don't worry. I've been traveling since I was an infant, and I've developed tricks of the trade when it comes to snagging the best deals on a hotel, from first-class resorts to budget motels.

 Understanding RevPAR

RevPAR stands for "revenue per available room" and is where a hotel estimates a month's revenue based on historical data. Assume that a 100-room hotel budgets $250,000 in revenue for June. The revPAR number would go like this: $250,000/(100 rooms × 30 days) = $83.33 revPAR. This is the minimum the hotel needs to charge for each room to meet its revenue plan.

First of all, don't just depend on online deals, whether it's through the hotel itself or through a third party. Online booking sites often guarantee the lowest rates, but let's compare the different prices you can find. I checked the rates on hotels in four cities: Chicago, Dayton, New York, and Phoenix. For each rate, I requested a Friday- and Saturday-night stay, 2 months in advance. I looked at: Hotels.com; an online travel booking Web site such as Expedia, Orbitz, or Travelocity; the hotel's direct Web site; and the hotel's reservation desk. I also tried to negotiate the rate for frequent visitors arranged through the hotel's director of sales.

Auction Web sites, like Priceline and Hotwire, are known as "opaque" sites. That means you won't know which hotel you've booked until after you've made your reservation based on price. These sites offer descriptions like "four-star hotel" . . . but there could easily be differences of opinion on what exactly a "four-star hotel" is. However, there are other auction Web sites like Sky Auctions and Luxury Link that let you see what you're getting before you book. These sites have auctions, but they show you the hotels involved.

❗ You've already learned that third-party hotel-booking Web sites aren't always the best option. Sometimes you can get a better deal by going to the hotel's Web site, and more often than that, you can negotiate a better rate by calling the hotel directly. The gist of it is that it's fine to utilize online travel sites to find out what the going rate is, whether there's a better deal than what the hotel is offering, and if you can negotiate a better rate by talking to a real human being.

❗ Be wary of special deals that you find online: That "third night free" option might wind up being more expensive than a regular booking, or that "honeymoon package" may charge you an extra $200 just for a bottle of champagne and chocolates on your pillow.

❗ When calling a hotel to make reservations, don't call the 800 number. That will go to a national center that has less wiggle room to give you a discounted rate. Call the hotel's direct line—when you call, don't ask for the reservation department, as they'll probably reroute you right back to the 800 number. Ask to speak to a manager on duty or a director of sales: They have insider knowledge to let you know if there is a wedding party taking over 90 percent of the hotel or if an impending rainstorm means that there will probably be a block of cancellations. That puts you in a better negotiating position.

COMPARISON SHOPPING: ONLINE OR ON THE PHONE?

	HOTELS.COM	OTHER WEB SITE
Marriot Marquis, New York	$449 per night plus taxes = $1,068	Travelocity: $449 per night plus taxes = $1,048
Wyndham Chicago	$247.50 per night plus taxes = $598.03	Orbitz: $258.75 per night plus taxes = $607.13
Country Inn Suites, Dayton, Ohio	$109 per night plus taxes = $255.14	Expedia: First the Web site asked me to "check back shortly." A few minutes later, it quoted $75 per night. Then it said that details are unavailable and to try again later. Not helpful.
Hilton Garden Inn, Scottsdale, Arizona	$153 per night plus taxes = $354.40	Orbitz.com: $169 per night plus taxes = $385.03

! The Web doesn't think creatively. While you may be getting the lowest-priced room in the house, there's nothing to indicate that your room faces a brick wall or overlooks the alley where trash is picked up at the crack of dawn. You don't necessarily need to talk to someone in reservations to find out that kind of information. Talk to someone at the bell desk, the concierge, or even housekeeping to get the real information. Hotels are spending $5 billion on renovations, so your odds of being near jackhammers and noisy trucks are pretty good. An important detail that most people don't know about is to find out what floors the booster pumps are on: Most high-rise hotels cannot maintain consistent strong water pressure, so if you get a room on the same floor as a booster pump, you're pretty much ensured good water pressure.

! Call ahead of time: The best time to call the hotel is around 4 p.m., local time, on a Sunday. That's when hotel revenue managers, who set and control room rates, aren't working. You're in a better position to negotiate since the hotel knows that an unsold room is revenue that they'll never recoup by the next morning.

HOTEL WEB SITE	HOTEL RESERVATION DESK	NEGOTIATED RATE
$429 per night plus taxes = $979.78	Reservation agent first quoted $449 per night, but when asked if that was the lowest rate, he quoted $429 per night.	Got the room for $375 a night when I spoke with the manager on duty.
"Webrate," which requires prepayment and is nonrefundable: $233 per night for a total of $537.60; lowest standard rate: $259 per night plus tax = $599.06	After being put on hold for several minutes, the lowest rate was $259.95 plus taxes = $599.96.	After talking with the hotel's sales manager, he dropped the rate to $190 a night.
$75 per night plus taxes = $170.25	After much confusion over what dates I was looking for, the receptionist quoted me a lowest price of $89 per night plus tax = $202.04.	Talked to the front desk clerk—also the manager— and snared the room for $85.
Prepaid, nonrefundable "Net direct rate": $152 per night; lowest standard rate: $169 per night plus taxes = $378.29	$169 per night plus taxes = $378.28	Got the room for $120 a night.

❗ Call at the last minute: Hotels may lower rates last minute if they're not fully booked. Here's a trick: Reserve at an inexpensive chain that allows cancellations up to the day you arrive. A day or two before arriving, call the hotel you would prefer to stay at and ask for their lowest rate—if you get a better deal, you can cancel your first hotel.

❗ If you're staying through the week, ask for a weekend rate for the entirety of your stay.

Hotel Loyalty by Credit

Did you know that you can hook up with a hotel loyalty program with a credit card? It works just like earning airline miles on the ground but can be a lot easier to redeem. Hilton, Marriott, Intercontinental, and Starwood cards are the biggest of the bunch, and using these cards can help push you up to elite status. Translation: room upgrades, free stays, and even cashing in on benefits with the hotel's partners such as airlines and car rental agencies.

! Watch out for hidden fees: Ask about all fees in advance of your stay. I've been hit for a "mandatory bellman charge" and for receiving a FedEx package. Other unexpected fees may include minibar restocking charges, in-room safe surcharges, resort amenity fees, baggage holding fees, cancellation fees, early departure/arrival fees, and Internet/telephone/fax charges. If you're not informed of these charges ahead of time, you can ask the hotel to remove them at the end of your stay.

! Before you take your room key, tell the front desk that you want your phone and Internet charges bundled—a flat fee of $10 or $15 a day for unlimited Internet and domestic long-distance calls. This also applies to other annoying charges like resort fees and use of the hotel gym.

! Talk to the bellhop. When he's showing you your room, ask him if he actually *likes* the room. In some cases, he can even arrange to change the room through his friend at the front desk.

! If the hotel is overbooked, ask the bellhop to show you a "suite connector room," which is the sitting room portion of a suite that isn't always sold along with the entire room, or an "out-of-order" room, which is a room that isn't deemed "ready" for the public. Something as small as a stained carpet or broken television can get you a discounted rate.

! Safety first: Everyday fears of crime and fire don't go away just because you're on vacation. Ask the hard questions before you book your room— find out whether the hotel requires proof of identification of all guests, if access to guest floors is restricted, and whether there are in-room safes or a hotel safe to store your valuables. It's okay to ask how many incidents of burglary and other crimes have occurred and if hotels perform background checks on their employees.

! When it comes to fire safety, you would be surprised how many smoke detectors don't work because guests remove the batteries. And although most states mandate use of sprinklers and smoke detectors, not every state mandates that *enough* of them be installed. Ask whether the rooms and public areas have sprinklers. A tip: When booking your room, stay on the ninth floor or below. There's not a firefighter who can fight a fire quickly above the ninth floor. This also applies to developing countries where fire-safety regulations and procedures aren't as strict as in the United States. I know this for a fact— I've been a volunteer New York firefighter since I was 18 years old.

Nickel-and-Diming

Once on a business trip to Arizona, I went to hotel called the Tempe Mission Palms, a building walking distance from my business meeting. The room rate was $200 a night, so I gave the clerk my credit card, filled out the registration card, and checked in.

Eight hours later, as I was getting ready to check out of the hotel, I noticed my bill, which had been slipped under my door. There was my $200 room charge, but there was also something else: a $9.95 charge listed as a "hospitality fee." But all I had done was sleep in the hotel.

I went down to the front desk and asked them to explain the charge. "It's our hospitality fee," the clerk deadpanned and then she handed me a slip of paper. The fee was assessed to all guests, and it allowed free local and toll-free numbers, transportation to the airport, and health club privileges.

The issue here wasn't what services the "hospitality fee" provided. The real concern is that the hotel had failed to disclose the charge when I had initially checked in. The clerk insisted that I was responsible for paying the charge. I argued that because the hotel had never informed me of the charge when I was checking in, I was required to dispute the charge. She removed it from my bill.

Less than a week later, I was in Hilton Head, South Carolina, staying at the Westin Resort for 1 night. And it happened again. My bill, slipped under my door, had a nearly $13 charge for a "resort" fee. And once again, the hotel had not disclosed the fee in advance. Again, I disputed the charge, and again, it was taken off my bill.

Perhaps the worst offender of the failure to disclose a hotel charge occurred last year in Phoenix, when I stayed at the Pointe Hotel. I checked in late at night and had only carry-on bags. So after showing my credit card and getting my key, I just walked to my room unassisted. And . . . you guessed it. The next morning, there was my bill, slipped under my door. The outrageous charge this time? A $10 "mandatory tip to bellman" charge. I never used a bellman. And if I had, I would have already tipped him anyway. How many other guests found this charge on their bill and just paid it? That's also outrageous.

A hotel must fully disclose all fees and charges at the time it quotes the room rate. All too often, hotels want to stay competitive on rates, so they conveniently forget to mention the hidden additional costs they will try to slip onto your bill. Even worse, charges that should be optional are levied as mandatory, when in fact there is no legal justification for those charges. If you're spending a considerable amount of money to stay at a hotel, why should you be charged $13 a night for a towel? This is nothing less than insulting nickel-and-diming.

In another situation, as reported by journalist Christopher Elliott, two friends were vacationing in the Bahamas at a hotel booked through Travelocity. While they were sleeping, their room was robbed of $640 in cash, jewelry, and a cell phone. After reporting the crime and giving statements, the duo asked the manager for some money for lunch or dinner. The manager refused but finally relented and gave them cash for breakfast. Another different staff member gave them $15 to get to the airport. Then, to add insult to injury, the hotel charged them a $14 resort fee per person, per night, without any disclosure from the hotel or Travelocity. Sure, the friends learned their lesson about traveling with cash and leaving jewelry in the room—but the hotel had a responsibility to take care of their guests who had been victimized.

While excess fees are a pain, they are usually easily handled by disputing the charges. But a recent study by the Wichita-based Corporate Lodging Consultants shows that the problem goes much deeper. The firm negotiates hotel rates for about 270 companies and reviewed the hotel bills for a major client over a 12-month period. The firm examined 624,606 nightly charges and found that 11.6 percent of the total charges varied from the negotiated room rate, for a total of $820,250. The average overcharge per room per night: $11.35. If you project this to all US business-travel lodging—1.4 million rooms a night—the annual overcharge would reach more than $500 million.

Here's a winning case: In 2004, a class action suit was filed against 11 different Hilton Resort hotels. The class action lawsuit alleged that customers who reserved a room were promised certain room rates by Hilton but incurred an additional "resort fee" that was not disclosed. Hilton settled in 2006 without admitting any wrongdoing. The agreement provided that each hotel had to discount its resort fee by 75 percent until it had "forgone a total of 22.5 percent of the total resort fee it collected in the years before January 1, 2004." The discount applied to all guests, but anyone who could prove that they stayed at any of those properties before that date and paid a resort fee would get that amount reimbursed. Not a huge win, but at least the public was made aware of the hotel's nickel-and-diming.

My advice: If a hotel tries to bill you for any undisclosed charge, you have the right—if not the obligation to your fellow travelers—to dispute that charge. If the charges aren't removed from your bill and/or reversed from your credit card bill, you have the additional responsibility to dispute that charge with your credit card company.

Concierge Kickbacks

In many cases, the concierge can be your best friend, supplying you with much-needed items, tips on getting a seat at the trendiest restaurants, and insider knowledge on which Broadway show is really worth the bucks.

But be wary: An increasing number of hotels are actually outsourcing their concierges. These third-party deals mean that your hotel concierge may actually be making money when you follow his advice on attending a particular restaurant or theater production or using a car rental agency. So unbeknownst to guests, the concierge has his own, and his employer's, best interests in mind—not yours.

The Web site Vegas.com, a destination travel Web site, operates Casino Travel & Tours, which has retail and concierge desk locations at the Palms, Paris, MGM Grand, Bally's, Mandalay Bay, Excalibur, New York–New York, Luxor, and Stardust hotels in Las Vegas. The online booking site Expedia.com has its own concierge desks at hotels in Hawaii, Mexico, and Vegas. In some cases, the desk or kiosk is clearly marked as an Expedia offshoot, whereas in other situations, the guests may not be aware that their concierge—who is booking restaurant reservations or offering advice on a show—is an Expedia employee.

The idea of concierges earning kickbacks isn't a new one. Even traditional concierges can receive commissions when guests take them up on certain recommendations. But the quality assurance behind that scenario is that if the concierge is employed by the hotel, it's in his best interest to keep the guests happy. When being paid by a third-party supplier, it's no longer as important to have the same satisfied guests returning to the hotel.

Other problems abound. For one thing, guests don't often know that the person they're seeking advice from is employed by a third party. If they get good advice, great. If not, then the hotel can simply say, "It's not our fault."

Unusual Concierges

When you come across a concierge who goes above and beyond the call of duty, it makes a lasting impression. Concierges have been known to come through in a pinch, providing travelers with unexpectedly needed items, like cameras, dry ice for breast milk, a denture repair kit, even a personal assistant! Some hotels have some very cute stories about concierges who really go out of their way to help out guests.

At the Muse Hotel in Manhattan, concierge Barbara is a native of Poland who came to the United States on summer vacation in 1994 and never left. She's been a concierge at the Muse for 4 years and has made many unforgettable impressions on her guests. When a woman and her husband spent a few days at the Muse, Barbara got to chatting with them about her ethnic roots. When the woman mentioned that she had never sampled Polish cooking, Barbara enlisted the help of her mother and baked a platter of traditional Polish doughnuts for the guest, who was incredibly touched by the gesture.

Even better, Barbara came to the rescue when a couple came to the hotel to celebrate their 40th anniversary. Before checking in, the stressed husband called up Barbara to get some help in planning a romantic stay. He wanted something more than flowers to celebrate the occasion, because apparently he gets them for his wife every other week or so! Barbara arranged for a balloon bouquet to be delivered to his wife the next morning. When the balloons arrived, the husband handed Barbara a handwritten poem, too shy to read it to his wife himself. Barbara took the lead and recited the poem, which was something to the effect of "Roses are red, violets are blue; after 40 wonderful years, I'm still completely in love with you."

The lesson is that in the highly competitive hotel business, the winning properties usually depend on extraspecial services to keep their guests happy. I'm not just talking about basic services like housekeeping, turndown, and room service. At some hotels, whatever you want, chances are there's a concierge dedicated to getting it.

Vibe Specialist

Okay, a vibe specialist? This is just one of a string of hotel promotion stunts to make you feel like you're getting your money's worth. At some hotels, there's a tanning butler, an oxygen butler—and I presume at some hotels there could possibly be a butler's butler. And in the latest gimmick, at the International House in New Orleans, you'll find the vibe specialist. The claim is that the vibe specialist can organize everything from a crawfish boil to a meeting with a local voodoo priestess—not exactly different from any dedicated concierge (except perhaps for the voodoo). Other hotels have been hopping on board this New Age train, with vibe specialists cropping up at

Miami's Hotel Victor, Loft 523 in New Orleans, and Chicago's Hard Rock Hotel. Just remember, these good "vibes" usually don't come for free.

Eco-Concierge

At 70 Park Avenue Hotel, eco-concierge Christal White helps guests go "green on the go." A victim of Hurricane Katrina, Christal moved from New Orleans to New York and has made it a mission to minimize her environmental impact and inspire others do the same. She may recommend that guests hail a pedicab over a Yellow Cab, give you an eco-friendly guide to shops and restaurants, or direct you to New York's eco-friendly volunteer opportunities. Christal has coordinated a green bridal shower for 10 women, which included hiring hybrid vehicles to take the ladies to an organic spa, creating handmade bowls made of recycled materials, and getting a gift card that plants a tree in the bridesmaids' names. An eco-friendly wedding proposal involved arranging for a pedicab to take the happy couple to an organic picnic (complete with organic champagne), plus a walking tour around Manhattan with a personal tour guide. www.70parkave.com

Golf Concierge

Many hotels are offering the services of a golf concierge, not only to help you arrange tee times, but also to set up lessons and even take you shopping for the right set of clubs. Golf concierges are most likely to pop up in the more upscale hotels, especially ones with a large number of nearby courses—San Diego, Chicago, Phoenix, and Toronto rank as the biggest golf destinations. Just outside Phoenix, the Fairmont Scottsdale Princess has a golf concierge, as does the more moderately priced Hilton Garden Inn in north Scottsdale. Rose Hall in Jamaica now offers golf concierges that are a combination of a caddie and a tour guide: Their knowledge of the golf course includes everything you need to negotiate the course's winds, elevation changes, and "deceptive greens." In addition, Priority Traveller offers a golf concierge service for its customers, as does Golfing Elite for its premium members, while GolfSwitch allows its members to make reservations for a number of courses worldwide.

Beach Butler

At most hotels, the most "service" you'll get on the beach will be either help in setting up an umbrella or perhaps fetching you a cool drink. But if you're willing to spend the money, a growing number of hotels are offering an ever-increasing variety of services beachside. Now you might find a sorbet butler, like at the Rosewood's Jumby Bay in Antigua. This "butler" strolls the beach handing out complimentary frosty treats to guests.

On Nantucket, the Veranda House offers a beach concierge, who helps guests choose one of the island's beaches (family friendly versus quiet and romantic, for example) and arranges for a taxi to get them there. The Beach concierge will pack your taxi with a picnic lunch, umbrella, sunscreen, or whatever else you might need for your time on the beach. And when you return at your preset time (just call the hotel if you want to come back earlier), he will put your gear away—leaving you free to continue relaxing back at the inn. The only work you'll have to do is haul your gear from the taxi onto the beach itself—and back.

High-Tech Concierge

Have you ever stayed at a sleek, modern hotel, one packed with amenities and gadgets and doodads—and you just couldn't figure out how to, say, flush the toilet or open the curtains? That's where the high-tech concierge comes in. The modern W Hotels offer this concierge service to help with your room's electronic gadgets. And if you need help accessing the hotel's wireless Internet system, the high-tech concierge should be able to oblige. Some W hotels also offer videoconferencing services through this concierge.

And then there's the St. Regis, which already offers butlers to many of its guests. So to take their offerings even further, they've added a new twist: the e-butler. These PDA-equipped butlers are able to answer guests' requests at any time with a quick e-mail. But really, the only real difference between an e-butler and a regular butler is that with an e-butler, you send an e-mail for your requests. With a regular butler, you'll have to pick up the phone— or perhaps ring a silver bell.

Boot Butler

Even elite Spanish hotels are getting in on the extraordinary-services bandwagon. The La Pleta Hotel & Spa in the Baqueira Region, Val d'Aran (Pyrenees), Spain, now has a boot butler for the winter and offers a "white glove" picnic to attract summer travelers. In the winter, skiers coming in from the slopes are met by the boot butler to whom they hand over their ski boots. The butler will clean, polish, sterilize, and dry the boots, leaving them ready for guests to use again in the morning. So thanks to the boot butler, your ski boots will at least look like new every morning—and the pool of dirty sludge that often accompanies their presence on the floor of your hotel room won't be there, either.

Sleep Concierge

At the Benjamin in New York, a sleep concierge helps guests choose from a pillow menu, including antisnoring, hypoallergenic, and water-filled pillows as well as a 5-foot body cushion. You can also opt for an evening massage and a bedtime snack of milk and cookies or borrow a white-noise machine to drown out the sounds of Manhattan.

Stargazing Specialists

While the title concierge doesn't exactly apply here, you may be surprised to learn how many hotels keep resident astronomers on hand to help guests learn about the night sky during their stay.

At the **Hyatt Regency Maui Resort and Spa**, you can gaze through "Great White," a 16-inch telescope that is located on the rooftop of the hotel. An on-site astronomer is there to help you locate planets, stars, and galaxies. Rates are $20 for adults and $10 for kids, or you can arrange a couples-only stargazing evening with champagne and chocolate-covered strawberries for $25 per person. 808-661-1234, http://maui.hyatt.com

With few lights and low humidity, the Australian Outback is perhaps one of the best places to explore the night sky. At the **Ayers Rock Resort**, the Sounds of Silence dinner features a 4-hour Northern Territory feast (get ready to dine on kangaroo and emu), after which a resident astronomer points out constellations and planets, while explaining ancient and Aboriginal stories of mythology and creation. Rates are $149 per adult and $75 for kids ages 10 to 12. 61-2-8296-8010, www.ayersrockresort.com.au/astronomy

Located on the cliffs of Big Sur, California, the **Post Ranch Inn** offers free guided stargazing sessions on the veranda, every night at 8 p.m., weather permitting. 831-667-2200, www.postranchinn.com

The sky is so clear over Kohala that even stargazing is one of the most popular activities available at nearby **Hapuna Beach Prince Hotel**. A high-powered telescope is set up for you to view the Hawaiian skies with the guidance of professional astronomers. Rates are $25 for adults and $12 for children, every Friday at 8 p.m. 888-977-4623, www.princeresortshawaii.com/big-island-recreation.php

Arizona's **Kitt Peak Visitor Center** offers an advanced observing program, which means overnight stays for would-be astronomers (no previous experience is necessary). It's geared toward anyone with an interest in observing the night sky at the world's largest optical observatory under some of North America's finest skies. Stargaze in the observatory for $375 a night, plus $75 per person for room and board. 520-318-8726, www.noao.edu/outreach/aop/

What Guests Steal

Those who balk at the $100 price tag of the Ritz bathrobes might take matters into their own hands, much to the chagrin of hotel managers and owners. Even though a number of hotels have gone so far as to bolt down their lamps and televisions, there's still a surprising amount of items taken from hotels each year.

Some of these are expected: towels, ashtrays, bathrobes. In fact, 9 out of 10 people surveyed by the Holiday Inn admit to stealing at least one of the hotel's signature green-and-white towels, causing the Holiday Inn to lose about 590,000 a year. Others consider themselves collectors of kitschy hotel items, like the man who collects nothing but "Do Not Disturb" signs.

The most recent case was in Kamogawa, Japan, where a bathtub worth nearly $1 million was stolen from the guest bathroom at the Kominato Hotel Mikazuki. The 18-karat gold tub weighed 176 pounds and was a primary feature in the hotel's shared bathroom.

It doesn't end there. At the Ramses Hilton in Cairo, the general manager discovered that a Japanese bathroom accessory manufacturer had stolen the

Unusual "Do Not Disturb" Signs

I have a growing collection of creative—and funny—hotel "Do Not Disturb" signs from around the word.

! The Parker Meridien hotel in New York has one of my favorite signs: FUGGHEDABOUDIT

! A hotel in Europe: DON'T EVEN THINK ABOUT IT. . .

! The Dylan Hotel in New York: A big red Z means that you don't want to be disturbed. When the cleaners are there, they hang up a red sign that says "styling your room."

! The Shoreham Hotel in New York has a sign that reads on one side "Dirty. That's me! aka Please clean my room" and "Try Next Door, I'm Busy!" on the other. When the room is being cleaned, a sign reads "Specialist at work. Makeover in progress."

! The Borgata Hotel Casino & Spa has a reversible sign: One side says "Tidy Up," and the other side says "Tied Up."

! The Abaco Club in the Bahamas has a two-sided sign that says "It's so much better in the Bahamas! Leave us alone!" and "We made a real mess, please send in the troops!"

hotel's Egyptian bidet faucets. At the Beverly Wilshire, a guest actually chiseled away the room's marble fireplace. And he didn't sneak it out of the building under his shirt—a bellman actually helped the guest leave with the fireplace because the man told him he was "just taking it to get repaired."

When the InterContinental London opened in 1975, the management fully expected items to be stolen. Indeed, the expected items made their way into guests' suitcases over the years, but hotel officials were a little surprised when a guest checked out with both his own baggage—and his bathroom door.

At the InterContinental Carlton in Cannes, bathrobes and pillows are favorite items of slippery-handed guests. But so was the Uma Thurman Suite sign from the seventh floor of the hotel. The InterContinental Athens may have had to rethink its generosity when lent laptops found their way into guests' suitcases, while in Prague the plastic ducks in the bathtubs found new homes (so did the hotel's toilet brushes).

Stuff Hotels Sell

The good news is that in most cases you won't need to resort to stealing those items that you love in hotels. Even if you're envious of the thick mattresses and plush carpets, some hotels have taken the initiative to turn a profit with their most coveted items.

I should know—after my Los Angeles home was severely damaged by the 1994 Northridge earthquake, I remodeled my entire home based on my favorite items from hotels I've visited. I wanted the king-size bed from the Four Seasons in New York, the tiles from the Four Seasons in Hawaii, the bathtub from the Peninsula in Hong Kong, a toilet like the one in Tokyo's Park Hyatt, a pool like the Westin Hotel in St. John, and even a sink like the one in Caesar's Palace. Since I had a direct line to the CEOs and general managers of all these hotels, all I had to do was ask to learn that I could buy these items. And so can anyone else.

The **Westin Hotels at Home** catalog offers items for beds, baths—and dogs. Customers can use their Starwood Preferred Guest StarPoints to purchase items from their hotel room. In fact, Starwood has sold more than 35,000 of its Heavenly Beds to date. After they introduced their signature White Tea scent in hotel lobbies, guests started clamoring to purchase it, so the chain developed its own home fragrance line. 877-777-5418, www.westin-hotelsathome.com

Post Ranch Inn in Big Sur, California, sells mattresses, bedding, handmade soaps, and bath accessories, as well as more alternative items like a fleece hoodie, a hemp baseball cap, and original sculptures. And some of the even more unusual requests? An iron frog pulling a snail shell that holds teaspoons and a pewter soap dispenser. Among their best sellers are an iron matchholder/striker that is placed on fireplace mantels and rock candleholders carved from Big Sur granite. Hotel execs were a little confused when guests asked to purchase the fruity scent in the room, until they discovered that the source was probably the citrus-based wood polish used in the room. 831-667-2795, www.postranchmercantile.com

At the **Hilton Garden Inn**, their most expensive item sold is the Hilton Serenity Mattress Collection, which tops off at more than $2,000. Guests have ordered this mattress from as far as remote islands off Maine as well as Romania, to fill a multiple-bedroom house. True road warriors will appreciate Hilton's new Cuisinart coffee makers, and the most unusual item they've sold to date is their curved shower rod. www.hiltontohome.com

Hampton Inn's Hampton Home Collection offers the Hampton Bed by Serta mattress and box spring, as well as numerous pillows, beds, bath products, lap desks, and even an alarm clock. Managers report that their hotels have received numerous calls from guests not just wanting the new Hampton bed but asking for the exact bed that they slept in in their guest room. www.hamptonhomecollection.com

The **Arizona Biltmore** is home to six Biltmore Sprites, slender statues that were conceived in 1914 by sculptor Alfonzo Iannelli for a Frank Lloyd Wright project. In fact, these sprites have been called the lost children of Frank Lloyd Wright. The Biltmore sells 12-inch replicas for $125 and 6-foot sprites for $3,000. www.arizonabiltmore.com

We've all heard about the Ritz-Carlton's famous bathrobes. But the **Ritz-Carlton Grand Cayman** reports that guests at the Periwinkle restaurant have actually finished their meal and asked their server to add the cost of the table setting to their check—the plates, place mats, cutlery, the little flowerpot in the center that grows . . . The hotel has also had guests request the sun hats worn by the water sports staff—since they're not sold at retail, staffers just took them from the uniform closet. However, the resort's gallery, which showcases art by local Caymanian artists, has sold paintings worth up to $8,000. Their biggest surprise? A "Do Not Disturb" sign that shows a lady napping in a hammock. They just let the guests have it. 345-943-9000, www. ritzcarlton.com/en/Properties/GrandCayman/Default.htm

If you see anything you like at the **Marriott,** you can probably buy it. That includes the Marriott bed, a line of bath and spa products, their exclusive red lamp, and even Zagat software for PDAs, with information on local restaurants and movies. Their most expensive item is the Kashwere Chenilla Chaise, which costs $1,695. www.shopmarriott.com.

The **W Hotels** store sells items that were designed exclusively for the hotel chain, including the Lauren Merkin W Hotels exclusive evening clutch (it's a red purse), an $1,800 Ole Mathiesen watch, and the kinky Mile High Mini Kit that includes a lipstick mirror, a mini-massager, two condoms, and a bottle of lubricant. And yes, Viagra is a common request among guests. www.whotelsthestore.com

Each **Best Western** is independently owned and operated, so some items may be exclusive to individual properties. But you can find NASCAR-themed items like a bed-in-a-bag and shower curtains, as well as unusual items like a 22-piece picnic-set backpack and a garment steamer. The Best Western Merry Manor in Portland, Maine, had requests from guests to purchase the in-room Human Touch electronic massage chairs and is now a distributor for those chairs. The Best Western Merrimack Valley in Haverhill, Massachusetts, has acrylic cotton ball/cotton swab holders that are available for $7.95 and sells a surprising two dozen per month. The Best Western River North Hotel in Chicago stocks each room with a logoed rubber duck, intending for guests to take them. The Best Western Salmon Rapids Lodge in Riggins, Idaho, sells original photographs of the Salmon River by longtime resident photographer Frank Mignerey and specially designed light sconces that feature two fish swimming across a wave. www. shopbestwestern.com

Kimpton Hotels' Kimpton Style program allows guests to purchase traditional items like the mattress and box spring sets, down comforters, and feather beds, as well as more unusual items like the hotel's signature animal print robes and recycled glassware. www.kimptonstyle.com

The Great Smokeout

Much to the chagrin of some smokers, many hotel chains are going the healthy route by going entirely smoke free. In the United States, smoking is already banned in hospitals, government buildings, museums, airplanes, theaters, and many restaurants, depending on where you live. It was only a matter of time before hotels joined in.

In 2005, Westin Hotels & Resorts snuffed out indoor smoking in all of its 77 properties in the United States, Canada, and the Caribbean. Less than a year later, Marriott Hotels followed suit; its 2,300 properties in the United States and Canada will be smoke free. In 2007, Choice Hotels International announced that all 433 Comfort Suites properties in the United States would go 100 percent nonsmoking.

Westin stated that it based its decision on its own customer research. According to Westin, 92 percent of its guests requested nonsmoking rooms and didn't smoke in any part of the hotel. Eighty-eight percent of its guests preferred restaurants and other enclosed public spaces to be free of cigar and cigarette smoke, and 81 percent disliked staying in rooms that smelled of smoke. Since launching this initiative, the company has also gone nonsmoking at the Westin Melbourne, the Westin Sydney, and the Westin Denarau Island Resort & Spa Fiji.

Marriott is the largest chain to ban smoking to date, having extended the rule to all 10 of its brands, including JW Marriott, the Ritz-Carlton, Renaissance, Fairfield Inn, TownePlace Suites, and Marriott ExecuStay.

For now, Marriott's international hotel brands in 67 countries and territories outside the United States and Canada won't be affected, although the company will look at each case on a country-by-country basis. For example, JW Marriott Dubai recently announced that the hotel has increased its number of nonsmoking rooms to 45 percent, adding 67 new nonsmoking rooms that have undergone refurbishing of upholstery, including curtains, beds, and linen.

To find out which hotels are smoke free, both major brands and independent hotels, visit **www.freshstay.com.**

But one important caution: Some hotels with even the most well-intentioned antismoking rules have loopholes. With Westin, for example, the rule says if you get caught, there's a room penalty and a possible cleanup charge. And yet, there's no rule that says you can't smoke out on your room balcony. And that's where the loophole kicks in. If you go out on your balcony and light up, guess where the smoke goes. Inside your room!

Housekeeping Etiquette

My first advice to everyone and anyone when it comes to hotel health: Take off that top comforter upon arrival. Toss it in a corner. Never look at it again.

Next, take the packet of disinfectant wipes that you should have carried with you (for the plane) and wipe down the doorknobs, telephone, and remote control. If you have to ask why, bring extra.

Ask housekeeping to bring extra pillows to your room and then swap them for the ones on your bed. Chances are, the new pillows from downstairs are fresher and cleaner than the ones that were already in your room. That goes double for the extra pillows in your closet.

Never put ice directly in the ice bucket. Always use the liner provided, because those ice buckets are rarely, if ever, washed. Now take a look at the coffeepot and cups and think about it. Then go find the drinking glasses in the bathroom . . . you get the point.

Even worse, think about how often the housekeepers scrub down the bathtubs and shower curtains. Your best bet is to fill up the bathtub with water for one last rinse before you step in.

As for those drinking glasses in the bathroom: Most hotel maids are responsible for cleaning between 12 and 16 rooms per 8-hour shift. These people are heavily tasked. And if your room happens to be among the last one or two of their shift, they have—almost by definition—run out of time. Do they replace the drinking glasses from the last guest? Sometimes yes, sometimes no. In many cases, they just do a cursory rinse and put them back on the sink. My advice: Just as a precaution, when checking into your hotel room, take the drinking glasses and run them under hot water for at least 3 minutes.

Unusual Hotels/Alternatives to Hotels

I could fill an entire book with options for alternative accommodations. From underground caves to tree houses, unusual lodging options are a great way to add a new experience dimension to your trip. A good first stop is **www.unusualhotelsoftheworld.com,** but here are some more options to get you started.

Lighthouses

Once used to mark dangerous coastlines and guide ships into the harbor, most lighthouses have been usurped by modern navigational aids—in the United States, there are only about 600 operational light stations remaining. But as an integral part of maritime history, lighthouses have gained a sort of romantic lore in our culture. "Lighthouses are really hot. In the last 25 years or so, there has been an incredible amount of interest in them," explains Wayne Wheeler, president of the San Francisco–based United States

Lighthouse Society (www.uslhs.org). "They're mysterious: It's the picket fence against that dark, dangerous sea; it's the last thing a sailor would see as he set off and the first thing he would see coming home. They're always in a spectacular setting, whether it's the Outer Banks of North Carolina or the craggy shores of Maine."

The good news? These days, many lighthouses are actually being maintained and restored as private or nonprofit bed-and-breakfasts. In many cases, you probably won't stay in the lighthouse itself but in attached lighthouse keeper accommodations. But you'll have access to what's probably the best view of the ocean anywhere around. For a complete list of lighthouses that offer overnight accommodations, you can visit www.lighthouse.cc/links/overnight.html. Meanwhile, here are a few options to see what they have to offer.

Keeper's House Inn, Isle au Haut, Maine. At this location, they weren't kidding about the no electricity, no phone, no television concept. Innkeepers Jeff and Judi Burke, once Berkeley activists in the '60s and '70s, proudly advertise this feature in their remote bed-and-breakfast. There is running hot water, but you can expect oil lanterns and candles to lead you around at night. The Burkes collect food from the sea and from their organic garden, make their own diesel fuel from vegetable oil, and even extract drinking water from the sea. There is no development surrounding this area—in fact, guests can only reach the lighthouse by mail boat ($16 each way), and in exchange, you'll get one of the closest and most unobstructed views of the ocean and its marine life. Weekly rates for two guests, plus bicycle rentals and a Wednesday-night lobster bake, are $1,750 in the spring and fall and $1,250 to $2,000 in the summer. 207-460-0257, www.keepershouse.com

Saugerties Lighthouse, Saugerties, New York. Lighthouse keeper Patrick Landewe actually keeps a blog of his experiences operating a the bed-and-breakfast/museum, so if you've ever wondered what it's like to live in a lighthouse . . . The lighthouse was saved from demolition by the local community in the 1970s, and the Saugerties Lighthouse Conservancy was formed in 1985. It was rededicated as an operational lighthouse in 1990 with a solar-powered automated beacon. Getting to the lighthouse requires walking along a half-mile trail, and the building has no air-conditioning and only one shared television. There are two bedrooms available for $160 a night. 845-247-0656, www.saugertieslighthouse.com

Browns Point Lighthouse, Tacoma, Washington. This 30-foot concrete structure on Commencement Bay is open for public tours, and the keeper's dwelling was recently restored by the Points Northeast Historical Society. The society has implemented a keeper program, in which guests act as the lighthouse keepers for a week—this includes light daily chores and conducting tours of the facility. This job is designed for at least two people, and six maximum, so it makes a good family experience. Rates range from $500 to $700 per week, plus a $20 family membership and a $200 refundable damage deposit. 253-927-2536, www.pointsnortheast.org

East Brother Light Station, Point Richmond, California. Located in the straits that separate San Francisco and San Pablo Bays, this is considered the crème de la crème of lighthouse bed-and-breakfasts. East Brother offers a high-end experience for visitors. For $266 to $415 a night, visitors get boat transportation from the Point San Pablo Yacht Harbor, a four-course gourmet dinner with wine, full breakfast, and a tour of the island. Built in 1873, this redwood structure was one of the second group of lighthouses to be built along the West Coast and is the oldest operational one around the San Francisco Bay. 510-233-2385, www.ebls.org

Cape Otway Lightstation, Apollo Bay, Victoria, Australia. Operating continuously since 1848, this is the oldest surviving lighthouse on the Australian mainland and contains the largest and oldest group of lighthouse keepers' quarters in the country. The head lightkeeper's house is spacious enough to fit up to 16 people. Beyond the seaside landscape, the Cape Otway region includes the Otways Ranges rain forest and waterfalls, volcanic lakes country, and the town of Colac. Rates start at about $180 per night for two guests. 61-3-5237-9240, www.lightstation.com

Branscombe Lodge Cottage, Portland Bill, Dorset, England. This garden cottage is located next to a squat little 18th-century lighthouse, which ceased functioning in 1906. Its rich history includes the fact that Dr. Marie Stopes, the pioneer of birth control, owned the lighthouse from 1923 to 1958 and entertained the likes of George Bernard Shaw, H. G. Wells, and Thomas Hardy. It was the first lighthouse to use Argand lamps and also the first in the world to have a true reflector. Surrounding the cottage is a garden with ornamental fishponds and outdoor furniture (even a barbecue), and guests have access to the tower observatory to see the famous Dorset sea view. 01305-822300, www.oldhigherlighthouse.com/accommodation.html

Cape Columbine Lighthouse, Western Cape Coast, South Africa. About an hour and a half outside of Cape Town, through Vredenburg and the fishing village of Paternoster, is the Cape Columbine Lighthouse. Built in 1936, this lighthouse was named after a ship that wrecked in this area in the 1820s. It is surrounded by the Columbine Nature Reserves, where you can find plenty of sea life as well as private game lodges. There are two keepers' cottages and a much more rustic backpacker's lodge, each of which sleeps two to six people. Recent upgrades include a large conference room and a swimming pool, as well as vast amounts of land that can hold events and weddings. Rates start at about $580 a night for the keeper's cottage and about $100 a night for the backpacker's lodge. 27-21-449-2400, http://www.npa.co.za/salato/Cape%20Columbine.htm

Outrageous Hotels

If you're looking for something totally different in a hotel, then these places prove that the accommodation is the experience. One disclaimer—from me: Most of these hotels prove the point that there's no explanation or accounting for bad taste, but there's no limit to the entertainment factor either.

Madonna Inn, San Luis Obispo, California. The Madonna Inn has garnered a lot of attention for its offbeat—practically gaudy—themed rooms. Alex Madonna, who passed away in 2004 at the age of 85, opened the inn with his wife, Phyllis, in 1958. With Phyllis at the helm of the interior design, the couple worked with artists and designers from around the world to create 109 eccentric, detailed, themed rooms. The pink-signed Madonna Inn is now one of the oldest continuously operated themed inns in the country, and in today's market of trendy boutique hotels and gargantuan chains, it represents sort of a tribute to old American kitsch. Try out the Caveman room, fashioned entirely out of stones, with a rock waterfall shower and leopard print furniture. If you're in the mood to really get away, you can opt for rooms like Paris Violets, Oriental Fantasy, Swiss Chalet, and even the Traveler's Yacht. Don't forget to go to the restrooms downstairs to check out the rock waterfall urinal and the child-size toilet and sink for little ones. Room rates start at $168 and go up to about $380 per night. 800-543-9666, www.madonnainn.com

Dog Bark Park Inn, Cottonwood, Idaho. If you're not ready to get the kids a dog, how about letting them sleep inside one? The world's largest beagle resides in Cottonwood, Idaho, where guests can sleep inside the belly of the beast (and lounge about in his muzzle). Toby, a 12-foot-tall beagle statue, and his smaller companion, Sweet Willy, were built by husband-and-wife team Dennis Sullivan and Frances Conklin, who specialize in chain saw art. Rates are $92 per night, including breakfast. You can also visit the studio where Dennis and Frances create chain-saw dog carvings that are available in their gift shop. 208-962-3647, www.dogbarkparkinn.com

Northern Rail Traincar B&B, Two Harbors, Minnesota. It may be hard to curb your kids' obsession with video games by pulling out your old train sets, but you can teach them about the old days by spending the night on a train. The train car hotel is made up of connected rail cars with 18 guest rooms. You can choose from Victorian, Asian, and safari-themed rooms. The Yardmaster condo is also available for short- and long-term rent, with a full kitchen, fireplace, and lake view. Located on 160 acres of forested land (about 25 minutes outside of Duluth), there's access to Lake Superior, Gooseberry Falls, hiking trails, snowmobiling, and golf. Room rates are about $110 to $180. 877-834-0955; www.northernrail.net

The Big Red Barn Getaway, Port Townsend, Washington. Located on Puget Sound, a ferry ride away from Seattle, the Big Red Barn Getaway offers a quirky little spot designed just for two. A real barn built in the 1890s, it has been renovated into a tiny inn surrounded by nature (you may actually catch sight of a bald eagle here) and small-town antique shops and galleries. Rates are about $139 per night. 360-301-1271, www.bigredbarngetaway.com

Anniversary Inn, Utah and Idaho. For the romantic couple with a sense of humor, the Anniversary Inn has five locations in Utah and Idaho, where only adults are allowed. Each suite is designed with an extravagant theme, like the biker roadhouse with a Harley-Davidson pinball machine and a leather bed, the mammoth ice cave done up with stalagmites and stalactites, and the ever-romantic Sleeping Beauty's Castle. Rates range from $139 to $289 per night. 800-324-4152, www.anniversaryinn.com

Tree Houses

If you have to struggle to get your kids to play outside, consider making them sleep outside. Sort of. The **Cedar Creek Treehouse** is a private mountain retreat at Mount Rainier, located 50 feet up in a 200-year-old western red cedar tree. Owner Bill Compher built the tree house himself, making it large enough to accommodate up to five people and featuring a bathroom, kitchen, and dining area, not to mention skylights and an observatory 100 feet up that offers great views from all around. Though it's a safe climb up, kids under 10 are not allowed inside the tree house. Rates are $300 for two people and $50 for each additional guest. 360-569-2991, www.cedarcreektreehouse.com

Most people know the **Post Ranch Inn** in Big Sur as a high-end luxury resort, but the place also includes seven single-unit tree houses built 9 feet off the ground on stilts. Each triangle-shaped room can accommodate two people, with a fireplace and a mountain view. The resort also features the Sierra Mar restaurant, spa treatments, and yoga classes, and the towns of Monterey and Carmel are a short drive away. Rates for the tree house units are $845 per night. 800-527-2200, www.postranchinn.com

The **Costa Rica Tree House Lodge** is a two-room, two-floor accommodation that sleeps up to six people. The complex, which also includes two beach houses and a house at the edge of the jungle, is located on a 10-acre ocean-front property on Punta Uva beach and offers private beach access. The bathroom is actually built around a 100-plus-year-old tree, which is still growing around the house. The tree house has been entirely built of sustain-

 Hotel Fun Facts

In 1941, El Rancho Vegas was the first resort to open on the Las Vegas Strip (across from what is now the Sahara).

It would take 288 years for someone to spend 1 night in every hotel room in Las Vegas.

Stephen King is said to have found inspiration for *The Shining* from the Stanley Hotel in Estes Park, Colorado.

The Hotel Monaco in Washington, DC, is housed in the original General Post Office Building and was the site of the first telegraph transmission and where the concepts of zip codes, home delivery, and the Pony Express were conceived.

The Williamsburg Inn in Williamsburg, Virginia, was John D. Rockefeller Jr.'s 1937 vision. He wanted to make a hotel as comfortable as a Virginia estate for discriminating guests. Not surprisingly, the inn was the first hotel in America to have air-conditioning.

At the Furnace Creek Inn in Death Valley, rainfall is 1.8 inches per year. The hotel's golf course is the world's lowest at 214 feet below sea level.

The Fairmount in San Antonio entered the *Guinness World Records* book in 1985 when the 3.2-million-pound hotel was moved intact to its current location.

The exterior of the Henley Park Hotel in Washington, DC, has more than 120 gargoyles. Two of the gargoyles have the faces of the hotel's architect and his wife.

able woods, which were salvaged from fallen trees. Rates start at $225 a day or $1,350 per week. 506-750-0706, www.costaricatreehouse.com

A treetop . . . spa? The **Out 'n' About Treesort** just outside of Cave Junction, Oregon, is an 18-tree-house complex for overnight stays and is presumably the world's largest clustering of tree houses. Guests can stay in "treesorts" like the Swiss Family Complex, which is two tree houses connected by a swinging bridge; the Treezebo, a wall-less structure with a toilet and sink; and the Treepee, an 18-foot tepee in the trees. Kids and adults get to play around the multiple forts, swinging bridges, ropes courses, and giant zipline. On the ground are a freshwater swimming pool, a performance stage, and barbecues, all located on 36 private acres of land. Recently added to the complex is Deva Spa, a full-service spa facility that is, yes, located on a treetop. Rates range from $120 to $220 for two to four guests. 541-592-2208, www.treehouses.com

Teniqua Treetops is upscale, eco-friendly lodging in South Africa, located in a forest canopy. Built on platforms, the tree house lodges include tented bedrooms, fully equipped kitchens, and bathrooms with functioning plumbing and hot water. Up in the tree you may be surrounded by fork-tail drongos and buzzards, while on the ground you can check out bushpigs, porcupines, and leopards. The lodge mostly uses dry toilet systems to process waste without threatening the local environment and filters washing water. The seven tree houses can fit two to four guests and range from $100 to $150 per night. 27-044-356-2868, www.teniquatreetops.co.za

At **Pezulu Tree House Game Lodge**, you can actually see herds of animals running below you from your private balcony. Located in the Limpopo Province of South Africa, the lodge is made up of seven thatch-and-reed tree houses, which can fit up to 14 people. The unit has been built around the trees with no nails going into the trees, and branches grow inside the lodges. Each tree house has electricity and does include a working bathroom. Rates range from $80 to $100 per night. 27-15-793-2724, www.pezulu.co.za

Green Magic Nature Resort in Kerala, India, has two lodges located 90 and 100 feet off the ground. Both were built by Paniya tribesmen from local materials, creating two-story structures with wraparound decks. There is functioning plumbing, and energy is produced by a combination of solar power and Gober gas from cow dung, as well as kerosene lamps. The resort is located on 500 acres of rain forest and coffee, cardamom, and pepper plantations. Meals are taken in a communal food court, using locally produced organic fruits and vegetables. Rates are about $200 per day for two guests, including all meals. www.hotelskerala.com/greenmagic

Yurts

How about a yurt? If you don't already know, a yurt is a modernized version of a shelter that was used by ancient Central Asian nomads. These round stationary structures are covered with fabric walls and usually come complete with bed, a table, and a small refrigerator or even a kitchenette. Yurts tend to be easier to pitch and more spacious than traditional tents, so you can have that outdoorsy feel without all the work. In general, though, you'll want to bring the same kind of amenities as if you're going camping, which includes hiking gear, warm and rainproof clothing, water filters, and small appliances like a Swiss Army knife.

Treebones Resort in Big Sur, California, has 16 yurts along the ridge above the Pacific Ocean, four of which can fit families. Rates are $175 to $270 for two to four people and include a waffle breakfast. Barbecue dinners cost extra (about $18 to $24) and can be taken in the main communal lodge or in an ocean-view bar. 877-424-4787, www.treebonesresort.com

Mary Rose Herb Farm and Retreat in Bristow, Indiana, rents out two yurts, each with two beds, antique furniture, electricity, and year-round climate control. Guests can also get herbal teas, fondue, and a pot of Mexican hot chocolate in the evenings and take advantage of the outdoor tubs and massage services. Rates are $70 for two people and $17.50 for each additional person. 812-357-2699, www.maryroseherbfarm.com/yurts.htm

Salt Creek Retreats in Salt Creek, Ohio, has both cabin and yurt rentals that sleep four (plus two on the floor). The yurts are made of wood with felt and woolen blankets covering the walls. There's no electricity or plumbing, but there's insulation and a propane heater for the winter and a solar shower in the summertime. The surrounding area is 40 acres of woodlands, with ample hiking. Rates are $50 to $65 per night for up to six people. 614-397-3422, www.saltcreekretreats.com

Falls Brook Yurts in Minerva, New York, offers 20-foot yurts that can fit up to eight guests, with propane heating and a kitchen with a gas stove. A sky dome allows for stargazing, and a private fire pit is available near each yurt for seasonal barbecues. Falls Brook, Minerva Creek, and Minerva Lake are all nearby. Winter activities include backcountry skiing and snowshoeing, and summertime allows for extensive hiking, swimming, tennis, and basketball. Rates are $95 for two people, plus $10 for each additional guest. 518-761-6187, www.fallsbrookyurts.com

Caves

Kokopelli's Cave Bed & Breakfast is carved into 65-million-year-old sandstone, located 70 feet underground in Farmington, New Mexico. The entrance is in the cliff face and is reached by walking down a sloping path and steps cut into the sandstone, down a short ladder, and into the cave. The one-bedroom cave room is furnished with carpeting and has electricity, hot and cold running water, and a waterfall-style shower. Because the cave is located in the Four Corners region, you can stand on an aboveground platform to watch the sun set over four different states—New Mexico, Arizona, Utah, and Colorado. Rooms are about $240 a night for two. 505-326-2461, www.bbonline.com/nm/kokopelli

Experience an authentic Australian outback dugout at the **Desert Cave Hotel**, located within the sandstone of Coober Pedy. There are 50 suites available in the hotel, 19 of which are underground. Also underground are casinos, shops featuring locally mined opals, and Aboriginal arts and crafts. Rooms are about $200 a night, not including meals or a cave tour. www.desertcave.com.au

There are several underground hotels in Cappadocia, Turkey, including the **Gamirasu Cave Hotel**, which is located inside a restored thousand-year-old Byzantine monastic retreat. There are 18 rooms, some of which were actually monk cells, which are carved into the cave or built with volcanic rock. Nearby Ayvali Village is a relatively untouristed area featuring the Goreme Open Air Museum, authentic shopping areas, and restaurants. Room rates range from $75 to $700, from single rooms to deluxe family suites. www.gamirasu.com

If you've already been there and done that with a French B&B, how about one that's carved out of rock? **Le Prince Noir** in Les Baux, Provence, is a tiny inn carved into a mountainside in one of the most attractive regions in the south of France. Though Les Baux tends to get heavy traffic during the daytime, your overnight stay ensures that you'll be able to experience the area with fewer visitors. Three rooms are available for rent, with functioning plumbing, accommodating up to 10 people. Prices range from $115 to $230, including breakfast, with a 2-night minimum stay. www.leprincenoir.com

Underwater

How about sleeping with the fishes—in an underwater hotel? Underwater hotels seem to be the, er, wave of the future. With massive, billion-dollar projects already under way, the underwater concept is certainly an exercise in ambition and architecture, but will these hyped-up concepts ultimately sink or swim?

The **Utter Inn** is a two-story, one-room house located 9 feet under Lake Mälaren in Västerås, Sweden (about an hour west of Stockholm). Designer Mikael Grenberg conceived it as an art project, designed as a traditional Swedish red house with white gables. Guests can arrive at the port of Västerås and travel out on the lake with an inflatable boat to enter the house on the water's surface. Two twin beds and a table are located downstairs, underwater, where you're essentially spending the night inside an aquarium with fish gazing at you while you sleep. Rates range from $250 to $350 per night, and the inn is generally closed in the winter. 0870-855-6912

The **Jules Verne Undersea Lodge** is a research lab located 30 feet underwater in Key Largo, Florida, that allows visitors to spend a night (although since it's only 600 square feet, you probably won't last more than a night or two). Overnight visits include diving gear and unlimited dives for certified divers (or you can get a PADI or NAUI certification during your stay). The only way to enter is by scuba diving in, but a 3-hour course trains even inexperienced divers to make their way down. The habitat includes electricity, hot water, and air-conditioning. Rates are about $445 per person, with breakfast and dinner included. 305-451-2353, www.jul.com

Currently in development is the **Hydropolis** in Dubai, a self-proclaimed 10-star hotel off the coast of Jumeirah Beach that will sit on the floor of the Persian Gulf, 66 feet below the surface. There have been some heavy delays over the cost ($500 million and counting) and concerns over the project's impact on marine life. The structure, which will be made from concrete, steel, and Plexiglas, will consist of 220 luxury suites. Visitors will enter the "land station," then take a train through a 1,700-foot-long tunnel into the hotel, where you'll find two translucent domes to view the underwater life. There will also be a concert auditorium and a ballroom, which emerge out of the water, and the bubble-shaped suites will feature clear glass walls. www.hydropolis.com

The **Hydropolis** in Qingdao, China, scheduled to open in 2009, will be located in the Yellow Sea, where guests will arrive via yacht. There will be 200 suites, what is expected to be the "world's largest underwater ballroom," an oceanic museum, and a revolving restaurant. A land-based HydroTower component is scheduled to be open for the 2008 Olympic Games in Beijing.

Crane Hotel. Have you ever considered sleeping 50 feet in the air . . . on a crane? That's right. Located in Harlingen in the Netherlands, the crane was built in 1967 and used to unload timber freight from Russia and Scandinavia. It opened its doors as a hotel in 2003, and today, for about $365 a night, you can sleep inside the 200-square-foot suite, complete with a sea view. The suite has all the amenities, including a plasma TV and air-conditioning. Best of all, you can sit in a chair to control the heavy machinery, rotating a full 360 degrees!

Prison Hotels

Spending the night in a prison? Why not, if you're looking for a truly offbeat, authentic experience. Some prison hotels are a little more luxurious than others, while others . . . well, read on.

Karosta is an old Soviet military jail on the west coast of Latvia and is known as "the prison that nobody escaped from." Although the prison closed in 1998, it now offers day and overnight experiences for guests who are interested in seeing what prison life is really like. Located in the town of Liepaja, the prison was built in 1905 by Czar Nicholas I and was later used by the Soviets. The hosts are a mix of ex-Soviet military personnel and hired tour guides, who spend the night shouting at, berating, and questioning the guests. You'll sleep in a prison bunk or iron bed and may even be forced to clean a bathroom with a toothbrush. Rates are about $15 per person. www.karostascietums.lv

The **Malmaison Hotel** in Oxford, England, takes pride in being the first prison in the United Kingdom to be converted into a hotel. You probably won't notice, what with the trendy decor, high-speed Internet, and hipster bar, but some rooms actually have the original iron cell doors and even iron bars on the windows. The prison was closed in 1996 and remodeled to contain 96 rooms (three cells equal one hotel room), plus a prison chapel now done up into a public lounge. Nightly rates range from $300 to $850. www.malmaison-oxford.com

Extended Stays

Whether you tuck a fragile family photo into a nest of T-shirts or squash a favorite pillow inside an already overstuffed suitcase, integrating the comforts of home into your extended-stay hotel can be a challenge. But for many frequent travelers, maintaining a connection with home is a necessity. And some extended-stay hotels are finally catching on.

ExecuStay. When your employer comes into a lease agreement with ExecuStay by Marriott, an account representative is assigned to take care of your housing needs. This point person will reach out for a pre-move-in conversation, to figure out what your particular needs and desires are and try to arrange for them. Want to bring your pet to Denver for a month? Your rep can get you a doggie bed, arrange for a regular dog walker, and point you in the direction of the local dog park. The rep can also be on hand if your family comes to town, figuring out activities for the kids and romantic restaurants to explore with your spouse.

ExecuStay also offers a personal photo service: After you e-mail them pictures of your family, you'll arrive to find they've been framed on your desk or stuck to the fridge with a magnet. When a group of businessmen from Texas stayed at ExecuStay in Sacramento, they found photos of Texas scattered around the apartment (and horseshoes over their doors). 888-340-2565; www.execustay.com

Homewood Suites. Hilton-owned Doubletree Guest Suites has offered incoming guests chocolate chip cookies that are baked on the premises—a practice that has been adopted by other hotels (800-222-8733, doubletree. hilton.com). Also owned by Hilton, Homewood Suites is offering a new grocery store service that allows guests to fill out a shopping list online, so that your kitchen will be fully stocked by the time you arrive. 800-225-5466, homewoodsuites.hilton.com

Candlewood Suites. Some extended-stay accommodations have stepped up their interior decorating skills to increase your comfort factor. Candlewood Suites has adopted the new tagline "Consider Us Home" and is embarking on a major upgrade project on their hotel interiors. These changes will feature warmer color schemes, as well as the addition of a leather recliner in each suite and residential-style bedding that includes new duvets and triple sheeting. 888-226-3539, www.candlewoodsuites.com

Homestead Studio Suites. This chain launched their new brand, Extended Stay Deluxe. Though pricier than their other residences, these 29 properties are designed to look and feel like real apartments. All are designed in earth tones, with oversized couches, ergonomic desk chairs, and contemporary artwork on the walls. Hopefully, moss green is your color of choice. 800-804-3724, www.homesteadhotels.com

If you find yourself homesick on your travels, here are a few tips on how to take advantage of an extended stay to feel closer to home.

! In an extended-stay hotel, there's plenty of space to stash your family or friends. Take advantage of your home away from home to entertain.

! You have a kitchen. Use it—and not just the microwave to reheat leftover Chinese food. Eating home-cooked meals is not only a more healthful way to travel but also a way to make your daily routine feel more like home.

! Whether it's a live Webcam or an online chat, you can be there for your family in real time. Most extended stays are fully equipped with high-speed Internet, and wireless is becoming increasingly available.

! One of the reasons business travel is so lonely is that your loved ones can't share the experience, and sometimes it's hard to say it all over the phone. A blog can instantly shoot off a recap of your day or delve into your innermost feelings, so everyone you care about can see what's going on in your life away from home.

Time-Shares

We've all heard horror stories about time-share properties. Your "free" weekend vacation gets usurped by sleazy salespeople who push you into 6-hour-long presentations, trying to get you to pay money to visit the same Florida resort for the same 2 weeks, year after year after year . . .

In general, time-sharing (also known as vacation ownership) is a shared ownership of vacation real estate where purchasers acquire a period of time (usually 1 week) in a condominium, apartment, or other type of vacation accommodation. Owners may share the same accommodation at different times, exchange accommodations, or split larger accommodations into smaller ones. Members usually make a onetime purchase of furnished resort accommodations at a fraction of whole ownership costs and pay an annual maintenance fee.

According to the American Resort Development Association (ARDA), as of 2006, 4.1 million American households owned one or more US time-share weekly intervals or points-equivalents, an increase of 5 percent from the previous year. On average, there are 25.6 owners per time-share unit, and there are 154,439 time-share units at 1,604 resorts in the United States. In terms of units, Florida is in the lead with 378 resorts; that's three times more than California, which has 123 time-share resorts. As you probably guessed from these two states, the most popular type of time-share is a seaside or ocean resort.

The truth is, when it comes to time-shares, the value is in the use. Consider the following caveats before you sign the papers.

! Watch out for superlatives or terms that sound too good to be true, such as the words *free, perfect, always,* or *never.*

! Don't consider it an investment. Time-shares are notoriously hard to turn over, and the rate doesn't always appreciate. Translation: You can deed it, put it in your will, give it as a gift. But the true resale value of most time-shares is the last reason you should ever buy one.

! Ideally, time-shares are designed to provide you a part-time vacation home at a lower rate. Figure out how many vacations you take per year and how much you would pay for a hotel, then take into consideration inflation rates over the years.

! Don't sign up right away. Sleep on it. Be realistic about how much time you can spend in your time-share and whether it's a location you're really interested in spending time in.

! Look at other listings for the property or nearby properties to compare with the rate you're getting.

! Ask for the contact information for other owners or previous owners. (Be wary if the sales agent doesn't want to provide this.) Find out if they're satisfied with the property and if they've experienced any issues during their ownership.

The following is a partial list of time-share terms from ARDA. Before you go into a time-share situation, it's a smart idea to arm yourself with all the jargon so that you don't get smooth-talked into something you don't want.

According to banking or deposit: depositing a week of time-share into an exchange system or inventory pool.

Biennial: use of a time-share week every other year. Owners are often referred to as either "odd" or "even" year owners.

Developer: the company owning the resort. Responsible for constructing the accommodations and selling the product.

Exchange company: the system that allows time-share owners to trade the accommodations they own for comparable accommodations or travel-related services. Most resort companies are affiliated with an exchange company. Many resort companies offer an internal exchange mechanism that allows owners to exchange to resorts within their company's portfolio of resorts.

Fixed week: a type of time-share ownership in which usage rights attach to a specific week of the year each year in perpetuity.

Floating week: a type of time-share ownership where the use rights are subject to the owner reserving his or her week within a season purchased (winter, summer, etc.) or sometimes throughout the year. A year-round "float" is most often found in resorts with similar seasons, like Hawaii or the Caribbean.

Fractional ownership: leisure real estate sold in intervals of more than 1 week and less than whole ownership. Fractionals are usually associated with the luxury segment of vacation ownership, offering greater services and amenities.

Home resort: the resort location where a new purchaser owns his or her week or designated as the home resort in a club or points-based program. Ownership is usually tied to this home resort and generally involves priority reservation rights in that location.

Lock-off: a type of time-share unit consisting of multiple living and sleeping quarters designed to function as two discrete units for purposes of occupancy and exchange. The unit can be combined to form one large unit or can be split or "locked off" into two or more separate units, allowing the owner to split the vacation into multiple stays or bank all or a portion for exchange purposes.

Points: a "currency" that represents time-share ownership and is used to establish value for seasons, unit sizes, and resort locations. Points are used by some developers for both internal and external exchange.

Points conversion program: an offering whereby owners of a time-share interval pay a fee to convert their interval for the equivalent in points.

Rescission: sometimes called a cancellation or cooling off period. This is a period of time during which a consumer has the right to cancel a purchase contract and obtain a full refund of his deposit with no penalty. Dictated by state statute and company policy, rescission periods vary from state to state but range on average from 5 to 7 days. This is another example of the strong consumer protections built into time-share sales.

Trading power: a term used for the value assigned for exchange purposes to a member's deposited vacation time.

Trial membership: a product offered after the initial sales tour consisting of travel-related products and services packaged with an opportunity to experience the resort developer's primary vacation ownership product within a defined period. Sometimes called a sampler program.

Source: *www.resortime.com/services/terms.asp*

▽ Resources

RedWeek: www.redweek.com

The Timeshares Users Group (TUG): 904-298-3185, www.tug2.com

Timeshare Insights: 407-361-0850, www.timeshareinsights.com

Partial Owner: sales@partialowner.com, www.partialowner.com

Residence Clubs

Fractional ownership resorts or destination clubs) are fractional vacation real estate developments owned by members. Each member owns a fraction, ranging from 4 to 12 owners per unit, of a club residence and an interest in the club facilities and common areas.

Fractional interests are usually sold in shares of 3 weeks or greater. These resorts are usually more "exclusive" than traditional time-shares, appealing to consumers who want a high-end vacation address but don't want to pay the million-dollar price tag. Residence club owners can also transfer or resell their interests as they would with real estate ownership.

PRCs are commonly located in popular vacation destinations such as mountain, beach, golf, or urban resorts. Standard amenities usually include pools and gyms, but there are often amenities to correspond with the location, such as a golf course, pro shop, boating dock, or tennis court.

When you buy a share in a vacation home, there is usually an up-front purchase price, which can cost hundreds of thousands of dollars. For example, the Four Seasons Residence Club Punta Mita, Mexico, starts at approximately $190,000 per fraction (and can go up to more than $400,000), with fractions sold in $\frac{1}{12}$ so owners can spend a total of 4 weeks at the property (3 weeks are guaranteed timing and 1 week is booked according to availability). More than likely, there will also be the annual maintenance fee. And don't think that "ownership" translates into "all-inclusive." There can be extra charges for everything from golf memberships to spa treatments, so check the fine print first.

Four Seasons Hotels & Resorts offers fractional interests in residence club villas. There are residence clubs in Aviara, California (near San Diego); Scottsdale, Arizona; Jackson Hole, Wyoming; Punta Mita, Mexico (near Puerto Vallerta); and Peninsula Papagayo in Costa Rica. One is currently in development in Vail, Colorado.

One of the benefits of joining a residence club is that you also have access to other residence clubs, as well as access to other resorts in the Interval International exchange network (www.intervalworld.com), and you receive Four Seasons "currency," which can be spent at select Four Seasons hotels or resorts. Reservations may also be split into one 4-night weekday visit and one 3-night weekend visit.

Four Seasons Residence Club accommodations are designed so that owners can divide villas into two separate units. Owners can exchange their extra space or use it at a later date, thereby acquiring 2 weeks of use for 1 week purchased. www.fourseasons.com

Marriott Grand Residence Clubs are available in Lake Tahoe, California; Keystone, Colorado; and London. The Lake Tahoe property works more like a real estate deed, offering 13-week interests with seasonal options that let you determine which weeks in each season you will have usage. The London property works more like a time-share, selling $\frac{1}{12}$ fractional interests, which allow 21 days of use per year. Grand Residence Club owners also have access to the exchange privileges offered by Interval International. www.grandresidenceclub.com

The **Ritz-Carlton Club**'s ownership ratios are 10 to 1 or 12 to 1, giving owners a minimum of 5 or 4 weeks a year, respectively. Each club has its own reservation system based on seasonality. In addition to their own private residence property, owners have reciprocal access to all current and future locations. Owners can also submit reservations to management for rental income or take advantage of special rates at other Ritz-Carlton properties. www.ritzcarltonclub.com

Condotels

Condotels (sometimes known as aparthotels) tend to be redeveloped historic buildings located in the middle of large cities with strong condominium markets and high hotel occupancy rates. Currently, most condotels are managed by luxury brands like Mandarin Oriental, Starwood's St. Regis, Marriott's Ritz-Carlton, and Hilton's Conrad division.

Recent developments include the W Hotel & Residences, set in Victory Park, a $3 billion urban construction (a virtual minicity) near downtown Dallas. But the hottest properties in town are the 66 condos atop the hotel, which range in price from $400,000 to $7 million. In White Sulphur Springs, West Virginia, the more than 200-year-old Greenbrier is getting into the ownership game with lots and homes ranging from $400,000 to $2 million. So is the Fontainebleau Hilton Resort in Miami Beach, which manages two condominium towers.

Fractional owners buy access to a specific hotel room for a designated number of days out of the year. A $\frac{1}{27}$ share buys 2 weeks; a $\frac{1}{12}$ share buys 4 weeks. This means you can buy a $\frac{1}{12}$ share of a $600,000 hotel room for $50,000 and stay there for 4 weeks out of the year.

Unlike a time-share, a fractionally owned room is real property that can be depreciated, resold, or passed on to heirs. Owners not in residence often elect to recoup a portion of their taxes and mortgage payments by putting their rooms into a rental pool managed by the hotel. Revenue generated by other guests staying in your room is split between the owner(s) of the room and the hotel, which maintains the property.

But the amenities and cachet of a luxury hotel do not come cheap. In addition to hefty management fees, owners pay a service charge when they occupy the room. Part of that money—but not all—is returned when a room in the rental pool is occupied by a paying hotel guest. Hotels normally take 50 percent of any rental income a privately owned condo generates, plus an additional 25 percent booking fee for handling the transaction.

▽ Resources

Condo Hotel Center: 305-944-3090, www.condohotelcenter.com

Victory Park: 214-303-5542, www.victorypark.com

Greenbrier: 304-536-1110, www.greenbrier.com/site

CondHotel: 786-276-6959, www.condhotels.com

Budget Accommodations

There was a time when budget travelers had limited, often grimy, options when it came to accommodations. Plenty of cities still boast cheap hotels and hostels with cell-like rooms or multiple bunk beds crammed into one corner, but these days, there are plenty of other alternatives that won't break the bank.

Monasteries

If you're willing to live the simple life, try spending the night in a monastery. It will probably cost a fraction of what you'd pay in even the sparsest hotel room.

Some overnight monasteries resemble spartan hotels designed for religious travelers who are on a pilgrimage or spiritual journey, while others are active monastic orders who believe in hospitality to strangers (and who rely on paying guests as part of their income). The latter are often less expensive than the former but have stricter rules for their guests. In either case, you can expect to find a single-size bed or two (even married couples often have to sleep on opposite sides of the room), vegetarian meals, and certainly no Internet, television, or, for that matter, in-room telephone. This is certainly no place for hard-partying summer backpackers, but it's perfect for those who are interested in soaking up the local culture while enjoying some spiritual silence.

A few things to keep in mind:

! Unlike backpacker-friendly youth hostels, monasteries and convents don't necessarily have English speakers on-site. It's a good idea to call, fax, or e-mail the location first to set up your reservation and find out whether there is someone with whom you can communicate. If there is no phone number available, contact the country's tourism office to see if they can help you arrange accommodations and determine prices.

! Some of these places don't take reservations and are first come first served. Find out if this is the case in advance. Make backup plans for alternative accommodations in case there are no rooms available upon your arrival.

! More often than not, religious institutions have very strict rules and regulations, and they require absolute compliance from guests. Use your common sense on this one—no drinking, smoking, or even breaking curfew (more than one tardy traveler has found himself locked out of the building at 3 a.m.). If the monastery has a vow of silence or observes periods of silence, you need to abide by this. If there are certain areas that are off-limits to visitors, don't let your wanderlust get the better of you. In the long term, you run the risk of paying dearly to a . . . higher authority. In the short term, you'll be asked, quietly but forcefully, to leave.

The New Camaldoli Hermitage, Big Sur, California. Located in the cliffs high above the Pacific Ocean just 25 miles south of Big Sur, this Camaldolese monastery offers private and group retreats, though all rooms are single occupancy, most with half baths. The nightly fee of $70 ($80 for trailer hermitages) includes meals, and rooms can be reserved up to 6 months in advance. This is a silent retreat; however, quiet speaking is permitted occasionally. Don't forget to order your brandy-dipped fruitcake or hand-made candle on the way home (made and sold by Camaldolese monks). 831-667-2456, www.contemplation.com/Hermitage/home.html

Abbey of New Clairvaux, Vina, California. This Cistercian monastery in the picturesque vineyards of Sacramento Valley offers private retreats for individuals, meals included, for a donation "according to the individual's means" to be used for those less fortunate. Guests can experience silence and solitude, separation from the outside world's distractions, and the daily monastic rhythm between communal and personal prayer and work. The monks make pottery and now wine from their own vineyards—both available for sale to guests. 530-839-2434, www.newclairvaux.org

Holy Trinity Monastery, St. David, Arizona. This "semicontemplative" Benedictine monastery in the high desert offers individual and group retreats (single or double occupancy). Guests are expected to participate in the monastic exercises of silence, solitude, simple living, and community and personal prayer. Your stay includes your room and meals (all silent) on 92 wooded acres. No radio or TV is allowed on the premises. As the monastery is supported by donations, they suggest giving anywhere from $40 to $70 per day, plus a donation for meals ($15 is suggested for three meals per day). 520-720-4016 or 520-720-4642, ext. 17, www.holytrinitymonastery.org/chronicles.html

Mepkin Abbey, Moncks Corner, South Carolina. This monastery offers accommodations for short-term (1 to 6 nights) retreats and long-term (30 days) stays. Visitors observe the same silence as the monks, eat the same vegetarian meals, and can take part in the prayer services. The monks of Mepkin Abbey belong to the worldwide Order of Cistercians of the Strict Observance. www.mepkinabbey.org

Istituto Maria Santissima Bambina, Vatican City, Italy. What better way to experience Vatican City than staying at a religious institution overlooking St. Peter's Basilica with a balcony overlooking the Square? A single bedroom with private facilities (i.e., no communal toilets) is about $60 a night, and a double is about $55 per person. This is more of the guesthouse variety of monasteries that can capitalize on their enviable location, so the rules may be a bit more lax than other places. You may find yourself mingling with other American travelers who are part of religious tour groups. 06-6989-3511, fax: 06-6989-3540, imbspietro@mariabambina.va (e-mail)

Casa San Filippo Neri, Florence, Italy. Travelers get to live among the priests in this Florentine monastery, and the location is ideal for first-time visitors to the city. It's located right in the center of Florence, near the Uffizi and Il Duomo. The facilities are quite rustic, with 21 beds in five single rooms and eight doubles with a common bathroom. Meals are not available, but there is a shared TV room. 39-075-5725919, fax: 39-075-5739948

Convitto della Calza, Florence, Italy. Travelers who are willing to pay a few more dollars for more posh facilities may want to check out this remodeled 14th-century Florentine convent. This is part of the Italian Association of Houses for Spiritual Exercise designed for church groups, religious conventions, and spiritual travelers; however, all paying visitors are welcome. It's located near the Palazzo Pitti, about a mile from Il Duomo, and has a private bathroom in each room. There are also a chapel, several meeting rooms, and playrooms for children, and it is even handicapped accessible. Rates start at about $80 a night for a single room and go up to about $135 for a triple. Visiting pilgrim groups can qualify for major discounts. 39-055-222287, www.calza.it

Hotel Hospederia dy Leyre, Navarra, Spain. Navarra, located near the French border, is a beautiful and peaceful region of Spain that combines the modern city of Pamplona with medieval elements from its ancient days. This lodging is actually a hotel located next to the monastery, and visitors are welcome to observe and participate in religious services and attend confession with the monks (you may be fortunate enough to hear the monks' Gregorian chants during your stay). Guests are asked to remain silent when walking to the church and refectory, avoid loud social interaction in the hotel rooms and hallways, and refrain from heated political or religious debates. Meals are served along with the monks at specified times. There are 32 rooms that include central heating and private baths. 948-884-100, fax: 948-884-137, www.monasteriodeleyre.com

Monasterio de San Benito de Montserrat, Spain. Montserrat is not actually a town but an entire Benedictine monastery on its own. It's about an hour's drive outside of Barcelona, which can be reached by car or by train and cable car. Guests can participate in any of the six daily prayer services and can expect to interact with monks, nuns, and other visitors looking for some spiritual rest. Children are not allowed, and while visitors don't need to maintain silence, they are asked to avoid making loud noises. Single rooms are about $25 a day. 34-938-350-078, 34-938-777-701

Benedictine Priory at Sacré-Coeur, Montmartre, Paris, France. This monastic community is always buzzing with out-of-towners, but the sisters there offer a retreat for those looking for some peace. Travelers can join any of the worship services in the morning and evening. The accommodations are quite sparse, but guests need pay only a few dollars for an overnight stay. 33-01-46-06-1474

Taize, France. Although not exactly a monastery, Taize is a tiny Christian community that openly welcomes travelers and pilgrims from all over the world. It's located in east central France, near the historical monastery of Cluny. You can meet thousands of other spiritual types or spend your days with prayer and meditation—there are three services a day for all worshippers. Overnight accommodations are available in this community for about $12 to $24 per person, or you can spend the night in nearby Cluny. 33-3-85-50-30-02 (Taize's English-speaking welcome service), www.taize.fr

Bachkovo Monastery, Bulgaria. Located about 20 miles southwest of Plovdiv on the bank of the Chepelare River, this monastery is one of the oldest in the region, having been built in the 11th century. It's noted for its exquisite architecture and intricate wall paintings and murals. There are about 200 beds available for guests, but it's recommended that you book in advance during the summer season. The main village is packed with shops and restaurants that have made this a rather popular tourist destination, plus there are several hiking trails that begin at the monastery. 359-03327-277

Rila Monastery, Bulgaria. Founded in the 10th century, the Rila Monastery is one of the most well-known Eastern Orthodox monasteries in the region. The area is made up of three sections: The main church was built in the middle of the 18th century, contains five domes and three altars, and is known for its intricate woodworked frescos. The museum section is most famous for its large cross made from just one piece of wood. The residential building is four stories tall, and visitors are welcome to stay overnight for about $15 a night. Religious services are at 7 a.m. and 4 p.m., or 8 a.m. and 5 p.m., depending on the time of year. Make sure you check out the library as well, which holds 250 old manuscripts. 359-70542-208

Ramet Monastery, Romania. Seated in the valley of the Geoagiu River in the Trascau Mountains, this 13th-century structure is one of the oldest Orthodox churches in Transylvania. It is a large complex, with two churches, a museum that showcases glass and wood icons, and living quarters that house 95 nuns and sisters. No contact information is available; to arrange accommodations, contact the Romanian tourism office at 212-545-8484.

Brâncoveanu Monastery, Romania. Founded in the 17th century, this large structure at the bottom of the Fagaras Mountains had suffered from Romania's ongoing battles but has been restructured to house modern and ancient elements. An on-site museum exhibits 18th- and 19th-century glass paintings and historical letters, documents, and items from the monks. There are already about 40 people of the religious order living in the monastery. Visitors can stay at the Academia de la Sâmbta, which contains 130 beds and a meeting room for religious conferences or dialogues. 40-0268-241237, www.manastireabrancoveanu.ro

Couch Swapping

This is an entirely different kind of religious experience. Traveling solo or on the cheap often requires the help of other experienced travelers, whether through local friends or professional guides, especially when searching for übercheap overnight accommodations. Back in the "old" days, solo travelers and backpackers usually had to depend on word of mouth, guidebooks, and loosely organized hospitality groups like Servas to find other like-minded travelers and locals who could help them out for the night. However, today there is a growing online presence of "hospitality exchange" Web sites that are bringing the global traveling community even closer.

A hospitality exchange Web site is an informal tool for travelers to secure what are perhaps the cheapest accommodations possible—someone else's couch. These sites are usually free to use and involve travelers who are interested in getting a taste of the local culture (as well as a free place to sleep) and hosts who are willing to share their couches, guest beds, or just floor space (think of it as "couch time-sharing"). The level of contact between the traveler and host is up to the individuals: Some hosts offer nothing more than a place to sleep, while others get fully involved with cooking meals, sightseeing, and socializing.

Of course, there is one question, first and foremost, on most travelers' minds: What about safety? Rule number one: There are no guarantees. But most Web sites do address the safety issue, as follows.

Couchsurfing.com has implemented a few safety precautions. Each user is linked to other users in the system, so references and testimonials are readily available. A vouching system means that a member can officially vouch for another host or traveler; only an already-vouched-for member can vouch for someone else; and the site cautions users to think carefully before putting their own reputations on the line by vouching for another. A verification system means that the user has paid $25 via credit card for the Web site administrators to check on the name and physical address and also that the user's name matches the credit card. Essentially it's just an extra step to show that the user is a serious Couchsurfing member. However, note that vouching and verification are only optional steps.

Servas.org is an accredited NGO (nongovernmental organization) recognized by the United Nations to promote global friendship "by opening doors to peace and understanding." (*Servas* means "to serve" in the international language of Esperanto.) Established in 1949, the organization brings together more than 13,000 homes in 130 countries. It's a little more structured than other hospitality Web sites, as host homes are divided into nine areas around the world, with a coordinator for each region. With an actual organization and contact person in place, security measures are supposedly a bit more stringent, and there is someone to contact with your questions and concerns. Servas also arranges events and meetings for members.

Hospitalityclub.org operates on a similar mission to build "intercultural understanding and peace through hospitality exchange." Members can offer each other travel help, whether it's free accommodations, a tour around town, or just a local friend to have coffee or dinner. To foster some security, guests are required to show their passports upon arrival, and the online feedback option allows the site's administrators to review individual memberships. The Web site was founded in 2000 by Veit Kühne, a German traveler who is active in both the hitchhiking community and the global volunteer organization AFS.

Globalfreeloaders.com. You gotta love this name alone! Founded by Australian traveler Adam Staines, the site requires that guests also offer to be hosts, to emphasize the give-and-take nature of hospitality communities.

Otherwise, it operates in pretty much the same manner as other exchange Web sites, though it hasn't implemented any specific safety measures.

Welcometraveller.org is the only one of these sites that charge for use: Members must pay $30 a year to use the site and $10 a night to the host as a courtesy, which of course is a far lower rate than most hostels or hotels. The site sorts posts into specific groups to bring together like-minded individuals; for example, there are sections for quilters and crafters, educators, and women only, to name a few (there is a general section as well). Guests are also strongly encouraged to offer accommodations to other travelers, even if it's just floor space. This company is newer than most, so it doesn't have the same user feedback and personal vouches as the other Web sites.

If you're traveling solo, here are a few tips to help ensure your safety.

- **!** Always let one or more people know exactly where you're staying each night, including the name and phone number of your host. If your plans change, alert someone of this.

- **!** Have a backup plan in case your host arrangement doesn't work out.

- **!** Always carry a list of emergency contacts.

- **!** Keep a photocopy of your passport and/or ID separate from the originals.

- **!** Bring two credit or check cards and store them in different places.

- **!** Provide feedback, positive or negative, about your host/guest to the organization that brought you together, so others can make an informed decision.

House Swapping

If you're intrigued by the idea of free accommodations, another popular option among budget travelers is house swapping. It's exactly what it sounds like—you and another homeowner agree to swap abodes for an agreed amount of time. In some cases, participants may swap a second home, so it doesn't need to be a simultaneous exchange, but the concept is still the same.

The fun part is that not only can you take advantage of free stays when you're traveling, but there are some unusual accommodations available out there. How about a castle in Scotland, a sheep farm in New Zealand, or a yurt in Washington?

There are several Web sites dedicated to facilitating home exchanges—

like Couchsurfing, these sites can't make any guarantees. They allow travelers to meet online, and then you handle the details yourself. Like online dating, the recommended protocol is that you communicate ahead of time by e-mail and phone, swap photos, and get some background information. Make sure you get pictures of the accommodations as well, so that you're not in for any ugly surprises when you get there. It's also important to discuss, and write down, all responsibilities and expectations for the stay: Is there a pet in the house? An alarm that needs to be set? Once the agreements are in place, it's a good idea to let trusted friends and neighbors know you're home swapping. Not only will your guests appreciate having a few local contacts, but you'll appreciate having peace of mind knowing your home is okay. And lastly, to be on the safe side, make sure your homeowner's insurance is paid up before you leave.

▽ Resources

International Home Exchange Network: www.ihen.com

Intervac: www.intervac.com

Home Exchange: www.homeexchange.com

Senior Home Exchange: www.seniorshomeexchange.com

Singles Home Exchange: www.singleshomeexchange.com

Home Link International: www.homelink.org

Capsule Hotels

When it comes to travel, there's style, and then there's substance. When it comes to efficiency and space, there's naval architecture. And finally, when it comes to minimalist square footage, no one has mastered hotel occupancy like the Japanese. If you haven't heard of "capsule hotels," you've probably seen parodies of them where dozens of businessmen snooze soundly in what looks like a chest of drawers.

There is some merit in choosing a capsule hotel. Depending on your schedule—as well as if you're traveling with someone or going solo—you need to be clear about why you need a hotel room in the first place. Are you planning on entertaining a delegation in your room? Catering a party?

In some cases, there's a reasonably good chance that you're only looking for a temporary place to sleep and shower. Welcome to the capsule hotel concept.

In reality, a capsule hotel has long provided sleeping quarters for business travelers. While not exactly drawers, they're rows of miniscule spaces (often stacked into two levels) that can be as small as 3 feet by 3 feet by 7 feet. That's basically the length of a sleeping human. What you may not expect is that these spaces often include a tiny mounted television, an alarm clock, and even a shelf for some belongings. In Japan, the idea behind these capsule hotels was to provide shelter for area businessmen who missed the last train of the night.

Sound pleasant? It's not, really, but the concept has its benefits. For one thing, a standard capsule hotel in Tokyo costs about $30 a night. For budget travelers, that's far more palatable than the $700 a night the Imperial Hotel in the same city charges for a room that's only slightly larger. If you're planning on only sleeping in your hotel room and expect to spend a night or two, it can be worth saving money on your accommodations (and splurge on that extra-fresh sushi dinner instead!)

The concept of capsule hotels is beginning to take hold outside of Japan. The philosophy is simple—microsize rooms equal lower prices, so it's win-win: The hotel has high occupancy and turnover, and you save significantly on your travels.

In London's Gatwick airport (specifically in the International Arrivals of the South Terminal), you can find something called the **Yotel**. Founded by Simon Woodroffe, who started the Yo! Sushi chain, Yotel is a capsule hotel with rooms for just £25 a night (about $50). Even better, travelers with long layovers can book a Yotel capsule by the hour. Standard rooms can fit "a cosy 2," with a single bed that's about 6 feet long and 3 feet wide—think of it like a cruise-ship cabin. The hotel maximizes on space by including a shower (no tub), a fold-out work desk, and overhead luggage storage. Don't worry about going stir-crazy (unless you're claustrophobic), as you can keep busy with free Internet, a television, iPod ports, and 24-hour room service. www.yotel.com

The folks who created EasyJet have opened up **EasyHotel** (Sir Stelios Haji-Ioanou's brand includes everything from EasyPizza to EasyJobs). Room rates start at £25 (about $50) in the London properties and £32 (about $65) in Zurich. The good news here—as opposed to his airline—is that at least you're not gouged for checked bags (see page 45). Locations throughout Germany, Budapest, and even expensive Dubai are in the works. One caution: We're still talking about miniscule rooms with en suite bathrooms—you can barely fit two people. The price makes it popular with budget travelers, but just like its cousin, EasyJet, which charges for everything short of its on-board toilet, EasyHotel charges you for everything from housekeeping to using the remote control! OK, you've been warned. www.easyhotel.com

If you kick the capsule hotel idea up a notch, you get the **Nitenite** in the Birmingham, England. The concept here is a "boutique budget" hotel where, again, you're sleeping in a room that's less than 100 square feet. The space is a little sleeker than the Yotels and EasyHotels of the world, not least of all due to the 42-inch plasma TVs. You can expect to pay about £35 (about $70) for prepaid, no-refund rates, and £54.95 (about $110) for flexible rates. No food, no mints on the pillow, but at least you've found a relatively decent place to sleep in the city center. 08458 90 90 99, www.nitenite.com

Last but not least, the mini-room hotel has made its way to New York. The **Pod Hotel** has taken over the former Pickwick Hotel in Manhattan. The 1930s building is centrally located, on East 51st Street in Midtown, which is walking distance to Broadway, Rockefeller Center, and plenty of other must-see spots in the city. The hotel markets itself as being a trendy, almost futuristic spot for young and budget-minded travelers—and it does have some stylish elements, with a hip decor, an iPod docking station, LCD-screen televisions, and free Wi-Fi. Most of the 347 rooms are just about 100 square feet—tiny even by New York standards. But there are some choices: Bunk bed rooms start at $89 a night (astonishing for Manhattan prices, but one caution—you'll be sharing a bathroom); a room with a double bed starts at $169; a full townhouse studio, which includes a living room, a queen and sofa bed, and a 25-inch television, is still a relatively modest $229. And what the rooms are lacking in view is more than made up for by the rooftop garden, where you can have a quiet respite with spectacular views of the city. 212-355-0300, www.thepodhotel.com

Hostels

Despite the name, a youth hostel is a great budget option for travelers of all ages. Many hostels don't have any kind of age limit and actually market themselves as a viable alternative for families and solo travelers. Youth hostels usually have amenities like communal kitchens, common rooms, Internet access, and information on local events and resources.

In Europe and Australia, particularly, hostels and backpacker lodges are relatively easy to come by. Hostelling International (formerly known as International Youth Hostel Federation, or IYHF) is a nonprofit organization composed of more than 90 different youth hostel associations representing over 4,500 youth hostels in more than 80 countries. They include the Youth Hostels Association (YHA) in England and Wales, the Scottish Youth Hostels Association (SYHA) in Scotland, and the American Youth Hostels.

Hostelling International members must adhere to standards, which helps ensure your comfort and peace of mind when traveling. For example, hostels must provide freshly washed bedding (you may have to pay a fee), lockers for your luggage and valuables, single-sex and mixed-sex dormitories, and meals (also for a fee). Beds may be located in large dormitory-style rooms, but hostels are increasingly turning toward smaller two- and four-bed rooms. Hostelling International offers memberships for reduced rates, plus some savings on travel insurance and phone cards.

Even if you choose an independent hostel that is not affiliated with a larger network, you can still have a positive experience. You may be able to show up at their doorstep to stay the night, but generally it's a good idea to call ahead for reservations since they tend to fill up during peak seasons. Some other tips to keep in mind:

- Hostels in more urban areas tend to be open 24 hours a day, but don't count on it. Call ahead, especially if you think you may arrive late at night.
- Pack lightly and don't carry valuables while you're traveling. The hostel should have a safe for important items like your passport if you choose not to keep it on you.
- Make sure that someone knows where you're staying, with all the contact information. If you decide to leave early or stay longer, make sure they're aware.
- If you're squeamish or on a budget, consider bringing a sleep sack or your own sheets.

! Be friendly. Hostels are filled with like-minded travelers, who are generally an open bunch. It's a great way to make friends with other travelers, but of course always use common sense when hanging out with strangers.

▽ Resources

Hostelling International: www.iyhf.org

US branch of Hostelling International: www.hiayh.org

Listings and online bookings for hostels and budget accommodations worldwide: www.hostelworld.com

Listings and booking for hostels worldwide: www.hostel.com

Worldwide hostel review: www.hostelz.com

CHAPTER 6

Cruises

⁦⁦ There was still room to turn around in, but not to swing a cat in,
at least with the entire security to the cat. ⁩⁩

—MARK TWAIN, ON THE SIZE OF A SHIP'S STATEROOM

As recently as a decade ago, cruise ship vacationing still conjured up images of hordes of elderly folks playing shuffleboard and taking afternoon tea on the promenade deck. Not true anymore. Cruise lines are actively targeting everyone from families and multigenerational travelers to singles, honeymooning couples, gay and lesbian travelers, and baby boomers. There are ships for 200 people and ships for 3,500 people, ranging from basic weekend party cruises to floating cities where the destination of the ship is more often than not incidental to the onboard experience.

And the industry continues to grow, almost exponentially. A hundred new ships will have debuted between 2000 and 2010—that's a record number. Seven new ships debuted in 2006, and another nine were scheduled for 2007. Recent statistics show that members of the Cruise Line Association (CLIA, the industry group representing US-based cruise lines) carried 12.1 million worldwide passengers in 2006, which was an 8.4 percent increase from the previous year. It was predicted that 12.6 million cruise passengers would set sail in 2007, an increase of approximately half a million guests from 2006. The three largest groups—Carnival, Royal Caribbean, and Star Cruises—control more than 125 mostly large cruise ships.

And that's not all of it. Besides CLIA members, there are about 200 other foreign cruise ships. On any given day, there are an estimated 150 to 200 cruise ships sailing—from large commercial ships to river boats and small expedition cruises.

Understanding the Industry

The real numbers are staggering. In the travel industry, the cruise line business is considered the most discretionary product consistently producing the most enviable profit margins. More and more big—and bigger—ships are being built. And the cruise lines are filling them.

Consider this: In 2005, Carnival Corporation generated a billion-dollar profit in a single quarter. In 2006, it broke that record with a $1.2 billion profit for the third quarter. There's a lot to be said for mass—Carnival, the largest cruise company in the world, has more than 81 ships sailing under more than 12 brands. Why did I say "more than"? Because by the time you read this, those numbers will likely have increased.

Cruising is a relatively new trend for travelers. Back in 1980, only 1.4 million people in North America had ever taken a cruise. By 2005, the number was up to 9.6 million. The cruising industry estimates that there will be 10.8 million passengers by 2010 in North America . . . and 16.4 million globally. Even with those impressive sounding numbers, it translates into only about 17 percent of the American population. It's a relatively young business. But it's a big business.

And the ships are big as well. The Royal Caribbean ship *Freedom of the Seas*—currently the biggest ship afloat, but not for long—has an atrium that soars 15 decks to a nighttime disco that juts out over the pool—well, one of the pools, since the ship has four. It has 10 restaurants. It has an ice-skating rink, a surfing machine, 16 bars and lounges, and an old-fashioned barber shop.

It also has a maximum capacity of 4,370 passengers. And every week, the ship is filled to capacity. If managing a hotel is complicated, if running a restaurant is challenging, and if operating a shipping business is intricate, imagine the complexity of doing all three simultaneously.

And how do cruise lines make money? By filling their cabins to capacity.

On airlines, breakeven might be a load factor of 68 percent. But in the cruise industry, it's an entirely different—and surprising—business model: 100 percent occupancy isn't a goal; it's a requirement.

In fact, ships often are filled to more than capacity, since cruise lines base 100 percent occupancy on the "lower berth" count of two beds per cabin. The "upper berth" count includes putting three and four passengers in cabins.

Think I'm kidding? Look at the financial statements of the three largest public cruise companies. In 2005, Carnival's 12 brands sailed at 105.6 percent occupancy, NCL Corporation operated its fleets at 106.1 percent occupancy, and Royal Caribbean Cruises operated at 106.6 percent occupancy.

And what you pay for your cabin is often unimportant and, in fact, often bears no resemblance to what you'll really pay by the time you're ready to disembark. It also has little to do with the profits the cruise lines make. It's the onboard revenue generated by each passenger that puts cruise lines in the black—big time. Shore excursions, onboard shopping, the spa, the casino, and let's not forget the liquor. Ka-ching!

That's huge, because when sailing at 100 percent capacity, operating costs are more than covered by the ticket price. And onboard revenue is the real make-or-break item—it drops straight to the bottom line.

Yes, there is the official pricing of cruise line cabins, which can be as confusing for cruise passengers as for airline passengers trying to find a deal on a plane ticket. For example, Royal Caribbean's *Freedom of the Seas* has up to 20 price categories for each of its 52 sailings every year.

And how are the cabins sold? It's just as much of a dark science as with the airline industry. In the airline and hotel businesses, it's called yield management. The cruise industry has a somewhat sexier term: "availability spill." What's that? The "spill" is what happens when there is no availability in a cabin category or a sailing that a customer wants. Then there's something called price spill—when the prospective cruise passenger decides not to buy because of price. The optimal situation for the cruise line is when spilled business results in replacing people who were looking for lower prices with consumers willing to pay more. In the grocery business, spillage is a bad thing. In the cruise line business, spillage is everything.

Add to that the cruise industry's notoriously draconian refund policies—and the 105 percent occupancy figure starts making a lot of sense.

It hasn't always been this way. In the 1970s and 1980s, the list prices in the cruise lines' brochures almost always reflected what people actually paid. The pricing was simplified and more or less inflexible. The price was the same whether a cabin was booked 1 week or 3 months before the sailing. There was no incentive for early booking and no distressed-inventory discount for last-minute booking. A flight from Seattle plus the cost of the cruise, known in cruise language as an air-sea ticket, was the same as an air-sea ticket from Atlanta, despite the difference in cost to the cruise line.

But then came the 1990s. And that's when the big shipbuilding push came. The cruise lines figured that if only a small percentage of Americans had ever taken a cruise, then an overwhelming majority was determined to go. It wasn't long before supply outpaced demand, and you know what that meant—the dreaded "d" word: *discounting.*

And in relatively short order, the cruise lines' pricing models started to mimic some of the airline pricing. Last-minute bookers were rewarded with better deals. The early-booking passengers were at a disadvantage.

Some cruise lines tried to change that last-minute-discount booking model. Royal Caribbean introduced something called breakthrough pricing. What they did was establish low-price months before a cruise to encourage demand and then continue to raise prices as the ships were filled. No more late-booking discounts. But that, of course, presumed that inventory would always tighten as the sailing departure date for each cruise approached.

On some very popular cruises—Christmas and New Year's, summer Alaska cruises, and the world cruises still offered by some lines—or whenever a line introduced a new ship, the concept of breakthrough pricing worked.

But the law of supply and demand is a law for a reason. If demand wasn't there, it was inevitably followed by discounting.

And as the new shipbuilding craze continued—almost unabated for a few years—so did discounting. On some itineraries, the discounting was so severe that one could argue—with proof—that it was cheaper to go for a week on a cruise ship than to stay at home, factoring in the cost of meals, transportation, and other goods and services.

And then came 9/11.

Ironically, 9/11 was perhaps the best thing that ever happened to the cruise industry. It was the only segment of the travel industry that could—literally—move its assets. With Americans terrified about flying—especially over bodies of water—the cruise industry literally moved their ships to

America, to 17 separate ports. Within weeks of the World Trade Center tragedy, the cruise industry made almost all of their ships drive-to destinations, a situation that remains to this day. It also changed the demographics of cruisers and opened up cruising to a whole new set of travelers.

This is cruising's "get out of jail free" card. If the Caribbean is soft, cruise lines redeploy ships to the Mediterranean. If the French Riviera gets crowded or loses its luster, lines send their vessels to Croatia. If Libya opens its ports to Americans, they put it in the itinerary. If it closes them again, they substitute Tunisia. And, of course, we can now all prepare for the inevitable—the big cruise line push to Cuba. Once again, the cruise lines will be perfectly positioned to be first in. In fact, the major US cruise lines have already charted what they consider to be eight "viable" Cuban ports, including Havana. The minute the US travel ban is lifted, I can guarantee you the ships will be running at 110 percent occupancy, as everyone wants to be first on his block into the once-forbidden destination.

And it will be easy. After all, you won't have to worry about ground infrastructure—the cruise ships are floating hotels. The only folks worrying will be other Caribbean cruise port destinations—rightfully concerned that the market, at least initially, will shift dramatically away from them.

One more note about profits. Here's an interesting statistic: Carnival Cruise Lines earned $11 billion in revenue in 2005. So did Marriott. But Carnival's net income on that revenue was $2.2 billion, a 20 percent profit margin; Marriott's was $669 million, a 5.8 percent profit margin. (One reason, but by no means the only reason, is that cruise lines accrue immense financial benefit from being foreign-flagged vessels, thus not paying the taxes and wages that US companies do.)

Fun Facts

Cruise Ship Genealogy

Your "brand-new" cruise ship may not be so new after all. Cruise ships often live several lifetimes under different names. For example, Windjammer Cruise's iconic ship the *Yankee Clipper* was actually built way back in 1927, as a private yacht named *Cressida*. After World War II, she was acquired by the Vanderbilt family and christened the *Pioneer,* and she was considered one of the fastest tall ships on the West Coast. It wasn't until 1965 that she joined Windjammer and was renamed the *Yankee Clipper.*

Check www.cybercruises.com/shiplist.htm for lists of ships owned by cruise companies, the number of passengers each can carry, and, in some cases, the ships' former names. For example, the Malaysian-based Star Cruises operates the *SuperStar Gemini,* which used to sail under the name *Crown Jewel* when it was owned by Cunard. Monarch Classic Cruises in Greece has a whole fleet of reappropriated ships, including the *Blue Monarch,* which used to be Elysian Cruises' *World Renaissance* ship. The *Ocean Countess* may win the award for having the most lives—it used to sail as the Cunard *Countess,* Awani *Dream II,* and Olympia *Countess.*

When you think about it, it makes sense—these large ships would take an awful lot of time and material to build from scratch. But think about it the next time you step on board the next "new" ship acquired by a cruise line and imagine all that she may have experienced over many lifetimes.

Cruise Ship Godmothers

You probably already know the tradition of breaking a bottle of champagne against the hull of a ship to christen it. What you may not know is that the person doing the smashing is just as important as the symbolic crashing itself. An honorary yet official title, a "cruise ship godmother" has few real responsibilities but carries a symbolic connection to the ship she christens. In other words, it's a marketing scheme but one that is steeped in tradition. Iconic actress Sophia Loren, for example, has christened nearly all of the ships belonging to MSC Cruises, whose slogan is "Beautiful. Passionate. Italian." Princess Cruises set up a dual christening ceremony in Santorini over Mother's Day weekend, where TV mothers and daughters broke the glass: Florence Henderson and Susan Olsen from *The Brady Bunch* and Marion Ross and Erin Moran of *Happy Days.* And the godmother of the *Disney Wonder*? Well, that would be the first animated godmother in cruise ship history: Tinker Bell.

They Just Keep on Getting Bigger

Although smaller ships are gaining popularity with travelers for their more intimate environments and ability to navigate lesser-known routes, the big ships just keep on getting bigger. For many years, the *Queen Mary 2* was the largest passenger ship ever built, at 148,000 tons. But in 2005, Royal Caribbean surpassed this with its new "ultra-voyager" *Freedom of the Seas,* a 160,000-ton behemoth (about the weight of 80,000 cars) that can carry 4,300 passengers. That's more than three times the size of the *Titanic.* She has 16 bars, 10 restaurants, three swimming pools, a water park, an ice-skating rink, something called a wave generator, and Wi-Fi throughout the ship. It costs about $1 million a day to keep this cruise ship operating, with 10 restaurants, 16 bars and lounges, and more than 250 waiters . . . not to mention 750,000 lightbulbs, 78,000 pounds of ice cubes produced per day, and 530,000 tons of water in the swimming pools!

But Royal Caribbean isn't stopping there: A new ship, called *Project Genesis,* is in the works to be completed by 2009. This will be the world's largest cruise ship, at 1,180 feet long, 154 feet wide at water level, and 240 feet high—and carrying up to 6,400 passengers. It will be the most expensive cruise ship, with a price tag of $1.2 billion.

Above and Beyond Amenities

Cruise lines are working hard to attract travelers with above-and-beyond amenities—oftentimes surpassing what you could expect to find in a traditional hotel or resort. Nowadays, it's old news for a cruise to have swimming pools, hot tubs, video game arcades, and family movie night. Cruise lines are going above and beyond to make sure that the ship is as much of a destination as the ports.

Carnival Cruise Lines, for example, operates the only ships at sea that offer wireless Internet access, from "bow to stern," aboard the *Valor, Liberty,* and *Freedom* ships. Celebrity Cruises features virtual golfing simulators and swing cages that help monitor your swing and improve your overall game. Norwegian Cruise Lines has recently installed the kid-friendly Wii systems on several of the ships. Families also may be impressed to know that Cunard's *Queen Mary* 2 includes the only planetarium at sea and the largest library afloat, with 8,000 volumes on board.

Packing Tips

Now that airlines have imposed a 50-pound limit on suitcases, my advice is to pack light. Dress codes on ships are usually very loose, including Norwegian's "Freestyle Cruising" policy, which recommends resort casual wear. However, formal standards are enforced on luxury lines like Crystal, Cunard, Regent, Seabourn, and Silversea. Dresses and sarongs are very light and easily packable. Rugged cruises, like to Alaska, may require hiking shoes and warm layers.

In the mood for some adventure? The *Costa Concordia* boasts a Grand Prix racing simulation, while Royal Caribbean's *Freedom of the Seas* includes a shipboard surf park and a full-size boxing ring. The SeaDream Yacht Club features retractable water-sports marinas for tubing, sailing, and kayaking. They also offer guests the use of a personal Segway to explore the ports in two-wheel style.

Something called freestyle dining has also grown increasingly popular on cruise lines. Rather than forcing you to sit for dinner at 5 p.m. or 8 p.m., additional specialty restaurants allow you to eat what you want, when you want. The *Norwegian Sun* was the first ship to feature this concept in 2001—at least four of the alternative dining venues don't have a surcharge, and you can choose from Italian, a buffet restaurant, a snack shop, and even a tapas bar. Other restaurants, including a steakhouse and French cuisine, will cost you up to $20 a person. Which brings me to my next point . . .

Pricey Amenities

One of the long-running myths about cruise ships is that they're all-inclusive. Sure, the buffet can be never ending and you can order limitless midnight hamburgers to your cabin. But if you're expecting the final price to be the same as what was originally quoted, think again—most of the important elements will come at a cost.

And, as you now know, even the so-called all-inclusive food doesn't always come for free. Many cruise ships now have cafés and ice cream shops that will cost you extra, and the trendy freestyle dining restaurants that are alternatives to traditional cruise dining usually charge a $20 to $30 cover charge per person. And don't forget that alcohol is rarely ever covered in the original price. For example, on Royal Caribbean, if you want to wash your many meals down with something other than juice, be prepared to pay up: Even sodas cost money, and alcoholic beverages will probably rack up your bill faster than you expect. Royal Caribbean does offer some packages to help offset the cost, like charging a flat fee for unlimited soda or a Wine and Dine deal that includes wine or champagne with your dinner (about $125 for a 7-day cruise).

Looking to get off the ship for a while? Get out your credit card. Most cruise lines don't include shore activities in their price: On Princess Cruises, a visit to a glacier and a salmon hatchery starts at $39 per person, while a helicopter tour starts at a whopping $395 per person. On a Royal Caribbean

Mexican Riviera cruise, you can take a tour of Puerto Vallerta for $28 per person ($18 for kids), take a cooking lesson for $34, or go for a bike ride . . . for $38. On Costa Cruises, a day tour of Reykjavik is $63, bathing in the Blue Lagoon is $85, and a Jeep tour of the island is $177.

The key here is to understand which shore excursions you need to book through the ship and which you can handle yourself. After all, if you need to pay $68 to go barhopping in Mexico, you're probably already inebriated! However, in Alaska, if you try to book a helicopter trip to the glaciers when more than one cruise ship is in port (and during the summer season, there can be as many as five ships docked at a time), you're out of luck. All the helicopter tours have been block-booked by the ships for months. If the ship is offering a walking tour, something tells me you can do that yourself, unless the guide is a real expert.

My other piece of advice: If you're traveling with one other couple or meet them on the ship, e-mail or call ahead to the best hotel in the port city you're visiting and ask the concierge to book you a car or minivan and a driver/guide. You'll see the destination at your own pace, won't get trapped either on a tour bus or inside an avoid-at-all-costs souvenir store, and have a much better experience. One caution: Watch the clock and get back to the ship no later than 90 minutes before sailing. If you do your own transportation and miss the ship, you will be hiring more than a car!

Money-Saving Deals

Despite their reputation, cruise ships don't have to be a pricey option. There are plenty of ways to save money on a cruise vacation, without sacrificing comfort and class for the sake of a few dollars. Here are a few tips for cruising on the cheap.

Alternative Ports

Royal Caribbean and Carnival Cruise Lines started sailing out of Galveston, Texas, in 2000, heading into Mexico, the western Caribbean, and Central America. www.portofgalveston.com

Norfolk, Virginia, has an 80,000-square-food cruise terminal for Carnival and Royal Caribbean cruises to Bermuda and the Bahamas. www.norfolkvisitor.com

In Bayonne, New Jersey, Cape Liberty Cruise Port opened for sailings in 2004. www.cruiseliberty.com

Repositioning Cruises

In some cases, you can find great discounts with something called a repositioning cruise. A repositioning cruise usually happens when a cruise line wants to change the main port of sailing for one of its ships and needs to move it from one place to another, often across an ocean or up or down the coast from a summer to a winter port. For example, you might depart Miami and sail across the Atlantic to a European port like Barcelona, Rome, or Athens. Such a cruise might stop in the Bahamas, Canary Islands, Azores, or Portugal en route, but it isn't likely that it would make more than a handful of port calls. Repositioning cruises are usually most prevalent in the spring and fall, as cruise lines rearrange their fleets to adjust to the changing seasons.

As a general rule, with repositioning cruises you get fewer port days and more days at sea. For cruisers looking for ample time to spend reading by the pool, exploring the ship, or playing shuffleboard, a repositioning cruise could be ideal. For the most part, repositioning cruises usually last longer than standard cruises, and it's rare to find one that's less than a full week long.

Note that because a repositioning cruise will drop you off in a different location than where you started, you may have to buy a one-way fare back home. Since one-way fares tend to be more expensive than round trips, this can tack on a significant fee to your travels. Also, since you may be spending more time on board the ship, expect to wind up paying for amenities like drinks, alternative dinners, massages, and manicures.

Cruising for Free

I always say if it sounds too good to be true, it is. But cruising for free really is a possibility . . . if you can convince 16 of your closest friends (that's eight cabins) to take a cruise. As a perk, cruise lines often throw in an extra room for the group leader. That's when bowling groups and canasta clubs come in handy.

Another option for cruising on the cheap is to become a gigolo. Okay, I'm not serious, but I'm close. You don't have to look like Richard Gere or dance like Fred Astaire, but if you're a man between the ages of 45 and 72 and if you can more or less navigate around a dance floor, you can cruise for free as a cruise ship "host." Cruise ship hosts are men who dance and socialize with guests for a few hours a night—that can mean charming the ladies at the dinner table, joining a tango lesson, or even accompanying a tour group on an excursion. For more information on how to apply, call 708-301-7535 or visit www.theworkingvacation.com/text/about2.html.

Specialty Cruises

One of the growing trends in cruising is the proliferation of "specialty cruises" or "participatory cruises." Whether you're into sports, cooking, or yoga, many cruises are including hands-on workshops, lectures, and excursions geared toward travelers who are interested in incorporating education with their cruising. Some themes involve outside organizations that block out large portions of an existing cruise voyage. So while there are special events going on for that group, you will generally be mixed in with other passengers. Others are itineraries coordinated by the cruise line itself, often bringing in experts and industry celebrities to draw in passengers.

Crystal Cruises offers dedicated golf cruises, currently on board the *Crystal Symphony*. An 11-day voyage leaves from London and offers passengers the option to play at St. Andrews' Jubilee Course in Edinburgh, Scotland, as well as several other courses in Ireland like the K Club in Dublin and the Harbour Point Golf Club in Cork. Onboard activities include lectures, golf clinics, and social gatherings featuring PGA pros and golf experts. 888-722-0211, www.crystalcruises.com

Silversea Cruises has several enrichment programs on various itineraries. A wine series includes guest lectures, tastings of vintage blends, and optional guided excursions to renowned wineries and cellars. The culinary arts series, which includes cruises from Nice to Athens and Barcelona to Rome, features chef lectures, demonstrations, gourmet meals, and hands-on instruction in the Viking Cooking School program. Other Silversea enrichment programs target history buffs, art aficionados, and nature lovers. 800-722-9955, www.silversea.com

Regent Seven Seas has many Spotlight and Circles of Interest cruises, both featuring lectures and workshops on various topics. For example, photography buffs can learn how to take the perfect picture, and public broadcasting

 **Budgeting**

One handy budget tool can be found at www.cruisetip.tpkeller.com. This cruise tip calculator can help you estimate how much you'll spend in tips alone on a cruise. Just click on the cruise line and plug in how many days you'll be on board; it breaks down the amount of tip per cruise ship staff. For example, on a 7-day Royal Caribbean cruise, one couple can expect to pay the waiter $49, the assistant waiter $28, the stateroom attendant $49, and the head waiter about $10.50, for a total of $136.50.

fans can participate in a PTV at Sea program with interactive panel discussions and private cocktail parties with PBS personalities. Antiques buffs shouldn't miss a cruise in China with *Antiques Roadshow*'s David Battie leading lectures and on-shore antiques shopping trips. 877-805-5370, www.rssc.com

Accessible Cruising

Please refer to "Accessible Travel" on page 328.

Safety Concerns

Between a cruise ship's sinking off the coast of Santorini, folks falling off cruise ships, and real-life missing persons at sea murder mysteries, cruise ship safety has made headline news once too often for some travelers. Are their concerns well founded, or is the biggest problem media hysteria? More to the point, how safe are cruises today?

A recent (some would say tidal) "wave" of publicity surrounded the 2005 disappearance of George Allen Smith IV, a honeymooning passenger on Royal Caribbean's *Brilliance of the Seas*. Though this was a rare instance of what is believed to be foul play, it triggered fears in travelers and attracted the attention of the federal government. In December 2005 and March 2006, Congress held two hearings to address the topic of cruise ship safety, with testimony from the FBI, cruise industry officials, and passengers and family of crime victims.

The Cruise Line Association (CLIA) released information in March 2006 regarding crime on board cruise ships prior to the second Congressional hearing. The industry data, based on 15 cruise lines' submissions, showed that there were 206 complaints from passengers and crew between 2003 and 2005. Out of 31 million passengers, there were 178 complaints of sexual assault, four robberies, and 24 missing persons during the 3-year period.

However, one of the major complaints raised by victims and their families is not the frequency of crimes on board cruise ships but the *reporting* of these crimes. Indeed, although serious crimes against US citizens on board a cruise ship are supposed to be reported to the FBI, crimes against noncitizens are not included, and the ship's security officers are often allowed to determine what constitutes a "serious" crime. Also, the statistics on these crimes, particularly sexual assault, may be deflated, because passengers may be unwilling to report an assault and are uncertain of what their rights are on international waters. All too often, if incidents are reported, they are reported (and subsequently recorded) in the port cities where the cruise ship may temporarily dock but not necessarily to US authorities. Bottom line: There is no central information repository for cruise ship crime information or current statistics.

In June 2006, Congressman Christopher Shays and Congresswoman Carolyn Mahoney announced the introduction of the bipartisan Cruise Line Accurate Safety Statistics Act (CLASS Act) to improve the reporting of cruise ship crimes. The act would have required the owners of cruise ships that call at US ports to report to the Department of Homeland Security (DHS) any crime, person overboard, or missing person incident that happens on board involving an American citizen.

Sounds like a great concept, right? But this bill was never brought to the House floor for debate.

Still, passengers are just as susceptible to crime on a cruise ship as anywhere else. Here are a few tips on traveling smartly and safely.

! Avoid drugs and limit your alcohol intake. Want to know why people "fell off" cruise ships in the last few years? I have one word to share with you: *alcohol!*

! Don't leave a public space like the pool deck with someone you don't know well.

! Avoid traveling alone on cruise ships that are known for their "party" atmosphere and are filled with young spring breakers.

! If you must bring valuables on board, insure them and store them in the ship's safe. There may also be a small safe inside your room, but it's probably not as secure.

! If you win big while gambling, don't make a spectacle of your success and do not store your cash in your cabin. Instead, put it in the ship's safe.

! Trust your gut. If someone is making you nervous or worried, extract yourself from the situation or notify onboard authorities.

! Most important (and this is just as true for women staying in hotels), no points will be deducted from your final score if you ask a uniformed crewmember to escort you down the corridor to your cabin.

Cruise Ship Health

Recent news stories of mass "stomach flu" outbreaks on cruise ships may also have some travelers concerned. Officially known as norovirus (abbreviated from Norwalk-like virus), symptoms include nausea, vomiting, diarrhea, and cramping, as well as low-grade fever, chills, headache, muscle aches, and general exhaustion. The sickness usually lasts 24 to 48 hours and is highly contagious—it can be contracted by eating or drinking contaminated food or liquids, touching contaminated surfaces and placing your hands in your mouth, or having direct contact with someone who is infected. The Centers for Disease Control and Prevention (CDC) estimates that 23 million Americans contract norovirus every year, which comes out to about 1 in every 12 people.

In February 2007, more than 100 passengers were stricken with norovirus on a Holland America cruise to the Caribbean, and 200-plus passengers on Royal Caribbean were afflicted in July 2006. The high volume of these cases made headlines, but in reality only about 1 percent of passengers suffer from the illness in a given year.

Cruise ships are prime locations for the rapid spread of norovirus due to close living quarters, buffets, public restrooms, and even elevator buttons—all of which are considered "high-touch areas." However, norovirus exists everywhere in society and runs in different cycles through various regions. Other closed environments like retirement homes and summer camps also tend to experience outbreaks.

Cruise ships are required to report cases of gastrointestinal illnesses (GI),

 CDC-Reported Norovirus Outbreaks in 2006

Royal Caribbean Cruise Lines: 8

Holland America Line: 7

Celebrity Cruises: 5

Princess Cruises: 5

Carnival Cruise Lines: 1

Norwegian Cruise Lines: 1

Source: *www.cdc.gov/nceh/vsp/surv/GIlist.htm*

which means that an unbalanced amount of media attention is thrust toward the cruising industry. Since these cases are in confined spaces with a shared medical resource, they're easier to track than land-based outbreaks. The CDC's Vessel Sanitation Program (VSP) means ships have to report any GI outbreaks if there are three or more episodes of loose stools in 24 hours or if there's vomiting and one additional symptom, including loose stools, abdominal cramps, headache, muscle aches, or fever, reported by a passenger or crewmember to the master.

Cruise lines work closely with the CDC and its VSP to minimize the risk of gastrointestinal illness on ships. The VSP inspects cruise ships with foreign itineraries that call on US ports and that carry 13 or more passengers. These ships are inspected twice a year, with criteria including the storage, distribution, and disinfection of the water supply; the filtration and disinfection of swimming pools and spas; food preparation, storage, and service; and employee hygiene. The VSP also trains the crew in proper public health techniques. When there is an outbreak on board or even just an increase in doctor visits, cruise lines increase sanitation procedures, encourage sick guests to remain in their rooms, and provide room service for the duration of the illness, which is usually a day or two.

Illnesses on Cruise Ships

Forget images of the doctor on the *Love Boat*. And don't think for a minute that you are cruising on a cutting-edge emergency room at sea. Yes, there is a ship's doctor and medical staff on board, but this is not a floating hospital, and it is not equipped as such.

Yes, the quality of medical care on board cruise ships has improved dramatically in the past 10 years. There was a time, in the not-too-distant past, when—all too often—the cruise ship doctor had questionable medical credentials. On some ships, the "doctors" were tantamount to escaped gynecologists, fugitives from justice, and, at least in one case, a door-to-door knife salesman with no medical training!

Multimillion-dollar negligence lawsuits changed all that. And now, US-based cruise ships carry doctors who are trained as emergency medicine practitioners as well. Still, you must remember, their primary job is to stabilize someone until they can get him to the closest port of call or until the nearest local Coast Guard can do a medical evacuation airlift.

It's heartening to note that the 16 largest passenger cruise lines that call on major ports in the United States and abroad agreed to meet or exceed the requirements of the American College of Emergency Physicians Health Care Guidelines on Cruise Ship Medical Facilities. The goals are: to provide reasonable emergency medical care for passengers and crew aboard cruise vessels; to stabilize patients and/or initiate reasonable diagnostic and therapeutic intervention; and to facilitate the evacuation of seriously ill or injured patients when deemed necessary by a shipboard physician. Guidelines include 24-hour medical facilities with basic pharmaceuticals and equipment, including an EKG machine, IV fluids and supplies, oxygen, and defibrillators. Doctors must have emergency experience; be fluent in the

Cruising Past Norovirus

To avoid contracting and spreading norovirus, the CDC recommends the following advice: Wash your hands. It's as simple as that.

Wash your hands after:
- Using the toilet
- Coughing or sneezing into your hands
- Engaging in any activity that may have contaminated your hands

Wash your hands before:
- Handling food
- Eating or drinking
- Smoking
- Brushing your teeth
- Engaging in any activity that involves hand-to-mouth contact

Wash your hands upon returning to your cabin.

Wash your hands frequently throughout the day even if you think they don't need to be washed.

Wash your hands using the following procedure.
1. Wet hands with warm water.
2. Apply a generous amount of soap and lather hands well.
3. Rub hands together for 20 seconds, paying special attention to the areas between fingers and under nails.
4. Rinse hands thoroughly with warm water.
5. Dry hands with a disposable towel.
6. Use the disposable towel to turn off the faucet and open the door.

official language of the cruise ship, crew, and most of the passengers; and have at least minor surgical skills. For a complete list of criteria, visit www. acep.org and type "Cruise" in the search box.

However, even though these facilities are available on board, it doesn't mean that they're necessarily equipped for serious emergencies. When passengers become seriously ill, whether it's a heart attack or a broken bone, oftentimes the ship's medical staff can only stabilize them until they can be treated elsewhere.

The Cost of Medical Care Onboard

Travelers should be aware that Medicare and some HMOs will not cover you outside of the United States. If you are seriously injured in or near a location that doesn't have suitable facilities, you may have to be airlifted back to the United States or another country that has suitable care. This is where insurance comes in, because emergency medical evacuation can cost tens of thousands of dollars for a patient and a family member. (See also the Travel Insurance chapter.)

To protect your health, here are some tips to think about before you travel.

! Pack all your prescription medications and a copy of your prescriptions, as well as any over-the-counter medicines you may need.

! Complete a personal medical information form, which can be found on the CDC Web page (www.cdc.gov). Bring one and leave another with an emergency contact.

! Call the cruise line ahead of time to discuss your health concerns and how the ship may handle them.

! Keep a phone card handy so that you can call your own doctor if necessary.

! Purchase travel insurance.

Cruise Ship Travel Insurance

Did you know that according to the US Travel Insurance Association, more than 70 percent of cruise ship travelers buy travel insurance? That's because cruises tend to fulfill all the criteria for why travel insurance is important: If you have to cancel your trip, you stand to lose a lot of money. If you become ill or injured on your trip, you may find yourself in the middle of an ocean or in a foreign country with substandard medical care.

I recommend that you purchase travel insurance when cruising, but keep these caveats in mind.

Some things may already be covered. Whether it's your homeowner's or renter's insurance, credit card coverage, or health insurance, you may be covered in more ways than you think. However, each one of these is specific, and you need to check with your policy to see what is actually covered. For example, homeowner's insurance may cover lost baggage but not a health emergency or trip cancellation. Your credit card may cover lost baggage or trip cancellation (if you purchased the trip with that card), but there may be limitations. If there is an impending hurricane that has already been identified and named by the National Weather Service, your cancellation policy may be voided. And lastly, your health insurance can get very, very sticky when you're overseas.

Basic trip cancellation and interruption insurance will cover you from the time that you purchase your cruise until you return from the trip. Some cruise lines offer cancellation waiver insurance, which is not the same thing as trip cancellation or interruption insurance. Waivers cost about $50, but you must cancel at least several days prior to the scheduled start of the trip (e.g., if you get sick or have an unexpected commitment). To be covered in both instances, you may need to purchase a combined waiver and cancellation/interruption insurance policy.

An important caution: Do *not* purchase insurance directly from the cruise line itself; instead, look for a third-party provider. Cruise ships almost always operate under foreign flags and travel on international waters, so if you are injured or ill, the cruise ship company may not be liable. The same thing applies if you suffer injuries during offshore excursions that you might opt to do yourself and are thus not affiliated with the cruise line.

If you don't want to buy a full travel insurance package, you may want to at least consider purchasing medical evacuation coverage. Cruise ships are only equipped to stabilize emergency situations, but major treatment has to be done at a nearby hospital. The cost of an airlift to a hospital, whether it's a local facility or one of your choice, can run into the tens of thousands of dollars. With medical evacuation, you are covered, even though you're traveling in the middle of the ocean.

Medjet Assist: This annual membership plan provides prepaid air ambulance transportation, including worldwide evacuation and repatriation to the member's hometown hospital. 800-963-3538, www.medjetassist.com

Air Ambulance Card: A prepaid air ambulance flies members to the US hospital of their choice if they are hospitalized more than 150 miles from home. It runs $195 per year for individuals and $295 per year for families. 877-424-7633, www.airambulancecard.com

Go to the Travel Insurance chapter for more information.

Cruise Food and Health

Of course, one of the reasons we love cruises is the abundance of food. From breakfast on the Lido deck to four-course dining room meals (and yes, you can order more than one entrée) to the infamous midnight buffet, cruising has often been synonymous with the 7-day weight-gain diet. For example, among the most popular statistics that have been thrown around in recent years is that, on a 1-week trip, passengers and crew of Royal Caribbean's *Mariner of the Seas* can consume 20,000 pounds of beef, 28,000 eggs, 8,000 gallons of ice cream, and 18,000 slices of pizza! Fortunately, health trends are catching up with cruising, so you won't need to crash diet before you cruise.

In a 2003 study by the Physicians Committee for Responsible Medicine (PCRM), dietitians reviewed the food options of 10 large-ship cruise lines, determining which ones had the healthiest options. Four out of 10 cruise lines received the maximum rating of four stars: Carnival, Norwegian, Royal Caribbean, and Windstar all had healthy options that were readily available to cruisers without having to give advance notice. These options included whole wheat toast, soups, tofu stir-fry, and wraps. Celebrity, Crystal, Holland America, and Princess failed to provide a nondairy vegetarian option at lunch and dinner but met all other PCRM criteria by having a low-fat, high-fiber entrée for each breakfast (usually oatmeal), a vegetarian option at lunch and dinner, and a choice of fruit for desserts and snacks. Still, these lines tended to have mostly higher-fat options for lunch and dinner, like cheeseburgers and lobster tail with butter. The cruise lines that received the lowest ranking of two stars were Disney and Delta Queen, which offered vegetarian options only if requested in advance, and even then, it's not guaranteed. For a complete report, visit www.pcrm.org/news/health030122report.html.

If you're trying to maintain or even lose weight on your cruise, there are options available.

! First off, skip the buffet. It's too difficult to maintain portion control, and there's little to stop you from going back for seconds . . . and thirds. Limit your eating to only the dining room or on excursions, so you don't find yourself snacking on hot dogs by the pool or nibbling late at night in your room.

! Get in at least one workout every 2 days. Most cruise ships offer group fitness classes, and the exercise amenities are growing every year. Practically every ship has a swimming pool, a track, and gym facilities. But if you're looking for something more unique, ships are now including rock-climbing walls, ice-skating rinks, and basketball courts.

! Choose more vigorous offshore activities. Instead of sampling local cuisine or lying on the beach, try scuba diving, walking on a glacier, or kayaking.

! Choose a specialty cruise with a fitness angle. Themed cruise ships are abundant these days, particularly focusing on health and fitness: Crystal has hosted a Caribbean cruise focusing on "Mind, Body, and Spirit," with aerobics, tai chi, and yoga classes led by fitness experts, as well as nutrition and prevention seminars. Costa Cruises takes the holistic approach by hosting a Taste of Health cruise, where experts in natural health and organic cooking lead lectures and workshops, and guests dine on organic meals.

Cruising and the Environment

One of the major concerns surrounding large-ship cruising is the amount of waste that is produced. As the industry grows, so are the cruise ships: Royal Caribbean's *Freedom of the Seas* is currently the world's largest passenger vessel, with 15 decks carrying more than 4,300 passengers and a crew of more than 1,300. According to the Bluewater Network, an environmental group designed to raise awareness and prevent environmental damage from vehicles and vessels, a typical ship in 1 week generates more than 50 tons of garbage, 1 million gallons of gray water (wastewater from sinks, showers, galleys, and laundry facilities), 210,000 gallons of sewage, and 35,000 gallons of oil-contaminated water. In addition, ships spew a range of pollutants into the air.

It's important to note, however, that such environmental effects aren't relegated solely to cruise ships. In fact, cruise ships make up less than 1 percent of the world's oceangoing vessels, but they are among the most high profile and are therefore looked upon to set environmental standards. The cruise industry has indeed made great strides in the past 5 years to reduce waste and protect the environment: This includes wastewater purification systems, and most have a zero-tolerance policy—no raw waste is dumped into oceans. For members of CLIA, the countries where vessels are registered have the responsibility to oversee that the ships comply with international environmental standards. While operating in the United States, ships have to follow laws such as the Clean Air Act, the Clean Water Act, the Refuse Act, and the Federal Water Pollution Control Act.

Does size matter? The International Ecotourism Society seems to think so. Here are some of their suggested tips for cruising more responsibly.

! Choose a small ship, under 150 guests.

! Check for certification or awards that the company has earned, particularly related to environmental practices.

! Ask how the company contributes to the economy of local communities it visits. Do they hire locally? Purchase locally?

! Find out about the staff it hires. Do trained interpreters offer onboard education to guests about local communities and their natural environment? Does the company follow labor laws and treat staff with respect?

! Ask what environmental policies and systems are in place to reduce the impact on coral reefs and reduce damage to marine life.

Small-Ship Cruising

While the large US-based cruise lines are growing increasingly popular to the mass market, don't be fooled into thinking that this is your only option. There are hundreds of smaller cruise lines out there beyond the Carnivals and Cunards of the world, many of which sail the world's rivers and canals. Most of these are not American owned and may offer a much more intimate, even more authentic, experience than the well-known cruise lines.

Small-ship cruising is a trend that has been holding its own over the past few years. According to the Niche Cruise Marketing Alliance (www. nichecruise.com), small ships carry about 625,000 passengers per year, almost half of which is through river cruising. Of course, this is still a tiny segment, compared with the 12.6 million total projected passengers in the entire cruising industry, but the small-ship business has actually doubled in the past 5 years. Small-ship cruising basically includes vessels, such as river-boats, yachtlike vessels, and barges, that carry 500 or fewer passengers.

One of the benefits of smaller-ship cruising is that vessels can traverse more remote destinations, through rivers, canals, and inlets that larger ships can't handle. You can travel along the Danube and sample four cities in one trip, visit the backcountry of Russia as you travel from St. Petersburg to Moscow via waterways, or explore the canals of Northern Holland. As a rule of thumb, yachtlike cruising caters to the high-end luxury crowd; river cruises cover a range of midprice to expensive; and expedition cruises, while not cheap, are often very rugged and adventurous.

Remember, though, that small ships don't come with all the amenities of larger cruise lines. There probably won't be any all-you-can-eat buffets or nightly entertainment. You can almost forget about a spa or massive onboard shopping opportunities. And don't go looking for the casino. There is also less anonymity than on a large cruise ship—a river cruise holds up to about 200 passengers. This can be a great way to avoid the party atmosphere of a larger ship, but younger travelers should remember that the age range tends to skew toward baby boomers and retirees. Also, call ahead to make sure the cruise line can accommodate any disabilities or special needs. (You can find a comprehensive list of accessible smaller ships at www.smallshipcruises. com/allwheelboats.shtml.)

River Cruises

Viking River Cruises has excursions throughout the world, including a 12-day tour of Shanghai and Beijing, with a 5-night Yangtze River cruise. The ship starts at the Three Gorges Dam and sails along the Three Gorges and Lesser Gorges before reaching Chongqing. Rates start at about $2,700 per person. 877-668-4546, www.vikingrivercruises.com

American Cruise Lines travels through rivers and inlets throughout the United States, including a tour of New England islands. Visit Martha's Vineyard, Nantucket, and Block Island. Onboard activities include lectures from naturalists and historians, as well as musical and theater performers from local towns. A 7-day cruise starts at about $2,600. 800-814-6880, www.americancruiselines.com

Imperial River Cruises travels from the Caspian Sea to Moscow, stopping in more than a dozen smaller cities and towns along the way, starting at $2,100 for 20 days. A shorter 12-day trip travels from the Ural Mountains to Moscow, with day tours in cities like Kazan and Uglitch, starting at $1,590. 866-922-4640, www.cruisebyriver.com

Norwegian Coastal Voyage not only takes you along the fjords of Norway but also offers hardy voyages like Buenos Aires to Santiago via Antarctica. A 19-day expedition includes visits to Half Moon Island and Port Lockroy, surrounded by mountains and glaciers, with sightings of humpback whales and penguins. Onboard activities include lectures on topics relating to Antarctica. Rates start at $6,999. 800-323-7436, www.norwegiancoastalvoyage.us

Yacht or Yachtlike Cruises

Bora Bora Cruises is a privately owned company in Tahiti that operates two high-end yachts—the *Ti'A Moana* and the *Tu Moana*—around the French Polynesian islands. The ships travel from island to island, navigating out-of-the-way lagoons and waterways, where you can Jet Ski and scuba dive or just hang out on the beach. A 6-day, 7-night cruise starts at $6,000. www.boraboracruises.com

SeaDream Yacht Club operates two vessels through the Caribbean, Mediterranean, and Atlantic. As discussed previously, the *SeaDream I* and *SeaDream II* are among the highest-end yachts out there, with unexpected amenities like a golf simulator, a full-service spa and fitness center, and use of your own personal Segway—a high-tech, two-wheeled, electric transporter—for tooling around the ports. A 5-day cruise between Nice, Monte Carlo, Cannes, and St. Tropez starts at $5,900, and a 14-day trip from Barbados to Portugal and Spain starts at $4,900. 800-707-4911, www.seadreamyachtclub.com

Seabourn Cruises travels to regions like the Mediterranean and the Caribbean but also to more unexpected locations like India and Asia. Three luxury ships carry 208 passengers. You have not only spa services and gourmet food but also a personal shopping specialist who can create a specialized tour of a destination's shopping areas, as well as dedicated enrichment programs that focus on culinary experiences, writing, and even opera. An 18-day tour of the Inca Coast, with stops in Costa Rica, Ecuador, Peru, and Chile, starts at about $7,500, and a 14-day excursion to Dubai, Oman, India, and Malaysia starts at about $6,500. 800-929-9391, www.seabourn.com

Expedition Cruises

Intrav's two clipper ships, the *Clipper Adventure* and the *Clipper Odyssey*, are able to navigate harsh environments, including Antarctica, Greenland, the Norwegian Fjords, Australia's Great Barrier Reef, and the Russian Far East. These ships accommodate 122 and 128 passengers, respectively, and include amenities like onboard e-mail access and a workout room. A clipper ship cruise includes an 11-day voyage along the Aegean Sea, traveling along the coastlines of Croatia, Montenegro, Albania, Greece, and Turkey. Rates start at $3,890. 800-456-8100, www.intrav.com

Natural Habitat Adventures offers expedition cruises to some of the most inhospitable regions of the world, including Iceland's fjords and glaciers and Spitsbergen, an island located just 600 miles from the North Pole and known as the European Arctic. These small-group voyages are unlike any other type of cruise, traversing rugged waters, dramatic marine life habitats, and massive glaciers. Rates start at $6,295 for an 11-day expedition. 800-543-8917, www.nathab.com

> The Queen Elizabeth 2 moves 6 inches for each gallon of diesel she burns.

Polar Cruises travels into Antarctica and the Arctic Circle on both first-class and luxury ships, as well as research vessels that have been converted to accommodate small groups (48 to 110 passengers). Trips extend throughout both regions, including crossing the Antarctic Circle and touring the Arctic, Russia's Far East, and Greenland. Rates range from $3,900 to $16,000 (for penthouse suites) for 14-day expeditions. 888-484-2244, www.polarcruises.com

Lindblad Expeditions sails small ships to off-the-beaten-path locations throughout the world, including Alaska, Antarctica, Central America, and the Mediterranean. Expedition leaders are trained naturalists, zoologists, and cultural anthropologists who provide hands-on learning and lectures on these tours. A 12-day cruise through Alaska, British Columbia, and the San Juan Islands ranges from $6,890 to $8,990. A 10-day tour of the Galapagos Islands starts at $4,150. 800-397-3348, www.expeditions.com

Barge Travel

If you want to go really small, consider traveling by barge. Barges are flat-bottomed boats designed to travel on canals and rivers and can carry anywhere from 4 to 11 passengers. Barging has long been an elegant way to see parts of Europe, offering access to small villages and countrysides. Barges tend to cover small areas in depth, traveling about 4 miles an hour and sailing only about 30 to 50 miles per week—it's so slow that not only will you avoid seasickness but you can actually walk alongside the boat on foot. Many barge operators also provide bicycles on board to explore the countryside as you stop from village to village. Vessels can range from very rustic to high end, so do your research—particularly if you have special needs. Generally, barges with overnight accommodations, meals, and planned itineraries are referred to as hotel barges, whereas others are self-drive or chartered for groups.

Many barges are foreign owned and operated, but US tour operators can coordinate the trip for you.

The Barge Lady has a comprehensive Web site with overviews of tested and recommended barge trips throughout Europe. Her trips include a barge called *Litote,* which travels through the many waterways of southern Burgundy. A maximum of 20 passengers can travel on board this first-class vessel, which goes along the Canal de Bourgogne. A 7-day excursion includes stops in famous Burgundy vineyards, gourmet meals prepared by a French chef, and optional walks through village markets. Rates start at $1,790. 800-880-0071, www.bargelady.com

Barge TravelPoints, a travel agency located in Boulder, Colorado, plans barging and river cruises throughout Europe. For example, the *Marjorie,* an eight-passenger barge that was originally built as a yacht, travels on a 6-day "tulip cruise" through Holland's canals, starting in Amsterdam and traveling to the Aalsmeer flower auction, through Rotterdam and the famous Keukenhof Gardens. Rates start at $1,899. 800-549-2575, www.bargetravelpoints.com

Barge Connection is a California-based company that specializes in European barge travel. A weeklong trip aboard *La Dolce Vita* traverses Venetian canals, covering sights in Venice as well as the outer islands of Torcello, Burano, and Murano and cruising the Brenta River. The vessel accommodates six passengers, starting at $2,750. 888-550-8580, www.bargeconnection.com

The Barge Experts, part of Elations Travel Group in Illinois, coordinates barge trips throughout Europe. An eight-passenger cruise aboard the

Scottish Highlander travels along the Great Glen, from Inverness to Fort Williams, and sails along various lochs and the Caledonian Canal. Rates start at $2,499 for 7 days. 800-584-0472, www.thebargeexperts.com

Overseas Adventure Travel offers barge trips throughout Burgundy, the South of France, and the canals of Holland and Belgium, with stops at various villages and towns to experience local gourmet food, wine tasting, and sightseeing. Rates start at $3,245 for a 12-day tour. 800-493-6824, www.oattravel.com

The Web site **BargesinFrance.com** is a one-stop shop for barge travel not just in France but in Holland, Belgium, England, Scotland, Ireland, and Germany. Voyages can take you through Paris on the Seine, along the Thames or Shannon river, and past the tulips of Holland in springtime. Chartered barges range from 6 to 22 people, with rates starting at $1,990. 877-642-2743, www.bargesinfrance.com

Freighter Travel

If traveling by sea is more about the journey than the destination, then you may want to consider taking "the slow boat" and hopping on board a freighter. As cargo ships sail between points to deliver products, a number of sea-loving travelers are allowed to go along for the ride.

More than likely, a cargo ship carries just a few passengers, plus anywhere from 10 to 25 crewmembers and officers. A freighter voyage can take anywhere from several days to several months, and travelers can pay about $100 per day to join the trip.

Itineraries usually include far-off regions that would otherwise be difficult to cover in one continuous trip. For example, the ship *Pugwash Senator* departs from New York to Norfolk, to Savannah, through the Panama Canal to Pusan (South Korea), then to Shanghai, Yantian, and Hong Kong, back to Pusan, and then to New York via the Panama Canal. The trip takes about 56 days and costs about $6,048 for double occupancy. However, if the idea of being at sea for so long sounds daunting, you can usually find shorter trips of about 1 to 2 weeks.

The size of these ships can vary greatly, but they're generally going to be much smaller than any standard cruise ship. The good news is that modern freighters have come a long way in terms of comfort. Today's freighters are generally spacious and clean, and rooms have private bathrooms, a small refrigerator, a couch, table, and desk—even a steward to clean up after you.

When it comes to food, your experience can be surprisingly good. Meals are prepared fresh, so really you just have to hope for the best when it comes to your chef's cooking skills. Don't expect gourmet meals, though; you'll probably be getting lots of meat and potatoes (not a lot of fruits and vegetables). There are usually self-service laundry facilities and small shops with drinks, toiletries, and cigarettes.

It's also important to keep in mind that traveling by freighter can also be an exercise in independence. You may be able to stop in ports for only 8 to 24 hours—and there's no guarantee that you'll even be there during daylight. A ship may arrive at midnight and depart at 8 a.m., leaving you no time to see the city. Longer-haul trips, especially around-the-world trips, tend to stop in ports for a few days at a time. Your port of call can change on a whim, based on weather conditions, port congestion, or other factors.

Most cargo ships have an upper age limit of 79 to 82 and require that passengers have a statement of good health signed by a physician. These ships aren't handicap accessible, and they often require climbing steep flights of stairs. Cargo ships don't have stabilizers, either, so there is the likelihood of getting seasick, especially while you're developing your sea legs.

Booking a trip through a travel agency is recommended, as an agent can walk you through details like health certificates and immunization requirements, as well as answer questions about the specifics of the ships.

Maris Freighter & Specialty Cruises offers both long- and shorter-term freight cruises, such as Los Angeles to Melbourne and Sydney, Australia; Tauranga, New Zealand; possibly Suva, Fiji, or Papeete, Tahiti; Ensenada, Mexico, and back to Los Angeles in 48 days. This trip accommodates six passengers and starts at $80 per day. 800-996-2747, www.freightercruises.com

Freighter World Cruises has multiple long-term trips, including a trip from New York to Norfolk or Savannah, on to Brazil and back to New York on a 35-day itinerary. Total price is about $3,920, and the ship includes a swimming pool, sauna, and sports room. 800-531-7774, www.freighterworld.com

▽ Resources

Cruise-addicts.com: You'll find not only cruise reviews and news but also uploaded videos of various excursions.

Cruisebrothers.com: Not surprisingly, this site is operated by . . . two brothers! Steve and Russ are cruise brokers who provide some of the better discounted rates and deals on the net.

Cruisecritic.com: Find a cruise based on cruise styles and destinations, with up-to-date news and ship reviews.

Cruisediva.com: This "cruise expert" offers advice for cruisers on everything from port security to parental consent forms, details on ships' amenities like restaurants and kids' programs, and fun facts (like that the captain of Windstar's *Wind Spirit* maintains an open-bridge policy and welcomes passengers to the navigation bridge anytime to watch).

Cruisemates.com: This informational site has daily updates on cruise news and ship reviews. The information is quite thorough, including reviews of ships' kids programs, general overviews of passenger demographics, and whether tipping is expected.

Gofox.com/cruises/shipstats.php provides information on a Cruise Line Association–member cruise ship's dimensions, when it was built, and number of crew members.

Note: Some cruise industry statistics provided courtesy of *Travel Weekly*.

CHAPTER 7

Frequent Flier Miles/Loyalty Programs

“ There's a sucker born every minute. ”

—P. T. BARNUM

Since they were first offered nearly 27 years ago, the frequent flier airline loyalty programs have been considered one of the more innovative, powerful marketing ideas of the 20th century. The result is that we've evolved into a country of mileage junkies. And, like addicts, that means we'll resort to just about anything to obtain those miles—we'll buy stuff we don't need, refinance our mortgage, even pay for our kids' weddings with a credit card just to earn extra miles.

The real truth is that more than 57 percent of all mileage earned these days is earned on the ground!

Now for the bad news. According to the annual 10K reports that airlines have to file with the Securities and Exchange Commission, there are more than 14 trillion outstanding miles floating around the United States. While the airlines claim that more miles were redeemed last year than ever before, the actual redemption percentage—that is, the percentage of eligible miles that were really redeemed by the airlines—hovered at slightly below 10 percent.

For the airlines, the mileage programs have become one of their few profitable divisions, so there's no chance of their going away anytime soon. Airlines sell miles to thousands of marketing partners, including restaurants, banks, gas stations, even florists. That means you can "earn" additional miles when you make purchases. Some frequent flier programs have as many as 200 partners, selling miles to these partners for a total of about $2 billion a year. Partners pay airlines between 1 and 2 cents per mile for each one they purchase. What's a mile worth? For airlines, a mile is worth about 1.7 cents in revenue. This is where customers get screwed: Since the airlines also manage and control redemption of those miles—without any oversight, regulation, or control—they build in a huge profit. They might as well be printing money.

The airlines will argue that their members are happy with their programs and their ability to redeem those miles. Really? Dig a little deeper and you'll find that what the airlines are *not* telling you is that the airlines are playing a little game of extortion—which they are allowed to do under deregulation. Since these programs aren't regulated, no airline is required to provide any seat free of charge in these programs—in much the same way as the airlines can advertise a discount fare without revealing how many seats are actually available at that fare.

Since airlines control that redemption, redemption levels remain pathetically low. And for consumers, that's an amazingly painful experience.

MILEAGE AWARD TICKETS REDEEMED

AIRLINE	2004	2005
American	2,600,000	2,600,000
Southwest	2,600,000	2,500,000
United	1,900,000	1,700,000
Northwest	1,492,000	1,380,000
Continental	1,400,000	1,200,00
US Airways	1,300,000	1,500,000
Alaska	750,000	631,000
America West	239,000	215,000

And this is a significant number: While reward redemption increased by 6.5 percent during 2005, total reward liability increased by an even greater 13.9 percent. The following table lists the reward liability assigned by the airlines to their 2005 and 2004 balance sheets.

REWARD LIABILITY BY AIRLINE

AIRLINE	2004	2005
American	$1,400,000,000	$1,500,000,000
United	$840,000,000	$923,000,000
Alaska	$409,000,000	$467,000,000
Northwest	$215,000,000	$248,000,000
Delta Air Lines	$211,000,000	$291,000,000
Continental	$195,000,000	$236,000,000
US Airways	$73,000,000	$147,000,000
America West	$13,000,000	$10,000,000

Here are the figures.

! In the beginning of 2006, the world's frequent flier programs boasted more than 180 million members, 120 million of whom were US residents, with 140 airlines.

! American AAdvantage is the largest frequent flier program in the world. It began with 283,000 members in 1981 and has grown to more than 46 million members. More than 11,000 new members enrolled in the program each day in 2001—20 years after the program started.

! Loyalty programs grow at a rate of 11 percent per year. The fastest-growing segment of these programs is "mileage consumers," not frequent fliers.

! Credit cards are the number one way to earn miles without flying.

! The average active member of a frequent flier program earns 11,364 miles per year.

! It is estimated that some 307,000 frequent fliers have earned at least 1 million miles in their programs. And as you may know, I have earned at least 1 million miles on every major US airline—and at American Airlines, more than 6 million miles.

According to our friends at SmarterTravel.com, foreign airlines give reduced mileage on their cheaper fares. For example:

! Air France gives only 50 percent of actual miles on tickets booked in G and U classes, 25 percent on L class, and none on A, O, and X classes.

! British Airways gives 25 percent of actual mileage on "lowest" economy fares.

- Cathay Pacific gives 50 percent of actual mileage on "discounted" economy tickets.

- Japan Airlines gives 70 percent of actual mileage on "discounted" economy tickets.

- Lufthansa gives 50 percent of actual mileage on tickets booked in S and W classes.

- Singapore gives no credit for tickets booked in V, Q, G, N, and T classes.

SmarterTravel.com also points out how US airlines that partner with foreign airlines have complicated mileage programs. Some examples are:

- American Airlines gives 25 percent of the full mileage for economy flights on British Airways classes K, L, M, N, O, R, E, G, Q, S, and V. It gives mileage for economy flights on Cathay Pacific only in classes B, Y, and H (pretty much full-fare classes). It gives 50 percent of full mileage on Qantas flights in M, V, L, R, G, O, and S classes.

- Delta (SkyTeam) gives no credit at all on a handful of fare classes on Air France, Alitalia, Emirates, KLM, Korean, Singapore, and others.

Redeeming Miles

As a whole, the airlines awarded 19 trillion miles in the past 26 years. Want to get really impressed? That's enough to circle the globe 760 *million* times.

What Are Miles Really Worth?

What are miles really costing you?

One last disheartening statistic: Since the airlines have to carry miles as a liability on their books, they also have to give the unredeemed miles a value. And you'd better sit down: Most airlines value their miles at 40 cents per 1,000 miles. How does that translate? Assuming the airline actually redeems your 25,000-mile award for a "free" domestic ticket and gives you a seat on the plane, you've already spent an average (in airfares and outside purchases on a 1 mile per $1 protocol) of $16,000 for that ticket. And in real dollars, what did it cost the airline to redeem those miles at 40 cents per 1,000 miles? *Ten dollars.* Now you understand why the mileage programs are often the most profitable divisions of the airlines!

One small problem with that gee-whiz statistic: It presumes those miles were redeemed for real flights. A majority of them weren't.

Almost all mileage programs of the major carriers get you to enroll by strongly implying in all of their advertisements and promotional materials that as soon as you get to the first redemption level—25,000 miles—you'll be sitting on a beach with a piña colada. But the reality is that, nowadays, airlines have doubled the ante. In almost all cases, when you call to redeem those 25,000 miles for a free coach domestic ticket or 35,000 for a free coach ticket to Hawaii, the airline then informs you that no seats are available at that level. But the airline somehow *does* have your seat for double that amount—50,000 or 70,000 miles! It's a clever but painful way for airlines to dispose of their mileage liabilities—and that's if they want to release any seats at all.

So what can you do? The answer is that you have to think outside the box, be a contrarian, and play the game.

On your primary carrier:

1. Pick alternate airports. Don't just look for award seats to Los Angeles International, for example, but to Burbank, Ontario, and Long Beach as well. Visit www.alternateairports.com for a listing of airports nationwide.

2. Pick alternate routings. Don't just think point-to-point or nonstop flights. Seats might not be available on nonstop flights, so make a stop in Chicago en route to San Francisco from Miami. Or, as was the case in our search for Hawaii flights, throw out the map entirely. On one routing offered to us to redeem our miles to Hawaii, United told me the only way they could get me there was Los Angeles to Denver to Chicago to Honolulu (ouch!).

If all else fails, look to mileage partners. Want to redeem your miles on a flight from Los Angeles to Frankfurt on United? No seats available. Then try flying United to Chicago and then Lufthansa to Germany (a United mileage partner). How about Los Angeles to Hong Kong? If there are no seats on American Airlines partner Cathay Pacific, try Qantas, another partner, through Sydney.

Here are the three major mileage partner programs.

Star Alliance: Air Canada, Air New Zealand, ANA, Asiana Airlines, Austrian Airlines, BMI, LOT Polish, Lufthansa, Scandinavian Airlines, Singapore Airlines, South African Airways, Spanair, Swiss International, TAP Portugal, THAI Airways, United Airlines, and US Airways

Oneworld: American Airlines, British Airways, Cathay Pacific, Finnair, Iberia, Japan Airlines, LAN, Malév, Qantas, Royal Jordanian

Skyteam: Aeoflot, AeroMexico, Air France–KLM, Alitalia, Continental, Czech Airlines, Delta, Korean Air, Northwest

In many cases, you may need to book as much as 320 days in advance to get those seats.

Some airlines, like Continental, offer a feature on their Web site that allows you to check mileage seat availability up to 11 months ahead. That's the good news. The bad news: You have the luxury of being disappointed online. But again, go to the partner airlines and see what's out there.

And if all else fails—and the reservations agent tells you there are no seats on any flight, on any route, to any nearby airport on your primary airline or any partner airline—it's time to speak to a supervisor. Why? The key reminder here is that loyalty programs are worthless if they don't reward you for your loyalty! In almost all cases, supervisors have the discretionary power to override computer blocks and release mileage seats.

What about that powerful Capital One card (and other similar credit cards) that offers no blackout periods for your miles? The answer is that these card/mileage programs are not affiliated with any airlines and are structured differently. The miles/points you earn relate to a dollar amount (roughly 20,000 miles equals about $190 in your account), and what that means is that the program actually goes out and uses the money in your account to buy you a full, purchased ticket.

But think about this math: If you get about 1 mile per $1 spent in the airline programs, and the lowest level for eligibility is 25,000 miles, and 57 percent of all miles earned are earned through nonflight activities such as credit card purchases, that means, at the very least, you've spent $14,000 for that "free coach ticket." And that doesn't include the money you spent for airfare to accrue the other 43 percent of your miles. That's one expensive "free" ticket. And when the airline then doubles the miles you need for that ticket, it could easily represent a $28,000 ticket! On the Capital One card, you've spent even more money for that ticket: If a round-trip ticket between New York and Los Angeles, for example, now sells for about $360, you've spent about $40,000 in purchases to get that ticket. We're definitely in the wrong business!

American Airlines is credited with having the world's first frequent flier program, established in 1981. It's true that American had the first computer-based system-wide program (AAdvantage), but the very first frequent flier program was created by California's Western Airlines in 1980. A $50 Travel Pass was offered between San Francisco and Los Angeles; travelers could collect these passes and use them to buy tickets.

If you're accumulating miles and having a hard time using them, you can donate your miles. Check www.miledonor.com, www.heromiles.org, www.redcross.org/donate/donatemiles.html, www.aa.com/milesforkids, www.aa.com/makeawish, and www.dreamfoundation.com.

You can transfer miles from one airline to another, but this is one of the trickiest options out there. For one thing, you have to do it through a middleman. For example, if you have miles with Continental, Amtrak Guest Rewards can convert them to United miles. Other middlemen offer more options but are more complex: For example, Diners Club Rewards lets you convert America Airlines AAdvantage miles into Club Rewards points, and then redeem those Club Rewards points for frequent flier miles in 20 participating frequent flier programs (including Delta SkyMiles and Virgin Atlantic's Flying Club). But the catch is that you get only half the worth of your miles—i.e., if you transfer 10,000 miles, you get only 5,000 in the new airline. Other middlemen like Hilton HHonors will cost you a whopping five-to-one conversion rate. To figure out how each airline transfers miles and what it will be worth, visit our friends at www.insideflyer.com/tools/mileage_converter.

You can transfer miles to a friend or family member's account, but remember that it's going to cost you, thereby depreciating the value of the miles. If you're paying $.0275 per mile, with a minimum of a 1,000-mile transfer, you may as well just buy a whole ticket.

And as a last resort—and I mean a *very* last resort—consider cashing in your miles for that magazine subscription or toaster. Sure, it's going to be one heck of an expensive kitchen appliance when you calculate the math, but at least you have something to show for all your work. Try visiting www.points.com to redeem your miles for store products. But don't say I didn't warn you that your *Reader's Digest* subscription ordered this way just cost you $14,000!

One last note: Don't forget to maintain activity on your account. If no miles are added or used within a certain period of time, your account can expire and you will lose all your accrued points.

! US Airways will delete all accounts with no activity in 18 months, down from 36 months.

! United Airlines will delete all accounts with no activity in 18 months, down from 36 months.

! Delta began deleting all accounts after 2 years, down from 36 months.

! Only Continental and Aloha miles don't expire at all.

! AirTran and JetBlue are the strictest, tolerating only 1 year of inactivity.

▽ Resources

www.milemaven.com: Through this resource, you can search for current travel offers by route. Type in your travel route and the double, triple, and other bonus-miles promotions will appear.

www.mileport.com: This Web site consolidates all your frequent flier points and account information—from more than 105 airline, hotel, and other points programs—into a single statement. If you're a frequent flier on multiple airlines, this is an easy way to track your miles and to arm yourself when trying to book on partner airlines.

CHAPTER 8

Online Booking

> *A computer can figure out all kinds of difficult problems, except the problem of how to pay for it.*
>
> —ANONYMOUS

Consider this one simple and powerful fact:

For the first time in history, more than half of all travel in the United States is purchased online.

A few years ago, when it became possible to book your flights, hotels, and car rentals online, travelers were wary. For technophobes, it seemed a lot safer and more efficient to call up the reservation line and book your travel, just as we had been doing for decades. But with the dotcom revolution, high-speed Internet, and increased transaction security, more and more travelers are turning toward the Internet from start to end.

As the story goes, Alaska Airlines was the first domestic airline site to sell tickets over the Internet at www.alaskaair.com. The airline introduced the site on December 28, 1995, and sold the first online ticket the same day to a family of four from Washington state. And travel booking life as we know it has never been the same.

According to a 2005 report from the Travel Industry Association (TIA), "Travelers' Use of the Internet," the Internet continues to grow as a major resource for booking travel and for marketing to travelers.

In fact, even though the number of US adult travelers using the Internet overall has plateaued, the number of travelers who use the Net to plan and book their trips grew significantly from 2004. The survey showed that 78 percent of 79 million "online travelers" used the Internet for travel information, a huge leap from the previous year's 65 percent rate. The survey also found that 82 percent of travelers who plan their trips online actually go ahead and book the reservations online, up from 70 percent in 2004.

Translation: Online travel is a $40 billion industry.

In 2006, some preliminary statistics (released by the TIA and D. K. Shifflet & Associates Ltd.) showed that in 2005, telephone reservations dropped drastically due to online booking. During that time, 35 percent of transportation reservations (planes, trains, buses, ships, etc.) were made online. That's a 25 percent increase from the previous year. The next most common method was calling a transportation carrier's toll-free telephone number, but that rate dropped 16 percent from 2004. Of all travelers who made transportation reservations in 2005, 4 percent used travel agents, which was similar to the 5 percent rate of 2004.

Even hotels are getting in on the action—late to the game, but players nonetheless. About 24 percent of travelers who booked accommodation reservations did so online in 2005, which was up from 9 percent the previous year. The first choice for travelers is to book through a hotel Web site, then

Who Is Booking through What?

The three most popular types of travel sites are:

Online travel agencies (such as Expedia.com, Travelocity.com, Priceline.com, Hotels.com): 67 percent

Search engines (such as Google.com, Yahoo.com): 64 percent

Company-owned Web sites (such as Continental.com, Marriott.com): 54 percent

But let's not forget the big search engines—Kayak.com and SideStep.com—and a UK-based site that's seeing growth in the United States: Cheapflights.com.

through online agencies like Expedia or Orbitz, and an almost equal amount of travelers used the hotel's 800 number. Only 4 percent of travelers used a travel agent.

Although travel agents may balk at this one, online booking is more lucrative for travel providers than the old way: Leisure travelers spent an average of $1,288 when booking their most recent trip online.

This, of course, proves my long-standing point that I prefer dealing with a human being. I have always done better when negotiating with a real live person than with the Internet. People think creatively; the Internet deals only in a linear way with limited flexibility. What do we give up when we choose the perceived expediency of the Web? In many cases, flexibility, choice, and (never underestimate this one) *mood*. Get a person on the phone in a bad mood, you can always hang up and call back until you get someone in a good mood. And a reservation agent in a good mood is far more likely to give you a deal than your computer is.

There's another plus in dealing with human beings. Once you book your flight, most airlines give you 24 hours in which to buy it. That benefits you in a number of ways, the most important being that you then have the option to surf the Web within the next 24 hours to see if you can beat the deal you negotiated on the phone or in person. If you can, you can book and buy it. If you can't, you still have your confirmed deal.

Reverse the process (as a majority of people do) and if you go right to the Web first, chances are you'll be trapped if you find a lower deal after you've hit that key and provided your credit card information.

Having said that, I'm also the first to acknowledge that the Web is an unstoppable steamroller, picking up speed almost exponentially.

Airline tickets, lodging, and rental cars continue to be the top three travel items booked online. But people are also booking more activities online (about 2.3) than they do offline (1.7), including cultural events, theme and amusement parks, travel packages, and sports events.

Regardless of whether Web sites have made last-minute travel an affordable possibility or whether procrastinators are fueling the fire of online travel sites, more and more travelers are waiting until the 11th hour to book their tickets. Priceline did a study of 1,000 consumers and found that 30 percent couldn't plan their travel more than 7 days in advance. Overscheduling was the most common complaint, and 13 percent said that financial concerns were the driving force behind waiting until the last minute. Twenty-seven percent were waiting to find better travel deals. Seventy percent said that they would stay 3 nights or fewer on a short-notice vacation—only 4 percent would stay 8 nights or longer. Of those polled, 59 percent would book a hotel room on short notice, 36 percent would book airline tickets, and 35 percent would book a rental car. However, only 10 percent would book a whole package, and 7 percent would book a cruise. Keep in mind that this is a study coming from a Web site that attracts last-minute buyers, so the sample demographic naturally skews the results.

The folks running these transactional Web sites, as well as executives at the big search engines, are starting to see the effects of this boom. Online-booking site Kayak reports that since its beta launch in 2004, it rapidly became one of the fastest-growing travel sites on the Web, about 20.5 percent per month. In January 2007 alone, the site received 11 million hits—that's more than Starwood Hotels, Northwest Airlines, and JetBlue combined.

Similarly, Hotwire recently touted itself as the highest-ranking independent travel site in online customer satisfaction. The independent study from J. D. Power and Associates measured the satisfaction of 6,800 travelers who booked airline, hotel, or car rental reservations between March and October 2006. The Web sites included were Hotwire, Expedia, Travelocity, Priceline, Cheaptickets, Yahoo!Travel, Orbitz, and Hotels.com. The criteria included competitiveness of price, ease of booking, usefulness of the information on the Web site, availability of booking options and travel packages, appearance and design of the site, and the ease of navigation.

A Word from Johnny Jet

Here's what our friend Johnny Jet (www.johnnyjet.com), one of the premier sources for online travel and a directory of more than 5,000 travel-friendly sites, has to say about booking travel through the Internet.

> *Booking travel is not rocket science. All it takes is time and tactics. The key to finding the best deal is flexibility and thoroughness. If you are flexible with your dates, times, or even airports, you could save a bundle. And no matter what your travel situation is, it's worth checking your options thoroughly. There is not one Web site out there that has the cheapest deals*

24/7. All the sites have negotiated deals with specific carriers, so you never know who has the absolute lowest, and besides, the fares are always changing. One minute the best deal could be found on Travelocity, while the next it's on Orbitz.

No matter what, before logging on to any Web site, find out base prices through your airline's toll-free number (I created AirlineNumbers.com just for this reason). If the agent quotes you a fair price, reserve it. You usually can hold reservations for 24 hours. Then log on to the Internet and search for a better deal online. If you find a better deal, book it and cancel the first one.

Everyone knows about the major online travel agencies like Expedia, Orbitz, and Travelocity . . . They spend lots of advertising dollars. However, some alternate sites you might not have heard of but are definitely worth checking out are Mobissimo, Kayak, and SideStep. These are called "metasearch" sites, and they scour dozens of other travel booking sites. When I buy a ticket online, I visit all of those sites; but instead of going crazy and reentering the same dates and cities, I first go to BookingBuddy.com or OneTime.com. That's because they search all the sites above as well as some others, and the best part is that you don't need to keep putting your dates and cities in over and over—you just do it once. On BookingBuddy, users need to click each provider individually, while OneTime users can check all the sites they want to check and click "search deals." Windows for each one will open up all at once, kind of like fireworks for your computer. I prefer OneTime because I have high-speed (and attention deficit disorder), so it saves me time.

No matter what, I always check alternate airports. Most online travel sites also offer this option, and it's worth selecting; if you're willing to drive a little, you can save a lot. For example, San Francisco's options include Oakland and San Jose. (Other cities' options are listed on another one of my Web sites, AlternateAirports.com.)

Because airfares always change, the big question is: "When should I book?" No one knows the answer. Certainly, the cheapest fares can be found 21, 14, or 7 days before departure. And Tuesdays, Wednesdays, Thursdays, and Saturdays are generally the cheapest days to fly. I don't recommend booking months in advance, unless you are traveling on a major holiday and are not flexible. And if, after shopping around, you find a deal that sounds great, grab it. Don't wait for it to go any lower—it could rise! Farecast.com is a Web site that actually predicts (and pretty accurately, using historical data) if the airfare is going to increase or not.

More often than not, I find myself using Travelocity, because they show me how I can save money if there's a lower fare on another date (usually a day before or after my original dates), and they do a nice job packaging trips together. Sometimes buying an airfare on Travelocity that includes a hotel or car rental could be cheaper than just the flight on its competitors. This happened to me on a Los Angeles to Aspen ticket—who would've thunk that getting a three-star hotel priced in with my plane ticket would be $100 cheaper? For those who want to save $5 to $10 on the agency's per-ticket service fee, book directly through the airline's Web site once you find out who has the cheapest deal.

I also like to use SideStep, because they have access to the low-fare airlines like Southwest and JetBlue, which most of the other online agencies don't. If you are booking with a low-fare carrier here or abroad, it's always best to book as far in advance as possible or jump on one of their sales (each airline offers fare alerts; or log on to SmarterTravel.com or AirFareWatchDog.com to sign up for their domestic specials). Some budget carriers in Europe sell tickets for 1 cent (not a typo), and even with their taxes and fees, it still sometimes comes out to just $30 one way. Just be sure to find out which airport you're departing from and arriving at (it may be an alternate airport like Stansted). And be sure not to pack too much—low-fare carriers tend to be strict about baggage allowance.

Budget Booking

While the number of low-cost airlines has proliferated in recent years, finding flights on them can still be a chore. The truth is, most major travel search engines have a very limited selection of flights from low-cost carriers. You won't find Southwest on search engines and metasearch engines, and JetBlue appears on only a few of them, which means you have to take several extra steps to compare prices between flights on budget airlines.

The good news is that some new Web sites have emerged, and some of the older Web sites have been retooled, making the task of finding cheap flights internationally a little bit easier. The following are a few you may want to check out.

The home of *OAG* (which stands for *Official Airline Guides*) on the Web, **oag.com** is a useful site in terms of discovering basic flights and flight information. You can find a searchable database, which answers questions like "Who flies where?" and brings up all the airlines that fly between two airports. Other topics such as "Where can I fly from here?" or even "What's the first flight of the day from this airport?" can come in handy as well. The Direct Flight Destination Finder brings up a list of every direct destination from that airport; just note that the site sometimes lumps direct (no plane change with stops) and nonstop flights together.

Whichbudget.com deals solely with low-budget airlines—111 of them, to be exact. This covers 120 countries, where you can find information on point-to-point routes. So, for example, if you want to fly out of Orlando, you can take Air Transat to Montreal or Toronto; Aer Lingus to Dublin; JetBlue to Bermuda, Puerto Rico, and several other cities; and Southwest to dozens of US locations. But it doesn't end there. Want to fly out of Saigon? You can take Jetstar to Australia, Tiger Airways to Singapore, and Pacific Airlines to Bangkok and cities within Vietnam.

Another option for finding cheap flights is **flycheapo.com**. Like WhichBudget, FlyCheapo relies almost exclusively on budget carriers for its flight options. However, this site has a design that's more similar to a typical travel search engine, especially the Route Search feature. Here you can select two airports and see which airlines offer budget flights between them. Note that most of the airports that FlyCheapo represents are in Europe, but the site does offer a useful news section that announces new budget flights and expansions and brings up all relevant city news and flight info when you click on a city name in the news section.

Online Booking Tips

You probably already know that flying midweek is an easy way to save money. But did you know that to get the best fares, you should also *book* your flight midweek? Airlines tend to raise their fares Friday and bring them back down on Monday. Another hint: Book your flight after the seventh of every month, as booking is busier right after payday on the first and fifteenth. Mondays and Tuesdays are the busiest days for bookings, so you'll save by searching for flights when no one else is, like very early or very late on Wednesdays and Thursdays. So if you're planning on purchasing your

Johnny Jet's 10 Wackiest and Most Useful Web sites

www.speakjamaican.com/glossary.html: If you've ever wanted to learn the exact meaning of "mon," check out this site, a comprehensive dictionary of Jamaican terms/words and their meanings. ("Mon" can represent every person in Jamaica—man, woman, and child. Yes, mon! Yes, man, woman, or child!)

www.whoissick.org/sickness: I'm not sure how accurate the information on this site is or even how useful you'll find it, but it's still interesting to see who's sick in the United States and what they've got (runny nose, cough, fever, headache). If you're a hypochondriac, then you can avoid traveling to these disease-infested places. Ha, ha, *ha*!

www.travbuddy.com: With just a few clicks—and no registration required—visitors can create a map of the world that includes the countries (and states) they have visited. There's even a URL and simple html code, so visitors can show their map off on their Web site or blog to friends and readers. TravBuddy also offers networking features with other members, but those require a 1-minute registration.

www.publictoilets.org: This Web site allows you to locate a public toilet in 19 countries (United States, Australia, New Zealand, and 16 in Europe) and obtain detailed information about the quality of the facility. (Some entries have photos and even provide the longitude and latitude for geocachers, those high-tech treasure hunters who rely on GPS to hide and find their secret stashes.)

www.menupages.com: This site has thousands of menus available online for Boston, Chicago, Los Angeles, New York, Philadelphia, San Francisco, and Washington, DC, restaurants. In New York, they've collected virtually every menu, from the swankiest places like Le Cirque 2000 (Midtown East) to the dive pizza joints like Don Filippo's (the best pizza on the Upper East Side). You can search easily by neighborhood or by typing in your favorite restaurant or type of food.

tickets online, book your flight between 10 p.m. Wednesday and 6 a.m. Thursday for a shot at the cheapest rates.

There are several different Web sites out there that can help you score better deals by providing you with as much information as possible. Here's the breakdown of what they are and what they can do for you.

Farecast.com answers the question "Should I buy my airline ticket now or later?" The site is still in beta testing but currently offers airfare predictions in more than 75 departure cities in the United States. The airfare prediction recommends whether you should purchase your ticket now, before it rises,

www.gotvoice.com: Now this is a handy one for travelers. Have your voice mails sent to your e-mail, so if you are overseas you don't need to make a long-distance call. Or if that someone special left you a message and you want to save it forever, sign up for this free service. Just log on, put in what kind of phone (cell or landline), which service provider, phone number, PIN, and which e-mail to send the voice mails to. You can set it to check your voice mail daily or on weekends or just when you log on and alert it to.

www.babelfish.altavista.com: This Web site should be bookmarked on every traveler's computer. Users can translate passages of text or entire Web pages in 11 languages (Chinese, Dutch, French, German, Greek, Italian, Japanese, Korean, Portuguese, Russian, Spanish) or quickly translate a page into their language of choice. The best part is that it's free and easy.

www.jiwire.com: This is one of the first places I go when looking for a wireless signal. Just type in your destination (domestic or international—it serves almost 100 countries), then click on the more than 60,000 free and commercial hotspot locations, as well as the address, cost, and provider.

www.timeanddate.com: Their world clock lists current local times around the world. It will fast become one of your most useful tools when you travel.

www.whatplug.info: This is a great one for international travelers. When you first log on, it will identify what country you are from (that's if you are logging on from home). The next page has all the countries divided by region (Europe, Americas, Africa, Asia, Oceania). Once you click your destination country, it will tell you the type of plug, socket, voltage, and hertz (only important if you are bringing a plug-in alarm clock, because some clocks use the frequency of electricity to measure time and could get messed up). Not only do they tell you what type of adapter you need bring but they will inform you if it's okay to just plug your equipment into the wall without a transformer—if the voltage is different, you can't.

Thomas Cook was the first modern travel agent. In 1938, he introduced 8-day package holidays from Britain to the French Riviera for about £8.50. In 1841, he arranged for a special train to be run to a religious meeting, which was probably the first time a train ride was advertised to the public. He led his first grand tour of Europe in 1856.

or wait until later, when it drops. For me to fly from Dallas–Fort Worth to Las Vegas, the Web site shows a graph predicting that, in the next month, the price will drop from about $450 to about $200 in about 20 days, spike to about $300 for a couple of days, and then drop back down at the end of the month. Even more dramatic is a flight from Los Angeles to Hartford, Connecticut—the spikes show prices dropping from $350 to $240 then jumping back up and back down again, all within the course of 1 week.

Farecast also recently launched "Farecast Deals," which culls through airfares each day to inform users of potential savings and whether you should snag the deal right away or wait; e.g., "$191 New York (JFK) to San Francisco (SFO) (Sat. 5/12–Tues. 5/15); fares rising, record low—act fast" or "$297 San Francisco (SFO) to Honolulu (HNL) (Wed. 5/9–Mon. 5/14); fares rising, save $116 off average low found today."

Farecompare.com lets you know if the price being quoted is reasonable, which can be a big help when you're flying an unfamiliar route. Using historical data over the last year, FareCompare shows monthly average prices, as well as the minimum, average, and maximum monthly low prices for specific routes. A flight from Chicago to Washington, DC (all airports), shows up as $179 from June through November and $168 from December through April. This is an average of all the airlines. But wait, click on "Add Row" and suddenly the average prices for Delta show up to see how much it varies from the total average price (it doesn't). Add another row and you can see that AirTran prices much higher, at $269. A further search shows that US Airways averages at $189. So now you know there are better deals out there—you just have to know how to find them.

Airfarewatchdog.com is one of the most innovative sites out there. Why? Because it uses humans, not algorithms. A team of "watchdogs" compiles the best fares out there, even catching "bloopers" like $0 fares that airlines have to honor once they're published. The site includes budget carriers Southwest and JetBlue, which rarely show up in travel search engines, and also smaller airlines that you may not even be aware of.

Flyspy.com can help you figure out which itinerary offers the best price. The graph shows you the predicted market for airfares over the next 30 days. You can change your trip length from 1 to 7 days and customize your departure time to see if that affects the price. Currently, the only city of origin is Minneapolis, but expect other cities to be added soon.

Tripstalker.com requires downloaded software that runs even when you're not online. Yes, it's a little creepy, but it will pop up low fares for your specific criteria, meaning that you don't have to spend hours a day trying to catch the cheapest rates. Other similar systems include **Southwest's DING!** program—if you're willing to fly Southwest, download the software and the site will literally make a "ding" sound every time the program thinks it's found a fare that you will like. **Kayak's Buzz** program does send weekly e-mail alerts based on your maximum desired price. **Expedia's Fare Tracker** will alert you via e-mail and on your personalized page for up to three different routes. **Yapta.com** is a newer site that can actually earn you money! You may not know this, but some airlines will refund the difference if a fare drops after you've purchased your ticket. Yapta will alert you to the price drop and help you figure out what refunds or vouchers you can get. Airlines that offer refunds include Alaska Air, JetBlue, Southwest, United, and US Airways.

Looking to save time? **Checkinsooner.com** does 24-hour-mark check-ins and e-mail boarding passes for American, Continental, Delta, United, and Southwest.

Did you know that you can even book a private jet online? **One Sky Jets** is a network of more than 1,500 private jets. If I want to fly from New York's La Guardia Airport to Omaha, Nebraska, and back, I can charter a five- to seven-passenger jet for about $26,000, which breaks down to about $3,800 per person; a turboprop can go for about $1,650 per person for 12 passengers. Not a bad deal when you think about the efficiency, comfort, and privacy involved. 866-663-7591, www.onesky.com

Internet Errors

If you're *really* vigilant (and lucky), you may win big in the online game. Why? Because Web sites are run by humans, and humans make mistakes. If a price is listed incorrectly, the carrier has to honor it—one traveler managed to book a room at the Holiday Inn Resort in Phuket, Thailand, for 3 cents a night after being tipped off in the message boards of **flyertalk.com.** And **airfarewatch-dog.com** spotted a fare on American Airlines from Milwaukee and Kansas

City to Acapulco for $0 (plus taxes and fees). There have been reports of a $51 flight to Fiji, a US Airways flight for $1.86 (the airline had to honor 1,000 tickets at that price), and hotels pricing at $25 rather than $250. If you have an eagle eye and a penchant for traveling on the fly, this is the strategy that—when it works—can pay off big.

Last-Minute Booking

Last-minute booking is often the best way to score the lowest prices. But, of course, it's last minute, which means that you'll need a flexible schedule and an ability to think out of the box in terms of where you travel and when.

For one thing, those e-mail blasts that you get every week *can* be useful. Just look carefully. Airlines started the trend of offering last-minute fares for weekend and off-season travel. If you have frequent flier miles, stick with just those airlines to maximize your earnings. The only major drawback is that you usually have to book quickly or the fares will disappear.

Last-minute Web sites are making waves in the travel industry. Such sites offer package vacations, which can include flights, hotels, and even car rentals, for up to 2 weeks in advance—which means you may have to drop everything and take off the very next day. **11thhourvacations.com** recently announced that it has offered more than 4 million vacation packages on its site. **Lastminutetravel.com** claims that it has provided travel savings of up to 80 percent from retail price, while **site59.com** promises to offer up to 70 percent in savings. Pay close attention to that "up to" caveat, but if you can be flexible and able to travel at the spur of the moment, you can really save yourself quite a bit on a perfectly great vacation. This especially holds true for cruise ships! At least 65 percent of a cruise ship is sold well in advance, and that usually covers the entire cost of the ship. The remaining 35 percent of sales is all about profit, so if those cabins aren't filled as the departure date comes closer, you may be able to score some last-minute savings.

Best Price Guarantees

Have you ever wondered if that "best price guarantee" that a number of travel companies offer is really worth it?

Some hotel companies have made the bold challenge that if you can find a lower price than the one offered on their own Web site, they'll give you a reward—free nights, or they'll match the rate, or, in one case, they'll give you a $50 US Savings Bond. When I asked the chairman of that hotel if there was any limit to the number of savings bonds I could get, he winced. The reason? He knew, and I knew, that the challenge was bogus. Of course I could get a lower rate—by calling one of his hotels directly and speaking with the manager on duty or the director of sales, the two people at the hotel who are always the best arbiters of their individual inventory. After all, if a wedding just canceled, the hotel chain's Web site won't reveal that sudden inventory surplus of rooms.

And many Internet companies claim that you can't find a lower price than the one they offer online, and hence the guarantees. Recently, I came across one traveler who had an illuminating "guarantee" experience at the online booking site Expedia.

First, some background: Expedia's guarantee essentially says that if you can find the same package on another site for less, Expedia will replicate the lower price and give you a $50 voucher for future travel.

Expedia also says that for the guarantee to kick in, you must find a lower price elsewhere within 24 hours of making the Expedia reservation and that the lower price must be verified by an Expedia representative.

And when one man, Ryan J., claimed he did find a lower price than the one he had already booked with Expedia, he followed Expedia's instructions regarding their price guarantee. He said he called well within 24 hours and found the exact same travel package for less money offered on rival site Travelocity.

Did he get the $50 voucher?

Not exactly. Expedia claimed it couldn't find the lower-priced package. No voucher.

It was only after I got in touch with Expedia that the travel site offered to make amends to Ryan. They were extremely apologetic, engaged in a lengthy conversation about how things might be improved, and even offered him a direct phone number that is staffed 24/7. Not a bad result, right?

While the company's seemingly sincere apology may be a good step in helping out future travelers, what are you supposed to do when booking online and you can't get a straight answer from a live person?

Your first step is to make sure you get that live person on the phone. The Web site **gethuman.com** tells you how to bypass the recorded messages so you can talk to a real human. The site includes online booking companies like Cheaptickets.com, Cheapflights.com, Orbitz.com, and Hotels.com.

The next step is to make sure that you're going straight to the top. Sure, everyone says that, but it's true: Don't take no for an answer from someone who doesn't have the authority to say yes in the first place. If that means writing a letter to the CEO, do it. You'd be surprised how quickly things get done when orders come from above.

Make sure there's a paper trail—that means printing out the receipts that are e-mailed to you, taking down the agent's first and last name and ID number (if applicable), the date that you spoke, and what was said. Trust me, if you get caught up in red tape when trying to resolve a problem, you'll be glad that you have something on paper to refer to.

Stay focused. It's easy to get caught up in the blame game, but be clear and firm about what the problem is and how *you* want it resolved. If that means you need your airline tickets refunded, ask for it. If you want your hotel rebooked for a future date, say so. Don't get swayed by $50 vouchers. At the same time, don't be greedy. Just because a Web site glitch or a space cadet ticket agent messed up your cruise cabin, it doesn't entitle you to a week's free vacation.

Don't be afraid to complain. That's what the Better Business Bureau (www.bbb.com) is there for. If you have an issue with a travel agent, file a complaint with the American Society of Travel Agents (www.astanet.com). You can also file complaints with Consumer Affairs, which are listed by individual city and state at www.consumeraction.gov/state.shtml.

Last but not least, since I presume you paid with a credit card and your dispute takes place within 60 days of the time you purchased the travel service, you can always dispute the charge with your credit card company.

And if all else fails, let me hear from you. Log on to www.petergreenberg. com and provide me with the details.

CHAPTER 9

Security and Terrorism

❝ **Those who would give up essential liberty to purchase . . .
safety deserve neither liberty nor safety.** ❞

—BENJAMIN FRANKLIN

Nothing is more counterintuitive than the airline business. Just about every time I fly, I am taken out of the security line for additional screening. Everything I own is inspected, and I am frisked, wanded, and scanned. I have also been told by the Transportation Security Administration (TSA) that I'm on the "no-fly" list. I'm tempted to create a "why fly?" list.

I fly 400,000 miles a year. I haven't checked a bag domestically since 3 years before 9/11. Like many frequent fliers, I make my reservations less than 24 hours before I travel, and in many cases, I fly on one-way tickets, because my itinerary changes so often. Under current profiling protocols, my first name might as well be Ahmed.

It's unfortunate enough that anyone named Ahmed will be stopped. Yet I apparently fit the profile, too. But let's look at that profile: no bags, one-way ticket, reservations made within 24 hours of scheduled flight . . . This doesn't describe a terrorist but a high-yield, frequent flier business traveler.

The TSA has two types of watch lists. The best known is the no-fly list, and the other is called the selectee list, which contains the names of people whose boarding passes are marked with an SSSS and who have to go through an extra screening process.

Consider this: In 1 week, I can fly on as many as 12 flights, many of them connecting. There was a week when I traveled from Los Angeles to Dallas, Dallas to New Orleans, and back. Then to Greenville and Spartanburg, South Carolina, and back. Then to New York. Then Westchester, New York, to Washington, DC. A few days later, Washington, DC, to Miami and back to the West Coast. And then to Buenos Aires. With only one exception, I was pulled out of line each time because the dreaded SSSS was printed on my boarding pass.

On almost every flight, this meant that I somehow fit the profile and that "secondary screening" was required. I was scanned, wanded, touched, and then touched again. My carry-on bags were unpacked and dissected. And in many cases, they were run through machines a second and—in one case—a third time.

On one flight, when one of my staffers was flying with me, she had the SSSS experience simply because she was flying with me.

This isn't effective profiling. This is a stressful waste of time, which could (at least in my case) qualify as harassment.

Recently, I was discussing my issue on the air from a remote broadcast in Minneapolis. "There's no intelligence and intuition being applied to airport security," I said. "When I finish this segment, I will go to the airport to fly to New York to be on the *Today* show tomorrow. I will have no bags, I have a one-way ticket to La Guardia, and my office just made my reservation 2 hours ago. And I will immediately be taken out of line as fitting the profile."

And of course, that's exactly what happened. I raced to the airport, got my boarding pass, showed my driver's license and boarding pass to the rent-a-cop at the beginning of the security line, and was told, "You have been selected for secondary screening." This time, when I started to laugh, I noticed some of the other TSA screeners were laughing too. What did they find so funny? They had just watched my segment on TV! "I'm sorry," one of them shrugged. "We think it's silly, too, but we have to do this. We don't have a choice."

But we *do* have a choice. It's called common sense. Before September 11, airport security was nothing more than an attempt to provide a psychological deterrent against truly emotionally disturbed people.

After September 11, airport and airline security is nothing more than an attempt to make people who don't fly very often feel better. But those of us who do fly often know better. More than 5 years after September 11, while the TSA is still strip-searching nuns, looking for tweezers, almost none of the cargo—carried directly below the passenger compartment in the baggage holds of commercial aircraft—is inspected. Neither is the mail carried on almost all passenger flights.

Then there's the Federal Air Marshal program. These men and women are supposed to fly incognito. Really? They always preboard the flight. Duh. They always sit in the same aisle seats, wear their Dockers and Pendleton shirts and fanny packs, read their Tom Clancy novels, and try to blend in. And worse, there are not enough of them. If we want real airline security, let's put a marshal in uniform in the jump seat next to the cockpit door facing the passengers.

It's basic common sense that terrorists don't follow the path of most resistance, but they aim for the path of least resistance. Sadly, we continue to fight the last war instead of anticipating and preparing for the next one. Less than 10 percent of all containers entering US ports are actually inspected (and with that figure I am being generous). Take the case of the Port of Los Angeles, the largest in America. More than 40 percent of everything that enters this country comes through Los Angeles.

Last year, the Department of Homeland Security gave city officials a $40 million grant to beef up port security in LA. Sound like a lot of money? To put things in perspective, that's the exact same amount we spend every day nationally on airport security screeners! And the overwhelming majority of those containers is still not being inspected.

If the TSA wants effective profiling, they should give their frontline people the respect and flexibility they deserve: to think, to use their intuition, and to ask appropriate, effective questions.

But that never happens. Even when authorities *do* ask questions, they're consistently stupid in their delivery, because they are robotic and the questions easily answered by "yes," "yes," and "no."

Did you pack your bags yourself? (Yes.)

Have they been in your possession since you packed them? (Yes.)

Did anyone give you anything to pack in your bags? (No.)

When these questions are asked, they are always asked in this order. So any dumb terrorist only needs to know it's two yeses and one no and . . . bye-bye.

Any good reporter or street cop will tell you that you never want to ask any question that can be answered by yes or no. Don't ask a suspected killer if he murdered his wife. You'll always get a no.

Instead, ask him what he did with the murder weapon. If he answers that question, you have your criminal. The same applies to airport and airline security. Just ask someone where he or she is going. And why. Or ask him what hotel he stayed in last night.

And you don't have to be a rocket scientist to ask the questions—or effectively interpret the answers. So let's allow our TSA folks to think, to use their intelligence and their intuition—and to embrace common sense.

Until then, SSSS means "stupid times four."

And to prove the point, let me share with you a story that can only be described as coming under the category of "you can't make this stuff up."

Herewith the story of Kenny, a professional musician, and his acoustic guitar. Kenny was traveling out of the Salt Lake City airport with one check-in bag and his acoustic guitar, packed safely in its case. He had been touring the country for years, always carrying his guitar on board, without incident—until that fateful day when he was at the counter at Delta Air Lines in Salt Lake.

The counter agent told him he could not travel with the guitar and claimed it was too big to be a carry-on. (Keep in mind he was not traveling with a cello but with a regular-size acoustic guitar.) Kenny was told he'd have to check the guitar. That was unacceptable to him (and to most sane people), and he tried to argue his case, but the Delta agent would hear none of it. Finally, Kenny asked if there were any other options.

Yes, the agent replied. There was one. He could buy a separate ticket and seat for the guitar. With time running out before departure time and left with no other choices, Kenny coughed up the extra money.

But when he tried to go through security, he was denied entry. While the guitar had a ticket (and, remember, I said you can't make this up), the first security agent stopped him because the guitar did not have a photo ID and there was no name on the ticket.

Kenny returned to the counter, where he proceeded to give the guitar a name: "Mr. Acoustic Guitar." Then he returned to the security checkpoint. Again he was denied, because the agent claimed there was still no government ID to match against Mr. Guitar.

On the third try, with a Delta agent as escort, Kenny was allowed to proceed to security. But he was stopped again at the x-ray machine. Why?

The guitar had been selected for secondary screening! Your tax dollars at work.

The lack of common sense with security also extends to US Customs and Immigration. And, as always, there appear to be some easy fixes. Consider the subject of. . .

Preclearance

Few things in the travel experience remind you of how far we haven't come than when, usually after a very long flight, you arrive at your foreign destination—or return from one—only to have to stand in a long (and lately, longer) line to go through immigration and customs "clearance."

But it's a problem with a very easy solution.

First, let's talk about staffing. When they built the international terminal at Los Angeles International in time for the 1984 Summer Olympics, airport authorities boasted that the facility would feature 70 inspection stations for immigration and customs officials to process arriving passengers.

One small problem—not once in the last 23 years have I ever seen more than 30 of these stations manned at any one time. The same is now true at Kennedy, Miami, and other major international gateway airports in the United States.

The result: lines of as much as an hour—or more—to present your documents, and that's even before you get your luggage and wait in another long line.

And because of new security protocols required by the Department of Homeland Security, it's even worse if you're not a US citizen. Not surprisingly, recent surveys of foreign passengers reveal a distinct drop in visitors to the United States—and one of the reasons cited is how difficult we make the initial "welcome."

It's just as bad overseas—for us. One trip, I landed in Buenos Aires at 10 a.m. I cleared customs at 11:45! There were 20 inspection stations for immigration and customs officers—only two were manned.

Okay, so much about staffing. Here's the most frustrating part. We already know that it is a time-consuming, time-wasting process. But it's made even more frustrating when you discover there is already an effective, efficient, and economic solution to that line.

And, believe it or not, it's not only been implemented for years but works perfectly. It's called preclearance. If you've ever flown to the United States from Canada, Bermuda, or the Bahamas, then you know all about preclearance.

Once you check in for your flight and your bags are tagged to your final destination, you walk through US customs and immigration already in place in *that* country. And once you're cleared there, you're cleared. Period. When you return to the United States, there are no lines. You simply go to baggage claim, get your bags, and go home or go to another gate and make your connecting flight. No more lines. You've saved nearly 2 hours in the process—because you consolidated all the lines into one—at your originating airport.

If security is part of that argument, consider this: Under current rules and regulations, before any international flight heading to the United States can take off, each airline is now required by the Department of Homeland Security to electronically transmit the passenger manifest to US security officials for inspection—to make sure no one on the no-fly list is on board. Conceivably, this same list (which also contains passport numbers recorded at the time each passenger checked in) can be shared with immigration and customs.

Once that happens, it's just a matter of staffing US customs and immigration officials overseas, just as we already do in the Bahamas, Bermuda, and Canada.

The actual cost of implementing these preclearance programs is more than offset by the savings to airlines and airports of misconnected passengers, misconnected and lost baggage, and expensive congestion at airports like JFK and, especially, Miami. How many more foreign visitors would then come and spend their money in the United States because they would be less intimidated by the mere process of arriving?

Remember, the preclearance system doesn't need to be tested. It already works.

The only line we should be standing on is the queue to lobby our elected representatives—many of whom get to bypass long lines when they fly—to convince them this approach is a win-win for all concerned. And in the end, it's not just about cost; it's about value and long-term good will.

It's one thing to say that the technology doesn't exist. But when it does exist, when it already works, when implementing it is easy, and when it makes our lives easier, has no security downside, and has a positive economic impact, there is no excuse for not marrying technology with common sense.

It's a hugely confusing topic. There isn't just one comprehensive government watch suspect list out there; in fact, there are several. There is the "big" government watch list, which can include everyone from the nun carrying tweezers to the current leader of Al Qaeda.

There is the no-fly list, which before September 11 had 16 names on it. These days, the total number is unknown; but when CBS's *60 Minutes* producers were able to review a recent list, they discovered to their surprise a bloated 540-page document with 44,000 names. The good news is, if you get a boarding pass, you're not on the no-fly list. Congratulations!

The government also keeps a "selectee list" of folks who get extraspecial security screening but aren't necessarily banned from flying (including me). CBS estimated that there are 75,000 names on that list. How many of them are dangerous terrorists? Just ask Senator Ted Kennedy, a senator's wife named Catherine Stevens (aka Cat Stevens), and a 40-something Jesuit priest—all of whom found themselves on this watch list. The list also

False Positives

I wanted to find out which facts about the no-fly list are made public, such as how many people are even on the list. The first move is a no-brainer. I called up the Transportation Security Administration (TSA) public affairs number that was listed on their press page. A nice young man named Michael answered. Then he said he was getting another call and put me on hold for several minutes. When he returned, I said I had questions about the no-fly list. He gave me another number to call. I called that number, and it was the Department of Homeland Security. The lovely lady who answered that call told me, "You need to call the TSA." I explained that it was the TSA that had transferred me to her. She was very confused, started typing on her keyboard, mumbling "no-fly list," and finally gave me an 866 number. When I asked what that number was, she said, "They deal with security and stuff." No way was I calling an 866 number, so I called back the TSA. The woman who answered asked where I was calling from—at that time I was in Los Angeles, so she gave me a West Coast press contact for the Department of Homeland Security. When I pointed out that it was not even 7 a.m. where I was and could I have an East Coast number, she said no, that I can only speak with the assigned representative. But "if he doesn't answer his Blackberry, call me back and I'll give you another number." She wound up giving me both numbers, both of which were West Coast. And that, folks, is a great example of how our government operates. (I will say this—the West Coast contact did return my call within 5 minutes but didn't have the answers I was looking for.)

included convicted terrorist Zacarias Moussaoui along with a whole host of dead people, including Saddam Hussein. You can also find about 400,000 names on the National Counterterrorism Center's Terrorist Identities Datamart Environment (TIDE), which is a central repository of international terrorist identities. About 100,000 of them are aliases and name variants.

If you find that you're constantly being pulled aside for extra security screening or if you can't print out your boarding pass online or at a kiosk, then you may be on a government watch list. But good luck confirming if your name is really on the list or if it resembles someone else's name. And most important, good luck getting yourself off that list. In this arena, at least, the government is trying to pare down the lists—the Department of Homeland Security (DHS) even has a new and improved Traveler Redress Inquiry Program (TRIP; www.dhs.gov/trip). But depending on *which* list you're on, you have to go through the agency that put you there in the first place. That can mean the DHS, the CIA, the FBI, the Terrorist Screening Center. . .

At one point, it was estimated that there were 15,000 people *a week* applying for redress. As for how many succeeded in getting off, who knows? It's likely that you'll never get off the list, but the TSA suggests that successfully applying for redress will "facilitate a more efficient check-in process."

Even scarier is something called the Automated Targeting System (ATS). The Department of Homeland Security has been quietly evaluating millions of Americans without their knowledge. When Congress passed the program back in 2001, it was mandated that "each air carrier and foreign air carrier operating a passenger flight in foreign air transportation to the United States shall provide to Customs an electronic transmission of a passenger manifest, and carriers shall make passenger name record information available to the Customs Service." The system since then has developed into one that looks at data of all who cross US borders and assigns them a number calculating their risk factor. Even worse, travelers are not allowed to see or even challenge these risk assessments, and yet that data can be shared with state, local, and foreign governments. Best of all? You'll be on that list for 40 years.

Failed Airport Screening

All too often, we hear news reports about airport screeners who fail random inspections, and it's not getting much better. In Newark Airport, screeners failed 20 of 22 security tests that were conducted by undercover US agents.

I'm talking about missing concealed bombs and guns that were placed in checkpoints in the airport's three terminals.

At Denver International Airport, checkpoint security screeners didn't find simulated weapons and explosives that undercover agents brought through security—even though the machines' alarms went off. The screeners didn't follow standard TSA procedures such as searching the luggage by hand or even patting down the agents.

In one recent report, investigators for the Government Accountability Office tested out the airlines under orders from Congress. The investigators looked up the recipes for homemade bombs and were able to bring those chemicals and ingredients through security screenings at 21 airports. Although what those ingredients are is proprietary information, you can probably let your imagination run wild with this one. And not one of those 21 airport screeners noticed anything wrong.

Liquid Bans and You

By now we've all been inconvenienced by the liquid ban that went into effect after the foiled terrorist plot in London in August 2006. For months, the rules kept changing; people had to throw out gallons of expensive lotions, perfumes, and solutions, not to mention gift bottles of wine. Finally, the regulations seem to have settled down into one semiconsistent format. Here are the rules as they currently stand, according to the TSA.

For simplicity sake, keep in mind the "3-1-1 rule" for liquids in carry-ons.

! 3-ounce or less bottles for all liquids, gels, and aerosols, placed in

! 1 quart-sized, clear, plastic, zipper-lock bag

! 1 bag per passenger placed separately in a security bin for x-ray screening

And for a more detailed description:

! All liquids, gels, and aerosols must be in 3-ounce or smaller containers. Larger containers that are half-full or toothpaste tubes rolled up are not allowed. Each container must be 3 ounces or smaller.

! All liquids, gels, and aerosols must be placed in a single, quart-sized, zipper-lock, clear plastic bag. Gallon-sized bags or bags that are not zipper-lock, such as fold-over sandwich bags, are not allowed. Each traveler can use only one approved bag.

! Each traveler must remove his quart-sized, plastic, zipper-lock bag from his carry-on bag and place it in a bin or on the conveyor belt for x-ray screening. X-raying separately will allow TSA security officers to more easily examine the declared items.

Sounds easy enough, right? Well, it is, until you consider that many travel items don't come in sizes that are 3 ounces or smaller. Think about contact-lens solution—the travel-size bottles are 4 ounces! Fortunately, companies are taking notice and resizing their travel items to comply with TSA standards. Bausch & Lomb, for example, conducted a study that found that one in three Americans is still confused about what's acceptable to bring on an airplane, and one in five Americans has had to throw away items at airport security. So the company introduced "TSA-approved sizes" for carry-on luggage, which included reducing that 4-ounce contact solution to 3 ounces. Travelon created its own clear, quart-sized, zipper-lock bag with 3-ounce bottles to carry your liquid products. La Fresh just introduced a new line of individually wrapped beauty and hygiene products, such as nail polish remover pads. You can also be a little creative and carry essential items in nonliquid form as well. There is dry powdered toothpaste out there and even prepasted disposable toothbrushes, not to mention baby wipes and lotion pads.

But what about those duty-free items that come in sizes that are far larger than 3 ounces? Although you're allowed to purchase liquids once you're past airport security and bring them on board, most people forget one major factor: connecting flights. If you buy a bottle of perfume in Munich, fly to New York, and then connect to a domestic flight to Tulsa, you're going to have to go through security all over again. And there goes your perfume. So when buying duty-free, keep in mind that you're likely going to have to fit it into your carry-on bag at some point.

And the real irony here? While the moisturizer and shaving cream detectives continue to enforce the rules, there is a definitional problem. What really constitutes a liquid or a cream? The answer varies by airport. Recently, a mother who packed a peanut butter and jelly sandwich for her 12-year-old son was stopped at security. The peanut butter was allowed. The jelly wasn't.

On a much sadder and serious note: While all of this scrutiny continues —however well intentioned—the nation's airlines are still not inspecting the cargo that is being shipped in the holds of passenger planes!

The Future of Airport Security

You may have already experienced what are popularly called puffer scanners—new airport security devices that shoot air onto travelers to check for the presence of explosives, among other things. These GE-made devices are being tested in a number of airports, from Miami to Indianapolis.

More and more new devices are beginning to roll out in airports across the country. In fact, whether you're a frequent flier or just an occasional traveler, you'll probably be seeing many of them in the coming years.

Exactly what are these new devices, and how do they work? While they may ultimately make us safer, many of them are raising new issues regarding privacy.

People Portal II

Step inside this futuristic device and you're enveloped in low-level microwaves that generate a wire-frame image of your person. The People Portal automatically detects threats and doesn't require an operator to look at the scan. From a security standpoint, this device is years ahead of the current metal detector technology.

People Portal scans can detect materials that aren't picked up by more traditional scans, such as nonmetal guns, explosives, and illegal drugs. Each of these items would likely not be detected with traditional methods. Basically, the People Portal detects anything that isn't clothing, flesh, or bone—whether it's ChapStick or plastic explosives.

Being both funded and tested by the Federal Aviation Administration, the People Portal attempts to sidestep privacy concerns since it doesn't generate pictures when it generates the scan.

Hand-Held Detection Systems

Future investments in security aren't limited to large, person-sized devices. In 2005, the Connecticut Center for Advanced Technology (CCAT) awarded a grant to Daylight Solutions to advance its Tiny Tunable device. A subsequent investment of $7.5 million in private venture capital is helping ensure that the company will bring its main products to market.

Officially a mid-infrared laser lens detector, the Tiny Tunable is roughly the size of a loaf of bread. Smaller devices like this one are not bound to a particular area and are meant to be used in a variety of situations.

According to CCAT, the technology employs Quantum Cascade Lasers that can be tuned across a large number of wavelengths to detect the tiny molecules of explosives, poisonous gases, or illegal drugs that might be on the person scanned. Not only that, but a Tiny Tunable could also theoretically be used to detect various molecules associated with diseases, potentially being very useful in preventing a pandemic. A suspected infected person, for example, could have his breath scanned for molecules associated with a disease to find out if he is contagious.

This device is projected to be completed and put into handheld form by the end of 2007. It may be a bit longer before it hits the commercial marketplace, but most of the necessary technology has already been developed. However, once it is eventually deployed, the potential uses for such a device are countless—from standard airline security purposes to testing for diseases at quarantine stations.

Laser and Passive Scanning

One of the most Big Brother–like new innovations, still being tested in the lab, uses lasers to scan travelers. This laser-mixing technology, being developed by Dr. William Tong at San Diego State University, analyzes the pattern created by the intersection of two laser beams during a scan to detect various particles and molecules.

The technology could theoretically detect even trace amounts of explosives or other illicit substances from a distance. That would make it nearly impossible for a terrorist to conceal a weapon or a dangerous substance. A grid of laser waves at the entrances to an airport, for example, could detect anyone bringing in explosives. The lasers would be practically invisible, and the person being scanned might not even be aware of that fact.

But for many privacy advocates, the scenario of being completely scanned for nearly any imaginable substance without noticing or giving consent is nightmarish. Fortunately, with the technology still a few years away from being perfected, there is time to assuage the concerns of privacy advocates and civil libertarians.

Ultimately, while the battle over privacy rights at the airport and beyond may be far from decided, one thing is certain: Advancing technology will almost certainly continue to produce such security and privacy conundrums.

Registered Traveler Program

The Clear Registered Traveler program has gotten the most press over the past couple of years. The Transportation Security Administration and private industry developed the program to provide expedited security screening, which is being unrolled in US airports.

For about $100 a year (that's the introductory rate), travelers would submit to a background check to become a registered traveler. Passengers who pass the background check, which includes checking the applicant's identity against terrorist-related, law enforcement, and immigration databases, get a personal smartcard that they can use in a reserved security lane.

The kiosk combines a shoe scanner, an explosives test, and a biometric scanner. Members of the Clear program step onto the shoe scanner, insert their registered traveler card, and place their hand on an explosives detector. Then, after an iris scan—and assuming the machine detects nothing out of the ordinary—travelers can go on their way. Registered travelers aren't exempt from random security screenings.

All in all, the process takes about 2 to 3 seconds in a laboratory setting and perhaps a second or two longer in real-life conditions. While accuracy is still being tested, the registered traveler kiosk does offer a level of security that is more comprehensive than the current system of photo ID checks and metal detectors. The iris scan establishes identity in a way that is theoretically far more difficult to fake than a passport or driver's license.

Clear lanes at security checkpoints are open every day at the following airports: Cincinnati/Northern Kentucky, Indianapolis, New York JFK

Checked Bags and (No) Security

Here's a little detail you may not be aware of: a woeful, if not downright terrifying, lack of security screening of check-in bags. That's right—even though your carry-on bags are treated like explosive devices, your toothpaste is considered to be a national threat, and you practically have to strip down to your skivvies to go through security, those suitcases that get loaded onto the belly of an airplane go through a screening process that is far from thorough. We're talking about 6 billion pounds of cargo that could carry any number of dangerous items. Currently, Congress is considering legislation that would require the TSA to screen all the cargo that goes onto an airplane, but this wouldn't go into effect until 2009 at the earliest. In 2006, a pilot program was implemented at San Francisco International Airport to inspect six times more cargo than is currently being screened. Even so, that's not a multilateral move; not all cargo will be inspected.

Terminals 4 and 7, Orlando, and San Jose. If you want to join, the Clear Registered Traveler program now has mobile enrollment kiosks at the Hyatt Regency Hotels in Santa Clara and San Francisco's Embarcadero Center. Additionally, San Francisco International Airport is planning on choosing a registered traveler vendor.

However, travelers aren't exactly clamoring for the opportunity. There are currently just 45,000 members of the Clear Registered Traveler program. A recent study by Deloitte & Touche, which commissioned a Tourism, Hospitality, and Leisure survey, found that 61 percent of the respondents were unaware of the program. Better yet, after reading about the program, 83 percent were *not* interested in enrolling.

For the moment, consider me part of that 83 percent. In theory, if you're a frequent flier, you have to love the Clear program. After all, anything that gets me through airport security faster is something I totally support. But there is continuing confusion, and a lack of integration with the program, between local airports, airlines, and the TSA. As a result, the implementation and success of the program work at some airports and not at others. Turf and money issues abound—after all, who is going to man and pay for the new Clear program passenger channels? In a number of cases, being a member of the Clear program often means you don't necessarily speed through security. Instead, you get to stand in a completely different line. And remember, TSA still reserves the right for secondary screening. So in my case—and many others—Clear is not an option.

Bus and Train Security

Essentially, it doesn't exist. Nothing more needs to be said. But so much needs to be done. . .

Cruise Ship Safety

We can debate airport security forever, but what people aren't talking about is security that is equally relevant. I'm talking about cruise ships.

Immediately after September 11, cruise lines implemented their highest level of security (Level 3, or "High Threat Level"), as defined by the US Coast Guard's "Security for Passenger Vessels and Passenger Terminals" regulations (ntl.bts.gov/DOCS/nvic396.html). These measures include:

! Restricted areas should have intrusion detection systems that activate an audible or visual alarm, or guards should be posted outside.

! All baggage, cargo, and stores should be screened.

! All passengers and carry-on items should be screened.

! Each entering passenger should be compared with the official passenger list prior to being allowed to board the vessel.

! Baggage should be compared against the official passenger list of the vessel prior to being loaded aboard the vessel.

One thing you can count on with a cruise ship is that it's a closed environment, and in theory that means it is relatively easy to contain. When a ship is in port, there are only one or two entrances and exits, and an ID and ticket check is almost always enforced, along with metal detection. Even before September 11, cruises have had a very good track record when it comes to terrorist acts—in 30 years, there has been only one passenger death due to terrorism. That took place on the cruise ship *Achille Lauro* in 1985, when a 69-year-old passenger was shot to death and pushed overboard by hijackers from the Palestine Liberation Front.

The cruise lines work closely with the Coast Guard, which is now part of the Department of Homeland Security. They also work in conjunction with the US Customs and Border Protection, the US Customs and Immigration Enforcement, the Transportation Security Administration, and the US Citizenship and Immigration Services. Point being, if you don't belong on the ship, chances are you won't be let on.

Cruise lines claim that baggage screening is also a high priority. But don't

Check-In at Home

One airline is trying to make check-in a little easier. The Israel-based El Al airline allows passengers to complete their security check at home. An agent actually comes to your home, hotel, or other agreed location between 6 and 24 hours prior to your flight. The agent checks your passport and ticket, puts you through a security screening, gives you your boarding pass, and transports your bags to the airport. The service costs $49 for up to four passengers, plus $5 for each additional passenger. Unfortunately for most travelers, this service is available only on El Al flights departing from Israel.

count on that. My experience is that x-ray machines near passenger boarding areas are more about showing security without really providing it—more about making people who don't travel very often feel better. But those of us who do travel often *know* better.

Cruise ships are also heavily monitored by surveillance cameras (bet you didn't know that). While there are no cameras in your room, you can expect them to be in the embarkation areas, hallways, common areas, and restricted areas for crew.

Since September 11, all US ports have a minimum 300-foot "no float zone," a security perimeter that prohibits private boats from coming near cruise ships.

▽ Resources

www.tsa.gov/travelers: the Transportation Security Administration's rules on what you can and cannot bring on board

www.dhs.gov/xtrvlsec: information on travel requirements and carry-on rules from the Department of Homeland Security

PART 2

IMPORTANT
FACTS

Presque Isle District Library
Rogers City Branch

181 East Erie Street
Rogers City, MI 49779
Phone: 989.734.2477   Fax: 989.734.4899

CHAPTER 10

Baggage

❝ With modern jets, you can have breakfast in Los Angeles, lunch in New York, dinner in London, and baggage in Rome. ❞

—ANONYMOUS

I've said it before and I'll say it again: As far as I'm concerned, there are only two kinds of airline bags: carry-on and lost. And in recent years, it's safe to say things have not gone from bad to worse—they've gone from worse to: Why are you checking your bags on domestic flights?

The baggage situation was bad before 9/11. It deteriorated after 9/11, and then came 8/10. I'm referring to August 10, 2006, when British security authorities supposedly foiled a terror plot on the United Kingdom. According to the official complaint, terrorists were plotting to board planes carrying chemical liquids and, sometime during their flight, go into the lavatories, mix their explosive brew, and detonate it at 37,000 feet.

At least, that was the official reason why—within 24 hours of the arrests—authorities on both sides of the Atlantic initiated harsh new rules about lotions, potions, moisturizers, toothpaste, bottled water, and in some cases even peanut butter and jelly. No more souvenir bottles of wine in your carry-on. In London, for a number of weeks after the arrests, the rules were even harder: *no* carry-on bags allowed.

And of course, the new rules changed the way we packed. And they certainly—and radically—revised our carry-on-bag protocols. Some might say it was all a conspiracy of the cosmetics and distilling industries. Either way, just imagine plane after packed plane disgorging disgruntled, angry, and unmoisturized women at remote gates after a long flight. Not a pretty scene.

But the new rules certainly represented a challenge for passengers and airlines alike. We were apparently up to the challenge to check more bags, since we no longer had a choice. The airlines were *not* up to the challenge, and they *did* have a choice. When more checked luggage presented the airlines with a huge capacity and weight problem, they simply chose not to board the bags in the aircraft holds—or in some cases, there simply wasn't room. As airlines reduced flight frequencies, that meant more planes were pushing back from their gates full. It also meant—in a growing number of cases—that the aircraft were so jammed that there were clearly more bags than the planes could hold. For example, I've always said that the Miami airport looks like Saigon 1975, with everyone scrambling for the last flight out. After August 10, 2006, the baggage stacked up at Miami resembled Saigon 1975 on PCP.

In 2006, lost luggage rates nationwide were nearly half a million higher than in 2005. And when the August 10 ban on carry-on liquids and gels kicked in, it caused a 30 percent increase in bags checked. And the result: There were 4,083,054 bags mishandled by the airlines in 2006 in the United States, which meant 340,255 mishandled bags per month, 11,186 per day, 466 per hour, 7.8 per minute, and 1 bag mishandled every 7.7 seconds! My position on baggage is simple: I won't check it. In fact, I haven't checked a bag domestically for 8 years. The expense of shipping my luggage is worth it, because I avoid the hassle of waiting around for lost luggage and hoping that the airline will ship it to the right destination. Perhaps most important, I save on average 2 hours of my life every time I fly—I don't have to schlep, I don't have to stand in line at the airline counter, I don't have to stand in line at the security checkpoint, and I don't have to stand around the baggage carousel. Where are my bags? In my hotel room.

You can ship your luggage via a freight company or through one of the major three shipping services, like FedEx, but there are more than 17 luggage shipping services available these days. The benefits of using one of these services: You can avoid the excess baggage fee; the company usually takes care of all the paperwork for you—including airbills and international customs forms; and they can pick up and drop off the luggage at your home or hotel.

Luggage Forward. The Boston-based company reported that bookings in the fourth quarter of 2006 increased by 500 percent! It has a domestic shipping guarantee that waives the shipping charge for any item that arrives late. They will also reimburse you for expenses deemed to be directly related to the delay, up to an amount of $500 per piece of luggage. If you are shipping sports equipment and your shipment is late, Luggage Forward will cover the cost of comparable rental equipment and arrange for those rentals to be waiting for you upon your arrival. Standard round-trip shipping, which takes about 4 days to arrive, for two medium (about 50 pounds) bags from New York to Los Angeles would cost approximately $570. Bulkier items, like a large bag (about 70 pounds) and a baby carriage, on the same trip would cost about $966. Each piece of shipped luggage gets $500 coverage, but you can purchase additional coverage up to $10,000, which provides protection against lost or damage bags beyond normal wear and tear. 866-416-7447, www.luggageforward.com

Luggage Club. Although they haven't released any statistics, the folks at the Luggage Club have stated that business "is going very nicely" over the past year. Two medium bags shipped 5-day economy service from New York to Los Angeles, round trip, cost about $336. You have to log in to the system to get a quote, but once you schedule a trip, the company will mail or e-mail you shipping labels and any appropriate paperwork (you just have to sign). Each shipped item is insured up to $1,000, and you can get additional insurance up to $10,000. 877-231-5131, www.theluggageclub.com

Sports Express. Two medium bags shipped from New York to Los Angeles, round trip, at a 3-day economy rate cost about $554. Preprinted airbills can be faxed or e-mailed to attach to your bag. Each item is insured for $500, and you can purchase additional insurance up to $5,000. But remember to check the fine print: You'll need to use a travel case that is "Sports Express–approved" or the company will not accept liability for damage. 800-357-4174, www.sportsexpress.com

Virtual Bellhop. Through Virtual Bellhop, shipping two medium bags cross-country costs about $403 round trip for 3- to 5-day service. The insurance included is $1,000 per item, with additional insurance available. 877-235-5467, www.virtualbellhop.com

ADDITIONAL PROVIDERS

Baggage Direct: 800-959-4424, baggagedirect.com

Excess International Movers: 800-260-8098, www.excess-baggage.com

First Luggage: 800-224-5781, www.firstluggage.com

Luggage Concierge: 800-288-9818, www.luggageconcierge.com

Luggage Express: 866-744-7224, www.usxpluggageexpress.com

Luggage Free: 800-361-6871, www.luggagefree.com

XS Baggage: 202-747-0487, www.xsbaggage.com

DHL: 800-225-5345, www.dhl-usa.com

FedEx: 800-463-3339, www.fedex.com/us

UPS: 800-742-5877, www.ups.com

And for those of you who are unlucky enough to lose your bags, there's a way you can try to visit your stuff and buy it back. The Unclaimed Baggage Center in Scottsboro, Alabama, is a block-long treasure trove of unclaimed items that can be purchased for discount prices, including clothing, artwork, luggage (of course), sporting goods, and cameras. Each day, the facility—it's about the size of a Wal-Mart Supercenter—puts out about 7,000 new items from 21,000 flights from all major US airlines. You can shop inside the center or online. 256-259-1525, www.unclaimedbaggage.com

Lost Baggage

If your bag does get lost, the first thing to know is that you do have rights. If you are without your bag for 24 hours, many airlines will reimburse you for some clothing and toiletries, *if* you keep your receipts. But know that what you get is all based on your class of service and your frequent flier status.

Currently, the airlines' maximum liability was raised by the Department of Transportation to $3,000—that's per incident, *not* per bag. And if the airline loses your bag forever, your claim is lessened by depreciated value. (It's amazing how quickly an airline depreciates your stuff.) I know of no one in recent years who ever got a check for the full $3,000 from any airline.

However, there is a little-known service that protects your bags over and above that $3,000 cap. The airlines don't publicize it; you won't find any signs at airport counters. We called dozens of airline reservations agents, and they claimed they'd never even heard of it. It's called *excess valuation*, and you have to ask for it at the check-in counter. It provides up to $5,000

> You've heard of the City of Lights (Paris). But what about the City of the Seven Hills (Rome), the City of a Hundred Spires (Prague), and the Heart-Shaped Land (Bosnia and Herzegovina)?

additional coverage, at a rate of approximately $1 per $100 in value. There are obvious exclusions (like jewelry and financial documents), but it's still a great deal, especially if you'll be changing planes in unfamiliar hub cities or changing airlines en route.

Another important thing to do is look through your bag before you leave the airport. Most people are usually so happy to see their bag moving around that carousel that they simply grab it and leave the airport. Bag thieves don't usually steal bags. They steal individual items from bags, and if you wait until you get home to discover something's missing, it's your word against the airline's and you usually lose.

Consider the recent story of the Delta Air Lines passenger who stupidly packed his brand-new digital camera inside his checked bag. It was only when he arrived home that he discovered the camera had been taken from his bag. When he called the airline, they essentially told him he had no standing because he hadn't filed a claim immediately upon landing.

So, was he out of luck? Normally, the answer would be yes. But in this case, the planets seemed to be in outrageously beneficial alignment. On a whim, the passenger went on eBay to see about buying a replacement camera. And what did he spot? *His* camera for sale!

It was sold before he could make his own bid, but he found out the name of the buyer and contacted him. Through the buyer, he got the name of the seller. He did a little more detective work. Guess where the "seller" worked? *Delta!*

He called Delta and told them proudly that he had solved the case. No response. And no reimbursement check, despite the fact that there was a very strong circumstantial case that it was a Delta employee stealing from Delta passengers.

So our passenger simply called the police and explained what he had discovered. The police took over and questioned the "seller," who immediately admitted stealing the camera. Upon further interrogation, authorities learned the Delta employee had quite a history of discount sales on eBay.

The man was arrested. Once again, the passenger called Delta and told them that not only had he solved the case but one of their employees had been arrested by the police and charged. And Delta *still* refused to compensate him. (It was only when he wrote to me and I made the call that Delta acted and wrote him a check.)

The bottom line here is that even when you go the distance—as this passenger did—to find your stolen stuff, most airlines will still make it difficult for you to get reasonable compensation (or in his case, compensation at all) if you don't play by their rules.

So here goes: When you're filing a lost-bag complaint, the airline normally gives you a lost-bag form to fill out with an 800 number to call to be able to check on the status of your lost/missing baggage. But if you just fill out the form and take that number, you aren't doing yourself any favors. Don't leave the office without getting the exact, direct-dial number of that specific office and the first and last name of the baggage claim agent who helped you.

Why? You need the agent to share your sense of urgency. Even if the airline does find your bag and they tell you that they will deliver it, that's only technically correct. In reality, the airline subcontracts out with a van/truck delivery service. And if you don't track the bag directly with the agent and ensure that the driver of the delivery vehicle also shares your sense of urgency, you might be last on his delivery list. This can be crucial if you're at a midpoint city about to continue your journey, and that truck delivery time can often mean the difference of making or missing your flight.

As already mentioned, if the airline loses your bag for good, they are only required to reimburse you up to $3,000 per incident, not per bag, and the amount is not based on depreciated value. For most international travel, liability is limited to $9.07 per pound for checked baggage and $400 per passenger for unchecked baggage, usually limited to 44 pounds. Remember, I know of *no* human alive who has ever gotten the full $3,000. And on international flights, do the math: If you're very, very lucky, you might get $350.

It's also important to note that exceptions are made on things like jewelry, electronics, furs, and negotiable documents. You can also go to your homeowner's policy after the airline settles with you to try to recoup the rest of your loss. If you're still not satisfied with the outcome—and increasingly, many people aren't—you have another option: small-claims court.

Excess Baggage

First it was charging you for headphones, then it was the food. And now, the luxury of checking your bags comes at a cost. More and more carriers are nickel-and-diming their customers by charging for each piece of checked luggage. European discount carrier Ryanair has been doing it for some time now, and Spirit Airlines is now charging passengers up to $10 for checked baggage as well as $1 for nonalcoholic drinks. To make it even more complicated, Spirit charges you $5 for the first bag, $10 for the second, and $100 for each additional bag.

Although other cash-strapped airlines haven't gone this far, they haven't stayed out of the game completely. Southwest originally allowed three checked items plus one piece of sporting equipment or infant item; however, they changed this to include that extra item in your allotted three. Anything additional will cost you $80 per piece, up to three pieces (it goes all the way up to $180). In October 2005, JetBlue changed their policy from three checked bags to two (but they can each weigh 70 pounds). US Airways/America West charges you $80 for your extra luggage, unless you're fortunate enough to be a Chairman's Preferred/Gold Preferred or Star Gold Member, who gets to check a third bag. And there is a checked-bag limit of 50 pounds with charges of $50 to $80 per overweight bag. The bottom line? Overpack for a long vacation and you could be facing some unexpectedly hefty charges.

Here's another bump in the road. If you're flying on British Airways (BA) from the United States, you're still allowed to check two bags on your flight. But if you break up your journey overseas and then want to fly BA on their other routes, you're allowed only one check-in bag, up to about 50 pounds. A second bag: Get out your wallet. The airline can charge you up to £120—that's $240—per bag, per flight! Totally absurd and enough to make me want to change airlines.

If you're like most American passengers, you'll board your flight with two carry-ons. No problem there, except if you're flying through London (not just Heathrow but Gatwick as well). If you're changing planes for your onward journey, the British Airports Authority will not allow you to enter the terminal with more than one carry-on bag. No exceptions. It's downright ugly. As a matter of policy now, unless I am required to go *to* London on a trip, I will *not* connect through Heathrow to go to my final destination. I will connect through Frankfurt, Amsterdam, even Paris before I'll endure the carry-on-bag abuse in London.

And one more thing: If you are changing planes in London and you've checked bags, be aware of a huge discrepancy in time deadlines. While your flight may require a 2-hour connect time from your outbound to your connecting flight, at airports like Heathrow the time allowance requirement for connecting *baggage* may be as much as 4 hours. Translation: When booking flights through Heathrow, make sure your flight connection is at least 4 hours or your bags may not make it. And the airlines don't often tell you that.

Airlines determine your checked-bag allowance in one of two ways. There is the "weight concept," which defines the amount entitled by pounds. This can vary based on your ticket—an economy-class ticket might allow you a total of 50 pounds, for example, while a first-class ticket might allow 60 pounds. There are also often size limits, which are measured in linear inches; i.e., the sum of length, width, and height. A bag that is 62 linear inches is the maximum size for checked baggage before you get charged an oversize fee. The "piece concept" is determined by the number of bags allowed but still takes into consideration the weight and dimensions of your bags. Again, an economy ticket might allow you two pieces of checked baggage, while first class might get three.

Most airlines will charge you a fee for extra, overweight, or oversized checked bags (although again, the grayer areas can be subjective, depending on the operator's mood that day). Believe it or not, some airlines, like United, charge extra for checking in . . . antlers. And Alaska Airways rakes in extra cash for salmon and halibut.

The one major change that's taken place in recent years in several airlines is a reduction in weight limits from 70 pounds per bag to 50 pounds for domestic flights. Airline officials have stated that the reasons behind this move were to save on fuel costs and to protect baggage handlers. In 2003, the International Airline Transportation Association (IATA) put forth the recommendation to limit the free-baggage allowance internationally to 50 pounds for all carriers, pointing out that baggage handlers are at high risk of on-the-job injury.

Depending on where you're leaving from and flying to—along with your class of service—the restrictions vary greatly. In the United States, Continental Airlines will no longer allow fliers to check any bag weighing more than 70 pounds. In other cases, the cost is based on weight; for example, Virgin flights to and from Australia, China, Dubai, Hong Kong, India, Japan, South Africa, and the United Kingdom base their excess-baggage charges on a percentage of the weight.

EXCESS-BAGGAGE COMPARISON

AIRLINE	CARRY-ON BAGS (PLUS ONE PERSONAL)	FREE CHECKED BAGS
American	1 piece, max 45 lin. in. and 40 lb.	2 bags, max 62 lin. in.
Continental	Departing from everywhere except Europe and India: 1 bag, max 51 lin. in. and 40 lb. Departing from Delhi: 1 bag, max 45 lin. in. and 40 lb. Departing from Europe, except the UK: 1 bag, max 45 lin. in. and 40 lb. Departing from the UK: **No personal items allowed**. 1 bag, max 45 lin. in. and 40 lb.	(Except for travel to Brazil) Economy class: 2 bags, max 62 lin. in. and 50 lb. OnePass Elite Members economy class: 2 bags, max 62 lin. in. and 50 lb. First class, BusinessFirst, and international business class: 3 bags, max 62 lin. in. and 70 lb.
JetBlue	1 piece, max 45 lin. in.	2 bags, max 62 lin. in. and 50 lb.
Northwest	1 piece, max 45 lin. in. and 70 lb. (transpacific: 100 lb.)	Domestic/international coach: 2 bags, max 62 lin. in. and 50 lb. Domestic/international first class: 3 checked bags. First 2 bags, max 62 lin. in. and 70 lb.; third bag, max 45 lin. in. and 40 lb.
Southwest	1 piece, max 50 lin. in.	3 bags, max 62 lin. in. and 50 lb.
United	1 piece, max 45 lin. in.	Economy class: 2 bags, max 50 lb. First or business class: 2 bags, max 70 lb. 1K, Premier Executive, and Star Alliance Gold Members: 3 bags, max 70 lb. Travel to/from Brazil, Japan, and the Philippines: max 70 lb.
US Airways/America West	1 piece, max 51 lin. in. (US Airways Express max 45 lin. in.)	Coach: 2 bags, max 62 lin. in. and 50 lb. First class and Envoy class: 2 bags, max 62 lin. in. and 70 lb.

OVERWEIGHT FEE	OVERSIZE FEE	EXCESS BAGGAGE FEE
For travel within the US and Canada, 50–70 lb.: $25 For travel within the US, 70–100 lb.: $50	Over 62 lin. in.: $100 Charge is in addition to any charge assessed for additional or overweight baggage. Over 115 lin. in. not accepted	$80 per piece for first 3 additional pieces $105 each for pieces 4–6 $180 each for pieces 7 and up
Economy class: 50–70 lb.: $25 Charge is in addition to any charge assessed for additional or oversized baggage. Over 70 lb. not accepted	Over 62 lin. in.: $80 Charge is in addition to any charge assessed for additional or overweight baggage. Over 115 lin. in. not accepted	$80 per piece for first 3 additional pieces $105 each for pieces 4–6 $180 each for pieces 7 and up
51–70 lb.: $20 71–99 lb.: $50 Over 99 lb. not accepted	63–80 lin. in.: $50 Over 80 lin. in. not accepted	$50 each
Domestic: 51–70 lb.: $25; over 70 lb. not accepted International: 51–70 lb.: $50; over 70 lb. not accepted	Fees vary by origin and destination cities: $168–$300	Fees vary by origin and destination cities: $84–$150
51–70 lb.: $25 71–100 lb.: $50 Over 100 lb. not accepted	Up to 80 lin. in.: $50 Over 80 lin. in. not accepted	$50 each for bags 1–9 $110 each for pieces 10 and up
51–100 lb.: $50 Over 100 lb. not accepted	Up to 115 lin. in.: $100 **Note: Customers checking antlers as baggage for travel within the US and to/from Canada will be charged $200 per set.**	$85 per piece for first 2 additional pieces $125 each for pieces 3 and 4 $200 each for pieces 5 and up
Coach: 51–70 lb.: $50; 71–100 lb.: $80 First class and Envoy class: 71–100 lb.: $80	Up to 80 lin. in.: $80 Over 80 lin. in. not accepted	$80 each for bags 1–9

Here are my tips to help prevent lost or mishandled luggage when you travel.

❗ On domestic flights, follow my lead. Don't check your bags. Pack light, taking only carry-on luggage.

❗ Ship your luggage ahead to your destination. It can cost $40 a bag and up, but it saves you hours of time. And if you plan properly, you can send the bags 3 days in advance for a discount. (And on your return flight, who says you need your dirty underwear by 10:30 the next morning? Again, use the 3-day discount provision.)

❗ For safety's sake, put only your name on the outside of your bag and your name and contact number on the *inside* of the bag. (Never put your address on the outside of your bag: It's a huge advertisement to burglars who now know your address *and* that you'll be out of town!)

❗ Put a copy of your itinerary inside the baggage—that will make it easier for an airline employee to find you if a bag does become lost.

❗ Take a photo of your bag with your cell phone before you check it, in case you need it later for show-and-tell.

❗ Consider buying baggage insurance. This is available as part of comprehensive trip cancellation and interruption travel insurance packages (see Travel Insurance chapter), which can cover loss or damage to your personal effects and reimburse you for purchasing necessities if your baggage is lost. Your credit card may also cover your baggage insurance: American Express, for example, includes baggage insurance up to $1,250 on many of its cards, as well as additional insurance for an additional fee of up to $9.95 per trip.

❗ Never pack items you must have within 24 hours—medicine, for example, or the suit you need for that presentation in the morning. And take photocopies of your prescriptions, in case you need more medicine or to prove to an overzealous customs agent that you're not a drug smuggler.

❗ Never pack valuable or precious items like jewelry, electronics, or cash in checked luggage, because if the bag is lost, you can't claim them. (Remember our Delta passenger?)

❗ After you've claimed your bag on the other side, don't just grab it and run. Open it and check it before you leave the baggage claim area just to make sure all your stuff is inside. If something is missing, it will be a lot easier to handle it directly at the airport than when you get home.

CHAPTER 11

Passport Rules

The world is a book, and those who do not travel, read only a page.

—ST. AUGUSTINE

I got my first passport when I was 12. It's one of the best things my parents ever gave me. Indeed, it was the gift that keeps on giving. If you define true luxury travel by the ability to keep your options, then a passport is clearly the enabler: It gives you those options.

Sadly, less than 30 percent of all Americans have passports. And while that number is now growing, it's still embarrassingly low.

And then there's something called the Western Hemisphere Travel Initiative (WHTI): In order to strengthen border security and facilitate entry into the United States, as of January 23, 2007, all people, including US citizens, traveling by air between the United States and Canada, Mexico, Central America, South America, the Caribbean, and Bermuda are now required to present a valid passport.

If you're traveling by sea or land (that means ferries, cars, trains, etc.) between the United States and those same areas, this law won't apply until January 1, 2008.

> You probably know that America was named after Amerigo Vespucci. But did you know that Saudi Arabia was named for Abdul Aziz ibn-Saud? And the Philippines was named after Philipp II.

As expected, the new law caused a massive number of people to scramble to get their passports in order, quickly. In 2006, the State Department issued 12 million passports. By the middle of 2007, it was expected that the State Department would issue 17 million passports—or more. More than 74 million Americans currently have passports, and more than 1 million get passports every month. This has created a huge backlog of passport applications, not to mention renewals from frequent travelers. Initially, the State Department said it might take up to 8 weeks to process a passport. Then that number went to 12 weeks. In reality, it ran closer to 16 and, in some cases, 17 weeks for a passport. Even today, if you're planning a trip outside the United States, you may be delayed waiting for that passport, so plan accordingly.

By midsummer 2007, the mess was so bad at the State Department that the rules changed almost weekly. First, the agency allowed folks who had applied for a passport and were still waiting to show a receipt from the State Department proving their application was still "in process" to fly without a passport. Then, it got even wilder. The deadline for those needing a passport to drive across the borders to either Canada or Mexico was extended a year, from January 2008 to January 2009. It's a perfectly sad—and still evolving—example of commerce trumping security. Still, that should not keep you from delaying applying for a new passport or renewing one about to expire. The waits are only going to get worse.

At the same time, you should also budget accordingly. A new standard 10-year-validity passport will run you $97 ($82 for children under 16)—that's nearly $400 for a family of four. And while that may seem expensive, amortized over 10 years, it's less than $10 a year to be able to see the world.

Passport Security

In an effort to improve security and prevent passport forgeries, the government has begun to issue a new biometric passport, which combines the traditional paper documents with electronic data. The new passport will be equipped with a radio frequency identification (RFID) chip. The chip stores the same data that is in a standard passport, along with digital image of the owner. The data isn't encrypted, but the information can't be read by just anyone—a State Department private key is used to encrypt a "hash" (a number generated from a string of text) of the information on the chip. A passport officer has to swipe the passport through an optical reader, scanning the text that's printed on the passport page below the photo. The hash creates a unique key that unlocks the data on the RFID chip. The passport includes a radio shield in the cover that protects the chip, but if the chip is broken, the passport is still valid.

If this all sounds too *Brave New World* for you, consider the fact that RFID chips are already being used in car keys to prevent theft, library books, airline baggage tracking, pharmaceuticals, ID badges, the American Express Blue credit card, and even in pets. Biometric passports are already in effect in Australia, Canada, and Singapore.

And then, once you get your passport, don't get stuck if you lose it. Before traveling, make a photocopy and digital scan of your passport and keep it in a separate location from the original. If you're not comfortable with e-mailing yourself your passport scan through a Web-based account, you can store it on www.passportsupport.com for $11 per year.

What the Government Doesn't Tell You

You may not know that you can be denied boarding or reentry into the United States if:

! Your passport is going to expire within 6 months.

! You don't have enough blank pages remaining on your passport.

Before you travel, make sure you have at least two blank pages on your passport to pass through customs in foreign countries. If your passport isn't expiring for a while, it's worth it to order extra pages from a passport office or American consulate.

Your passport can't expire while you're out of the country, and a general rule of thumb is that you should have at least 6 months remaining on your passport, beyond the stay of your travels (so if you're traveling from April 15 to May 15, your passport shouldn't expire before November 15, 6 months after your return). This varies country by country (and customs agent by customs agent)—you can usually get away with it if you have 6 months remaining from when you depart the United States, not when you return.

Children and Passports

Children of all ages are required to have a passport for international travel. A 2001 law states that when applying for a US passport for a child under 14, both parents must provide proof of consent or the applying parent must have sole authority to obtain the passport. What constitutes proof of consent? For starters, my advice is to get a notarized letter of permission—actually two individual notarized letters, one from each parent—giving the other parent permission to take the child out of the country. Without that letter, it is highly likely that your kid won't be allowed to board an international flight from the United States. This law was passed to decrease the possibility of international child abduction by a parent. For more information on how to apply for a passport for a minor, visit travel.state.gov/passport/get/minors/minors_834.html or call the Office of Children's Issues in the Bureau of Consular Affairs at 202-501-4444.

Obtaining a Passport

For information on how to obtain a passport, visit travel.state.gov/passport. Or check the Travel Industry Association's site, www.getapassportnow.com.

To obtain a first-time passport, you'll need proof of US citizenship (preferably a birth certificate) and proof of identity such as a driver's license or military ID. You need to fill out Form DS-11. You must apply in person at a

You Need a Passport in Texas?

A 2007 survey conducted by the online booking agent Kayak.com found that Americans are woefully uneducated when it comes to passport rules. In a survey of more than 1,000 respondents, 26 percent thought that Americans would need a passport when returning from Maui, Hawaii, and a surprising 50 percent thought that a passport was required to return from South Padre Island—in Texas. About 48 percent thought that it would take 3 or more months for an average citizen to get a passport (although 51 percent thought that members of Congress who applied for a new passport would be able to jump the line and get one in a single day). One in three people plan to apply for a passport now that it's mandatory when returning from Canada, Mexico, and parts of the Caribbean. But fewer than 1 in 20 had actually started the application process.

passport acceptance facility, including post offices; libraries; federal, state, and probate courts; and county and municipal offices. You need to provide two identical color passport photos, taken within 6 months of applying. (The fee for a person over age 16 is $97, and for kids under 16 it is $82.)

If you're renewing a passport, the process is a little easier, as you can do this by mail (unless your passport has been damaged or altered, in which case it needs to be done in person). You'll have to mail in your old passport, two new passport photos, and a fee of $67. Keep in mind, however, that the time frame for renewing an expired or an almost-expired passport is the same as if you were obtaining a first-time passport.

Expedited Passports

Obtaining a new passport can take up to 6 weeks, and expedited services can take 2 weeks. But February through April is the busiest time of year for Passport Services, due to spring break and summer trips. In special cases, like when the new passport law came into effect, services can be delayed. During that crunch period, passport applications were flooding the State Department at a rate of one million a month. Between October 2006 and March 2007, applications were up 44 percent from the previous year. According to the State Department, processing both new and renewed passports took up to 10 weeks for standard service and 4 weeks for expedited service, but now you know better—it can be up to 17 weeks.

One handy tip is that if you're applying for an expedited passport, write "EXPEDITE" on the outside of the envelope containing your application. To obtain a new passport or visa and to check the status of your application, call the National Passport Information Center at 877-487-2778 or visit travel.state.gov/passport.

If you need to obtain a passport or visa quickly (even within 24 hours), you can use an authorized expedited passport service. But be prepared to pony up serious money for it—count on $200 or more. But if time is money (and remember that 17-week wait for everyone else), it's a no-brainer: Do it. *An important note:* You need to provide "proof" that you are actually leaving within a short time window. My advice is to go out and purchase a fully refundable full coach ticket to London leaving in 10 days and present that as proof. In almost all cases, they'll need to see that ticket. Then get your passport and refund the ticket.

▽ Resources

It's Easy Passport: 866-487-3279, www.itseasypassport.com

Passport Plus: 800-367-1818, www.passportplus.net (New Yorkers call 212-759-5540)

Passports and Visas: 800-860-8610, www.passportsandvisas.com

Passport Express: 800-362-8196, www.passportexpress.com

Zierer Visa Services: 866-788-1100, www.zvs.com

Fun Fact

The new passport rules really threatened a number of Caribbean destinations that rely so much on US tourists. For example, 80 percent of the Americans visiting Jamaica had always just presented their birth certificates in lieu of a passport. So the new rules could have potentially resulted in a huge drop in arrivals.

As a result, a number of hotels and resorts in the region began offering to pay for your passport as an incentive to get you to come back to their country. For example, SuperClubs' "Passport Included" promotion paid the fee for clients up to $97 per person as part of their all-inclusive Caribbean vacation. Westin Aruba Resort, Renaissance Aruba Resort & Casino, Amsterdam Manor Beach Resort, MVC Eagle Beach, Boardwalk Boutique Hotel Aruba, and CheapCaribbean were all involved with coupons, credit, and vouchers to cover the cost of a passport. Jamaica also offered in-kind dollar credits at a number of hotels equal to the amount of money you spent for your passport. In Anguilla, the Arawak Beach Inn offered a special rate and a free day trip to

 Passport Confusion

If the recent passport rules have you confused, you're not alone. The Travel Industry Association and Yesawich, Pepperdine, Brown & Russell released a survey of 1,980 American adults, more than half of which (56 percent) could not correctly answer a question about the countries from which a passport is now required for all US citizens returning by air (the answer is all of them). Twenty-two percent weren't sure about the requirements, and 7 percent thought that no passport was required for any returning resident regardless of which country was visited.

a private island if you could arrive showing that Anguilla was the first stamp on your new passport.

While these were limited-time promotions, the real bottom line here is that if you call these hotels ahead of time and tell them you just got a new passport in order to visit them, you might be surprised at how many will still step up to the plate and offer you a real dollar incentive to visit them first.

Visa Requirements by Country

Having a passport is only the beginning. Many countries still require you to get a visa, which—attached to your passport—allows you to enter a specific country during a given period of time for a certain purpose. There are different kinds of visas—tourism, business, student. And it can be a confusing process. Visa rules and how to obtain them can differ wildly between countries, so do your research well in advance of your travel plans.

Passport and Visa Requirements

The following is a partial list of international passport and visa requirements. In researching this book, I asked the State Department to provide me with the phone number for each country's embassy. And guess what? At least 30 of those numbers were wrong! Here's the right information for you (and if you're willing to risk it, visit this site: http://travel.state.gov/travel/tips/brochures/brochures_1229.html).

Afghanistan: Passport and visa required. Embassy of Afghanistan, 202-483-6410, www.embassyofafghanistan.org

Albania: Passport with minimum validity of 6 months required. No visa required. Embassy of the Republic of Albania, 202-223-4942

Algeria: Passport and visa required. Visa required for stays up to 90 days. Consular Section of the Embassy of the People's Democratic Republic of Algeria, 202-265-2800, www.algeria-us.org

Antigua and Barbuda: Passport with minimum validity of 6 months or proof of US citizenship such as certified birth certificate along with picture ID required. Onward/return ticket and proof of funds required for tourist stay of up to 6 months. Embassy of Antigua and Barbuda, 202-362-5122

Argentina: Passport required. Visa not required for business/tourist stay of up to 90 days. Argentine Embassy, 202-238-6400, www.embassyofargentina-usa.org

Armenia: Passport and visa required. Visa for stay of up to 21 days requires application form, one photo, and $60 to $95 processing fee (fees vary according to processing time). Embassy of the Republic of Armenia, 202-319-1976, www.armeniaemb.org

Aruba: Passport or proof of US citizenship (original official birth or naturalization certificate and photo ID) required. Visa not required for tourist/business visit of up to 90 days. Proof of onward/return ticket or sufficient funds for stay may be required. Airport facility charge is $32, paid upon departure. Royal Netherlands Embassy, 202-244-5300, www.netherlands-embassy.org

Australia: Passport, Electronic Travel Authority (ETA) or nonelectronic label visa, proof of onward/return ticket, and sufficient funds required. Embassy of Australia, 202-797-3000, www.austemb.org

Austria: Passport required. Visa not required for tourist stay of up to 90 days. Embassy of Austria, 202-895-6700, www.austria.org

Bahamas: Proof of US citizenship, i.e., a passport (if you are using an expired passport, it cannot be expired more than 5 years) or original or certified copy of a birth certificate with a photo ID, and onward/return ticket required for stay of up to 8 months. Proof of sufficient funds required. Embassy of the Commonwealth of the Bahamas, 202-319-2660, www.bahamas.gov.bs

Bangladesh: Passport, visa, and onward/return ticket required. Embassy of the People's Republic of Bangladesh, 202-244-0183, www.bangladoot.org

Barbados: Passport and proof of sufficient funds required. Cruise passengers planning to disembark in Barbados must have a valid passport. Visa not required for stays up to 6 months. Departure tax of $12.50 paid at the airport. Embassy of Barbados, 202-939-9200

Belgium: Passport required. Visa not required for business/tourist stay of up to 90 days. Embassy of Belgium, 202-333-6900, www.diplobel.us

Belize: Passport, onward/return ticket, and sufficient funds required. Visa not required for stay of up to 30 days. Embassy of Belize, 202-332-6888, www.embassyofbelize.org

Bermuda: Passport (or proof of US citizenship with photo ID) and onward/return ticket required for tourist stay of up to 3 months. Departure tax of $10 is paid at airport. British Embassy, 202-588-7800, www.immigration.gov.bm

Bolivia: Passport required. Visa not required for tourist stay of up to 30 days. Consular Section of the Embassy of Bolivia, 202-232-4827, 202-232-4828, www.bolivia-usa.org

Bosnia and Herzegovina: Passport required. Visa not required for tourist stays of up to 3 months. Embassy of Bosnia and Herzegovina, 202-337-1500, www.bhembassy.org

Botswana: Passport, onward/return ticket, and proof of sufficient funds required. Visa not required for stays up to 90 days. Embassy of the Republic of Botswana, 202-244-4990, www.botswanaembassy.org

Brazil: Passport with minimum validity of 6 months and visa required. Brazilian Embassy, 202-238-2700, www.brasilemb.org

Bulgaria: Passport required. Visa not required for tourist stays of up to 90 days. Consular Section of the Embassy of the Republic of Bulgaria, 202-483-1386, www.bulgaria-embassy.org

Burma (Myanmar): Passport and visa required. Embassy of the Union of Myanmar, 202-332-3344, www.mewashingtondc.com

Cambodia: Passport and visa required. Visa requires application, one current passport-sized photo, and passport with minimum validity of 3 months. 202-726-7742, www.embassyofcambodia.org

Cameroon: Passport and visa required. Yellow fever and cholera immunizations are required. Embassy of the Republic of Cameroon, 202-265-8790

Canada: Passport or proof of US citizenship such as a birth certificate, naturalization certificate, and photo ID required. Visas are not required. Canadian Embassy, 202-682-1740, www.canadianembassy.org

Central African Republic: Passport and visa required. Embassy of Central African Republic, 202-483-7800

Chile: Passport required. Visa not required for stay of up to 90 days. Entry fee of $100 charged at airport. Embassy of Chile, 202-530-4106, www.chile-usa.org

China, People's Republic of: Passport and visa required. Due to tightened visa policy, travelers may be required to undergo a personal interview. Transit visa required for any stop (even if you do not exit the plane or train) in China. Business travelers are required to obtain formal invitation from their Chinese business contact. Tourist visas are issued only after receipt of a confirmation letter from a Chinese tour agency or letter of invitation from a relative in China. Chinese Embassy, 202-328-2500, www.china-embassy.org

Colombia: Passport and proof of onward/return ticket required for tourist stay of up to 180 days. Upon arrival, the Colombian Immigration authority stamps a stay authorization, normally no longer than 90 days (extendable up to 180 days). Colombian Embassy, 202-387-8338, www.colombiaemb.org

Congo, Democratic Republic of the (Kinshasa): Passport and visa required. Evidence of yellow fever vaccination required for entry. Embassy of the Democratic Republic of the Congo, 202-234-7690/7691

Congo, Republic of the (Brazzaville): Passport and visa required. Evidence of yellow fever vaccination is required for entry. Embassy of the Republic of the Congo, 202-726-5500, www.embassyofcongo.org

Costa Rica: Passport and onward/return ticket required. For stays exceeding 90 days, apply for an extension within the first week of visit with the Costa Rican Immigration Department; after 90 days, obtain an exit visa. Consular Section of the Embassy of Costa Rica, 202-238-2291, www.costarica-embassy.org

Côte d'Ivoire (Ivory Coast): Passport required. US citizens traveling to Côte d'Ivoire for business or tourism do not require visas for stays of up to 90 days. An international health certificate showing current yellow fever immunization is required. Embassy of the Republic of Côte d'Ivoire, 202-797-0300

Croatia: Passport and onward/return ticket required. Visa not required for tourist/business stay of up to 90 days. Embassy of Croatia, 202-588-5899, www.croatiaemb.org

Cuba: Passport and visa required. Cuban Interests Section, 202-797-8518. HIV test required for those staying longer than 90 days. US citizens need a US Treasury Department license in order to engage in any transactions related to travel to and within Cuba (this includes the use of US currency). Licensing Division, Office of Foreign Assets Control, US Department of Treasury, 202-622-2480, www.treas.gov/ofac

Cyprus: Passport and round-trip ticket required. Visa not required for tourist/business stay of up to 3 months. Embassy of the Republic of Cyprus, 202-462-5772, www.cyprusembassy.net

Czech Republic: Passport required. Visa not required for business and tourist stay of up to 90 days. Embassy of the Czech Republic, 202-274-9100, www.mzv.cz/washington

Denmark (including Greenland): Passport required. Visa not required for a stay of up to 90 days. Royal Danish Embassy, 202-234-4300, www.ambwashington.um.dk

Dominican Republic: Passport is strongly recommended, but tourists may enter with birth certificate and photo ID. A tourist card is required and can be purchased for $10 at consulate or Dominican airports at entry points. Embassy of the Dominican Republic, 202-332-6280, www.domrep.org

Ecuador (including the Galapagos Islands): Passport with minimum validity of 6 months required. Visa not required for a stay of up to 90 days. Embassy of Ecuador, 202-234-7166

Egypt: Passport and visa required. Visas may be obtained upon entry from the Entry Visa Department at the Travel Documents, Immigration, and Nationality Administration or most major ports of entry. HIV test required for study and work permits. Embassy of the Arab Republic of Egypt, 202-895-5400, www.egyptembassy.net

El Salvador: Passport and single-entry tourist card required. The tourist card may be obtained from immigration officials for $10 upon arrival in country. An exit tax of $32 must be paid. Embassy of El Salvador, 202-337-4032, www.elsalvador.org

Estonia: Passport required. Visas are not required for stays of up to 90 days. Estonian Embassy, 202-588-0101 or the Consulate General of Estonia, 212-883-0636, www.nyc.estemb.org

Ethiopia: Passport and visa required. Yellow fever immunization is recommended. Embassy of Ethiopia, 202-364-1200, www.ethiopianembassy.org

Fiji: Passport with minimum validity of 3 months, proof of sufficient funds, and onward/return ticket required. Visa not required for stay of up to 4 months. All visitors over age 12 are required to pay $25 departure tax. HIV testing required for stays exceeding 6 months. Embassy of the Republic of the Fiji Islands, 202-337-8320, www.fijiembassy.org

Finland: Passport required. Tourist/business visa not required for stay of up to 90 days. Embassy of Finland, 202-298-5800, www.finland.org

France: Passport required. Visa not required for tourist/business stay of up to 90 days in France, Andorra, Monaco, and Corsica and 1 month in French Polynesia. Consulate General of France, 202-944-6195, www.info-france-usa.org

French Polynesia: Includes Society Islands, French Southern and Antarctic Lands, Tuamotu, Gambier, French Austral, Marquesas, Kerguelen, Crozet, New Caledonia, Tahiti, Wallis, and Furtuna Islands. Passport required. Visa not required for visit of up to 1 month. Consulate General of France, 202-944-6195, www.info-france-usa.org

Germany: Passport required (must not expire before end of trip). Tourist/business visa not required for stay of up to 90 days. Embassy of the Federal Republic of Germany, 202-298-4393, www.germany-info.org

Ghana: Passport and visa required. Proof of yellow fever vaccination required. Tourist visa required for stay of up to 30 days (extendable). Embassy of Ghana, 202-686-4520, www.ghana-embassy.org

Greece: Passport required. Visa not required for tourist/business stay of up to 90 days. Embassy of Greece, 202-939-1333, www.greekembassy.org

Grenada: Passport recommended, but tourists may enter with birth certificate, photo ID, and onward/return ticket. Visa not required for tourist stay of up to 3 months; may be extended to maximum of 6 months. Consulate General of Grenada, 202-265-2468, www.grenadaembassyusa.org

Guatemala: Passport required for stay of up to 90 days. Embassy of Guatemala, 202-745-4952, www.guatemala-embassy.org

Haiti: Passport required. Visa not required for tourist/ business stay of up to 90 days; compulsory for longer stays. Visas are available at port of entry. Embassy of Haiti, 202-332-4090, www.haiti.org

Honduras: Passport and onward/return ticket required. Visa not required for stay of up to 90 days; holders of US passports are issued a 30-day permit, which can be renewed every 30 days for up to a maximum 90-day stay. Departure tax $30. Consular Section of the Embassy of Honduras, 202-966-7702, www.hondurasemb.org

Hong Kong, Special Administrative Region: Passport and onward/return transportation by sea/air required. Visa not required for tourist/business stay of up to 90 days. Visa Section of the Embassy of the People's Republic of China, 202-328-2500, www.china-embassy.org

Hungary: Passport, onward/return ticket, and proof of sufficient funds required. Visa not required for stay of up to 90 days. HIV test required for persons staying longer than 1 year. Embassy of the Republic of Hungary, 202-362-6730, www.huembwas.org

Iceland: Passport required. Visa not required for stay of up to 90 days. Embassy of Iceland, 202-265-6653, www.iceland.org/us

India: Passport and visa required. HIV test required for all students and anyone over 18 staying 1 year or more. Embassy of India, 202-939-7000, www.indianembassy.org

Indonesia: Passport and visa required. Embassy of the Republic of Indonesia, 202-775-5200, www.embassyofindonesia.org

Iran, Islamic Republic of: Passport and visa required. The United States does not maintain diplomatic or consular relations with Iran. Embassy of Pakistan, Iranian Interests Section, 202-965-4990, www.daftar.org. Attention: US citizens may need a US Treasury Department license in order to engage in any transactions related to travel to and within Iran. Before planning any travel to Iran, US citizens should contact the Licensing Division, Office of

Foreign Assets Control, US Department of Treasury, 202-622-2480, www. treas.gov/ofac. Authorities may confiscate US passports of US–Iranian dual nationals upon arrival. Therefore, the State Department suggests leaving US passports at the nearest US Embassy or Consulate overseas prior to entering Iran and to use an Iranian passport to enter.

Iraq: The Iraqi government is currently reviewing entry requirements. Iraq requires HIV test results for residency/exit permits. Embassy of Iraq, 202-483-7500, www.iraqiembassy.org

Ireland: Passport required. Tourists are not required to obtain visas for stays less than 90 days but may be asked to show onward/return ticket. Embassy of Ireland, 202-462-3939, www.irelandemb.org

Israel: Passport, onward/return ticket, and proof of sufficient funds required. Visa not required for tourist or business stay of up to 90 days. Ministry of Interior reserves the right to deny entry to aliens claiming to be HIV positive. Consular Section of the Embassy of Israel, 202-364-5527, www.israelemb.org

Italy: Passport required. Visa not required for tourist or business stays up to 90 days. Within 8 days of arrival, visitors are required to register with local police and obtain a permit to stay, regardless of length of visit. Proof of sufficient financial support may be required. Embassy of Italy, 202-328-5500, www.italyemb.org

Jamaica: Passport or original birth or naturalization certificate and valid driver's license or state-issued photo ID, onward/return ticket, and proof of sufficient funds required. Embassy of Jamaica, 212-935-9000, www. congenjamaica-ny.org

Japan: Passport and onward/return ticket required. Visa not required for tourist/commercial business stay of up to 90 days. Americans cannot work on a 90-day "visa-free" entry. Embassy of Japan, 202-238-6800, www. us.emb-japan.go.jp

Jordan: Passport and visa required. Visitors may obtain a visa, for a fee, at most international ports of entry upon arrival, except at the King Hussein/Allenby Bridge. HIV testing required for stays exceeding 6 months. Embassy of the Hashemite Kingdom of Jordan, 202-966-2664, www.jordanembassyus.org

Kazakhstan: Passport, onward/return ticket, and visa required. Embassy of the Republic of Kazakhstan, 202-232-5488, www.kazakhembus.com

Kenya: Passport, visa, and onward/return ticket required. Travelers who opt to obtain an airport visa should expect delays upon arrival. Evidence of yellow fever immunization may be requested. Airport departure tax $40. Embassy of Kenya, 202-387-6101, www.kenyaembassy.com

Korea, Democratic People's Republic of (North Korea): Passport and visa required. The United States currently does not maintain diplomatic or consular relations with North Korea. For visa information, contact the Permanent Representative of the Democratic People's Republic of Korea to the United Nations, 212-972-3105. US citizens may need a US Treasury Department license in order to engage in any transactions related to travel to and within North Korea. Before planning any travel to North Korea, US citizens should contact the Licensing Division, Office of Foreign Assets Control, US Department of the Treasury, 202-622-2480 or www.treas.gov/ofac. As most travelers enter from China, travelers may need to obtain a two-entry visa for China. The visa is essential for departing from North Korea at the end of a visit or in an emergency.

Korea, Republic of (South Korea): Passport and onward/return ticket required. A visa is not required for a tourist stay of up to 30 days. HIV test required for persons working as entertainers and staying longer than 90 days. Consular Section of the Embassy of the Republic of Korea, 202-939-5653, www.koreaembassyusa.org

Kuwait: Passport and visa required. Visa issued at port of entry. Embassy of the State of Kuwait, 202-966-0702, www.kuwaitembassy.org.

Laos: Passport with minimum validity of 6 months and visa required. Visa available for stay of up to 15 days, extendable. Consular Section of the Embassy of the Lao People's Democratic Republic, 202-332-6416, www.laoembassy.com

Latvia: Passport with minimum validity of 3 months required. Visa not required for stay of up to 90 days. Valid health insurance policy (policy should cover all costs relating to medical care during stay) required for all visitors. Embassy of Latvia, 202-328-2840, www.latvia-usa.org

Lebanon: Passport and visa required. Note: All visa applicants holding an Israeli visa on their passport, at the time of applying for visa or arrival in Lebanon, will not be granted a visa and/or be admitted to Lebanon without the prior approval of the Lebanese Immigration Authorities. Embassy of Lebanon, 202-939-6300, www.lebanonembassyus.org

Liberia: Passport, visa, and evidence of a yellow fever vaccination required. There is a $100 airport tax on departing passengers. Embassy of the Republic of Liberia, 202-723-0437, www.embassyofliberia.org

Libya: Passport and visa required. Restrictions on the use of a US passport for travel to, in, or through Libya have been lifted as of February 2004. At this time, neither Libya nor the United States provides visa services in each other's countries; US visitors to Libya should therefore plan to obtain a visa via a third country. Within 3 days of arrival, visitors must register at the police station nearest where they will be residing. Libyan Mission to the United Nations, 202-752-5775. Attention: US citizens need a US Treasury Department license in order to engage in any transactions related to travel to and within Libya. Before planning any travel to Libya, US citizens should contact the Licensing Division, Office of Foreign Assets Control, US Department of Treasury, 202-622-2480, www.treas.gov/ofac

Lithuania: Passport required. Visa not required for tourist/business stay of up to 90 days. All visitors to Lithuania must have a valid health insurance policy or contract that covers all health expenses during their stay. Embassy of Lithuania, 202-234-5860, www.ltembassyus.org

Madagascar, Republic of: Passport and visa required. Embassy of Madagascar, 202-265-5525, www.embassy.org/madagascar

Malawi: Passport required. US passport holders do not require a visa to enter Malawi. A 30-day visa, which can be extended up to an additional 60 days, issued at point of entry. There is a $30 airport departure tax. Embassy of Malawi, 202-797-1007

Malaysia: Passport with minimum validity of 6 months required. Visa not required for stay of up to 3 months, extendable for 2 months. Embassy of Malaysia, 202-572-9700, www.kln.gov.my/mission/washington

Maldives: Valid passport, along with an onward/return ticket, proof of hotel reservations, and sufficient funds, required. Tourist visa issued upon arrival for 30 days validity. All visitors departing the Republic of the Maldives (except diplomats and certain exempted travelers) must pay an airport departure tax. Travelers need a yellow fever immunization if they are arriving from an infected area. Maldives Mission, 212-599-6195, www.un.int/maldives

Malta: Passport with minimum validity of 6 months required. Visa not required for stay of up to 90 days. Embassy of Malta, 202-462-3611/3612

Mexico: Passport or proof of citizenship (such as original birth or naturalization certificate) and photo ID. Tourist card required. Visa not required for US citizens for tourist/transit stay of up to 30 days. Obtain tourist cards in advance from consulate or tourism office or from most airlines serving Mexico upon arrival. Embassy of Mexico, 202-728-1600, www.embassyofmexico.org

Micronesia, Federated States of: Includes Chuuk, Kosrae, Pohnpei, and Yap. Passport (must be valid for at least 120 days beyond the date of departure), birth certificate, or FSM entry permit required. Sufficient funds and onward/return ticket required. Departure fee for Chuuk, Kosrae, and Pohnpei is $10; for Yap, $5. Health certificate may be required if traveling from infected area. HIV test required if staying over 90 days. Embassy of the Federated States of Micronesia, 202-223-4383, www.fsmembassydc.org

Monaco: Passport required. Visa not required for stay up to 90 days. Consulate General of Monaco, 212-286-0500, www.monaco-consulate.com

Mongolia: Passport required. Visa not required for tourist and private business stays of less than 90 days. Tourist/business travelers may be asked to show letter of invitation or a letter from a Mongolian company and onward/return ticket. Visitors planning to stay for more than 1 month are required to register with the Immigration, Naturalization, and Foreign Citizens Agency within 7 days of arrival. Embassy of Mongolia, 202-333-7117, www.mongolianembassy.us

Morocco: Passport required. Visa not required for stays of up to 3 months. Embassy of Morocco, 202-462-7980, http://moroccoembassy.com

Mozambique: Passport and visa required. Visa must be obtained in advance, or tourist visa can be obtained at some borders in Mozambique. Embassy of the Republic of Mozambique, 202-293-7146, www.mozambiqueembassy.com; New York residents: Mozambique Consulate, 212-644-5965

Namibia: Passport, onward/return ticket, and proof of sufficient funds required. Visa not required for tourist stay of up to 90 days. Embassy of Namibia, 202-986-0540, www.namibiaembassyusa.org

Nepal: Passport with minimum validity of 6 months and visa required, visa extendable. Tourist visas can be purchased upon arrival at Tribhuvan International Airport in Kathmandu and at all other ports of entry. Royal Nepalese Embassy, 202-667-4550, www.nepalembassyusa.org

Netherlands: Passport required. Visa not required for tourist/business visit of up to 90 days. Tourists may be asked to show onward/return ticket, proof of sufficient funds, health insurance coverage, and that there is adequate housing available for length of stay. Royal Netherlands Embassy, 202-244-5300, www.netherlands-embassy.org

Netherlands Antilles: Islands include Bonaire, Curaçao, Saba, St. Eustatius, and St. Martin. Passport or proof of US citizenship (i.e., certified birth certificate or voter registration card with photo ID) required. Visa not required for tourist/business visit of up to 90 days. Departure tax $20 when leaving Bonaire, $20 in Curaçao, $25 in St. Eustatius, $20 in St. Martin. Royal Netherlands Embassy, 202-244-5300, www.netherlands-embassy.org

New Zealand: Passport required. Visa not required for tourist/business visits or consultations stay of up to 3 months. Must have onward/return ticket, visa for next destination, and proof of sufficient funds. Embassy of New Zealand, 202-328-4800, www.nzembassy.com/usa

Nicaragua: Valid passport, onward/return ticket, proof of sufficient funds, and entry fee required for stay of up to 30 days. A visa is not required for US citizens; however, a tourist card must be purchased ($5) upon arrival. Airport departure tax of $32. Consulate of Nicaragua, 202-939-6570

Nigeria: Passport with minimum validity of 6 months and visa required. Tourists must submit copies of hotel reservations. Embassy of the Republic of Nigeria, 202-986-8400, www.nigeriaembassyusa.org

Norway: Passport required. Visa not required for stay of up to 90 days. Royal Norwegian Embassy, 202-333-6000, www.norway.org

Oman: Passport with minimum validity of 6 months and visa required. Proof of sufficient funds and proof of onward/return ticket, though not required, are strongly recommended. Proof of yellow fever immunization required if entering from infected area. Embassy of the Sultanate of Oman, 202-387-1980

Pakistan: Passport and visa required. Obtain visa before arrival. Consular Section of the Embassy of Pakistan, 202-243-6500, www.pakistan-embassy.org

Panama: Passport or proof of US citizenship and photo ID plus visa and tourist card required. Also proof of sufficient funds and onward/return ticket. Visa and tourist card valid for 30 days. Embassy of Panama, 202-483-1407, www.embassyofpanama.org

Papua New Guinea: Passport, visa, onward/return ticket, and proof of sufficient funds required. Tourist/business visas for a stay of up to 60 days (extendable). Embassy of Papua New Guinea, 202-745-3680, www.pngembassy.org

Paraguay: Passport and visa are required. Paraguayan Embassy, 202-483-6960, www.embaparusa.gov.py

Peru: Passport required. Visa not required for tourist stay of up to 90 days, extendable after arrival; onward/return ticket required. Embassy of Peru, 202-833-9860, www.peruvianembassy.us

Philippines: Passport and onward/return ticket required. For entry through all international ports of entry, visa not required for transit/tourist stay of up to 21 days. A passenger service charge of $11 must be paid when departing the country from international airports. Embassy of the Philippines, 202-467-9300, www.philippineembassy-usa.org

Poland: Passport and proof of sufficient funds required. Visa not required for tourist/business stay of up to 90 days. Visitors must register at a hotel or with local authorities within 48 hours after arrival. Embassy of the Republic of Poland, 202-234-3800, www.polandembassy.org

Portugal: Includes travel to the Azores and Madeira Islands. Passport required. Visa not required for visit up to 90 days. Embassy of Portugal, 202-328-8610, www.portugalemb.org

Romania: Passport with minimum validity of 6 months after trip required. Visa not required for a stay of up to 90 days. Embassy of Romania, 202-332-4846, www.roembus.org

Russia: Passport and visa required. Tourist visa valid for 30 days. HIV test certificate required for anyone staying over 3 months. Consular Section of the Embassy of Russia, 202-298-5700,www.russianembassy.org

Rwanda: Passport required. Visa not required for stay of up to 90 days. Yellow fever immunization required. Departure tax is $20. Embassy of the Republic of Rwanda, 202-232-2882, www.rwandaembassy.org

Saint Lucia: Passport or proof of US citizenship, photo ID, and onward/return ticket required for stay of up to 6 months. Embassy of Saint Lucia, 202-364-6792

Saint Vincent and the Grenadines: Proof of US citizenship, a certified US birth certificate, ID photo, and onward/return ticket and/or proof of sufficient funds required for tourist stay of up to 6 months. Embassy of Saint Vincent and the Grenadines, 202-364-6730, www.embsvg.com

Samoa: Passport and onward/return ticket required. Visa not required for stay of up to 60 days. Departure tax is $30. Independent State of Samoa Embassy, 212-599-6196

San Marino: Passport required. Visa not required for tourist stay of up to 90 days. Honorary Consulate of the Republic of San Marino, 202-223-3517

Saudi Arabia: Passport and visa required. Individual tourist visas are not available for travel to Saudi Arabia. Visitors must obtain meningitis vaccination prior to arrival. Royal Embassy of Saudi Arabia, 202-342-3800, www.saudiembassy.net

Senegal: Passport and onward/return ticket required. Visa not needed for stay of up to 90 days. Senegalese health officials may request a WHO vaccination card with current yellow fever and cholera vaccinations if the traveler is arriving from an endemic area. Embassy of the Republic of Senegal, 202-234-0540, www.senegal-tourism.com

Sierra Leone: Passport and visa required. Proof of yellow fever and cholera vaccination required. Embassy of Sierra Leone, 202-939-9261, www.embassyofsierraleone.org

Singapore: Passport with minimum validity of 6 months, proof of sufficient funds for stay, and onward/return ticket required. Visa not required for tourist/business stays, length determined at the discretion of immigration officer, normally 30 days. Embassy of Singapore, 202-537-3100, www.mfa.gov.sg/washington

Slovak Republic: Passport and proof of sufficient health insurance coverage and funds required. Visa not required for business/tourist stay of up to 90 days. Embassy of the Slovak Republic, 202-237-1054, www.slovakembassy-us.org

Slovenia: Passport required. Visa not required for tourist/business stay of up to 90 days. Embassy of the Republic of Slovenia, 202-667-5363, www.washington.embassy.si

Somalia: Passport required. Consulate of the Somali Democratic Republic in New York, 212-688-9410

South Africa: Passport, onward/return ticket, and proof of sufficient funds required. Tourist or business visa not required for stay of up to 90 days. Embassy of South Africa's Consular Office, 202-232-4400, www.saembassy.org

Spain: Passport required. Visa not required for tourist/business stay of up to 90 days. Embassy of Spain, 202-452-0100, www.spainemb.org

Sri Lanka: Passport, onward/return ticket, and proof of sufficient funds required. Tourist visa not required for stay of up to 30 days (extendable in Sri Lanka). Embassy of Sri Lanka, 202-483-4025, www.slembassyusa.org

Sudan: Passport and visa required. Transit visa valid for up to 7 days. Tourist/business visa required for single-entry visit lasting 8 days up to 3 months. Yellow fever and cholera vaccinations are recommended. Embassy of the Republic of Sudan, 202-338-8565, www.sudanembassy.org

Swaziland: Passport required. Visa not required for stay of up to 60 days. Visitors must report to immigration authorities or police station within 48 hours, unless lodging in a hotel. Embassy of the Kingdom of Swaziland, 202-362-6683

Sweden: Passport required. Visa not required for stay of up to 90 days. Embassy of Sweden, 202-467-2600, www.swedenny.com

Switzerland: Passport required (with minimum validity of 3 months after leaving country). Visa not required for tourism/study stay of less than 90 days. Embassy of Switzerland, 202-745-7900, www.swissemb.org

Syria: Passport and visa required. Embassy of the Syrian Arab Republic, 202-232-6313, www.syrianembassy.us

Taiwan: Passport, onward/return ticket, and valid visa for next destination, if applicable, required. Visa not required for stay of up to 30 days; no extensions if traveling on the visa waiver program. Taipei Economic and Cultural Representative Office, 202-895-1800, www.taipei.org or www.boca.gov.tw

Tanzania: Passport and visa required. Embassy of Tanzania, 202-939-6125, www.tanzaniaembassy-us.org

Thailand: Passport required. Visa not required for stay of up to 30 days. Royal Thai Embassy, 202-944-3600, www.thaiembdc.org

Tonga: Passport and onward/return ticket required. Visa not required for stay of up to 30 days. HIV testing required for stays exceeding 6 months. Tonga collects a departure tax. Consulate General of Tonga, 415-781-0365

Trinidad and Tobago: Passport and onward/return ticket required. Visa not required for tourist/business stay of up to 90 days. Embassy of Trinidad and Tobago, 202-467-6490

Tunisia: Passport and onward/return ticket required. Visa not required for tourist/business stay of up to 4 months. Embassy of Tunisia, 202-862-1850, www.tunisiaembassy.org

Turkey: Passport and visa required. Visa can be obtained at Turkish border crossing points for tourist/business visits of up to 3 months or through a Turkish consular office in the United States. Consular Office of the Embassy of the Republic of Turkey, 202-612-6700, www.turkishembassy.org

Uganda: Valid passport and visa required. Visa should be obtained in advance. Yellow fever and cholera vaccination certificate required. Embassy of the Republic of Uganda, 202-726-7100, www.ugandaembassy.com

Ukraine: Passport required. Visa not required for tourist/business/private stay of up to 90 days. Consular Office of the Embassy of Ukraine, 202-333-0606, www.mfa.gov.ua/usa/en

United Arab Emirates: Passport required. Visa and fee not required for stay of up to 30 days. Embassy of the United Arab Emirates, 202-243-2400, www.uae-embassy.org

United Kingdom: Includes England, Northern Ireland, Scotland, and Wales. Passport required. Visa not required for stay of up to 6 months. 202-588-7800, www.britainusa.com/embassy

Uruguay: Passport required. Visa not required for tourist/business stay of up to 90 days. Embassy of Uruguay, 202-331-1313, www.uruwashi.org

Uzbekistan: Passport and visa required. Invitation letter from a sponsoring organization or individual required. Consular Section of the Embassy of the Republic of Uzbekistan, 202-887-5300, www.uzbekistan.org

Venezuela: Passport, onward/return ticket, and proof of sufficient funds required. Visa not required for stay of up to 90 days. Embassy of Venezuela, 202-342-2214, www.embavenez-us.org

Vietnam: Passport and visa required. Embassy of Vietnam, 202-861-0737, www.vietnamembassy-usa.org

Virgin Islands, British: Islands include Anegarda, Jost van Dyke, Tortola, and Virgin Gorda. Proof of US citizenship, photo ID, onward/return ticket, and sufficient funds required for tourist stay of up to 6 months. British Embassy, 202-588-7800, www.britain-info.org

West Indies, British: Islands include Anguilla, Montserrat, Cayman Islands, Turks and Caicos. Passport, onward/return ticket, and sufficient funds required for tourist stay of up to 3 months. British Embassy, 202-588-7800, www.britishembassy.ie

West Indies, French: Islands include Guadeloupe, Isles des Saintes, La Desirade, Marie Galante, St. Barthelemy, St. Martin, and Martinique: Passport required. Visa not required for tourist/business stay of up to 90 days. Embassy of France, 202-944-6195, www.info-france-usa.org

Yemen, Republic of: Passport and visa required. Prior to visiting Yemen, it is necessary to visit a medical clinic. Embassy of the Republic of Yemen, 202-965-4760, www.yemenembassy.org

Zambia: Passport and visa required. Embassy of the Republic of Zambia, 202-265-9717, www.zambiaembassy.org

Zimbabwe: Passport, visa, onward/return ticket, and proof of sufficient funds required for stay of up to 6 months. Visa issued upon arrival. Antimalarial pills are recommended. $30 exit fee paid at airport. Embassy of Zimbabwe, 202-332-7100, www.zimbabwe-embassy.us

CHAPTER 12

❝ There is no such uncertainty as a sure thing. ❞

—ROBERT BURNS

How much do you know about travel insurance? How much do you *want* to know? If you're like most travelers, the sad answer to both questions is: not much. But what you don't know—or don't want to know—can definitely hurt you.

A couple on an Alaskan cruise got off the ship when it pulled into Juneau. As they walked near the ship, they approached a person in a moose costume. Thinking it was a cute animal character out to greet cruise ship passengers, they asked to have a photo taken with the moose and were held up at gunpoint instead.

Two friends were driving in a rental car through Hawaii. As they were enjoying the scenery, a huge wild pig suddenly ran in front of the car. The automobile was totaled.

And of course there is always the seasonal story of the honeymooning couple on a Caribbean island, stranded by a hurricane that destroyed their hotel.

In each of these scenarios, travel insurance saved the day.

Having said that, consider this: Only about 30 percent of Americans purchase travel insurance, which is a drastic increase since 9/11, when less than 10 percent of travelers were insured. Today, we spend about $1.3 billion on different—and differing—travel insurance policies. Some of these policies presumably offer peace of mind. Others are actually meaningful. It's a confusing world to navigate—and if you're not careful, even those of you with the best of intentions about being responsible travelers will make foolish insurance investments.

Top 10 Reasons for Travel Insurance

Since I'm an advocate of purchasing travel insurance, people are always coming up to me asking, Why? Which is why I've come up with my list of the top 10 situations in which travel insurance can come in handy.

! Your flight has been canceled.

! Your bags are lost and your medication is in them. You need to have an emergency prescription filled.

! Your passport and wallet are stolen, and you need emergency cash and a replacement passport.

! You're involved in an accident, and adequate medical treatment is not available. You need medical evacuation.

! You need to cancel your trip due to illness.

! Your cruise line, airline, or tour operator goes bankrupt. You need to have your nonrefundable expenses covered and to get to your destination.

! You have a medical emergency in a foreign country.

! A terrorist incident occurs in the city where you're planning to visit, and you want to cancel your trip.

! A hurricane forces you to evacuate your resort, hotel, or cruise ship.

! And finally? It's simply worth the extra few dollars to ensure your peace of mind. Trust me, it will make the days leading up to your trip and throughout your travels a little less stressful.

Even if you think you're familiar with the basic concept of travel insurance, an overwhelming majority of travelers do not know the important distinctions between flight insurance, trip cancellation insurance, travel health insurance, baggage coverage, and, perhaps most important, medical evacuation insurance.

Here's a breakdown of travel insurance and some stuff that you may not know.

First, some definitions of terms.

Insurance Terms Defined

Flight insurance. Many of us grew up noticing those insurance kiosks at airports. They offered to pay out big bucks if you bought the insurance, the plane crashed, and you were on it. Advice: This is not necessary. In fact, if you annualized the premium, it's the most expensive kind of travel insurance you can buy and probably the least necessary.

Trip cancellation and interruption insurance. This is a biggie. The key here is price point. If you're flying on a $59 Southwest Airlines ticket from Burbank to Las Vegas, you have an incredibly small investment to protect. You shouldn't buy trip cancellation and interruption insurance. A $15,000 once-in-a-lifetime cruise vacation? Yes. If you get sick or miss your trip or if the travel provider (airline, cruise line, bus transfer company) goes out of business, you're not left high and dry. You're covered. But do not buy this insurance from the individual travel provider, meaning don't buy your cruise trip insurance from the cruise ship company. Why? If that company goes out of business, chances are so does their insurance.

Health care insurance. This is perhaps the most confusing area. Most people think they are covered if they already have existing health care insurance. Within the United States, that's true. Outside the United States, however, is a big *if*. And in some cases, your insurance won't even cover you if you're traveling on a foreign-flagged vessel. This is a huge red flag, since most cruise ships, even those cruising US waters, are not flagged in the United States. And then there's another reason for getting this coverage: If you're in a foreign country, particularly a developing country, many hospitals will admit you without caring about coverage, but they won't let you leave until you pay. Travel insurance can help facilitate payment and act as an advocate so that you're not overcharged because you're an American.

Baggage insurance. Many trip cancellation and interruption policies also provide coverage for lost, damaged, delayed, or stolen bags. And this is especially necessary if you're flying overseas and checking bags. Why?

Because of a nasty little thing called the Warsaw Convention. The old Warsaw Convention limits liability to approximately $9.07 per pound for checked baggage and $400 per passenger for unchecked baggage. Do the math. If you're allowed only 44 pounds of baggage as a coach passenger, you're not getting a fat check.

If you're just flying between US cities, you might think you have no need for a larger trip cancellation and interruption policy because you are simply covered by the airlines' published limits of liability when it comes to lost, stolen, delayed, or damaged bags. Think again.

On the surface at least, there appears to be good news. As of February 28, 2007, US airlines' liability for lost or damaged luggage increased to $3,000 per passenger from the previous limit of $2,800. According to the Department of Transportation, the change was made to address increases in the consumer price index. Small air taxis and commuter air carriers are exempt from the rule. Sounds good, right? Well, let's talk about that limit in realistic terms: There's an entire list of excluded items not covered (jewels, furs, negotiable financial documents, et al.), and your compensation is all based on depreciated value. I would almost bet that *no one* has ever received the full amount (short of going to small-claims court).

But there *is* a little-known insurance provision you've probably never heard about. It applies to domestic US flights. And the airlines aren't exactly rushing to tell you about it. In fact, not one single airline even advertises this provision, even though it's available to every single passenger. It's something called **excess valuation**.

When you get to the airport, ask the counter agent for this little-known option. The counter agent will generally not be in a good mood when you ask for excess valuation, since it involves some paperwork. But it provides up to $5,000 additional coverage, at a rate of about $1 per $100 in value. If you purchase excess valuation, you will be asked to describe the contents of the bag. It's well worth it if the airline does lose your bags.

Nonrefundable insurance. Some policies also offer straight coverage if you buy the nonrefundable airline ticket and then can't use it and don't want to be hit with the minimum $100 change fee. This runs about $13 per $100 of coverage. It's an expensive premium but still worth it if you really think you might have to change your trip once you purchase your ticket.

In addition to trip cancellation and interruption, the more comprehensive travel insurance plans available today may also cover:

- Emergency medical expenses

- Emergency medical transportation, when ordered by a doctor, to the nearest adequate medical facility

- Reimbursement for accommodations and expenses incurred due to travel delays; reimbursement for the purchase of essential items if baggage is delayed

- Coverage against lost, stolen, or damaged baggage

Travel insurance plans typically fall into two categories.

- Per trip packaged plans are designed for travelers going on a single trip. This is the more popular choice among travelers.

- Annual plans provide coverage for multiple trips throughout the year.

The cost of travel insurance is usually based on your age and the cost of your trip. As a general rule, one can estimate the cost at 5 to 7 percent of the trip's total cost.

Tips on Travel Insurance

- While many cruise passengers buy trip insurance in case of emergencies, that insurance doesn't always offer the protection they need. For instance, some cruise ship companies may not be liable for injuries suffered during offshore excursions that are not affiliated with the cruise. This is one of the major reasons why you should buy travel insurance from a third party and not from the tour operator itself.

- Compare the cost of the trip versus the cost of the policy. If you just bought a $200 airline ticket, is that worth covering? If you paid for it with a credit card and the airline ceases to operate before your flight, you're already covered—under federal credit laws—by your own credit card company, since you bought or contracted for a service that you didn't get.

- Look for a policy with a travel insurer that is not only independent from your tour operator but also licensed by your state. Many cruise lines and tour operators offer insurance, often at lower premiums than those charged by outside insurers. But if the cruise line or tour company goes out of business, there may not be money to cover your claim.

- If flight or cruise delays make you want to cancel, you may be out of luck. Read the fine print; with some policies, more than half of your vacation has to be delayed before you can cancel and be covered.

And last but not least, remember full disclosure. If you have a preexisting medical condition and don't list it on your policy application, your entire claim could be denied, even if your medical condition wasn't a factor in the cancellation.

Travel Insurance and Terrorism

Traditionally, this falls under "trip cancellation interruption" (TCI) insurance. But terrorism may be covered under these policies. Coverages are still evolving, and it really gets down to a definition of terms. For example, many policies refer to an "incident" or "outbreak." And many of the policies didn't cover travelers stranded after the August 10, 2006, events in London, because there was no terrorist incident or outbreak under their definition. Bottom line: For the moment, terrorist attacks are not always covered by these policies. However, some insurance policies, like one from Travel Safe, allow you to cancel a trip for any reason. And the 2006 events in London certainly were covered under that policy. But buyer beware: The cost for these policies generally ranges 40 percent higher than normal TCI policies. And almost no travel insurance policies cover your general fear or state of mind.

Terrorism Tips

! Read the policy wording carefully. If war breaks out or there is a terrorist act, are there clauses that essentially void your policy? Very few policies cover trip cancellation for reasons of any kind. Most policies now include "force majeure" clauses. For example, most policies now still cover trip cancellation if the US State Department issues a travel warning. Also, many policies cover you for your trip only if an act of terrorism occurs in the specific country you're traveling to or from. And they set limits on how close an attack has to be to your destination before it goes into effect. You generally must buy the policy before violence erupts to be covered. But almost all policies will not cover any losses caused by war or threat of war.

! Call and talk to the agency personally. Ask them the specific questions you have before your trip to put your mind at ease. Some insurance plans cover you only if a travel company formally files for bankruptcy protection. (Not every policy covers every bankruptcy.) Other policies leave it up to the US State Department, law enforcement agencies, or news media outlets—not you—to define what constitutes a terrorist attack, foreign or domestic.

❗ Understand that most insurance policies won't cover last-minute anxiety. After the September 11 attacks, for example, AIG Travel Guard reimbursed customers who canceled trips because they were afraid to fly. While Travel Guard felt it was the right thing to do, it's unlikely the insurer will do it again. It was the costliest event in the history of that company.

Natural Disasters

The 2005 hurricane season, which ran from June 1 through November 30, made travelers think long and hard about purchasing travel insurance. That season was the most active Atlantic tropical storm season on record, with 28 named storms and 15 hurricanes.

The frequency and severity of hurricanes in 2005 were certainly felt by the travel insurance industry. According to AIG Travel Guard, the combined claims that resulted from hurricanes Katrina and Wilma surpassed those resulting from 9/11—the costliest event in the history of the travel insurance industry.

While the most recent hurricane seasons haven't been as active as 2005, that doesn't mean you shouldn't consider travel insurance before you go. If you're headed to a hurricane-prone region like the Caribbean or Florida, travel insurance seems like a sensible purchase. But you must remember that timing is everything. So is full disclosure.

You must buy your policy before the National Weather Service (www.nws.noaa.gov) actually names a storm.

❗ A hurricane is defined/validated by the National Hurricane Center, typically a tropical cyclone in which the maximum sustained surface wind is 74 mph (64 knots) or greater.

❗ Insurers will pay only when travel gets delayed or canceled due to severe weather. If the airlines and the cruise ships are operating, you can either go on the vacation or lose your money. When a port is expecting a rough storm, cruise lines often substitute a different port where the weather is more promising. If the cruise takes place—even if the new ports are second rate—the insurance company doesn't owe you a dime. Plead with the cruise line instead; it might give out vouchers for future cruises.

! Benefits don't kick in the moment your flight is delayed. Instead, there's a waiting period—typically 5 to 12 hours, depending on the policy—before you can book a hotel for the night and expect to get reimbursed.

! If flight or cruise delays make you want to cancel, you may be out of luck. Read the fine print; with some policies, more than half of your vacation has to be delayed before you can cancel and be covered.

! You cannot buy your travel insurance after a hurricane has been named. As I said earlier, insurance must be purchased 24 hours prior to when the hurricane is named. Once the hurricane has been named, Trip Cancellation and Interruption losses resulting from the hurricane are excluded from the coverage of the policy.

! If you choose to cancel a trip based on what you *think* might happen, you're not going to be covered. So if you cancel your trip because you are worried that a named hurricane might affect your destination, you're out of luck.

! Suppose your hotel has been destroyed in a hurricane. If flights are running on your departure date, insurance might not do you any good. One exception is from Travel Guard, which words its policy more broadly than others and ponies up if the destination is ruined.

Following are a few scenarios of how travel insurance and travel assistance can help.

! A hurricane hits before trip departure, forcing trip cancellation. Travel insurance will provide reimbursement for nonrefundable expenses, up to the limit of coverage purchased.

! Hurricane forces a traveler to evacuate during vacation. All trip expenses will be covered as well.

! Don't go hungry or sleep in the airport. Travel insurance companies will often cover charges for food purchases, hotels, and alternate means of transportation if a traveler's flight is canceled or delayed.

Hurricane Guarantees

After the disastrous effects of the 2005 hurricane season, some hotels and resorts kicked in to keep the travelers coming. "Hurricane guarantees" offered

> In Vietnam, there are no streetlights, crosswalks, or stop signs, and motorbikes have the right of way. Local etiquette dictates that you walk straight ahead without pausing or changing direction and let the bikes maneuver around you.

travelers refunds and rain checks if their trips were cut short or canceled by a hurricane, as determined by the National Hurricane Center. Here are just a few of the resorts that have made the effort to help out travelers during the hurricane season. Keep in mind that these policies may have very specific limitations, such as the airport must be completely shut down—specific airlines that are delayed or canceled may not count toward this. Check in advance to make sure that you are covered in this kind of situation.

Sixteen resorts in Bermuda guarantee that if a storm is predicted to pass within 200 miles of the island, guests will be able to cancel their reservations without penalty within 5 days. If a hurricane strikes during a stay, the room, food, and beverages are provided for free until normal operations can resume. If the hotel is damaged and unable to resume normal operations, guests have a year from the property's reopening to resume their vacation. For more information on participating resorts, visit www.bermudatourism.com.

The Westin Casuarina Resort and Spa Grand Cayman offers to replace the guest's vacation for the entire duration of the reservation. If there's a category 3 or higher hurricane, the hotel will waive any early-departure fees. If a guest can't travel to the resort because the airport or resort is closed, he will be given the option of a full refund or a one-room-category upgrade.

Other hotels involved with hurricane guarantees are the Reef Resort Cayman Island, 16 Marriott resorts in nine Caribbean and Mexican beach sites, the Westin Rio Mar Beach Golf Resort & Spa, and the Westin and Sheraton Grand Bahama Island Our Lucaya Resort.

Some of the guarantee restrictions are reasonable. Others are laughable. Some resorts, while agreeing to give you a replacement vacation in the event of a hurricane, also insert: "blackout dates apply." You need to negotiate these potential blackout dates up front—or there's little point to the guarantee.

One additional important note: Just because the hotel or resort or destination itself offered hurricane guarantees in previous years does not mean it will offer them in the year when you're ready to travel. You need to ask up front—before you book your trip—and get the guarantee in writing from the particular travel provider or destination.

Medical Evacuation

Even if you are covered for basic emergency care overseas (again, a big *if*), in almost all cases your current health insurance does *not* cover to evacuate you and repatriate you back to the United States. Medical evacuation can easily cost $10,000 and up (emphasis on the word *up*), depending on your location and medical condition. Other health insurance plans may reimburse medical evacuation costs on a case-by-case basis but generally cover the full cost of a medical evacuation to the United States only when an injury or illness threatens the life of an insured person.

This is where "medical evacuation and repatriation" insurance comes into play. I believe this is essential for anyone who travels. It's an insurance program (usually an annual premium, not often purchased on a per trip basis), and here's how it works: If you get sick or injured overseas, the policy will get you treated, stabilized, and flown back to the United States. There are a number of good companies that provide this plan, two of which are Travel Guard and MedJet Assist. The annual premium is about $300, and it's the card you hope you never have to use. After the events of September 11, MedJet reported that its membership increased 23 percent to 25 percent per year.

One important caveat is to always read the fine print. With Travel Guard and MedJet Assist, these policies provide that they will get you initially treated and stabilized and then send a medically equipped and staffed jet to fly you to the doctor and medical facility of *your* choice. This is crucial. Outside of Travel Guard and MedJet Assist, many other companies that offer this insurance will fly you to the doctor and medical facility of *their* choice. Do you really want to end up in a lowest-bidder auction for your care? You do *not* want to find yourself at a bad HMO in Rwanda.

Medical evacuation can come in handy on cruises, which are short-term trips that may stop in ports with lower medical standards. And unlike basic travel insurance, these medical evacuation policies do not have terrorism exclusions (i.e., if the US State Department issues a travel advisory in a particular country, your traditional insurance may be void).

 Activities Coverage

You can also purchase extra insurance for golf travel, which protects against equipment loss and delay. There is additional adventure and extreme sports travel insurance, and even professional sporting event coverage, which provides protection where most basic insurance doesn't.

There are some unusual situations that may arise as well: In one case, a man on a dogsled expedition across the Arctic got stuck in a crevice. He contacted MedJet from a satellite phone. A companion got him to a weather station near Eureka, the northernmost outpost, where a MedJet Canadian affiliate airlifted him out.

In another, even more dramatic situation, two men from Nashville and a videographer from Canada were sheep hunting on a mountain in Kyrgyzstan. A snowstorm caught them, and the government sent a helicopter to rescue them. However, the helicopter was overloaded, and sensing that something was about to go wrong, the three men jumped out of the helicopter while it was still 40 feet in the air—just moments before it crashed. The videographer got to a mountain station and called MedJet. An avalanche was blocking the way, and it took MedJet 3 days to reach them, after hiring 50 to 60 locals to shovel the runway. The three guys (who were in stable condition) were flown for medical care. Now that's customer service.

What May Already Be Covered

There is one major reason *not* to get travel insurance. And that is, if you are already covered.

Credit Card Coverage

If you book your trip on a credit card, you may already be covered in many cases. But more often than not, your basic credit card coverage will be limited to flight accident insurance, "secondary" rental car insurance, or limited baggage insurance. Be sure to read your card's terms and conditions or call your credit card provider's toll-free line for guidance.

For example, according to American Express, even if you have a basic card, you automatically receive at no cost:

BENEFITS	BASIC	PLATINUM	CENTURION
Global Assist Hotline—24/7 emergency service to local medical and legal providers and information on passports, visas, etc.	Yes	Yes	Yes
Travel Accident Insurance—provides accidental death and dismemberment coverage for card members and dependents while traveling on a plane, train, ship, or bus	Yes	Yes	Yes

BENEFITS	BASIC	PLATINUM	CENTURION
Assured Reservations—ensures the booked room will be held for late arrivals up to checkout time the next day	Yes	Yes	Yes
Car Rental Loss and Damage Insurance— secondary coverage for damage to or theft of a rental car; covers rental cars with an original manufacturer's suggested retail price not exceeding $50,000 (not available in Australia, Ireland, Israel, Italy, Jamaica, and New Zealand)	Yes	Yes	Yes
Secondary car insurance coverage for damage to or theft of personal property, excess medical expense coverage, and accidental death and dismemberment benefits	No	Yes	Yes
Emergency medical transportation assistance	No	Yes	Yes
Baggage Insurance Plan—provides coverage for loss and damage to carry-on baggage up to $1,250 at no extra cost and provides secondary coverage for checked baggage up to $500 (in excess of the carrier's coverage)	Yes	Yes	Yes

According to Visa, its holders also have:

BENEFITS	VISA CLASSIC	VISA SECURED	VISA GOLD	VISA PLATINUM	VISA SIGNATURE
Auto Rental Collision Damage Waiver	Yes	Yes	Yes	Yes	Yes
Cardholder Inquiry Service	Yes	Yes	Yes	Yes	Yes
Emergency Cash Disbursement and Card Replacement	Yes	Yes	Yes	Yes	Yes
Lost/Stolen Card Reporting	Yes	Yes	Yes	Yes	Yes
Zero Liability	Yes	Yes	Yes	Yes	Yes

(continued)

Credit Card Coverage—*Continued*

BENEFITS	VISA CLASSIC	VISA SECURED	VISA GOLD	VISA PLATINUM	VISA SIGNATURE
Lost Luggage Reimbursement	Yes	Yes	Yes	Yes	Yes
Purchase Security	No	No	No	No	Yes
Rewards Program	No	No	No	No	Yes
Roadside Dispatch	No	No	No	No	Yes
Travel and Emergency Assistance Services	No	No	No	No	Yes
Travel Accident Insurance	No	No	No	No	Yes
Visa Signature Access	No	No	No	No	Yes
Visa Signature Concierge	No	No	No	No	Yes
Visa Signature Dining	No	No	No	No	Yes
Visa Signature Privileges	No	No	No	No	Yes
Warranty Manager Service	No	No	No	No	Yes
Year-End Summary Statement	No	No	No	No	Yes

But you must always check with your individual card issuer—Visa Signature cardholders, as well as American Express Platinum and Centurion cardholders, have additional benefits. Also, when renting a car, be advised that most credit card rental car "insurance" is known as secondary insurance. The coverage under secondary insurance kicks in only when the policy limits of the primary coverage are exhausted. If you don't have primary insurance, secondary insurance is meaningless. Always check with your own auto insurance company first to determine if you're already covered if you rent a car—as well as the dollar liability and collision limits.

Health Care

More often than not, your standard health insurance is still officially in effect when you travel. However, in many companies, this only applies to "customary and reasonable" hospital costs, so major surgery and emergency services beyond basic attempts at stabilization may be out. Some major providers, such as Aetna and Cigna, will cover your medical emergency overseas, but as always, there are plenty of caveats. For one thing, the definition of "emergency" is up for grabs. If it's believed that your condition could lead to permanent injury or death, then the emergency may be covered—that means something like severe chest pains or a broken leg. But if you contract a major rash or a severe flu, you probably won't be covered.

If you require serious medical attention and you're not in a location where that can happen, few insurance policies will pay for your medical evacuation back to the United States. Some companies may not cover you at all if you're over 100 miles away from home. And here's a particularly painful exclusion found on some health insurance policies—you may not be covered if you're cruising on a foreign flagged ship (and most cruise ships do not fly the US flag) or if you're a passenger on a foreign-based international airline.

Medicare members should be aware that their insurance generally does not apply outside the United States and its territories. There are only three exceptions: One, which covers travelers, is for medical emergencies arising in Canada for those who can document that they are traveling the most direct route between the continental United States and Alaska; second is when an emergency occurs and a Canadian or Mexican hospital is closer than any in the United States; and third, when someone's home is closer to a Canadian or Mexican hospital than to one in the United States.

If you're in a foreign country, particularly a developing country, many hospitals will admit you without caring about coverage, but they won't let you leave until you pay. Travel insurance companies can help facilitate payment and act as an advocate on your behalf so that you're not overcharged because you're an American.

One last tip: If you're concerned about finding a qualified doctor while traveling, ask your medical and/or travel insurer for a list of prescreened doctors and hospitals that meet US standards.

▽ Resources

Compare national plans, based on what they cost, what they cover and payouts at **www.insuremytrip.com.**

You can find comparisons and user testimonials at **www.tripinsurancestore. com.** You can also sign up for a plan through the site.

MedJet Assist: This annual membership plan provides prepaid air ambulance transportation, including worldwide evacuation and repatriation to the member's hometown hospital. 800-527-7478, www.medjetassist.com

Air Ambulance Card: A prepaid air ambulance flies members to the US hospital of their choice if they are hospitalized more than 150 miles from home; $195 per year for individuals and $295 per year for families. www. airambulancecard.com

Travel Guard International: 800-826-4919, www.travelguard.com

Access America: 800-729-6021, www.accessamerica.com

Travelex Insurance Services: 800-228-9792, www.travelex-insurance.com

International Medical Group: 800-628-4664, www.imglobal.com

HTH Worldwide: 888-243-2358, www.highwaytohealth.com

Travel Insured International: 800-243-3174, www.travelinsured.com

Global Travel Insurance: 800-232-9415, www.globaltravelinsurance.com

CHAPTER 13

Cell Phones

" Technology improves things so fast that by the time we can afford
the best, there's something better. "

—ANONYMOUS

I am always surprised—okay, if truth be told, I'm usually shocked—when I
open up my cell phone when traveling abroad and find out that it works.
Then comes the, uh, unpleasantness—when I get my bill in the mail. The
good news is that cell phone technology is getting better on an almost daily
basis. Not only is the technology improving, but competition for your business is intensifying. Translation: Sky-high roaming rates when you are traveling are beginning to disappear.

First, some background.

The United States has its own digital cellular technology, called Code-
Division Multiple Access (CDMA). But most countries (more than 200, in
fact) use something called Global System for Mobile communications
(GSM). You'll find GSM in all of Europe and throughout Asia, Africa, and
Australia.

The thing about GSM phones is that they're locked into a frequency that matches the area they come from. For example, most GSM phones that are used in Australia, New Zealand, and Europe operate on the 900 and 1800 megahertz (MHz) frequencies. In the United States and Canada, the 1900 MHz frequency is used.

Long story short: If you want to use a cell phone abroad without getting nailed by excess charges, you have some options.

Your Own Phone

If you have a GSM phone, it should be at least "tri-band" or "quad-band," which refers to how many bandwidths your phone is equipped to pick up. You can use a tri-band phone in most GSM countries, and a quad-band phone is universally global.

Companies like T-Mobile and AT&T use GSM, so their phones can be used in hundreds of countries. Verizon and Sprint are CDMA equipment, which means that they can only be used in about 26 countries. You can simply tell your provider that you will be using your cell phone abroad, and the international roaming feature will be added to your account. The catch? Your roaming rates can be as high as $4.99 a minute.

The good news is that you can swap out your SIM (subscriber identity module) card with one that is appropriate to the country that you are visiting. This is a removable "smart card," which is what provides the cellular service, voice mail, and Internet service on your phone. In order to do this, your phone must be "unlocked," so that it will recognize a SIM card from any carrier; a locked phone will recognize only a SIM card from a particular carrier, which is often the case with free or deeply discounted phones from a provider. Even better, you can swap out the card yourself.

You can buy a SIM card—and these are usually available from your cell phone provider—that offers reduced per-minute rates. Best of all, your incoming calls are free. You can purchase prepaid SIM cards from a company like Cellular Abroad or get them in an airport shop, local convenience store, or kiosks in the United States or at your destination. Most of the time, SIM cards come with a certain amount of time—say, 30 minutes—which allows you to make calls for what is usually a low rate (calls from the United Kingdom to the United States, for example, can be as low as 5 cents a minute). If you run out of minutes, you can purchase prepaid time by calling your service or buying another card.

The drawback is that if you're planning on traveling from country to country, you have to buy a new SIM card and prepaid minutes in each. That means you'll have a different phone number each time, which can be a hassle if you're traveling for any long period of time.

Cellular Rentals and Purchases

If you can't swap out your SIM card and you're planning on being in the same country for a few weeks at a time, renting or purchasing an international cell phone is usually a good option. You can rent or purchase a cell phone in the United States before you travel or find a cell phone company in your destination country (they're usually in the airport). Do the math and figure out if purchasing a new phone is a better deal than the weekly or monthly rental rates.

The benefit of renting or purchasing in the United States before you go (rather than in the local country) is that you can have the phone up and running the minute you get off the plane. Also, if you're traveling to a country where English isn't the first language, setting up a phone rental can be a hassle.

Sprint and **Verizon** customers can rent or purchase phones from those providers. Sprint rents a Motorola Razr for $58 for the first week and $70 for 2 weeks, plus $1.29 to $4.99 a minute of airtime. Verizon charges $3.99 a day to rent, plus $1.49 to $4.99 a minute. Verizon also sells three combo CDMA-GSM models, priced from $150 to $600 with a 2-year contract.

Cellular Abroad recently launched a new service with *National Geographic* called the National Geographic Talk Abroad Travel Phone. This phone picks up local services, so you can use it in more than 100 countries. The phone number is based in the United Kingdom and stays the same no matter where you travel.

Cellular Abroad will give you a start-up kit that claims to be easy to use, even for the technologically challenged. The phone is an unlocked quad-band GSM cell phone and battery—just insert the included SIM card. The band switch should be set to "auto," so that the phone can scan for the right frequency when you're traveling from country to country.

Since the phone number is based in the United Kingdom, making calls outside the country will require an international dialing code and a country code (visit www.countrycallingcodes.com). With the purchased phone package, dialing out seems seamless; but with a rental package, the Talk Abroad service will ring you back to complete the connection. For incoming service, callers will have to dial your UK number, regardless of where you are.

A minimum rental is 1 week for about $50, or you can purchase the phone for about $200. Included is English-language voice mail, SMS text messaging, a universal wall charger, an international plug adapter, and unlimited free incoming calls from 65 countries. With the purchase, you also get more than 30 minutes of outgoing talk time.

The per-minute rate varies, based on which zone (there are four) the outgoing or incoming call is coming from and whether you're calling a landline, cell, or another Travel Phone. For example, calling from Zone 1 (including Europe, Saudi Arabia, and Egypt, among others) to a US landline costs $0.90 per minute; calling a US cell phone is $1.25 per minute; and calling another Travel Phone in Zone 1 is $1.25 per minute. Calling from the United States (Zone 4) to a New Zealand landline (Zone 2) is $3.25 per minute, and calling a New Zealand cell phone is $3.50 a minute.

Cellular Abroad also offers satellite phone rentals if you're traveling to a location where an international cell phone can't be used—this can include cruise ships, mountain locations, or countries where there is unreliable or no cellular coverage. Remember that you'll need to be outside for the satellite service to work. www.cellularabroad.com/travelphone

Cellhire has a few different options: Like Cellular Abroad, an international cell phone rental works in more than 170 countries, with a single phone number based in the United Kingdom. As with Cellular Abroad's phone, you'll have to dial the country code if calling outside of the United Kingdom, and callers will have to dial your international number. The phone will automatically scan for the right frequency depending on what country you travel to and will work off whatever is the strongest signal.

Rates for your international cell phone vary based on the country where incoming calls are originating or where you are calling from. For example, calling the United States from the United Kingdom is $1.29 a minute; incoming calls while you're in the United Kingdom are free (since you have a UK number); and calling someone within the United Kingdom is $0.09 a minute. A call from China is $2.29 per minute; a call from China to the United States is $3.09 a minute; and calls within China are $1.29 a minute.

If you're planning on staying in one country for a long period or if you make multiple trips to one country, a local airtime solution may be your best option. Cellhire can set up a local phone number in about 24 countries, including the United Kingdom, Italy, France, Ireland, Argentina, the Netherlands, Australia, Brazil, India, and China. That means that making locals calls in that country are at a low rate, and almost all incoming calls are free from anywhere (certain areas are excluded, such as if you're located outside of New Delhi, India, or outside of Rio de Janeiro, Brazil). Calls to the United States range from $1.29 per minute to $4.64 per minute, depending on where you're located, and local calls within that country range from $0.50 to $2.55 per minute. However, if you take this phone out of the country, expect much higher rates.

Cellhire's Follow Me program allows you to keep your own phone number when you travel out of the country. Since US cell phone numbers can't be forwarded to an international number, the company allocates a toll-free number to you. Callers just need to dial your usual number, which gets forwarded to the Cellhire center; from there, the call is forwarded to your cell phone for a fee, ranging from $0.79 to $2.77 per minute. However, remember that not all US cell phones can be retrofitted for use abroad.

Cellhire also rents BlackBerry units overseas, with a single UK number. The data on your home BlackBerry can be synchronized with the rented version, so that your e-mails can be rolled over (when you go back home, everything can be rolled back to your original phone). The flat rental rate of $99 per week or $299 per month includes unlimited e-mail and Web browsing. (Cellhire is the only company right now that offers BlackBerry service in Japan.)

You can also rent a satellite phone through Cellhire. Outgoing calls cost $2 to $3 per minute, and all incoming calls are free. Rates are $125 per week or $350 a month. www.cellhire.com

WorldCell also rents out international cell phones, BlackBerrys, and satellite phones.

Their international GSM cell phone gives you one number that is based in Iceland. The first week is $39.95, and each week thereafter is $35, or $5 per day. You can also opt for insurance for $2 per day. Rates in France, Germany, Italy, Spain, and the United Kingdom are $2.29 to $2.49 per minute when calling the United States. Local calls within those countries are $0.99 per minute. Incoming calls are free in Italy and the United Kingdom and run $0.99 per minute in France, Germany, and Italy. In Asia

(China, Hong Kong, Japan, Korea, and Taiwan), calls to the United States range from $2.49 to $3.99 per minute; local calls range from $0.99 to $1.99 per minute. Incoming calls are free in Japan and Korea and cost $1.49 to $1.99 per minute elsewhere. In South America (Argentina, Brazil, and Colombia), calls to the United States are $4.99 to $5.99 per minute. Local calls are $2.59 to $3.99 per minute, and incoming calls are $2.59 to $2.99 per minute.

Satellite phone rentals are $175 for the first week and $60 for each week thereafter, or $9 per day. All incoming calls are free, and per-minute rates range from $0.99 to $10. www.worldcell.com

Thanks to eBay's recent purchase of a service called Skype, many people have now heard of **VoIP** (Voice over Internet Protocol) phones. The concept of VoIP is that your voice carries through the Internet, not through a phone; you can rely on a computer-to-computer or a phone-to-computer conversation at prices that are usually far cheaper than cell phones or calling cards.

You'll need a high-speed Internet connection (bad news for dial-up users). This can be through a cable modem, DSL, or a local area network. Some VoIP services only work over your computer or a special VoIP phone, while other services allow you to use a traditional phone connected to a VoIP adapter. If you use your computer, you will need some software and a microphone and speakers (which may be included in your computer). Special VoIP phones plug directly into your broadband connection and operate largely like a traditional telephone.

Right now, Skype is probably the most popular VoIP service out there, due to the fact that it's cheap and easy to use. All you have to do is download the free software onto your computer (Mac, PC, or Linux-friendly). Then, plug in headphones, microphone, and speakers or a USB phone (a special phone that plugs into a computer's USB port) and you're all set. A global directory can help you locate your friends and family who also use Skype.

It's free to call up other Skype users and includes video calls, group chats, and conference calls with up to nine people. Paid services come in when you want to call up phones, send and receive voice mails, or send SMS text messages. Currently, Skype Unlimited costs $29.95 per year for unlimited calls to any phone in the United States and Canada. You can also choose to pay a per-minute fee for international calls or purchase prepaid Skype credit for a per-minute rate.

Something called SkypeIn allows you to create a regular phone number linked to your Skype account. For example, you can choose to have a SkypeIn number in the Kansas City area. Non-Skype users in Kansas City will be charged local rates (by the local phone company, not Skype), callers from New York will be charged long-distance rates (again, not by Skype)—but both calls will be routed to you when you use your Skype account from anywhere in the world. A 12-month subscription costs $38, or $12 for 3 months. www.skype.com

When you sign up for **Vonage,** the company sends a free adapter that connects any phone to your high-speed Internet connection. Simply connect and use your phone just as you always have—only this time your voice is going over the Internet instead of through an actual telephone line. Packages start at $14.95 a month, which includes 500 minutes for calls in the United States, Canada, and Puerto Rico. Calls to the United Kingdom are $0.04 a minute, and calls to Shanghai are $0.10 a minute. www.vonage.com

Even **Yahoo** now offers free voice services. Yahoo Messenger with Voice is essentially a souped-up version of Yahoo's popular, free instant-messaging service. You get free PC-to-PC calling for people who have Yahoo Messenger, plus free voice mail and call history. However, you can't use Yahoo Messenger to make calls to regular phones from your computer. www.messenger.yahoo.com/feat_voice.php

Microsoft purchased VoIP provider Teleo and began integrating its technology into its **MSN Messenger** program. Microsoft's VoIP service adds voice services on top of a traditional instant-messaging service (MSN Messenger, in this case). As with other VoIP services, simply download the appropriate software for free and you're ready to get started. You get free PC-to-PC calls among people who have MSN Messenger, unlimited file and picture sharing, free text messaging to mobile phones (this may incur a charge for the receiver), and videoconferencing. If you and the person you're connected to via MSN Messenger have Webcams or similar video equipment, you'll be able to have a "Video Conversation" in real time. MSN Messenger is available for Mac users. www.join.msn.com/messenger/overview/

Cell Phones on Planes

Years of conditioning has led travelers to believe that turning on a cell phone or BlackBerry will cause a plane to crash and burn. I've been busting this myth for years. The Federal Aviation Administration (FAA) has been researching this for more than 25 years and has found no specific evidence that radio frequency (RF) interference from electronic devices does anything. However, a 2006 study done by Carnegie Mellon University in Pittsburgh found that on a number of planes they analyzed, if many passengers made cell phone calls at the same time, it might—in rare cases—interfere with the GPS navigational system. But for RF interference with BlackBerrys, Game Boys, and other personal electronic devices? Not likely.

That said, I can't imagine anything more annoying than a planeload of passengers chatting on their cell phones for the entire flight. Despite the Carnegie Mellon study, cell phone usage on airplanes is pretty much inevitable. In fact, for a while there, it was just around the corner: In 2006, the Federal Communications Commission (FCC) auctioned off air-to-ground broadband frequencies, offering the highest bidder a license to operate cellular service and wireless Internet service on airplanes. The highest bidders were a JetBlue subsidiary called LiveTV and a company called AirCell. JetBlue is focusing on "silent" options like text messaging and Internet access on BlackBerrys and PDAs. AirCell had planned to roll out cellular services by 2008, but that may no longer be the case.

The FAA recently announced that it would continue to uphold the ban on using cell phones on airplanes (causing thousands of passengers—including me—to breathe a sigh of relief). According to the FAA, their decision was based on the fact that "insufficient technical information" was available on whether airborne cell phone calls would affect the networks below. The agency told Congress that each airline would have to demonstrate that each and every type of cell phone wouldn't interfere with any type of aircraft.

The FAA also admits that they've been flooded with calls and e-mails from air travelers who steadfastly do not want cell phones on board. And that's not anything new. A 2005 poll sponsored by the Association of Flight Attendants–CWA and the National Consumers League showed that 63 percent of respondents were against allowing cell phones on airplanes; only 21 percent were in support of it. In 2006, a poll by the International Airline Passengers Association found that only half of the respondents would find cell phones useful on a flight and thought that allowing the practice would lead to "air rage."

That doesn't mean the issue is entirely closed. The FAA stated that it might "reconsider this issue in the future if appropriate technical data is available for our review."

> Now that you can rent or buy cell phones abroad, do you know how to call for help? In Australia, the number for police and ambulance is 000. In France, the police are 17, and an ambulance is 15. In Germany, you can call the cops at 110 and get an ambulance at 112.

Even the technology companies are finding it hard to stay in the game. You might remember that not too long ago, Wi-Fi was available on Lufthansa, SAS, Japan Airlines, ANA, Singapore Airlines, China Airlines, Korean Air, Asiana Airlines, and El Al. The service was provided by Connexions by Boeing, which used satellites to get air passengers online for about $30 a flight—but as of 2006, Boeing unplugged its Connexions service, leaving the airlines Wi-Fi free.

You might have also noticed that Airfones, those ridiculously expensive line-of-sight radio phones in the back of each seat, are almost extinct. The idea was to upgrade the system by offering two-way wireless communications in which Verizon customers could have calls from their cell phones forwarded to seat-back Airfones. However, Verizon backed out of the FCC auction quite early and, by the end of 2006, shut down that branch of the business.

But it's not over yet. In 2005, SITA, a Geneva-based company, teamed up with Airbus to form a new company, OnAir. The broadband satellite-enabled Mobile OnAir service supports inflight voice, SMS, and e-mail services over passengers' personal cell phones, as well as other electronic devices like the BlackBerry and Treo.

The OnAir system is designed for use with both Airbus and Boeing aircrafts. In early 2007, Air France was the first airline to introduce the OnAir service. The equipment is being installed as an in-line fit on an Airbus A318 aircraft. The Mobile OnAir installation is expected to have the first large-scale retro-fit on Ryanair's entire fleet of more than two hundred 757 Boeing aircrafts.

And lastly, leave it to Dubai to try to break the mold. Even though cell phone use on planes is currently in limbo, the Dubai-based Emirates is still claiming that it will be the first airline in the world to allow cell phone usage on planes. Using technology from a company called AeroMobile, Emirates expects to roll out the service on its Asian and/or Australian flights, but that's all still dependent on what the regulations are. To save our sanity, the system will allow the cabin crew to control the system at any time, as well as choose operating modes for particular flights—for example, they may disable voice service and select text-only operation mode for overnight flights. Passengers will be instructed and encouraged to switch phones to silent or vibrate mode at all times throughout the flight. And only five calls or fewer can be made at any one time, the same number as for the current in-seat phones used regularly by Emirates' passengers. Whether this latest plan in cell phone technology on airplanes will actually come to fruition remains to be seen.

Cell Phone Etiquette Abroad

It's probably no surprise that, like cuisine and customs, cell phone etiquette differs from culture to culture. So concludes a rather entertaining study conducted from 2001 to 2004 by Dr. Amparo Lasen at the University of Surrey that compared cell phone usage in London, Paris, and Madrid and discovered that there were significant cultural differences among the residents of these three European cities.

According to Lasen's study, mobile users in Paris and Madrid seemed more willing to gab in the streets; however, Parisians often sought out quiet back alleys to have their conversations. In London, the researchers noted the formation of a "sort of improvised open-air wireless phone booth." Londoners tend to gather with other people talking on their cellular phones and mutually ignore one another in a stationary cluster while talking. This happened most often in busy, transient public places, like Underground entrances and in front of large, busy department stores. But while Londoners treasure privacy while talking on their mobiles, a Spaniard may answer his cell phone when he's talking to you or out with a group of his friends. But according to the behavior Lasen's team observed in Madrid, you should be offended only if he doesn't then immediately try to bring you into the conversation he's having with the person on his mobile. The denizens of Madrid also give priority to their calls, answering them with the most frequency in cafés, on the streets, in class, and on public transport, the researchers discovered through interviews.

In Japan, it's common for mobile users, especially younger ones, to first send a text message to the person they need to contact before actually calling. This determines the availability of the intended recipient of a call and prevents the potential disruption caused by a sudden phone call. Nearly all Japanese phones are equipped with a button that may be translated as either "manners" or "polite" that instantly switches the phone to silent or vibrate mode. And as might be expected, many young, tech-savvy, highly connected Japanese consider it "a new taboo" to leave one's mobile phone, or keitai, at home or to let the battery die.

Elsewhere in the world, Moroccans seem to be enamored of caller ID, with one reporter even watching the prime minister screen his calls (answering one of eight) during an interview. Frequently, Moroccans will answer only when they know the person calling and need to speak with him. Otherwise, they're perfectly content with letting calls go to voice mail.

Here in the United States, about 70 percent of respondents in a recent poll by market research group Synovate reported a lack of cell phone manners. (Are you surprised?) The most common example of poor etiquette was the "cell yell" or loud cellular conversation in public, reported 72 percent of the respondents.

As cellular phone usage continues to climb in both the United States and abroad, these incidents seem certain to increase. To prevent a cell phone faux pas, respect local customs regarding public usage.

If in doubt, take cues from those around you. As the European researchers concluded: "In general . . . when the mobile phone use is discrete enough, when the user is not shouting, or when their use is not unusual in any way, like someone talking in a foreign language, nobody seems to pay attention." www.dwrc. surrey.ac.uk/Portals/0/CompStudy.pdf

Overseas Fees

Traveling abroad is costly enough, what with the sky-high airfares, costly hotels, and overpriced car rentals. The last thing you want to do is come home to a credit card statement with some shocking and unexpected charges. So what's going on here? It's a dirty little secret that most credit card companies won't tell you about: the overseas transaction and conversion fees.

When you use your credit card abroad, you may be charged up to 3 percent for any transactions. For example, MasterCard charges a standard 1 percent fee for foreign purchases, and American Express charges 2 percent. It's a foreign conversion rate that the credit card company levies for converting local currency into US dollars. The fee is issued on the day that you make the purchase, based on that day's exchange rate. And now, many banks are issuing a currency conversion fee *on top* of the credit card fee. So, for example, your Bank of America MasterCard will charge you 3 percent of your total purchase—2 percent for Bank of America and 1 percent for MasterCard.

To make it even more confusing, the policies keep changing. Visa, for example, used to charge a 1 percent currency conversion fee. But in 2005 they changed this to something called an International Service Assessment—a charge to issuing banks when transactions use the global payment system. While Visa claims that this charge is not passed on to cardholders, the issuing bank may do so.

Your ATM card isn't exempt from fees either. You can be charged up to $5 per transaction or up to 3 percent of the withdrawn amount—or *both*—every time you withdraw money from a foreign bank. (Even if you're traveling in the United States and can't find your bank of choice, you'll have to pay for the service. In fact, one study by Bankrate.com estimates that Americans pay up to $4.2 billion a year in fees from using competitors' ATMs.)

If you try to cash a traveler's check in a foreign bank, you can expect to pay up to 10 percent in fees, and you may get ripped off by unfavorable exchange rates. As for money exchange places? Don't even go there. (If you do *have* go there, avoid kiosks at the airport or train station—use a bank. And change only as much as you need for the moment, not large quantities.)

So short of walking around town with a wad of local currency, what are your options?

Well, it turns out the best bet is to use your credit card, despite the percentage fees. A 2005 *Consumer Reports* survey of transaction costs found that converting dollars into euros at an exchange bureau cost 10 percent more than using a Wells Fargo Visa with a 3 percent conversion fee. Exchanging dollars at a five-star hotel cost 22 percent more!

Your second best bet is to get cash from ATMs, particularly if you're only paying a flat fee, not a percentage. Just make sure you don't hit the ATM too often, or that $1 to $5 fee will start to hurt. If you do use an automated teller, avoid the independent machine that will most likely charge you even more than a bank machine. Even better: If you can find it, use the ATM for your own bank, not a competitor—otherwise you'll probably get charged a transaction fee by both banks. And lastly, if you take out a lot of money at once, consider stashing some of it in a hotel safe.

Don't get a cash advance from your credit card. You'll be hit with a triple header of the ATM fee, a cash advance fee, and the currency exchange fee.

Get as much information as possible in advance. That means calling your credit card company and bank to find out whether they charge a flat fee or a percentage fee and what the charges are for. Don't forget to check in with your hotel and restaurants to find out if they also add a fee for credit card transactions to cover their authorization fees.

Our friends at Bankrate.com put together this handy chart of foreign conversion fees and transaction fees. This chart is current as of May 2007, but keep in mind that this information can change frequently, so always check with your credit card company and bank first.

CURRENCY CONVERSION

FEE FOR CREDIT CARD PURCHASE MADE IN FOREIGN CURRENCY	FEE FOR A DEBIT CARD PURCHASE MADE IN FOREIGN CURRENCY	FEE FOR AN ATM CARD WITHDRAWAL MADE IN A FOREIGN COUNTRY/ CURRENCY
American Express		
2 percent charge on point-of-sale purchases after conversion to US dollars	No debit cards	No ATM cards
Bank of America		
3 percent on point-of-sale credit card purchases after conversion to US dollars (includes 1 percent for Visa or MasterCard)	3 percent on point-of-sale debit card purchases after conversion to US dollars (includes 1 percent for Visa or MasterCard)	$5 fee and 1 percent of amount withdrawn; waived if using a Global ATM Alliance machine

(continued)

Capital One

Does not pass along the 1 percent charged by Visa and MasterCard	Does not pass along the 1 percent charged by Visa and MasterCard	No fee

Citibank

3 percent of credit card purchase after conversion to US dollars (includes 1 percent for Visa or MasterCard)	3 percent on point-of-sale debit card purchases after conversion to US dollars (includes 1 percent for Visa or MasterCard); 1 percent charge on Citigold accounts	3 percent of the withdrawal at non-Citibank ATMs; 1 percent charge on Citigold account; no fee for Citibank ATMs

Discover

0 percent charged for credit card purchases	No debit cards	No ATM cards; 3 percent standard on cash advances

FifthThird Bank

3 percent of credit card purchase after conversion to US dollars (includes 1 percent for Visa or MasterCard)	3 percent of debit card purchase after conversion to US dollars (includes 1 percent for Visa or MasterCard)	3 percent of withdrawal

JP Morgan Chase

3 percent on point-of-sale purchases after conversion to US dollars (includes 1 percent for Visa or MasterCard)	3 percent on point-of-sale purchases after conversion to US dollars (includes 1 percent for Visa or MasterCard)	3 percent of withdrawal

Simmons Bank

3 percent of credit card transactions (includes 1 percent for Visa or MasterCard)	No fee for debit or ATM transaction except for 1 percent charged by Visa or MasterCard	No fee for withdrawal except the network charge

Wachovia

1 percent of credit card purchase charged by Visa or MasterCard	1 percent of debit card purchase charged by Visa or MasterCard	1 percent charged by PLUS network

Washington Mutual

1 percent of credit card purchase charged by Visa or MasterCard	1 percent of debit card purchase charged by Visa or MasterCard	3 percent transaction fee on each ATM withdrawal plus 1 percent for Visa or MasterCard

Wells Fargo

3 percent of credit card purchase (includes 1 percent for Visa or MasterCard)	3 percent of debit card purchase (includes 1 percent for Visa or MasterCard)	$5 per withdrawal

Source: *Bankrate Inc., used by permission*

CHAPTER 14

Travel Health

❝ **Anybody who doesn't like this book is healthy.** ❞

—GROUCHO MARX

In the air, on the ground, and on the water . . .

Airplanes

If you're afraid to fly, you may have good reason. Airplane travel is stressful on your body, and even the healthiest of travelers can't escape that. Just take a look at your water bottle after a flight and imagine what's going on inside your body. Airlines are notorious for having low barometric and oxygen pressure, extremely low humidity, poor air quality, and, of course, cramped seats in economy class. All this can add up to a trip that wreaks havoc on your body.

Oxygen

Lowered oxygen levels on airlines continue to cause problems. Because there is not enough oxygen in the air above 10,000 feet for you to survive, aircraft cabins are pressurized to 8,000-foot altitudes. But even if you're flying at that 8,000-foot atmosphere inside the cabin, you might be getting as little as three-quarters of the oxygen you get at sea level. Some might argue that this is really no different than living in a high-altitude environment (think Colorado), but a flight of any length simply isn't long enough to get acclimated to these lower levels of oxygen. A tip? Ask how many air packs are operating on your flight—air packs provide the fresh air that is circulated in the plane. The Federal Aviation Administration (FAA) states that an airliner's ventilation system must be designed to provide each passenger and crew member with at least 0.55 pounds of fresh air per minute. The average ratio of fresh to recycled air is about 50-50. Most wide-body aircraft carry three air packs. But many airlines, in an attempt to save money, operate only two—unless you ask. So the next time you board your flight, before turning right, turn left (momentarily) and ask the flight attendant to check with the cockpit crew to make sure all the air packs are operating. It can make a huge difference.

Some good news on the horizon: The new Boeing 787 Dreamliner has been designed to adjust the pressure to a more comfortable 6,000 feet.

Humidity

One thing we can all agree on. Airplanes are *dry*. When you're 35,000 feet in the air, humidity levels can drop to as low as 10 percent of what you're getting on the ground. With such low levels of humidity, your breathing passages can dry out, making your system more susceptible to disease, especially colds and flu. There's no way for you to change the humidity levels on the planes you fly, so you have to change your own hydration—and that's why aeromedicine specialists have suggested you drink as much water as possible throughout the flight and stay away from drying agents like caffeine and alcohol. For long—or longer—flights, use a saline nasal spray and eyedrops as needed.

Air Quality

A 2002 report from the National Research Council addressed the issue of air quality within airplanes. Aircraft cabins are enclosed environments in which passengers are totally dependent on the air provided by the environmental control system. This means that air is recirculated, with some ventilation to help eliminate contaminant buildup in the cabin. Fumes can spread throughout the cabin when a plane is being deiced, and in some instances, oil or hydraulic fluids can leak or spill into the aircraft's air supply system. All of this can result in the spread of toxic chemicals and carbon monoxide throughout the cabin. Chances are you won't notice any immediate bad effects after a flight, but you may hear a different story from flight attendants.

In 1999, 26 flight attendants filed a civil lawsuit claiming that poor maintenance on MD-80 aircraft operated by Alaska Airlines was causing toxic fumes to enter the cabins, endangering the health of crew and passengers onboard. The Flight Attendants Association also filed suit against the airplane and engine manufacturers.

The plaintiffs' complaints included unusual odors on the planes, noxious fumes, and occasional mists inside the aircraft cabins. Their health complaints included nausea, dizziness, blurred vision, or disorientation, and two of the 26 flight attendants were women in their midthirties who claimed to be permanently disabled with body tremors. In 2001, the case against the airline itself was settled out of court for $725,000, with the airlines admitting no responsibility. Net result: No legal precedent was set, and no criteria were established for the measurement of these fumes, acceptable levels, or enforcement.

But it's not just fumes you have to worry about. Arguably the worst culprits inside an airplane cabin are other passengers! You're sitting inside an enclosed aluminum tube with dozens of other people where the air is essentially recirculated for hours. That means germs, bacteria, viruses, and lots of gases other than oxygen are swirling around the cabin. And while most planes are set up to ventilate cabins with some outside air, there is no standard applied to how much ventilation is required. Most newer airplanes have HEPA filters, though they aren't required, but filters can trap only solid particles in the air, not toxic gases.

Does this mean you should board your flight with an oxygen mask and tank? If you have an acute respiratory condition, perhaps. (Or in some cases, don't get on the plane, period.) But for the rest of us, it does mean we should board forewarned (especially about the air packs).

And in a move that has pet lovers barking mad, Air Canada has taken steps to clean out the air in its planes by banning all animals from the cabins. Stating that pets can trigger allergic attacks in passengers, Air Canada now only allows animals to be transported in the cargo hold (not an option that I recommend).

Deep-Vein Thrombosis

One of the dangers of traveling via aircraft is a condition called deep-vein thrombosis (DVT)—otherwise known as economy passenger syndrome. It's real. And it generally occurs on long-haul flights (or car, train, or bus trips) of 4 hours or more, when you are undergoing long periods of immobility. This can result in a blood clot that restricts bloodflow in your veins, usually in the lower leg, and can cause pain and swelling in your calf. Usually, the body is able to break down the clot gradually, but it has the potential to lead to a pulmonary embolism, a clot of an artery in the lung that affects about 10 percent of DVT suffers. Blood clots can also lead to post-thrombotic syndrome, which occurs if the valves in the vein are damaged. Translation: Instead of flowing upward, the blood pools in the lower leg. This may occur in up to 23 percent of DVT patients over time and can cause edema (water retention), hyperpigmentation (increase in skin color), and skin ulceration.

The actual rate of DVT cases from airplanes is relatively low: about 1 percent, according to a 2003 study published in the *South African Medical Journal*. But some might argue that the low percentage is misleading because not everyone who gets DVT understands it or reports it. In fact, about 8 percent of the long-haul participants in that study had abnormally elevated levels of D-dimers in their blood, suggesting that they may have developed small unrecognizable clots. And that was thought to be a result of immobility, as only 6 percent of passengers reported exercising during the flight.

There are some preexisting conditions that can increase the risk of developing DVT. These include: advanced age, recent surgery, cancer and accompanying treatments, a past history or family history of DVT, obesity, immobility, pregnancy, taking birth control that contains a high dose of estrogen, hormone replacement therapy, circulation problems, or heart problems. (Translation: If you're old, fat, and sitting in 35E on an 11-hour flight, watch out!)

To reduce the risk of developing even minor blood clots while traveling, try to exercise your legs at least every 2 to 3 hours during your flight. This can include walking up and down the aisle, flexing your feet by pulling your toes toward your knees, and also raising your heels while pressing the balls of your feet down. Once again, water is involved: You should also keep well hydrated—as dehydration occurs, your blood thickens, which increases the risk of clots. Consider wearing compression stockings, which are made partly of Lycra, rubber, or Spandex, to help prevent blood from pooling and increase circulation.

Special Needs on Airplanes

Traveling by air is enough hassle for most of us. If you have any special needs, whether it's special medication or bulky equipment, your travels can easily become much more complicated. Airlines aren't exactly forthcoming with the kind of specific information you really need, and oftentimes the reservation agent on the other end of the line has little idea of how you can deal with your situation. Here's what you should know (and the next time you call the airlines, you might want to share the information with *them*!).

Oxygen Tanks

Travelers who are oxygen-dependent often have a difficult time flying—not with the flying itself but with individual airline regulations concerning the use of oxygen tanks. Because oxygen tanks are considered a hazard on board, most airlines have ruled that you cannot bring your own tanks on the plane. First, make sure that your airline provides tanks on board—but also remember that it's not legally required of them. You need to get a prescription from your physician that describes the proper levels of oxygen that you require, and arrange with your oxygen provider to have the tanks available at your destination. However, last year, the FAA approved a new oxygen device called a portable oxygen concentrator for use on planes, which produces oxygen by filtering out nitrogen from the air, rather than storing it in containers. These devices can be plugged into a wall outlet or run for short periods on rechargeable lithium ion batteries. Again, assumption is the mother of all misunderstanding—always check with your individual airline before ever heading to the airport, to make sure you're flying within their oxygen tank rules.

Medicine

Despite the post–August 10, 2006, regulations concerning carry-on lotions and potions, the Transportation Security Administration (TSA) still allows passengers to bring prescription medicine on board. Make sure that you have your prescription on you and that the name on your prescription and medicine matches the name on your passport or ID. Essential nonprescription medicines like insulin (and accompanying needles) are also permitted. Liquid medications and other liquids needed by people with disabilities and medical conditions are also permitted in 3-ounce containers inside a clear, plastic, quart-size bag. This includes:

! All prescription and over-the-counter medications (liquids, gels, and aerosols), including eyedrops and saline solution for medical purposes

- **!** Liquids, including water, juice, or liquid nutrition or gels, for passengers with a disability or medical condition
- **!** Life-support and life-sustaining liquids, such as bone marrow, blood products, and transplant organs
- **!** Items used to augment the body for medical or cosmetic reasons, such as mastectomy products, prosthetic breasts, bras or shells containing gels, saline solution, or other liquids
- **!** Gels or frozen liquids needed to cool disability or medically related items used by persons with disabilities or medical conditions

However, if the liquid medications are larger than 3 ounces, they *must* be declared to the Transportation Security Officer. A declaration can be made verbally, in writing, or by a person's companion, caregiver, interpreter, or family member. These declared liquids must be kept separate from all other property that goes through the x-ray machine. **Important caution:** Since TSA enforcement of these regulations is hardly uniform from airport to airport, allow plenty of extra time for you to have a calm, *informed* discussion with the TSA officer. In fact, you should photocopy this page and bring it with you!

Lifesaving Devices on Airplanes

Who would have thought that one of the best places to have a heart attack is on an airplane? The American Heart Association estimates that 95 percent of sudden cardiac arrest victims die before reaching the hospital. But when defibrillation is provided within 5 to 7 minutes, the survival rate jumps to almost 50 percent. In September 1996, the FDA approved an automatic external defibrillator (AED) for in-flight use. While defibrillators have been used in ambulances and other nonhospital settings for decades, testing was required in airplanes to make sure the equipment could withstand the unique environment and not interfere with airplane instruments.

In 1997, American Airlines became the first US carrier to equip its fleet with AEDs and trains all of its flight attendants in AED use and CPR. The airline claims that its survival rate of sudden cardiac arrest victims is now 63 percent and that 76 lives have been saved in the 10 years since installing the equipment. The first life saved? And this comes under the category of "you can't make this stuff up": the very man who lobbied the airline to install the systems!

Peanut Allergies on Airplanes

For some air travelers, anxiety doesn't come in the form of fear of terrorists or plane malfunction but, rather, from the fear that a certain killer will be on their flight: peanuts.

According to the Food Allergy and Anaphylaxis Network (FAAN), some 1.8 million people in the United States have peanut allergies (all potentially anaphylactic), most of them children. Anaphylaxis is described as "a sudden, severe, potentially fatal, systemic allergic reaction that can involve various areas of the body (such as the skin, respiratory tract, gastrointestinal tract, and cardiovascular system)."

And while to date, no deaths have been reported as a result of someone simply inhaling peanut dust on an airplane, there has been enough concern that some airlines have made changes in their onboard snack service.

As of June 2006, US Airways and America West joined the list of airlines that are now serving only nonpeanut snacks. That list also includes: Air Canada, Air France, American, ATA, British Airways, Frontier, JetBlue, Northwest, Qantas, Spirit, United, and Virgin Atlantic. Southwest still serves peanuts on their flights (the peanuts are almost part of the airline's brand), but if a passenger calls ahead, they will remove peanuts from that particular flight. (Passengers should also alert the gate attendant of the allergy before boarding.) Alaska Airlines also serves peanuts, but if contacted ahead of time, they will create a three-row "peanut buffer zone" for passengers with peanut allergies (for instructions, see their Web site, www.alaskaair.com).

There are a number of airlines that continue to serve peanuts, including Aloha, Cathay Pacific, Continental, Delta, Horizon, and Mexicana. Swiss serves peanut snacks, but passengers can preorder peanut-free meals.

Do note, however, that even with those airlines that might not serve peanuts as snacks on planes, there can be no guarantees that the flight itself will be completely peanut free (as in other peanut-packing passengers). Remember, the FAA does not regulate which foods airlines serve. Instead, the government agency recommends that passengers should carry medication if they have a severe allergy.

If you carry an epinephrine auto injector or other prescription medication, be sure that the pharmacy label is attached and that the name matches the passenger's identification. It's a good idea to carry a letter from your doctor explaining the need for the medication (you can see a sample letter on the Web site www.foodallergy.org). If you are taking a liquid medication such as

Benadryl, ask your doctor if you can switch to self-dissolving tablets.

Take these steps to ensure your safety.

! Call the airline in advance and ask about their individual peanut policy. (Do not wait until the day before your flight—it will be too late to change to other airlines without ticket penalties.)

! Wear long sleeves and pants (or dress your child in same) to minimize possible contact with peanut particles.

! If you are the parent of an allergic child, board early and wipe down the seat arms and tray table before your child boards.

! *Always* carry your (or your child's) allergy medication with you—e.g., an EpiPen or Twinject—in case of an emergency.

! If you or your child begins to develop symptoms, notify the flight attendant immediately so that the crew can monitor the situation—and if necessary, have the pilot make an emergency landing.

! If a reaction does occur or the airline does not live up to its promise, report the incident in writing to the airline's CEO and to the Aviation Consumer Protection Division (ACPD), which keeps track of air travel problems experienced by consumers. Guidelines for writing to the ACPD can be found at http://airconsumer.ost.dot.gov/problems.htm.

For additional tips on air travel for those with allergies, see www.foodallergy.org.

 Fast Food Nations

It's tempting to go for fast food when you're on the go, but remember that rules and regulations vary from country to country. Although the United States is making a push to ban trans fats, that's not necessarily the case elsewhere. A group of Danish doctors conducted a study of fried fast food in 20 countries. A large fries and chicken McNuggets from McDonald's in Denmark, where trans fats are restricted by law, had just 0.3 gram of trans fat per serving. In Spain, Russia, and the Czech Republic, the meal had about 3 grams of trans fat. Alarmingly, in New York, there were a whopping 10.3 grams. At Kentucky Fried Chicken in Poland and Hungary, a large order of hot wings and french fries had 19 grams of trans fat, whereas a similar meal in Germany, Russia, and Aberdeen, Scotland, had less than 1 gram.

Deep Cleaning on Airplanes

Before you settle down into your cramped airplane seat, consider this statistic: At any given time, an estimated 70,000 people have sat on the seat before you! And those blankets . . . well, there are no federal guidelines on how often airlines need to clean (or more appropriately, disinfect) their blankets, and when you think of the hundreds—maybe thousands—of people who used the blanket before you, it's enough to make you never want to even *touch* an airline blanket again.

American Airlines, for example, says that cleaning crews remove only blankets that are *visibly* dirty after each flight. JetBlue says it washes blankets left on the seats after each flight but may reuse blankets that appear to be unused. Continental says that they wash their blankets on a regular basis (whatever that means). Delta has now accelerated the deep cleaning cycle for many of its airplanes, and flight attendants and passengers alike (myself included) applauded the move. In fact, I flew down to Atlanta and participated in a late-night—all-night—cleaning of a 757, and what came off that aircraft was nothing short of . . . unmentionable. But at least, it came off!

A study from San Diego State University recently revealed even more squirm-inducing figures—not about the blankets but about the lavatories. Their bottom line: Airplane bathrooms are basically flying cubicles of germs. A sampling of airlines and airplanes found that bathrooms contained pathogens like strep and staph, which can cause anything from mild strep throat to fatal bacterial infections.

There are now plenty of gimmicks and gadgets on the market that promise to combat the unhealthy environment in airplanes—these range from portable airplane seat covers you bring with you and your own lightweight disposable blankets to sanitary wipes, booties, and even face masks. And you can even purchase a neck pillow with a built-in ionizer. But none of these gadgets can ever take the place of basic common sense: Stay hydrated, and wash your hands often and well.

Water on Planes

I've said it before, and I'll say it again. Bring your own bottled water on the plane. (With new TSA regulations, this means you need to buy it after you clear security.) Why? Unless you can see the flight attendant open the bottle of water and actually hear the crack of a newly opened bottle cap, skip the water that's offered to passengers. Airlines just don't stock enough bottled water for passengers on flights. And flight attendants have been known to refill empty bottles of mineral water with tap water from the airplane's disgusting holding tanks. You know what they call it? Tappian.

And it's not a pretty picture.

In August and September 2004, the EPA tested drinking water aboard 327 randomly chosen airplanes, from small commuter aircrafts to jumbo jets, in 19 airports, with some distasteful results. Fully 13 percent of tested aircraft water failed to meet EPA standards and tested positive for total coliform bacteria, signaling the possible presence of other harmful bacteria. Two planes actually tested positive for *E. coli* bacteria in their water!

As a result of the 2004 study, the EPA announced commitments from 11 domestic airlines and 13 smaller and low-cost airlines to implement new aircraft testing and disinfection protocols. The problem is that airlines are required to provide only total coliform and disinfectant residual samples from at least one galley and one lavatory—once a year. And there are no penalties against the airlines. Totally meaningless.

And to prove the point, when the EPA made the agreement with the airlines, the agency issued the following disclaimer:

> *Passengers with suppressed immune systems or others concerned should request bottled or canned beverages while on the aircraft and refrain from drinking tea or coffee that does not use bottled water . . . The water used to prepare coffee and tea aboard a plane is not generally brought to a sufficiently high temperature to guarantee that pathogens are killed.*

Another important caution: In the United States, aircraft water comes from public water systems that are regulated by state and federal authorities. But on international flights, a majority of aircrafts get water from foreign sources that don't have to follow EPA standards.

In Case of Emergency

When you're traveling, there's a very simple way to make sure that your next of kin can be notified if you are injured or fall ill. Just store that person's phone number in your cell phone under the name ICE, for "In Case of Emergency," to make sure that hospital staff can contact them quickly. If you have more one contact, simply store them as ICE1, ICE2, and so on.

Airport Health

There's some good news about health care at airports. There are now express health care clinics *inside* some airports to help you out. In Newark, Terminal C offers a health center, a full-service pharmacy, and a retail store. A nurse practitioner on staff can even write prescriptions.

Vancouver International Airport has not only a health clinic but also a walk-in dental clinic and pharmacy. The center is located before security in the Domestic Terminal Building.

There's a full-service dental clinic at JFK as well.

The medical clinic at San Francisco International Airport provides travel medicine, urgent care, and occupation health services. The clinic is located in the arrivals/baggage claim level in Terminal 2.

The Atlas Travel Clinic in London's Gatwick Airport offers travel health advice on travel immunizations, occupational health support, and general health services for travelers.

Eating at Airports

Hopefully, you've already read my book *The Traveler's Diet: Eating Right and Staying Fit on the Road,* but I'll share a few tips with you here as well.

My rules of thumb are as follows:

! Don't starve yourself. Cutting calories before or while you travel will put your body into starvation mode, which means it will burn fewer calories to conserve energy.

! Choose your airport food carefully. With the drastic reduction in airline food, airports are reaping the benefits as travelers crowd around chain restaurants, fast-food counters, and snack kiosks. Here are some examples of good choices.

> • **Chicago O'Hare:** vegetable chow mein with steamed rice at Panda Express in Terminals 1 and 3; veggie focaccia at Vienna Beef Hot Dogs in Terminals 1 and 2
>
> • **Detroit Metropolitan:** Philly veggie sandwich at Charley's Grilled Subs in the McNamara Terminal; grilled chicken and veggie sub at Quiznos in the Smith Terminal
>
> • **San Francisco:** smoky split pea soup and green salad at the San Francisco Soup Company in Terminal 3; udon noodles and veggie sushi at Ebisu in the International terminal

- **JFK:** mixed vegetables, tofu, and rice at Wok 'n' Roll in Terminals 1, 2, and 8; spaghetti with marinara sauce at Sbarro in Terminals 3, 4, and 8; sushi and edamame at Deep Blue Sushi in Terminal 6; roasted vegetable panini at Atlantic Bar & Lounge in Terminal 7
- **Dallas-Fort Worth:** bean burrito without cheese at Taco Bell in Terminals A, C, and E; gardenburger at T.G.I. Friday's in Terminals A, D, and E
- **Denver:** veggie taco with beans and rice at Cantina Grill Express in Concourses A, B, and C; portobello mushroom sandwich at Lefty's Colorado Trails Bar and Grill in Concourse A; spinach pizza without cheese at Wolfgang Puck Express in Concourse B

! Choose your airline food wisely, as well. Airplane food is generally loaded with sauces and sodium. Those snack packs for purchase are often filled with items like cookies, crackers with processed cheese, and candy. You may be better off bringing your own food on board. At www.airlinemeals. net, you can see more than 3,300 pictures of airline food served on more than 250 airlines, as well as photos and menus of airline food from the 1950s and beyond.

! Again, drink water: Studies show that H_2O can not only curb your appetite but also increase metabolic rate—water is crucial to maintaining liver health, which in turn is what converts and utilizes fat into energy. Stay away from alcohol.

! Exercise wherever and whenever you can. There are plenty of options that you may not have even thought about—like the airport. Check out www.airportgyms.com to see a list of US and Canadian airports with gyms either inside a terminal or in a nearby location. McCarran International in Las Vegas has a 24 Hour Fitness gym on site, which costs $10 per workout. In Munich, you can take a dunk in the lap pool, with a locker and towels costing $18. At New York's JFK, you can take a free shuttle to Cross Island Sports & Fitness, which costs $20 per day.

Don't just sit there. You can squeeze in a lot of exercise by walking in an airport with long distances between terminals. Terminal 3 at O'Hare is roughly a mile long to the end of each of the four concourses and back. Outside of security, you can walk the length of all three terminals, which is about 3 miles, round-trip. At Newark in New Jersey, the walk from Terminal A to C is nearly a mile long, and at Houston's Bush Intercontinental, the walk along the interterminal train is a 2-mile trip from one end to the other.

Hotel Health

When you enter a hotel room, there are three things you should immediately do: Take out the sanitizing wipes that you should have packed in your suitcase and use them to wipe down the remote control and phone handset, the two biggest carriers of bacteria in your room. Then walk over to the bed, pull off the bedspread, and throw it into the corner of a room. Never look at it again; never touch it again. Then go into the bathroom—turn on the hot water faucet and place the water glasses under it for at least 3 minutes. Why the water glasses? Maids at hotels are heavily tasked, often having to clean between 12 and 16 rooms per shift. And by the time they get to the 13th or 14th room, they're running very short on time. And when they get to those bathrooms, they've been known to not replace the drinking glasses but simply rinse them and put them back on the sink. That's why you're running the hot water in those glasses. You never know if your room was first or 16th!

Most recently, the latest concern over hotel health is something even more squirm-inducing—bedbugs.

Between 2000 and 2006, pest control companies have reported a whopping 71 percent increase in cases of bedbugs. The National Pest Management Association reports that pest control companies that originally received only about one or two bedbug calls a year are now reporting one or two each week overall. Looking at specific companies, the numbers get even more dramatic: At Terminix, their incoming reports of bedbugs increased 150 percent between 2005 and 2006! The pest control company has seen bedbugs in all 46 states that it services.

The Traveling Flu

Scientists have found that restricting air travel can actually have an effect on the spread of influenza. After air travel dropped in the weeks after the attacks of September 11, 2001, the winter flu season was delayed by about 2 weeks.

The word *malaria* comes from the words *mal* and *aria*, which mean "bad" and "air." This derives from the old days when it was thought that all diseases are caused by bad or dirty air.

However, there is good news. According to the Centers for Disease Control and Prevention (CDC), bedbugs are not a source of infectious disease. So while they certainly may be undesirable, there is no reason to panic. Having said that, here's what you need to know about bedbugs.

The creepy little critters (adults are reddish and about the size of an apple seed; eggs are about a millimeter and pale) were essentially eradicated in the 1940s due to the powerful pesticide DDT. However, these nocturnal blood-suckers continued to thrive in most other countries. Over the past several years, bedbugs have swarmed into the United States on a national scale, and they're not just targeting fleabag motels. One woman is suing the Nevele Hotel in Ellenville, New York, for $20 million after waking up one morning with more than 500 bedbug bites. A Florida couple claims to have been bitten while on a Royal Caribbean cruise ship. Although officials haven't yet determined the exact causes of the recent bedbug cases, they point to an increase in inter-national business and military travel, paired with the 1971 ban on DDT and recent use of milder, shorter-lasting pesticides applied in more focused areas.

Infestations have primarily taken over hotels and large cities, which see heavy traffic, but they've also been seen in hospitals, apartments, and even single-family homes. Bedbugs are hardy creatures that can live for a year or more without feeding on "blood meals" and can withstand temperatures from nearly freezing to almost 113°F. That means that hotels can't just shut the door and hope that they die out.

While bedbugs can't be managed with over-the-counter bug sprays or disinfectants, the good news is that they *can* be exterminated with the efforts of a trained professional. A pest control company will generally wash the bedding and put it in a commercial dryer for at least an hour at the highest heat setting. The bed is taken apart completely and the mattress vacuumed and steamed. They also clean and steam the headboard and nightstand, and they examine the carpets, draperies, and wallpaper to see if they need to be treated as well.

Here are some tips to keep bedbugs from ruining your travels.

- Before booking, check to see if there is an infestation alert for your hotel at www.bedbugregistry.com.

- Check around headboards, mattresses, and box springs for bedbugs and the dark blood spots they leave behind.

- Hang all clothing. Leave nothing lying on the bed or furniture.

- Avoid unpacking clothing and storing them in the hotel's furniture drawers.

- Don't allow your baggage to sit on the floor. Store it on a luggage rack as far from the bed as possible.

- If you notice evidence of bedbugs, request another room or change hotels.

- When returning home, leave luggage in the garage or basement until you are able to thoroughly inspect it for bedbugs.

- Vacuum suitcases when returning from trips and immediately wash clothing in hot water.

Hotels and Allergies

Air quality can be adversely affected by invisible toxins, such as mold spores, dust particles, and volatile organic compounds (VOCs) that emanate from many common household items. Just think about what kind of toxins you might find in the harsh cleaning supplies used by many hotels or what exactly might be trapped in the musty old drapes in your room. The good news is that some hotels are going completely natural, while many others are offering choices to make your stay as healthy as possible.

The **Hilton O'Hare** in Chicago has implemented a pilot program of 18 "enviro-rooms." In order to improve overall air quality, the rooms were stripped down (everything from carpets and drapes to wallpaper and bedding) and completely remodeled to reduce mites, spores, and VOCs. The rooms now consist of hardwood flooring, water-based stain, and breathable, nonvinyl wallpaper, and each room is equipped with a high-powered air purifier. The cleaning products, shampoos, soaps, and lotions are furnished by Free and Clear and are fragrance and chemical free. Even the bedding is made of all-natural cotton. Rates for the enviro-rooms are higher than a standard room, and Hilton is assessing the demand for such rooms to determine if they should embark on a larger-scale renovation. 800-445-8667, www.hilton.com

In the Kimpton Hotel chain, the environmentally friendly **Hotel Triton** in San Francisco has been such a success that they're spreading the program to all 39 of its properties. All of the rooms are cleaned with products such as Sierra Environmental Technologies and Ecolab Green Seals. While these products are not necessarily fragrance free for highly sensitive guests, they use all-natural ingredients and do not release carcinogens or toxins. Kimpton has taken its environmental stance to even higher levels, using only soy inks and recycled paper in its hotels and corporate offices, providing organic coffee, and installing low-flow faucets and toilets. 800-546-7866, www.kimptonhotels.com

A New York–based company called **Pure Solutions** has worked with several properties worldwide, including Marriott, Doubletree, and Sheraton, to clean out rooms to be allergy friendly (aka Pure Rooms). The company cleaned up allergens like mold, dust, and pollen; added air purifiers to the rooms; and use mold- and spore-proof bedding. At the Premier hotel in Times Square, for example, you'll find elements like tea tree oil inserted into the heating and cooking unit and dust-mite protectors on the mattresses and pillowcases. The total cost for the hotel to convert three floors: $30,000. Some properties are charging between 5 and 10 percent extra for the Pure Rooms, while others, like the Premier, are maintaining the same rate. You can find a list of hotels that Pure Solutions has worked with at www.pureroom.com/hotels.

There are also several independently owned lodges that have gone all natural. **The Natural Place** in Deerfield Beach, Florida (two blocks from Boca Raton), is an eco-friendly, chemical-free hotel that caters specifically to guests who suffer from multiple chemical sensitivity (MCS). Although MCS is not recognized by the American Medical Association, it is thought that sufferers experience a wide range of symptoms from exposure to substances in doses that are far below what are normally considered "safe" levels. These symptoms can include fatigue, irritability, depression, and tension. Some common culprits are cleaning products, shampoos, and fabric softeners, all items usually found in a standard hotel—even wall-to-wall carpeting can cause a reaction. Rates are about $60 to $80 a night for various-sized apartments, and there are also longer-term residences available. 954-428-5438; www.thenaturalplace.com

Tucson Natural Bed and Breakfast in Arizona is a four-room lodge founded about 13 years ago. The owners use only chemical-free cleaning supplies (preferring Seventh Generation brand) and keep a strict no-smoking, no-pets, and no-shoes policy. In keeping with the all-natural lifestyle choices, Tucson Natural also provides healthful, mostly vegetarian breakfasts and can cater to vegan, organic, and other special dietary needs. Rates are about $75 for a single room and $90 for a double. 888-295-8500, www. tucsonnatural.com

If you're in a standard hotel that doesn't have any chemical-free or allergy-friendly rooms, there are still some steps you can take to protect your health.

! Pick a hotel that is *not* pet friendly. Also, try to stay in a nonsmoking hotel room or, better yet, a smoke-free hotel. Visit www.smoke-freehotels. com for a comprehensive list of nonsmoking hotels.

! Make sure that the room you choose has central air, and ask the concierge to change the filter in the air-conditioner unit before you arrive.

! Avoid rooms near indoor pools, especially if you are sensitive to mold. If you are staying in a cabin or cottage near a beach or in the mountains, have it cleaned and aired out before you get there.

! Most hotels have foam pillows available. Check your closet first, and if there are none, you can call the front desk to have one brought up.

! The same applies to hotel closets and drawers, if you're sensitive to mold. They're great breeding grounds for spores.

! Carpeting and drapes are big-time attractions for dust mites, so see if you can have your room vacuumed before you get there. Better yet, pick a room with wood floors and blinds or shades.

! If you aren't in a hotel that provides allergy-proof bedding, bring your own. The effort it takes to change the sheets beats waking up with a stuffy nose and itchy eyes. (Just remember to alert the maid know or remove the sheets before your room is cleaned to avoid someone running off with your sheets!)

! Pack your own allergy-friendly pillow covers and fragrance-free shampoo and soap.

! Finally, always bring plenty of your own allergy medication and the name and number of a local allergist as well as your own doctor, in case of a severe allergic reaction.

Travelers' Diseases

No one hates fear mongering more than I do, but it goes without saying that travel does come with some potential risks. Getting sick is one of them, so here's what you should know about staying healthy on the road.

Norovirus

You may have heard the horror stories of hundreds of cruise ship passengers coming down with flulike symptoms. In February 2007, 100 passengers were stricken with norovirus—often dubbed the cruise ship virus—on a Holland America cruise. Another 200-plus passengers were afflicted on a Royal Caribbean ship in July 2006. Despite its ominous-sounding name, norovirus is really nothing more than the stomach flu. And the best way to combat it? Wash your hands. It's as simple as that.

I have a theory—and one that is only intuitive and impossible to prove—about how the norovirus gets on cruise ships. And it all has something to do with cruise lines and their draconian refund policies. Usually, if you want or need to cancel your cruise plans within 30 days of sailing, a cruise line contract specifies you get *no* refund, even if the cruise line can easily go out and resell your cabin. Result: A lot of people who'd want to cancel a cruise because they have the stomach flu *don't* cancel, because they don't want to lose their money, and they board the ship already infected. Again, it's my own theory, impossible to prove, but I'm putting it out there anyway. Makes sense, doesn't it? And once on that enclosed metal floating petri dish otherwise known as a cruise ship, the infected passenger doesn't take long to infect others. (For more on norovirus, see "Cruise Ship Health" in Chapter 6.)

Avian Flu

First there was SARS, and now it's the notorious "bird flu" virus, also known as avian flu or H5N1. What makes avian flu so scary to travelers? Although there has been only the rare case of the virus spreading from one ill person to another, so far it hasn't spread beyond one person. However, the big fear is that the more human cases occur, the more likely it is that this flu could mutate into a strain that is contagious between humans, in which case a worldwide epidemic is terrifyingly possible. There have been three influenza pandemics in modern times: The 1918 Spanish flu killed 500,000 people in the United States and 50 million to 100 million worldwide, nearly half of whom were between 20 and 40 years old. The 1957 Asian flu and 1968 Hong Kong flu pandemics killed two million and one million people worldwide, respectively.

In the past 10 years, there have been some high-profile reports about avian flu deaths. In 1997, avian flu was discovered in Hong Kong, where 6 out of 18 cases died. In 2006 in Indonesia, the World Health Organization reported evidence of human-to-human spread, when eight people in one family were infected. The first family member is thought to have become ill through contact with infected poultry and then infected six family members, and one of the six infected his father. One of the most recent deaths was reported in January 2007 in Nigeria; the deadly strain was first detected a year earlier on a farm outside the northern city of Kaduna, Nigeria, from where it spread to at least 19 states in Africa. Since 2003, there have been 166 deaths out of 272 cases. The hardest hit countries have been Vietnam, Indonesia, and Thailand.

Avian flu is caused by viruses that occur naturally among birds. It can be highly contagious among birds, spread through saliva, mucus, and feces. There is a mild form, which causes very little damage (like ruffled feathers and lowered egg production), and a much more dangerous form that can spread very rapidly among flocks. The stronger version can affect multiple internal organs and has a mortality rate of about 90 to 100 percent within 45 hours. Bird flu within poultry is now found in Africa, Eurasia, Egypt, Iraq, Iran, and Israel.

AVIAN FLU CASES AROUND THE WORLD

COUNTRY	2003*		2004		2005		2006		2007		TOTAL	
	CASES**	DEATHS	CASES	DEATHS	CASES	DEATHS	CASES	DEATHS	CASES	DEATHS	CASES	DEATHS
Azerbaijan	0	0	0	0	0	0	8	5	0	0	8	5
Cambodia	0	0	0	0	4	4	2	2	0	0	6	6
China	1	1	0	0	8	5	13	8	0	0	22	14
Djibouti	0	0	0	0	0	0	1	0	0	0	1	0
Egypt	0	0	0	0	0	0	18	10	2	2	20	12
Indonesia	0	0	0	0	19	12	56	46	6	5	81	63
Iraq	0	0	0	0	0	0	3	2	0	0	3	2
Nigeria	0	0	0	0	0	0	0	0	1	1	1	1
Thailand	0	0	17	12	5	2	3	3	0	0	25	17
Turkey	0	0	0	0	0	0	12	4	0	0	12	4
Vietnam	3	3	29	20	61	19	0	0	0	0	93	42
Total†	4	4	46	32	97	42	116	80	9	8	272	166

*All dates refer to onset of illness.

**World Health Organization reports only laboratory-confirmed cases.

†Total number of cases includes number of deaths.

Source: www.who.int/csr/disease/avian_influenza/country/cases_table_2007_02_06/en/index.html

Human-contracted bird flu is rare and comes from directly contacting infected birds or surfaces that are contaminated with secretions and/or excretions of infected birds. This can involve slaughtering, defeathering, or butchering poultry. Fortunately, the virus is not airborne, as it concentrates itself too deeply in the respiratory tract to be spread by coughing or sneezing. So unless you're traveling overseas to start up-close and personal work at a chicken ranch, you're probably not in line to contract avian flu.

Right now, there is no cure or vaccination for avian flu. However, in the United States, the National Institutes of Health has already developed and tested a vaccine against the virus. Eight million doses have been produced, but the drug is still in clinical trials, so it's not yet being distributed. A second vaccine is currently under development.

One of the major concerns about avian flu, and to a lesser extent SARS, has travelers wondering how safe travel is. If a disease becomes highly contagious, it will most likely be carried over from one country to another via aircraft.

Currently, there are 25 quarantine stations being opened or expanded at airports where two-thirds of US international travelers pass through each year. These quarantine stations are usually nothing more than an examination room, not vessels for mass evacuations or quarantines. However, these locations have CDC health officers who monitor for avian flu and other infectious diseases. There are currently 18 stations open in the United States. For more information, visit www.cdc.gov/ncidod/dq/quarantine_stations.htm.

CDC QUICK REFERENCE GUIDE

QUARANTINE STATION	DAYTIME PHONE	AFTER-HOURS PHONE
Anchorage	907-271-6301	907-271-6301
Atlanta	404-639-1220	404-639-1220
Boston	617-561-5701	617-561-5701
Chicago	773-894-2960	773-894-2960
Detroit	734-955-6197	734-955-6197
El Paso	915-351-2930	915-543-2829
Honolulu	808-861-8530	808-861-8530
Houston	281-230-3874	281-230-3874
Los Angeles	310-215-2365	310-215-2365
Miami	305-526-2910	305-526-2910
Minneapolis	612-725-3005	612-725-3005
Newark	973-368-6200	973-368-6200

QUARANTINE STATION	DAYTIME PHONE	AFTER-HOURS PHONE
New York	718-553-1685	718-553-1685
San Diego	619-692-5665	858-565-5255
San Francisco	650-876-2872	650-876-2872
San Juan	787-774-7812	787-774-7812
Seattle	206-553-4519	206-553-4519
Washington, DC	703-661-1320	703-661-1320

Plans are under way for the same type of facilities in at least six more cities, including Charlotte, Dallas, Denver, New Orleans, Philadelphia, and Phoenix.

Some airports have pinpointed locations where they can quarantine larger groups of people, but studies tell us that airports aren't as prepared as they could be. In the case of Los Angeles' LAX, for example, a vacant maintenance hangar can be used to hold large groups, but there is no plumbing or other amenities to keep people there for long stretches. Translation: We're not really adequately prepared.

Even though the World Health Organization has not issued any warnings about travel to countries affected by avian flu, there are still some steps you can take to protect yourself. The virus can be killed by heat, so make sure that any poultry or poultry-related food you eat is properly and thoroughly cooked to at least at 158°F. Be aware of cross contamination—be sure that the restaurant you're eating at (or whoever is preparing your food) properly scrubs and disinfects its cooking surfaces with soap and hot water. Also:

! Avoid contact with live markets and poultry farms. Even free-range poultry is at risk for developing bird flu.

! If you're planning to have fresh poultry, have the bird slaughtered at the market rather than doing it yourself.

! Wash your hands thoroughly with hot water and soap often or keep a bottle of antiseptic hand rinse with you.

Tuberculosis

A case of a highly infectious tuberculosis patient recently made headlines and had a lot of travelers worried. Andrew Speaker, a 31-year-old Atlanta attorney, was suffering from extremely drug-resistant tuberculosis (XDR-TB). Although advised not to travel, he flew from Atlanta to Paris, then to Greece to be married, and *then* to Rome for his honeymoon, where he was contacted by the CDC and urged to report to Italian authorities for treatment. He and his wife ignored that call and headed off to Prague and flew to Montreal. They entered the United States in Champlain, New York, by rented car, despite the fact that his passport was flagged on the US Customs and Border Patrol's computer system.

Tuberculosis (TB) is a bacterial infection that usually attacks the lungs. It is spread through the air and can lead to symptoms such as chest pain and coughing up blood. There were an estimated 1.6 million deaths from TB in 2005, according to the World Health Organization (WHO). There have been 17 US cases of the extremely drug-resistant TB since 2000, according to the CDC. This rare form of tuberculosis means the disease is resistant to the two first-line antibiotics that are commonly used for treatment: isoniazid and rifampin, and at least one of three second-line drugs.

WHO strongly advises that "persons known to have infectious TB should remain in isolation at home or at hospital, depending on the policies of the national programme, until no longer infectious. When travel is necessary while a person is still infectious, commercial carriers or other public transportation should not be used. Alternative private transportation (e.g., ground transportation, air ambulance, etc.) could be used instead."

Also according to WHO, all new commercial jet aircraft recirculate air, and many older aircrafts built before the late 1980s have been retrofitted to do so. About 10 to 50 percent of cabin air is filtered, mixed with fresh air and reintroduced into the cabin. "Generally, the first filter traps the largest particles. On most modern aircraft, before reentering the passenger cabin, the air passes through a high-efficiency particulate air (HEPA) filter, which can capture material as small as 0.3 microns." Tuberculosis bacteria are about 0.5 to 1 micron in size.

The CDC officially stated that the patient probably was not highly contagious, despite having a rare strain. He was asymptomic at the time, and to date no surrounding passengers have been diagnosed with the disease. Of course, the larger concern for many travelers is not the spread of tuberculosis from this incident but how this passenger was able to exit and reenter the country despite the fact that his passport was flagged. US Customs and Border Protection had been informed by the CDC that the passenger (patient) had a highly infectious disease. A warning was issued that agents should "isolate, detain or call the public health service" if Speaker attempted to cross the border. Human error and poor judgment are being blamed, as it's believed that an agent at the border crossing in New York let him through because he didn't appear to be ill. Now there's something to help you sleep at night.

Malaria

This parasitic disease has been a part of human society for more than 50,000 years. WHO estimates that each year 300 million to 500 million cases of malaria occur and more than one million people die of malaria, making it the leading cause of death and disease worldwide. Malaria was eradicated from the United States in the 1950s, but travelers to developing countries with warm climates are still at risk of contracting the disease.

The countries most at risk include Africa, Central and South America, Haiti and the Dominican Republic, Africa, the Indian subcontinent, Southeast Asia, the Middle East, and Oceania. (There is very little to no risk of contracting malaria in Japan, Taiwan, Hong Kong, Macau, and Mongolia.) Symptoms include headache, vomiting, fatigue, muscle pain, and shivering.

Check with your physician 4 to 6 weeks before traveling to any of these regions to determine if you're going to a high-risk area and if you need to go on a regimen of antimalarial pills. Don't stop taking the pills when you get back home, as symptoms can take months to appear. Malaria is spread by female anopheles mosquitoes that bite only from dusk till dawn. Wear long-sleeved clothing and socks to cover your ankles. Choose a mosquito repellent with DEET (20 percent to 30 percent is more effective, but the United States imposes a 10 percent limit on children). Make sure there's a mosquito net around the bed, preferably treated with insecticide. If your room is air-conditioned with no net, spray your sleeping area with insecticide.

If you become ill with a fever or suffer from flulike symptoms while traveling in a risky area or after you return home for up to a year, seek medical attention immediately.

For more information on malaria and prevention, visit the CDC at www.cdc.gov/malaria.

One additional note about malaria prevention. Many doctors—even those at the CDC—recommend that you take Larium before your trip as a defense against malaria. I'm not a doctor and don't play one on television, but I *can* tell you that a substantial number of travelers experience an adverse reaction to this drug. I've actually been in parts of Kenya when fellow travelers have had to be evacuated—not because of malaria but because of their intense reaction to Larium. Again, consult your doctor before you take Larium and see if you can pursue another alternative drug. Okay, you've been warned.

Dengue Fever

Like malaria, dengue fever is transmitted by mosquitoes. Whereas malaria is a parasitic disease, dengue is viral—however, it cannot be transmitted from human to human. Symptoms include a sudden fever, severe headache, body aches and muscle pain, a decrease in white blood cells or platelets, and even hemorrhaging in some cases. Dengue hemorrhagic fever (DHF) is a more severe form of dengue and is fatal in about 5 percent of cases. Although there is no vaccine or cure for dengue, treatment includes pain relievers and plenty of fluids or fluid replacement therapy in the case of DHF.

The CDC estimates that globally there are 50 million to 100 million cases of dengue fever in the world, and several hundred thousand cases each year. Recently, Venezuela's Health Ministry reported that there were 9,986 cases of dengue fever, an increase of 42.8 percent from the year before. Rarotonga, in the Cook Islands, was recently hit by an epidemic, with 900 nonfatal cases as of March 2007.

Because dengue is a mosquito-borne virus, prevention is similar to that of malaria: use air-conditioning, make sure that open doors or windows have screens, and make sure there is a mosquito net around your bed that is treated with mosquito repellent that contains DEET. See www.cdc.gov/ncidod/dvbid/dengue for more information.

Typhoid

Typhoid fever is a bacterial illness that affects about 21.5 million people every year, according to the CDC. It is still common in developing nations and can be spread by ingesting contaminated food or drinks. Symptoms include high fever, stomachache, headache, or decreased appetite—this can be tricky as these symptoms can be attributed to other illnesses, and you could still be carrying the bacteria even if your symptoms disappear. Typhoid can only be diagnosed through stool or blood samples and can be treated with antibiotics. If you haven't already been vaccinated for typhoid fever, with regular booster shots, talk to your doctor before you travel.

Because typhoid exists in so many parts of the world, it's a good idea to follow general commonsense guidelines when traveling. That includes drinking boiled or bottled water, avoiding iced drinks, avoiding raw fruits and vegetables, making sure your food—especially meat—has been thoroughly cooked, and avoiding food from street vendors.

Drinking-Water Problems

We've already covered the issue of drinking water on airplanes, but if you're traveling to a country with impure water sources, you are at increased risk of getting ill. Untreated water can be contaminated with bacteria that lead to deadly diseases like typhoid, dysentery, and cholera; viruses that cause polio and hepatitis; and parasites that cause diarrhea and abdominal cramps. According to the CDC, you'll find the highest risk of contaminated water in Africa, Mexico, Central America, South America, most of Asia, and the Middle East, particularly in rural areas. There's an intermediate risk in South Africa, Eastern Europe, and Southern Europe. Low-risk countries include the United States, Canada, Japan, Northern European nations, and Australia.

The most effective methods to purify water are boiling, filtering, distilling, and employing iodine and ultraviolet purification.

There are a number of travel gadgets on the market—many of them portable—to help you filter water.

Water purification tablets, which contain iodine, halazone, or chlorine, will kill most waterborne bacteria. Simply drop one tablet (8 milligrams) into a quart or liter of water and let it stand 10 minutes; add 10 minutes if the water is cold and an additional 10 minutes if it's discolored.

There are several brands of **water filters and purifiers** on the market, of varying sizes, water output, and portability. Both filters and purifiers remove bacteria from water particles using a mechanical process of pumping, then forcing water through a filtering device. However, purifiers have the additional ability to kill viruses through a chemical or electrostatic process. You should look for a "pore size" of 0.2 micron, which is the industry standard for the smallest filtering capability.

SteriPEN is a portable water purifier that uses ultraviolet light to destroy waterborne viruses, bacteria, and protozoans. Insert the pen-shaped object into water (up to a liter at a time) and it will kill microbes in about 48 seconds. www.hydro-photon.com

But in the absence of tablets, filters, and the SteriPEN, you can also follow these tips to avoid getting sick.

- While the drink may be purified, remember that the ice may not be. Avoid iced drinks or ask if the ice has been made from purified water.
- Use bottled or purified water when brushing your teeth.
- Avoid beer taps and soda fountains.
- Wipe bottles and cans dry before drinking, as they may be kept cold in tubs of impure ice water.
- If you purchase a bottle of water, make sure that the cap is sealed. Some unscrupulous dealers may refill used bottles with tap water.

Waterborne Illnesses

When summertime approaches or you're on vacation at a beach resort, it's impossible not to think about diving headfirst into the pool or ocean. But there are some issues to be aware of when it comes to the integrity of the water you're swimming in. Summer heat can turn stagnant water such as lakes and ponds into a bacterial stew. At the same time, ocean beaches around the country are closing down due to unclean waters.

Recreational water illness (RWI) is spread by swallowing, breathing, or having contact with contaminated water from swimming pools, spas, lakes, rivers, or oceans. This is not a specific condition but can result in a wide variety of symptoms; the most common complaint is diarrhea, followed by skin, ear, respiratory, and eye infections.

The most common cause of diarrhea comes from *Cryptosporidium parvum* (aka crypto), a microscopic parasite that can live in the intestines of humans and animals and is passed through stool. The parasite is found in every region in the country, and symptoms probably won't show up for 2 to 10 days after infection. When it comes to bacterial maintenance in pools and hot tubs, chlorine usually does a good job of killing germs. But crypto can live for long periods outside the body, and it can take a few days before it can be killed by chlorine. Most other germs and parasites can be killed in about a hour, but it's important to make sure that chlorine levels are at the recommended levels, about 1 to 3 parts per million. Factors like sunlight, dirt, and improper pH levels (between 7.2 and 7.8) can lower chlorine levels in pool water.

So what does this mean for swimmers? Quite simply, don't swim if you're suffering from diarrhea. Even if you don't have an "accident," you can still pass along the parasite that may affect other swimmers. This rule is especially important for young children and toddlers in diapers. It is also key to teach kids to avoid swallowing water; in fact, they should try not to get water in their mouths at all (this goes for everyone). Finally, you can help reduce germs in swimming pools by showering before swimming and washing your hands after using the bathroom.

The next rule is to stay out of oceans, lakes, and rivers for at least 2 days after it rains. The reason for this is that bacterial levels tend to be high after rain, especially in ocean waters that are adjacent to storm drains, creeks, and rivers. In many cities, sewer pipes carry used water and sewage, as well as storm water, during a heavy rain. The pipes may get too full and start to overflow into lakes, rivers, and oceans, creating what is called a combined sewer overflow. These elevated bacterial levels can continue for up to 3 days. In fact, avid swimmers and surfers have complained about flulike symptoms when swimming after heavy rainfalls.

Interestingly, a recent study has shown that you may also want to avoid moonlight swims. Apparently, it's possible for bacterial levels to rise during a full or new moon. The study examined 60 beaches from Point Zuma to Corona del Mar in Southern California and showed that one type of bacteria, enterococcus, associated with human sewage, rises during these points of the lunar cycle. This effect is thought to be widespread. It is further possible that lunar tides churn up bacteria in the sand to lead to these elevated levels, but the effect is considered too small to warrant closing beaches.

Specifically about Hot Tubs and Saunas

Finally, you may have heard about something called hot tub rash, which is another one of the more common RWIs. Hot tub rash is caused by a germ called *Pseudomonas aeruginosa,* which can live for long periods in improperly maintained pools and hot tubs. Because hot tub waters are warmer than regular swimming pools, chlorine levels can evaporate more quickly, possibly leading to unpleasant skin rashes. This condition usually clears up on its own within a few days. But to prevent it from happening at all, rely on common sense. A well-chlorinated spa should have little odor, while a strong chemical smell indicates poor maintenance. The sides of the spa should be smooth, not sticky or slippery. Lastly, talk to the staff about the water's temperature (it shouldn't go above 104°F), chlorine, and pH level and find out how frequently these levels are checked and maintained.

▽ Resources

These are the important health contacts to know when you are traveling.

Agricultural Department: Animal Production and Health Division: 202-653-2400, www.fao.org

Centers for Disease Control: 800-311-3435 or 888-246-2675, www.cdc.gov

United States Department of Health and Human Services: 877-696-6775, www.hhs.gov

World Health Organization: +41 22 791 2111, www.who.int

Sleep Aids

I travel 400,000 miles a year, and I never suffer from jet lag. I'll even go so far as to say I don't believe in it. But for thousands of travelers who experience sleeplessness while flying and then later on the ground, jet lag is a very real concern. And some doctors would argue it's a recognized, bona fide medical malady.

Many travelers turn to sleep aids to get them through the agony of long flights and to help reset their body clocks once reaching their destination. In the past, sleep medicines had a stigma of being habit-forming, particularly benzodiazepines like Valium and Xanax. These days, many pill manufacturers boast that new techniques have allowed them to create "nonaddictive" medication with no morning-after grogginess.

However, physicians still worry about psychological dependence and note that you should only use sleeping pills for about a week to 10 days. If you end up taking sleeping pills on a regular basis, be aware that suddenly discontinuing use can cause rebound insomnia, meaning that for a night or two, it's even more difficult than before to fall sleep.

One of the major concerns with sleep aids for travelers is that these medicines can actually cause temporary bouts of amnesia, meaning that you can't remember what happened for several hours after taking the pill. If you're already in bed, this usually isn't a problem because you can sleep through the effects of the medication. But if you're on an airplane and have only a few hours to doze, you might be forced to wake up while the pill is still active in your system. This "traveler's amnesia" means your memory could be wiped clean of landing, gathering your luggage, and, scariest of all, driving yourself to the hotel.

Only a physician can determine whether you ought to be taking a sleeping pill in the first place, especially if you are taking other medications, are pregnant, or are at risk for dependence. Here is a rundown of some of the more common sleep aids on the market today.

Ambien: The latest version of this popular pill, called Ambien CR, has an extended-release double layer, which clinical trials have shown helps you sleep through the night without interruption. This means you need at least 7 hours to devote to sleep to avoid traveler's amnesia. Studies support that Ambien CR is not physically addictive, but it is recommended for only short-term use. It is available in both 5- and 10-milligram pills; most people take the higher dose, but it's a good idea to start slowly and see how your body reacts to it. It works quickly, between 15 and 30 minutes, so it's recommended that you take it as soon as you're ready to go to sleep.

Lunesta: This pill launched in April 2005, and its manufacturers embarked on an aggressive marketing campaign. Their hook is that it is the "first and only" pill approved for long-term use—the actual meaning behind this is that a 6-month study showed that the pill didn't lose its effectiveness over that period and had almost no rebound insomnia. Some critics worry that the medicine hit the market after only 6 months of study without knowledge about long-term effects. Users also complain about a bitter, metallic taste in their mouths associated with the pill. Lunesta comes in 1-, 2-, and 3-milligram pills, and the recommended starting dose is 2 milligrams.

Sonata: This sleeping pill is similar to Ambien and Lunesta but wears off in about 4 hours. This can be effective in warding off traveler's amnesia if you're trying to sleep on the airplane or have an early-morning meeting. Sonata doesn't appear to be as effective as others in increasing total sleep time or decreasing the number of times a user wakes up after falling asleep.

If you decide that prescription medication is not for you, there are also a number of alternative sleep remedies available. Note that these aids are not FDA approved, are not regulated for quality or consistency, and do not have long-term studies to determine their effects.

Melatonin: At night, our pineal glands secrete melatonin to help our bodies regulate our sleep-wake cycles. As we grow older, our bodies produce less. Melatonin, available in 1.5- and 3-milligram pills, stormed the market in 1995, touted as a natural sleep aid with few to no side effects. However, some users have complained of nightmares, morning grogginess, and stomach discomfort.

Valerian: This herb has been known to help relax the central nervous system and decrease anxiety. It does not seem to cause morning grogginess and is nonaddictive, but studies show that its effects are most beneficial only when taken nightly for 1 to 2 weeks.

Kava: This herbal remedy, popular in communities throughout the Pacific, has a tranquilizing effect and has been used to treat ailments like anxiety and depression more than sleeplessness. There are some concerns over the possibility of liver toxicity with the use of kava.

If you're plagued by sleep troubles or jet lag when you travel, here are a few tips to help you out.

! Try to arrange for early-evening arrivals so you can sleep the night in your hotel.

! Set your watch to the destination time zone when you get on the airplane.

! Flying west to east is harder on your body clock, so prepare yourself by waking up and going to bed earlier for a few days before your trip.

! Try to get into the sun whenever possible to shut off melatonin production in your body and reset your body clock.

! A light box can help regulate your body clock if it's not possible to get sunlight.

! Avoid heavy meals, nicotine, alcohol, and caffeine (including chocolate) at least 2 hours before bedtime.

Fear of Flying

File this one under "mental health" while traveling. If you love to travel but hate to fly, don't worry—you're in good company. Millions of Americans have some anxiety over flying, with symptoms ranging from mild concern to paralyzing panic attacks.

To begin with, the fear of flying isn't always about crashing. Many people tend to be claustrophobic and fear having a panic attack on the plane. Other issues that can cause panic on flights include a fear of heights or simply a lack of control. Some of the symptoms of these panic attacks include heart palpitations, sweating, shaking, shortness of breath, and chest pain. Situations such as turbulence and takeoff—or simply hearing inexplicable noises on the aircraft—tend to cause the most anxiety.

Statistically speaking, you would have to fly every day for 32,000 years before you're in a fatal crash. In fact, statistics compiled by www. planecrashinfo.com state that the odds of being killed on a single flight, out of the top 25 airlines with the best records, are 1 in 6.3 million; for the bottom 25 airlines with the worst records, the odds are 1 in 543,000. But no matter how comforting these numbers may be to some, chances are they are not going to make a big difference to those with a significant fear of flying.

At the **Anxiety Treatment Center** near Chicago, psychologists specialize in helping people deal with anxiety and fear. For flying phobias, group therapy sessions meet for 90 minutes once a week, for about 6 weeks. For the final session, the group flies out of Chicago to nearby cities like St. Louis or Detroit. The cost of the course is $425 plus airfare. 847-481-5251, www. anxietycoach.com.

At the **Anxiety and Stress Disorder Institute of Maryland,** a therapist runs a support group for a total of 16 hours. During the group sessions, clients are taught how to embrace and cope with their fear, rather than trying to suppress it. Clients can also visit Baltimore/Washington International airport, tour the facility, and sit inside an aircraft if one is available. At the end of the course, the group takes an hour-long flight to a city, incorporating a fun activity with the flying exercise. A monthly follow-up meeting is available for those who have finished the course and want to continue treatments. The program cost is $600, including airfare, plus $20 for each monthly group. 410-938-8449, www.anxietyandstress.com

At the **Center for Virtual Reality Therapy**, doctors do things a little differently, using virtual reality treatment to simulate a flying experience. They run individual treatment sessions and boast a 93 percent success rate to overcome the fear of flying. They teach breathing techniques and physical relaxation to manage anxiety, and they work on redirecting irrational thoughts like plane crashes or terrorist attacks. Once those techniques are in place, patients use the virtual reality machine, which simulates flying on a plane. The actual view is a little cartoonish, but the seats simulate real movements of an airplane, from takeoff to landing. If a client doesn't suffer any anxiety while in the virtual reality machine, then the program may not be the best choice. Sessions are 1 hour for 8 to 10 weeks and cost $225. 818-222-8355, www.fearofflyingcure.com

If you're not in town to take a course, here are a few other helpful resources.

Captain Meryl Getline is a retired pilot from United Airlines whose humorous attitude has made her quite well known in the travel industry. Her book, *The World at My Feet: The True (and Sometimes Hilarious) Adventures of a Lady Airline Captain*, tells her story—from her days in the army to becoming the first female to ever get a DC-10 Type (Captain) rating, to her career as a pilot at a major airline. Through her Web site, you can order her 10 tips on what every "Anxious, Fearful, or Just Plane Curious Flyer" should know. You can also order her CD, *Ground School for Passengers* ($67), a collection of the concerns and issues that she addressed during her years as *USA Today*'s "Ask the Captain" travel columnist and from her own Web site. She also offers personal consultations for $250. www.flyingfearless.com or www.fromthecockpit.com

Captain Ron Nielsen of America West operates fearless-flight.com, which offers several options for dealing with flight fears. "*Chicken Soup for the Soul* Presents *The Fearless FlightKit*" includes a book of stories from other fearful fliers and a CD of soothing prose, music, and poetry to allay your anxieties ($24). Captain Ron also offers seminars to overcome your fears that are held live in Phoenix and can also be taken at home via teleclass. Basic classes are free and are held at Sky Harbor Airport, while advanced classes are $180 and include a round-trip flight to Los Angeles. The Web site also offers helpful information like the cause of air turbulence, along with research compiled from former clients. www.fearless-flight.com

Captain Stacey Chance is a 20-year airline veteran from American Airlines who runs an online self-help course. You can download the audio course ($9.98) or order it on CD ($14.95). Captain Chance has also just released a *Prepare to Fly* video, which you can download ($29.99) or order on DVD ($39.99). This package includes an explanation of the fear of flying, remedies for anxiety symptoms, a lesson on the various people who are involved in aviation (like air traffic controllers and mechanics), the basics of an aircraft and its environment, and explanations of turbulence. www.fearofflyinghelp.com

Tips to Handle Fear of Flying

! Try "belly breathing." Poor breathing can lead to more physiological symptoms that may increase panic. Inhale through your nose and exhale out your mouth, taking deep breaths into your belly (place your hand on your stomach to make sure it's rising and falling).

! Educate yourself on the mechanics of airplanes and the effects of weather. The more you know about strange noises and movements, the less uncomfortable you'll be.

! Arrive early. Check-in and security lines can be long, and being late for a flight will most likely increase anyone's anxieties, not just those with phobias.

! Avoid caffeine and other stimulants that can make you jittery while on the plane.

! If you have a long flight planned for an upcoming event, try a shorter practice flight in advance, if possible, to get yourself comfortable with the situation.

! Know that practically everyone on the airplane experiences some degree of fear. It's a natural instinct to avoid perceived danger—the trick is managing your fears while on the flight. Once you get through it, you'll probably feel much better prepared for your next flight . . . and the next.

PART 3

TRAVEL BY LIFESTYLE

CHAPTER 15

Accessible Travel

Do not follow where the path may lead. Go, instead, where there is no path and leave a trail.

—SOURCE UNKNOWN

The numbers are both staggering and impressive. And for years, the travel industry essentially ignored them. Consider this: If you include hearing impairment, sight impairment, and physical mobility issues, there are an estimated 49 million people, almost 20 percent of the US population, with a physical disability.

And like everyone else, people who have a disability are just as determined as you are to travel—perhaps even more so.

But obstacles and challenges to travel remain. If you have any sort of physical disability, planning is essential before taking a trip. It's best to talk with your airline, hotel, cruise, or destination, as well as with the Transportation Security Administration (TSA) to find out what your rights and responsibilities are as a traveler.

And also remember (perhaps you might even remind travel providers directly) that there are 49 million people who will vote with their wallets if their basic travel rights are themselves impaired.

Travel by Air

By law, no air carrier may discriminate against any otherwise qualified individual with a disability. You can obtain a booklet from the US Department of Transportation (DOT) called "New Horizons for the Air Traveler with a Disability," which includes information on the accessibility of airports and aircrafts; requirements for advance notice, attendants, and medical certificates; and how to file a complaint. airconsumer.ost.dot.gov/publications/horizons.htm

There are an estimated 17 million disabled passengers flying each year, according to the DOT. Statistics from 2005, the most recent yearlong comprehensive report, showed a total of 13,584 complaints, led by American Airlines (2,616), followed by Delta (1,699) and United (1,294). With all three airlines, the majority of complaints dealt with the airline's failure to provide assistance to passengers in wheelchairs. Similar complaints had to do with the failure to provide assistance to passengers with other disabilities (such as visual and hearing impairment), those with assisted oxygen, and travelers with allergies. Other filed complaints among all airlines include an inaccessible aircraft, damage to an assistive device, and long waiting periods to get assistive devices upon landing. And then there is the continuing confusion over passengers with breathing problems who need to travel with oxygen (more on that later).

Check out this Web site: airconsumer.ost.dot.gov/publications/gateway1.htm. This report contains a tabulation of complaints filed with the DOT regarding the treatment of passengers with disabilities.

If you have mobility problems, call the airline ahead of time and request wheelchair assistance. Don't expect the information to be communicated from one part of the airport to the next—you may need to let them know that you'll need assistance from when you check in to when you're getting off the plane. On flights that require passengers to walk onto the runway and up steps to get onto the flight, there should be a lift to take disabled travelers up and down. Again, make sure the airline is aware of this in advance.

Sometimes, the basic design of the airport is a huge obstacle. For instance, at the Bob Hope Airport in Burbank, California, there are no jetways. A wheelchair-assisted passenger boards the plane using an awkward, embarrassing, and potentially dangerous cherry-picker lift.

Keep in mind that some airlines may not be able to provide "lift-on" assistance inside the aircraft. For example, Air New Zealand uses an onboard skychair (a specially designed onboard wheelchair) to get you to your seat. Qantas offers crew assistance to get you in and out of your seat but provides onboard wheelchairs to transport you to and from the restrooms. However, many airlines note that if you have a mobility impairment so severe that it requires two-person assistance or a mechanical lifting device or you cannot evacuate yourself in case of emergency, you may need to travel with a caregiver. JetBlue, for example, states this in its contract of carriage: "Carrier may require that a Qualified Disabled Individual be accompanied by an attendant as a condition of being provided air transportation under the following circumstances [including] . . . a person with a mobility impairment so severe that the person is unable to assist in his or her own evacuation of the aircraft."

And then there is the huge challenge for travelers with breathing problems and the need for oxygen. There are approximately 1.6 million Americans who are oxygen-dependent, and that number is growing. But only about 5 percent of them travel by air because it's always so difficult to do so.

In most cases, if you know you'll need oxygen on board, you must first get a prescription from your doctor. You then must make your reservation with an airline that provides oxygen tanks on board—not every airline does—and make that reservation at least 48 hours in advance. Oxygen-dependent travelers are not allowed to bring their own oxygen on board.

This problem is now being addressed with new devices approved by the Federal Aviation Administration (FAA). For example, there's now an FAA-approved Portable Oxygen Concentrator (POC) for use on planes. And systems can be rented. (Check with www.oxygentogo.com.)

If you are hearing-impaired, talk to someone at the check-in gate and your flight attendant so that you will be notified of any emergency or other announcements. Some US airports have already installed assistive listening systems to help remedy this problem, and visual notice boards listing arrivals, departures, and gate numbers are required under the 1990 Americans with Disabilities Act (ADA) for all US depots and terminals.

Disabled air travelers can call a toll-free disability hotline for more assistance and information on travelers' rights. The hotline is staffed from 7 a.m. to 5 p.m. EST, Monday through Friday, 800-778-4838 (voice) or 800-455-9880 (TTY text telephone).

Hope for the Future

On its new 787 Dreamliner, Boeing is offering two wheelchair-accessible lavatories on each plane. Partnering with Oregon State University's National Center for Accessible Transportation (a great resource for anyone with a physical disability who needs to travel), Boeing designed interior and exterior door handles that are easier to use for people with limited hand movement, as well as touchless controls for faucets, toilet flushing, and waste flaps.

Service Dogs
Travelers with service dogs should be aware that some countries have restrictions on animals traveling through or arriving in their countries. Check on possible restrictions with the country's embassy or consulate and be clear about quarantine or vaccination requirements. Find out what documents are needed, including international health certificates and rabies inoculation certificates, and whether the documents need to be translated. Talk with your vet about how to travel with your dog and how travel will affect the dog (see "Pet Travel" on page 424).

The Million-Mile Dog
From the "you can't make this stuff up" department comes this piece of frequent flier news: A dog has just passed the million-mile mark in an airline's loyalty program. Nesbit, along with his owner, George Kerscher, received a special Delta award for his Million Miler status recently. You see, Nesbit happens to be the guide dog for Kerscher, a senior officer for Recording for the Blind and Dyslexic, and they have been traveling together, mostly on business, for 8 years. As part of Delta's service to its disabled travelers, the airline accommodated Nesbit on the flights at no additional cost, as the guide dog companion to Platinum Medallion SkyMiles member Kerscher. Of course, now that Nesbit has earned all those miles, he'll be faced with his greatest challenge: Like his human counterparts, he'll have to figure out how to redeem them. (Also see "Pet Travel" for how you can get miles for your dog regardless of your own condition.)

Accessible Cruising
Travelers with special needs, particularly those with mobility problems, can face challenges when traveling by sea. Cruise ships are often sprawling, multi-level vessels, and shore excursions are often not designed with accessibility in mind. However, many of the major lines are taking this population of travelers into consideration and have installed amenities to help make the trip a little easier. Still, most cruise ships allocate only about 6 percent of all cabins to disabled cruisers, when in fact the number of passengers with a physical disability is usually triple that on any one cruise.

Disabled cruisers won a small battle in 2005 as the US Supreme Court issued a 6–3 decision extending the reach of the ADA to foreign cruise lines sailing in US waters. The case was originally brought against Norwegian Cruise Line in 2000 for charging disabled passengers higher fares and extra surcharges and then not providing equivalent access to facilities on the ship.

As a result of the court's verdict, foreign-flag ships are obligated to abide by ADA requirements unless changes interfere with internal affairs of foreign-flag ships or conflict with international safety requirements. However, since many of the industry's ships are registered in countries outside of the United States, such as the Bahamas, Liberia, and Panama, it remains to be seen what actual changes will take place.

In general, US cruise lines claim they are working to make their ships more accessible. At the very least, ships should have roll-in showers, a mechanism to help wheelchair passengers on and off the gangway, and visual alert kits such as telephone amplifiers, visual smoke detectors, door knocker sensors, text telephones, and other aids for hearing and visually impaired passengers. New ships joining the fleets have more accessible cabins, and the public areas are designed to be more accessible. Cabins with roll-in showers are now available in a wide range of categories, and equipment for passengers who are deaf or hard of hearing is available on many ships.

You can visit www.access-able.com/dBase/cruise.cfm for a list of major cruise lines with accessible ships. Some listings have user reviews that help discern whether the ship's accessibility is functional in practice. For example:

Cunard's *Queen Elizabeth 2* (*QE2*) has only four fully accessible cabins and many more that are partially accessible. All decks are accessible, except the Signal and Sun Decks. There are accessible public restrooms. Still, it is a ship not very suitable for wheelchair users and not at all for scooter users. "The adaptations are small ramps on either side of 'doors' but still leave a ridge to be gotten over, and the hatchways are very narrow, not suitable to moving oneself through in a wheelchair. And I don't believe a scooter would fit at all," wrote one disabled passenger. "Elevators are small, old, and slow, and there are only four of them on the whole ship. Only someone with a companion who could push them over the 'humps' or maneuver them through doorways without ramps would be able to get about successfully."

In fairness, the *QE2* was built in the late 1960s. But what about newer ships? Princess Cruises' *Sun Princess* has 19 accessible staterooms, with bathrooms that have roll-in showers with seats, handheld showerheads, and grab bars. All decks are accessible, as are the public restrooms, which have distress alarms. The elevators have braille numbers on all decks, and the floor indicator is audio. Service dogs are permitted. One passenger recently wrote, "My 83-year-old father (disabled) and I had the pleasure of cruising on the *Sun Princess* in late April/early May from Fort Lauderdale to Victoria. The disabled room provided was excellent. The care, attention, and service we received were first class. The *Sun Princess* is very user-friendly. Getting ashore was never a problem. Their caring staff make it that way. This ship is no problem to anyone using a wheelchair or scooter. The only drawback—and the most common one—is that there are not enough of these rooms available, so book early. Happy sailing."

However, one of the biggest issues still confronting the cruise industry—and you need to be very careful about this when booking your cruise—is that while the ship may be accessible, the ports may *not* always be accessible. It has always astounded me that cruise lines have never taken a more proactive, determined stand to make ports accessible to *all* of their passengers. I am convinced that if a cruise line announced that it would no longer sail to ports that were not accessible to every one of its passengers, the countries in question would rebuild their port facilities overnight in order to be in compliance. It's a no-brainer . . . but then again, I don't really think the cruise lines realize how many of their passengers—or potential passengers—really are disabled and would take a cruise tomorrow if they could be assured of accessibility.

In the meantime, and until the cruise lines come to their senses, check in with your travel agent or contact the cruise line directly to find out which shore excursions are accessible and if there is accessible transportation available to even get off the ship at some ports. In some cases, passengers may be taken on and off shore by a small boat, and it's possible that the crew may deny you boarding due to bad weather conditions.

One company that makes scooters (www.scootaround.com, 888-441-7575) can help you out in a number of cruise ship ports. You can have a scooter or wheelchair delivered to you at the port, hotel, convention center, or even home. This is a great situation for slow walkers or people with mobility problems who may not need assisted transportation in everyday life but may have problems walking the long distances that go with travel.

Hotels and Accessibility

Enacted in 1990, the ADA hotel guidelines require that all hotels and motels make their facilities equally accessible to those with physical disabilities.

A property with 25 or fewer rooms needs to have at least one handicap-accessible room, and a hotel with 500 or fewer rooms needs to have nine accessible rooms. For guests with hearing impairment, hotels are required to equip rooms with notification devices, telephone amplifiers, and TDDs (telecommunications devices for the deaf).

When booking your room, make sure that you ask for it to be *reserved and guaranteed,* not just requested. It's also a good idea to call ahead to confirm that the hotel is conforming to ADA standards, which means a strobe light in your room so that you can be alerted when the phone rings or someone knocks at the door. Or ask if there is braille signage that you can find in an appropriate manner to be able to locate your own room. Also remember to contact the hotel to make sure your service dog can be accommodated.

Don't forget that a hotel concierge can be your best friend—you can find out whether the area has high curbs and crosswalks, how accessible the public transportation is, and whether there are amenities like restaurants and shops nearby.

Some hotels are being proactive in the accessibility movement: Inspired by a relationship with the Little People of America, Carlson Hotels, Microtel Inns & Suites, and Hawthorn Suites are now offering an "in-room assistive convenience kit" to aid the 1.2 million Americans who are short in stature (4 feet 10 inches or shorter) or who have a form of dwarfism. The kit includes a step stool, a reaching tool, and a bar to lower the clothes rack.

Accessibility Abroad

Since the ADA doesn't apply to other countries, dealing with disabilities when traveling abroad can often be a challenge. Foreign airlines may not be equipped to deal with disabled travelers, and hotels can be located in inaccessible areas or have steps with no ramps or elevators. Remember that European countries and developing nations may have difficulty retrofitting their streets and buildings to deal with accessibility issues.

If you're looking for a hotel that's wheelchair-friendly overseas, try www.laterooms.com (click on "Search" and then on the Disabled Access button and you'll see hundreds of hotels that are accessible). What about renting a villa? Check out www.ownersdirect.co.uk and go to the wheelchair-friendly section, where you can select by country and then by region or town.

In some cases, a DIY trip may be a complicated feat, between seeking out accessible hotels, finding neighborhoods without steep curbs, and navigating transportation between sights. There are several tour groups that offer trips to accommodate disabled travelers. The benefit of arranging through these companies is that these agents and tour operators have some expertise about the region's accessibility, so most of the work is taken out of your hands.

Accessible Journeys focuses on tour packages around the world for travelers in wheelchairs and their companions, as well as mature travelers and slow walkers. This includes wheelchair-accessible vans and motor coaches, luggage assistance, full-time tour operators, and stays in fully accessible hotels. Tours include a visit to the Canadian Rockies and Glacier National Park, a South African safari, trekking through India and Nepal, and a tour and cruise through Australia and New Zealand. Rates range from about $2,000 to $8,000 per person, from 1 to 3 weeks. 800-846-4537, www. disabilitytravel.com

Flying Wheels Travel offers escorted tours and cruises worldwide. International trips feature an auto tour of France, including Paris, Bordeaux, and Provence; a cultural tour of Spain; and a tour of Egypt and the Nile. Prices range from about $1,500 to $3,500 per person. 507-451-5005, www.flyingwheelstravel.com

The Guided Tour offers tours for travelers with both developmental and physical challenges. Most trips have a staff-to-traveler ratio of 1 to 3, including nurses who are trained to deal with specific disabilities as well as administering insulin shots or medication. If a traveler is in a wheelchair, is a slow walker, or is visually impaired, the staff ratio is usually 1 to 1. Trips include tours of Ireland, Nova Scotia, and Bermuda, with several US trips including Walt Disney World, Nashville, and Atlantic City. 800-783-5841, www.guidedtour.com

Endeavour Travels is a Southern Africa tour and safari company specializing in accessible travel and catering to people with mobility, visual, and hearing impairments as well as those who require oxygen or kidney dialysis. 27-21-556-6114, www.endeavour-safaris.com

And, if you're just visiting a city and want to enjoy local outdoor areas that are also accessible, check out www.boundlessplaygrounds.org for a list of areas that may have wheelchair-friendly trails or accessible outdoor playgrounds for children with disabilities. 860-243-8315

Adaptive Sports

Travelers who have mobility problems or other physical disabilities can face some serious challenges when heading into the great outdoors. Fortunately, an increasing number of destinations are now more equipped to deal with special needs. Whether it's skiing, sailing, or hiking, there are outdoor activities and specialized equipment available for disabled travelers.

You may have heard of the Paralympics, in which traditional Olympic sports were adapted to accommodate various disabilities, including spinal cord injuries, amputated limbs, cerebral palsy, dwarfism, and mental handicaps. The first Paralympics took place in Rome in 1960, a week after the Olympic Games, and the first Winter Paralympics were held in Örnsköldsvik, Sweden, in 1976. With the Paralympics serving as a model for ski resorts, parks, and other destinations, disabled travelers now have several options when it comes to outdoor sports.

Adaptive cycling, for instance, may include the handcycle, a three-wheeled hand-propelled bike for athletes with lower mobility problems. Blind and visually impaired cyclists may race on tandem bikes with a sighted partner, while cyclists with cerebral palsy or head injury may use both standard bikes and tricycles.

In Vancouver, British Columbia, hiking has become more accessible thanks to the Trail Rider, a device that enables people with significant or severe mobility problems to access trails that would otherwise be too rough. These Trail Riders resemble a sort of wheelbarrow-meets-rickshaw, with two volunteer "Sherpas"—one pulling in the front, the other pushing from the back—providing momentum. www.disabilityfoundation.org/bcmos

In Portland, Oregon, the Adventurer hiker's chair makes hiking on a non–wheelchair accessible trail easier. The 42-pound device can be wheeled through unsteady terrain, with one person pushing and one person pulling. www.ezhiker.com

In skiing, visually impaired skiers can be guided through the course by sighted guides using voice signals to indicate the course. As for equipment, the mono-ski is designed for skiers with disabilities like spinal cord injury or leg amputation in which they have use of their upper body. The bi-ski offers a wider base and better balance for those with less or no mobility in their upper body or those with conditions like cerebral palsy. The sit-ski is preferred by those who have significant physical limitations.

More options for skiers:

The Tahoe Adaptive Ski School, located in the Alpine Meadows ski resort, offers private lessons for adaptive skiing and caters to skiers with not just physical limitations but also cognitive and behavioral ones, like autism and attention deficit disorder. Instructors are certified through the Professional Ski Instructors of America, with a specialized certification in adaptive ski instruction. Because the program is part of Disabled Sports USA Far West organization, it is subsidized by grants and private funding, which translates into less-expensive lessons. 530-581-4161, www.dsusafw.org/sports.html

Snowbird Resort in Utah is completely wheelchair accessible, including a low-impact, barrier-free trail and an aerial tram that carries riders to the 11,000-foot Hidden Peak. Also at Snowbird, Wasatch Adaptive Sports operates year-round and provides activities like skiing, snowshoeing, and adaptive hockey in the winter; hiking, fishing, orienteering, bicycling, tram rides, and frequent special events during the summer; and adaptive horseback riding and bowling on a year-round basis. 800-232-9542, www.snowbird.com

Waterville Valley in New Hampshire offers the Waterville Valley Adaptive Snowsports Program under the nonprofit organization AbilityPlus, with more than 80 volunteer ski guides. www.waterville.com/winter/adaptive.html

The **Breckenridge Outdoor Education Center** in Breckenridge, Colorado—in association with Breckenridge, Keystone, and Copper Mountain resorts—offers adaptive private skiing, rafting, wilderness camping, climbing, and cycling. 800-222-7275, www.boec.org

Through the National Ability Center, Utah's **Park City Mountain Resort** offers adaptive skiing and snowboarding lessons with trained guides. 435-649-8111, www.parkcitymountain.com/winter/school/national_ability_center/index.html

The **Adaptive Ski Program,** New Mexico, offers ski lessons at Sandia Peak and Ski Santa Fe. 505-995-9858, www.adaptiveski.org

For more information on various types of adaptive sports, visit Disabled Sports USA at www.dsusa.org.

Special-Needs Summer Camps

According to Paula Goldberg, executive director of the PACER Center, a national resource center for professionals and parents of children with disabilities, there are about 6.5 million kids in this country who receive special education for disabilities like autism, learning disabilities, and Down syndrome. While there is no overall statistic regarding the number of pediatric patients with medical conditions, we do know that there are more than 8,500 kids under the age of 15 that are diagnosed with cancer each year and about 570,000 kids under the age of 13 living with HIV/AIDS. Add in other conditions like chronic asthma, blood disorders, and attention deficit disorder (ADD), and you have a pretty sobering number of kids who might have a hard time in traditional summer camps.

There are now a number of overnight camps that are designed especially for children who have special needs and that address a variety of physical, medical, behavioral, and mental challenges. While a parent's anxiety will probably never disappear altogether, these camps are generally staffed with trained counselors and medical experts who know how to deal with specific conditions.

You can also find a list of special-needs camps that are accredited by the American Camp Association at www.aca-camps.org, 765-342-8456. When you're researching camps for your special-needs child, don't be afraid to ask questions. Find out what the counselor-to-camper ratio is—ideally it should be about 3 to 1. Learn about what kind of medical staff is available and how close the camp is to a hospital. Also, be aware that some camps are specialized toward specific needs, while others are more encompassing of different disabilities.

Arizona Camp Sunrise is sponsored by the American Cancer Society for kids 8 to 16 who have or have had cancer. The camp is free of charge, relying heavily on donations from individuals. It has a ratio of four counselors to every camper, but those who need more attention than others will receive it. A 24-hour medical staff is on hand for all campers. Activities include many of the traditional camp fun things, like archery, arts and crafts, and drama. The camp also sponsors Sidekicks camp, designed for children who have siblings with cancer, allowing them the opportunity to meet and support other siblings going through a similar situation. 602-952-7550, www.azcampsunrise.org

Camp Heartland offers four weeklong programs in Minnesota and one weeklong program in Southern California for children ages 7 to 15 who are living with or affected by HIV/AIDS. Youths 16 to 21 can participate in the fall Youth Retreat programs. The fee is $50 per child (or a $100 maximum fee per multiple children) but can be waived for those in financial need. Besides traditional camp activities, the campers can sign up for discussion groups to talk to their peers as well as professional nurses, social workers, and psychologists about their condition. A physician is always available on-site or at a nearby clinic, and there are usually about five or six medical volunteers as well. Each nurse is assigned to one or two cabin groups to dispense medications and monitor each camper's health. 800-724-4673, www.campheartland.org

For kids with behavioral problems or learning disabilities, traditional camp often doesn't provide them with the patient, individualized attention that they may need. The following camps can rectify that.

Camp Kodiak in Ontario, Canada, is for children ages 6 to 18 who have learning disabilities, attention deficit disorder, and attention deficit hyperactivity disorder (ADHD). There is an hour of academic tutoring each day, and the rest of the day is spent building social skills through outdoor sports, along with a more focused approach through activities like drama and music. The ratio of campers to counselors is 2 to 1, so that each child can get the attention he needs. There are 3- to 7-week programs available, with fees between $2,875 and $6,175. 877-569-7595, www.campkodiak.com

The **Learning Camp** in Vail, Colorado, also deals with kids ages 7 to 14 with learning disabilities, ADD, and ADHD. The student-to-counselor ratio is 3 to 1. The program combines academics that are tailored to each child, with traditional outdoor camp activities. Classes are held outdoors and there is no homework, but lessons do last several hours each day. Two-week sessions are available throughout the summer and cost $2,900. 970-524-2706, www.learningcamp.com

Talisman Camps in the mountains of western North Carolina deals with children 8 to 17 with learning disabilities and ADD, as well as those with high-functioning autism and Asperger's syndrome. The camper-to-staff ratio is about 2 to 1, and there are several programs available for different conditions and age groups. Programs for children with Asperger's syndrome or high-functioning autism focus on activities like rope-climbing courses to build social skills and emotional management. The ADD and learning-disabled program may include a mix of academics and outdoor activities, as well as pioneering adventures. Two-week programs take place throughout the summer and cost $1,400 to $2,900. 888-458-8226, www.talismancamps.com

Many special-needs camps are more generalized, bringing together campers with a variety of physical, behavioral, and medical conditions like Down syndrome, cerebral palsy, spina bifida, ADHD, cancer, and diabetes.

Albrecht Acres of the Midwest in Iowa is a summer camp for both children and adults with different conditions. There is 24-hour nursing service and a 3-to-1 camper-to-counselor ratio (1-to-1 when needed). The price is $425 per week and $170 per weekend, but there is financial aid available. The camp fee for a weeklong (Sunday through Friday) program is $440; for a weekend stay (Friday through Sunday), the fee is $170. Camp season starts mid-June and runs to mid-August. 563-552-1771, www.albrechtacres.com

Camp Aldersgate, located on 120 acres in Arkansas, has three types of short-term programs available throughout the year. Their medical camps serve children with all sorts of disabilities and work with the organization

Med Camps of Arkansas to provide volunteer physicians on-site. Respite Care takes place several weekends throughout the year in order to give parents and caretakers a temporary break. Kota Camps are weekend or week-long programs designed for campers with disabilities along with their siblings and friends, to promote special-needs awareness and understanding. 501-225-1444, www.campaldersgate.net

A Community Comes Together

Chances are you've probably never been to the quiet little village of Jackson, New Hampshire (population 835). This small town borders nearly 750,000 acres of the White Mountain National Forest, just south of Mount Washington and the Presidential Range. Jackson is a place where you won't find any name-brand chain hotels or restaurants. There's a small historic library, a town hall, and a white steepled church. The main access to the village is through a historical covered bridge built in 1876 that crosses the nationally preserved Wildcat River.

But every year, something remarkable happens in Jackson, New Hampshire. This small New England community becomes a travel capital of sorts. The entire village opens its doors, bedrooms, and restaurants to welcome guests living with multiple sclerosis (MS) to enjoy a special free week of relaxation, rest, workshops, networking, and socialization. More than 10 country inns, bed-and-breakfasts, and grand hotels have hosted individuals living with multiple sclerosis.

The story started back in 2000, when Don and Joyce Bilger decided to quit the high-tension, fast-paced corporate life and move to small town America to pursue their dream of running a small bed-and-breakfast. And they restored the Inn at Jackson.

The idea that prompted the abrupt shift in lifestyle was that Joyce had been diagnosed with multiple sclerosis, and their lives changed forever. As the couple learned more about the crippling disease, they realized how many other people were in similar situations and needed information and support.

In 2006, they opened their inn to welcome folks with MS to attend a series of workshops, learn, and yes, even relax. The concept was simple and powerful: There are no charges for lodging, breakfast, or workshops. Participants are welcome to make a donation to the National MS Society in lieu of payment for the lodging and workshops, but this is not required.

The idea was so popular that the inn was soon filled. Eventually a random drawing had to be held to determine who could be accommo-

▽ Resources

Society for Accessible Travel and Hospitality offers news, tips, and resources for accessible travel issues. Topics include traveling by wheelchair, sight or hearing impairment, diabetes, and much more. 212-447-7284, **www. sath.org**

dated. Due to the overwhelming response to the event, other inns in Jackson were inspired to step forward to help meet the high demand for lodging. Soon the entire village became involved, with local specialty shops offering discounts to MS participants and dining establishments hosting benefit dinners for the National MS Society.

The Bilgers' dream has now turned into a town's mission to help those living with multiple sclerosis.

Before long, others in town climbed on board. Soon, more than 45 rooms were being offered free to MS patients. Then came the challenge of scheduling the programs, which included morning seminars, discussion groups, workshops, and professional medical speakers.

In 2007, 90 rooms throughout the village were made available, and the local restaurants of Jackson threw open their doors as well. Workshop topics included "Understanding Depression and MS," "Complementary and Alternative Medicine," and "Financial Planning," all subjects of vital interest to so many MS patients.

The Jackson village program has quickly become a model for other destinations and resorts to follow. More than anything else, it has united an entire community in a single cause and a great display of hospitality—a travel story with a purpose that goes way beyond simply visiting a destination.

One additional note: The Bilgers and the village of Jackson aren't the only ones giving deserving folks a much-needed break. In Glenwood Springs, Colorado, you'll find Bob Johnson, a real estate broker who also runs Operation Vacation, which awards three-day weekend getaways to soldiers returning from—or in the midst of—tours of duty in Iraq or Afghanistan. As in Jackson, New Hampshire, the resort town came together to put these special trips together.

The US Government also has a Web page with tips for travelers with disabilities. **www.travel.state.gov/travel/tips/brochures/brochures_1228.html**

Travel information for mature and special-needs travel, including worldwide listings of accessible cruise ships, accommodations, public transportation, attractions, tours, and medical resources: **www.Access-able.com**

Disabled Travelers offers a resource of businesses that specialize in accessible travel, including tour operators and travel agents, as well as airline policies and an online travel community. (Note that some links are no longer working) **www.disabledtravelers.com**

Mobility International USA works with disabled individuals worldwide and offers international exchanges, international development, and accessible volunteer and intern opportunities. 541-343-1284, **www.miusa.org**

Boundless Playgrounds is a nonprofit organization that specializes in creating playgrounds around the nation that are accessible to everyone. 860-243-8315, **www.boundlessplaygrounds.org**

Disabled Sports USA: **www.dsusa.org**

Adaptive Sports Association: 970-769-1991, **www.asadurango.org**

 Some Surprises

Amtrak offers a reduced fare for travel attendants, if you need to bring someone with you. Some Broadway shows give deep discount tickets (as much as 50 percent off) for disabled theatergoers and their companions.

CHAPTER 16

📖 **There are millions of Americans who are clever and fearless, but the trouble is that they are only four years old.** 🔖

—ANONYMOUS

In 2005, Americans took more than 200 million leisure trips with minors. American Express polled travel agents nationwide and found that 79 percent of them saw an increase in family travel—however, families are skipping the traditional routes and opting for more meaningful and active vacations. The poll found that 81 percent of agents are booking family trips that include multigenerational trips, which often include grandparents.

According to the 2004 Domestic Market Report from the Travel Industry Association (TIA), one in four household trips in the United States includes children under the age of 18. According to the TIA study, the most common activities on trips with children include shopping (32 percent), attending a social/family event (31 percent), engaging in an outdoor activity (14 percent), going to the beach (12 percent), and going to a theme/amusement park (12 percent). But the real question: Is that what your kids really want?

Consider this: The California-based KSL Resorts, which manages six resorts in California, Colorado, Texas, and Virginia, studied family travel and found that 70 percent of respondents would rather play with their kids instead of engaging in more "grown-up" activities like golf or spending the day at the spa. The study found that parents and grandparents actually want to go sightseeing and explore towns with the kids—but again, ask the kids first . . . a whopping 90 percent of the kids would rather hang out at the pool over the 43 percent who enjoy sightseeing.

Marketing agency Yesawich Pepperdine Brown and Russell (YPB&R) actually went directly to children for their answers. They polled 800 kids ages 6 to 17 and came out with some interesting results: 71 percent of the kids said they needed a vacation, citing the stresses of school and extracurricular activities. Theme parks came out on top; beach or lake vacations came in second place, followed by cruises. Fully 80 percent of the kids wanted to go swimming, 78 percent looked forward to eating in restaurants, and 76 percent simply liked the idea of staying in a hotel or resort. As for what they didn't like? No surprises here: 52 percent didn't want to get up early, and 34 percent didn't want to play golf. Surprisingly, 36 percent didn't want to ride in a car, which may put a damper on your upcoming family road trip—and don't make any special stops at any museums, according to 31 percent of the kids.

You may also be familiar with a new trend called multigenerational travel. That can involve all three (or sometimes four) generations hitting the road together or can mean kids traveling with their grandparents—without the parents! A 2006 study by YPB&R found that 28 percent of grandparents have traveled with their grandkids on one or more leisure trips in the previous 12 months, and nearly 60 percent of kids ages 6 to 17 say they'd like to vacation with their grandparents.

And finally, a 2006 study by American Express found that family travel is on the rise and also that traditional getaways are including more involved and meaningful activities. That means not just driving by the sites and pointing at the landmarks but actually digging in deep for hands-on experiences, educational learning, and most of all, making it fun!

Flying with Children

An estimated 4.5 million children under the age of 2 fly each year. At this time—and I consider this to be a major breach of common sense and responsibility—the Federal Aviation Administration (FAA) does not require infants and toddlers to be restrained or secured on aircraft during takeoff, landing, and turbulence but instead permits them to be held on an adult's lap, free of charge. However, both the National Transportation Safety Board (NTSB) and the American Academy of Pediatrics (AAP) have deemed this unacceptable and are strongly supporting a mandatory federal requirement for restraint use for children on aircraft, calling for the use of automobile-style, FAA-approved child safety seats during flights.

The common argument is that if a plane crashes, passengers are unlikely to survive no matter how well they are secured. But even this argument lacks common sense because it ignores what are called survivable "hard landings" and CAT (clear air turbulence). The real concern here is *avoidable* injury and fatality. Think about it: before takeoff and landing and when the plane hits turbulence, you have to buckle up, put away your laptop, and stay in your seat; flight attendants stow away the food carts and lock up the coffeepots—why? So that these items don't go flying around the cabin. So why would you keep a child unsecured on your lap?

There have been cases in which unsecured children and infants have sustained injury during heavy turbulence. Between 1970 and 1994, 23 lap-held children were injured or killed during a flight. The case in 1994 involved a 9-month-old infant who was held on her mother's lap and sustained fatal injuries. The mother was unable to hold on to her baby during the turbulence, and the child struck several seats. The NTSB believes that if the child had been properly restrained in a child-restraint system, she may have survived.

In 2005, the FAA withdrew its support of child restraint seats (CRS) for children under the age of 2 in aircraft during all phases of flight. The FAA argued that forcing parents to buy a separate plane ticket for a child will only add to the total cost of travel, meaning that if the airlines were forced to provide the restraint seats, it would result in higher airfares and more families would then choose the riskier option to drive rather than fly. Statistically speaking, the risk of fatalities and injuries to families is significantly higher on the road than in the air—in 2005, nearly 43,000 people died on US highways, as compared with 13 on commercial flights. Still, when I want the FAA to talk about highway safety, I'll ask those folks. We're talking about airline safety!

If you do choose to purchase an extra airplane seat for your child's FAA-approved safety seat, the following guidelines may help.

! Children weighing less than 20 pounds should be restrained in an approved rear-facing CRS—a hard-backed seat that is approved by the government for use in both motor vehicles and aircraft.

- ! Children weighing 20 to 40 pounds should be restrained in an approved forward-facing CRS.

- ! Children weighing more than 40 pounds should use the standard lap belt that is attached to all airline seats.

- ! Ask your airline for a discounted fare. Many airlines now offer discounts of up to 50 percent for children less than 2 years old who have their own seats.

If you choose not to purchase a second seat for a child, ask the flight attendant if there's a seat belt extension, which can secure the child to your lap—most airlines should have one available. The FAA has also approved a new harness-type device appropriate for children weighing between 22 and 44 pounds. The harness, cleverly named CARES (for Child Aviation Restraint System), attaches directly to the airplane seat belt. It is the first child safety restraint system to be approved by the FAA during taxiing, takeoff, turbulence, and landing. For more information, call 800-299-6249 or visit www.kidsflysafe.com.

Kids and Passports

If you are taking a child other than your own across the border or if it's your own child without your spouse, you need to have a notarized note from the parent(s) giving you permission to take the child out of the country. Be sure the note specifies the dates of travel and is signed and notarized. This is void if there is a court order that grants a parent sole custody. You can find a parental consent form at www.notary.org.

If a parent fears that a child might be taken abroad by the other parent without the mutual consent of both parents, the child's name can be put in the US passport name check system. If an application is received, the requesting parent will be informed before issuance of the passport.

For more information on children and passports, visit www.travel.state.gov/passport.

Childproofing Hotel Rooms

When traveling with children, it's essential to remember that hotel rooms aren't childproofed like your own home. Back in 2000, the US Consumer Product Safety Commission actually did spot-checks on hotels across the country, and what they found was disturbing. They visited more than 90 hotels in 27 states and found woefully inadequate situations with children's cribs. If the crib mattress isn't supported properly, it could fall through, and it could suffocate a child, as could pillows. Then there are problems with loose hardware and jagged edges.

But it's not just cribs that are an issue. There are potential dangers when it comes to electrical sockets, sharp corners on tables, sliding doors, windows, and open balconies.

The good news is that if a room isn't kid-friendly, you can take measures to childproof the room yourself. First, ask the hotel what facilities it has to childproof your room. Many hotel chains, such as Loews, Four Seasons, Westin, and the Nickelodeon Family Suites by Holiday Inn, actually provide a childproofing kit—this can include doorknob covers, electrical outlet covers, and drawer latches. But you've got to ask first. Or you can make your own kit, using masking tape or, preferably, duct tape (masking tape is easy for kids to remove). The tape is used to seal windows and latches, especially sliding doors, and to put together your own buffer for certain sharp areas like a table corner where you don't have bumpers. And to cover electrical outlets, use the appropriate plastic outlet covers or the tape itself.

One of the things you need to do when you check into a room, as a parent, is to get down on your hands and knees and literally crawl the room at the same height as your child might be so you can actually see those hazards. Often we take so much for granted and forget what is within their reach. In the bathrooms, always check the water temperature because kids can get easily burned when you just turn that faucet on.

Even cruise lines are childproofing. On Disney, for example, which caters to kids, you won't find any square or rough edges around the cabins. Every piece of furniture in a Disney cabin is rounded. The designers did that intentionally because of so many small children onboard.

Bottom line is that while hotels and cruise lines are getting smarter, you can't expect them to always do it for you. You have to be responsible and take the necessary precautions.

In the Room

❗ Move furniture away from the windows.

❗ Furniture needs to be stable and sturdy to avoid tipping over.

- ! Doorknobs should be tight so your children will not remove them (and put them in their mouths).
- ! Make sure that doors and windows are securely locked.
- ! Tie up any loose cords, such as on window blinds, to prevent possible strangulation.
- ! Cover unused electrical outlets.
- ! Tables with sharp edges should be removed or edges should be covered (washcloths are a perfect solution).
- ! Remove any tablecloths.
- ! With very small children, just because a hotel or motel might provide a crib, that doesn't mean you don't need to inspect it carefully. Make sure that it is up to standards with the Consumer Product Safety Commission: Slats should not be more than $2\frac{3}{8}$ inches apart.
- ! Remove any pillows or blankets that may cause suffocation.

In the Bathroom

- ! Never leave your child alone in the bathroom.
- ! When giving your child a bath, the water should not reach more than 120°F; try to keep it between 96° and 100°F.
- ! Unplug any electrical appliances, such as a hairdryer, and store them in a locked drawer.
- ! Make sure there are decals or a nonslip mat on the bathtub floor.
- ! Check to see if the bathroom mat has a stable backing to prevent slips.
- ! Any hazardous products should be put away: mouthwash, shampoo, cosmetics.

Last but not least, beware of hotel balconies. While the railings may be high enough to prevent a child from leaning or falling over, the real danger is the space between the iron bars or wooden slats. Some hotels, like the Four Seasons in Maui, provide plastic mesh that fits in front of the bars to make sure your child can't slip between or through the bars and fall off the balcony. But most hotels do not provide this. Your solution: Either bring your own mesh (with that all-purpose duct tape) or lock the balcony door.

Getting Good Service with Kids

This does not have to be a mutually exclusive situation. You *can* get good service with kids, but you need to know how to finesse the situation. Let's start with the obvious: The truth is, when restaurant managers, gate attendants, and front desk clerks see little people in your party, they often typecast you, whether they will admit it or not. And unfortunately, that can mean poor service for you.

Of course, you can't really blame them. There are the kids who disrupt romantic dinners by throwing the contents of their breadbasket at dining couples . . . the kids who have hours-long screaming tantrums on airplanes . . . the pack of mini-hooligans in the room next to yours who jump on the bed all night to Barney vocals.

Does that mean you should suffer? Of course not—if you can help it. To that end, here are some tips to help you get great service, even with the kids in tow.

In a Restaurant

❗ **Be realistic.** Before you book your table, decide what kind of atmosphere you want for yourself and the kids. If it's a special occasion, you may want a fine-dining establishment. Just make sure your children are up to the task. While you and your 10-year-old may be perfectly fine with a 3-hour, four-course meal, it will most likely be misery for your 2-year-old. When dining with very young children, pick an establishment that is at the very least kid-friendly. In general, restaurants that actually have a kids' menu are a good choice.

❗ **Call ahead.** When making your reservations, be honest about your expectations. If you want the coveted table by the fireplace and are bringing a well-behaved child, there should be no reason why you shouldn't get it. Just make sure you speak to the manager about your expectations ahead of time so that there are no ugly surprises when you show up. Explain that it is a special occasion, you are a repeat customer (even if you are not), and that you are bringing a child (or children)—but that you would like the same treatment you always get when dining at this particular establishment.

❗ **Request a specific table.** Many customers request "special" tables when making a reservation. Try to get a reservation confirmation number when doing this and make sure to get the name of the person you are speaking to.

! **Stand your ground.** If you have made your phone calling requesting a specific table and are still ushered to the table near the kitchen, kindly tell the maître d' that you arranged for a different table ahead of time. Invoke your confirmation number, request to speak to the manager, and explain again that this is a special occasion and you would like the table you reserved.

If all of the above fails, try not to have a temper tantrum yourself—you will only be validating their fears that children (and those who dare to bring them to a restaurant) are not suited for their establishment. Either accept the table they give you (with a strong letter to follow) or leave. There are many other establishments that will undoubtedly appreciate your business.

At the Airport

For starters, there is not a whole lot you can do in an arena where passengers—with and without children—are regularly abused. But here are a few ideas.

! **Don't tell them ahead.** If you are looking to get upgraded, don't drag the kids up to the gate agent. That's right, leave them seated nearby with another responsible adult, walk up to the gate agent alone, and ask that you and your "seat companions" please be upgraded with your certificates.

! **Appeal to the agent's sympathy.** If you are a mom en route to Chicago with a 2-year-old, let the agent know that you have been having a hard day and that getting upgraded or, at the very least, sitting in a decent section of coach would really make your day. Remember, that gate agent has the power (providing that seats are available), so be really, really nice.

! **Dress for success.** If you're looking to get upgraded and you're flying with children, you may want to spiff up a bit. Sure, if you happen to be a hit TV series producer or a famous actress, by all means, show up in crummy jeans and a sweatshirt—you'll still be treated like a king. Just don't expect the same treatment if you're a mom traveling with two toddlers.

At the Hotel

Everyone, even people with kids, deserves to get a good night's sleep. Here's how not to get the room next to that noisy ice machine or even next to someone else's annoying kids.

! **Put the kids on best behavior.** At least for the 10 minutes you'll be checking in, ask your kids (bribe them, if necessary) to be polite little angels. Have them play the Quiet Game, if you must, promising the winner a reward like a room service milkshake.

‼ Talk to the manager. If the front desk clerk insists there are only rooms next to the vending machine, immediately ask for the hotel manager. If you're polite and stand your ground, you should be able to land a nice room.

‼ Lastly, don't forget to be considerate of others. If your child does start screaming in a restaurant or hotel, you owe it to yourself, not to mention your fellow diners/travelers, to take the little darling outside until the tantrum is over.

Kid-Friendly Resorts and Hotels

Back in the old days, a "kid-friendly" hotel meant that the closest restaurant served chicken fingers, the pool had a lifeguard who was occasionally on duty, and, if you were really lucky, the lobby had a video game arcade. But today, more and more hotels, resorts, and cruises are catering to families with innovative kids' programs that let the parents wander free for a while, family-friendly food, and amenities to make your lives a little easier. In fact, a study by KSL Resorts in conjunction with Equation Research found that while a swimming pool is really the number-one feature that makes kids happy (92 percent), a kids activity center is hugely popular—79 percent of respondents would prefer to have one available, far surpassing the 19 percent who appreciate a traditional day-care option.

All-inclusive resorts and cruises are often better options for families—kids can go off and do their own thing while you lounge around the pool sipping mai tais, with no fear of anyone getting lost. When it comes to hotels that claim to be kid friendly, make sure that they offer more than just a few board games or a library of old books. Organized activities with supervised staff will likely cost $50 or more a day, but the benefit is that the kids won't just be stuck in the room with a babysitter, and you can have your alone time sans children.

Before you book a family vacation, here are some key questions to ask in advance.

‼ Is there a childproofing kit available?

‼ Do kids under a certain age stay for free?

! Can you get adjoining rooms? If so, ask for a discount.

! Are kid-friendly meals available at or near the hotel? Room service?

! Does the pool have a lifeguard and is it locked at night?

! Are there supervised, organized activities for kids? Find out the ratio of supervisors to children (preferably 4 to 1 or less). Do they offer babysitting services with pre-approved, qualified babysitters? (If there are no babysitting services, check www.sittercity.com for local babysitters where you're traveling—definitely schedule a phone interview, ask for references, and talk to the customer service reps if you have any concerns at 888-748-2489.)

It should come as no surprise that **Disney Cruises** offers some of the most kid-friendly programs out there. The ships are swarming with costumed characters ready to pose with your kids, and each night there are lavish stage performances such as a musical based on the "Cinderella" story with both new and old songs. Daytime activities abound, with programs for the little ones including puppet shows, play areas, and kiddie pools; travelers ages 13 to 17 have their own teen room with a soda bar, Internet kiosk, plasma TVs, video games, and music. There are also counselors on board who organize activities like pool parties, movie-making classes, and excursions to Disney's own private island, Castaway Cay. 800-951-3532, www.disneycruise.disney.go.com

Carnival Cruise Lines is also one of the more family-friendly lines available—the price includes admission to Camp Carnival, which offers activities that are tailored toward toddlers, juniors, preteens, and teens (keeping them out of your hair while you grab a little private time). Shore excursions can be a great way to bring about a little family bonding; even the surliest teens may wind up oohing and ahhing over the wiggling little creatures under a glass-bottom boat or crack a smile when they parasail over the Bahamas. 888-227-64825, www.carnival.com

At the **Ritz-Carlton,** the chain has a Ritz Kids program that varies by hotel. Some are pretty hokey, like a Bath Butler drawing a bath for babies, complete with rubber duckies, in the Hong Kong property. In Sarasota, Florida, kids have their own beachfront club, with organized activities like arts and crafts, scavenger hunts, and group swimming. The Ritz-Carlton, Kapalua is a full resort with activities for grown-ups and kids: Both full- and half-day programs include exploring the island, playing on a nine-hole putting green,

The Chinese government is cracking down on the use of "Chinglish"—opaque road signs that translate into some amusing phrases. Before long, you may not see signs like "the slippery are very crafty" or trash cans labeled "fruit leather suitcase." You also won't be able to visit "Racist Park" (more accurately identified as the Park of Ethnic Minorities) in Beijing, and the dish "old woman chicken" will be stricken from menus.

and storytelling at the Ritz Kids Room. On Amelia Island in northeast Florida, the resort holds tight to a pirate theme, where counselors dress like pirates or their princess companions for sing-alongs and storytime by a bonfire. In Paris, the Ritz offers a kids-only cooking course. www.ritzcarlton.com and www.ritzparis.com

Sixteen **Hyatt** locations offer Camp Hyatt, which offers organized events for kids ages 3 to 12: In San Antonio, kids can say yee-haw as they hunt for authentic arrowheads, listen to cowboy stories, and splash around in the river pool. On the island of Maui, kids participate in cultural themes such as making leis, Hawaiian storytelling, and hula lessons. In Lake Tahoe, kids can spend the day playing in the lake and go stargazing at night—this location also offers winter programs with sledding, snowshoeing, and making snow sculptures. www.hyatt.com

Kimpton Group's boutique hotels have always operated with a family-friendly vibe—kids get milk and cookies upon arrival, and parents will appreciate the free wine in the lobby. Individual hotels also offer several family-friendly packages throughout the 42 properties. In New York, the 70 Park Avenue Hotel's Kids Rule package includes cooking lessons for the kids and a 2-hour chauffeured shopping trip for the parents; at night, Mom and Dad can dine in the Silverleaf Tavern while the kids get an in-room pizza party with a babysitter, plus milk and cookies turndown service. The Hotel George in Washington, DC, offers the Undercover Washington package, which includes an official spy packet upon arrival, a visit to the International Spy Museum, a map to tour sites where famous spies lived, and a Spymaster Skills Exam. www.kimptongroup.com

The all-inclusive **Club Med** was once a mecca for swinging singles, but as it turns out, families are a lucrative market. Club Med's Passworld Club is dedicated solely to teenagers and tweens. There are supervised programs for two separate age groups—11 to 13 years old, and 14 to 17. Hands-on activities include theater productions, sound-mixing classes, jewelry making, and even graffiti classes. Other group activities, based on your location, include bungee jumping, windsurfing, waterskiing, hiking and camping, movies on the beach, and dance parties. Currently there are 12 Club Med resorts worldwide that have a Passworld Club, including properties in Cancun, Sicily, the Dominican Republic, Malaysia, the French Alps, and Morocco. 888-932-2582, www.clubmed.us

Sheraton Kauai Resort and students from Kauai High School's Academy of Hospitality and Tourism developed the Teen Concierge Program, inviting teen guests to participate in Hawaiian cultural activities that were planned by the students themselves. Activities include making leis, Hawaiian food tasting, surfing lessons, and a big screen movie under the stars. 808-742-1661, www.sheraton-kauai.com

The Breakers in Palm Beach, Florida, has long been known as a family-friendly destination—parents can reserve up to five adjoining rooms, and kids under 16 stay free in the room with their parents. Rooms can be childproofed, with covered electrical outlets, protected table corners, and plastic bags removed from garbage cans. There are toddlers' playrooms, a video game arcade, a movie room, and the Coconut Crew Interactive Camp for kids ages 3 to 12. On Fridays, a special Night Out event for families features a themed dinner party, like Breakers Survivor and Palm Beach Rodeo. 888-273-2537, www.thebreakers.com

Even though Las Vegas has dropped its family marketing campaign, plenty of the hotels still maintain a family-friendly vibe. The **Excalibur Hotel and Casino** has the usual slots for grown-ups, and the medieval theme attracts the kids—the Court Jester's Stage has puppetry, juggling, and music, while the Tournament of Kings jousting dinner show features dragons and fire. The Medieval Village is filled with themed shops, restaurants, a food court, and entertainers walking around for photo ops. 877-750-5464, www.excalibur.com

La Costa Resort and Spa in Carlsbad, California, recently opened a state-of-the-art kids club, Kidtopia, and a teen lounge, Vibz. Kidtopia is 6,000 square feet with a separate section for infants and toddlers featuring slides and soft toys, a movie lounge, a building-block area, a 7-foot treehouse, and a 600-gallon saltwater aquarium. The teen lounge includes a video game center, a mini bowling alley, pool, and air hockey tables. 800-854-5000, www.lacosta.com

Kid-Friendly Airports

Cheapflights.com is now offering a "Kids Airport Diversion Guide," which you can download at www.cheapflights.com/guides. The guide includes kid-friendly diversions at 22 US airports—everything from Kidports at the Boston Logan and Cincinnati–Northern Kentucky airports, to the Kids on the Fly exhibit at the Chicago O'Hare International Airport, to Dallas–Fort Worth Airport's Junior Flyer Clubs. For more on this, check out "Family-Friendly Airports" on page 16.

Familymoons

You may have already heard the term "babymoons," in which couples go away for some quality alone time before the baby is born. But many couples getting married today are also opting for the "familymoon," a honeymoon that the whole family can enjoy.

Let's face it: Marriage isn't always just about the loving couple anymore. Call it the Brady Bunch Syndrome—one or both of you may have children from a previous relationship, and the idea is that after the wedding, you'll be one big happy family. That, of course, is a lot easier than it sounds, especially when you factor in sullen teenagers, shared custody, and the always-complicated role of a brand-new stepparent. That's where the familymoon fits in. Now rather than leaving everyone behind to dash off to your romantic honeymoon, you can choose to bring the kids along for the ride—without compromising the romance.

In theory, the familymoon is just another concept dreamed up by the travel industry to create enticing hotel and vacation packages. But in practice, it can actually be quite useful. You get the benefits of a family-oriented vacation but with some of the perks of a romantic getaway—all in the hopes of making everyone feel happy and included. The following are a few places that are offering familymoons, along with a few tips on how you can create your own getaway with your brand-new, ready-made family.

Since Hawaii is one of the top honeymoon destinations for Americans, who better to create a familymoon package than the **Sheraton Keauhou**? This deal offers up to 50 percent discounts on second and third rooms that are connecting or adjacent, so you can stash the kids safely next door for some private time. Even better, you get supervised child care for up to 2 hours a day, plus an evening of babysitting service for up to four children. In the meantime, you or your sweetie can take advantage of a complimentary 40-minute massage at the hotel spa. As for family bonding, you can stop by the Keiki Club Keauhou Activity Center (a supervising adult is required), which has activities for kids ages 3 to 12. Rates range from $466 to $670 for the first room and $250 to $340 for the second or third room. www.starwoodhotels.com/hawaii

If a Caribbean romance is what you're dreaming of, head to the **Bolongo Bay Beach Resort.** Located on the waterfront, it's where you can let the kids run free while you spend some quality time with your honey; or the whole family can dive into the ocean at once. The resort's familymoon package includes 5 nights' accommodation for four people in a two-bedroom condominium—grown-ups get the master bedroom, and kids get two twin beds in the other room. As is de rigueur with honeymoon suites, your bedroom will be strewn with rose petals, and a bottle of champagne and chocolate-dipped pineapple will be waiting for you. The package also includes 4 hours of babysitting and a four-course dinner for two (plus a bottle of wine) at the Beach House. Rates range from $2,440 to $3,017. 800-524-4746, www.bolongobay.com/html/hmypkg.html

Looking for a slightly more rugged honeymoon adventure? Try the **Hyatt Regency Tamaya Resort & Spa** in New Mexico, a 500-acre resort owned by the Santa Ana tribe, where you can skip the deep-sea diving and instead take in the southwest Native American experience. The familymoon package includes 3 nights' accommodations and breakfast for up to four people. Kids ages 3 to 12 get two half-day or evening sessions at the on-site Camp Tamaya, where they can try out making traditional adobes, creating sand paintings, and learning Native American games. Honeymooners get a $250 credit toward spa treatments, golf, or trail riding, plus wine and cheese for the grown-ups and milk and cookies for the kids. Rates start at $1,765. 505-867-1234, www.tamaya.hyatt.com/hyatt/hotels/index.jsp.

Single with Kid

With more than 16.5 million single parent households in the United States, the definition of a traditional family is changing fast, and the resort industry is only now huffing and puffing to catch up. In fact, according to the Travel Industry Association, in general single parent family travel has increased by more than 25 percent in the last 10 years. Even if you're not looking for love, traveling with other single parents and their kids can be a great way to meet other like-minded people and even make connections for future travels.

Single Parent Tours arranges trips for single parent families to Jamaica, Turks and Caicos, and Rocking Horse River Ranch in Nevada as well as a cruise to New Brunswick. Tours include activities for parents to do together with their children and adult-only activities for single parents to mingle. Rates for one adult and one child start at $573 and go up to $900 for one adult and three children. 888-277-8543, www.singleparenttours.com

Parents Without Partners, a support organization for single parents and their kids, sponsors several conventions for members and their families. Recent trips include a 2-day cruise from New York to Nova Scotia and a weeklong Caribbean cruise. 800-637-7974, www.parentswithoutpartners.org

Family Volunteer Vacations

I can't think of any better way to promote family bonding than a volunteer vacation. It's a great way to show your kids the world while avoiding their complaints over sightseeing and museum trips; you'll be so busy building homes or working with local kids that the family squabbles will subside, and hopefully, the experience can bring you all a little closer together. If a volunteer organization doesn't have a specific family program, you can usually join an existing group as a family or even customize a trip—just make sure you ask questions beforehand to determine if there is a minimum age, if the work is appropriate for younger children, and if they'll need any vaccinations or immunization shots.

Earthwatch Institute has family-oriented expeditions with half-day hands-on science programs led by scientists. On a mission to Barnegat Bay in New Jersey, families can capture and tag the diamondback terrapin turtles, plus engage in activities like canoeing, hiking, and swimming along the coast. A visit to Puerto Rico gives kids the real perspective on saving the rain forests by harvesting the trees without harming the ecosystem and planting new seedlings, as well as monitoring the local tree frog. Program rates are about $1,950 per person. 978-461-0081, www.earthwatch.org

I-to-I welcomes families on several of its programs: One weeklong trip, open to children ages 15 and older, takes you to Costa Rica, where you'll work with a rural housing association to build homes. On a 2-week trip to India, kids ages 10 and older can volunteer with the community in Bangalore, with opportunities like working with a YMCA homeless shelter, volunteering with hearing impaired children, or teaching carpentry skills. Children as young as 3 can travel to Sri Lanka and Bolivia (the youngest age to participate is 10). Rates start at about $1,100 for a weeklong program, with supplements for each additional week. 800-985-4582, www.i-to-i.com

The **Sierra Club** offers service vacations for families, such as a trail outing in Snowmass, Colorado. Families with kids ages 7 and older can get involved with creating new trails on the Elk Mountain range, building winter habitats for small animals, and trail clearing and maintenance. A program in Bryce, Utah, invites families to participate in various projects such as landscaping, revegetation, and monitoring threatened species. Prices start at $395 for adults and $295 for children. 415-977-5500, www.sierraclub.org

Road Tripping with Kids

The family road trip is as American as apple pie. But if you're not careful, your educational exploration of our great country can turn into a stressful, exhausting experience for both parents and kids. In this case, planning is essential: Keep plenty of (healthy) snacks on hand to avoid fast-food stops; bring along books on CD; carry a portable DVD player (just limit the length of time kids can watch it); plan ahead for food, bathroom, and gas breaks, keeping in mind that kids need breaks as often as every 2 hours. Look for parks and scenic points where you can stretch your legs. Consider breaking up your trip by spending a night in a hotel. Most of all, don't forget that the journey is as important as the destination.

! Roadtrip America is a good one-stop resource of attractions, itineraries, seasonal travel, and food options on the road. www.roadtripamerica.com

! Skip the fast-food and chain restaurants. One of the best parts about traveling is experiencing local food. The Web site www.roadfood.com is a resource of more than 1,000 restaurants and food stops along highways, in small towns, and in city neighborhoods. The listings tend to feature homestyle food, making it easy to please kids.

! Microsoft Streets & Trips 2006 software can help customize the right trip for you and your family. You can customize your profile, like preferred driving speed, desired frequency of rest stops, and your car's fuel tank size and gas mileage. You'll then get a personalized travel route based on your preferences and a database of 1.8 million businesses, indicating when you should stop for food, gas, or a bathroom.

Car Safety

Most parents are already familiar with car seat rules, but it's important to reiterate the facts. The National Highway Traffic Safety Administration reports that car safety seats are 71 percent effective in reducing deaths for infants and 54 percent effective in reducing deaths for children ages 1 to 4 years. Belt-positioning booster seats reduce the risk of injury by 59 percent for children ages 4 through 7. Infants should ride in rear-facing child safety seats in the back seat until at least age 1 and at least 20 pounds.

Visit www.seatcheck.org for safety tips, state laws, and a list of Certified Child Passenger Safety Technicians than can help install car safety seats properly. 866-732-8243

Family Summer Camp

Summer camp isn't just for the kids anymore. These days, families can join in the fun of canoeing, tennis, archery, yoga, and even wine tasting, in what can turn out to be a relatively low-cost, all-inclusive vacation.

The Appalachian Mountain Club sponsors 5-day family camps in several locations throughout the Appalachian Mountains. Their programs are designed for parents and kids ages 5 to 12 with optional itineraries like hiking with a geologist, a picnic lunch, arts and crafts, nature journaling, and an evening campfire. 617-523-0636, www.outdoors.org/lodging/adventure-camps.cfm

Medomak Family Vacation Camp, in Washington, Maine, offers weeklong family programs all summer, combining traditional activities with more progressive excursions like yoga, museum visits, and tastings of Maine cheese and beer. 207-845-6001, www.medomakcamp.com

Located on a California ranch in the Shasta-Trinity National Forest, **Bar 717 Ranch** rustles it up family style with weeklong programs in August. Kids (and grown-ups) can really rough it by waking at dawn to feed the farm animals and milk the cows. 530-628-5992, www.bar717.com

Nontraditional families can get in on the fun at **Rainbow Families** camp in Saugatuck, Michigan, where gay and lesbian parents and their children can gather. 616-218-9679, www.rfgl.org

Kids' Cooking Schools

Surprisingly, a new favorite in kids activities is . . . cooking. The likely culprit? Television cooking shows. From filets to flans, those TV demonstrations with celebrity chefs are attracting kids' attention these days, spurring interest in learning how to cook and bake on their own. That said, why not incorporate an educational hobby with your next vacation?

If you want to start off right, you may as well go straight to the culinary source. The **Ecole Ritz Escoffier** offers cooking lessons with Les Petits Marmitons du Ritz, for kids ages 6 to 12. Rabbits in chocolate and roasted wild duck, anyone? 01-43-16-30-30, www.ritzparis.com

Italy and food are practically synonymous, and the options throughout the countryside are practically limitless. **Fontana del Papa Monti della Tolfa,** in Northern Lazio Rome, has organic cooking classes for children, where the kids can prepare dinner for Mom and Dad. A day class is about $280. www.cookitaly.it/kids.htm

Le Manoir aux Quat'Saisons in Oxford, England, offers half-day cooking classes, where kids can get a behind-the-scenes tour and participate in an herb-tasting competition and dessert making, followed by a tea party with their parents. A day class is about $280. www.manoir.com

Miette Culinary Studio in Greenwich Village, New York, is located in a 19th-century townhouse. A 2½-hour cooking program for parents and kids teaches them to use organic ingredients to prepare healthy, gourmet meals and snacks. $75. 212-460-9322, www.mietteculinarystudio.com

Chef Eric's **Culinary Classroom** in Santa Monica, California, hosts 4-day child and teen cooking courses, where they create a different dish each day. $300 to $350. 310-470-2640, www.culinaryclassroom.com

Young Chefs Academy is a national franchise with multiple locations in 17 states across the country. Courses vary by location but include themes like All-American Cuisine, Texas Camp-Out Cooking, and Now That's Italian. www.youngchefsacademy.com

Interactive Animal Tours

Forcing your kids into an educational tour can result in some grumpy travelers. But when you incorporate something that kids love, like swimming and animals, you can sneak in some education without them even knowing it.

Dolphins Plus in Key Largo, Florida, is an education, research, and experiential learning and environmental-awareness facility, where you can swim in natural sea water with 14 Atlantic bottlenose dolphins and two California sea lions. www.dolphinsplus.com

The **Dolphin Connection** at the Sheraton Waikiki allows guests to swim with Atlantic and Pacific bottlenose dolphins and the rare wholphin, a cross between a false killer whale and a dolphin. www.sheraton-waikiki.com/wn_dolphin.htm

Wildquest offers weeklong Human-Dolphin Connection retreats on a Bahamian island, where visitors can swim with wild dolphins. Keep in mind that this is not a traditional Bahamian resort, as there is not much else beyond this activity on the island. 800-326-1618, www.wildquest.com/dolphin-swim-programs.html

Dolphin World offers swimming programs in Mexico, the Bahamas, and Florida. Dolphin encounters start at $76 per person and allow guests to swim with trained or wild bottlenose dolphins as well as experience an in-depth program of wading with the dolphins to learn how trainers handle the animals. 866-630-9868, www.dolphinworld.org

Sheraton Keauhou Bay Resort in Hawaii is a feeding ground for native manta rays (not to be confused with stingrays; manta rays have no stingers). With wingspans of more than 20 feet, manta rays feed at night in what is known as the "manta ray ballet." Guests can learn about manta rays from a local expert and view their feeding from balconies and special viewing areas. 866-718-8109, www.sheratonkeauhou.com/mantarayexperience.htm

Safari's Exotic Wildlife Sanctuary in Broken Arrow, Oklahoma, houses 200 animals that were abused, unwanted, or the result of overbreeding from zoos. Kids can come face-to-face and help feed big cats, wolves, bears, zebras, and reptiles, as well as little guys like pigs, sheep, and even African hedgehogs. More threatening animals are kept behind a perimeter fence about 6 feet away from guests, which still offers a much closer view than a traditional zoo. 918-357-5683, www.safariszoo.com

If you happen to be visiting Dollywood, swing by the **Smoky Mountain Deer Farm & Exotic Petting Zoo.** This is more of a tourist attraction than an animal sanctuary, and the animals are kept in pens throughout the day. However, in the evenings after the business is closed, the animals roam freely about the pastures of this 143-acre farm. The farm is home to animals like zebras, zonkeys (exactly what you think), camels, reindeer, wallabies, and miniature horses. 865-428-3337, www.deerfarmzoo.com

If your kids' interest in animals extends beyond just petting and feeding them, you may consider going all-star at the **Exotic Animal Training School** in Los Angeles. This school is home to exotic animals like tigers, lions, and elephants and uses a positive reinforcement method to train the animals for working in the entertainment industry. Kids over 12 can participate in the Trainer for a Day program. 323-665-9500, www.animalschool.net

Hands-On Museums

Do your kids yawn at the notion of going to a museum? Rather than dragging them all the way to Paris to fight the hordes of tourists gawking at the *Mona Lisa,* you can stay local and get them involved with an interactive children's museum.

The Children's Museum of Denver has several interactive play areas designed for kids from newborns to 8 years old. A playscape for babies and toddlers simulates the great outdoors, exercising their large motor skills and sensory awareness; older kids can don their fire hats and learn the inner working of a fire station, from handling the equipment to working as a team to save victims. A mini grocery store will teach children the ins and outs of healthy eating as they roll their carts down the aisle, and a kid-sized basketball court will have them shooting hoops all day long. 303-433-7444, www.cmdenver.org

Kids will be blown away at the **Children's Museum of Indianapolis,** where a 43-foot-tall blown-glass sculpture reaches the ceiling, and families take a tour to view the glassblowing process. They can travel back in time in the Age of Steam room, where there is an old steam engine and kids can sell railroad tickets from Madison to Indianapolis or send Morse code messages to other train stations. The Dinosphere is one of the largest displays of real juvenile and family dinosaur fossils in the country, with a working paleo-lab and a hands-on dig. A planetarium and live theater bring everyone together for family fun. 317-334-3322, www.childrensmuseum.org

The **Long Island Children's Museum** in New York is a hands-on museum for children and adults. It offers Early Childhood Programs, including Creative Connections and Messy Afternoons, where kids can experience hands-on art and exploration activities. Exhibits include the Communication Station, where kids can learn about communication from the days of the caves to the Internet, and Sandy Island, where they can make sand dunes with wind or form a beach with rolling waves. You can even rent the museum for private celebrations. 516-224-5800, www.licm.com.

At the **Guggenheim Museum** in New York, kids can get hands-on art lessons. www.learningthroughart.org

The **Arizona Science Center** features camps, classes, and more than 300 interactive exhibits for children to learn about science. Summer camps include

Camp Seafari, where children can learn about marine life and how to save the ocean and its inhabitants. There's also the Biotechnology Medical Institute at Barrow Neurological Institute of St. Joseph's Hospital and Medical Center, where kids ages 12 to 14 can extract DNA from plant tissue and help research a cure for cancer. 602-716-2000, www.azscience.org

Imagine It! Children's Museum of Atlanta lets kids step inside the world of *Sesame Street,* where they can learn their ABCs and 1-2-3s in a hands-on playground, read a book in Big Bird's Nest, watch educational videos at Oscar's Newsstand, and write a message for their favorite character. Kids can learn the "Cooperation" song, make their own puppets, and join in Boogie Time and a retro dance party. 404-659-5437, www.imagineit-cma.org/home.asp

In Cincinnati's Union Station, kids can visit the Museum of Natural History, an IMAX theater, and the Cincinnati History Museum in the same complex as the **Duke Energy Children's Museum.** At the Duke museum, Kid's Town lets the little ones take charge at a mini grocery store, veterinary clinic, diner, and post office. A farmyard is open for toddlers to sort fruits and vegetables in the garden, fish from a row boat, play at a sand table, and create their own puppet shows. 800-733-2077, www.cincymuseum.org/explore_our_sites/childrens_museum

At the **Philadelphia Please Touch Museum,** children can slide down the rabbit hole to discover the world of Alice in Wonderland, sipping tea with the Mad Hatter and playing croquet with the Queen of Hearts. In the Maurice Sendak exhibition, kids can go "Where the Wild Things Are"; in more everyday exhibits, they can grab a shopping cart and hit the grocery store or put on their tool belts to do construction projects, build a tree house, or work in a garage. 215-963-0667, www.pleasetouchmuseum.org

The **Santa Fe Children's Museum** has multiple hands-on exhibits, including bubble making, creating art from recycled materials, a toddler climbing structure, and a climbing wall for bigger kids. Other activities include face painting, scavenger hunts, and building fantasy cities with blocks and Legos. 505-989-8359, www.santafechildrensmuseum.org

The **Children's Discovery Museum** in San Jose, California, offers 150 interactive exhibits in more than 28,000 square feet. Inside the Wonder Cabinet, kids can crawl through a tunnel, explore the woodland puppet forest, and experiment in the sand science laboratory; a kids' bank teaches the value of a dollar with cash deposits and withdrawals, while an interactive garden offers a cool break in the shade by a pond filled with goldfish. 408-298-5437, www.cdm.org

The **Exploratorium** in San Francisco is located in the Palace of Fine Arts and is a collage of hands-on science projects and human perception exhibits. Kids can learn about the essential elements of life, DNA, energy, and sound. There's also an exhibit where you can "explore in the dark" and learn to use your tactile senses. 415-561-0362, www.exploratorium.edu

The Lawrence Hall of Science at the University of Berkeley, California, features hands-on exhibits, events, and classes. One of its recent exhibits is Circus! Science under the Big Top, which allows children to walk a tightrope to learn about balance and the body's reaction to different stimuli, become an acrobat to learn about momentum, and squeeze into a tiny space to see how our tendons and ligaments work to hold our skeletal system up. 510-642-5132, www.lhs.berkeley.edu

The Tech Museum of Innovation in San Jose, California, features themed galleries with hands-on exhibits. Also featured at the Tech are the newest gadgets out of Silicon Valley. The NetPl@net Exhibit allows you to arm wrestle (virtually) with museum visitors in New York or Alaska. The Innovation Exhibit features the chance to design your own roller coaster or build a microchip—even to get a three-dimensional self-portrait. 408-294-8324, www.thetech.org

The **Museum of Discovery and Science** in Fort Lauderdale, Florida, aims to provide experimental trails for adults and children to learn about science using hands-on exhibits, films, and programs. One such exhibit is the Living in the Everglades exhibit, where you can actually walk through an 11,000-square-foot outdoor trail to see the various ecosystems in the Everglades, while learning about the history and present of the Everglades. There are also hands-on discovery lab programs and live demonstrations for children in kindergarten to eighth grade. 954-467-6637, www.mods.org

Olympia, Washington, is home to the **Hands-On Museum,** featuring six galleries with interactive exhibits. Kids can try their hands at construction: designing and drafting their own building plans, loading and operating a dump truck, and using a crane to transfer cargo. There is a "working" waterfront, backyard wilderness, and a Young Arts Studio with an enormous array of new and recycled art supplies. 360-956-0818, www.hocm.org

HABITOT Children's Museum in Berkeley, California, has a drop-in art center for kids and grownups to really get their hands dirty (and finally get to fingerpaint on the walls!), as well as age-specific workshops and camps where they can dance, cook, and create art without Mom and Dad cramping their style. 510-647-1111, www.habitot.org

Young at Art Children's Museum, located in Florida, is a place where kids can drop in for workshops in dancing, singing, science education, and hands-on arts projects. Ongoing exhibitions include climbing in and around a recycling sorting center and a psychedelic room of "pop-surrealistic" art. 954-424-0085, www.youngatartmuseum.org

The **Satrosphere Science Centre** in Aberdeen, Scotland, features the Exhibition Hall, where kids can learn all about science and technology with interactive exhibits. There are several interactive workshops available, which last about 45 minutes each. In the Renewables Workshop, kids are taught about how energy is reused, through the building of a windmill that produces energy. The Electricity Workshop allows children to build a circuit using a bulb, switch, and buzzer. The Centre is open daily from 10 a.m. to 5 p.m. 01224-640340, www.satrosphere.net

The **Questacon National Science and Technology Centre** in Canberra in the Australian Capital Territory features various hands-on exhibits for children and teens alike. The Top Secret—License to Spy exhibit allows your child to become a secret agent. Children can learn all about the history of spy technology with their personalized mission file and disguise, as they collect intelligence from 23 interactive exhibits using secret codes and laser beams. Similar programs teach children about the history of music, sports, sound, the digital world, and the earth, all through innovatively entertaining ways. 02-6270-2800, www.questacon.edu.au

The **National Space Science Centre** in Leicester, United Kingdom, features hundreds of interactive hands-on activities for kids of all ages to learn about the science of space. The Human Spaceflight: Lunar Base 2025 allows visitors to test their mental and physical ability to survive a flight into space. 0116-261-0261, www.spacecentre.co.uk

Aquariums

The **Georgia Aquarium** is considered to be the world's largest aquarium, with over 8 million gallons of fresh and marine water and more than 100,000 creatures from 500 species around the world. General admission is $25 for adults, $20 for seniors over age 55, and $18 for kids ages 3 to 12. Some of the exhibits include the Cold Water Quest, which features marine life from cold-water areas throughout the world and is intended to educate people about the perils of poor ocean source management; and the Tropical Diver—The Coral Kingdom, which presents a display of tropical coral reefs along with the underwater creatures that sustain coral life. The Georgia Aquarium even has an Ocean's Ballroom, available for special events. The ballroom features aquarium viewing windows and can accommodate anywhere from 1,100 to 1,600 people, catered by Wolfgang Puck. 404-581-4000, www.georgiaaquarium.org

The **Shedd Aquarium** in Chicago is the second largest aquarium in the world. The aquarium offers family overnight visits, which include animal encounters, a marine mammal presentation, and dancing. The Asleep with the Fishes program is available for community groups with kids from kindergarten to sixth grade. Program rates are $25 per person ($20 for members). 312-939-2438, www.sheddaquarium.org

The **Aquarium of the Pacific** in Long Beach, California, features creatures from all over the world's largest ocean. See the 10,000-square-foot Shark Lagoon exhibit, with more than 150 bull, whitetip, zebra, bamboo, and epaulette sharks. The Shorebird Sanctuary is an emulation of a wetland, home to shorebirds, fish, and plants. Also featured at the aquarium are 3-D films exploring the deep sea. 562-590-3100, www.aquariumofpacific.org

The **New England Aquarium,** located in Boston, incorporates field trips and unique programs as a way of teaching about underwater life. Admission is $17.95 for adults and $9.95 for children ages 3 to 11. Board a catamaran and travel 30 miles east of Boston to the Stellwagen Bank whale feeding grounds. For $150, you can participate in the Trainer for an Afternoon program, in which you'll learn what it takes to be a Marine Mammal Trainer. The aquarium also rents out its facilities for private events such as weddings or receptions. 617-973-5200, www.neaq.org

The **Dallas World Aquarium and Zoological Garden** in Texas emulates a South American rain forest. A Mayan Performance Troupe performs for visitors on weekends, adding a unique touch to the aquarium and zoo experience. Also present at the aquarium is an emulation of a South African lagoon, complete with plants and animals from the original area. 214-720-2224, www.dwazoo.com

The **Monterey Bay Aquarium** in California is unique for a section of its aquarium that connects directly with the Pacific Ocean. Its Life on the Bay exhibit takes you to see the more than 30 species that pass through the Monterey Bay. It also has a SplashZone, where kids and families can see penguins, clams, and moray eels up close. The Monterey Bay Aquarium has several conservation and research programs taking place, some of which you can take a part in to help save endangered species and areas. Among these programs is the Student Oceanography Club, in which kids ages 11 to 14 can learn firsthand about marine science and conservation through field experiences and other club events. 831-648-4800, www.mbayaq.org

The **uShaka Marine World Aquarium** in Darban, South Africa, incorporates tourism and education to make up the aquarium experience. The Sea World and Dolphin World comprise an indoor-and-outdoor saltwater aquarium with a dolphin stadium and a chance at an "edutainment tour," in which guests may learn about the marine life through snorkeling and scuba diving. uShaka even has the Wet 'n Wild World, a water amusement park for kids and adults, featuring water slides, pools, and rides. There are special tours offered, educating guests on how the aquarium rehabilitates injured marine life and how the aquarium itself works. 031-337-8099, www.ushakamarineworld.co.za

You'd never guess that under the Mall of America in Bloomington, Minnesota, is the world's largest underground aquarium, the **Underwater Adventures Aquarium.** The aquarium features four exhibits: the Wild Woods, showcasing freshwater creatures of the Minnesota forest; the Tunnel, which allows you to walk through a tunnel 14 feet underground to see sea life from the world over; the SeaCrits Gallery, featuring celebrity sea life from Hollywood movies; and the Starfish Beach, where you can touch a real shark and then take a ride on a virtual submarine. 952-883-0202, www.sharky.tv/index.html

The **Aquarium of Western Australia** proclaims that you can see 12,000 kilometers of Australia's Western Coastline in just one day. It has five main exhibits focusing on Australia's different coasts, allowing you to do just that—Great Southern Coast, Perth Coast, Marmion Marine Park, Shipwreck Coast, and Far North. The facility features the largest aquarium and underwater tunnel and the world's largest collection of Western Australian marine life. AQWA Adventures is a program provided by the aquarium to allow you to snorkel or dive with the sharks. You can also explore the reef, sea stingrays, turtles, and fish in its Shipwreck Coast Aquarium. 61-8-9447-7500, www.aqwa.com.au

Ocean Park Hong Kong is one of the largest ocean parks in the world, taking up over 170 miles of land in Aberdeen, Hong Kong. Ocean Park incorporates tourist attractions with entertainment and education to attract multitudes of visitors each year. The park consists of two parts— the headlands of Mount Nanlang and the Huang Zhu Keng Valley lowlands. Among some of the featured exhibits are the Panda Habitat, the

Dinosaur: Now and Then exhibits, and the Dolphin Breeding Center. There's also the Butterfly House and the Goldfish Pagoda, among the wildlife exhibits that educate people on the importance of taking care of endangered species. The Atoll Reef allows visitors to see the reef and other marine life, and the Shark Aquarium features an underwater tunnel that allows guests to view sharks. The Ocean Theater is an open-air theater where dolphins and sea lions put on a performance for guests. There's also an area of the Ocean Park that features thrill rides and roller coasters. 852-2552-0291, www.oceanpark.com.hk/f_index.html

Sleepover Programs

Are your kids so enthralled by the zoo that you can't get them to leave? Some aquariums, museums, and zoos have solved this problem by inviting kids to grab their sleeping bags and sleep with the fishes (and lions and dinosaurs . . .).

The Field Museum in Chicago welcomes families for Dozin' with the Dinos. Wander the ancient Egyptian exhibit by flashlight, prowl through the African savannah with lions roaring in the distance, and discover new information about ancient dinosaurs. Program fees are $47 per person. 312-922-9410, www.fmnh.org

The **Memphis Zoo** invites kids to a Zoo Snooze, where they can meet the animals up close, go on a moonlight safari, and get a behind-the-scenes look at the zoo animals' nutrition center. Prices are $45 per person for a minimum of 15 and include snacks, a pizza dinner, breakfast, and free entrance to the zoo the next day. 901-276-9453, www.memphiszoo.org

The **Smithsonian's National Zoo**'s Snore & Roar sleepover program includes a nocturnal hike through the zoo, followed by a "campout" on Lion/Tiger Hill in four-person tents. A family experience is $65 per person, and a special adults-only program is $75 to $100. 202-633-4800, natzoo.si.edu

The **San Francisco Zoo**'s Wild Nights program means you can sleep under the stars, and you're almost guaranteed to wake up to the roaring of a lion. 415-753-7080, www.sfzoo.org/education/groupOvernights.htm

The **¡Explora! Museum** in Albuquerque, New Mexico, has an Overnight Camp-In program, where kids can learn all about science with more than 250 interactive science, technology, and arts exhibits. You can head to the RoboLab, where kids can design, build, program, and play with their very own robot. The overnight program is intended for third to ninth graders and costs $35 per person, including snacks, a pizza dinner, breakfast, and a souvenir patch. 505-224-8300, www.explora.us

Take your kids to the **Kidspace Museum** in Pasadena, California, for an Overnight Nature Retreat. For $45 (or $40 if you're a Kidspace Member), you can be one with nature as you hold giant millipedes and tarantulas, learn a bee dance, and learn all about nature as you sleep under the stars. 626-449-9144, www.kidspacemuseum.org

The **Battleship *New Jersey*** in Camden, New Jersey, is a fun and interactive way of teaching kids about the history of World War II. A night aboard this Iowa-class battleship goes for $49.95 a person, with the cost including a ride on a 4D Flight Simulator and the chance to spend the night in authentic sailor fashion. 856-966-1652, www.battleshipnewjersey.org

Take your budding marine biologist to the **USS *Blueback,*** a Barbel-class fast-attack submarine at the Oregon Museum of Science & Industry in Portland. Here your child can spend the night learning how a submarine works. An overnight stay costs $51 per person and includes snacks, breakfast, and a planetarium show. 503-797-6674, www.omsi.edu

Your kids can Roar and Snore at the **San Diego Zoo Wild Animal Park** in California. Kids ages 4 to 7 can camp out near the East Africa Field Exhibit and interact with different animals. Prices start at $89 per person from November through March and $109 from April through October. Fees include dinner and a pancake breakfast. 619-231-1515, www.sandiegozoo.org

For up-and-coming paleontologists, take your kids to the **Natural History Museum** in Los Angeles. For $43 a person, kids age 5 and up can camp overnight at one of several exhibitions, learning about fossils. Included in the cost is a museum patch for the children and free admission into the museum the following day. 213-763-3466, www.nhm.org

At the **Philadelphia Zoo** in Pennsylvania, your kids can camp out for the Night Flight Overnight Program, where they'll spend the night in a tree house, watching animals in "night mode." The program is intended for children ages 6 to 12 and costs $45 a child. Activities include a theater presentation and a live animal presentation, along with free admission to the zoo the next day. 215-243-1100, www.philadelphiazoo.org

Have your kids' Sleepover by the Sea at the **Children's Museum of Portsmouth** in New Hampshire. The cost is $25 per person, and included in the overnight program is a museum patch, an evening snack, and a continental breakfast. At the program, kids can participate in art and science activities and a scavenger hunt. 603-436-3853, www.childrens-museum.org

▽ Resources

www.kids.nationalgeographic.com: One of the premiere sites on the Web for kid-friendly travel articles, educational games, printable coloring books, and even an interactive family trip planner.

www.travelforkids.com: This site provides tips for travel by location, lists of family-friendly hotels, and children's book recommendations that highlight various countries and nationalities.

www.tablethotels.com: This online booking site matches travelers with their hotels based on preferences, and has launched a family-friendly section. The hotels listed tend to fall into "sophisticated" or "luxury" categories, and you can specify what amenities you need such as babysitting services or a kid-friendly restaurant.

www.bbonline.com/kidfriendly.html: This one-stop resource list of B and Bs and country inns has a page that provides links to accommodations that welcome children.

www.takingthekids.com: A nationally syndicated column with weekly travel stories, ideas for traveling with kids, and tips on family travel.

www.nps.gov/learn/gozone.htm: The National Park Service provides information, quizzes, factoids, and downloadable coloring books to help kids learn more about the national park that you're planning to visit.

CHAPTER 17

Women's Travel

❝ If you want anything said, ask a man. If you
want anything done, ask a woman. ❞

—MARGARET THATCHER

When Calgon isn't enough to take you away, it may be time to take a trip into no-man's land . . . and no kids. The concept of women's travel may once have been just a marketing scheme for spas to offer two-for-one pedicures or hotels to promote "girl getaway" packages by throwing in a bottle of champagne or painting the walls on a dedicated floor a pathetic lavender color. But these days, the travel industry is starting to notice the growing force of women travelers—and that includes women of all ages, whether they're single, married, or divorced, and whether they're traveling for business or pleasure.

According to a 2002 Travel Industry Association (TIA) survey, an estimated 32 million single American women traveled at least once in the previous year, and about 3 in 10 traveled five times or more in that year. In most households, women are the primary trip planners, and almost 40 percent of women over the age of 35 don't have a built-in travel partner. In fact, out of the 34.8 million US adults who have traveled solo in the past 3 years, 47 percent are female. A 2006 survey released by the Adventure Travel Trade Association reports that women comprise 52 percent of adventure travelers.

So what does all of this mean? Women travelers are rapidly altering the travel industry's old preconceptions of the "typical" traveler, in both business and leisure, so the choices in destinations and experiences for women are growing exponentially.

Women's Travel Clubs

Women know that much of life is about compromise; but when you're embarking on a travel adventure, why play by everyone else's rules? If you're a single woman eyeing that Alaskan cruise, you're probably also dreading the singles mixers. If you're a married mom packing up the family's bags for a European expedition, you can pretty much forget about leisurely museum strolls or gourmet dinners. Sometimes, when you embark on a travel adventure, you want to be able to do what you want to do, which is where the all-important "girlfriend getaways" come in.

An increasing number of companies are creating women-only tours that mean no husbands, boyfriends, or young kids are allowed. Some tours integrate traditional sightseeing with female-friendly activities like antiquing, wine tasting, shopping, and spa visits, while others have created outdoor adventure packages for women only.

Most of these clubs offer a yearly membership for about $40, which takes care of administrative costs and usually gets you reduced prices on airfare and lodging. With the benefit of group discounts, trip organizers can create specific itineraries that include meals, hotels, and guided tours, while adding on all the female-friendly frills. The average age of participants ranges from 30 to the 60s, and the majority of travelers are unmarried or divorced, followed by married women and widows. Most participants tend to go solo, without a friend or relative in tow, but if you are traveling alone, my advice is to hook up with another traveler to share a room—single-supplement fees still apply in these groups, and they can tack on another 50 percent to the total cost. Here are a few companies that might offer what you're looking for in a women-only vacation.

Adventure Women: Although Adventure Women offers some heartier experiences than some other companies, don't worry about being left behind. Trips are ranked by activity level—from easy to high energy—so you won't find yourself desperately gasping for breath or, alternatively, traipsing miles ahead of the pack. The groups tend to be small, about 12 women, and the company organizes several domestic and international trips each year. 800-804-8686, www.adventurewomen.com

The Women's Travel Club: Based in Florida, this club offers small-group, women-only trips throughout North America, Asia, Europe, Africa, the Middle East, and Central and South America. An 11-day trip to Peru includes city tours, a night on Machu Picchu, five-star accommodations, and a ride on the Orient Express; starting at $3,369. A trek through Kenya and Tanzania runs for 13 days and includes safari and game tours, visits to local women's groups, and a trip down into Ngorongoro Crater; starting at $3,999. 800-480-4448, www.womenstravelclub.com

Gutsy Women Travel: A division of Gate 1 Travel, Gutsy Women Travel coordinates trips worldwide, from adventure travel to cruises and spa trips. An 8-day river cruise along the Danube travels over Christmastime, when the cities and villages are decked for the holidays; starting at $1,439. An 8-day spa package in Sedona, Arizona, includes a meditation session and a Jeep tour through the red rock region; starting at $1,899. 866-464-8879, www.gutsywomentravel.com

Women Traveling Together: This company arranges trips worldwide for groups of 10 to 20 women. Tours range from adventurous, like a 7-day Grand Canyon rafting excursion or a 10-day African safari, to tamer events like a Holland tour during tulip season. Tours are rated by their activity levels, from easy to strenuous, with tips on what kinds of activities to expect at each level—ranging from a leisurely pace with frequent rests all the way up to lengthy uphill hiking treks. Rates go from $1,489 for a New England sampler to $6,696 for an African safari. 410-956-5250, www.women-traveling.com

Adventurous Wench: You can get in touch with your inner wench with this company that combines outdoorsy adventures of varying intensity, like hiking and Jeep tours, with more relaxing activities like massages and gallery hopping. An 8-day trip through Alaska and the Yukon starts at $3,195, and an 8-day trip through Ireland starts at $3,249. 866-419-3624, www.adventurouswench.com

Sierra Wilderness: Women with an adventurous streak can dig in their heels on Sierra Wilderness' women-only hiking and climbing expeditions. Many trips are short term in areas like Mount Shasta and Yosemite, but there are also longer rain forest treks into Peru. Keep in mind that many of these tours are high intensity, so check in advance to see what kind of physical requirements may be involved. A 2-day climb up Mount Shasta starts at $425 and includes how-to instructions on using a crampon, ice axes, and basic mountain safety before you climb. 888-797-6867, www.swsmtns.com/womens_adventures/index.html

Canyon Calling Adventures for Women: This company focuses on outdoor adventure trips like sand tobogganing in Fiji and white-water rafting in the Alps. However, only a moderate level of fitness is required, and no experience is necessary to participate in these activities. Some trips are coed for couples, but the majority are geared solely toward women. Domestic trips in Sedona start at $1,595, and an excursion to New Zealand via Fiji starts at $4,395. 928-282-0916, www.canyoncalling.com

Adventure Travel Associates: This tour company has been operating for more than 20 years, arranging small-group women-only and coed tours worldwide. Some favorite adventure trips include a 3-day whale-watching kayak tour of the San Juan Islands (starting at $475), an 8-day cultural immersion tour of Tanzania (starting at $2,720), and an 11-day tour of Peru that includes 4 days of hiking up to the ancient ruins of Machu Picchu (starting at $2,395). 888-532-8352, www.adventureassociates.net

DIY Women's Getaways

If you'd rather gather up your girlfriends and skip the organized tours, here's how you can hang 10 and stay loose on a do-it-yourself getaway. These are also great options for mother-daughter vacations, as they usually involve some sort of hands-on educational element. I have no statistics to back this up, but rumor has it that long, lazy days tend to promote bickering among mothers and daughters—so keep busy and get bonding!

Hang 10

Surf Divas, located in La Jolla, California, introduces women of all ages to surfing in a fun and nonintimidating all-women environment. They offer everything from competitive coaching and beginner lessons to corporate team-building clinics and bachelorette parties, even surf diva wear. Weekend clinics and weeklong surf safaris in Los Olas, Mexico, are also available. 858-454-8273, www.surfdiva.com

From 40th-birthday gatherings to bachelorette parties, **The Saltwater Cow-**

girls Surf Camp deals primarily with women who have never surfed before, which alleviates some of the anxiety that would-be surfers feel the first few times out in the ocean. 904-242-9380, www.saltwatercowgirls.com

For a more far-flung vacation, **Pura Vida Adventures** is an all-woman surfing camp in Costa Rica. Along with daily surfing lessons with women of all levels, the camp offers yoga and cultural immersion activities like Tropicana salsa night and basic Spanish lessons. A 7-day camp starts at $1,540 per person in a shared bungalow. 415-465-2162, www.puravidaadventures.com

If you prefer the rush of the river over crashing ocean waves, you and your girls may want to spend the afternoons casting your rods with fly-fishing. **Ms. Guided Fly Fishing** offers 4-hour workshops in the Virginia and Maryland areas for women and practices a catch-and-release philosophy with all fish. 703-893-7020, www.msguidedflyfishing.net

Nature Getaways

The Miami Bombshells aren't a women's basketball team. They're a team of ladies who believe that a "bombshell" is a courageous woman who loves herself from the inside out. They arrange weekend camps around the country for women to play, leaving the men, the makeup, and the stresses behind. Take part in pie-eating contests, rock climbing, zip lines, and bonding over wine and s'mores while clad in sweatpants. A mother-daughter camp getaway near Orlando brings moms and girls over the age of 13 together for team-building exercises like obstacle courses and war games, plus bonding experiences like journal writing and cooking lessons, starting at $549 for 2 nights. 305-965-7561, www.miamibombshells.com

Ski resorts aren't always about skiing. **Breckenridge, Colorado,** offers hiking, biking, and golf all summer long. Women's mountain-biking trips take place on weekends throughout the summer, geared toward women of all skill levels. Weekends include bike maintenance clinics, daily guided tours, training, and nutrition, and you can even add on spa treatments at the end of the day. Weekend rates start at $200. 888-251-2417, www. gobreck.com

Just because it's called a dude ranch doesn't mean that it's all about the guys. More and more ranches are catering to gals who are looking for down-and-dirty outdoor adventure with a feminine twist. No cowboys allowed. The **Lazy K Bar Guest Ranch** in the Tucson Mountains offers adult cowgirls a true West experience. The 4-day adventure starts with a margarita party and line dancing, followed by lessons on horse physiology and handling and a mini-rodeo with events like barrel racing, team penning, robo roping, and trail riding. 800-321-7018, www.lazykbar.com/cowgirl.htm

One ranch is going all out with a Girlfriends with Guns package: That's right, you get to hoist a shotgun on this long weekend getaway. At **Teton Ridge Ranch** in Idaho, women can try the traditional horseback riding, fly-fishing, and an old-school hayride, as well as learning the art of clay shooting. Rates start at $495 for 3 days. 800-926-3579, www.tetonridge.com

---

"Qantas" is a former acronym for Queensland and Northern Territories Air Service.

For the less hardy but still outdoorsy, **The Hills Health Ranch** in British Columbia combines outdoor activity with wellness and weight-loss techniques. Whether you spend the day horseback riding or hiking, you can cap it off with a massage or Pilates class or dine on a low-fat meal. A 2-night riding and spa package starts at $479, and a 3-night hike and spa treatment vacation is $747. 800-668-2233, www.thehillshealthranch.com

Spa Culinary Classes

When you're going solo or getting away with girlfriends, it's always a boon to surround yourself with like-minded travelers. A spa cooking vacation is a great way for women to gather around a common interest, while getting a hands-on learning experience in a relaxing environment.

Budding chefs can put their skills to the test with **The Sagamore**'s Chef for a Day program. Located on a 70-acre island on Lake George in the heart of the Adirondack Mountains, this 3½-hour culinary experience allows guests to work side-by-side with some of the resort's finest chefs. Students can prepare daily specials and participate in preparing dinner service at the four-diamond Trillium restaurant. A weekend package starts at $460, including accommodations, culinary class, and dinner. 866-385-6221, www.thesagamore.com

Wellness spa **Canyon Ranch** has had a long tradition of promoting healthier lifestyles through nutrition and fitness programs. The ranch offers daily cooking classes run by Executive Chef Shawn Brisby (under the tutelage of Corporate Chef Scott Uehlein), as well as daily "lunch and learn" demos.

Hands-on cooking classes cost $110; demos are included in an all-inclusive rate, which starts at $3,280 for a 4-night stay in the Tucson property and $2,470 for a 3-night stay in the Lenox, Massachusetts, property. 800-742-9000, www. canyonranch.com

Lake Austin Spa Resort in Texas offers cooking lessons 3 days a week and a monthly Culinary Experience program—this weeklong getaway features renowned restaurateurs and cookbook authors, with daily cooking demos, wine seminars, and cheese tastings. A 3-night package begins at $1,455. 800-847-5637, www.lakeaustin.com

Claiming to be the world's first fitness spa is **Rancho La Puerta** in Baja, Mexico. The spa and culinary school focuses primarily on organic produce and natural foods, having created hundreds of recipes since it was founded in 1940. The spa is located on a 6-acre organic farm, where guests can pick their own produce and prepare dishes in the 4,500-square-foot, hands-on kitchen. A 1-week all-inclusive stay begins at $2,535. 800-443-7565, www. rancholapuerta.com

Red Mountain Spa in Saint George, Utah, has a small-group, 5-night culinary program each month. This includes 8 hours of private cooking instructions to teach guests how to prepare healthful meals at home, along with classes on healthier living, guided hikes, and fitness classes. Culinary experiences range from basic bread making to cooking with game. A 7-day package starts at $2,298. 800-407-3002, www.redmountainspa.com

Pregnancy Spas

What's a girl getaway without a visit to the spa? Well, when you're pregnant, you may feel like you have to skip out on the massages due to health and safety reasons for both you and your baby. But these days, prenatal spas can help pregnant women enjoy the benefits without having to worry about the risks—your swollen feet will thank you!

In the spa-heavy region of Scottsdale, Arizona, **Bei Bella** pregnancy spa aims to help moms-to-be make informed decisions about their pregnancy as well as nurturing their changing bodies, from prenatal yoga and spin classes to seminars about circumcision and natural childbirth. 480-990-9642, www.beibella.com

New York City's **Mama Spa** is a traveling prenatal spa that will visit Manhattanites with a variety of treatments. Prenatal massage, reflexology, "mama-cures," and pedicures are all available for expectant moms from the comfort of their own couches. 212-252-5471, www.mamaspa.com

Barefoot & Pregnant at Soul Water Day Spa in Mill Valley, California, pampers and preps pregnant women for motherhood. Fitness courses like yoga and Pilates, prenatal massages, and even acupuncture are sure to help mothers relax and rejuvenate their changing bodies. 415-388-1777, www.barefootandpregnant.com

Edamame Spa aims to ease the changes that occur in a woman's body during pregnancy, like bloating, swollen feet, and stretch marks. Edamame Spa currently operates maternity spas in New York, New Jersey, Massachusetts, and North Carolina. 877-646-4666, www.edamamespa.com

Indigenous Spas

Even chronic spa junkies can get overwhelmed when facing an array of massages, facials, and body wraps. A volcanic ash body scrub? A Dead Sea mud facial? Depending on where you are in the world, you may find that they want to slather some rather unusual items on your body. For example, in Maine you could come across an antioxidant blueberry facial. In Hawaii they might promise that pumice from nearby volcanoes will set your skin aglow. And in Arizona? Chances are you'll find cactus extract somewhere in their services. Welcome to the ever-growing industry of the indigenous spa.

At **La Posada de Santa Fe Resort & Spa,** the locally grown chile peppers star in the specialty treatment. The chocolate-chile wrap consists of covering your whole body in a spicy-sweet blend mixed with adobe clay mud. At $120 for a 50-minute session, some guests might wind up wishing they could eat the product rather than be wrapped in it. So is it really worth it? Well, the reason that Santa Fe's chile peppers burn your tongue so viciously is an ingredient called capsaicin, the same ingredient used in treatments like Icy Hot that help relieve pain in your muscles or joints. In smaller doses, it can act as a stimulant for your skin. So bring it on. 866-331-7625, www.laposada.rockresorts.com

Spa Luana at the Turtle Bay Resort in Oahu offers something called a Polynesian Sea Salt Scrub ($105 for 50 minutes). The purpose is to exfoliate the dead cells from your skin, leaving behind softer, smoother skin. Polynesian sea salt certainly sounds ancient and exotic, but does that mean it has magical properties? Not exactly magical, say some dermatology professionals. Dead Sea salt and Great Lake salt (and technically even generic table salt) can offer similar exfoliating properties, but the mineral content of Polynesian sea salt has long been used by locals to increase circulation, draw out toxins, and even heal bruises. 808-293-6000, www.turtlebayresort.com

In Corona, California, **Glen Ivy Hot Spring** offers its signature red clay mud bath—which uses red clay from nearby Temescal Canyon mixed with mineral water—where you can wallow around like a gleeful kid. The spa claims that its local clay absorbs impurities from your pores, removes dead skin cells, and improves circulation. What it isn't able to explain is what the specific mineral content is that causes this effect. 888-258-2683, www.glenivy.com

Safety Tips and Topics

Whether traveling in a pack to taste wine throughout Italy, backpacking solo through New Zealand, or lounging in a desert spa, women travelers always need to remember to take safety precautions. Even in destinations that promote themselves to be "safe" for women, basic common sense should always be first and foremost.

According to the 2006 National Business Travel Monitor from Yesawich, Pepperdine, Brown & Russell, 88 percent of women business travelers (compared with 71 percent of men) are likely to consider measures that ensure their personal safety when it comes to choosing a hotel room.

There are even a few hotels out there that offer women-only floors. The **JW Marriott** in Grand Rapids, Michigan, made headlines with the announcement that the 19th floor of the hotel would be for ladies only—the floor would have boasted enhanced security and a private bar and lounge for women. The announcement actually sparked a debate within the industry and drew the attention of attorney Gloria Allred, who condemned the idea and compared it with a "whites-only floor for Ku Klux Klan members." She noted that a floor reserved exclusively for women could only spur the push for men-only floors and lounges. Well, as it turns out, the public outcry was enough for Marriott to scrap the idea entirely.

But it's not as if the Marriott is the first hotel to come up with this idea. **The Park Lane Hilton** in London and the **Jumeirah Emirates Tower** in Dubai currently offer women-only floors. Parents may be relieved to know that plenty of youth hostels and guesthouses around the world have women's sections for female travelers.

The Mermaid Hotel in Wellington, New Zealand, is a women-owned and

-operated guesthouse that allows only women travelers to stay in the four-bedroom home. www.mermaid.co.nz

In Berlin, the **Artemisia Hotel** is a 12-room accommodation reserved exclusively for women, located in the West City. www.frauenhotel-berlin.de

Some Tips for Women Travelers

! Familiarize yourself with the area by studying maps before you get there. Avoid reading maps and guidebooks out in the street or in public areas; you'll look confused or lost.

! If your hotel doesn't offer information, ask a local female employee whether she walks in the area at night.

! In countries that aren't as welcoming to large groups of women, consider having male guides or allowing male travelers to join the group.

! If you must ask directions, ask other women, families, or women with children.

! Consider renting a cell phone when you're abroad, so you can keep in touch with other travelers or friends and family back home.

! Stick with a friend or groups. Even if you're traveling solo, there's safety in numbers, so join up with another traveler or group for parts of your journey.

! Take cultural cues from those around you—for example, if other women don't make eye contact or smile at others when in a bar, don't do so.

! No hitchhiking.

! Keep with you a small light and/or whistle, but avoid potentially illegal items like pepper spray or Mace. Use common sense and avoid dark streets and empty neighborhoods at night.

! Stay alert in crowded areas like marketplaces and public transportation. These are easy locations for pickpocketing and even sexual assault.

▽ Resources

www.aa.com/women: American Airlines is the first airline site to provide a page specifically designed for women travelers. How useful this page is remains to be seen, but it does provide travel ideas (including the requisite "girlfriend getaways,"), book recommendations, and links to women's networks.

www.gutsytraveler.com: Check out this one-stop shop of women's travel statistics, resource books, and recommended links.

www.journeywoman.com: You'll find travel tips, resources, and stories written for women by women.

www.travel.state.gov/travel/tips/brochures/brochures_1227.html: The State Department has put together a handy guide of tips for women traveling alone.

www.womentraveltips.com: This resource guide is packed with safety tips for women, teens, solo travelers, and other travelers.

CHAPTER 18

Gay and Lesbian Travel

If you judge people, you have no time to love them.

—MOTHER TERESA

In recent years, the travel industry received the big wake-up call. And it's all about chasing the "pink dollar." After discriminating against gays and lesbians for two centuries, hotels, airlines, cruise lines, and other travel providers had to come face-to-face with a powerful economic reality: the travel purchasing power of the gay and lesbian community. Few groups spend as much money. Few are more loyal to travel providers. The gay consumer market and its purchasing power with travel and leisure activities is nothing short of staggering. A 2006 survey by Community Marketing, Inc., found that gay travelers spend about $64 billion a year on travel.

As a result, is it any wonder that there's been a quantum shift in the travel industry toward gay-friendly resorts and activities? The pink dollar is talking.

The concept of an all-gay or gay-friendly destination is not to exclude others but to provide a safe and comfortable experience for openly gay travelers. Popular cities, resorts, and cruises have shifted their attitude toward homosexuality—not always willingly—and the result is more gay-friendly and gay-owned travel businesses.

According to the Travel Industry Association, the top destinations for gay and lesbian travelers in 2006 were:

San Francisco

Key West

New York City

Fire Island (part of Long Island)

Provincetown, Massachusetts

Los Angeles

Miami–South Beach

Las Vegas

New Orleans

Palm Springs–Palm Desert

And then there are some surprises. Even Disney has changed its policy to allow same-sex couples to have their Fairy Tale Wedding at Disneyland and Disney World, as well as on its cruises. If you shell out enough money, you can even arrive at the ceremony in the Cinderella coach, heralded by costumed trumpeters.

In **Portland, Oregon,** there is not only a bevy of bars and clubs in the "pink triangle" neighborhood but also a doughnut shop that performs same-sex weddings. Also in Portland, an openly gay city commissioner, Sam Adams, blogs about his political views on gay and lesbian issues.

Vancouver, British Columbia, has recently made a push to attract gay visitors, especially since the government legalized gay marriage in 2003. The city boasts the largest gay population in western Canada, and its gay scene is mostly centered around the West End, especially along Davie Street. And best of all, you don't need to be a resident to tie the knot.

While Sydney has long been a mecca for gay travelers, **Melbourne** has its own scene to brag about (as locals like to say, "Melbourne is the lady; Sydney is the whore"). There are two separate gay-friendly neighborhoods—Prahran/South Yarra and Collingwood, which are divided by the Yarra River. Melbourne is also the home to a huge gay-oriented arts and culture event every January called the Midsumma Festival.

In **Osaka,** Japan's gay neighborhood, Doyama-cho, has more than 20 gay bars and several nightclubs tucked among trendy restaurants and shops. The year 2006 was momentous, as Osaka hosted its first Gay Pride, with more than 900 marchers taking to the streets.

As one recent news story suggests, even cities that are considered to be gay friendly can have the random act of homophobia. Travelers Anthony Niedwiecki and Waymon Hudson arrived at the Fort Lauderdale airport on a flight from Chicago just past midnight and heard something that shocked them. According to Niedwiecki and Hudson, a Biblical passage condemning homosexuality was read—at least twice—over the public-address system in the baggage claim area.

The Old Testament passage, oft cited by antigay advocates, is Leviticus 20:13, which is usually translated as "If a man lies with a man as one lies with a woman, both of them have done what is detestable. They must be put to death."

The Broward County administrator vowed to fire any county employees who may have been involved. After an investigation, county officials discovered that the person responsible was actually a skycap working for

Some Interesting Gay Travel Statistics

Gay men traveling alone reported that they spent nearly a third more on their total trip expense ($800 on average) than heterosexuals traveling alone ($540). When gay men reported their last trip traveling as a group, the average spending of their entire party was $3,070, while heterosexual groups spent an average of $2,870; lesbians traveling together spent an average of $2,740.

The Travel Industry Association, in partnership with Harris Interactive and Witeck-Combs Communications, conducted a national survey among 2,020 self-identified gay US travelers and 1,010 self-identified hetero-sexuals, ages 21 and above, who have taken at least one leisure trip within the past year. Nearly half of all gay men (48 percent) and lesbians (47 percent) surveyed said that a destination's gay friendliness is an important factor when making leisure travel choices. About 27 percent of gay men and 28 percent of lesbians said that gay friendliness is "extremely" or "very" important as a consideration in travel planning, while more than half of gay travelers and two-thirds of lesbian travelers desired a place where they could hold their partner's hand without fear of harassment.

an independent company at the airport, not a Broward County employee. The confessor claimed that he had only played the Bible verses (downloaded onto his phone) because he was bored. He was subsequently fired, and an apology was issued to the offended couple.

But despite this rather ugly incident, the Fort Lauderdale and Broward County area largely remains a welcoming destination for gay travelers. It has been cited as a top gay destination by outlets as diverse as Gay.com and the Travel Industry Association. In fact, in 2006, 950,000 lesbian, gay, bisexual, and transgender (LGBT) travelers visited the area, according to the International Gay and Lesbian Travel Association.

While this may have been less than 10 percent of the 10.4 million visitors to the area (according to the Greater Fort Lauderdale Convention and Visitors Bureau), LGBT visitors contributed almost 15 percent of the $8.8 billion in travel-related revenues the area received.

Official support for the community is strong: The Convention and Visitors Bureau spends about $350,000 yearly in cooperation with local businesses to target gay travelers. And with a recent Community Marketing survey showing Fort Lauderdale moving ahead of traditional Florida gay hot spots like Miami and Key West in terms of interest from gay travelers, the area looks poised to welcome even more gay and lesbian visitors.

What's the point here? Difficult, uncomfortable, and even offensive situations can arise almost anywhere, even in cities that claim to be the most gay friendly in the world. You can find a gay enclave or, at the very least, a gay bar or two in most major cities. Before you choose a destination solely based on its gay-friendly reputation, remember that there are always off-the-beaten-path options as well. Do your research about local attitudes toward homosexuality or where there have been recent cases of homophobic attacks—Jamaica, for example, has had several widely publicized cases of violence against gay men, and gay sex between males is illegal. Visit the site **www.sodomylaws.org** to find out local laws against homosexual relationships and same-sex marriage around the world, as well as links to major news stories about legal matters.

Gay-Friendly Airlines

When it comes to booking an airline, you'll probably want to consider issues like redeemable miles, nonstop flights, and whether you'll have to pay $7 for a stale sandwich. But for some travelers, an airline's attitude toward the gay community may also be added to the criteria when deciding where you want to spend your travel dollars.

In February 2007, British Airways issued an apology when a British businessman filed sexual discrimination claims with the Human Rights Commission (HRC). On a British Airways Comair flight from Cape Town to Johannesburg, a flight attendant brought over a blanket to a man who was holding his boyfriend. The flight attendant asked the two men to cover themselves up, claiming that some passengers had been complaining. Although a Comair spokesperson maintained that it does not condone any type of "sensual behavior," regardless of gender, airline representatives did publicly apologize.

Most travelers wouldn't consider this kind of incident as a make-or-break issue when choosing an airline, but unlike with some bars, restaurants, and destinations, it's not easy to determine whether or not an airline is gay friendly. That's when we have to look at the bottom line: Where is the airline spending its own dollars?

United Airlines made headlines in 1999 when it became the first US airline to come out with benefits for domestic partners. Within a week, American Airlines followed suit, and then US Airways joined in just one day after that.

You can also check out the HRC's Web site, where it tracks how airlines are advertising in the gay media, whether they provide benefits for their LGBT employees and their domestic partners, and if diversity training involving sexual orientation and gender identity is required. According to HRC, American Airlines is the winner, with US Airways coming a close second. Both companies rated 100 percent on the HRC 2006 Corporate Equality Index. www.hrc.org, click on Workplace.

In North Korea, tipping is illegal.

American also has pages on its Web site that court gay travelers. The pages offer discounts and tour packages to gay-friendly destinations like Province-town and San Francisco, and they also offer a calendar of events geared toward gay participants. www.aa.com/rainbow, www.aavacations.com/rainbow

In 1993, a group of American Airlines and American Eagle employees formed GLEAM, an advocacy group for gay, lesbian, and transgendered associates, which offers information on domestic partnership benefits and acts as a liaison between employees, management, and community groups. www.amrgleam.com

Low-cost carrier Southwest is also holding its own against legacy carriers, having improved its policies on gay issues. It covers a nondiscrimination policy toward sexual orientation and gender identity in its employee handbook and requires employees to attend diversity training to deal with these topics. Health benefits also extend to same-sex partners, although not in the case of COBRA-like benefits, which apply to spouses only. Southwest also does not include any coverage or short-term disability for sex-reassignment surgery or treatment.

Gay Travel Marketing

Studies show that when it's done right, affinity marketing works. The 11th Annual Gay & Lesbian Travel Survey in 2007 asked 7,500 LGBT consumers where they would be likely to visit in the coming year. Greater Phoenix showed an expected 79 percent increase in gay and lesbian travelers, which followed an active marketing push to this demographic. The Central Visitors' Bureau worked with the city's Gay and Lesbian Chamber of Commerce, advertised in the gay travel magazine *Passport,* and attended gay and lesbian travel conferences for greater visibility.

You may remember that, a few years ago, the city of Philadelphia released a commercial featuring gay couples and inviting travelers to "Come to Philadelphia. Get your history straight and your nightlife gay." The multimillion-dollar campaign was based on Greater Philadelphia Tourism Marketing Corporation studies that showed just how lucrative the gay dollar is, and with that came targeted gay travel promotions.

Even more recent is the introduction of microsites—gay-oriented pages within mainstream travel sites. Targeting the gay community, these links offer information on tour packages, deals, and tips on major destinations, all with a gay twist. Orbitz and Travelocity, for example, have added gay microsites to their services. These sites feature travel deals, event guides in gay-friendly destinations, and searches for gay-friendly hotels. www.orbitz.com/gay, www.travelocity.com/gaytravel

Gay-friendly hotels have also jumped on board the online microsites, to target gay and lesbian travelers. Sure, there's some pandering involved, but the

(continued on page 390)

Pride Festivals Around the World

You can find gay pride festivals practically year-round, sometimes in the most unexpected destinations.

January

Melbourne, www.pridemarch.com.au

February

Cape Town, www.capetownpride.co.za

March

Phuket, Thailand, www.phuketpride.org

April

Mobile, www.mobilealabamapride.com

Phoenix, www.phoenixpride.org

May

Long Beach, California, www.longbeachpride.com

Northampton, Massachusetts, www.northamptonpride.org

June

Albuquerque, www.abqpride.com

Atlanta, www.atlantapride.org

Austin, Texas, www.austinprideparade.org

Boston, www.bostonpride.org

Brooklyn, www.brooklynpride.org

Charleston, West Virginia, www.pridewv.org

Chicago, www.chicagopride.com

Cincinnati, www.prideisalive.com

Detroit, www.pridesource.com

Fresno, www.fresnopride.com

Hamilton, Ontario, www.hamiltonpride.com

Hartford, Connecticut, www.connecticutpride.org

Houston, www.pridehouston.org

Indianapolis, www.indyprideinc.com

Lansing, www.michiganpride.org

Little Rock, www.littlerockpride.com

London, www.pridelondon.org

Los Angeles, www.lapride.org

Louisville, Kentucky, www.kentuckianapridefestival.com

Memphis, www.midsouthpride.org

Milwaukee, www.pridefest.com

Minneapolis, www.tcpride.com

New York City, www.nycpride.org

Omaha, www.ongp.com

Pittsburgh, www.glccpgh.org

Portland, Oregon, www.pridenw.org

San Antonio, www.alamopridefest.org

San Francisco, www.sfpride.org

Seattle, www.seattlepride.org

Sonoma, California, www.sonomacountypride.org

Spokane, www.outspokane.com

St. Louis, www.pridestl.org

St. Petersburg, www.stpetepride.com

Syracuse, www.cnypride.org

Toronto, www.pridetoronto.com

Tulsa, www.tohr.org

Wilton Manors, Florida, www.stonewallstreetfestival.com

Zurich, www.csdzurich.ch

July

Bismarck, North Dakota, www.dakotaoutright.org

Fort Wayne, Indiana, www.fortwaynepride.org

Rio de Janeiro, www.arco-iris.org.br (in Portuguese)

San Diego, www.sandiegopride.org

São Paulo, www.v-brazil.com/tourism/sao-paulo/gay-parade.html

Vancouver, British Columbia, www.vancouverpride.ca

Windsor, Ontario, www.windsorpride.com

(continued)

Pride Festivals Around the World—*Continued*

August

Charlotte, North Carolina, www.pridecharlotte.com

Eugene, Oregon, www.eugenepride.org

Galway, Ireland, www.brodireland.com

Montreal, www.diverscite.org/anglais

Munich, www.csd-munich.de (in German)

Reykjavik, Iceland, www.gaypride.is/english

September

Cornwall, Ontario, www.pridecornwall.com

Dallas, www.dallasprideparade.com

message is a good one. Kimpton Hotels, which launched its LGBT travel program early in 2007, describes how it has created packages for newly married same-sex couples and for various gay prides www.kimptonhotels.com/glbt

Wyndham Hotels highlights its gay friendliness on its site. Okay, this one is funny: "In addition to trendy restaurants, upscale accommodations, and world-class spa services, Wyndham hotels and resorts also provide bath amenities, plush bathrobes, and other special touches that appeal to the highly sophisticated gay and lesbian traveler." www.wyndham.com/locator/gay_lesbian/main.wnt

LGBT Travel Companies

Atlantis Events is one of the leading gay travel companies, creating all-gay and all-lesbian group tours, cruises, and resorts. A 2-week all-inclusive stay at the Club Atlantis Vallarta, a gay beach resort, starts at $1,199. An all-gay cruise from Athens to Venice starts at $1,669 for 9 nights. 800-628-5268, www.atlantisevents.com

Odysseus Travel has been arranging tours for gay and lesbian travelers since 1984. A 7-day Greek Island Cruise from Nexus Gay Sailing starts at $1,595. Odysseus offers a Travel Planner Guide, with suggestions for gay-friendly hotels, clubs, resorts, health spas, and tour destinations in 116

October

> Johannesburg, www.joburgpride.org.za
>
> Tucson, www.tucsonpride.com

November

> Buenos Aires, www.marchadelorgullo.org.ar

Source: *www.gay.com/pride/calendar*

countries. The guide costs $31 and is also available on CD. 800-257-5344, www.odyusa.com

RSVP Vacations, owned by the PlanetOut media company, organizes gay and lesbian cruises and river boat excursions around the world. The Olde World River Journey lets you explore Eastern Europe in true gay fashion, from Budapest to Vienna to Prague. You'll spend 7 nights on the *River Empress*, then 4 nights total in select cities, with short stops along the way. Rates begin at $2,695. www.rsvpvacations.com

Olivia Cruises caters to lesbian travelers, including cruise and resort packages, adventure trips, and family vacations. The Passage to India is an 8-day adventure that takes you through the backroads of the typical tourist path, including a special event at the Taj Mahal. You'll stay in five-star hotel accommodations for $7,149, with an early-bird price of $5,499. 800-631-6277, www.oliviacruises.com

▽ Resources

International Gay and Lesbian Travel Association, www.iglata.com: This national organization has a database of hundreds of gay-owned and gay-friendly travel businesses, including destinations, tour operators, accommodations, airlines, cruise lines, and car rental companies.

Some countries have dedicated Web sites that list **gay-owned and gay-friendly accommodations**: Try New Zealand's www.gaystay.co.nz and Australia's www.gaystay.com.au. For parts of Europe, check out www.pinktravel. com.

365gay.com: This media and entertainment site, owned by parent company Logo Online, offers destination pieces on gay-friendly cities, including Boston, the capital of "America's gay marriage state," plus listings on gay prides around the world.

Damron, www.damron.com: These travel guidebooks cater to gay and lesbian travelers and include a guide to 75 cities around the world.

Gay.com, www.gay.com/travel: This travel portal offers destination guides, expert advice, and listings for LGBT travelers.

Gaytravel.com: Here's a one-stop shop for gay packaged tours and gay-friendly hotels and businesses.

Gaywired.com (click Travel): This site provides features on gay-friendly destinations, special events, and stories on other travel-related topics.

Lesbian and gay hospitality exchange international, www.lghei.org/English.htm: This is a network of gay and lesbian hosts and travelers who offer free accommodations to other members. There are currently more than 500 listings in over 30 countries.

Planetout, www.planetout.com/travel: This leading media and entertainment company targets gay consumers—the travel portal offers information on hot gay destinations, off-the-beaten-path travel, listings of gay tours, and operators.

Purple Roofs, www.purpleroofs.com: The site offers listings of gay- and lesbian-owned/friendly accommodations worldwide.

CHAPTER 19

🙶 Old age is always fifteen years older than I am.🙷

—BERNARD BARUCH

The 2000 Census found that people ages 65 and over make up 12.4 percent of the population (34,991,753). If it's hard to wrap your head around that number, think of it this way: This is equivalent to the entire populations of New York, Connecticut, Massachusetts, and Washington state. Even more astounding is that the number of mature Americans, age 65-plus, is expected to double to 70.3 million by 2030.

Now, wrap your head around this fact: More seniors than ever are traveling—they are more active, spending more money, and often going way beyond traditional destinations and experiences. When my mother turned 80, I wanted to send her on a cruise with a close friend. She balked: "I don't want to go on some boat with a lot of old people," she said. She didn't perceive herself as that old. And she was in good company. A growing number of senior travelers are dramatically changing the demographics of cruising—they are skewing younger when it comes to their destination, as well as their travel experience choices.

While older travelers have historically represented the smallest proportion of domestic leisure trips—about 25 percent (with baby boomers the largest among this percentage)—seniors are considered great money generators. Why? Because they're more likely to travel farther from home than the younger set and travel longer than any other age group (the perks of retirement).

Senior Tour Companies

While most tour companies don't have an age limit, operators that are geared toward older travelers have proliferated. Don't think that these tours involve riding a coach for 2 weeks—the current senior tour operators travel to far-flung corners of the world and can be just as adventurous and active as a traditional tour group. The benefits of going with companies that target seniors are that you'll be surrounded by like-minded travelers who share your interests and experiences, and the pace of these tours can also be flexible, ranging from easy to strenuous, based on the group's needs. Of course, you should check with your doctor before traveling and make the travel company aware of any special needs you may have.

ElderTreks is an adventure tour company designed exclusively for travelers ages 50 and over, providing small-group trips in more than 50 countries. Trips range from "soft adventure" tours of South America and "high arctic adventures" in Russia's Far East, Greenland, or the North Pole to a grizzly bear wildlife sanctuary on Canada's west coast. Try a 10-day trip through Costa Rica that includes outdoor activities such as hiking, visits to hot springs, and horseback riding, starting at about $3,000. A 15-day cruise around French Polynesia features excursions to several islands led by expert naturalists, visits to local artisans, and plenty of swimming and diving, beginning at about $2,200. 800-741-7956, www.eldertreks.com

Elderhostel is a nonprofit organization providing educational experiences for travelers ages 55 and over. There are trips throughout the United States and into 90 countries, ranging from whitewater rafting in Colorado to an archaeological tour of Turkey. A South African safari runs for 15 days and includes city tours of Johannesburg and Cape Town, starting at about $5,000. Elderhostel offers detailed information on how strenuous the trips are: whether there is easy or moderate hiking, extreme weather, or rough travel conditions. 800-454-5768, www.elderhostel.org

Even if your 40th high school reunion is coming up, that's all the more reason to keep on learning. **Senior Summer School** is a year-round program offering learning experiences throughout the United States and Canada. Summer sessions are 2 to 6 weeks, with classes taught by a mix of teachers and local professionals. Shorter fall and winter programs feature lectures and discussions, such as the Life and Times of Georgia O'Keeffe and Cloning and Stem Cell Therapy. 800-847-2466, www.seniorsummerschool.com

The Canadian-based **Good Earth Travel** arranges tours throughout the Canadian Rockies and the Pacific West Coast. A special section for travelers ages 55 and older tailors trips based on your needs and abilities—whether you're a slower walker or simply want a more luxurious experience than a standard package. One of the most popular trips among this age group includes a tour of southern Vancouver Island, where you can go whale watching from your boat or take a cooking class with a local island chef. Starts at about $2,000 for 7 days. 888-979-9797, www.goodearthtravel.com

 Where Are Seniors Traveling?

A 2006 study by Yesawich, Pepperdine, Brown & Russell (YPB&R) compared "mature" travelers (born in 1945 or before) with baby boomers (born between 1946 and 1964) and Gen-Xers (born between 1965 and 1978). According to the study, matures are more likely to take a trip to visit friends or relatives (68 percent), a general sightseeing trip (31 percent), a cruise (20 percent), a trip to a city (17 percent), or a gambling trip (13 percent, which was equivalent to baby boomers).

According to a 2001 study by the Travel Industry Association, favorite activities among mature travelers include shopping (29 percent), visiting historical places or museums (15 percent), attending cultural events or festivals (12 percent), gambling (11 percent), doing outdoor activities (11 percent), visiting national or state parks (8 percent), and going to the beach (7 percent). Another 3 percent of all mature trips include golf, tennis, or skiing.

Warm climates are always a draw for senior travelers, especially for those who live in harsh winter climates. Seniors are traveling to Mexico, Canada, the United Kingdom, France, Italy, and Germany. However, out of 28 domestic locations, YPB&R found that matures most preferred to visit national parks like the Grand Canyon and Yellowstone, followed by Hawaiian islands such as Maui and Kauai. But I bet you can't guess the place that scored the biggest statistical difference between matures and any other age group: It's Branson, Missouri. A good 39 percent of matures chose Branson as a desirable location versus 27 percent of baby boomers and 15 percent of Xers.

Volunteering for Seniors

I've always been a big supporter of combining your vacation with volunteer services, so if you're retired, this is really an optimal travel/experience opportunity. Most volunteer organizations point out that a majority of their participants are over 50: Mature travelers have real-world work experience that can be applied to their volunteer services. And since these programs aren't necessarily cheap (though they are tax-deductible), they attract those who have the time and resources to travel for anywhere from a week to several weeks at a time. Even if you haven't been involved with hands-on volunteer experience before, don't worry—volunteer programs are open about details such as how strenuous their activities are, how comfortable the accommodations will be (it could be anything from camping to a homestay to a standard hotel), and whether there is a cook traveling with the group. Just ask the right questions and you'll be able to find a program that suits your interests, needs, and abilities.

Earthwatch Institute encourages seniors to join its hands-on adventure programs; in fact, its primary pool of volunteers tends to be baby boomers. Volunteers can survey Ecuador's cloud forest birds, tag 1,000-pound sea turtles, and go on archaeological digs in Peru. Earthwatch will inform you ahead of time how tough the trip will be—whether you'll have a private chef or be expected to help cook, whether you'll be camping out in a cave or a dormitory, and even how much weight you'll have to carry in your backpack. 800-776-0188, www.earthwatch.org.

Global Volunteers brings together small-group teams for 1- to 3-week programs in 19 countries. About 40 percent of its volunteers are over the age of 60 and of varying skill levels. Skilled volunteers like medical professionals are welcome to provide patient examinations and screenings, while general volunteer programs include teaching English and providing child care. 800-487-1074, www.globalvolunteers.org

International Executive Service Corps relies on high-level business experts and professionals and matches their skills for development and economic programs abroad that can last several weeks to several months. Programs can include helping private business become more competitive, working with the local chamber of commerce to improve its marketing strategies, or coordinating with the ministry of tourism to increase visibility. 202-589-2600, www.iesc.org

Amizade provides community service opportunities both domestically and abroad to promote cross-cultural awareness. Many of their programs are in partnership with other organizations. For example, in Bolivia you can work alongside employees of Millennium, a nonprofit organization created by doctors and psychologists to provide health and mental care to orphanages in Cochabamba. In the greater Yellowstone region of Montana, Amizade has partnered with the USDA Forestry Service to clean up debris, repair buildings, and maintain trails. 888-973-4443, www. amizade.org

I-to-I offers a Premier Pack for travelers ages 50 and older, which provides more upscale, private accommodations with air-conditioning, en suite bathrooms, and prepared meals—all the luxuries that aren't guaranteed with I-to-I's other packages. Volunteer opportunities include helping to build homes for underprivileged families in Costa Rica (no previous building experience necessary) and teaching English in Moshi, Tanzania. Program rates start at $1,345. 800-985-4852, www.i-to-i.com

Grandtravel

In the past, it was a no-brainer to leave the kids home with their grandparents while Mom and Dad headed off for some alone time. But these days, with the older generation growing increasingly active and interested in travel, something called multigenerational travel, or "grandtravel," is striking a chord. Grandtravel can refer to all three generations traveling together or, even better, grandparents traveling with their grandkids—without the parents getting in the way!

Grandparents are at the forefront of the latest travel trend—heading to resorts, exotic locations, and adventure trips with their grandchildren in tow. Grandtravel is popular because it offers something for everyone, even for the parents who are not involved. Grandparents and grandchildren are able to spend quality time together, without interference from the parents, and the parents are able to relax, knowing their children are with someone they know and trust. It's a win-win for all three generations.

A 2006 study by YPB&R found that 28 percent of grandparents traveled with their grandkids on one or more leisure trips in the previous 12 months. Even more significant is that almost 60 percent of kids ages 6 to 17 say they'd like to vacation with their grandparents. Why? Because grandparents are more democratic with the kids than their parents are. Although the

Former French President Jacques Chirac once insulted Britain by saying: "The only thing they've ever done for European agriculture is mad cow."

grandparents are more likely to make the logistical decisions like where and when they're traveling, how much money to spend, and which hotel to stay in, the kids have a voice when it comes to what they do when they arrive at their destinations. That includes activities and restaurants, and, of course, grandparents love to spoil their grandkids with everything from ice cream sundaes to pricey souvenirs.

Disney may still be a top pick for a kids' vacation, but kid-friendly resorts and adventure vacations are becoming increasingly popular, especially with multigenerational travel.

Here are some of the many choices available for grandtravel throughout the world.

I've already mentioned **Elderhostel**'s catering to the mature crowd, but on some of their trips, the kids are invited as well. An intergenerational camping trip in Highlands, North Carolina, brings together grandparents and grandkids ages 8 to 12 for 5 days of hiking, swimming, craft making, and singing around the campfire in the Appalachian wilderness (starting at $585). A seashore adventure on Prince Edward Island will probably appeal to young girls who fell in love with the *Anne of Green Gables* series, so activities have a nostalgic flair, like picking berries, making ice cream, and taking a wagon ride, topped off with a musical version of the famous books (starting at about $900). 800-454-5768, www.elderhostel.org

Generations Touring Company offers worldwide adventure-oriented opportunities for grandparents and their grandkids. You can stay in your own backyard and take a tour of Boston and New York City to follow in the footsteps of great baseball history—including a tour of the Baseball Hall of Fame, behind-the-scenes tours of the baseball fields, and, naturally, plenty of game watching. If you'd prefer to travel a little further afield, try a multi-generational trip to Vietnam, Peru, or the Galapagos with the young ones in tow. And last but not least, a volunteer vacation in New Orleans can bring generations together like nothing else. Program rates start at about $1,600. 888-415-9100, www.generationstouringcompany.com

Grandtravel is a company that specializes in creating packages designed to appeal to both generations. From the American West to a Kenyan safari, no parents are allowed on these adventures. On a weeklong trip to Hawaii, grandparents and kids can try hula dancing, diving deep underwater in a submarine, and dolphin watching from a sailboat to Lanai. A trip to London and Paris includes the high-speed train through the Chunnel and all the fancy food and cultural excursions you can handle (note: listen to the kids if they're sick of museuming; they'll thank you for it later). Rates range from about $5,000 to $8,000. 800-247-7651, www. grandtrvl.com

In addition to tour companies, many hotels, spas, and even trains are catering to grandparents traveling with their grandkids.

GrandLuxe Railways, part of the American Orient Express family, welcomes grandparents and grandkids on the National Parks of the West rail journey. Grandparents traveling with children save up to 12 percent of their tickets for a 9-day tour of Grand Teton Park, the Grand Canyon, Yellowstone, and Zion National Park onboard a luxury train. Packages include five-course gourmet meals and guided tours. Rates for one cabin for one grandparent and one child start at $7,857 and rise to $15,715 for four passengers in two cabins. 800-320-4206, www.americanorientexpress.com

The Sierra Club periodically offers trips reserved exclusively for grandparents and grandkids, which include adventure and educational programs. A trip to Tahoe National Forest invites older travelers with children ages 6 and older to stay in the Sierra Club's own lodge outside of Lake Tahoe. Activities include hiking, bird watching, games, and movie nights, with family-style meals for the whole group. Starting at $525 for adults and $425 for children. 415-977-5500, www.sierraclub.org

The **Banana Courtyard** is a bed-and-breakfast, located in the French Quarter of New Orleans, that offers a grandparent/grandchild Explore New Orleans package, available year-round. Kids get to stay in the pirate's attic room, next to their grandparents. For $495, visitors can take a kid-friendly tour of New Orleans, including tickets to the Aquarium of the Americas, the Audubon Zoo, the Children's Museum, and a round-trip cruise from the French Quarter to the zoo on a Mississippi riverboat. Regular low-season rates for the B and B start at $60 a night. 800-842-4748, www.bananacourtyard.com

The **Safety Harbor Resort and Spa,** located on the Tampa Bay coastline in Florida, is based around a 2,000-year-old natural mineral springs. The grandmother/granddaughter package includes a 4-night stay in premium accommodations (a bay view with a balcony) and spa treatments, starting at $754. 888-237-8772, www.safetyharborspa.com

Senior Discounts

There are financial positives and negatives to traveling as a senior. The bad news is that your travel insurance is almost always going to be higher, regardless of your health. With advancing age, however, comes the once-coveted senior discount—okay, so it's usually only about a 10 percent savings. And you need to be careful here—a growing number of senior "discounts" offer 10 to 20 percent savings but only from the highest retail prices. Savvy seniors can often get better deals without playing the age card.

The basic rule of thumb about senior discounts is that you have to ask for them—no one is going to offer them up-front (be flattered). The next rule is that you should check your other options as well: If you have AARP or AAA membership, you might get an even steeper discount, and if there are any ongoing specials, those prices may actually beat what you would get with a discount.

Your first stop should be www.seniordiscounts.com. You can access its free database of more than 125,000 available discounts for travelers ages 50 and older. You can build your trip around discounts for airlines, car rentals, public transportation, and hotels (note that while the Web site operators try to keep the ongoing discounts as accurate as possible, you may need to verify with the companies directly). The site also sells a senior discount card for $12.95 a year, which includes a guidebook on obtaining discounts and some deeper discounts for members.

Members can find discounted travel packages through **AARP's Passport Program**, which has established partnerships with airlines, hotels, and car rental companies specifically for seniors (booking goes through Travelocity). There are also travel tips and features to help you find the right kind of trip for you, with links to everything from literary adventures in Dublin to all you need to know about RV travel. 888-687-2277, www.aarp.org

The **American Automobile Association** gives seniors an extra 10 percent discount on top of regular AAA discounts, based on a variety of partnerships with airlines, hotels, and car rental companies. www.aaa.com

Airline Discounts

The golden years of the senior discounts on airlines are waning. When US Airways and America West merged in 2006, their senior discount programs were discontinued. Northwest Airlines has also discontinued its 10 percent senior discount program, and Delta halted its Young at Heart program back in 2001. On airlines that do still offer discounts, they are usually not readily apparent or even available online and often have stringent requirements that make the 10 percent not worth the hassle. It's best to call the airlines directly to ask about their senior discount program and compare that rate with their lowest available fare—chances are, the regularly discounted fare will beat out the senior discount. However, here are some existing airline discount programs to be aware of.

Southwest Airlines has one of the best policies for senior travelers ages 65 and older. There is no advance purchase required, and tickets are both refundable and changeable. There is an upper limit to how much a senior will pay for a ticket—Southwest reports this cap to be $149, but in a call to the airline, a cross-country flight from Hartford to Los Angeles wound up pricing at $154 each way. In any case, the same rule of doing your homework still applies, as you may find a cheaper fare even without the senior pricing. 800-435-9792, www.southwest.com

American Airlines, American Eagle, and **AmericanConnection** offer senior discounts of 10 percent on some fares for passengers 65 and older. These discounts are available only over the phone, must be booked 14 days in advance, and include a Saturday night stayover. 800-433-7300, www.aa.com

United Airlines has a Silver Wings program for travelers ages 55 and over that includes more than $300 in travel credits each year (promising that these credits will be easy to redeem) and double miles on Mileage Plus flights. Membership is $240 per year. 800-864-8331, www.united.com

Air Canada gives 10 percent discounts to fliers ages 60 and over (plus a companion) on domestic and some international routes. Note that this discount can't be accessed online. 888-247-2262, www.aircanada.ca

Continental Airlines offers travelers 65 and older 10 percent discounts off many domestic and international fares with 14-day advance purchase. Bookings may be made online or by phone. 800-525-0280, www.continental.com

Trains

Amtrak travelers ages 62 years and older can get a 15 percent discount on adult fares. This discount doesn't apply to sleeper accommodations, the auto train, the weekday Acela Express, or the weekday Metroliner. Seniors can also receive a 10 percent discount on the North American Rail Pass, a 30-day rail pass through the United States and Canada. 800-872-7245, www.amtrak.com

Car Rentals

Alamo, Avis, and **Budget** offer discounts of up to 10 percent for Senior Discount Card members. www.seniordiscounts.com

Hertz, National, and **Dollar** offer discounted rates of 5 to 25 percent for AARP members, which varies by location.

Hotels

Most hotels offer a 10 percent discount for seniors (although the definition of "senior" can vary from 55 to 65), but some hotels offer even steeper discounts for AARP members. Remember that rates vary by location and there may be qualifications such as booking well in advance and getting no refunds if you cancel.

Choice Hotels (which includes Clarion Hotels, Quality Inns, Sleep Inns, Friendship Inns, Rodeway Inns, and Econo Lodges) offers 10 percent off for travelers ages 50 and older and 20 to 30 percent off if you're 60 or older, with advance reservations. Note that this discount is available only if you call the 800 number, not the direct location—always call the location itself to see if you can negotiate a better rate. 877-424-6423, www.choicehotels.com

At more than 2,000 **Marriott** hotels worldwide (that includes Fairfield Inns, Courtyards, and Residence Inns), seniors ages 62 and older can get up to 15 percent off the room rate. 888-236-2427, www.marriott.com

At the **Days Inn,** seniors ages 60 and older receive 10 percent off the room rate, and AARP members can save up to 15 percent. 800-329-7466, www.daysinn.com

Motel 6 gives 10 percent off for all travelers ages 60 and older in the United States and Canada. 800-466-8356, www.motel6.com

Tips for Senior Travel

! Remember that airline restrictions apply to prescriptions or over-the-counter medication in liquid, gel, or aerosol form. Travelers are allowed to carry liquids in 3-ounce bottles or smaller. These items must be kept in a single quart-sized, clear plastic, sealable bag.

! If you're bringing medication on board, the Transportation Security Administration requires that each medication be properly labeled with a professionally printed label identifying the medication and manufacturer's name or pharmaceutical label. The prescription medicine must match the name on the passenger's ticket.

! If you require more than 3 ounces of medications in your carry-on bag, they may not be placed in the quart-sized bag and must be declared to a Transportation Security officer. A declaration can be made verbally, in writing, or by a companion, caregiver, interpreter, or family member. Declared liquid medications and other liquids for disabilities and medical conditions must be kept separate from all other property submitted for x-ray screening.

! Travelers can bring beverages and other items purchased in the secure boarding area on board the aircraft. This includes water and juices for medical purposes.

! You are allowed to bring onboard life-support and life-sustaining liquids such as bone marrow, blood products, transplant organs, and gels or frozen liquids needed to cool disability-related or medically related items.

! If you require disability-related equipment such as wheelchairs, canes, prosthetic devices, personal oxygen, and supplies related to diabetes, they are allowed through security checkpoints once cleared through screening. The carry-on luggage limit does not apply to these devices. Make sure all of these items have ID tags if applicable.

! If you would like to have a family member or friend accompany you to your gate, they'll need to obtain a gate pass. Request one at the ticket counter when you check in. (Your family member or friend will need to show identification as well.)

 Driving Miss Daisy

An innovative program called the Independent Transportation Network (ITN) is putting some seniors into the passenger's seat. In regions where public transportation is lacking, ITN volunteers drive seniors who are no longer able to get behind the wheel themselves. This "dignified transportation for seniors" program originated in Portland, Maine, and now has affiliates in South Carolina, Florida, and California. 207-857-9001, www. itnamerica.org

CHAPTER 20

Solo Travel

❝ **It is better to travel alone than with a bad companion.** ❞

—AFRICAN PROVERB

When it comes to travel, those who go solo often get the short end of the stick, in terms of prices, service, and even experience. Hotels and cruises often charge what's known as a "single-supplement fee," claiming that they need to make up the cost of that extra bed in the room—always, always beware of that "double occupancy" fine print when comparing prices. Restaurants may overlook lone diners in favor of higher-revenue couples and groups. And then there are just basic personality obstacles when it comes to solo travelers—if you're not the outgoing type, it can be easy to get lost in the crowd of other travelers.

But if you know how to work around the system, the pluses of traveling alone are often more desirable. Traveling solo means you can go where you want, when you want. You can join up with other solo travelers or groups or separate yourself from the crowd. As someone who travels alone a majority of the time, I can tell you that there is no better way to get lost in a culture and truly experience the world.

The 2006 National Leisure Travel Monitor polled the travel habits of 4,354 Americans ages 16 and older. Across all age groups, 29 percent of travelers took a trip alone in 2006, up from 26 percent the previous year. By age, 34 percent of echo-boomers (born between 1979 and 1988) traveled alone, as well as 28 percent of Gen-Xers (born between 1965 and 1978), 27 percent of baby boomers (born between 1946 and 1964), and 30 percent of matures (born in 1945 or earlier).

Even more dramatic was a 2005 study by Fodor's Travel Publications, which found that one in four Americans had traveled alone for pleasure for 2 or more nights in the previous 3 years, saying that solo leisure travel would allow them more freedom and flexibility.

So how is the travel industry responding? Travel providers are slowly but surely recognizing the solo traveler as a potent source of revenue, and for once, there are now hotels, destinations, tour operators, cruise lines, and travel services that are becoming more single friendly—which means that they've eliminated or reduced single-supplement fees or that they offer reasonably priced single-occupancy rooms or that they provide a guaranteed share option for solo travelers to bunk together. If your operator isn't deemed single friendly, remind the agent that an unsold room is revenue they'll never recoup once the sun rises or the ship sails . . . and with growing purchasing clout, you might be surprised at the deals you can get.

Tour Companies

As a solo traveler, one of your options is to join an existing tour group. Chances are, the dreaded double occupancy will still apply here; you'll have to room with a stranger to avoid the single supplement, but often the tour operator will make a match based on your gender, interests, smoking preferences, and even sleeping habits. It's important to research the makeup of these groups, as swinging singles may not want to join a senior citizen tour, and elderly travelers may want to avoid crowds of rowdy spring breakers. One thing you can be sure of: no honeymooning couples allowed!

All Singles Travel, a division of Travel Services Worldwide, puts together travel groups made entirely of solo travelers. The optional roommate matching service means that you can avoid the single supplement, which can save hundreds of dollars in hotel and cruise fees. Organized activities such as cocktail parties and group dinners also take the stress out of making your own social plans, but you do have the option of doing your own thing if you want. There are also specialized trips for Jewish, Christian, and senior singles, although the company makes it clear that its tours are not designed to be a dating service (but that's optional too!). Trips include a 10-day tour through Italy and a biannual Costa Rican adventure, with prices averaging $2,000 to $3,000. 800-717-3231, www.allsinglestravel.com

Travel Buddies Worldwide was founded by a widower who was looking to save costs on solo travel. The organization offers free membership and arranges small-group trips with an optional roommate matching service to avoid the single-supplement fee. A 9-day tour of Istanbul and Kusadasi is about $1,200, with a relatively low $160 single-supplement fee if you choose to go without a roommate. A 16-day trip to Costa Rica is about $2,300 to $3,400, depending on the number of roommates, airfare not included. 800-998-9099, www.travelbuddiesworldwide.com

O Solo Mio arranges about 20 trips a year in small groups of 10 to 24 that are exclusively for its members. It also offers cruises for single travel in a group setting but leaves time for your own explorations. Travelers are matched with roommates on all trips by gender, smoking and sleeping habits, and age. Upcoming trips include Greek island-hopping and a sojourn from Paris to Provence. Average prices are about $3,000. 800-959-8568, www.osolomio.com

Some all-inclusive resorts also cater to solo travelers, like the classic Club Med. With more than 100 villages in more than 40 countries worldwide, most resorts welcome lone travelers, but **Club Med's Solo Rendezvous** on Lindeman Island has grown into a legendary excursion for singles ages 30 and older. Single supplements still apply unless you opt to room with another traveler. A 7-day vacation starts at about $1,250, and since Club Med is all inclusive, this takes care of your airfare, accommodations, meals, and even alcohol. 888-932-2582, www.clubmed.com

Adventures for Singles has been operating since 1990, providing international travel packages for solo and single travelers. A trip to visit Singapore and the orangutans of Borneo or a tango and samba trip through Buenos Aires is about $2,200. 877-813-9421, www.adventuresforsingles.com

Cruise Lines

Cruises have long been a popular choice for single and solo passengers, especially now that entertainment options extend far beyond the traditional shuffleboard and bingo. However, cruises are also notorious for their single-supplement charges, sometimes charging as much as 200 percent(!) of the base price.

Some lines will open up double cabins to single travelers when they are having trouble filling a cruise, particularly during the off-season. Often, you'll pay a reduced supplement or, sometimes, no supplement at all. But you have to ask—this isn't a deal that cruise operators are eager to let out.

Your other best bet is to bunk up with a roommate to avoid the fees. And whether you're traveling solo or as a couple, one principle remains that I must remind you of: How much time are you really going to spend in your cabin, other than sleeping and showering? Once you understand that, it makes a big difference as to the cabin you choose (and the price you pay) or whether, as a solo passenger, you choose to have a roommate to save on those single-supplement costs.

When considering a cruise, first try asking the cruise line to hook you up with another solo passenger of the same sex—although this practice isn't very common, it's almost always worth a shot, and you may even have a chance for your own room without the extra fee if they can't find anyone. Otherwise, a tour company can help match you up with another traveler who books through them. Here are a few that specialize in solo traveler cruises.

Singles Travel International specializes in group travel for singles. On cruises, they guarantee to find you a roommate or they'll cover the supplement fee themselves. Trips include a Caribbean vacation on the *Queen Mary 2,* starting at $899 a person, and a tour of Italy for singles in their 30s and 40s, starting at $1,626. There are optional group events like predinner cocktails and singles-only seating at dinner. 877-765-6874, www.singlestravelintl.com

Solo Cruiser offers a "lower single supplement" on various cruise lines. The discounts are available only if you book through Solo Cruiser—by booking group departures, the company qualifies for free cabins, which they turn around to offer savings for solo cruisers. The company also offers themed cruises for special interests like culinary arts and photography, cruises for single mature travelers ages 55 and older, and all-inclusive cruises that include gratuities, alcohol, and some shore excursions. 888-765-6278, www.solocruiser.com

CruiseMates, the online cruise publication, offers a free message board for cruisers seeking roommates. The publication also devotes an entire section to solo cruisers with tips, articles, and stories. www.cruisemates.com

While many travelers prefer the solo experience for what it is, there are plenty of singles who are hoping to find love on the high seas. **Cruising for Love** offers cruises throughout the Caribbean, Mexico, and Canada, where there is ample opportunity to meet plenty of like-minded singles. Predeparture dinners and organized activities like poolside cocktails and beach olympics keep the social vibes flowing. Cruises range from $300 to $800, not including airfare. 866-451-5027, www.cruisingforlove.com

> The Scottish Tourism Board will let you "Date a Hot Scot." Vote online for the hottest guy in a kilt, and a winner will be chosen to fly to Scotland to party with the Scots.

The Real Love Boats

Wanted: single men 45 and over who can dance and socialize and who understand the lost art of chivalry.

No, this isn't one woman's personal ad, but it is what Lauretta Blake, owner of the Working Vacation and the Gentlemen Host Program, is looking for. This is an ad to find men, known as "social hosts," to take a cruise for free in exchange for dancing with the single women on board. Call it *American Gigolo* for the new millennium.

The trend actually began in 1982 when Royal Cruise Line (now part of Norwegian Cruise Line) began recruiting bachelors to dance with the large number of single women who take cruise vacations. Each host must pass a background check ($75) and a "dance test" ($25 to $50) covering the five basics: waltz, fox-trot, rumba, cha-cha, and swing (jitterbug).

Men must be between the ages of 45 and 72 and can apply directly to some cruise lines through the Working Vacation. If accepted, the applicant will then be flown to the departing port of the cruise ship. While cabin and meals are free, a placement fee of $28 a day applies. The good news for men: The costs are dramatically cheaper than paying the regular cruise fare. And for women, the good news is obvious.

But for prospective male applicants, some important cautions:

Your schedule needs to be flexible. You should be prepared to sail for a minimum of 21 days, though some hosts spend an entire year afloat. On board, hosts are very active, working about 50 hours per week. They dance and socialize with guests for 3 to 4 hours per night, host tables for dinner, participate in daytime activities, and assist with special events and shore excursions. Most ships allow hosts to accept gratuities and join shore excursions for a reduced or no cost. While physical involvement between passengers and hosts is officially not allowed, in real life romance happens.

For a listing of upcoming cruises looking for hosts, call 708-301-7535 or visit www.theworkingvacation.com/text/about2.html.

Social Networks

One of the best parts of being a solo traveler is discovering that you're not alone after all. There are now several social Web sites that are designed to link up solo travelers, whether you're looking for an activity partner or a long-term travel companion or you simply need some travel tips before embarking on an experience.

Deemed the MySpace for travelers, the free Web site **www.tripup.com** utilizes popular social features like online profiles and discussion groups. There are also travel blogs and worldwide reviews of restaurants, hotels, shopping, parties, sights, and activities. In addition, the site's trip planning tool allows solo travelers to check out trips that others are setting up or, alternatively, to set up their own itinerary that they might invite others to join. One unique feature of TripUp is that you can become a Travel Guru for a specific destination. Whether it's your hometown or a favorite destination, you can act as an information source for that place.

Another site, **www.triphub.com,** is designed for both existing groups and solo travelers who want to form or join a group—you can use the site to extend invitations to others to join your trip and to set up a TripHub homepage to coordinate all the details like dates, hotels, who's coming, and who's driving.

The oldest of the meet-and-greet trip-planning sites is **www.travelchums. com,** a travel companion matching site. With more than 35,000 members, TravelChums boasts a fairly diverse range of ages and backgrounds. Solo travelers may enjoy browsing the tips and member profiles; however, only paid subscribers can send out e-mails—free users can only respond to any subscribers who might write to them.

Travelocity's "Meet Me In . . . " feature offers mainly discounted, last-minute packages for solo travelers to meet up in a particular destination. These prepackaged offers cover more than 170 international and domestic destinations from about 150 different departure cities, with prices starting at around $200 for short domestic jaunts. By coordinating flight itineraries,

Meet Me In . . . can help maximize the time travelers spend together and even offers a "time together" calculation that shows, to the minute, how long you and your travel partner will be in your destination together. www.travelocity.com/meetmein

The old notion of meeting your partner while on an airplane is a romantic one, so of course now there's a Web site to help move things along: **www.airintroductions.com** allows members to create a personal profile and seats you next to someone with similar interests. Love matches aren't guaranteed, but it might make for a great story to tell the grandkids.

The social networking site **www.whereareyounow.com** allows you to connect with others who live or will be traveling where you're going—and allows you to post photos and journals and to chat with others via texting.

Safety Issues When Traveling Solo

It should come as no surprise that traveling solo can make you more vulnerable to "dangerous elements." Without a travel buddy by your side, you can become a target for petty crime. Solo travelers ought to at least have one contact on the ground who is aware of their comings and goings—and will know if they fail to arrive at a destination. Thankfully, as international cell phones become inexpensive and commonplace, it's easier than ever to keep in touch with a point person.

The US Department of State has up-to-date information on travel warnings and security risks in foreign countries at www.travel.state.gov. And while I suggest you consult this site, I also suggest you don't get frightened by it. There is no such thing as a crime-free destination. You just need to pack a little extra common sense.

Trains

Some bad news to report. Travel crime—especially against solo travelers—is increasing in places where you might not expect it. European trains are a great example. The image of rolling through the European countryside while staring wistfully at the farmsteads trundling by is an iconic one for most. But travelers on European trains would be wise to pay attention on their journeys. Thieves are now often targeting solo travelers. My advice: Make friends quickly on your train trip or never leave your seat. More and more solo travelers are reporting all their luggage missing after they return from the restroom or take long naps.

Cabs

Taxicabs are often the most convenient method of transport in many cities. But cabs can present some extra security risks for solo travelers in particular. For example, in India, solo travelers should avoid just walking out of the airport into the street looking for transportation. This is a great way to become prey not only for pickpockets but for unscrupulous cabdrivers as well. Instead, go to the designated cab stands inside most Indian airports. This will result in a safe, registered cab with a standardized prepaid fare. Go outside and you'll certainly pay more, and your arrival isn't guaranteed.

As a corollary to this, avoid hailing cabs off the street, especially in Mexico City. Criminals have been known to impersonate taxi drivers, pick up unsuspecting tourists, and force them to withdraw money from ATMs. While this can happen to groups, it's even more prevalent among solo travelers. So instead, use designated taxi stands at hotels and inside (or just outside, in some cases) airports. Also, when being dropped off after taking a reputable cab from your hotel, make sure you have the number for the taxi company so you can call them to come back.

Airports

The airlines aren't the only ones who might lose your bags. If you're not careful, you might lose them before you even get to the gate. It's easy to become a victim of something called a crime of distraction. And one common airport crime for which solo travelers are especially at risk is what's known as the mustard trick. In this one, perpetrated by two thieves, the first "accidentally" spills mustard (or any other messy substance) on the victim's clothing. While the first thief distracts the victim by helping clean up the mess, the second will make off with the solo traveler's unattended bag. To prevent this scenario, always keep your bags right between your legs whenever you set them down, even to do something as simple as making a phone call.

Also watch out for the escalator trick, which occurs both in airports and, sometimes, in heavily trafficked shopping malls. In this one, the perpetrator reaches across to the oncoming escalator and nabs a victim's purse or bag. The hapless victim is left going the wrong way, while the thief gets away. In this case, always keep purses and shopping bags on the opposite side of your body from the oncoming escalator to make it difficult or impossible for the thief to reach over. Generally, being aware of your possessions can actually help ward off potential thieves, as an alert traveler is always a tougher target than an inattentive one.

Go Local

A solo tourist sticks out like a sore thumb—or a big target. So be a solo traveler, instead. Try to blend in as best you can by taking cues from those around you. This doesn't necessarily mean going as far as traditional dress, but for men, avoiding baseball caps, shorts, and tennis shoes can go a long way toward making you look more like a local instead of an American. For women, dressing appropriately to the culture is always the best option. In both cases, taking note of those around you is the best way to blend.

▽Resources

Connecting: Solo Travel Network is an organization dedicated to helping single travelers. A 1-year online membership costs $30 and includes access to a bimonthly newsletter featuring solo travel tips and stories, tour listings, and recommendations, plus a copy of the Single-Friendly Travel Directory, which lists more than 250 travel suppliers. 604-886-9099, www.cstn.org

Safety Text: Developed by a father whose daughter was murdered while traveling in Tokyo, Safety Text involves sending a text message saying where you're going, with whom, and when you're expected back. The message is stored in a system—when you return from your trip, you can cancel the text; but if you don't return by that date, the text is sent to your emergency contact at home. www.safetytext.com

Solotravel.org is an online resource for solo and women travelers, with safety tips, links to tours, and personal stories. www.solotravel.org

CHAPTER 21

Student Travel

“ **Education is too important to be left soley to the educators.** ”

—FRANCIS KEPPEL

Ten years ago, only about 76,000 US students studied abroad. Today, we're talking about more than 200,000 students—that's more than a 250 percent increase in study-abroad participation in the last decade alone. About 40 percent of students go abroad during their junior year in college; the rest are dispersed primarily between summer school programs and the spring of sophomore year. (And a number of high schools are now actively involved in summer study programs abroad.)

Of course, the idea of one's child, even a 20-year-old college student, simply taking off and flying to a foreign country might strike fear in any parent's heart. But in a survey conducted by the Institute for the International Education of Students of alumni who had participated in study-abroad programs between 1950 and 1999, the benefits are clear: Alumni reported increased self-confidence, a broadened interest in seeking more diverse friendships, increased interest in academics, and invaluable help in defining their future career path.

Bottom line: If you want to become streetwise—worldwide (hint: you do)—then do your best to spend at least 1 year studying overseas.

These study programs have been evolving rapidly over the past 10 years as study-abroad participation has grown exponentially. The old philosophy was simply to send students to a college in a foreign country and hope that, by diving in headfirst, they would quickly assimilate and integrate into a new culture. Not exactly an easy task, and students often found themselves battling loneliness, unexpected culture shock, and, in a worst-case scenario, risks to their safety.

It's important to ask questions about the program's level of immersion and enrichment, to make sure that your child isn't just being placed into a

The Top 20 Destinations for US Students Studying Abroad

RANK	DESTINATION	2003–2004	2004–2005
	TOTAL	191,321	205,983
1	United Kingdom	32,237	32,071
2	Italy	21,922	24,858
3	Spain	20,080	20,806
4	France	13,718	15,374
5	Australia	11,418	10,813
6	Mexico	9,293	9,244
7	Germany	5,985	6,557
8	China	4,737	6,389
9	Ireland	5,198	5,083
10	Costa Rica	4,510	4,887
11	Japan	3,707	4,100
12	Austria	2,444	2,757
13	New Zealand	2,369	2,657
14	Czech Republic	2,089	2,494
15	Greece	2,099	2,445
16	Chile	2,135	2,393
17	South Africa	2,009	2,304
18	Argentina	1,315	2,013
19	Brazil	1,554	1,994
20	India	1,157	1,767

Source: *Open Doors 2006 Report on International Educational Exchange*

foreign school and ignored until the return home. Look beyond the brochures and PowerPoint presentations that claim the program is nothing but fun, growth, and personal satisfaction. It's not unreasonable to expect the same level of education and opportunities as a student's home university—and the same levels of risk and concern.

! Are the study-abroad classes contributing to the student's major? Sure, traveling abroad is an educational experience, but it may not be worth it if it means graduating a semester or year late.

! Is there an orientation to prepare students for cultural changes?

! Is there a point person on campus or nearby who can deal with personal issues?

! Can study-abroad students join the host school's team sports and other extracurricular activities?

Of course, the biggest fear for parents is that their child may be harmed while abroad. Some of the biggest risks students face while living abroad include drug and alcohol abuse, physical assault, sexual harassment, theft, and exposure to diseases or illnesses in the destination country.

One tragedy happened back in 1996, when four students were killed while visiting India on their semester at sea. A scheduling mix-up put the students on a plane from Varanasi to Delhi, rather than to Agra to see the Taj Mahal as planned. The students were put on buses from Delhi to Agra—about a 6-hour ride on some rough terrain. One of the buses, carrying 27 Americans, swerved and careened into a ditch, killing four students along with three other passengers.

More recently, in March 2007, a student at the University of Minnesota went public with claims that she repeatedly endured sexual assault and harassment while studying at the University of Dar es Salaam in Tanzania. She alleged that the man in the office where she registered for classes refused to let her register until she agreed to a "date," which she says was a metaphor for sex; she states that handwritten research papers were stolen by another student who demanded sex in exchange for their return; and a man at the office for foreign students asked uncomfortable questions about her sexual habits. The student has also publicly criticized the university's study-abroad office for its response to her allegations.

Does all of this mean you need to lock your child in his dorm room for 4 years? Of course not, but you need to be aware of any risks and learn how to ask the right questions when arranging for a study-abroad program, whether it's by sea or by land.

These days, many study programs claim that they're putting more emphasis on supporting students throughout the whole travel/educational experience, not just prepping them before they leave or when they first arrive. That early preparation is important, of course, for alerting students to potential cultural and linguistic differences (in England, don't call it a "fanny pack"; and in parts of Italy and Greece, skip the thumbs-up sign). But beyond that is where many programs fail to protect their students. This is where it's crucial for parents to get involved . . . this is the time to ask the hard questions.

! Find out what kind of insurance the college has. Is there insurance to evacuate a student or group of students if necessary?

! Is there a point person on-site to deal with medical, security, and personal issues?

! Find out any details on crime, illness, accidents, and other issues that have occurred on campus in the recent past.

! Find out how locals and local laws deal with crime and sexual assault.

! If applicable, get background information on host families.

! Find out how you can get your child released from the program if necessary.

Study-Abroad Programs

Many programs are sponsored by universities that have relationships with institutions abroad. However, if a student wants to study in a country or city that isn't available through his or her own school, it's still possible to go through another accredited US institution. There are also several independent organizations that can arrange a program abroad.

Global Learning Semesters operates 35 study-abroad programs, hosted at five foreign universities: Intercollege, University of Paris IV (Sorbonne), University of Alcala, London Metropolitan University, and Galen University. 877-300-7010, www.globalsemesters.com

EF International Language Schools have programs for high schoolers and adults as well as college students. College semesters are available for 6- and 9-month periods in France, Germany, Italy, Spain, Ecuador, Costa Rica, and China. 800-992-1892, www.ef.com

Council on International Educational Exchange has 95 programs for high school and college students in more than 33 host countries. 800-407-8839, www.ciee.org

Semester at Sea

If the ocean is calling, a semester at sea may be the answer. The following programs offer students the opportunity to have both classroom and experiential learning while traveling around the world.

Semester at Sea sponsors ocean-bound travel education for college students (as well as law school students, teachers, nonstudents, and seniors). A sample 110-day itinerary starts in the Bahamas with likely stops in San Juan; Salvador, Brazil; Cape Town; Port Louis, Mauritius; Chennai, India; Yangon, Myanmar; Ho Chi Minh City; Hong Kong; Qindao, China; Kobe, Japan; and Seattle. 800-854-0195, www.semesteratsea.com

SEA Education Association program offers a 12-week hands-on oceanography course for a semester credit from Boston University. Students spend the first 6 weeks in Woods Hole on Cape Cod studying oceans and then sail 134-foot vessels in the Atlantic/Caribbean or in the Pacific, depending on the season. 800-552-3633, www.sea.edu

Sea-mester Programs focus on the shipboard experience for students who are interested in marine and nautical sciences. Their 80-day excursions begin with 10 days in the British Virgin Islands and then continue with 7 weeks of sailing the Caribbean. 800-317-6789, www.scamester.com

The Scholar Ship, a new program, is accepting a significant number of international students and staff in order to enhance the global experience on board. The curriculum will also include leadership training and courses led by business leaders from organizations. 410-962-7344, www.thescholarship.com

▽ Resources

GoAbroad.com: Choose from a variety of study-abroad programs, plus links to jobs, volunteer opportunities, and internships.

IEE Passport, www.studyabroadfunding.org: Plan your trip based on this database of study- and teach-abroad programs, as well as information on scholarship programs, fellowships, and grants.

Institute of International Education, www.iie.org: You'll find a database of scholarships, fellowships, and grants for US and international students that allows you to search by subject or location.

Studyabroad.com: You'll find a directory of intensive language, study, summer, internship, and volunteer-abroad programs, organized by subject, country, or city.

Studyabroaddirectory.com: This is a directory of high school and college, volunteer, internship, and teaching-abroad programs; language schools; eco and adventure travel; and TEFL certification, as well as travel guides and contact information for embassies and consulates.

Transitions Abroad, www.transitionsabroad.com: This is one of the premier publications for living abroad, whether it's for study, work, or volunteering. The Web site is a great resource for programs, accommodations, tips, and personal anecdotes.

Working Abroad

Studying abroad doesn't always have to involve an academic curriculum. Learning about life in another country can also involve volunteering, internships, and paid positions. Teaching English as a foreign language is a popular choice, particularly in Asia and Africa, while au pair work is commonly found in Europe and Australia. Farm areas around the world often require seasonal help. Do your research carefully on this one, as these programs tend to be more independent than studying abroad: If accommodations are provided, make sure that they're in a safe area and satisfy basic standards in health and comfort. If a host family is involved, get in contact with them beforehand and don't be afraid to say "never mind" or cut the stay short. All the commonsense rules about behavior in a foreign country apply here.

Workingabroad.com is a great resource for au pair positions and jobs teaching English abroad. Teaching English in Madrid and the surrounding suburbs starts at $695, which includes a 1- to 3-month stay with a host family and discounted accident and sickness insurance. Au pair placements usually require a 9- to 12-month commitment of 30 hours of child care per week; duties may include dropping off children and picking them up at school, helping with homework, and light housework.

Transitionsabroad.com provides links to all kinds of work, internship, and volunteer-placement services, from jobs on cruise lines to working on an organic farm in New Zealand.

Student Discounts

To card or not to card? Student discount cards promise savings on everything from youth hostels, plane tickets, and language classes to camel treks, diving excursions, and massages . . . but the trick is that you have to remember to use them. Often these cards get pulled out for the first couple of weeks abroad and then get tossed aside. Another benefit of these cards is that they provide international identification, so students don't need to get stuck carting around their passports. Besides, they're not terribly expensive, so the general theory is: It can't hurt.

International Security Exchange card is internationally recognized for identification and worldwide discounts for students ages 12 and older. $25. 800-255-8000, www.isecard.com

International Student Identification Card offers global discounts, as well as access to a 24-hour emergency help line, which can refer you to legal, medical, or travel advisors; can send urgent messages to your family at home; and can help you to replace lost or stolen travel documents. $22. Available through STA Travel: 800-781-4040, www.isic.org, www.statravel.com.

STA Travel is the largest student travel agency in the world, having been around since 1979, with 400 branches around the globe and more than 70 in North America alone. One of the benefits of STA Travel is that it can be a one-stop shop for all components of your travels, including trains, planes, buses, car rentals, hostel and hotel bookings, insurance plans, and even phone services, usually for discounted rates.

For example, students can book a round-trip flight to Australia from Los Angeles, plus flights between Brisbane, Melbourne, Tasmania, and Sydney, for $999. A similar itinerary on Qantas was quoted as at least $200 more. Once you're in Australia, STA has connections with a slew of low-cost hostels and hotels, like the Bakpak Hotel in Melbourne, which starts at $22 a night (as compared with the lowest-price hotel found online: the Easystay, which starts at $83 a night).

STA's Travel Connect plan offers global cell phones starting at $29, which is heavily discounted from the original $89 price tag, and includes $10 of call time. The phone works in more than 100 countries and can receive toll-free calls. 800-781-4040, www.statravel.com

Launched in 1992, **Student Universe** is now an exclusively online service that has paired with Orbitz to find discounted student fares on airlines and rail carriers. For example, a student fare from New York's JFK airport to

> Don't miss the Montana Testicle Festival that takes place every August. Chowing down on bull testicles, or "Rocky Mountain oysters," is the main event, along with wet T-shirt contests and hairiest chest contests.

Madrid has prices from $580 to $676; the same standard itinerary search on Orbitz costs $687 to $1,075. Once you arrive in Madrid, you can find your already-booked hostel, hotel, or apartment with rates running from $18 to $146 per night. Student Universe has partnered with Patriot Travel Medical Insurance, Insuractive, Travel Guard, and Travelex to offer student rates on varying insurance plans. 617-321-3100, www.studentuniverse.com

United College Plus is **United Airlines**' frequent flier program for college students. Students who are already members of United's Mileage Plus program can earn additional travel miles by charging their tuition to a United College Plus Visa card, and they can receive 10,000 miles upon graduation. 800-241-6522, www.united.com/page/middlepage/0,6823,1271,00.html

Southwest Airlines offers youth fares for passengers 12 to 21 years old. The discounts may not save as much as standard discounted tickets and special deals, but these fares are unrestricted, which means there's no extra fee for last-minute bookings or trip cancellations. These fares are available only through bookings made on the phone. 800-435-9792, www.southwest.com

Lufthansa has a Generation Fly program aimed at students, which offers discounted rates available online. Travelers must register for an account using a valid college e-mail address to verify that they are students. 800-399-5838, www.generationfly.com

Amtrak offers 15 percent off the best available fare to all Student Advantage Card holders. However, this does not apply to weekday Metroliner or Acela Express service, connections to non-Amtrak carriers, or upgrades. And it can't be combined with other discounts. 800-872-7245, www.amtrak.com

Greyhound offers 15 percent off normal fares and 50 percent off package shipping sent through Greyhound PackageXpress for Student Advantage Card holders. 800-231-2222, www.greyhound.com/deals/student_discount.shtml

Insurance

These days, many study-abroad programs have optional or mandatory health insurance provided by the affiliated American university. If the student is traveling independently, make sure that he is covered, either through family insurance or student travel insurance. If he's traveling to a country with lower medical standards and procedures, remember that it can cost more than $10,000 to evacuate a student out of the country and back to the United States, so health insurance or medical evacuation coverage is important.

Travel insurance is generally a good idea for long-term plans, particularly if the student is planning to travel to various countries during his stint abroad.

There are several companies that offer plans specifically for traveling students that cover both travel and health issues. When you're researching plans, there are two major things to look at: the amount of money being covered and the policy's exclusions. For example, in the case of medical evacuation, a $20,000 policy isn't going to cover much if a student is being flown from one country to another with an accompanying medical team. And it's common for insurance policies to exclude injuries from sports outside of university-sponsored activities. The following are some key terms that you should look for.

Trip cancellation or interruption: You may get reimbursed up to the full cost of your trip due to illness, injury, or death to you, a traveling companion, or a covered family member. Other possible terms can include jury duty, subpoena, having a home made uninhabitable by a natural disaster, hijacking, and being involved in a documented traffic accident en route to departure.

Trip delay: Additional accommodations, meals, and transportation expenses due to delays caused by the carrier or other covered reasons are often reimbursed.

Baggage protection: This offers reimbursement for the loss, damage, or theft of baggage or personal effects during a trip or while in transit. This benefit may include baggage delay protection, covering the purchase of necessary items if your luggage is delayed.

Medical protection: This includes coverage for medical expenses if you become ill or are injured while on your trip.

Emergency evacuation: You may receive emergency medical transportation to the nearest appropriate medical facility in the case of illness or injury.

Emergency reunion benefit: In the case of emergency medical evacuation, this covers the expenses of travel and lodging for a family member if a doctor determines it would be beneficial for the covered person to have a family member at his or her side during transport.

Repatriation of remains: In the event of death while under the plan, this is coverage to return a person's body to his or her home country. Covered expenses may include embalming, cremation, coffin, and transportation.

24-hour worldwide emergency assistance: Telephone assistance hotline for medical and travel-related emergencies, ranging from cash transfer; legal, dental, or medical referral; and lost travel documents assistance as well as medical consultation and monitoring.

Insurance for students traveling abroad is available from the following companies.

Council on International Educational Exchange recommends purchasing the International Student Identity Card and will extend the medical evacuation and 24-hour emergency help line coverage 2 weeks before and 2 weeks after the program dates to cover participants who may want to travel beyond school dates. 800-407-8839, www.ciee.org

STA Travel provides coverage through BerkeleyCare. Travel insurance plans start at $48 for an 8-day trip, which includes coverage for trip cancellation, interruption, or delay; lost, stolen, or delayed baggage; sickness or accidents; emergency evacuation; accidental death and dismemberment; 24-hour travel and medical emergency assistance; and emergency cash transfer services. 800-781-4040, www.statravel.com

International Student offers coverage from Student Secure, Atlas America, Atlas International, and International Citizens. www.internationalstudent. com/insurance

American Institution for Foreign Study offers insurance from Cultural Insurance Service International. 800-303-8120 extension 5181, www. culturalinsurance.com

Some Tips for Students

! Study up on local maps and public transportation before you go. Getting adjusted to a new city is much easier when you have your bearings.

! Don't be taken by surprise when it comes to the cost of living. Learn the prices of everyday items in advance.

- Find a local authority figure in your dorm or near your residence who is accessible and approachable.

- At night, stick to well-lit streets and avoid empty areas.

- Whenever possible, travel with a group.

- Tell someone where you are going, especially if traveling alone.

- Get contact information for American embassies and consulates.

- Photocopy and scan your passport, tickets, health insurance card, school ID, and driver's license. Store this information separately from the originals and give a copy to your parents or emergency contact.

- Don't wear "ugly American" clothing that identifies you as an American, such as "I Love NY" T-shirts, college sweatshirts, blue jeans, baseball hats, and white athletic shoes.

- No, fanny packs and neck pouches aren't cool, but they are handy for keeping your money and documents safe.

- Know the local laws, especially when it comes to drugs and alcohol.

- Alcohol plays a major factor in threatening or dangerous situations. Make sure your kids are aware of the risks of abusing alcohol or drugs, especially in a neighborhood they aren't familiar with. This especially holds true in countries where there may be a language barrier or in cultures that frown upon public drinking.

- Female students, in particular, need to be made aware of the risks of traveling in a foreign country. Be aware of behaving appropriately in a bar or at a party—cultural cues differ by country, so while smiling at strangers and looking people in the eye may be considered harmless behavior at home, it may have a much different meaning abroad. Dress appropriately and be aware of the culture's attitudes when it comes to clothes.

CHAPTER 22

❝ **Our perfect companions never have fewer than four feet.** ❞

—COLETTE

Let's start with a basic given. Our pets are our families. And when we travel, we do everything we possibly can (sometimes within reason, many times without) to have our pets travel with us. Not surprisingly, dogs and cats are the most popular travel companions—14 percent of all US adults (29.1 million) say they have traveled with a pet on a trip of 50 miles or more, one way, away from home in the past 3 years. Dogs are the most common type of pet to take along (78 percent). Cats come in a distant second, with 15 percent of travelers taking their favorite feline friend along. Only 2 percent travel with their birds, and 3 percent report taking their ferret, rabbit, and even their fish along for the ride. One of the fastest-growing figures—and rising: 29 percent of those who travel with a pet stay at a hotel or motel.

General Transportation Issues

On the surface, it does seem more humane for you to share your vacation with your favorite pet. The alternative: asking a friend or family member to watch the animal or stashing it in an expensive kennel for days, perhaps weeks. If you are a pet owner, you must put your animal first. It's crucial that you consider your pet in all aspects of your trip planning, including whether or not it's even the smartest option to take him at all.

First off, think about transportation. Are you flying or driving? Flying in the cargo hold of an airplane can be an incredibly stressful, and sometimes dangerous, experience, depending on which hold your animal is placed in, as well as the duration of the flight—both scheduled and real. Is it a long-haul trip, or can it be broken into segments? Is your hotel pet friendly? Are there open spaces for your pet to get regular exercise? What about exotic pets? Are your activities and excursions pet friendly, or will you have to leave him in an unfamiliar environment? Remember, many pets depend on a consistent schedule, and the disruption may be more dangerous than you think.

Pets on Airlines

Each airline has different rules and regulations when it comes to flying animals. The two options: Bring your pet into the cabin—of course, that only applies to animals that are small enough (usually under 20 pounds) to fit into a crate that can be stored under the seat. If your pet is too large to fit under the seat in front of you and inside its container, your only other option is relegating your pet to the cargo hold. And trust me, at that point, airlines officially and legally define your pet not as a passenger but as a checked bag.

The bottom line is that when you're shipping an animal as airline cargo, there are absolutely no guarantees for its safety. Current laws and regulations protect transported animals only as much as they do your luggage—and that means airlines have limited liability if something goes wrong. Even if the airline is held responsible, monetary compensation for the loss or injury of a pet is the same as for lost or damaged luggage, which usually caps at $3,000 per passenger for domestic flights or $9.07 a pound for international flights.

As of May 2005, the Department of Transportation (DOT) requires that US airlines submit reports whenever there is a loss, injury, or death of an animal during air travel. According to the Air Transport Association, more than 500,000 pets are transported by air each year, and they estimate that 1 percent of these animals suffer "complications."

However, the numbers of animal incidents still may be skewed, as the

DOT does not require airlines to file reports of losses, injuries, or deaths if the animals are not kept as pets by a household in the United States (e.g., transporting zoo animals), if they are carried on an all-cargo or unscheduled flight, or if they are being carried on a flight that is operated by a foreign airline—and that includes when the foreign flight is code sharing with a US carrier.

Of course, the first step is that owners need to take responsibility by deciding whether their pets can handle the stressful environment of a cargo hold. Last year, American Airlines reported that a boxer was deceased upon arrival, which was later attributed to a preexisting heart condition. American also reported that a 14-year-old pug was found dead upon arrival in Dallas from West Palm Beach—although the cause of death was determined to be his advanced age coupled with a stressful environment, the report notes that the flight was delayed by almost 5 hours, during which the animals were watered and placed near an open door. Both dogs were short-nosed, which made them high-risk travelers, as it can be difficult to breathe at high altitudes and in closed environments.

Many incidents involve pets that are injured, go missing, or are killed when they escape or try to escape from their kennels. A golden retriever named Skipper, flying from Newark to Seattle on Continental, tried to chew and scratch his way out of the crate, causing him to cut his gums and lose several teeth and toenails. Because the wounds were self-inflicted, the airline was not held responsible. In December 2006, Alaska Airlines reported two injuries on recent flights: The first was a dog that escaped its crate and broke its leg in the process; the second injury involved a small greyhound that got her jaws locked while biting the wire crate door.

Consider the case of Pumpkin the cat. She apparently escaped from her cage in the cargo hold of a United Airlines flight heading from Manchester, England, to Washington, DC. When the plane landed more than 7 hours later, the orange cat was nowhere to be found, despite an exhaustive search of the airplane.

She turned up 3 weeks later in Denver! No one knows how many cities, or even countries, Pumpkin visited during that time. She was finally found having survived extreme dehydration and malnourishment, along with very cold temperatures. Such stories are—sadly—not uncommon.

According to the Web site ThirdAmendment.com, which has compiled all the animal incident reports from the Department of Transportation, the statistics are sobering.

PET INCIDENTS ON AIRLINES, MAY 2005 TO FEBRUARY 2007

AIRLINE	DEATH	INJURY	LOSS
Alaska Airlines	4	6	1
American Airlines	10	0	0
ATA Airlines	0	0	2
Atlantic Southeast	1	0	0
Comair	0	1	0
Continental Airlines	17	11	0
Delta Air Lines	3	0	4
Frontier Airlines	0	2	0
Hawaiian Airlines	1	3	1
Horizon Airlines	2	1	0
Midwest Airlines	2	1	0
Northwest Airlines	0	2	4
Pinnacle Airlines	0	2	0
Shuttle America	1	0	1
SkyWest Airlines	1	0	0
United Airlines	8	0	3
US Airways	1	1	1
Total	51	30	17

Of the deaths, 43 involved dogs, 5 involved cats, 2 involved birds, and 1 involved a rat. Of the injuries, 23 involved dogs and 7 involved cats. Of the losses, 3 involved dogs, 13 involved cats, and 1 involved a bird. One of the lost dogs and a lost cat were reported recovered, while three of the injured dogs subsequently died of their injuries.

You can see complete reports of incidents and apparent causes, broken down by individual airline, at airconsumer.ost.dot.gov/reports/index.htm.

Pets in the Cabin

You have to check with your airline to determine whether a small pet can travel in the cabin with you. Some have limits on how long a flight (more than 6 hours is usually not allowed). Many airlines only allow one pet per passenger and a maximum of two pets per cabin, so it's crucial to let the agent know that you will be bringing a pet on board when making your reservations.

! All pets must be in a container approved by the International Air Transport Association (IATA). The problem is that only a couple of companies make these carriers, so don't be fooled by discount products or carriers that have a picture of an airplane on them. Sherpa Products and PetFlys make IATA-approved containers.

! This container must fit under the seat in front of you and must have a waterproof bottom.

Pets as Baggage

So what are the risks you should consider when transporting an animal as baggage?

! Cargo holds are very dark, with strange noises and smells that can distress sensitive animals.

! Although the holds are pressurized and temperature controlled, animals can suffer from extreme temperatures during the loading and unloading process or if they escape from their crates or if the airplane is delayed for long periods. Many airlines will not transport pets during summer months, usually between May 15 and September 15, specifically for this reason.

! Human error is always a risk. There have been cases in which animals were mistakenly put into the unpressurized cargo holds, in which temperatures can reach deadly levels (although one case resulted in a dog's arriving "cold and shivering" but otherwise okay). Other situations can include baggage handlers who forget to load a pet onto a connecting flight and animals that are left unattended in the "lost baggage" section of an airport.

! External factors can also play a part in an animal's injury or death, at which point the airline may not claim any responsibility. An incident in April 2006 involved a cat named Ginxie that was scheduled to travel on United from Chicago to Charlotte. The cat escaped from its crate while on a cart to the aircraft and was subsequently struck and killed by an oncoming tractor. No fault was found with the crate, and because United followed all standard procedures, no corrective action was taken.

! Flying in the cargo hold can exacerbate any preexisting conditions. For example, in October 2005 a Boston terrier named Baxter flew on American Airlines from Dallas to San Francisco and was found dead on arrival. It was determined that the dog died of a preexisting heart condition and that the stress of flying caused him to hyperventilate and triggered a cardiac episode.

! It's especially recommended that snub-nosed cats and pug-nosed dogs, like Pekingese, bulldogs, and pugs, don't fly, as they can have difficulty breathing, especially at high altitudes and in hot environments.

But the tips don't stop there. People for the Ethical Treatment of Animals (PETA) also makes the following suggestions:

! The animals must be in an IATA-approved container and meet certain other requirements. The container must be large enough for the animal to stand, turn around, and lie down. The crate must be made of sturdy plastic and have a secure locking system. If the container has wheels, they must be removed or taped securely so that the crate cannot roll. The crate must be ventilated on all sides, and have *live animal* stickers on the top and sides at least 1 inch tall. Make sure you mark the container with the animal's name and your name, address, phone number, and destination.

! Pets should be at least 8 weeks old before traveling.

! Always try to book a nonstop flight. During transfers, animals are at an increased risk for accidents, trauma, and escape. If you must transfer, ask about the airline's transfer policy. Most will not transfer animals to a connecting flight; you will need to retrieve them at the baggage claim area and recheck them.

! Avoid traveling in extreme temperatures. In the summer months, try to fly as early in the day as possible; in winter months, try to fly in the afternoon.

! Avoid tranquilizing your pet. According to the American Veterinary Medical Association, oversedation is the most frequent cause of animal deaths during airline transport and accounts for almost half of all deaths.

! Verify that the crate's baggage claim tag shows the correct destination and is securely attached.

! Fill your animal's water dish with ice cubes instead of water, which can easily spill.

! When you check in, ask the gate agent if you can speak to the ramp supervisor for your flight to offer that person any information you think may be useful about the handling of your animal.

! If the flight is delayed, inform the crew that an animal is on board and ask that the captain be informed. If the delay is lengthy, your animal must be removed from the plane until flight time. Insist on this. You are the only person who is going to protect your animal.

! Watch as your animal is loaded into the cargo area to ensure that he or she is on your flight. If you cannot see the loading of the cargo, ask the flight attendant to phone the cargo area to make sure that your animal is on the flight before you board.

! When you reach your destination, retrieve your animal immediately. If you notice anything wrong, get your pet to a veterinarian as soon as possible.

! Consider an insurance policy for your pet, to prevent sticker shock if you should need to get him emergency medical treatment while traveling. A company like Veterinary Pet Insurance (www.petinsurance.com) can provide this for an annual fee. Keep a file of your pet's medical records and information on any preexisting conditions.

For more information on pet transport laws and regulations, visit www.doglaw.hugpug.com/doglaw_041.html.

For a complete list of airlines and pet regulations, visit www.pettravel.com/airline_rules.cfm.

The following table outlines general rules and prices for transporting dogs and cats on airlines. Other animals may be allowed on the flight, so check with the airline to find out any further rules and restrictions. Service animals do not have to follow the same restrictions as pets.

Air Canada	As of September 2006, pets can no longer travel in the cabin on Air Canada. Pets traveling as cargo cost $91 to the United States and $213 internationally.
American Airlines	Pets traveling in the cabin domestically are $80 each way. Checked pets between the United States and Canada, Central America, South America, or the Caribbean are $100 each way. Other international rates vary by destination.
British Airways	BA follows the Pet Travel Scheme, which states that pets are not allowed to travel in the cabin. Their World Cargo allows pets to travel as cargo. The base price is $750, which includes handling fees, and the price goes up depending on the size of the container and destination. The Pets Passport desk can be reached at 888-578-4806.
Continental Airlines	Continental's PetSafe program has a dedicated 24-hour Live Animal Desk (800-575-3335). Pets traveling in the cabin are $80 each way, and international rates vary by destination.
Delta Air Lines	Delta's Pet First program allows pets to travel domestically for $50 in the cabin and $100 as cargo. International rates vary by weight and destination, starting at $153.
JetBlue	Pets are allowed to travel in the cabin for $50 each way.
Lufthansa	Pets are allowed to travel in the cabin. Prices range from about $68 to about $205.

Midwest Airlines	Pets can travel in the cabin for $100 each way and as cargo for $130 to $319, depending on the size of the crate.
Northwest Airlines	Pets are allowed to travel domestically in the cabin for $80 each way. Pets can travel as checked luggage for both domestic and international flights; rates are based on excess baggage fees, which depend on the size and weight of the carrier.
Southwest Airlines	Southwest does not allow pets to travel in the cabin or as cargo.
Spirit Airlines	Pets can travel in the cabin or as cargo for $75 each way.
United Airlines	United allows pets to travel in the cabin for $80 one way on domestic flights. Pets as checked luggage are $100 for small and medium crates and $200 for intermediate and extra-large crates. International rates vary by destination.
US Airways/America West	Pets are able to travel in the cabin for $80 one way. International rates vary by destination.
Virgin	The UK's Pet Travel Scheme allows pets to travel on Virgin in the cargo hold to and from Boston, Los Angeles, Miami, New York, Newark, Orlando, San Francisco, and Washington, DC. Pets can also travel to Johannesburg, although this is not part of the Pet Travel Scheme. Prices start at $245 and increase based on handling fees, weight, and dimensions.

Pets Flying Overseas

If you're planning on traveling overseas, it's even less recommended to take your pet along with you. However, if it's unavoidable, here is some important information.

Most countries have two standard requirements for your pet to enter their borders: a microchip implant and a rabies vaccination. The microchip, embedded with a unique identification number, must meet international standards so that your pet can be scanned properly at any location. The chip is usually implanted at the base of the skull, between the shoulder blades, but check with your vet first. If your pet had a chip implanted several years ago, it might have moved out of place, making it impossible to scan. Costs vary by veterinarian, but expect to pay about $55 to $60. When it comes to rabies shots, make sure you leave plenty of time to get the job done: It takes about 30 days for your pet to develop antibodies, and then your vet will send a blood sample to get tested. This test is done in only two labs in the country—in Texas and Kansas—so turnaround can take up to 30 days. While rabies shots themselves are relatively inexpensive, especially in clinics and pet stores, the test will cost you about $150. Timewise, keep in mind that there are travel certificates that need to be endorsed by your vet and the US Department of Agriculture within 10 days of traveling.

Once you've cleared these hurdles, things start to get even more complicated. Every destination has its own specific rules on importing pets, but countries like the UK, South Africa, and Australia have some of the toughest procedures. These are rabies-free zones, and they want to keep it that way. The UK, which up until recently had a waiting period of 180 days from the date that the blood was received at the rabies testing lab, recently implemented the Pet Travel Scheme. This scheme eases some of the tough restrictions and allows pets to skip the lengthy quarantine, but each step must be followed to the letter . . . or your pet may still be quarantined (see www.defra.gov.uk/animalh/quarantine for more information). South Africa requires that your pet be tested for a whole assortment of infectious diseases, from common heartworms to tropical diseases like leishmania, which isn't even found in the United States. In Australia, after jumping through a similar set of vaccination hoops, your pet will still be quarantined for 30 to 115 days upon arrival.

For quite a long time, bringing your pet to Hawaii was a hassle. Your pet had to stay in quarantine for at least 4 months, which was hard on the wallet (more than $1,000) and your peace of mind. The state changed its rules in 2003, so pets can be released within 5 days at the Honolulu International Airport, as long as other measures are taken to ensure that your pet is free of rabies. That means proving your pet has had a microchip implanted, two rabies vaccinations (the last vaccination should be administered at most 12 months before arriving for a 1-year vaccine and 18 months prior for a 3-year vaccine), and a blood test to determine that there is a sufficient level of rabies antibodies in your pet. There's a 120-day prearrival waiting period between the time the lab receives the blood sample and the earliest date the pet can enter the state. The fee for this program is $224 for up to 5 days of quarantine and $165 for direct release from airport. As a result, the number of cats and dogs arriving in the island is up 30 percent in 3 years. The US Department of Agriculture (USDA) reports that nearly 9,000 pets arrived in Hawaii last year, up from 7,650 in 2005 and 6,800 in 2004.

Pet Insurance
Now here's something you may not have thought of: pet insurance. Consider the astronomical prices for state-of-the-art veterinary treatments. In

2006, Americans spent more than $9.4 billion in vet bills, according to the American Pet Products Manufacturers Association. Out of 163 million pets in the United States, only about 3 percent of dogs and 1 percent of cats have insurance. Recently, the Leading Hotels of the World and Travel Guard International paired up to provide a travel insurance plan that includes "Pet Care Home Alone" coverage. The plan pays up to $25 a day (up to $200) to cover any additional boarding fees for your pet if your return is delayed due to any in-patient medical treatment you're receiving yourself.

Some Tips

- To learn specific regulations and requirements, from Algeria to Zimbabwe, visit the USDA at www.aphis.usda.gov/vs/ncie/iregs/animals.
- Talk to your vet! Some animals may not meet traveling regulations, due to age, compromised health, or breed.
- Call your airline to make sure of its specific rules and prices. Many airlines require that your pet has a "fit to fly" letter from your vet; others may require that animals travel in the cargo hold and not in the cabin, etc.

Pet Frequent Flier Miles

Talk about pet friendly. Some airlines are going the extra mile and offering frequent flier miles . . . for pets! United Airlines launched its United Pet Class, which gives extra frequent flier miles to owners who have their pets fly with them. Virgin Atlantic has a slightly more extravagant pet program in which frequent flier miles are applicable to the pet or the owner, and your pooch will even get his own Pet Passport. In Midwest Airlines' Premier Pet Program, for every three paid round-trips (or six paid one-way trips) that pets fly with their owners, they earn one free round-trip. And owners who are Midwest Miles members can earn a free round-trip for their pets by redeeming 15,000 Midwest Miles. El Al's Points for Pets club gives a free round-trip ticket to Israel for any three round-trips within a 3-year period.

Pet Shippers

If you're traveling for a long period or moving overseas, a good option is to have your pet sent via a professional pet shipper or pet travel agent. These shippers are aware of all the ins and outs of airline restrictions and quarantine requirements, and they can deal with oversized or unusual pets (sometimes llamas need to get places too!).

These agents can educate you on specific airline rules and international restrictions as well as make sure that your pet is contained in an airline-approved crate. Check with the Independent Pet and Animal Transportation Association (IPATA) at www.ipata.com or 903-769-2267 for a comprehensive list of professional pet shippers.

Road-Tripping

Driving with your pet is usually your best option. Still, there are plenty of considerations to keep in mind.

- Practice riding in the car before taking a long trip.
- Bring your pet's favorite blanket or towel to place in or around the crate.
- If your pet is on any medication, ask your vet to write an extra prescription slip, just in case.
- Bring along your dog's vaccination papers, as requirements may vary from state to state.
- Bring along a first aid kit, tick removers, flea prevention products, etc.
- Bring along bottles of the water that your pet is used to drinking, as new water can make him sick.
- Put ice cubes instead of water in his bowl; they'll splash less, and the water will stay cool for your pup.
- Consider a doggy seat harness so he can stay in place in the car, without distracting you.
- A dog with bad manners may have problems dealing with an unfamiliar city and strangers.
- Never park in the sun, as animals tend to overheat inside vehicles.
- Call ahead to hotels to make sure that your pet is welcome or you may find yourself stranded without accommodations.

Car Rentals

There is no standard set of rules when it comes to pets and car rental companies, but usually with a well-behaved animal and a damage deposit, they're welcome. You may end up paying extra if your dog or cat sheds excessively or causes damage to the interior. When calling ahead for information, call the direct location, not the national car rental number, as rules on pets are different at many individual locations.

Pet Kennels

So, is it worth it to show your pet some TLC while you're away? In most cities, you have plenty of options on what kind of facility you want for your pet. They range from standard kenneling to cage-free farms to decadent overnight spas. Figure out what fits your budget and how much you want to spoil your pet while you're away. If a little extra something is what they need, here are some kennels around the country that offer surprising treats to make your pooch's stay one that he'll remember for a lifetime.

When you're considering a boarding facility for your pet, there are several things you need to keep in mind. Your first stop should be the American Boarding Kennel Association's Web site, www.abka.com, which provides much of the information that you'll need. Here are some tips to get you started.

- ! Call ahead to make sure the kennel can handle your particular pet. Some have restrictions on large dogs or young puppies.
- ! Visit the kennel to make sure it's well run and sanitary. Use your common sense on this one: Does the place look and smell good? Is there fresh water? Is it temperature controlled between 68 and 72 degrees?
- ! Many kennels don't allow human visitors in order to prevent aggression from the dogs. But there should at least be a viewing window so you can see the inside of the facilities or play area. Here are some things to watch for.
  - The sleeping and playing areas must be free of sharp objects or ones that can be swallowed.
  - Playtime should be in groups of other dogs that are a similar size and temperament. If your dog doesn't get along well with others, the facility should be able to accommodate that.
  - Cats should be in closed facilities, away from the dogs.

The owners of these facilities supposedly know how much you love your pet, so many of them are spicing up their services to make a buck. But you still need to do your own research to see if they're charging extra for services like doggy treats or if paying for the Penthouse Suite accommodations really means just an extra square foot of space. If you're not careful, you might end up spending more on Fido's boarding, manicures, and treats than on your own vacation.

PetSmart has opened a PetsHotel division, which provides day and overnight care for dogs and cats. There are currently several dozen hotels open around the country, with new locations in Massachusetts, Michigan, New Jersey, Pennsylvania, and Illinois. www.petsmart.com/petshotel

Located in Virginia, **Olde Towne Pet Resort** is a full-service spa that offers the option of bedding your pup down with a TV so he can watch his favorite show on Animal Planet, as well as including a video camera in the kennel so he can wave hello to you over the Internet. 703-455-9000, www.oldetownepetresort.com

Show him some southern comfort in the 33-acre **Eureka Farm** in Georgia, where pets reside in a home, not a kennel, with constant supervision. They can sit at the kitchen table, take a swim in the lake, and hang out in the garden for some bird-watching. Your dog will get to try out different rooms to see which one he likes best. Kennels are available to keep cats separate from the dog population. 912-658-4242, www.eurekafarm.com

LA Dogworks is where Hollywood celebrities take their favorite arm candy to be spoiled. It has a 2,500-square-foot indoor dog park and spa treatments that you've never even tried yourself. Is it all just hype? Decide for yourself after checking out the Hydrosurge, a handheld massage sprayer, and the Zen Den, "a simple, Eastern retreat for your dog to relax and indulge." 323-461-5151, www.ladogworks.com

At the **Cozy Inn Pet Resort and Orchid Spa** in Pennsylvania, your pup's chi will be in good shape, as feng shui is used to provide a "relaxing and comforting environment." Skylights, music therapy, color stimulation, and food-scented aromatherapy are used throughout the facility, as well as 12 Zen gardens. 412-798-5297, www.cozyinnpetresort.com

Dog-Friendly Cities

Some cities are more dog friendly than others, when you take into consideration factors like available hiking trails, pet-friendly accommodations, outdoor restaurants, and even accessible transportation. In Boston, for example, the subway system allows leashed dogs of all sizes during nonrush hours. In

San Francisco, dogs can ride the cable cars and even hop on board the BART trains, and of course the popular outdoor café culture means plenty of dog-friendly eateries.

Here are some of the more pet-friendly cities. Some you may expect, and others might be a bit of a surprise.

Napa, California

"But my dog doesn't drink," you argue. No worries. While you're lapping up the region's top-notch wine, your canine pal will have plenty of things to do. First off, **Europeds** has recently introduced a Dog Walking Tour through the wine country, which offers the two of you quality bonding time while also allowing you to explore some humans-only activities. For $2,500 per person (plus one dog), the tour includes accommodations in pet-friendly hotels, meals, and even visits to local wineries that welcome pooches. On some portions of the trip, the Europeds leaders will take care of your pup while you go off for spa treatments or shopping excursions. 415-388-2853, www.europeds.com

If you're planning a DIY walking tour, here are some places that will accommodate you and your dog.

Cuvaison Winery: Well-behaved dogs on leashes are allowed to join you in the small tasting room and in the three outdoor picnic areas. 707-942-6266, www.cuvaison.com

Clos du Val Winery: Dogs on leashes are allowed in the enormous tasting room and on the property. 800-993-9463, www.closduval.com

Hillcrest Country Inn: Host Debbie O'Gorman runs this country home with her three dogs—Taz, Debo, and Bamboo—who are friendly and welcoming to other canine friends. The antiques-filled home is located on a hilltop with an unbeatable view of Napa Valley. You and your pup can romp around the 36-acre property, where there is swimming, hiking, and fishing, and then he has the option of staying in your room or in a large outdoor kennel. 707-942-6334, www.bnbweb.com/hillcrest

The Beazley House: At this downtown Napa bed-and-breakfast, you'll be able to play with resident golden retrievers Sissy and Autumn Beazley, and you'll even receive a doggy welcome basket with a bowl, doggy beer, bones, and cleanup baggies. Three rooms open out into the gardens. There is a $25 per day per dog charge, with a maximum of two dogs per room. 800-559-1649, www.beazleyhouse.com

Aspen, Colorado

If you can take your pup to wine country, why not to the slopes? They probably don't make skis to fit all four paws, but there are lots of other options for the two of you. Colorado is a pretty dog-friendly state for outdoorsy folks, but Aspen really has some puppy loving going on. Many hotels are open to pets, and dogs are welcome to wander the pedestrian-friendly area.

The resort's hardy mountain trails are open to adventurous dogs and their friends: From June to August, the Silver Queen Gondola can take you and your dog up Aspen Mountain, and you can even buy a souvenir dog gondola pass with his mug on it for $5. Your dog doesn't need to be leashed, but it's recommended along the hiking trails and loops. Other popular dog hiking trails are the Rio Grande, Hunter Creek/Hunter Valley, and Sunnyside. Each of these is accessible by foot and under 10 miles long.

The Little Nell: This small hotel is located just a couple feet away from the Silver Queen Gondola and offers a doggy menu with treats like chicken breast and beef tenderloin. 970-920-4600, www.littlenell.com

The Sky Hotel: This groovy boutique hotel welcomes dogs of all sizes and will even offer them a fire-hydrant treat when they check in. 800-882-2582, www.theskyhotel.com

Ajax Tavern: Dogs are allowed at the outdoor tables on leashes at this casual Aspen eatery that is famous for its stunning view. 970-920-9333

One important note: The local humane society will actually "lend" you a dog for your stay. Of course, there's a worthy ulterior motive—in 80 percent of the "loan" cases, these dogs get adopted. An honorable mention goes to the **Ritz-Carlton, Bachelor Gulch** hotel in Colorado: It offers a "loan-a-Lab" program—yes, you get their yellow Lab for the day and evening. www.ritzcarlton.com

New York City

With more than 120,000 licensed dogs in the city, it's no surprise that New York makes our list of dog-friendly cities. But did you know that you can actually give your four-legged friend some education on your trip? Susan and Art Zuckerman offer canine walking tours of New York that give you a history of specific neighborhoods while showcasing some of the local hot spots for both humans and dogs. On the Greenwich Village Tour, you can check out Washington Square Park, one of the best dog runs in the city, or take a stroll through one of the largest toilets in the world (at least from your dog's point of view!)—Central Park. 914-633-7397

The Regency: According to the "Loews Loves Pets" program, Loews hotels don't just welcome pets; they love them. Your pup will get amenities like the hotel's signature dog bowl, a mat, doggy treats, and a room service menu (including vegetarian options, bottled water, and milk for feline companions). The hotel concierge can also recommend local dog-walking routes and pet-friendly restaurants and will arrange for walking and sitting services. The hotels offer items you may have forgotten or lost. The Puppy Pager allows hotel staff to contact you immediately for emergencies (like an excessively barking pup). Note that you may be charged $25 for room cleaning. 800-563-9712, www.loewshotels.com

Le Parker Meridien: This upscale midtown hotel has hosted a whole menagerie of animals, including a camel in the conference room. The staff admits the camel got a little rowdy, so they won't be inviting him back, but dogs are perfectly welcome. Their "Feed the Party Animal" menu even offers fancy treats like steak tartare. 800-543-4300 www.parkermeridien.com

The Benjamin indulges your pets with its Dream Dog program. Upon check-in, your dog gets a welcome note from the general manager, his own bed, food and water bowls, a bathrobe, toys, treats and homemade "Canine Cuisine," and a doggy DVD. Optional extras include a daytime doggy spa, dog walking and grooming, and even a consultation with a pet psychic. If that's not enough, you can buy your pooch a Cane and Able Dog Spa gift basket. 212-715-2500, www.thebenjamin.com

Long Beach, California

Los Angeles already has a reputation for being a dog-friendly city, but its neighbor down south is taking steps to become the next hot dog spot in Southern California. Long Beach is a coastal city that has opened 3 acres of its beach in Belmont Shore as an off-leash area, aka The Dog Zone. The Dog Zone starts at 4800 East Ocean Boulevard, between Roycroft and Argonne avenues.

Also in Long Beach is the very active Haute Dogs organization, which arranges several doggy-centered events in Belmont Shore all year long. The Haute (pronounced "hot") Dog Easter Parade features hundreds of dogs marching along in bonnets and Easter outfits, while the Howl'oween Parade and Canine Costume Contest includes an adoption fair, a bulldog kissing booth, and dancing dog demonstrations. If that's not doggone wacky enough, stick around Long Beach for the Haute Dog poetry contest and bulldog beauty contest. www.hautedogs.org

Several restaurants and shops along the busy Second Street in Belmont Shore offer water bowls to welcome pets. Pet-friendly accommodations are rather scarce (you may be better off making Long Beach doggy festivities part of a day trip), but you can try the **Renaissance Long Beach Hotel.** This luxury hotel welcomes dogs of any size for a $75 nonrefundable fee. 562-437-5900

More Pet-Friendly Hotels

These days, still more hotels are realizing that happy pets mean happy guests, so they're opening their doors to our furry friends. Some are even going the extra distance: At the Fairmont Copley Hotel in Boston, the hotel has its own "canine ambassador" named Catie Copley, a 68-pound chocolate Labrador who serves as the hotel's official greeter.

Starwood Hotels and Resorts, which include Sheraton, Westin, and W Hotels, allow dogs and cats in all locations throughout the United States and Canada. Their decision was made after learning that 76 percent of pet owners interviewed would be more loyal to a hotel chain that accepted pets. The Westin now offers a dog version of the hotel's branded Heavenly Bed, along with food bowls, turndown biscuits, and even room service menu choices including German Shepherd Pie and Schnauzer Sausage Pasta. The Sheraton counters with its canine Sweet Sleeper Bed, doggy toys, and doggy massages. Dogs over 40 pounds may be allowed at the hotel's discretion and should be discussed with the general manager prior to accepting the reservation. Your pet should be kept on a leash or in a carrier while in public areas and kept out of all food and beverage areas. You can leave the pet unattended in your room, but notify the front desk when you're leaving. The hotel will provide you with a "Pet in Room" sign to alert housekeeping and other guests. www.starwoodhotels.com

Depending on locations, you may be able to find pet-friendly accommodations at more budget-minded hotels, including Holiday Inn, Days Inn, Best Western, Econo Lodge, and Comfort Inn.

Before you check in, here are some questions to ask.

! Are dog-walking or dog-sitting services offered?

! Is there a security deposit or fee, and if so, is it refundable?

! Is there a dog park or common area for pets?

! Are there size or weight restrictions?

! What amenities are offered?

! Is your pet allowed to stay in the room alone?

For a database of pet-friendly accommodations in the United States and Canada, visit www.petswelcome.com. For worldwide listings, visit www.travelpets.com.

Of course, what this also means is that if you're allergic to dogs or cats, this database can also be helpful in showing you which hotels to avoid.

▽ Resources

US Department of Transportation, airconsumer.ost.dot.gov/reports/index.htm: Find the monthly airline incident and accident reports broken down by airline.

US Department of Agriculture, www.aphis.usda.gov/vs/ncic/iregs/animals: This government site lists all the current quarantine regulations and restrictions by country.

American Animal Hospital Association's Animal Hospital Locator, www.healthypet.com/hospital_search.aspx: Find a nearby veterinarian wherever you're traveling in the United States.

Dog Law, www.doglaw.hugpug.com/doglaw_041.html: Confused about transport laws and regulations? This site explains it all in comprehensive terms.

Dogfriendly.com: Here are listings of pet-friendly accommodations, city guides, hiking guides, and outdoor dining guides.

Independent Pet and Animal Transportation Association, 903-769-2267, www.ipata.com: The professional pet shipper association can walk you through all the steps on how to safely transport your pet.

Pet Travel, www.pettravel.com/airline_rules.cfm: Learn about the regulations for pet travel broken down by airline.

Petflight.com: This site lists all of the pet travel incidents (including fatalities) dating back to May 2005.

Petsonthego.com: Get information on pet-friendly hotels, tips on travel, and blogs.

Petswelcome.com: Find listings of more than 25,000 pet-friendly hotels, B and Bs, ski resorts, campgrounds, and beaches worldwide.

Takeyourpet.com: Check directories of pet-friendly accommodations, boarding facilities, kennels, and a community bulletin board.

Travelpets.com: Here are listings of pet-friendly hotels, B and Bs, and cabin rentals for you and your pup.

Tripswithpets.com: This site has listings of pet-friendly lodgings, campgrounds, resorts, and restaurants, plus activities and airline regulations.

PART 4

ACTIVE
TRAVEL

CHAPTER 23

“ When I see an adult on a bicycle, I do not despair for the human race. ”

—H. G. WELLS

The beauty of biking during your travels is that you can get a real feel for the region's landscape, people, and sights—you can stray farther off the beaten path than on a tour bus and cover far more distance than on a walking tour. Whether you're spending a half day cycling the trails of your local park or vineyard-hopping along the Italian countryside, a bicycle adventure can be not only a healthy alternative to the traditional methods of travel but more often than not more culturally rewarding.

If you're planning to take a bicycle tour of an unfamiliar region, an organized trip can be one of the best ways to take advantage of all the sights and activities. For one thing, you don't have to schlep your own baggage—it's transferred from point to point. You can cycle alongside other travelers whose pace matches yours; your nightly accommodations and meals are already arranged; and a tour leader can take you to the area sights and activities. Self-guided tours are also another option: They tend to be less expensive and allow you the flexibility to go at your own pace and choose where you want to go within a route. The company will outfit you with all the maps and routes, sightseeing recommendations, and information on your lodging and meals, as well as emergency services. Most tour companies will inform you in advance of how strenuous the terrain is (rugged and uphill or paved and flat) and how many miles you're expected to cycle a day. As always, make sure to inform the company of any special needs you may have, and it's imperative that you check with your physician before embarking on any physically active tour.

Europe has long been considered to be a far more bike-friendly culture than the United States. Countries like the Netherlands and Denmark lead the pack, with nearly half of their residents commuting to work by bicycle. We're talking about people riding their bikes while drinking coffee, eating breakfast, and talking on their cell phones—now that takes some skill. Dedicated bike paths and parking spaces help promote bike riding over driving or even public transportation and help keep these cities cleaner, less congested, and easier to navigate. So how does the United States stack up against Europe?

The League of American Bicyclists, an advocacy group that represents the 57 million cyclists in the United States, ranks the top American bicycle-friendly communities based on "engineering, education, encouragement, enforcement, and evaluation and planning." The top cities are currently:

Tucson, Arizona
Davis, Palo Alto, and San Francisco, California
Boulder, Colorado
Corvallis and Portland, Oregon
Madison, Wisconsin

Find out more bicycle-friendly communities on the League's Web site, www.bikeleague.org.

Bicycle Tours

Backroads arranges biking and walking tours at more than 90 destinations in 40 countries worldwide. You can choose from lightweight titanium bikes to rugged mountain bikes, as well as innovative two-seat, two-pedal bikes for adults and children to ride in tandem. A 9-day bike tour of Bryce, Zion, and Grand Canyon national parks takes you from the red rock country of Utah to the desert land of Arizona, stopping at mountain lodges and park inns each night. If you'd rather stray a little farther from home, an inn-to-inn bike tour along New Zealand's South Island takes you along the west coast, through the Franz Josef Glacier, along Lake Wanaka, and into the adventure capital of Queenstown. Rates in the United States begin at $2,000, and international tours are about $4,000. 800-462-2848, www.backroads.com

For active travel with a luxurious spin, **Butterfield & Robinson** arranges bike tours throughout the world with high-end accommodations and gourmet meals, plus several options for family-friendly travel. A 7-day trip through the Loire Valley takes you through French villages, sunflower fields, and vineyards, with plenty of opportunities to stop at the wineries along the way (rates start at $6,195). A family trip through South Africa allows kids ages 12 and over to join their parents as they travel from Cape Town to Port Elizabeth. The 10-day tour includes 3 days each of bike riding, walking, and safari, for an up-close look at the cities, orchards, vineyards, and animals that flourish in the region (starting at $8,795). 866-551-9090, www.butterfield.com

Leading bicycle tour company **Bike Tours Direct** offers several options throughout Europe, both guided and self-guided. One of the more unusual tours combines bicycling and boating—a 7-night, easy route from Amsterdam to Brussels involves sailing from one town to another, where you can explore the countryside by bicycle for up to 30 miles a day. A wine and wellness bike

Biking Stats Today

From mountain biking to BMX racing, bicycling is considered the number one sport among outdoor enthusiasts (38.2 percent), followed by fishing (34.5 percent) and hiking (34.2 percent), according to the Outdoor Industry Association (OIA).

The OIA has tracked bicycle statistics since 1998: The sport hit its peak in 2001 with 4,949 participants (over the age of 16) but has declined slightly over the past several years. There was actually a significant decline in bicycling from 2004 to 2005: Biking participants took an average of 45 outings in 2004 compared with 36 outings in 2005 and dropped from 3,885 participants to 3,123. The cause of this is unknown, but industry experts suspect that extreme weather conditions may have been a factor—2005 was the year of massive hurricanes in the south-central region, bitter cold in the Northeast, and late snows in the Midwest.

tour takes you through Austria, where you can bicycle up to 35 miles a day from one vineyard to the next, through thermal spa towns and into farms where you can sample home-cooked meals. Rates start at $800 for a week. 877-462-2423, www.biketoursdirect.com

Adventure Travel Group offers fully guided tours through Canada, Europe, and South America. This company has the unusual benefit that it also caters to noncyclists—most tours include 2 or 3 nights' stay in one location, and noncyclist companions have the option of traveling in the support van (bikers who need a break can also catch a ride in the van). A 6-day bike tour of the Piedmont region in Italy includes lots of wine tasting and stops among the lakeside villages of the region. A bike tour of Chile and Argentina's lake district takes you through the volcanic terrain, into the Southern Andes, and includes a half day of white-water rafting. Trip rates start at about $2,300. 858-232-0362, www.adventuretravelgroup.com

Trek Travel offers a variety of cycling vacations, including the leisurely classic rides as well as lower-budget, family-friendly, higher-intensity, and weekend trips. An intensive ride through Santa Barbara brings together bike enthusiasts with pro cyclist Kevin Livingston to learn fitness training, cycling goals, and climbing techniques; you'll ride about 45 to 80 miles a day. An adventurous family trip through Costa Rica includes hiking, biking, and kayaking in the jungles. Rates range from about $2,500 to $4,000 for longer trips, and 3-day weekend trips start at $1,400. 866-464-8735, www.trektravel.com

Northern California's wine country is an ideal location for bike tours, especially if you're there to take in the sights or sample the wares. **Escape SF Tours** coordinates bicycling-only and multisport (cycling, kayaking, and hiking) tours in Sonoma, with stops among multiple wineries for tastings and tours, plus vineyard lunches and options. Prices range from $860 to $1,200. 866-372-2735, www.escapesftours.com

Join the millions of Chinese who use bikes as their main form of transport. **Bike China** offers tours that range from easy-to-moderate 8-day rides to extremely challenging 30-day adventures. Regions include the provinces of Fujian, Gansu, Hunan, and Hainan, among others, traveling across mountain terrains, along the Yangtze River, and through villages and cities. This is my favorite way to see China. Riders average about 30 miles per day, with overnight stops in cabins and lodges. An 8-day tour is about $2,500. 800-818-1778, www.bikechina.com

Why not take the easy route and bike downhill all the way? **Maui Downhill** offers visitors to the island a variety of biking tours through spectacular landscapes, including the ever-popular Haleakala trek where you downhill from the summit of the world's largest resting volcano. Sunset tours are also available for those who have packed their day with activities. Prices range from $100 to $150 per 7- to 10-hour session. 800-535-2453, www.mauidownhill.com

Escape Adventures has several mountain-biking and road-cycling excursions in the western United States, including Bryce and Zion national parks in Utah, hot springs in Idaho, the Grand Canyon North Rim, and the Mojave Desert. There are also limited trips in Hawaii and Alaska. The new trend this year is that many of the support vehicles will be fueled by vegetable oil to make it an even more eco-friendly vacation. Overnight options include camping or inn to inn, and most trips run from 4 to 6 days. Prices range from $790 to $2,290 per person. 800-596-2953, www.escapeadventures.com

> The Pony Express, which connected 1,800 miles between Missouri and California, lasted only 18 months.

Bike Riders has cycling trips in New England, Canada, and Europe, following lesser-trafficked routes to capture the local flavor. Both guided and self-guided tours are offered, including a 6-day biking and hiking tour of Umbria, Italy; biking and whale watching on the north coast of Canada's Cape Breton Island; and a family island-hopping tour of Martha's Vineyard and Nantucket. Overnight accommodations tend to be historic inns and higher-end hotels. Prices run from about $2,300 to $4,200. 800-473-7040, www.bikeriderstours.com

Global Adventure Guide, a New Zealand–based company, offers mountain-biking trips throughout the world. A 17-day South African ride starts at Kruger National Park, then on to the Umfolozi-Hluhluwe National Park (where you'll find the highest concentration of rhinos in the world), through the famous Garden Route, and ending in the Western Cape. The route involves riding 12 to 30 miles per day, plus short walks throughout the country; $2850. A 9- or 14-day mountain-bike ride through Vietnam takes you through the ancient cities of Hanoi and Saigon as well as along the Red River Delta and Cuu Long—and gives your legs a rest by kayaking on the

Halong Bay. Rates range from about $2,000 to $4,500—just remember that the company is based in New Zealand, so a US bike trip may be pricey. 800-732-0861, www.globaladventureguide.com

DIY Bike Tours

If you're planning a do-it-yourself bicycle tour through America's trails, there are plenty of issues to keep in mind. It's important to do some heavy research beforehand so that you don't find yourself stuck out in the rain or thwarted by unmanageable terrain.

Your first stop should be the **Adventure Cycling Association**'s Web site, which is a solid resource for bicyclists of all experience levels. Here you can find guided bike tours, a "companions wanted" section, and social gatherings. You can also find cycling maps that show details like the locations of campgrounds, hostels, motels, gas stations, groceries, restaurants, post offices, and bike shops; turn-by-turn instructions; contour lines to illustrate elevation profiles; a weather chart; and summaries of riding conditions providing info on road surfaces, traffic volumes, and areas of caution. 800-755-2453, www.adventurecycling.org

On the Web site **www.pedaling.com,** you can define the parameters of your ride: what state, how much incline, what kind of environment (desert, woods, seashore), and how long—to come up with a route that works for you. For example, in Michigan, a 5- to 20-mile lake ride comes up with five options, with details on the terrain, local bike shops, and light commentary on the views.

If you're not planning on camping out, visit **Bed, Breakfast and Biking** at www.bbbiking.com. This is a hugely comprehensive resource of bike-friendly B and Bs and inns along or near the bike trails and byways throughout all 50 states. Major bike trails and lesser-known ones are covered here. The innkeepers tend to be knowledgeable about the area, so you may be able to get some insider knowledge of local trails, back routes, and must-see scenery.

The following are routes that are defined and named by the Adventure Cycling Association.

Pacific Coast Highway: Pedaling the Pacific Coast Highway offers some of the best views in the country. For example, the route from San Francisco south to Santa Barbara is 378 miles. The route takes you along the Monterey Peninsula, the 17-Mile Drive, Big Sur, and the Hearst Castle. Remember that winter months tend to be rainy, and in the summertime, the roads get crowded with travelers, so April and May are a good time to arrange a bike ride. www.adventurecycling.org/routes/pacificcoast.cfm

Atlantic Coast Route: Broken into two sections, this route travels from Bar Harbor, Maine, to Richmond and from Richmond to Key West, for a total of 2,535 miles. The northern section covers some rough terrain but takes you through picturesque and historical parts of the coast, through Maine, Boston, Connecticut, and Philadelphia. This is definitely where you can find some spectacular fall foliage. The southern route takes you through the farmland and swamps of Virginia, North Carolina, and Georgia and into the beaches of Florida. www.adventurecycling.org/routes/atlanticcoast.cfm

Utah Cliffs Loop: This is *the* place to see the incredible red rock cliffs of southern Utah. Starting and ending in Saint George, the route travels through Snow Canyon State Park, into Pine Valley, and up to the high elevations of the Markagunt Plateau of the Dixie National Forest and Navajo Lake. www.adventurecycling.org/routes/utahcliffsloop.cfm

The Great Divide: The Adventure Cycling Association refers to this route, which covers 2,490 miles between Roosville, Montana, and Antelope Wells, New Mexico (maps are broken into six sections), as "remote," which also translates into "amazing scenery." However, it also can mean rough terrain, harsh weather, and little access to medical help or even civilization at some points—however, there are shuttle services available at various points to help you out. www.adventurecycling.org/routes/greatdivide.cfm

Safety Tips

Traveling safely is always a first priority, but when cycling, it's crucial to keep your wits about you. According to the National Highway Traffic Safety Administration (NHTSA), 725 bicyclists were killed in 2004 and an additional 41,000 were injured in traffic crashes. Kids ages 14 and under accounted for 18 percent of these deaths (130), making it one of the most common causes of injury-related death for children. Here are some safety tips to keep in mind on your next bicycle travels.

! Always wear a helmet. The NHTSA has found that nearly 70 percent of all fatal bicycle crashes involve head injuries. It's estimated that bicycle helmet use in kids ages 4 to 15 would prevent up to 45,000 head injuries and up to 55,000 scalp and facial injuries each year.

! If you're riding in traffic, never pass on the right and always go in the direction of traffic.

! On trails, cyclists should yield to all other trail users, and hikers should yield to equestrians.

! Obey all signs. Riding off trails can damage the ground, create erosion, and disturb local wildlife. And depending on the type of bike you're riding, it can also damage the bike and seriously injure the rider . . . meaning *you*.

! Before you go, plan out your route carefully and try to locate alternate routes in case you're not able to follow your original path.

▽ Resources

Adventure Cycling Association: The association Web site provides information on routes and maps, guided tours, and volunteer opportunities around the country. 800-755-2453, www.adventurecycling.org

Bicycletour.com: You'll find a comprehensive directory of bicycle tours and events around the United States.

Bicyclingworld.com: Find bicycle tours and events worldwide.

Bikeaccess.net: Bike enthusiasts sound off and share their experiences with sending their bikes via airlines, trains, and shipping services.

Bikely.com: Figure out which paths are best for you based on real user reviews and recommendations.

GORP: The adventure travel Web site offers information on popular, off-the-beaten-path, and "epic" bike paths and tour groups around the world. http://gorp.away.com/gorp/activity/biking.htm

League of American Bicyclists: The organization can help you find local bike clubs and provides educational resources and tips. 202-822-1333, www.bikeleague.org

National Highway Traffic Safety Administration: Find out the latest statistics and safety tips for bicyclists on the road. 888-327-4236, www.nhtsa.com

Routeslip.com: Cycling fans share information on favorite bike rides, elevation profiles, and more.

CHAPTER 24

Camping, RVing, and Boating Safety

> GG Camping is an outdoor vacation during which you have a great time in great discomfort. JJ

—ANONYMOUS

Whether you prefer sleeping under the stars or holing yourself up in a five-bedroom RV, camping is one of those all-American traditions that bring together family and friends in an environment that's free from the stresses and distractions of daily life.

According to the Outdoor Recreation Participation Study for 2005, camping was the fourth most popular outdoor vacation activity (among Americans 16 and older), behind bicycling, fishing, and hiking. In 2005, there were a total of 347 million outings, including those who camped out only once in the year (33 percent) and those who camped three to six times (33 percent). Camping is also one of those gender-equal outdoor activities, making up an almost even split across all age groups (slightly favoring men). As a family activity, it's a hit: More than 81 percent of "car campers" (camping out within a quarter mile of the car) went with family members. As you may expect, campers also tend to be enthusiasts of other outdoor activities like hiking, biking, and fishing.

And if you have any preconceptions about traveling to campgrounds—or just traveling throughout the United States by RV, throw them away. Recreational vehicles are not just for your grandparents anymore. According to a University of Michigan study, the typical RV owner is 49, is married, owns a home, and has an annual household income of $68,000. There has been a recent surge in RV travel over the past few years, resulting in an increase in camping appeal. The Recreation Vehicle Industry Association (RVIA) estimates that there are more than 30 million RVers in the United States. That's 10 percent of the population! Today nearly 8 million US households own at least one RV, which is a 15 percent increase over the past 4 years and a significant 58 percent rise since 1980. RVIA says that only about 1 million of those actually live in their RV full-time; the rest use their RV for vacation, for about 42 days per summer, covering 4,000 to 5,000 miles per year.

And a statistic that can only be described as counterintuitive but true—despite gas prices that have been hovering near, and sometimes above, $4 a gallon—RV sales are actually increasing, which proves a more general (and powerful) point about Americans and travel. Yes, an RV might be described as a gas station on four wheels, but this hasn't stopped us. We will not be denied, when it comes to travel as well as *how* we travel!

One in 12 US vehicle-owning households has an RV. That statistic alone is perhaps the biggest surprise. And with other travel costs rising—airline tickets, hotel room rates—the RV has enjoyed a new popularity among travelers who no longer need an airline ticket or a hotel room. Multiply that by four (typical family size) and it suddenly becomes economically viable.

Destinations

There are more than 16,000 commercial and public campgrounds in the United States, located all across the country, from national parks and forests to popular tourist attractions to the sides of highways, and even in cities and small towns. Noncampers may be surprised to learn that camping doesn't necessarily mean roughing it—many campgrounds and RV parks have at least the basic amenities of hot showers, kitchens, and even laundry facilities. Nowadays, you can even find destinations with high-speed Internet and

Wi-Fi, golf courses, and spas. Of course, if you're not sure what kind of campground you're looking for, a good rule of thumb is to determine whether your campground has a "flush" toilet versus a "pit" and go from there . . .

As you may expect, some of the most frequently visited campgrounds are located in the popular national parks, such as Yellowstone, Grand Canyon, and Yosemite. Here is a sampling of the campgrounds you can find in these areas.

YELLOWSTONE NATIONAL PARK, 307-344-7381, WWW.NPS.GOV/YELL

Bridge Bay: Open May through September. Reservations are required. $17 per night.

Canyon: Open June through September. Reservations are required. $17 per night.

Fishing Bridge RV: The only campground that is hooked up with electricity, sewer, and water. Only hard-sided camping units are permitted, no tents. Reservations are required. $35 or more per night.

Grant Village: Open June through September. Reservations are required. $17 per night.

Indian Creek: Open June through September. $12 per night.

Lewis Lake: Open June through November. $12 per night.

Madison: Open May through October. Reservations required. $17 per night.

Mammoth: Open year-round. $14 per night.

Norris: Open May through September. $14 per night.

Pebble Creek: Open June through September. $12 per night.

Slough Creek: Open May through October. $12 per night.

Tower Falls: Open May through September. $12 per night.

Source: *www.yellowstone-natl-park.com/camping.htm*

GRAND CANYON, 928-638-7888, WWW.NPS.GOV/GRCA

Desert View: Open mid-May through mid-October. $12 per night.

Mather: Open year-round. Reservations are recommended from March through November. $18 per night.

Trailer Village: An RV park adjacent to Mather Campground; includes hookups. Advance reservations are required. Rate is $28 per night, double occupancy.

Source: *www.nps.gov/grca/planyourvisit/cg-sr.htm*

YOSEMITE, 209-372-0200, www.nps.gov/yose/planyourvisit/camping.htm

Bridalveil Creek: Open July through September. No reservations. $14 per night.

Camp 4: Open all year. Does not require reservations. Trailers and RVs are not permitted. $5 per person.

Crane Flat: Open July through September. Reservations are required. $20 per night.

Hodgdon Meadow: Open all year. Reservations required from approximately mid-April through mid-October. $20 per night.

Lower Pines: Open March through October. Reservations are required. $20 per night.

North Pines: Open April through September. Reservations are required. $20 per night.

Porcupine Flat: Open July through October. $10 per night.

Tamarack Flat: Open June through September. RVs and trailers are not recommended. $10 per night.

Tuolumne Meadows: July through September. Reservations are available online for half of all campsites. The other half of the campsites are available on a first-come, first-served basis. $20 per night.

Upper Pines: Open all year. Requires reservations. $20 per night.

Wawona: Open all year. Reservations are usually required May through September. $14 to $20 per night.

White Wolf: Open July through September. $14 per night.

Yosemite Creek: Open July through September. RVs and trailers are not recommended. $10 per night.

Source: *www.nps.gov/yose/planyourvisit/campground.htm*

Remember, even if you're not visiting a national monument, you may find yourself enjoying equally spectacular views with fewer crowds if you travel a little off the beaten path (just carry a map!). Want to travel to a lava field that can only be reached by boat? Try visiting California's Ahjumawi Lava Springs, an isolated 6,000 acres that's partially covered by black volcanic rock, surrounding forests, and several lakes and rivers, with views of Mount Shasta and Mount Lassen. The campgrounds are primitive, at best, but it's an ideal location for boating, kayaking, hiking, and swimming.

Want a lakeside campground with gourmet food, magic shows, and haunted hayrides, plus happy hour every night? Visit the Acres of Wildlife campground in southern Maine. Even your trip to a Hawaiian paradise can be free from luaus and pig roasts if you camp out beachside on one of the island's state parks or private campgrounds. The point is, while the most popular camping spots in the United States receive millions of travelers every year, the alternatives are plentiful. The campground and RV park resources below are the best places to start searching for locations where you're interested in traveling.

Luxury Camping

Let's face it—some people are just not made to rough it on vacation. Battling mosquitoes and walking outside to use the restroom are not everyone's idea of a good time (and also not mine), and of course, let's not forget some of the other creature comforts that may be missing, like air-conditioning. But it's not all bad news. There are now hotels all over the country offering a rustic experience that even the refined can enjoy. Although you may still have to contend with bugs and inclement weather, at least you'll have fine food, champagne, linens, and maybe even a real bed (what a concept).

It's hard to believe you're camping when massages and a heated pool are involved. However, the Safari Tent at the **El Capitan Canyon** is technically a tent, albeit with down-comforter bedding and carpeting on the floor. And you do have to walk to the bathrooms and zip the canvas flap closed at night, as well as grill your own meals, but otherwise, consider yourself spoiled. Just 20 miles north of Santa Barbara, activities include yoga, swimming, kayaking, hiking, and horseback riding. And if you have your own horse, you can put it up at the full-service El Capitan Ranch. Safari tents run $135 per night. 866-352-2729, www.elcapitancanyon.com

Costanoa has accommodations ranging from a lodge to fir cabins and tent bungalows, or you can bring your own tent to share on a wood platform. But you can take advantage of the real simple pleasures in life at the Spa at Costanoa, which offers a selection of massages, or order from a gourmet deli to take along for a day hike or beachcombing. 650-879-1100, www.costanoa.com

If you're looking to set up camp outside of the United States, take a look at **Luxury Camps & Lodges of the World,** a comprehensive overview of high-end, eco-friendly accommodations worldwide. Highlights include the Phinda Rock Lodge on the Phinda Private Game Reserve in South Africa, which has four cottages designed for families or small groups and is close to a watering hole frequented by wildlife. Or there's the Aman-i-Khas in the Ranthambore National Park in India, which has tents complete with living rooms, four-poster beds, air-conditioning, and even a beauty salon. 39-06-6780231, www.lclworld.com

Green RVing

If you're an RVer, chances are you have an affinity for simple living in our natural environment—the sheer mass of an RV can get some eco-travelers cringing, but there is good news. At this writing, although the technology exists, the industry has still not introduced a hybrid RV (and it should).

But until that happens, there are some other beneficial counterbalances. Because of the limited space on an RV, campers often shop only for what they need, reuse containers, and conserve water in their travels. There's also a considerable number of companies aimed at helping RVers go green, including those producing biodegradable products for toilet holding tanks and solar and wind power kits. RV manufacturers are helping out by offering more aerodynamic—and therefore more fuel-efficient—travel trailers, better insulation to make cooling and heating more energy efficient, and diesel engines that are being converted to biodiesel, a cleaner-burning fuel

RV Travel

With RV travel growing in popularity, there are also more options than ever. Whether you're looking at brands like Winnebago, Airstream, or Fleetwood, RVs come in all sizes and are packed with amenities to make a traveling home that suits all sorts of budgets. You can go from a cheapie $4,000 folding camping trailer up to the big daddy of the type A motorhome that will cost you between $58,000 and $400,000! Somewhere in between are sport-utility RVs (ranging from $21,000 to $58,000), which are popular among younger buyers and outdoor enthusiasts for bringing along an ATV, motorcycle, or Jet Skis. A type C motorhome has all the amenities of home fitting into a compact space—even smaller type C units have recently come on the market that are more fuel efficient and range from $48,000 to $140,000. A conventional travel trailer comes in all sizes, ranging anywhere from $8,000 to $65,000.

made from natural renewable sources such as vegetable oils.

Here are some eco-friendly tips for greener RVing.

! If you burn diesel, check out www.biodiesel.com to see if there is a station with biodiesel fuel on your route.

! Use eco-friendly holding-tank products.

! Keep your tires well inflated to save on fuel.

! Travel light—you'll be amazed at how much stuff you can do without.

! Keep to the speed limit to conserve fuel.

! Use alternative power—wind and solar—when possible.

! Conserve water.

! Visit farmers' markets and buy local and organic produce.

! Recycle. Many grocery stores have recycling facilities for aluminum and plastic. Campsites also often have recycling facilities.

! Cut back on trash. Don't use disposable dishes, do mix drinks from powder rather than buying in cans or bottles, and reuse whatever you can.

RVing Abroad

Traveling by RV is an excellent way to experience sprawling countrysides when you're abroad. Not only are you saving on hotels and airfare, but you get to experience a foreign destination in a way that is more intimate than traditional travel methods. You can pack up a whole family and all your luggage into an RV, drive the back roads or change your route on a whim, pay about $15 to $20 a night for parking, and live among the locals in a campground.

! When it comes to traveling safely by RV, it pays to arm yourself with knowledge first. Knowing the rules of the road is key, and remember that crossing borders may mean a whole new set of laws.

! Next up, you'll need a comprehensive map of the area that you're traveling to—terrain can change unpredictably, and some areas may not be accessible to large vehicles.

! Stock up on supplies, as roadside assistance may not be as easily accessible when you're traveling abroad.

! There aren't really any international RV companies that allow one-way drop-offs. So, for example, if you're traveling through Europe, you'll probably need to return your vehicle to the country in which you picked it up. Traveling a loop is an easy way to solve this problem.

Camping/Hiking Safety Tips

Whenever you travel, it's important to keep safety issues in mind. But this becomes especially important when you're planning to be camping away from civilization for any length of time. The American Red Cross has the following guidelines for safety when camping and hiking.

! If you have any medical conditions, discuss your plans with your health-care provider and get approval before departing.

! Review the equipment, supplies, and skills that you'll need. Consider what emergencies could arise and how you would deal with those situations. What if you got lost or were unexpectedly confronted by an animal? What if someone became ill or injured? What kind of weather might you encounter?

! Make sure you have the skills you need for your camping or hiking adventure. You may need to know how to read a compass, erect a temporary shelter, or give first aid.

! Leave a copy of your itinerary with a friend or local camp ranger. Include such details as the make, year, and license plate of your vehicle, the equipment you're bringing, the weather you've anticipated, and when you plan to return. Include a map with your intended route highlighted.

! Get trained in American Red Cross first aid before starting out and bring at least a basic first-aid kit with you.

! If your trip will be strenuous, get into good physical condition before setting out. If you plan to climb or travel to high altitudes, make plans for proper acclimatization to the altitude.

! It's safest to hike or camp with at least one companion. If you'll be entering a remote area, your group should have a minimum of four people; this way, if one is hurt, another can stay with the victim while two go for help. If you'll be going into an area that is unfamiliar to you, take along someone who knows the area or at least speak with those who do before you set out.

! Some areas require you to have reservations or certain permits—campgrounds that are on a first-come, first-served basis tend to fill up early in the day. If an area is closed, don't try to skirt around authority and stay there anyway.

❗ Find out in advance about any regulations—there may be rules about campfires or guidelines about wildlife.

❗ Find out in advance if there are any restrictions on pets. If pets are allowed, in most cases they will need to be leashed.

❗ Pack emergency signaling devices and know ahead of time the location of the nearest telephone or ranger station in case an emergency does occur on your trip. Remember that your cell phone may not work when you're out in the wilderness.

▽ Campground Resources

Camping.com: The site allows users to make reservations in camping grounds, RV parks, and cabins around the country. There are also very general travel guides and ideas in every state.

Gocampingamerica.com: You'll see a comprehensive database of parks and campgrounds around the United States and a useful "plan your trip" guide and checklist.

Koa.com: The Kampgrounds of America site lets you make reservations in the United States and Canada, as well as find trip planners and peruse an informative blog.

Lovetheoutdoors.com: Find links to national and state park campgrounds, hiking and camping checklists, clubs and associations, and a few readers' stories.

Woodalls.com: This is the online source for *Woodall's Campground Directory,* which has listings for RV parks, campgrounds, RV dealers, service centers, camping activities, attractions, and more.

▽ RV Resources

Arvc.org: The National Association of RV Parks and Campgrounds offers facts and figures plus industry news.

Autoeurope.com: This company rents motorhomes in Australia and New Zealand as well as European locations like France, Germany, and Spain. One-way rentals are available for a fee, and rates include unlimited mileage, cooking utensils, vehicle kit, public liability insurance, fire insurance, theft protection, and collision damage waiver.

Campertour.com: Camper Tour and Touristik Service is a German-based company that rents out vehicles in Europe, including some unexpected places like Finland, Norway, Sweden, and Sicily.

Campervan.co.nz: United Campervans in New Zealand has two locations— Auckland on the North Island and Christchurch on the South Island—for campers traveling throughout New Zealand.

Gocampingamerica.com/gorving: Check out this resource of RV campgrounds, from rustic to luxury, across the United States.

Gorving.com: This is a great resource for all things RV. There are descriptions and price ranges for RV types, insurance options, and a database of 3,600 RV dealers and campgrounds.

 Packing List

Being prepared is crucial when it comes to camping and RVing safely. Gorving.com has the following suggestions for necessary items when traveling. Of course, not all these items will be feasible if you're back-packing it, but use your judgment and plan ahead for all potential situations and emergencies.

Batteries	Matches and lighter
Binoculars	Nature field guides
Blankets	Picnic basket
Bottle/can opener	Pillow
Camera and film	Plastic bags
Dishes and cooking utensils	Road flares
Firewood	Rope, cords, or wire
First-aid supplies	Shovel (small folding type)
Fishing gear	Soap
Flashlights and lanterns	Sports equipment
Folding chairs	Sunscreen
Games	Tool kit
Grill and fuel	Towels
Insect repellent	Trash bags
Jacket/raincoat	Umbrellas
Maps and road atlas	Water hose
Marine toilet paper	

Rentaholidaycaravan.com: Rent a Holiday Caravan leases motorhomes throughout Great Britain, including all corners of the United Kingdom, Ireland, Scotland, and various parts of Wales.

rversonline.org/RVMFHSE.html: RV parks are going wireless. You can find out which parks are hooked up at this site.

Rvia.org: The Recreation Vehicle Industry Association, a national trade group, offers facts and figures on RV travel.

Topographic Maps

Topographic maps use contour lines to show a region's roads, rivers, and lakes, as well as its elevation above sea level, vegetation, and pipelines. If you're not used to reading a "topo map," check out this Web site to figure out common symbols and terms: erg.usgs.gov/isb/pubs/booklets/symbols. Other useful sites:

US Geological Survey, topomaps.usgs.gov: Find topographic maps and information on the history of topography.

National Geographic Outdoor Recreation Software, maps.nationalgeographic. com/topo: You can purchase handy topography software as well as illustrated maps on this official *National Geographic* site.

Topozone.com: This is thought to be the first online topographic mapping service and provides not just topo maps but also street maps and aerial shots.

Trails.com/maps.asp: Find topographic, aerial, and GPS maps on this handy section of Trails.com.

Boating Safety

Millions of Americans hit the water each year on boats, Jet Skis, canoes—if it floats on the water, we'll be on it. But there's a serious and growing problem out there—boating accidents and the lack of proper education and training. With recreational boating becoming more and more popular, more and more people are operating motorcraft with little or no training, and what's worse, in most US states, they're not even required to be trained. As a result, a beautiful day on the water can quickly turn tragic.

It might surprise you to learn that more people die every year in boating accidents than in trains or buses. There are 13 million registered boats out in the United States. And according to the US Coast Guard, in 2006 there

462

were nearly 5,000 boating accidents last year, resulting in 710 deaths.

The major cause of death? Drowning. Nine out of ten victims were not wearing a life jacket.

The recent death of New England Patriots player Marquise Hill offers a lesson for boaters everywhere. Hill was not wearing a life jacket when he fell from his Jet Ski.

Another serious problem? BUI—or boating under the influence. It accounts for at least 20 percent of all fatal boating accidents each year.

And here's the most serious underlying problem: Just about anyone can operate a boat; most states don't even mandate a license or a minimum age to get behind the wheel. (About 36 states require a "certificate" of competency, but none of those certificates require—or reflect—on-the-water, hands-on training.)

Although there are numerous boating safety courses offered across America by the nonprofit group US Power Squadrons, the programs are not mandatory, while most safety officials think they're essential.

The US Coast Guard Auxiliary also offers boating classes and instruction. So do some marine retail stores, like West Marine (the chain offers life-jacket seminars, as well as free vessel-safety inspections). And it is easily argued that taking just one of these courses could help save lives. In 2005, nearly 70 percent of all reported deaths occured on boats where the driver had not recieved any boating instruction.

Then there's the problem of proper equipment. It's not enough just to carry the required number of PFDs (personal flotation devices). You need to wear them. Reaching for a life preserver after an accident is like trying to fasten your seat belt after your car hits a wall.

Also know where fire extinguishers are. Don't just carry one—carry two.

Then there's the problem of boating under the influence. You'd better have a designated driver who knows how to safely operate a boat—especially if you're out on the water and drinking. One thing is for sure: The US Coast Guard as well as local marine police will be making many more random stops and searches on the water, checking for alcohol as well as safety equipment on board.

In the long term, the US Coast Guard Commandant, Admiral Thad Allen, wants to have all recreational boaters required to have state-issued boaters' licenses—not just because it's a safety issue. Allen argues it is also a homeland security issue. As part of this initiative, the Coast Guard is seeking authority from Congress that could lead to a national standard on boating education. Under the proposal, Congress would amend a section of the

United States Code to give the secretary of transportation the power to establish minimum requirements for recreational boater proficiency.

▽ Resources

US Coast Guard Office of Boating Safety, www.uscgboating.org: Find safety tips, federal regulations, and complete reports of boating accidents.

North American Safe Boating Campaign, www.safeboatingcampaign.net: See boating accident statistics, educational resources, and more on this national campaign site.

Safe Boating Kidsite, www.boatingsidekicks.com: This is a kid-friendly boating safety site, featuring the ongoing "Saved by the Jacket" life jacket campaign and other safety tips.

Boat Ed, www.boat-ed.com: This is where you'll find up-to-date information on boating certification requirements by state, as well as online safety courses and handbooks.

 Some Sobering Statistics

Each state is required to submit an accident report to the Coast Guard regarding boating accident statistics. Their findings are sobering: In 2005, there were 4,969 boating accidents, resulting in 697 fatalities and 3,451 injuries. That means that there were 5.4 fatalities per every 100,000 boats (there are 12,942,414 registered boats in the United States). The reports for 2005 show that 21 children ages 12 and under died while boating, compared to 14 children in 2004. Across the board, the 2005 statistics demonstrate that there was a slight increase in boating fatalities (676 in 2004), injuries (3,363 in 2004), and accidents (4,904 in 2004). However, compared to the stats from 10 years ago, registered boating has become increasingly safer. In 1995 there were 829 fatalities, 4,141 injuries, and 8,019 accidents. Florida, California, and Louisiana lead the way in the annual boating deaths because they have a high level of year-round boating activity.

The scariest part about all this? Not one state requires that people be licensed to drive a boat. Many states do require certification, which requires an in-class or online boating education course followed by a test. But no one can take that certificate away from you if you operate a boat recklessly. In some states, like Illinois and Kentucky, kids as young as 12 can operate a motorized boat. And in Arizona, California, Idaho, North Dakota, and Wyoming, no certification is required at all.

CHAPTER 25

❝ When you're safe at home, you wish you were having
an adventure; when you're having an adventure,
you wish you were safe at home. ❞

—THORNTON WILDER

When it comes to outdoor activities, hiking ranks in the top three favorites, following bicycling and fishing, according to the 2005 Outdoor Recreation Participation Study. The American Hiking Society reports that 76.7 million Americans are hikers, and 13.5 million are backpackers. (Hiking is defined as traveling through nature areas on an unpaved surface, while backpackers are hikers that camp out overnight. Backpacking usually means carrying your tent, sleeping bag, food, etc., to be able to stay in the wild for an extended period of time.) In 2005, Americans went hiking (not including backpacking) a total of 844 million times, with the average hiker heading out between 3 and 10 times per year.

Since trails often crosscut both federally managed and private land, it's difficult to determine just how many miles are out there, but it's estimated that there are 200,000 miles of trail in the United States.

More than you thought, right?

So now, it's just about access.

America's Trails

Some of the most popular trails:

❗ **Appalachian National Scenic Trail** is a 2,175-mile trail that runs from Maine to Georgia. It's estimated that 3 million to 4 million visitors hike a portion of the Appalachian Trail each year, and since 1936, more than 9,000 hike completions have been recorded by the Appalachian Trail Conservancy. The trail runs from the rugged White Mountains of Maine, through the Blue Ridge Mountains, and onto Clingman's Dome in the Great Smoky Mountains National Park. www.appalachiantrail.org

❗ **Continental Divide National Scenic Trail** runs 3,100 miles, from the Mexican border to the Canadian border along the "backbone" of America. The trail passes through Glacier National Park, the Chinese Wall in the Rocky Mountains, and the Red Rock Lakes National Wildlife Refuge. www.cdtrail.org

❗ **Pacific Crest National Scenic Trail** runs 2,650 miles, from Mexico into California, Oregon, and Washington, including Yosemite National Park, Mount Shasta, and the remote Northern Cascades. www.pcta.org

> In 2005, a man named Matt "Squeaky" Hazley hiked up the Pacific Crest trail, down the Continental Divide trail, and up the Appalachian trail, all in succession—that's 7,925 miles through 22 states! He was only the third person to hike each of the three US National Scenic Trails in a calendar year and the first to do it in only 240 days. To complete all three trails is called a Triple Crown.

Who Likes to Hike?

According to the Outdoor Recreation Participation Study of 2005, 161.6 million (72.1 percent) Americans ages 16 and older participated in an outdoor activity that year. The top five outdoor activities were bicycling (38 percent), fishing (34.5 percent), hiking (34.2 percent), camping (30.4 percent), and trail running (18 percent).

Over 160 million Americans participate in outdoor activities, but only 59.5 million took a vacation specifically to participate in an outdoor activity. Outdoor adventure travel is still something of an untapped market.

About 78 percent of Americans living in the West participate in outdoor activities. Those living in the Northeast are least likely to participate in outdoor activities.

Lesser-Known Trails

As any avid hiker can tell you, some of the best trails can be found in—or very near—your own backyard. The key is to figure out what type of trail is best for your level of fitness, what sort of terrain you want to travel, and what kind of scenery inspires you. Looking to catch a spectacular sunset as you hike along the beach? Try hiking the demanding Olympic Coastal Strip section in Olympic National Park. Looking to take a dip under a roaring waterfall? Try heading to North Carolina. To get you started, visit www.americanhiking.org, www.trails.com, or www.localhikes.com to see what kind of natural beauty you can find on your next hike.

According to the American Hiking Society, the National Landscape Conservation System (NLCS), established by the Bureau of Land Management in 2000, encompasses 26 million acres of the best lands and waters in the West. The organization recently put together a list of "The Best Unknown Rivers and Trails of the NLCS." The top trails are as follows.

1. **Chain of Craters Area—New Mexico:** This section of the Continental Divide National Scenic Trail crosses New Mexico's volcanic badlands, offering views of lava fields and volcanic calderas.

2. **Little Blitzen Gorge Trail—Oregon:** This path is less challenging, taking you through wildflower meadows and into a gorge of heavy waterfalls.

3. **Lost Coast Trail—California:** Part of the California Coastal Trail, this beachside walk passes by old lighthouse ruins and provides a view of the 4,087-foot-high King's Peak.

4. **Paria Canyon—Arizona:** The Vermillion Cliffs Wilderness Trail is cut by the Paria River, which created a 38-mile-long canyon suitable for moderate hiking.

5. **Pinnel Mountain Trail—Alaska:** Here is where you can take a summer hike to a view of the White and Crazy mountains under Alaska's midnight sun.

The American Hiking Society also explored trails throughout the United States to put together its own lists of top hiking spots.

10 GREAT TRAILS FOR A GREAT WORKOUT

1. **Red Trail—Albany, New York:** 1.2-mile loop, 15 miles southwest of Albany. The trail alternates between woodlands and marsh and is

generally moderate in nature. It also provides outstanding views. The area is acknowledged as one of the richest fossil-bearing formations in the world.

2. **Barton Creek Greenbelt—Austin, Texas:** 7.9-mile trail in the heart of Austin. There are five access points along the route so that trips of varying lengths are possible. The trail follows spring-fed Barton Creek through lush foliage, past a cavern and below steep cliffs. Along the route, the stream is crossed several times. During the spring and early summer, the trail features swimming holes. There is some moderate elevation change on the trail.

3. **Rock Circuit Trail—Boston:** 3.7-mile loop 20 minutes north of downtown Boston. New England trails tend to be rugged, and these are no exception. Expect a good workout and expect to cover only 1 to 1.5 miles per hour of walking.

4. **Sand Creek Greenway—Denver:** This almost 14-mile public greenway connects the High Line Canal in Aurora, Colorado, with the Platte River Greenway in Commerce City. Along the way, it passes through Denver and the former Stapleton International Airport site. www.sandcreekgreenway.org

5. **Burke Lake Trail—Greater Metro Washington, DC (Fairfax/Northern Virginia):** Located 25 minutes from Washington, DC, this level trail runs in a loop for 4.7 miles around Burke Lake and follows mostly a fine gravel surface. www.rundc.com/trails/va/burkelakemap.htm

6. **Indiana Central Canal Towpath—Indianapolis:** The towpath runs for 5 miles and links directly to two other trails. This towpath follows the route of the Indiana Central Canal. The soft limestone surface is good for either walking or running, and the numerous access points make trips of any length possible.

7. **The Long Path—Greater Metro New York City (New Jersey):** This 3.3-mile segment of the 350-mile Long Path runs from Fort Lee Historic Park to the Rockefeller Lookout. Much of the route lies atop the palisades of the Hudson River, providing stunning views of the New York skyline and the George Washington Bridge. Along the way, a short side trail leads to High Tor promontory and more great views.

8. **Black Rock Loop—Phoenix:** There are 26 miles of trails in the 30,000-acre park. Black Rock Loop and the Waterfall Trail interconnect and

provide 2.7 miles of pedestrian-only trail. When the rains do come, the results are amazing: Wildflowers burst out everywhere.

9. **Guy Fleming Trails—San Diego:** Located 20 minutes north of the center of town in Carlsbad, this 0.6-mile loop passes through the forest; bluffs reveal sandstone formations and ocean views with the possibility of sighting dolphins or gray whales.

10. **Coastal Trail—San Francisco:** This trail is located right in San Francisco, with views of the Pacific Ocean, the Marin Headlands, and the Golden Gate Bridge. The featured segment is 3 miles long and stretches from Baker Beach to the Golden Gate. The trail makes a direct connection to the bridge, allowing hikers to cross the 1.7-mile-long span.

Family-Friendly Trails

These were chosen based on the trails' accessibility to a major city, ease, and amenities.

1. **Lizzy's Trail—Boston:** Located 45 minutes from downtown Boston, this hike covers about 2 miles along the Ipswich River. The first section, Lizzy's Trail, is named for Lizzy Heerlein, a local resident.

2. **Illinois & Michigan Canal—Chicago:** About 45 minutes from downtown Chicago is the 3-mile trail segment from Channahon to McKinley Woods.

3. **Ohio & Erie Canal Trail—Cleveland:** The 4.3-mile segment from Boston Store to Station Road Bridge is 30 minutes from downtown Cleveland. Highlights include the Boston Store constructed in 1836 and the 1881 bridge.

4. **The Long Path—New York/New Jersey:** Most of the Long Path is in New York, but the 3.3-mile section from Fort Lee to Rockefeller Lookout takes you along the palisades of the Hudson River in New Jersey, overlooking Manhattan.

5. **Florida Trail—Orlando:** About 20 minutes from downtown Orlando is the 4.8-mile trail (round-trip) from Barr Street trailhead. This trail is a haven for wildlife, including fox, otters, bobcats, sandhill cranes, wild turkeys, bald eagles, and osprey.

6. **Great Allegheny Passage—Pittsburgh:** About 20 minutes from downtown Pittsburgh is the 2.3-mile Dead Man's Hollow Hike, which

runs north from Boston on the Youghiogheny River Trail. This grade and others are being linked together to form a 150-mile trail called the Great Allegheny Passage.

7. **Horsetail & Ponytail Falls—Portland, Oregon:** Located 45 minutes from downtown Portland is this 2.7-mile loop beginning at Old Columbia Highway. The hike is located in a scenic area of the Columbia River Gorge known as "waterfall alley."

8. **Katy Trail—St. Louis:** This 5.7-mile linear hike follows the Katy rail-trail, 50 minutes from downtown St. Louis. When complete, 247 miles of trail will be available for recreation.

9. **Point Reyes—San Francisco Bay Area:** The Laguna Loop is a 5-mile gentle walk through coastal scrub and grasslands 45 minutes from downtown San Francisco.

10. **Chesapeake & Ohio Canal—Greater Metro Washington, DC:** About 20 minutes from downtown Washington, DC, is this 2.3-mile hike starting from Angler's Inn toward Great Falls Tavern. The Billy Goat Trail and the Washington Aqueduct provide opportunities for loop hikes in the area.

Tour Companies

Although many hikers venture out into the wilderness on their own or with friends, a hiking vacation is a great way to meet others in the great outdoors. Hiking tours often run from day trips to several-night excursions—do plenty of research beforehand to determine if a particular tour is right for your level of experience. Some companies offer both guided and self-guided tours; some involve roughing it outdoors, while others travel inn-to-inn, staying the night in hotels, lodges, or mountain retreats. Be clear with your operator how heavy duty the hiking tour is: Most tours are divided into levels of difficulty, like easy, moderate, difficult, and strenuous. Are you expected to provide your own tent and materials? How much weight will you be carrying in your backpack? How many miles will you be hiking per day? How high an altitude will you reach? And, of course, check with your doctor before departing and make sure your tour operator knows of any preexisting conditions or injuries.

Mountain Travel Sobek offers hiking and outdoor adventures around the world—a trip through the Swiss Alps involves hiking the Haute Route, a trail that offers astonishing views of Mont Blanc, the Matterhorn, and the Dent Blanche. Hiking the Inca Trail in Machu Picchu, stopping at inns each night, is an experience in overnight hiking without having to camp—and you'll get a glimpse of one of the most spectacular views in the world. You can also find hikes in the Himalayas, Galapagos, and Alaska. Rates range from $3,000 to $4,000. 888-687-6235, www.mtsobek.com

Glacier Wilderness Guides & Montana Raft Company is a multiadventure tour company that offers experiences in rafting, hiking, and fishing. Try a 3-hour white-water rafting trip along the Middle Fork of the Flathead River or a full-day adventure of a 6-mile hike followed by an afternoon of white-water rafting. Rates start at about $85 and go up to about $1,500, depending on the activity and trip length. 800-521-7238, www.glacierguides.com

Wild Horizons Expeditions arranges small-group (10 people or fewer) hikes through the wilderness of Wyoming, southern Utah, and Arizona. A 5-day trip starts at about $1,100, including backpacks, tents, sleeping bags, and meals prepared by the guides. 888-734-4453, www.wildhorizonsexpd.com

Whether it's making your way through Yosemite, biking into Italian vineyards, or strolling through Costa Rican rain forests, **Backroads** offers hiking and bike tours throughout North America, Latin America, Europe, and Asia. Packages cost from $1,000 to $5,000 per 3- to 5-day trip. 800-462-2848, www.backroads.com

Country Walkers travels to 29 countries throughout the world, focusing on morning and afternoon hikes and walks that run from 4 to 14 miles per day. Activities include wine tasting and stopping at a local farmers' market, along with adventure sports like rafting, kayaking, and horseback riding. Prices range from about $2,000 to $5,000 for 6- to 12-day trips. 800-464-9255, www.countrywalkers.com

The World Outdoors has hiking and camping trips worldwide. You can trek through domestic spots with the Grand Canyon Classic Hiker and the New England Fall Foliage Hiker trips, or you can travel abroad to Peru and Machu Picchu, Iceland, and Kilimanjaro. Trips average about $2,500 for 6- to 9-night stays. 800-488-8483, www.theworldoutdoors.com

The Wildland Trekking Company hosts guided hiking trips with both overnight camping and inn-to-inn stays, with destinations in the Grand Canyon, Utah, Yellowstone, the Canadian Rockies, the Peruvian Andes, and the Austrian Alps. Prices range from $850 to $4,300 for 3- to 8-day excursions. 800-715-4453, www.wildlandtrekking.com

Distant Journeys offers hiking and walking tours throughout Europe, Norway, and Iceland. Trips include a strenuous hike on Mont Blanc, stopping at hotels and mountain refuges in France, Italy, and Switzerland, and trekking northern England from coast to coast. Prices range from $1,600 to $3,700, depending on destination, trip length, and whether the tour is guided or self-guided. 888-845-5781, www.distantjourneys.com

Leave No Trace

The "Leave No Trace" principles come from the Leave No Trace Center for Outdoor Ethics (www.lnt.org), an international nonprofit organization dedicated to building awareness about responsible outdoor activities.

1. **Plan ahead and prepare:** Know the type of terrain and possible weather conditions you might encounter. Minimize impact by keeping groups small.

2. **Travel and camp on dependable surfaces:** Focus activity on resilient ground. Surfaces consisting of sand, gravel, rock, snow, or dry grass are durable and can withstand heavy use. Walking single file and avoiding shortcuts limits damage to the trail and surrounding ecosystems. Walk through mud and puddles to avoid widening the trail.

3. **Dispose of waste properly:** Pack it in. Pack it out! Clean up all trash and leftover food and properly dispose of human waste. Leave the areas you enjoy as good as, if not better than, you found them.

4. **Leave what you find:** You can look, but don't take. Leave everything that you find in the wilderness where it belongs. Take pictures instead; this allows others to enjoy the same experience.

5. **Minimize campfire impacts:** Keep your campfire small—or go without. Use previously constructed fire rings or mounds. Be aware of the level of fire danger of the area. Burn all wood and coals to ash, put campfires out completely, then scatter the cool ashes.

6. **Respect wildlife:** Never feed animals! Let the wild be wild. Keep your distance and do not attract or approach them.

7. **Be considerate of other visitors:** Show respect for other trail users. Keep voices and other noises from getting intrusively loud. Be courteous and yield to other users on the trail.

Packing List

The American Red Cross suggests you bring along these items when you're hiking, regardless of how long you're planning on being away. For more information, visit www.redcross.org/services/hss/tips/hiking.html.

Candles and matches

Cell phone

Clothing (always bring something warm, extra socks, and rain gear)

Compass

First-aid kit

Food (bring extra)

Flashlight

Foil (to use as a cup or signaling device)

Hat

Insect repellent

Map

Nylon filament

Pocketknife

Pocket mirror (to use as a signaling device)

Prescription glasses (an extra pair)

Prescription medications for ongoing medical conditions

Radio with batteries

Space blanket or a piece of plastic (to use for warmth or shelter)

Sunglasses

Sunscreen

Trash bag (makes an adequate poncho)

Water

Waterproof matches or matches in a waterproof tin

Water purification tablets

Whistle (to scare off animals or to use as a signaling device)

Always allow for bad weather and for the possibility that you may be forced to spend a night outdoors unexpectedly.

It's a good idea to assemble a separate "survival pack" for each hiker to have at all times. In a small waterproof container, place a pocketknife, compass, whistle, space blanket, nylon filament, water purification tablets, matches, and candle. With these items, the chances of being able to survive in the wild are greatly increased.

▽ Resources

A hiking club is a great way to get to know your local trails and gain experience from other like-minded travelers. You can find a database of regional hiking clubs at **www.hikingandbackpacking.com/hiking_clubs.html**.

American Hiking Society, www.americanhiking.org: The national organization is dedicated to promoting and protecting America's hiking trails and the natural areas surrounding them. Its Web site offers information on hikes, trail events, and volunteer opportunities in your state.

Gorp.com: This portal of Orbitz Worldwide is an outdoor adventure resource with links to national parks, monuments, trails, and rivers, plus features on activities and destinations.

Localhikes.com: You can find information on local hiking opportunities near metropolitan areas across the United States.

National Forest Service, www.fs.fed.us: The service manages public lands in national forests and grasslands, which encompass 193 million acres. The Web site includes links to scenic byways, national trails, and wild and scenic rivers.

National Park Service, www.nps.gov: The service's official Web site provides information on each unit within the system, with links on protecting natural sources and activities for kids and teachers.

Trails.com: This is a comprehensive collection of descriptions and maps for more than 38,000 trails in the United States and Canada. Find the "top 100 trails," city trails and parks, state and national parks, and a community message board.

Busting Some Common Travel Myths

If you use your BlackBerry, the plane will crash. Recirculated cabin air on planes will make you sick. Cruise ships are all-inclusive. If you rent a car with a credit card, you don't need additional insurance. Taking the train in Europe is cheaper than flying. X-ray machines at airport security checkpoints can erase your computer's hard drive. And your hotel card key can be used to steal your identity.

These are just some of the things many travelers believe to be true. And, in fact, they are nothing more than this year's batch of travel myths.

! **Let's start with the BlackBerry myth.** Every airline flight attendant makes more or less the same announcement, insisting you turn off your cell phones and BlackBerries, blueberries, strawberries, and other personal electronic devices "because they interfere with the plane's navigational systems." And if you ask if it is a rule, the flight attendant will tell you it's Federal Aviation Administration (FAA) policy. True or false?

False on both counts. First, the FAA has tested personal electronic devices—from Walkmans to Game Boys to laptop computers. Their scientists—for more than 25 years now—have bumped up the radio-frequency interference these devices give off, up to 100 times their normal levels at distances of less than 3 feet from sensitive cockpit avionics. And guess what? Nothing happened. Nothing has ever happened. So did the FAA make a rule? Or a policy? Not exactly. Instead, under the current federal air regulations, the FAA simply states that since it was unable to prove any connection or link between operating these devices and airplane system interference, it hasn't made a rule and is leaving it up to each individual airline to set policy. So, if you insist on ignoring the flight attendant and using your BlackBerry, you are in violation of an airline policy (and subject to arrest for interfering with a flight crew), but the plane won't crash because you were sending e-mails.

! **Recirculated cabin air can make you sick.** True or false? In my experience, the answer is a qualified yes, but there is no scientific proof. First, let's talk about the cabin air. Modern jet planes were designed to bring in air from the outside at high altitudes. In theory, the extremely cold air (about 40° to 60°F below zero) is then heated by the aircraft engines and brought into the cabin. And the old air is purged. But there's a problem. That exchange costs fuel, and fuel costs money, so many airlines simply recirculate the air already on board the plane and bring in precious little new air. So although it can be argued that if the person in seat 2B has the flu you'll be breathing his air back in 35E, to date there have been no definitive scientific studies to prove that allegation. Still, my advice is to hydrate yourself and wash your hands often on the plane, and if you turn off the air vent over your head, you'll not only avoid a frozen neck but keep the air around you—not someone else's—longer.

! **Your "all-inclusive" cruise means you can put your wallet away for a week.** Think again. Not that long ago, what you paid for your cruise (exclusive of liquor) was what you paid. Not anymore. Consider cruise ships today to be nothing less than multiple floating revenue centers. Some cruise lines now charge a flat fee for unlimited soda or offer a Wine and Dine deal that includes wine or champagne with your dinner (about $125 for a 7-day cruise). But the key to cruise ship profitability can be summed up in two words: onboard revenue. A new rule of thumb for budgeting your next cruise: Take the basic cruise fare and multiply it by 1.75. And that's what you'll pay per person.

! **My personal auto insurance covers me if I rent a car.** The answer, in most cases, is true—but with a big warning from me. You need to check your policy limits. If your personal car is worth only $5,000 and you total a car worth $20,000, you're out $15,000.

What's worse, many credit card companies promote that if you rent a car using their card, your rental car insurance is covered. As a result, a number of unsuspecting renters, who don't own a car and thus don't have insurance, think they are covered. Another myth. Almost all credit card companies offer something called "secondary insurance." And therein lies the problem: Secondary insurance kicks in *only* when you've exhausted all the limits of your primary policy. And if you don't have a primary policy, then you are not covered at all.

! **X-ray machines at security checkpoints can erase the hard drive on your laptop.** Another myth. Even though x-rays are a form of electromagnetic energy, this doesn't mean that they are magnetically charged. This electromagnetic energy is basically like light but more energetic (and in much the same way, it will expose your camera film). But sending your laptop through the x-ray machine won't damage it.

You can, however, damage your computer in the unlikely scenario of sending it through the metal detector or examining it with a metal wand. These detectors send out a strong magnetic pulse that can damage hard drive data.

! **Lower fares are available only if you stop over on a Saturday night.** Not too long ago, this one wasn't a myth, and in a very few cases it's still in effect. The Saturday night–stay rule was implemented to separate business from leisure travelers. Business travelers tend to fly on short notice during the week. Many airlines prefer that reservations be made in advance so they can manage their pricing and seating effectively and penalize last-minute fliers. As a result, business travelers—and others who didn't stay over on a Saturday—were forced to purchase more expensive tickets, sometimes double or triple the original price.

But these days, there are more options available to business travelers: Telecommuting became a more popular business model, and lower-cost carriers like JetBlue, AirTran, Frontier, and Southwest never implemented the Saturday night rule. The Saturday night stay became a less efficient and less cost-effective strategy for airlines. United ended its restriction in 2001, America West announced the same in 2002, Alaska Airlines eliminated the policy for advance purchases in 2004, and Delta and American eliminated it on most markets in 2005.

Still, keep in mind that in some cases, the Saturday night stay is still in effect, so do some price comparisons before you book. For example, Delta's SimpliFare applies only to travel in the United States and does not apply to flights that are operated by SkyWest, Northwest, Continental, or Alaska Airlines.

So what does that mean for an international flight? On Delta, a flight from New York's JFK to London's Gatwick costs $2,079 if you fly out Thursday and return on Saturday. But if you stay until Sunday? It drops down significantly to $849. On Air France, a flight from New York to Dubai costs $490 to fly out on Thursday, and a return on Saturday costs $3,127, for a grand total of $3,617. A return on Sunday costs $1,322, for a total of $1,812.

In some cases, one-way flights may suit your travel needs, while simultaneously avoiding any Saturday night issues. In some markets, low-cost carriers have driven down the prices of major airlines. For example, JetBlue flies from JFK to Washington, DC, starting at $50 one way (with 14-day purchases). The same route on Delta is $50 after fees and taxes. JetBlue's Boston to Orlando leg starts at $99, while US Airways' same flight is just a few dollars more at $103. On Southwest, the Oakland to Portland flight starts at $79 one way, while both Alaska Airlines and American Airlines charge a comparable $109. Southwest's Fort Lauderdale to Phoenix route starts at $119, while Continental offers a similar fee of $135.

! **Trains are the way to go within Europe if you want to save money.** While I have always been in love with trains, and I think back fondly to my days using a student Eurailpass, the dollars-and-sense truth exposes this as myth. Low-cost European airlines now occupy the low-fare throne for intra-European travel.

On Ryanair, a round-trip flight in early September from Rome (Ciampino) to Frankfurt is about $90. Or you can fly from Rome to

Berlin for about $128. By comparison, a point-to-point train ticket from Rome to Frankfurt *starts* at $326 each way and takes about 12 hours of travel time. However, there's a *very* important caution: Both Ryanair and EasyJet will absolutely gouge you if you have any bags weighing more than 15 or 20 kilograms, respectively. Travel extremely light or be prepared to enter the usurious world of excessive excess-baggage charges.

! **Your plastic hotel key card can be used to steal your identity and credit card account information.** It's another rumor floating around the Internet: Supposedly, a Pasadena, California, police officer is warning travelers about their plastic hotel card keys. According to this message, a local Doubletree Hotel had key cards that contained encoded personal information such as your name, a partial home address, the hotel room number, your check-out date . . . and your credit card number. Well, simply put, hotels do *not* put your personal information on the card. At the most, they'll put the room number and activation date. Another travel myth busted.

CHAPTER 26

National/State Parks

💬 Some national parks have long waiting lists for camping
reservations. When you have to wait a year to
sleep next to a tree, something is wrong. 💬

—GEORGE CARLIN

Although the National Park System wasn't created until 1916, the first
national park in the United States was Yellowstone, which was designated
in 1872. The system consists of 391 "units," covering more than 84 million
acres in nearly every state (a unit also includes protected areas like a
National Battlefield, a National Seashore, or a National Scenic Trail).

The beauty of the system is that you can find nearly every type of geographical landscape and ecosystem within a nationally protected park: Two
national parks are located north of the Arctic Circle in Alaska (Gates of the
Arctic National Park and the Kobuk Valley National Park), while another is
home to a tropical rain forest (National Park of American Samoa). Many
others encompass spectacular desert scenery (Death Valley and the Mojave
Desert National Preserve in California).

According to a 2004 study of national parks travelers by the Travel Industry
Association (TIA), the majority of travelers stay in a national park for a few

days—7 percent do day trips, 26 percent stay 1 or 2 nights, 39 percent stay 3 to 6 nights, and 28 percent stay 7 nights or more. About 46 percent of national park trips are taken by households headed by baby boomers. Another 25 percent of national park trips are taken by households headed by someone in Gen X or Y (ages 18 to 34), while 22 percent are taken by households headed by "mature" travelers, ages 55 or older.

When you take a look at our country's state parks, your options for travel expand dramatically. According to the National Association of State Park Directors (www.naspd.org), as of 2004 there were 5,842 state park areas comprising more than 13 million acres in all 50 states. This included 5,875 trails, 208,849 campsites, 129 golf courses, and 48 ski slopes. State parks are primarily a daytime destination.

At last count in 2001, there were 735 million visitors to state parks, the vast majority of them (91 percent) daytime users. And that number is growing.

If you're considering camping out in a national or state park, remember that many campsites are first-come, first-served. Some campgrounds that offer advance reservations also include campsites that are not reserved—space may be available at the last minute, even after all "reservable" units are filled. And another option: A number of well-known, crowded national parks border lesser-known, uncongested state parks that also offer camping sites.

One caution: Keep in mind that, although the great outdoors seems like a great place to bring your pet, national parks aren't necessarily pet friendly. Some hiking trails prohibit all pets, while others require that they remain leashed or caged. If you're camping, a small animal can become prey to bears, wolves, and mountain lions.

Not surprisingly, according to the TIA study, sporting activities like hiking, fishing, and biking are the most popular reasons to visit a national park (44 percent), followed by recreational activities like barbecues, camping, and simply taking pictures (39 percent). But did you know that you can also take a dunk in thermal hot springs at the Hot Springs National Park in Arkansas? Or view more than 300 glaciers in North Cascades National Park in Washington? Check out these fun facts about some of our lesser-known, less-crowded parks.

Avoiding Crowds

If you can't deal with the crowds of the major national parks, you have a few options. First, try visiting during "shoulder season," which is that period between high and low season, when crowds are thinner, prices are lower, and the weather is still (hopefully) holding up. Call up the parks ahead of time to find out what their patterns of visitation are—for example, parks in the northern part of the United States, like Yosemite, tend to experience heavy traffic in June and July. More southerly locations, like Texas and Florida, have an opposite schedule. Shoulder season tends to fall in unwieldy months, which makes it tough for families with children and other travelers with less flexible schedules. But if you have the freedom to steer clear of traditional travel months, you can reap the benefits.

Another option to avoid getting caught in major crowds is to sneak around the more trafficked areas. The National Park Service Web site, www.nps.gov, is a very comprehensive and complete resource, with interactive maps of each section of the parks. If there are alternative entrances into the parks, this is where you'll find them—in Yellowstone, for example, Old Faithful is most

 **Fun Facts**

! Olympic National Park, Washington, encompasses three distinctly different ecosystems: glacier-capped mountains, old growth and temperate rain forests, and more than 60 miles of wild Pacific coast.

! Craters of the Moon National Monument, Idaho, contains three lava fields, 25 volcanic cones, and 60 lava flows covering 618 square miles.

! Biscayne National Park, Florida, is 95 percent under water.

! Thaddeus Kosciuszko National Memorial, Pennsylvania, is the smallest national park at 0.02 acre.

! Wrangell–St. Elias National Park and Preserve, Alaska, is the largest national park at more than 8.3 million acres.

! Mammoth Cave National Park, Kentucky, is the longest cave system in the world, with more than 360 miles mapped.

! You can be the first in the United States to see the sunrise atop Cadillac Mountain in Acadia National Park, Maine.

! Sequoia National Park, California, is the site of the General Sherman Tree, the largest (by volume) tree in the world.

! Mount Diablo State Park in the Bay Area offers one of the most sweeping views of the world—the 3,849-foot summit shows more of the earth's surface than any other peak in the world, except for Kilimanjaro in Africa.

accessible via the west and south entrances, but there are three other entrances into the park that involve longer drives but possibly lesser crowds.

Here's a Yosemite tip: Consider renting a separate car once you get to the park. Not just any car but a Model T convertible. You won't go more than 20 mph, but this tour isn't about speed. In fact, you'll travel the way many Americans did—slow enough to actually see things! You can rent top-down Model Ts and Model A Roadsters between June and October, starting at $400 a day, up to $5,500 for the "ultimate" tour, which also includes 2 nights in a hotel and a tram ride in the Yosemite Valley. Model T-Tours is the name of the company. 866-488-6877, www.driveamodelt.com

Lastly, travelers can also follow my philosophy, which is to explore alternative parks beyond the "Big 10." In 2005, about 273 million people visited sites within the National Park System, but out of 391 units, only the top 10 received roughly 31 percent of the total visitors—that's a significant number clustering together.

Lesser-Known Parks Worth Visiting

Aside from the 391 units within the National Park System, there are also hundreds of state parks to choose from. These parks, rivers, trails, and historical sites are open to visitors, and you can have a great experience in your

Top 10 Most Visited National Parks (2006)

1. Great Smoky Mountains National Park, 865-436-1200, www.nps.gov/grsm
2. Grand Canyon National Park, 928-638-7888, www.nps.gov/grca
3. Yosemite National Park, 209-372-0200, www.nps.gov/yose
4. Olympic National Park, 360-565-3130, www.nps.gov/olym
5. Rocky Mountain National Park, 970-586-1206, www.nps.gov/romo
6. Yellowstone National Park, 307-344-7381, www.nps.gov/yell
7. Zion National Park, 435-772-3256, www.nps.gov/zion
8. Cuyahoga Valley National Park, 216-524-1497, www.nps.gov/cuva
9. Grand Teton National Park, 307-739-3300, www.nps.gov/grte
10. Acadia National Park, 207-288-3338, www.nps.gov/acad

own backyard. Don't want to deal with the crowds around Old Faithful? Green River State Park in Utah has the vibrantly colorful Crystal Geyser, which erupts twice a day. Here are a few options of some parks that are well worth the visit.

Mesa Verde National Park, Colorado: The ancient Pueblo people lived on this piece of land from A.D. 600 to 1300, and today the park protects more than 4,000 archaeological sites. One of the most notable aspects is that there are more than 600 preserved cliff dwellings. The largest in the country is Cliff Palace, a 150-room ancient mansion made of sandstone, mortar, and wooden beams. In 2006, the park celebrated its centennial as the first national park set aside to preserve "works created by humankind." 970-529-4465, www.nps.gov/meve

Cumberland Gap National Historical Park, Kentucky, Tennessee, and Virginia: With 20,000 acres of protected land, Cumberland Gap offers outdoor activities with a nod toward the westward pioneers who traveled through this region. There are more than 70 miles of hiking trails, ranging from short quarter-milers to the 21-mile Ridge Trail, backcountry camping, and guided cave tours. Indoor events include an interactive museum, a Pioneer Playhouse for kids, and short films chronicling the migration of pioneers and early settlers. 606-248-2817, www.nps.gov/cuga

Big Bend National Park, Texas: Big Bend is made up of a massive 800,000 acres of land, bordered by the Rio Grande for 118 miles and featuring the grand Chisos Mountains breaking up the desert terrain. You can choose between backcountry and mountain camping, while water lovers can take in the spectacular canyon scenery while floating along the river. 432-477-2251, www.nps.gov/bibe

Crater of Diamonds State Park, Arkansas: Have you ever thought of going to Arkansas to hunt for . . . diamonds? Situated among the 888 acres of pine forests in southwest Arkansas is a rare 35-acre field where visitors can actually search for diamonds. The plowed field is the eroded surface of an ancient volcanic pipe and is the only diamond area in North America that is open to the public. More than 70,000 diamonds have been found here, including an enormous rock that weighed in at 40.2 carats (dubbed Uncle Sam). Others include the Star of Murfreesboro (34.2 carats), the Star of Arkansas (15.3 carats), and the Amarillo Starlight (16.3 carats). If diamonds aren't your best friend, you can also find semiprecious gems like amethyst, quartz, and agate. 870-285-3113, www.craterofdiamondsstatepark.com

Cumberland Falls State Resort Park, Kentucky: In southern Kentucky, Cumberland Falls is home to a 125-foot-wide, 60-foot-tall waterfall that has earned it the nickname the "Niagara of the South." Not only is the size of this waterfall crashing over the boulders a stunning sight, but it is also one

More Lesser-Known Parks

My good friend Bill Wade, from the Coalition of National Park Service Retirees, has his own top-10 list of lesser-known parks that are well worth a visit.

Tuskegee Airmen National Historic Site, Alabama. Learn the story of the Tuskegee Airmen, our country's first African-American military pilots, who were trained in 1940s Alabama in what became known as the famous Tuskegee Experience. Kids can take part in educational scavenger hunts, and on Memorial Day weekend, the Tuskegee Airmen Fly-In features historic aircraft, military fly-bys, and aerial aerobatics. 334-724-0922, www.nps.gov/tuai

Lake Clark National Park, Alaska. This park has some of the most spectacular scenery in the United States, with active volcanoes, icy glaciers, and waterfalls. Visitors come here for kayaking and hiking in the Alaskan wilderness, and you may just catch sight of wild caribou, moose, and even whales swimming in the bays. 907-644-3626, www.nps.gov/lacl

Chiricahua National Monument, Arizona. Explore Arizona's "Wonderland of Rocks," where spires of rocks were formed millions of years ago by the volcanic eruptions. Visitors can ride along the 8 miles of scenic driveways and hike the 18 miles of hiking trails. 520-824-3560, www.nps.gov/chir

Lava Beds National Monument, California. Millions of years of volcanic eruptions have transformed this spot into a dramatic, rugged scene with more than 600 caves, craters, and blackened landscape. 530-667-8100, www.nps.gov/labe

Dry Tortugas National Park, Florida. Outside of Key West are the Dry Tortugas, seven islands made up of coral reefs and sand. Try snorkeling, diving, or boating to catch sight of some wonderful marine life and underwater scenery, and spend a night or two on these little-known islands. 305-242-7700, www.nps.gov/drto

of the few places in the world where you can catch a glimpse of something called a "moonbow." This natural phenomenon, also known as a lunar rainbow or a white rainbow, occurs at night from the faint light of the moon. 800-325-0063, www.parks.ky.gov

Andersonville National Historic Site, Georgia. Home to the National Prisoners of War Museum and the prison of Camp Sumpter, this is the only park unit that serves as a memorial to all American prisoners of war, from the Revolutionary War to today. 229-924-0343, www.nps.gov/ande

Puʻuhonua o Hōnaunau National Historic Park, Hawaii. This sanctuary is filled with a sense of history. Generations ago in Hawaii, criminals sentenced to death escaped to a "puʻuhonua," a place of refuge. Here, you can walk the Royal Grounds and visit ancient temples and wooden structures. 808-328-2326, www.nps.gov/puho

Saint-Gaudens National Historic Site, New Hampshire. This is the home and studio of famed sculptor Augustus Saint-Gaudens. Not only can visitors catch a glimpse of more than 100 of his pieces, but they can also participate in hands-on sculpting workshops. 603-675-2175, www.nps.gov/saga

Women's Rights National Historical Park, New York. The park commemorates the first Women's Rights Convention in 1848, held in Seneca Falls, New York, where Elizabeth Cady Stanton and other leaders inspired 100 people to commit to the women's suffrage movement. Visitors can also see a station on the Underground Railroad and learn about the Quaker influence on the women's rights and abolitionist movements. 315-568-0024, www.nps.gov/wori

Capitol Reef National Park, Utah. You've heard of a wrinkle in time—but what about a wrinkle in the earth? The Waterpocket Fold is a 100-mile-long "wrinkle" in the earth's crust that is now protected within the National Park System. There is ample opportunity for hiking, rock climbing, and backcountry camping in the beautiful Utah wilderness. 435-425-3791, www.nps.gov/care

PART 5

TRAVEL
WITH A
PURPOSE

CHAPTER 27

Responsible Travel

❝ **It is better to be a nobody who accomplishes something than a somebody who accomplishes nothing.** ❞

—ANONYMOUS

Vacations with a purpose. Doing the right thing. Being a socially, environmentally, culturally responsible traveler.

All the right buzzwords.

Indeed, there's no question that responsible travel is booming. After the United Nations declared 2002 the International Year of Ecotourism, the World Tourism Association found that ecotourism was growing three times faster than the tourism industry as a whole. In addition, about 13 percent of the 18.6 million leisure travelers leaving the country can be regarded as ecotourists, according to a 2002 study by the US Department of Commerce. The following year, a survey by the Travel Industry Association and *National Geographic Traveler* found that 55.1 million US travelers are classified as "geotourists," or interested in nature, culture, and heritage tourism.

Whether it's helping to rebuild homes after Hurricane Katrina, observing and protecting cheetahs in the wild, or weaving baskets with local tribal women, the terms "responsible," "sustainable," and "eco" are overtaking the travel industry.

But beware. There is no industry standard among all these buzzwords, but the following definitions are a start, courtesy of the International Ecotourism Society.

Certification: procedure that assesses, audits, and gives written assurance that a facility, product, process, or service meets specific standards; awards a marketable logo to those that meet or exceed baseline standards

Ecotourism: responsible travel to natural areas that conserves the environment and improves the welfare of local people

Geotourism: tourism that sustains or enhances the geographical character of a place—its environment, heritage, aesthetics, and culture—and the well-being of its residents

Mass tourism: large-scale tourism, typically associated with "sea, sand, sun" resorts and characteristics such as transnational ownership, minimal direct economic benefit to destination communities, seasonality, and package tours

Nature-based tourism: any form of tourism that relies primarily on the natural environment for its attractions or settings

Pro-poor tourism: tourism that results in increased net benefit for the poor people (money spent goes directly back to the communities)

Responsible tourism: tourism that maximizes the benefits to local communities, minimizes negative social or environmental impacts, and helps local people conserve fragile cultures and habitats or species

Sustainable tourism: tourism that meets the needs of present tourists and host regions while protecting and enhancing opportunities for the future

❗ Sustainability principles should apply to all types of tourism activities, operations, establishments, and projects, including conventional and alternative forms.

❗ Sustainable tourism practices promote management of all resources in such a way that economic, social, and aesthetic needs can be fulfilled while maintaining cultural integrity, essential ecological processes, biological diversity, and life support systems.

❗ The goal is to achieve a "triple bottom line," meaning to make businesses sustainable in terms of their environmental, social/cultural, and economic practices.

Confused yet? In the travel industry, these words get thrown around so much that they've become interchangeable and, in some cases, useless. Nowadays, it seems like any hotel with a pond is an ecolodge, and buying a handmade rug in Turkey constitutes sustainable tourism. It's easy to confuse a nature holiday with ecotourism. That hike you took in the Grand Canyon is a healthy and adventurous activity but is probably not doing a whole lot to protect the environment. Meanwhile, many tour operators and hotels are getting very skilled in the art of "greenwashing," where they claim to be eco-friendly, even if they only put it into practice by not washing your sheets every day. Wow . . . are you impressed yet?

It's not always easy to spot a legitimately responsible destination, resort, or hotel. There are five questions that I always ask a place that claims to be eco-friendly or sustainable.

1. How do you conserve resources? That can mean using renewable and efficient energy, practicing water conservation, using chemical-free cleaning agents, using recycled materials inside the building, and even encouraging guests to bike or walk instead of driving their vehicles.

2. How do you give back to the community? This includes hiring local staff at fair wages, supporting the community through charitable donations, or teaching employees self-sustaining skills like craftmaking or farming.

3. How do you protect the local flora and fauna? Resorts often encroach on natural space, so the criteria here include not overbuilding in a specific property. Other eco-friendly activities can include growing organic fruits and vegetables on the property and using them in the kitchen, as well as keeping pedestrians and cyclists on marked trails and roads rather than letting them go off into unprotected areas.

4. What responsible activities can guests partake in? Can guests actually get hands-on experiences in the garden, volunteering with locals, building homes?

5. Has the resort/hotel won any awards or been certified by a "green" program? Keep in mind that there are more than 100 certification programs around the world, each one claiming to be socially and/or environmentally responsible, so don't fall for just any stamp of approval.

Why Ecotourism?

When it comes to ecotravel, one of the first places to come to mind is the Galapagos Islands, the chain of volcanic islands near Ecuador that has remained relatively untainted by the massive amounts of visitors who arrive each year. Travelers must follow a very specific set of rules when visiting the islands. Although these rules aren't as strictly observed in most other natural locations, they serve as a great example of how you can "tread lightly" on your travels.

! When visiting the Galapagos, you must be accompanied by a qualified guide approved by the National Park.

! Visitors may not stray from marked trails.

! There is absolutely no feeding or touching of animals—even gentle handling could cause irreparable harm, as baby sea lions and chicks can be abandoned by their mother if she smells a human scent on her offspring.

! There is, of course, no littering allowed at all.

! Visitors cannot bring their own food to the islands (water bottles are allowed) and may not bring any live materials like pets, insects, or seeds.

! You cannot disturb or remove any natural object on the islands, including plants, rocks, bones, coral, and shells.

The Galapagos is just one destination where mass tourism could easily destroy the fragile ecosystem if it's not heavily regulated. Unfortunately, there are plenty of other places where mass tourism is having ill effects on the region—it's a vicious cycle in which an economy depends on tourists visiting the region for its natural beauty, ancient ruins, beautiful architecture, or traditional cultures; but left unregulated, tourism destroys those elements that made it so attractive in the first place. Natural coastlines become overbuilt with hotels and resorts (think the Mediterranean). Local infrastructures can be heavily stressed, perhaps taking away resources and necessities such as piped water from the local community in favor of hotels and resorts (this happened in Goa, India). Native traditions become an on-demand performance, while visitors trample on sacred grounds. And even animals in their natural habitats become a hands-on exhibit . . . just ask the manatees in Florida.

Certification Programs

The current gold standard is the Environmental Protection Agency's US Green Buildings Council, which has a rating system for **Leadership in Energy and Environmental Design**. This deals with the design, construction, and operation of a green building, but that doesn't necessarily apply to a particular resort's practices or philosophies outside of the building. www.usgbc.org

Green Globe is an environment certification program based on the Agenda 21 Principles for Sustainable Development endorsed by almost 200 heads of state at the United Nations Rio de Janeiro summit. Fancy jargon, but the bottom line is Green Globe 21 aims to set global environmental standards for the travel industry as a whole. Go online to check out what hotels and tour operators are participating in the certification program and how you can be more environmentally aware when you hit the road. www.greenglobe.com

The International Ecotourism Society's **Travel Choice Directory** is a network of tour operators, agents, lodgings, and transportation companies that have passed a Code of Conduct, which determines that they follow the guidelines of responsible ecotourism travel. www.ecotourism.org

The **Green Hotels Association** organizes hundreds of independent hotels and major chains that have pledged to uphold green practices. There isn't a hard set of criteria that members have to follow, but recommended practices include use of low-flow showers and toilets, bulk dispensers for toiletries (instead of those tiny bottles), recycled paper, and natural cleaning products. www.greenhotels.com

Sustainable Travel International has an **Eco-Certification Program** with a database of approved companies. Its criteria are based on several principles from organizations such as Agenda 21 Principles for Sustainable Development, Costa Rica's Certification for Sustainable Tourism, the European Voluntary Initiative for Sustainability in Tourism, and Leave No Trace Center for Outdoor Ethics. You can also find information on carbon offsetting and fair-trade shopping. www.sustainabletravel.com

Responsible Hotels and Resorts

Nowhere in travel has ecotourism taken hold more than in the hospitality industry. Green measures have made their way into major hotel chains, boutique hotels, and bed-and-breakfasts. And with good reasons: A study by the American Hotel & Lodging Association found that the average hotel consumes about 209 gallons of water per occupied hotel room each day. California Green Lodging reports that waste generation can be as high as 30 pounds per room per day, even though as much as 80 percent of these materials could be recycled.

Groups like the Green Hotels Association and California Green Lodging have brought together hotels that are interested in pursuing more eco-friendly practices. This might be as small as placing cards to encourage guests to reuse their linens and towels (hundreds of hotel chains are doing this now). It can also include heavy-duty recycling programs, installing water-saving devices, and going all natural with cleaning supplies and bathroom products.

To get you started, here are a few resorts and hotels that are making the effort to go responsible.

Kimpton Hotels: The boutique hotel chain began its EarthCare initiative in San Francisco's Hotel Triton and has rolled out the program in all 42 of its properties. The program uses water-saving devices in all the rooms, air- and water-filtration systems, and nontoxic products for cleaning. They recycle about 60 percent of their waste. Even their paper is printed on recycled paper and uses soy-based ink. 800-546-7866, www.kimptonhotels.com

Fairmont Hotels & Resorts: Fairmont has been putting in eco-friendly measures since the '90s and has launched something called Eco-Meet for businesses to hold green conferences. That includes local, organically grown food and beverages served with nondisposable items; edible, organic, or reused centerpieces; white boards instead of paper presentations; energy-efficient lighting; and the now-ubiquitous optional sheet and towel laundering. 416-874-2415, www.fairmont.com/ecomeet

El Monte Sagrado Living Resort and Spa: The 4-acre high-end resort in downtown Taos, New Mexico, pays homage to the region's Native American heritage and incorporates locally produced materials and eco-friendly elements. About 60 percent of the complex is geothermally heated, and other areas use photovoltaic installation and smaller solar panels. The spa uses filtered rainwater, and storm water is utilized in ponds and waterfalls. 800-828-8267, www.elmontesagrado.com

Danzante: This is a 10-acre resort near Danzante Island in the Sea of Cortez, Mexico. It's 100 percent solar powered and employs only native villagers from the immediate area to cook meals made from local produce and the resort's organic garden. The villagers are also trained as local naturalist guides. The owners provide no-interest loans for area families to develop solar power for their own homes. 408-354-0042, www.danzante.com

Lapa Rios: You'll find a 1,000-acre private rain forest reserve on Costa Rica's remote Osa Peninsula. Designed to help sustain the local rain forest, the main lodge is made of native, natural materials. Exotic plants were removed in favor of native flora, and the founders help to fund and build a public school in the remote region. 506-735-5130, www.laparios.com

Spice Island Beach Resort: The Grenadian resort launched a $12 million rebuilding project in the aftermath of Hurricane Ivan. Already Green Globe–certified, the resort has many new features that are environmentally conscious, with solar rooftop heaters, nonchlorine swimming pools, and a heavy reusing and recycling program that includes composting and grinding partially used soaps for laundry detergent. 473-444-4258, www.spicebeachresort.com

King Pacific Lodge: This is a floating wilderness resort in British Columbia accessible only by boat or floatplane. Each May, the whole lodge is hauled 75 miles to Barnard Harbour, where it remains for the summer before being towed back to storage in September—along with all the waste, sewage, and dirty water. 888-592-5464, www.kingpacificlodge.com

Omni Hotels of California: In Los Angeles, San Diego, and San Francisco, Omni has partnered with Habitat for Humanity with a Groups for Giving package. This allows groups holding conventions or meetings in these hotels to spend a day working with Habitat to build a new home. The hotel provides boxed lunches, water, and hard hats for participating guests. 888-444-6664, www.omnihotels.com

Punta Islita: Green travel is not uncommon in Costa Rica, but with heavy tourism comes the threat of environmental disaster. Located on the Guanacaste Peninsula, Punta Islita is dedicated to environmental sustainability, with reforestation and conservation as its main priority. There are separate bins for organic and inorganic materials, solar-heated pools, and organic food. Visitors can catch a glimpse of the protected sea turtle–nesting habitat and learn firsthand about the preservation of Costa Rica. 506-290-4259, www.hotelpuntaislita.com

Moonlight Head: In Australia, ecoresorts are flourishing, as you can see in this upscale villa. Located in Victoria, the four-room villa is built entirely out of sustainable materials such as volcanic rock, but it's the luxury amenities that are drawing in visitors. Guided nature walks, spa services, and even a ride on a mountain bike are all just part of the everyday experience here. 61-3-523-75208, www.moonlighthead.com

Charity Hotels

If you want to "donate while you sleep," sometimes all you have to do is pick the right hotel: a charity hotel. Visit **www.charityhotels.org** and you can choose from a list of major hotels that will donate 5 percent of your nightly rate to one of several charities, including the American Red Cross, Oxfam, and the World Wildlife Fund.

Airlines

In 2006, Virgin Atlantic billionaire Richard Branson brought worldwide attention to fuel conservation by pledging to reduce carbon-dioxide emissions on the ground by towing his aircraft to the runways. Other airlines have tried to save fuel by lightening the load on aircraft, by decreasing the weight limit of checked bags from 70 pounds to 50 pounds, by using lighter food carts, and even by removing magazines from the cabin (it saved Alaska Airlines $10,000 a year in fuel costs).

You can also help make a difference by choosing an airline that acts responsibly, so that your travel dollars can have a positive impact.

Founded in 1996 by a former flight attendant, **Airline Ambassadors** is a network of airline employees and others who volunteer as Ambassadors of Goodwill in their home communities and abroad. Volunteers have hand delivered over $34 million worth of medicine, school supplies, clothing, and food around the world and have escorted more than 1,000 children to new homes or to facilities where they could receive medical care not available in their home countries. Participating airline members include American, America West, Cathay Pacific, Continental, JetBlue, Northwest, Southwest, Spirit, TACA, and United. www.airlineamb.org

American Airlines and UNICEF have developed the **Change for Good Program,** which asks travelers on international flights to donate their unused currency. The program has raised more than $60 million worldwide for children whose lives have been impacted by natural disaster, conflict, and lack of basic education, nutrition, and immunization. The **Champions for Children** program has flight attendants collecting donations on American's international flights, while **Admirals Club Champions** collect donations at some Admirals Club locations.

If you're a Northwest Airlines WorldPerks member, you can receive 500 WorldPerks miles by making a $50 contribution to the **Marine Toys for Tots**

Foundation. Send a $50 check made out to "Toys for Tots Foundation" to Major Bill Grein, Marine Toys for Tots Foundation, P.O. Box 1947, Marine Corps Base, Quantico, VA 22134.

WorldPerks members can also donate miles to Northwest's **KidCares** program. Created in 1999, the program provides travel to children 18 and under (plus one adult) who are unable to receive the needed medical treatment in their home area. The KidCares program accepts mileage donations only, no monetary donations. 800-328-2881, www.nwa.com

You can participate by donating your unused frequent flier miles to the **Make-A-Wish Foundation.** The foundation uses about a billion miles a year to help make the wishes of seriously ill children come true. 800-722-9474, www.wish.org

Responsible Tour Companies

World Wildlife Fund: This is one of the largest conservation organizations and hosts wildlife-watching tours throughout the world. An 8-day cruise to Alaska on a 64-passenger ship travels along the southeast coast: View humpback whales, hike through forests with naturalists, and watch bald eagles along Glacier Bay National Park; starts at $4,840. A trip to watch the polar bears in Canada travels along the bears' migratory path for 6 or 7 days; about $3,700. 202-293-4800, www.worldwildlife.org/travel

Across the Divide: The UK-based company specializes in planning charity fund-raising expeditions. For example, you can hike across Greenland, trek through Peru, or climb Kilimanjaro while sponsorships help raise money for causes like cancer research or fighting poverty in Africa. 44-0-1460-30456, www.acrossthedivide.com

Hills of Africa: The North Carolina–based company arranges tours throughout South Africa, working solely with lodges, safaris, and other institutions that have received a stamp of approval from Fair Trade in Tourism South Africa. A 12-night tour that includes Cape Town, Mozambique, and a safari begins at about $6,000, and a family-oriented trip combining Johannesburg, Botswana, and a safari is about $4,500 for adults and $3,500 for children. 877-845-4802, www.hillsofafrica.com

Intrepid Travel: Winner of the UK's 2006 Responsible Tourism Award, the Australia-based company offers soft-adventure tours worldwide, with a focus on "responsible travel." This involves using public transportation, staying with local families, patronizing small locally owned establishments, and educating locals on sustainable tourism practices. 866-847-8192, www. intrepidtravel.com

Responsible Travel: This online portal has waged a campaign against mass tourism, those large-scale packaged tours that tend to leave locals out of the picture. For example, in an all-inclusive holiday, most of your money goes to the tour operator in your home country, the air carrier, insurance, and commissions, leaving very little for the hotel and even less for the hotel staff. Through this site, you can contact prescreened-holiday companies that function in a responsible manner by working closely with local operators and employees—includes adventure tours, budget travel, safaris, and volunteer vacations. 44-0-1273-600030, www.responsibletravel.com

Fair-Trade Tourism

This is one area that has been overlooked far too long in the responsible-travel surge. And I think it's one of the most important. Fair-trade tourism attempts to maximize the benefits of tourism for the local destination. This usually means hiring local employees, providing fair wages and benefits to those employees, providing training for career advancement, using locally produced resources such as food and textiles, and putting the money earned through local tourism back into the community. It sounds simple enough; however, fair-trade tourism can be difficult to execute. Lodge operators, tour guides, and expedition operators must find a way to engage in fair trade, while still turning enough profit to sustain their business.

For less-developed countries, it can be difficult to promote tourism as a viable resource without exploiting their local people, land, and culture. According to Tourism Concern, a London-based organization that is campaigning for ethical and fairly traded tourism, several nations are under scrutiny for the mistreatment of their tourism employees for the sake of promoting the industry. The Sun, Sea, Sand, and Sweatshops campaign is raising awareness of the appalling working conditions in various highly visited destinations; in resort areas like Cancún and the Maya Riviera, average salaries rarely go above $4 a day, while apartment rental for a local worker can cost $150 a month. In the Maldives, Tourism Concern has launched a Lost in Paradise campaign: The idyllic environment belies the fact that nearly half of the population is living on just over $1 a day, while amenities like fresh fruit and vegetables go directly to the tourist destinations (a recent study found that more than 30 percent of Maldivian children under 5 are suffering from malnutrition).

And these injustices aren't only taking place in tropical resorts. While it may be inspiring to hear those triumphant stories of people conquering the Himalayas, we forget about the porters who also have to scale the mountains—while carrying all the equipment. Those hardy climbers aren't immune to conditions like frostbite and altitude sickness. In the Himalayas, the traditional Sherpa is usually from a high-altitude area, but many porters are farmers from lowland areas and are unaccustomed to mountain conditions.

In June 2002, South Africa initiated Fair Trade in Tourism South Africa (FTTSA), the very first "trademark" in the fair-trade movement. Various South African tourism establishments, including game parks, lodges, and adventure tours, have since been accredited with the FTTSA stamp, meaning that these places fulfill the criteria of fair wages and working conditions (e.g., hiring local workers, using local resources, maintaining safe working conditions and practices, protecting young workers, conserving the environment, and establishing reliable services to visitors). For responsible travelers, this can make it easier to identify those businesses that practice fair-trade tourism.

And now that the FTTSA has taken a stand, hopefully the word is spreading to make it even easier for you to plan your own fair-trade tour. For example, Hills of Africa is one of the first in the United States to associate solely with FTTSA-accredited institutions.

Klippe Rivier Country House in South Africa is an example of how to execute fair trade in tourism. They not only hire locals to work in the guesthouse but also give every employee an interest-free loan to purchase a home—while working out individualized payment plans on those loans. The way it works is that travelers pay rates that are based upon a first-world travel experience, but business operation costs are third world. Employees make what is considered a fair wage there, but it's not at first-world standards—so the guesthouse absorbs the difference on these loans. www.klipperivier.com

For a complete list of FTTSA-approved businesses, visit the organization's Web site at www.fairtourismsa.org.za.

Fair-Trade Shopping
If it's not the right time to plan a trip abroad, you can still support local communities by shopping in American stores that sell fair-trade products. What

is fair-trade shopping? Basically, fair-trade certification means that when you purchase agricultural products from a fair-trade farm (this includes coffee, tea, herbs, cocoa, chocolate, fruit, sugar, rice, and spices), you are benefiting the farmers and farm workers. Fair-trade certification currently benefits more than 1 million people in 58 developing countries across Africa, Asia, and Latin America. Below are some of the principles behind fair trade.

Fair prices: Farmer groups receive a guaranteed minimum price for products and an additional amount for certified organic products.

Fair labor conditions: Workers are provided with safe working conditions and fair living wages. Forced child labor is strictly prohibited.

Direct trade: Importers purchase from fair-trade groups as directly as possible, which eliminates unnecessary middlemen.

Democratic and transparent organizations: Fair-trade farmers and farm workers decide together how to use their revenues.

Community development: Farmers and farm workers invest in local projects, such as scholarship programs, quality improvement training, and organic certification.

Environmental sustainability: The fair-trade certification system prohibits the use of genetically modified organisms and limits the use of harmful agrochemicals in favor of farming methods that protect farmers' health and preserve the ecosystem.

When you're in the United States, you can help the fair-trade cause by searching online for shops that carry fair-trade certified products at www.transfairusa.org. However, the philosophies behind the official fair-trade movement can apply to your shopping habits abroad as well.

The fair-trade shopping movement is being promoted to help bolster the economy in developing nations. Various social uplift programs involve providing craft materials to locals who are employed by the programs— they create the handicrafts, which the employers purchase at a fair price to sell in their own stores. Some programs also have an educational element, including business and literacy training to empower locals to continue providing for themselves.

In South Africa, for example, the unemployment rate is about 29 percent, and one-third of its population of 45 million people survive on just a couple dollars a day. In Cape Town, a shop called Streetwires showcases local artisans creating funky jewelry, handbags, and household items out of wire, beads, and metal. In the KwaZulu-Natal Province of South Africa, an Oxfam shop called the Bat Shop involves more than 120 craftspeople who transform traditional Zulu designs into baskets made from telephone wire and beadwork. Proceeds support a fund to assist the dependents of victims of HIV/AIDS. www.oxfamshop.org.au/retail

You can find a list of fair-trade companies at Global Exchange (www.globalexchange.org). The organization also has its own fair-trade stores in San Francisco, Berkeley, and Portland, Oregon.

Carbon Offsetting

Air travel is one of the most polluting forms of transport. Consider this: According to the Federal Aviation Administration, the average domestic flight is roughly 1,660 miles long. Each flight belches close to a half-ton of carbon dioxide into the atmosphere. According to the International Air Transport Association, although today's jet engines are about 40 percent more fuel efficient than those designed in the '60s, this improvement is negated by the fact that a staggering 85,000 commercial aircraft take off each day—and this figure is expected to double by the year 2050. Now throw in the fuel used by your rental car and the energy spent by your hotel, and that's a lot of environmental impact caused by just one trip.

The concept of *carbon offsetting* allows travelers to calculate the amount of carbon dioxide used by traveling and make up for it by contributing to the planet's health.

According to *Travel Weekly*, the European Commission has "acted to reduce greenhouse gas emissions from aircraft by including commercial aviation in an evolving European Union carbon-trading plan" that would take effect as early as 2012. *Carbon trading* means that a cap is placed on the amount of greenhouse gas that participating companies can produce. Companies can buy allowances from or sell them to each other.

While some European airlines are complaining that this will cost the industry up to $5.4 billion a year, more and more airlines are getting into the carbon offsetting game. British Airways was the first major carrier to offer tickets with optional carbon-offsetting fees—the airline partnered with Climate Care, so passengers can click on the carbon calculator and opt to pay the cost to offset the carbon output of their flight. Delta and Air Canada followed suit with similar programs, and Continental wasn't far behind. Silverjet, the all-business-class British airline, advertises itself as a "carbon-neutral airline," with the carbon-offsetting fee built into the price of your ticket.

You may have already come across carbon offsetting in your everyday life. At Whole Foods, a "wind-power card" costs $5 or $15, with proceeds going to support wind farms. If you book your vacation through Travelocity, for an extra few dollars the company will donate money to the Conservation Fund to plant trees.

Even hotels are getting into the act. The Rezidor Hotel Group—which operates Radisson SAS Hotels & Resorts, Regent Hotels & Resorts, Park Inn, and Country Inns & Suites in Europe, the Middle East, and Africa—has partnered with the CarbonNeutral Company. Guests can join Rezidor's free loyalty program, Goldpoints, and allocate a portion of their points toward offsetting greenhouse gas emissions. For example, staying 1 night at a Radisson SAS Hotel collects about 3,000 Gold Points, and 1,000 of those points go to programs like a wind-power project in India and methane-capturing projects in the United States.

Some of these carbon-offsetting projects have already sparked a backlash. Several of the carbon-offsetting companies are for-profit, which casts a shadow on their philanthropic mission. And because this is a relatively new enterprise, there aren't any standardized criteria that companies need to follow—they can pocket as much as they want, and individual travelers have little idea whether their money is actually being used effectively in these projects.

Fellow travel journalist Don George (donsplace.adventurecollection.com) notes some of the thornier issues of carbon offsetting for travelers. For one thing, he points out that the accuracy of carbon calculators can vary greatly among Web sites. Secondly, he explains that the long-term effects of these programs, whether they're wind-power, methane-energy, or tree-planting programs, are still unknown. In some cases, there have even been harmful effects—a *New York Times* report points to a tree-planting program in Uganda that resulted in villagers being hurt over land disputes. Finally, George points out that travelers may become complacent over responsible travel if they think that throwing a few dollars at a wind-power program is enough action.

When it comes to donating your dollars to offset your carbon usage, find out what percentage of your money actually goes into a project and how much goes toward administrative costs. Learn about the background of the project you're donating to. How long has it been around, who is sponsoring it, and is there a projected end date?

American Forests: This is considered to be the oldest nonprofit citizens' conservation organization in the United States that will plant trees with your dollars. Taking the average domestic flight of 1,660 miles will set you back only half a tree, but you might as well have a whole one planted for $15. 202-737-1944, www.americanforests.org

Better World Club: Based in Portland, Oregon, Better World takes $11 for domestic flights and $22 for international to invest in tree planting, reforestation, and wind-power projects or to install energy-efficient heating/cooling systems in public buildings. You can also book a trip through the company and take advantage of its roadside bicycle assistance and discounts for hybrid car owners. 866-238-1137, www.betterworldclub.com

TerraPass: This organization sells a yearly pass for $25.95 to $79.95 to offset your carbon output. TerraPass uses a portion of its proceeds to support programs like wind farms as well as to donate to dairy farmers so they can install digesters on farms to control methane emissions. The company has also partnered with Expedia—when you buy a $6 voucher on the online travel site, TerraPass commits to offsetting 1,000 pounds of carbon emissions within 90 days of purchase. 877-210-9581, www.terrapass.com

Native Energy: Primarily owned by the Intertribal Council on Utility Policy, a Native American nonprofit, the organization promotes renewable energy. You can calculate your usage of carbon and purchase your offset points for projects like WindBuilders and Remooable Energy (methane gas). 800-924-6826, www.nativeenergy.com

Carbon Fund: Your donated money is put into wind farms, solar energy, and reforestation projects, and the site has a calculator to help you offset your entire family's carbon usage. 240-556-1908, www.carbonfund.org

Climate Care: The organization donates money to energy-saving programs such as installing low-energy lighting in low-income households in South Africa and funding wind programs in India. 503-238-1915, www.climatecare.org/guardian

Carbon Counter: The Web site helps you to calculate your carbon usage and donates to localized projects like reducing truck diesel engine idling through truck stop electrification and reducing emissions in Portland, Oregon, from grid power, natural gas, and fuel oil. 800-429-5660, www.carboncounter.org

Conservation International: The organizations carbon calculator puts your carbon-offsetting points to use helping to protect the 832,000-acre Makira Forest in northeast Madagascar. www.conservation.org/carboncalculator

Driving Green: Figure out how to offset not only your travels but also your next Super Bowl party and other social events. 321-429-5660 www.drivinggreen.com

Agritourism

Agritourism encourages travelers to lend a hand in the local community's natural environment. Usually this means working on a farm or in a vineyard, but it can also include restoring village homes or helping out local fishermen. In many cases, you're able to exchange your help for free room and board, and if you're lucky, you may wind up reaping the benefits of your harvest. For travelers who are tired of the cityscapes and museum-hopping, this kind of outdoorsy, hands-on experience can be a great way to soak up local culture and be part of developing sustainable tourism within a community. And best of all, agritourism is catching on in rural areas around the world, so you have your pick of places to visit.

Of course, nothing comes with a guarantee. Without the luxury of knowing much about the environment that you're going into, you could very well end up in a one-room farmhouse with no electricity and surly hosts. Fortunately, these are volunteer positions, so you're free to leave at will. Most agritourism arrangements include a minimum commitment of a few days, but if you're uncomfortable with a situation, there's no reason you can't move on. However, it's important to keep in mind that in many cases, the organization that sponsors agritourism acts only as a go-between in this host/worker arrangement—they won't be able to help you out with any conflicts that arise during your travels.

If you're planning on getting involved with an agritourism venture, do as much homework as possible in advance.

❗ Gather any available past information about your host family from the sponsoring organization. Find out if there have been any complaints or concerns in the past.

❗ Be as clear as possible about the terms of engagement with your host family to avoid conflicts during your stay. Discuss how many hours per day or week you're expected to work, the conditions of your accommodations, whether the family has any restrictions on alcohol or tobacco, etc.

❗ Secure the correct visa for your travels. Depending on the country and your length of stay, you may not need one at all, or you may qualify for a working visa (even though it's a volunteer position, you're still receiving accommodations and meals for your labor).

❗ Make sure you're insured for health, travel, and liability. Chances are you'll be in a remote location, and your host family is not responsible for your safety, even if you're working on their property.

! Locate the American embassy in your host country in case any issues arise during your stay.

In many cases, the word "agritourism" is used simply to refer to working farms that welcome visitors for a fee—like quaint bed-and-breakfasts. But finding a farm that will trade free room and meals for your labor is a little trickier. Here are a few organizations that can connect you with hands-on agritourism opportunities.

Worldwide Opportunities on Organic Farms: Established in the United Kingdom in 1971, this is one of the longest-running agritourism connection services, consisting of several autonomous organizations throughout the world. Each group compiles and posts a list of organic farms that welcome volunteers, and it's up to you to contact the farm to make your arrangements. Through these groups, you can find placements like spending a week on a Czech farm breeding goats and donkeys or living in a Japanese temple and yoga center tending to the local garden. Keep in mind that while most farms are organic or are working toward that, there are varying levels of how eco-friendly and sustainable each place actually is. www.wwoof.org

Service Civil International: This Virginia-based organization works through various international nonprofits to send more than 5,000 volunteers around the world for short-term work camps. While this group sponsors a variety of activities—from rebuilding India's flooded regions and teaching theater in impoverished Chinese communities to working with the Irish Wheelchair Association—there are several farm-oriented opportunities available. Check carefully, as some hosts may expect you to stay off-site in a local hostel or campsite. The fee to join is $80 for US-based programs and $195 for programs abroad. www.sci-ivs.org/workcamps.htm

National Association of Rural, Ecological, and Cultural Tourism: This Romanian organization operates a network of more than 600 farms and rural communities that welcome guests. Some offer free room and board in exchange for a helping hand, while others may charge about $15 a night for your visit. www.antrec.ro

Vacation Jobs in Ecuador: This organization compiles various month-long volunteer opportunities, requiring 25 hours a week, in exchange for free room and meals. Among the offerings: Web-site translation and design, carpentry and bricklaying, and tending the organic garden and pastures at Finca Colibri vacation farm in the Pululahua Crater. www.ecuador-travel.net/job.htm

CHAPTER 28

Weather Vacations

> ❝I like weather rather than climate.❞

—JOHN STEINBECK

If you're a self-proclaimed "weather nerd," you probably already know about the concept of storm chasing. For everyone else, you probably got your first glimpse of storm chasers in the movie *Twister*. A storm chaser is basically anyone, whether a trained meteorologist or a curious observer, who tracks down where and when a tornado (in some cases, a hurricane) is going to hit and follows it to catch sight and take photos and video of the spectacle. Although catching a storm can't be guaranteed on a daily basis, storm chasers are mostly active across the so-called Tornado Alley in the Great Plains. Generally, storm chasing occurs in late April and May in the southern plains of Kansas, Oklahoma, and Texas; in June and July, the storms are in the northern plains of North Dakota, South Dakota, Nebraska, and Iowa.

If you haven't participated in storm chasing before, remember that there can be some dangers involved. Putting yourself directly in the path of flooding, hail, lightning, and twisters—not to mention slippery road conditions—

is a risk in any situation. Since storm chasing often involves driving long distances, checking weather data, and trying to capture the moment, the hazards increase tremendously. That said, there are now a few companies that arrange organized tours with experts leading travelers who may be inexperienced in the art of storm chasing.

Tempest Tours is made up of a team of veteran chasers and tornado scientists, arranging seven storm-chasing tours in May and June in the Great Plains. The base cities are generally Dallas, Oklahoma City, and Denver, but tours travel by van to different regions, depending on the weather forecast, and spend nights in local motels. Because of the fickle nature of tornadoes, you probably won't know where you're headed until the night before, or even the morning of, each chase day. The teams ride almost anywhere in the Great Plains, covering about 100 to 600 miles from Texas to the Dakotas and from the Rocky Mountains to the Mississippi River. Groups intercept the storms from a distance to view the event and take photographs, and they may stay in place to catch nighttime lightning storms. Tours range from 6 to 10 days and run from $1,995 to $2,795, including an Independence Day tour that features fireworks along with your chase. 817-274-9313, www. tempesttours.com

Storm Chasing Adventure Tours arranges nine storm-chasing tours in May and June. Base camps are located in Oklahoma City in the spring and in Denver in the summertime. The groups depart each day via SUV to a location, usually about 200 to 400 miles away, that's determined in the morning via analytics and forecasts. This company has linked up with Doppler on Wheels to help determine where the best storms will be happening. Storm watching usually takes place in the late afternoon and goes on until the night hours if there is a good lightning show in the area. Tours are $2,300 for 6 days or $4,000 for a 12-day back-to-back excursion. 303-888-8629, www.stormchasing.com

TRADD (Tornado Research and Defense Development) has 5-day storm-chasing tours in May and June, which you can extend for as many weeks as you want. The home base is in Dallas, and daily storm watching usually takes place between 3 p.m. and 9 p.m., after which you retire to a motel for the night. The good news is that if you wind up with a bum day where no tornado is likely, you can visit the *Twister* movie museum in Wakita, Oklahoma, which holds some of the props and equipment used in the film. TRADD also offers a guarantee that if you don't catch two storms in a weeklong trip, you get a $200 discount off your next trip. Rates are $1,699 for 5 days and $2,899 for 10 days. www.traddtornadochasingtours.com

Tornado Express has 6- and 7-day trips, 12- and 13-day mega trips, and "follow-along" tours in which you travel in your own car behind a storm-chasing van (you get a two-way radio to keep in touch). Home bases are located in Omaha and Oklahoma City. Rates are $1,750 for the shorter guided trips and $2,800 for the longer ones; follow-along tours are $150 per day with no hotel or $1,100 for a 6-day tour with hotel. 866-578-6767, www.tornadoexpress.com

Cloud 9 Tours has three trips per year, starting out in Oklahoma City. Your storm-chasing excursions can stretch from the Mexican border to the Canadian border and between the Rockies and Indiana, depending on the daily forecast. Rates are $2,600 for 2-week tours. 405-323-1145, www. cloud9tours.com

Silver Lining Tours has both 6-day tours starting in Denver and 10-day tours starting in Oklahoma City. Silver Lining also has several other options available: There are annual tours in the Canadian Prairies, from the foothills of the Canadian Rockies in western Alberta eastward across the lakes of Ontario. You can also be a part of Silver Lining's "on-call" storm chasing— short-notice trips that operate in the earlier part of tornado season and invite you to drop everything and chase a storm at a moment's notice. Real weather buffs can also join a Master Class Storm-Chasing Workshop, an interactive course on the fundamentals of forecasting, chasing strategies, and observation techniques. Rates start at $2,000, depending on the length and intensity of the tour. 281-759-4181, www.silverliningtours.com

Stargazing Vacations

If you're fascinated by the sky but would prefer to avoid getting caught in a twister, how about a stargazing vacation? Between light pollution in cities and suburbs, smoggy skies, and your own hectic schedule, opportunities to appreciate the stars are few and far between. That's where hotels are now stepping in, offering on-site astronomers to take you on a guided tour of the night skies.

At the **Hyatt Regency Maui Resort and Spa,** you can view those stars and much more using Hawaii's only recreational telescope, Great White. This 16-inch reflector telescope sits more than nine stories up, on a remote site of the hotel rooftop. The hotel's director of astronomy uses a computer to select an agenda and locate and identify 1,000 objects in the sky, including stars, planets, galaxies, and nebulae. Participants learn to interpret the sky first with the unaided eye, then with giant astronomy binoculars, and ultimately with Great White. Rates are $20 for adults and $10 for kids, or you can arrange a couples-only night under the stars with champagne and chocolate-covered strawberries for $25 per person. 808-667-4727, www.maui.hyatt.com

With few lights and low humidity, the Australian Outback is perhaps one of the best places to explore the night sky. At the **Ayers Rock Resort,** the Sounds of Silence dinner features a 4-hour Northern Territory feast (get ready to dine on kangaroo and emu), after which a resident astronomer points out constellations and planets, while explaining ancient and Aboriginal stories of mythology and creation. Rates are $145 per adult and $73 for kids ages 10 to 15. 61-2-8296-8010, www.ayersrockresort.com.au/astronomy

Located on the cliffs of Big Sur, California, the **Post Ranch Inn** offers guided stargazing hikes every night at 8 p.m., weather permitting. This hike is open to all hotel guests and restaurant patrons and features amateur astronomers leading the group throughout the property. 800-527-2200, www.postranchinn.com

The sky is so consistently clear over Kohala that stargazing is one of the most popular activities available at nearby **Hapuna Beach Prince Hotel.** A high-powered telescope is set up for you to view the Hawaiian skies with the guidance of professional astronomers. Rates are $25 for adults and $12 for children, every Friday at 8 p.m. 888-977-4623, www.princeresortshawaii.com

Arizona's **Kitt Peak Visitor Center** offers an advanced observing program, which means overnight stays for would-be astronomers (no previous experience necessary). You can observe at the world's largest optical observatory under some of North America's finest skies and sleep in the observatory for $375 a night. 520-318-8728, www.noao.edu/outreach/aop

Fall Foliage

When September rolls around, many travelers engage in the time-honored tradition of following the fall foliage. There's no doubt that a trip through New England yields some of the most brilliant shows of color in the country. But did you know that you can also track the changing of the leaves in Missouri? Iowa? Even sunny California has spectacular vistas where the fall colors put on a memorable show.

This might surprise you, but beautiful fall foliage can be found in all 50 of the United States. It's all about the deciduous trees, those broad-leaved trees like maples, oaks, and elms that lose their leaves in the fall. The other key to finding the best fall colors is to head to places where there is a pronounced cold snap; in the more southerly or western regions, where weather tends to cool down more slowly, leaves tend to hang on a little bit longer and turn dry and brown.

The turning of the leaves usually follows a very regular pattern, which means that ideal viewing time can run from mid-September all the way to mid-November, depending on where you're traveling. Leaf changing starts in the Northeast in the highland regions and moves both down south and downslope (from higher elevations).

Up high in the Canadian Rockies and in Colorado, the foliage turns in mid-September, draping the foothills with stunning yellow and gold colors from the quaking aspen trees. The Wichita Mountains, south of the Ozarks in Oklahoma, get the last of the foliage season from late October to mid-November. Did you ever think of traveling even farther east than New England? Nova Scotia and Prince Edward Island have late foliage, because the Atlantic Ocean keeps the weather more temperate and delays the changing of the leaves to late October. Michigan's Upper Peninsula, Wisconsin, and Minnesota have spectacular changes from late September to early October. Even in the rolling plains of the Midwest, there are beautiful deciduous trees in localized areas.

The traditional ways of viewing fall foliage are still some of the best, whether it's hiking through forests or bicycling along the New England coast. But there are also some spectacular views from less-traditional activities. Fast-moving vehicles like trains and cruise ships aren't the best way to get up close and personal with the trees, but they're great for soaking in the overall hues. A ride in a hot-air balloon or a vintage biplane? You get an entirely different, and often glorious, perspective. And if you do decide to go for the old standby of trekking through the forests, don't just stick to the guidebook routes—go out and get lost and see what kind of foliage you can find.

By Air

Snoopy would be envious. **Red Baron Rides** in Chicago takes you on a 50-minute biplane ride to the Chain O'Lakes area, where you can fly low over and around the lakes and park areas to see the fall colors. For an authentic experience, each passenger gets to strap on a leather helmet before climbing into the vintage-era biplane. Rates are $435 per couple, including a stop at

Pilot Pete's restaurant at the Schaumburg Airport. 847-466-3848, www.redbaronrides.com/theride.html

For the more independent minded, hang gliding and paragliding from 1,100 feet off **Buffalo Mountain,** located east of Talihina, Oklahoma, is the way to go. Late October to early November is peak season for catching sight of the cottonwoods and willow trees bursting into their fall colors. This is an advanced gliding site (rated Class 3), and since there are no instructors here, hang gliders need to be trained before flying. 918-567-3434, www.ouachitahanggliding.com

The **Great Smoky Mountains** are often awash in brilliant autumn colors, with hundreds of native deciduous trees changing hues. At the highest elevations, between 4,500 and 6,000 feet, leaves begin to change in mid-September with the yellow birch, American beech, and mountain maple; they peak in late October when the sugar maple, scarlet oak, sweetgum, and dogwood turn to gold, orange, and deep red. Since much of the national park gets jammed with travelers, a hot-air balloon ride in and around the mountains is a great way to capture the views. A 1-hour sunrise or sunset ride is $550 per couple. 828-667-9943, www.ashevillehotairballoons.com

Napa Valley is famous for its wine, and autumn is one of the most pleasant times to visit. During harvest season, the grapes are plucked and the grapevine leaves change to red and yellow. A hot-air balloon ride over Napa offers sky-high views of rolling vineyards and old oak trees that populate the area. Fall foliage rides run from October to November for $225 per person. 800-253-2224, www.napavalleyballoons.com

Hang gliders flock to Arkansas's highest point, the 2,753-foot **Mount Magazine** in the Ouachita Mountains. The colors change in this region within a week or so after the Ozarks start changing, usually early to mid-October and peaking in early November. Rising above the Petit Jean River Valley and Arkansas River Valley, you'll see maple, sumac, oak, sassafras, and hickory trees changing into all colors of the fall spectrum. Hang gliders must be Class 4 certified to fly alone, and a Class 3 flier can fly with a Class 4. 877-665-6343, www.mountmagazinestatepark.com/adventure-activities/hand-gliding

By Chair

Ski resorts aren't only for winter sports, you know. Going to a mountain peak is one of the best ways to see fall foliage in panoramic, sweeping views. And that doesn't mean you have to scale the mountain—many resorts operate their chairlifts in the fall just to catch the changing of the leaves!

They don't call it Aspen for nothing. At **Aspen/Snowmass** ski resort in Colorado, the month of September is the best time to see the leaves turning golden yellow. To take in the changing of the leaves, you can ride the Burlingame Lift in Snowmass Village or the Silver Queen Gondola in Aspen up the mountain and hike down to enjoy the scenery. 800-525-6200, www.aspensnowmass.com/summer_rec

In **Taos Ski Valley**, the aspens turn gold between mid-September and mid-October, and you can capture a beautiful view by taking a chairlift up the mountain and hiking or horseback riding down. Go during the local Oktoberfest and you can celebrate your hike down with bratwurst and beer. 505-776-8220, www.vtsv.org

The **Giant Steps Chairlift** in southern Utah (about 4 hours from Salt Lake City) carries you up to the top of Brian Head Peak for a view of the Parowan Valley, surrounded by the red rock landscapes. The chairlift operates weekends and holidays through the end of September, when you can catch sight of the vivid reds and yellows throughout the valley. 800-354-4848, www.scenicsouthernutah.com

Virginia's **Wintergreen Resort** on the eastern slopes of the Blue Ridge Mountains offers truly stunning views. The foliage starts to turn in October, covering the entire spectrum of brilliant colors. The Acorn Ski Lift can take you up to the top of Crawford's Knob for a view of 6,000 acres of mountain trees. On Saturdays in October and during Fall Foliage Fest, $5 gets you unlimited rides all day. 800-926-3723, www.wintergreenresort.com

By Foot

Nothing is more satisfying than crunching on autumn leaves (except maybe drinking hot cider while doing it). A hike through the woods is a time-honored tradition that is probably the most popular way to cozy up to the fall foliage. Here are a few places that you might not expect to have fall colors.

Mount Charleston is the highest point of the Spring Mountain Range in southern Nevada, about 20 miles north of Las Vegas. Take a drive along Route 157 in Kyle Canyon, one of Nevada's Scenic Byways, for 17 miles. You'll ascend 8,500 feet, passing every kind of environment from desert to forest. At the end of the road is a 9-mile trail that takes you to the top of Charleston Peak, where aspen, cottonwood, and mountain mahogany turn to red and gold. 800-955-1314, www.mtcharlestonlodge.com

Fall foliage in . . . Oklahoma? That's right, even the Plains states have spots with deciduous trees. Take a walk around the gardens of the **Philbrook Museum of Art** in Tulsa for a great view of scarlet and gold leaves. Guests can take an audio tour of the gardens to learn about the native Oklahoma plants and landscape architecture, or they can simply wander through the pathways, past the sculpture, and along the creek. 918-749-7941, www. philbrook.org

In October, Maryland is awash in fall colors—try a hike through **Seneca Creek State Park** in Gaithersburg (near DC and Baltimore), a 6,300-acre forest that winds toward the Potomac River. The 16½-mile Seneca Creek Greenway Trail follows the river, where you are surrounded by the fiery autumn trees. 301-924-2127, www.dnr.state.md.us/publiclands/senecaguide.html

▽ Resources

The Foliage Network has collects and analyzes data from "foliage spotters" twice a week, to give you accurate reporting of where to find foliage throughout the United States. **www.foliagenetwork.com**

The USDA Forest Services maintains its own site to provide information on where the leaves are turning throughout the United States, as well as links to regional resources. **www.fs.fed.us/news/fallcolors**

Weather.com has a fall foliage page with maps, destination guides and seasonal events to help plan your leaf-peeping travels. **www.weather.com/ activities/driving/fallfoliage**

CHAPTER 29

❝ Meals make the society, hold the fabric together in lots of ways that were charming and interesting and intoxicating to me. The perfect meal, or the best meals, occur in a context that frequently has very little to do with the food itself. ❞

—ANTHONY BOURDAIN

Whether you're a professional gourmet, a devoted oenophile, or simply someone who enjoys a good meal out, food and travel have become virtually synonymous. When you hear "culinary travel," your first thoughts may go to cooking lessons in the hills of Tuscany or to a roaming tour of Provence to dine in every Michelin-starred restaurant along the way. But a culinary experience can also involve haggling over the price of produce in a Mexican food market, stuffing yourself silly on street food in Bangkok, or driving an RV through Texas Hill Country to sample the region's wines (yes . . . wines). No matter where you travel, experiencing the local cuisine is really one of the best ways to immerse yourself in a culture. Think about it: You have to eat, so why not take some risks?

Culinary travel has grown so popular that the Travel Industry Association just released the very first study on this niche market. According to the 2007 study (in partnership with *Gourmet* magazine and the International Culinary Tourism Association), 17 percent of US leisure travelers (about 27 million Americans) have incorporated wine or culinary activities while traveling within the past 3 years. A stunning 60 percent of travelers are interested in pursuing culinary travel in the near future—these travelers tend to be younger, more affluent, and better educated than nonculinary travelers.

The study showed that, on average, culinary travelers spent $1,194 per trip, with about 36 percent of their travel budget going toward food-related activities. Dedicated culinary travelers—those who are visiting a region specifically to learn about its food or wine—spent even more: about 50 percent of their $1,271 travel budget. Wine travelers spent, on average, $973 per trip, with about 23 percent of their budget going toward wine-specific activities, while dedicated wine travelers spent 36 percent of their $950 budget.

We're also putting more and more importance on food—I actually think I'm the only person who *doesn't* have his own TV cooking show. We've got Emeril, Mario, Rachael, not to mention the continuing spotlight on celebrity chefs like Joël Robuchon and Alain Ducasse. And let's not forget the invention of celebrity chef–branded restaurants (hello, Wolfgang) and celebrity chefs running hotel restaurants (just go to Vegas to see what I mean). As a result, diners are eating out more and spending more money. Zagat Survey released the results of its 2007 America's Top Restaurants Survey (based on 21 million meals experienced by more than 123,000 surveyors in 42 US cities). Nearly 83 percent of respondents say they are eating out as often as or more often than they did 2 years ago. And 67 percent say they are spending more per meal.

One thing about Americans when it comes to food and wine: We're very susceptible to outside influences. You might remember the film *Sideways,* in which Paul Giamatti's character expressed a notable preference for pinot noir and a disdain for merlot. Well, it affected the wine industry. Merlot took a beating, and pinot sales soared 18 percent. Does this mean you have to follow the trend? Absolutely not. Be a contrarian. There are now some excellent (and moderately priced) merlots on the market as a result. But when eating out, should you order the house wine? It's a gray area, because at many restaurants, the choices have been traditionally limited to one brand of white and one red. Not much imagination there. However, a growing number of restaurants are offering a choice of different house wines by the glass. These are usually moderately priced, quality wines, and you should definitely try them.

Americans are also eating out more than ever, and they're spending more than ever before. The nation's 935,000 restaurants are expected to hit $537 billion in 2007 sales—only the second time in history that sales will exceed half a trillion dollars. The American adult is expected to spend nearly 48 percent of his food budget in restaurants.

New York City leads the way as the most costly US restaurant city, with an average meal tab of $39.43 per person. In second place is Palm Beach at $38.56. However, ultra-high costs of dining in Tokyo ($73.69), London ($71.19), and Paris ($65.85) make US prices seem like a steal. And thanks to the rise of the British pound against the dollar, London will soon take over as the costliest dining-out city in the world.

What's In and Out

Here are the National Restaurant Association's top 20 lists of hot and cool (passé) culinary trends for 2007.

Hot Items	Cool/Passé Items
1. Bite-size desserts	1. Scandinavian cuisine
2. Locally grown produce	2. Starfruit
3. Organic produce	3. Organ meats/sweetbreads
4. Flatbread	4. Ethiopian cuisine
5. Bottled water	5. Kiwi
6. Specialty sandwiches	6. Edible flowers/rose petals
7. Asian appetizers	7. Blackened items
8. Espresso/specialty coffees	8. Low-carb dough
9. Whole-grain bread	9. Soda bread
10. Mediterranean cuisine	10. Fruit soups
11. Pan-seared items	11. German cuisine
12. Fresh herbs	12. Taro
13. Latin American cuisine	13. Low-carb items
14. Exotic mushrooms	14. Foams
15. Salts	15. Okra
16. Grilled items	16. Vichyssoise
17. Pomegranates	17. Meat salad
18. Grass-fed items	18. Consommé
19. Free-range items	19. Catfish
20. Pan-Asian cuisine	20. Cold soups

Source: *National Restaurant Association survey of 1,146 members of the American Culinary Federation, October 2006*

One of the reasons the tabs are up has something to do with menu psychology. Smart chefs (or their menu consultants) know that when most of you open a menu, your eyes go right to the top of the page. And armed with that knowledge, chefs place the menu item that will give them the most profit at the top of the page. (And hence, it soon becomes their biggest seller.) Then, your eyes normally drift to the center of the page. And that's where many chefs place their absolutely most expensive item. But they do that not because they expect you to buy that item but because the psychology of menus indicates you'll probably then look at the items immediately above and below the high-ticket item and order one of those. My advice? The next time you look at a menu, take a deep breath and actually look around the menu. You—and your wallet—will be glad you did.

Last but not least, there's a growing trend toward serving locally grown, sustainable produce, meats, and cheeses. You've heard of carnivores and herbivores. Get ready for a new one: locavores—people who want to eat from the region they're visiting. The hot buzzwords include "organic, locally grown produce, sustainable farming, and all natural" (not necessarily in that order). The next time you look at a restaurant menu, ask where the lettuce, the cheese, and the cured meats come from. You might be surprised to learn it's usually from within a 100-mile radius of the restaurant. And it's a win-win situation: It supports local farmers and ranchers, and you get to eat fresh. This has become such an important part of the restaurant industry that some chefs have even bought their own farms—they want a guarantee of locally grown, fresh produce.

Culinary Schools

Once you sample the rich sauces of Parisian restaurants and organic meals in Sonoma Valley, there's an unfortunate downside: Those flavors that once danced on your palate become just a memory . . . that is, unless you learn how to do it all on your own. Plenty of destinations offer cooking classes for travelers to learn the secrets of their local cuisine and bring it home for good. And even these schools have changed—from demonstration-oriented teaching to up close and personal participation for culinary students.

You can visit www.cookingschools.com for a database of worldwide cooking schools and classes, for both novices and career-minded chefs. In the meantime, here's information to get you started.

Domestic Classes

Ramekins Sonoma Valley Culinary School, located just off Sonoma's Historical Plaza, has two teaching kitchens: one for culinary demonstrations and the other—a full restaurant kitchen—for hands-on classes. Professional chefs guide you in specific culinary themes such as Provençal cuisine, flatbreads of the world, and how to get your risotto as fluffy as the Italians do. Rates are $75 to $80 for a day class. 707-933-0450, www.ramekins.com

In Napa Valley, **Casa Lana** offers several classes to fit your schedule—whether you want to spend 3 hours cooking your lunch, spend a weekend preparing for your next dinner party, or immerse yourself in a 5-day course. A Mediterranean weekend features dishes from Spain, France, Italy, and Greece; a Thai class uncovers all the secrets of lemongrass. A 5-day course is about $1,000. 707-942-0615, www.gourmetretreats.com

Respected restaurants often open their kitchens to teach guests how to create their favorite dishes. In New York's Greenwich Village, chef-owner Abby Hitchcock of **Camaje** restaurant offers several hands-on cooking courses. Ranging from sushi basics and making your own pasta to figuring out how to handle a knife properly, classes provide a chance to learn a variety of dishes in a working kitchen. Day classes are about $85. 212-673-8184, www.camaje.com

If you want to experience what the professionals do, try heading to the **Institute of Culinary Education** in New York, where budding chefs are invited to 1- to 5-day cooking courses. With nine kitchens to choose from, you can specialize in anything you crave, from traditional Thai cuisine to gourmet French. One-day courses are about $85, while a 3-day class starts at $275. 800-522-4610, www.iceculinary.com

Eating and Drinking in the United States

The top 10 domestic destinations for food-related travel, according to the Travel Industry Association's 2007 Culinary Travel Report:

California 14 percent, Florida 10 percent, New York 7 percent, Texas 6 percent, North Carolina 4 percent, Georgia 4 percent, Louisiana 3 percent, Illinois 3 percent, Nevada 3 percent, Pennsylvania 3 percent

The top 10 domestic destinations for wine-related travel:

California 31 percent, New York 10 percent, Missouri 5 percent, North Carolina 5 percent, Oregon 5 percent, Pennsylvania 5 percent, Washington 4 percent, Virginia 4 percent, Texas 4 percent, Florida 2 percent

Even cruise ships are jumping on board the culinary craze. **Radisson's Seven Seas** ships offer several themed cruises, including a comprehensive cooking school—it's not the old-school demonstration cooking that you often see on cruises but a hands-on, fully participatory experience. Cruisers go with the chefs to local markets when the ship is in port and then head into the galley to create full menus. 877-505-5370, www.rssc.com

Classes Abroad

Near the French city of Bordeaux, **Two Bordelais** teaches would-be chefs the secrets of French cuisine—you can learn in a 300-year-old farmhouse, focusing on homey meals of duck, seafood, fresh fish, and locally grown vegetables. You can also study in a separate château kitchen to create more upscale meals and menus. The experience includes wine and cheese tasting and visits to the local markets. Rates are about $3,000 for a 5-day course. 510-848-8741, www.twobordelais.com

In the town of Nyons in Provence, chef Lydie Marshall invites eight guests for 5 days to study food and cooking at **A La Bonne Cocotte.** The focus is on traditional Provençal cooking, which highlights fresh garden vegetables with farm-raised meats, prepared with a Mediterranean twist. Excursions include the local Nyons market and wine tasting in Gigondas. 4-75-26-45-3, www.lydiemarshall.com

In Italy, **Food Artisans** offers weeklong hands-on classes in Campania, Tuscany, Piedmont, and Emilia-Romagna. If you're less into the cooking and more into eating, try tooling around Northern Italy in vintage Italian cars (like a 1969 Alfa Romeo or a 1976 Fiat), sampling artisan foods throughout the region. Rates are about $4,500 for a week of driving and dining. 805-963-7289, www.foodartisans.com

You may have heard of the famous cooking course at the Oriental Hotel in Bangkok, but Chiang Mai is considered to be another one of Thailand's food capitals. The **Four Seasons** offers a participatory culinary class for $150 ($675 if you stay in the ultra-luxury resort). You'll haggle over goods at the local food market, learn to make Thai curries from scratch, and even learn the art of fancy fruit carving. 800-819-5053, www.fourseasons.com/chiangmai

For an authentic Indian experience, head to family-owned **Philipkutty's Farm** in the backwaters of Kerala. The 50-acre farm is home to an immersive cooking course, where you can learn the traditions of Kerala cuisine—fresh fish, poultry, farm-grown vegetables, and, of course, lots of spices are the key ingredients here. Villa accommodations are about $200 a night, plus

$12 for cooking lessons. 91-4829-276529, www.philipkuttysfarm.com

It goes without saying that food and wine go hand in hand, so the Culinary Institute of America and Viking Life have partnered to create **Worlds of Flavor** food and wine tours. Regions visited include Napa Valley, Italy, Spain, India, Morocco, and Thailand, where you can sample regional cuisine and experience hands-on cooking classes. On a trip to Tuscany and Umbria, you can hunt for truffles, taste wines from local vineyards, visit cheese artisans, and meet the chefs in village restaurants. A culinary tour of India skips the wine but includes lessons from local tandoor masters and spice experts. 800-961-9239, www.worldsofflavor.com

Also see "Kids' Cooking Schools" on page 359 and "Spa Culinary Classes" on page 376.

Chocolate Vacations

For some, chocolate supersedes all other forms of entertainment. Why waste time on museums and monuments when you can surround yourself with chocolate, chocolate, and more chocolate?

If chocolate is your sole reason for traveling, try an intensive chocolate-making course at **Cuisine et Tradition School of Provençale Cuisine** in Arles, France. This 3-day private workshop is taught by maître-pâtissier Guy LeBlanc and includes hands-on chocolate-making classes and visits to other chocolate stores for "research," as well as tours to the local market and vineyards. Rates start at about $2,000. 33-0-4-90-49-69-20, www.cuisineprovencale.com

JS Bonbons is an intimate boutique in Toronto where you can learn to create unusual chocolate flavors like lemon, thyme, coriander, lime, lavender, Earl Grey tea, and rosemary. A more intensive 3-day workshop covers chocolate-tempering techniques, how to create special effects and textures with chocolate, and how to draft a showpiece design. The advanced workshop costs about $735. 416-920-0274, www.jsbonbons.com

K̆ Chocolatier in Beverly Hills has long attracted fans like Jackie Kennedy, Katharine Hepburn, Andy Warhol, Henry Ford, and Walter Cronkite. While the owners do not disclose their five-generation-old Hungarian recipes from Tom's great-grandfather (chocolate maker to Emperor Franz Joseph of Austro-Hungary), they do teach practical, do-it-at-home techniques. For $105 to $110, you will learn how to artistically dip fruit into chocolate and how to use chocolate molds. Best of all? You can bring your own wine to pair with the fruits of your labor. 310-248-2626, www.dianekronchocolates.com

According to a study by Forbes and Zagat, one of the most expensive restaurants in the world is Aragawa in Tokyo, which costs about $277 a person and is considered to be the best place in the city for Kobe beef.

InTrend International Travel specializes in 7-day chocolate tours through Belgium. Not for the fainthearted, these tours include chocolate-making demonstrations, gourmet chocolate desserts, and gift boxes. Sure, there's sightseeing and concerts, but that's all optional. 845-510-9630, www.intrend.com

"Living the sweet life in Paris" is the motto of **David Lebovitz**'s Chocolate Walks and Chocolate Exploration Tours. Spend a week on VIP tours of Parisian chocolate shops, indulge in private tastings, and join a hands-on chocolate-making demonstration. Your culinary experience isn't limited to just bonbons—don't forget to taste *pain au chocolat,* buttery caramels, and, when you need a break, a bite of a madeleine. Starting at $3,876. www.davidlebovitz.com/tours.html

Chocolate connoisseurs can discover Melbourne's secret stash of petits fours, hot chocolate, ice cream, and truffles with **Chocoholic Tours.** You can choose from among several options, including the Chocolate Indulgence Walk and the Chocolate and Historical Treats Afternoon Walk. 03-9686-4655, www.chocoholictours.com.au

You can't travel to Perugia without tasting the famous chocolate. A factory tour of **Stabilimento Nestlé** in San Sisto will spoil you for life with free samples of Perugina Baci (those chocolate kisses in blue-starred silver wrappers). 075-527-66-35

Off-the-Beaten-Path Wine Regions

Mention the idea of wine travel, and most people harbor images of sun-kissed Napa Valley vines, the rolling fields of Bordeaux, or the sprawling vineyards of Tuscany. All of these are spectacular ways to experience wine culture, but if you want to beat the crowds, you can easily travel to some lesser-known wine regions of the world.

Our colder northern neighbor seems an odd place to find a good glass of wine, but **Canada** has turned what it knows well—freezing temperatures—into renowned ice wines. These dessert wines are made from frozen grapes left on the vine well into winter, which are handpicked and pressed in the extreme cold. For more information about wine tours around Ontario,

Niagara, and the Okanogan Valley, visit www.winesofontario.org.

In **Hungary,** the climate is surprisingly supportive of both red and white varietals. The industry was neglected during the Communist regime, but over the past 10 years or so, Hungary has been working to make a name for itself in the wine community—some are familiar flavors like pinot gris and muscat, while others are more foreign, like Kadarka, a traditional Balkan red. www.winesofhungary.com

Traditionally, in **Israel,** Israeli wine—synonymous with kosher wine—has had a poor reputation. For a wine to be kosher, according to more conservative and observant Jews, the grapes may never be handled by anyone but a Jew, the wine can't be made by anyone who isn't Jewish, and the wine has to be boiled, which affects the flavor. However, kosher wine can now be zapped with a laser, which brings it to a boil for a nanosecond, thus preserving the flavor of the wine. *Le chaim!*

Legend has it that Dionysus himself brought grapes to **Croatia** from ancient Greece across the Adriatic; the zinfandel grape, long thought to be native to the Americas, was actually brought over from Croatia. During the winter months, vines are routinely blessed so that they will produce a fruitful spring. The two wine regions of Croatia, the coastal and the continental, produce a wide variety of both white and red wines. www.mycroatia.co.uk

Domestic Wines

Did you know that wine is produced in all 50 states in this country? But you need to put that fact into proper perspective. **California** produces 90 percent of the wine, followed by Washington and New York, which together produce about 8 percent. So, basically, the remaining 47 states combined produce only about 2 percent of the total.

Still, there is at least one winery in every state. The number of US wineries increased by over 500 percent to more than 4,000 in the past 30 years.

Washington State, the second largest wine producer in the country, has more than 450 wineries in nine regions. Washington is also known for having a significant number of women-owned wineries, a rarity in the industry. www.washingtonwine.org

New York State is another top wine producer. It has several wine-making regions, including Erie and Niagara, the Finger Lakes region, Hudson Valley, and Long Island. Get a taste of everything at the Finger Lakes Wine Festival (www.flwinefest.com) and find the popular wine trails throughout the region (www.newyorkwines.org).

Oregon's 40-year wine industry has grown rapidly over the past few years, from 47 wineries in 1986 to more than 300 today. The state produces 72 grape varieties, particularly in the Willamette Valley that stretches from Portland to Eugene. www.oregonwine.org

In 30 years, **Virginia** has grown from having six wineries to more than 100 throughout the state, offering both red and white varieties, as well as wines made from other fruits like blackberries, raspberries, and blueberries. www.virginiawines.org

The Lone Star state is full of surprises when it comes to wine. The **Texas** wine industry has grown from 54 wineries to 85 within 2 years, ranging from the Hill Country to the Gulf Coast. www.texaswine.com

Wine-Making Vacations

If you've had enough of trekking from one wine-tasting room to the next, maybe it's time to try getting your hands (or in some cases, your feet) wet with the art of wine making.

Wine making is seasonal, so these experiences generally take place in the fall (for harvesting) or spring (for bottling). As to how involved your wine making will be, it depends on the winery; some may welcome you for both seasons, while others focus on the grape picking and crushing or on the blending and bottling processes.

Michigan's wine industry has been booming over the past decade or so. In fact, a 2005 study showed that the amount of Michigan wine sold locally rose 84 percent over the previous 8 years, while the number of wineries in the state grew from 17 in 1995 to 50 today. The **Round Barn Winery, Distillery & Brewery** is a family-owned and -operated business where you can pick your own grapes, taste various wines, and determine what style and flavor you prefer. Return in the spring to taste your aged wine and take home two cases of your very own label. 800-716-9463, www.roundbarnwinery.com

In France, you can make your own barrel of Bordeaux in a weeklong wine-making course at **Château du Seuil.** Pick your own grapes, learn the process of fermentation, conduct lots of market research in local wineries, and sample the grape juice fermenting in the wine cave. After 2 years, you'll get an entire barrel of Bordeaux—that's 300 bottles(!) bottled and labeled with your name. 650-464-9408, www.winevillas.com

Long Island's North Fork wine region is one of the better-kept secrets of the East Coast wine industry, as it's usually overshadowed by upstate New York's Finger Lakes region or Virginia's wine country. But North Fork's climate is actually comparable to Bordeaux, often producing lighter, less acidic wines than those found in California. **Long Island Wine Camp** is a 4-day wine event with nine wineries in the area—you can experience grape harvesting, grafting and planting vines, fermentation, and blending and/or bottling. At the end of your visit, you go home with a case of local wine. 631-495-9744, www. winecamp.org

If you've got the money to spend, a super-VIP wine tour may be the way to go. At **Amici Cellars** in Napa Valley, you can spend $32,000 and come home with your own barrel of wine! That's right, we're talking about 288 bottles that retail at $89 per bottle. When you arrive at the exclusive winery, you get to live in the lap of luxury with wine tastings, gourmet meals, cheese sampling, and spa visits . . . but you can also get your hands dirty by picking grapes in the field and participating in the fermentation process firsthand. You'll get instant gratification with two bottles of Amici Cellars cabernet sauvignon to bring home immediately, and then in 18 to 24 months, you'll get your specially labeled and bottled wines sent to your home. 707-967-9560, www.amicicellars.com

Every fall, **Olympic Cellars Winery** in Washington State hosts an annual grape-stomping contest to "Stomp Out Child Abuse." Included are grape tossing and a harvest costume competition. 360-452-0160, www.olympic-cellars.com/eventsroot/grapestomp

> If you thought your grocery bill was high, you probably haven't ordered a $125 burger—a DB Burger Royale—at DB Bistro Moderne in New York. The burger is stuffed with foie gras and black truffles. At Brûlée in Atlantic City, you can get a $1,000 brownie—the French chocolate is flavored with two forms of Italian hazelnuts, finished with edible gold dust, and served with 1996 Quinta do Noval, a vintage port that is misted on your tongue to maximize the sensation of port and chocolate together. The $750 crystal atomizer is yours to keep.

Sonoma Harvest Fair features a grape-stomping contest, as well as the Great American Pumpkin Toss, scarecrow-building contests, and the classic grape-spitting contest. 707-545-4200, www.harvestfair.org

Each September, Arkansas celebrates its Swiss wine-making heritage in its annual **Wiederkehr Village Weinfest**. Along with its championship grape stomp, you can also join a conga line through the wine cellars, a German-English singalong, polka lessons, and free wine-tasting tours. 800-622-9463, www. wiederkehrwines.com/fest.html

Tea Plantation Tours

Did you know that it takes about 5 pounds of fresh tea leaves to make 1 pound of tea (about 200 cups' worth), and about 35 billion pounds of leaves are harvested in a year, almost all by hand? Tea plantations can be found in 35 different countries, usually in areas with tropical or subtropical climates and high altitudes, which can translate into a prime vacation spot if you go at the right time. India is the largest tea exporter in the world, followed by Sri Lanka, China, and Kenya.

The famous Darjeeling tea comes from a region of the same name, located at the bottom of the Himalayas in India. **Goomtree Tea Resort** invites visitors to stay in its four-bedroom Heritage Bungalow for a private tea experience. Your stay includes a tour of the tea garden and factory, where you can watch workers pick leaves (harvesting takes place between March and November) and learn about the multistep process of making raw leaves into consumable tea. www.darjeelingteas.com

Located about 4,000 feet above sea level in the Bogawantalawa Valley of central Sri Lanka, **Ceylon Tea Trails** offers guided tours of a tea estate and factory, four-course dinners, personal butler service, and, of course, morning and afternoon tea. www.teatrails.com

Illinois-based **The Tea House** hosts a packaged tour through China, visiting various factories and teahouses in the region. Highlights include the Lao She Tea House in Beijing, samples of "butter tea" in Tibet, and a visit to the Tea Research Institute in the Wuui Mountains. 630-961-0877, www.theteahouse.com/tourpage.htm

Not planning to travel abroad right away? The **Bigelow Tea** plantation on Wadmalaw Island in South Carolina is the only tea garden in the country. The 127-acre plantation holds hundreds of thousands of tea bushes, plus a new factory that has a 125-foot-long window gallery so you can see how tea is made. www.bigelowtea.com/act

Coffee Tours

Feed your addiction and go straight to the source on a coffee tour. As with wine tours, the experience can be as simple as wandering through a plantation and tasting varieties of brew or as involved as high-end educational experiences where you really learn the history and process of coffee making.

Hawaii's world-famous Kona coffee has broken many a budget. You can get up close to this favorite bean on a tour of **Kona Lea Plantation.** The family-owned, certified-organic estate has free daily tours of the plantation, on-site roasting facilities, and a tasting room to round out the experience. 808-322-9937, www.konalea.com

If you can't get enough, the **Kona Coffee Living History Farm** is a 7-acre spread on the Big Island, where you tour the coffee orchards, the farmhouse, a Japanese bathhouse, a coffee-processing mill, and drying platforms before getting your cup of Kona coffee. 808-323-2006, www.konahistorical.org

On a **Café Britt** coffee tour, you can experience coffee from the plantation to your cup. A tour in Heredia, Costa Rica, takes you through an organic coffee plantation and nursery, where the seed is fermented and dried, and a roasting factory, where the bean is brewed before your eyes. Also included are a lesson on the history of coffee and, naturally, a taste-testing session. Day tours begin at $47. 800-462-7488, www.cafebritt.com

Here's your chance to learn all about yet another world-famous brew, Jamaica's Blue Mountain Coffee. The aptly named **Blue Mountain Tours** start you out by driving to the highest point that you can reach by vehicle, called Hardware Gap. There, you'll embark on the longest downhill bicycle tour. You'll be surrounded by rain forest and coffee plantations, where you'll see a demonstration of how coffee is processed and sample a cup during an outdoor brunch. Rates start at $78. 876-974-7075, www.bmtoursja.com

▽ Resources

When you're traveling in a new city, you don't want to waste any time dining on sub-par food. Here are a few resources to help you find what you want to eat, anytime and anyplace.

FOOD DELIVERY SERVICE

Road warriors know that dining out in restaurants every night can get tiresome, and room service can be a pricey option. This is where food delivery services have stepped in, bringing prepared meals to your home, hotel, or extended-stay accommodations.

Dine Wise, 800-749-1170, www.dinewise.com: The company delivers frozen cooked meals to your door for you to microwave in about 10 minutes. Meal plans start at $199 for 13 to 21 meals per package, with different combinations of main courses, sides, and desserts.

Family Chef, 888-612-9264, www.familychef.com: You can order 6, 10, or 12 "meal packs," each serving two people, as well as options for "mega meals" with cake included. Prices start at $139.

Zone Delivery USA, 866-343-8321, www.zonedeliveryusa.com: You can get 3 days' worth of meals anywhere in the country for $99.99 plus shipping. Meals arrive in a thermal shipping box and can remain fresh for several days if refrigerated. All meals follow the Zone diet's 40–30–30 ratio of carbohydrates, proteins, and fat.

REVIEWS AND LISTINGS

Chowhound.com: Here's a community message board for foodies to share their dining experiences, plus feature articles and recipes.

Citysearch.com: This is considered to be one of the most dependable resources of bar and restaurant listings, reviews, and recommendations in more than 40 US cities as well as locations in Canada, Australia, and Sweden.

If you're in New York, you can text **GONYC (46692)** to have local restaurant and bar information sent to your cell phone from *New York* magazine. Text "food," the type of cuisine, and the zip code, neighborhood, or borough. You also text **GOOGL (46645)** for a listing of restaurants and bars nearby. Just text the city or zip code and the type of cuisine or the name of a restaurant to locate it. Here's a handy tip: With this SMS service, you can find out any information you'd get through Google online. Try texting "Driving directions Los Angeles to San Diego" or "translate dog in French" (*chien*) or "height of Mount Everest" (8,850 meters).

RESTAURANT RESERVATIONS

Reserving tables online is steadily becoming more popular. On average, 78 percent of Americans still call the restaurant; however, 8 percent are now using the Internet.

Cuisinenet.co.uk: You can make reservations and take-out and delivery orders throughout the United Kingdom.

Eat2eat.com: Check out restaurant reviews and reservations throughout Asia Pacific.

Menupages.com: Find thousands of menus for restaurants in Manhattan, San Francisco, Los Angeles, Philadelphia, Boston, Chicago, and Washington, DC.

Opentable.com: You can book your restaurant reservations online in 46 US states, as well as in Puerto Rico, the Virgin Islands, Canada, Hong Kong, Japan, Mexico, Singapore, and the United Kingdom.

Restaurantrow.com: Make reservations and get take-out and delivery orders in 170,000 restaurants, covering more than 13,000 cities and towns worldwide.

Toptable.co.uk: Make restaurant reservations throughout the United Kingdom.

DIETARY NEEDS

Vegetarian, vegan, and kosher diners can have a difficult time finding restaurants that are diet friendly. Check out the following resources for restaurants in the United States and abroad.

Happycow.com: This is a guide to raw-food restaurants, with more than 6,000 listings in 96 countries.

Kashrut.com/travel: You can find more than 2,500 listings for kosher restaurants in over 50 countries.

Vegdining.com: Find a worldwide guide to vegetarian restaurants, with more than 1,000 listings and 2,000 reviews.

Vegsource.com/travel: Message board users offer advice and tips on vegetarian restaurants worldwide.

Vegtravel.com: This online travel agency specializes in packages for vegetarian/vegan/eco travelers.

CHAPTER 30

Volunteer Vacations

❝ Be the change you want to see in the world. ❞

—MAHATMA GANDI

It is, perhaps, the fastest-growing segment in the US travel industry—trips with a purpose, or volunteer vacations. More and more of us are looking to travel in different ways that benefit not just us but others. And more and more of us are looking to do this—where possible—in a multigenerational approach: involving our families.

A 2006 study by the Travel Industry Association confirmed the trend: 24 percent of travelers said they were currently interested in taking a volunteer or service-based vacation. More than 1 in 10 travelers (11 percent) said they were more interested now compared with 5 years ago in taking a volunteer or service-based vacation. Interest was especially strong among baby boomers, with the largest share (47 percent) of those falling into the 35- to 54-year-old age range.

You may have heard the terms "voluntourism" and "volunteer vacations" being used interchangeably. In the aftermath of Hurricane Katrina, the concepts became even more popular. While they're similar, voluntourism involves lending a helping hand on your travels, which can be anything from spending a few hours out of a week assisting with disaster relief to dedicating your entire trip to working in a local clinic. But the idea behind voluntourism is that you don't have to donate your *entire* time to the cause—leaving time for additional activities that will help you immerse yourself in the culture, visit sites, or simply spend time with the locals in a social capacity. After Hurricane Katrina, volunteers were actively encouraged to go out on the town after volunteering, to help stimulate the economy.

An increasing number of organizations are also widening their programs to attract regular travelers who want to help and give back. That often means shorter, 1- or 2-week stints, which fit into your work schedule. There are also more family volunteer vacation opportunities—many organizations allow children as young as age 3 so that families can work together and share the experience (do your research first, though, as minimum ages vary).

When researching the type of trip that appeals to you, remember that several of these projects take place in remote locations in developing regions, which means that your surroundings may be very rustic and basic. Ask lots of questions beforehand, like what kind of accommodations to expect, whether there is hot running water, what kind of food will be provided, and what kind of transportation is available nearby. Also check with the State Department to determine if there's any activity in the area that you should be aware of. If your vacation plans don't include traveling a long distance, no problem—with so many options to choose from, you'll probably be able to find an opportunity in your own backyard.

▽ Resources

Idealist.org is a good place to start your research, as it offers a comprehensive list of global volunteer opportunities posted by various nonprofit organizations and communities.

Givespot.com provides links for projects around the world, including trips for teens and kids. The site also has a charity evaluation function, which gives ratings from the Better Business Bureau, access to nonprofits' tax forms, and criteria from the American Institute of Philanthropy.

Charityguide.org/volunteer/vacations.htm offers information on volunteer projects around the world, as well as some paid positions and additional tips on how to make a difference in the world.

Ciee.org (Council on International Educational Exchange) lists dozens of International Volunteer Projects for college-aged people throughout the world. Projects, which range from serving as an assistant at a summer camp for people with disabilities to helping to restore a medieval castle, are typically scheduled for the summer months and last 2 to 4 weeks.

Volunteer.cheaptickets.com is a Cheaptickets.com Web page that helps travelers find volunteer opportunities in the United States and shares blogs written by volunteers.

Volunteermatch.org can pair you up with a project that suits your interests, schedule, and location if you're not sure what you want to do.

Volunteer Vacation Organizations

Airline Ambassadors International (AAI) is an amazingly effective nonprofit organization that is affiliated with the United Nations. This network started with a few dozen airline employees—such as flight attendants, pilots, and others in the travel industry—volunteering as Ambassadors of Goodwill both domestically and internationally. (The membership now totals in the thousands and is open to all.) And, in the interest of full disclosure, I also serve on AAI's board of directors. At least eight times a month, AAI runs missions to orphanages around the world. And in times of immediate need—a tsunami in Asia or Hurricane Katrina in the Gulf—AAI is on the ground, often within hours, to provide aid, equipment, and supplies. The way it works is that Airline Ambassadors partners with nongovernmental organizations, schools, churches, and other institutions, and members use their position in the travel industry to make a difference. Regular travelers pay a nominal donation fee, cover their own airfare and hotels (usually discounted), and get hands-on experience around the world. Projects include escorting children into the United States for medical treatment, constructing medical clinics in developing nations, and traveling to orphanages to work with kids and provide assistance. Airline Ambassadors has also teamed up with UNICEF and American Airlines to relaunch the Change for Good Program, which collects money from American Airlines international flights to support children worldwide. 650-728-7844, www.airlineamb.org

  Earthwatch Institute organizes volunteer expeditions to mine data in rain forest ecology, wildlife conservation, marine science, archaeology, and more.

In north-central Namibia, where the world's largest remaining cheetah population exists, you can work on a farm at the headquarters of the Cheetah Conservation Fund, which involves participating in wildlife surveys, feeding and caring for captive cheetahs, and collecting biodata samples to assess the health of wild cheetahs. Dolphin lovers can head to the Alboran Sea near Spain. Participants travel on board a historic Norwegian fishing vessel to observe common dolphins, filming their underwater behavior, helping with photo identification, and tracking their movements over an extended period. Earthwatch projects are usually 10 to 14 days long, but there are also 1-week, 3-week, and weekend opportunities, plus programs geared toward families and teenagers. Program rates vary between $2,000 and $3,500. 800-776-0188, www.earthwatch.org

GlobeAware offers 1-week volunteer vacations in Costa Rica, Cuba, Brazil, Peru, Nepal, Thailand, Cambodia, Laos, and Vietnam, with the goal of developing cultural awareness and sustainability. The programs include both volunteer projects and cultural immersion activities, such as visiting a hospital clinic, horseback riding through the jungle, and sharing meals with local families. A trip to a remote village in Peru allows volunteers to work with local children to teach them English and computer skills, as well as coordinate community building and repair projects. A program in Siem Reap, Cambodia, brings together volunteers to assemble wheelchairs from recycled parts, to assist those who have been injured or maimed by land mines. Rates are about $1,200 to $1,300 for a weeklong program, plus a $325 registration fee. 877-588-4562, www.globeaware.org

Cross Cultural Solutions has programs that run from 1 to 12 weeks. There are English teaching programs in multiple countries, including Brazil, Costa Rica, India, Tanzania, and Thailand. Treatment services for children living with HIV/AIDS can involve supporting medical professionals, assisting in-home nurses, or managing training seminars in Brazil, Costa Rica, South Africa, and Tanzania. Women's empowerment programs involve running support groups, teaching basic English, and assisting with small local businesses. Volunteer experiences also include cultural activities, which may involve a regional culinary class or visits to historic heritage sites. Teen programs and internships are also available. Program rates range from $1,595 for 1 week to $5,206 for 12 weeks. 800-380-4777, www.crossculturalsolutions.org

Amizade has partnerships with 13 sites in 11 countries, including the United States, Brazil, India, and Tanzania. In Germany, volunteers can work on the grounds of the Auschwitz Museum and participate in preservation, documentation, and archive projects. Volunteers to the Karagwe area of Tanzania stay in a remote mountain town and work with one of three community-based organizations, including a local hospital, a family alliance program that helps empower local community members, and a women's organization that helps local women through legal support and training programs. US-based programs include tutoring students on a Navajo reservation and working with the homeless in Washington, DC. Program rates range from $610 to $1,810. 888-973-4443, www.amizade.org

Global Citizens Network sponsors teams of volunteers to work in developing communities where rural people are involved in grassroots efforts. Participating nations include Ecuador, Guatemala, Kenya, Nepal, Peru, Tanzania, and Thailand, as well as several locations in North America. 800-644-9292, www.globalcitizens.org

I-to-I creates programs for travelers ages 16 and older, sending more than 5,000 people each year to volunteer vacations. With more than 500 projects in 30 different countries, chance are you'll find a suitable trip. You can teach English in a rural village in Mexico or in the cosmopolitan city of Buenos Aires. Community work in Mombasa, Africa, may involve play, teaching, and counseling local children, as well as maintenance of the community center. Animal rescue work in India may deal with rounding up and caring for stray dogs, coordinating adoption programs, or assisting in public awareness programs. Most stays are a minimum of 3 weeks, starting at $1,745. 800-985-4852, www.i-to-i.com

Foundation for Sustainable Development (FSD) holds internship programs that center on educating people about economic problems around the world, particularly in developing countries. Interns may include students and professionals, and internships last 6 to 10 weeks and take place in the summer months (the foundation has short-term volunteer programs, as well). You can be a citizen of any country and must be at least 18 years old to participate. FSD has programs available in Bolivia, Ecuador, Nicaragua, Peru, Tanzania, and Uganda. All FSD interns receive a $200 mini-grant toward a project. The Pilot Project of Childcare Center in Pro Mujer Masaya, for example, focuses on promoting the positive development of women. The project also focuses on health and community development; FSD provides a grant of $670. 415-283-4873, www.fsdinternational.org

USA Freedom Corps (USAFC) was created after September 11 to promote and expand volunteer service in America as a way of honoring those who have sacrificed their lives for America's freedom. USAFC partners with national service programs around the country such as the Peace Corps and the Corporation for National and Community Service, and it focuses on building a culture of service, citizenship, and responsibility. USAFC connects volunteers with appropriate programs so that they may maximize their potential to help restore America's sovereignty in the world. 877-872-2677, www.usafreedomcorps.gov

Mobility International USA (MIUSA) is a group based in Eugene, Oregon, that focuses on making international volunteer vacations possible for those who are physically challenged. MIUSA offers intern, volunteer, and exchange programs, all intended to empower the disabled. Full scholarships are available. Past programs have included a US-Japan Cross-Cultural Perspectives on Disability Exchange Program in Tokyo, in which 12 young adults attended cultural events and workshops on education and disability laws. Another past program was the Women's Institute on Leadership and Disability held in Oregon, in which women leaders with disabilities came together to build networks of support for other disabled women. 541-343-1284, www.miusa.org

Global Volunteers sponsors programs designed to further develop communities in need. Volunteers can participate for 1, 2, or 3 weeks. Global Volunteers also offers an extended 40-week program. Projects are available in 19 countries worldwide, including Peru, Poland, Romania, Brazil, and China. You can care for orphaned and abandoned children in India for $1,995 (for a 2 -week program) or $2,095 (for 3 weeks). Volunteer here in America for $795 for a 1-week program. You can help to restore the communities and people of the Mississippi Delta or volunteer for labor and education projects. Discounts are available for students and returning volunteers. 800-487-1074, www.globalvolunteers.org

Volunteers for Peace (VFP) is a nonprofit membership organization that promotes international voluntary service projects, the premise of which is to exchange volunteers worldwide to raise intercultural awareness. VFP offers placement in over 3,400 projects in more than 100 countries annually, including over 40 in the United States. Registration fees include room and board and usually recreational activities. Unless otherwise noted, fees are $250 per project and $500 for volunteers under age 18. You can assist in teaching English in Indonesia for 6 months or help take care of asylum seekers at the Centre for Refugees in Rixensart, Belgium. 802-259-2759, www.vfp.org

Council on International Education Exchange (CIEE) is a nongovernmental international education organization that creates programs allowing students and educators to study and teach abroad. Headquartered in Portland (Maine), Boston, and Tokyo, CIEE administers 95 study-abroad programs in over 33 host countries and has teaching programs in Chile, China, Spain, Thailand, and elsewhere. Educators can participate in 26 summer seminars in 29 countries. Study-abroad programs for college students include semester programs in Gaborone, Botswana. If you have $10,800 for a semester (or $19,800 for a year) and a GPA of over 2.75, you can take part in this program. Students participate in excursions and activities designed to introduce them to the local culture as well as Botswana's rich environmental biodiversity. There are also countless opportunities for students to conduct independent research. Alternatively, there are teach-abroad programs, such as Teach in Thailand. Teachers are placed with either primary or secondary schools, with a typical load of 22 classes per week. 207-553-7600, www.ciee.org

La Sabranenque is a nonprofit organization based in Provence, France, that puts together volunteer restoration programs with an emphasis on the rural Mediterranean. Summer volunteer programs are available from June through September and focus on the preservation and restoration of typical sites. Restoration work takes place in the mornings and occasional afternoons, followed by free time to explore the surrounding area and meet with other participants. Such free visits are organized to take place at least one day during each 2-week session. For example, you can spend a weekend surveying the markets of Uzès or see the Pont du Gard, a Roman aqueduct that crosses the Gardon River. In April, May, and October, you can participate in Volunteer and Visit, Hike, Discover programs, consisting of 1-week sessions that combine restoration work (in the mornings) with afternoon outings three times a week. Some examples of the type of work needed for restoration projects include clearing of rubble, roof tiling, stone cutting, plastering, and path paving. www.sabranenque.com

Habitat for Humanity is a nonprofit, ecumenical Christian housing ministry whose purpose is to eliminate poverty and homelessness throughout the world. Although Habitat is operated through volunteer work and donations for materials, houses are not "given away"—the new homeowners spend much of their own time contributing work on their homes as well as on the homes of others. Habitat has several volunteer programs from which you can choose, including Global Village Programs, Disaster Response Programs, and programs specifically made for youths or women. Some places in which Global Programs take place are Russia, Armenia, Thailand, and Jordan. These programs typically take place over 9 to 14 days and allow volunteers to work alongside members of another culture in restoring communities. Programs range from $1,000 to $2,200. Habitat's Summer Youth Blitz Program gathers youths ages 16 to 18 from high schools and organizations around the United States to work on a Habitat house for 2 weeks, starting at $500. 229-924-6935, www.habitat.org

Ambassadors for Children is a nonprofit organization that provides hands-on interaction for children in need around the world. Volunteers can help the children by assisting in construction projects, delivering and distributing school supplies, supervising activities, and teaching English. Volunteers can work in an orphanage in Malawi, work with refugees in Jordan, and work with schoolchildren in Guatemala, along with many other opportunities in India, Serbia, Nepal, El Salvador, Costa Rica, and Kenya. Program rates start at $799 for double occupancy. 866-338-3468, www.ambassadorsforchildren.org

Relief Riders International (RRI) is a humanitarian adventure company that organizes horseback rides throughout developing countries. The program addresses the needs of the local economy—in particular, medical needs, as RRI has an extensive medical program. One typical journey lasts 15 days and takes you to five remote villages around Rajasthan, India. For $6,300, you ride 4 to 6 hours per day for 11 days, while interacting with the local people, distributing supplies, aiding the medical team, or helping to organize the caravan. You'll help struggling economies while taking in the rich culture and wildlife of the land. Space is limited to 12 riders, from beginner to advanced. 413-329-5876, www.reliefridersinternational.com

Why not spend your vacation working beachside in the Caribbean? **Caribbean Volunteer Expedition** runs 1-week programs from November to March to help preserve the region's cultural heritage. Volunteers participate on various islands to reconstruct cemeteries, historic buildings, gardens, and tropical forests, as well as working with museums managing collections. 607-962-7846, www.cvexp.org

Tropical Adventures coordinates volunteer programs in Costa Rica and recently introduced its new Chocolate Factory program. For a minimum of 2 weeks, volunteers live among the Bribi and Cabeca indigenous tribes and work with land cultivation for growing cacao, instruct on the marketing and sales of chocolate, and get involved with actual chocolate production. Average program prices are about $1,000 for 2 weeks, not including airfare. 800-832-9419, www.mytropicaladventure.com

Volunthai brings volunteers to Thailand to teach English in remote areas. Currently, there are 200 schools in rural provinces where volunteers live with a Thai family or in their own home within the community.

The organization is quite small, based on a network of schools with which the operators are personally involved. www.volunthai.com

Friendship Ambassadors Foundation hosts cultural exchange programs throughout the world. It even offered programs in Communist countries back when no other tour groups were doing the same. Besides cultural tours, the foundation also coordinates musical performances to foster cultural exchange and disaster relief. After Hurricane Katrina, the Youth Symphony and a school choir traveled to New Orleans to perform in parks, museums, and public areas to help revitalize the region. 800-526-2908, www.faf.org

Room to Read is a San Francisco–based NGO that is currently building libraries and schools in developing nations in Asia, Africa, and Latin America. Over the course of 7 years, the organization has opened 287 schools and established more than 3,600 libraries and 110 computer and language rooms. The ongoing Students Helping Students initiative involves taking American kids abroad to build schools and raise funds at home. 415-561-3331, www.roomtoread.org

Environmental Aid

Sierra Club is a grassroots environmental organization that is dedicated to conserving nature through education, in particular educational trips. They have over 100 years of wilderness travel experience and offer around 90 service trips a year throughout the United States, Canada, and Puerto Rico. Their Multigenerational Trail Work in Aspen, Colorado, is designed for families (children, parents, and grandparents) to contribute valuable work in the wilderness and to learn more about the importance of protecting open spaces. Most service trips last 1 week; the average price for a trip is $350 to $600, with some trips as low as $255. The trips run throughout the year in a variety of national parks, wildlife refuges, and other wilderness areas, and they offer something for everyone. 415-977-5500, www.sierraclub.org

Appalachian Mountain Club is dedicated to conserving the mountains, rivers, and trails of the Northeast. The club offers worldwide programs for children, teens, and adults that focus on teaching people how to be safe outdoors while maintaining and caring for nature. The Mountain Watch program invites hikers to help collect data out in the wilderness, and trail volunteers can get their hands (really) dirty by helping to maintain and restore trails throughout the United States. 617-523-0655, www.outdoors.org

Lack of funding, staff, and resources makes managing and protecting America's hiking trails difficult. **American Hiking Society** has implemented a program to support trail maintenance and repair. When a federal agency has a trail-building or maintenance project, it can request a Volunteer Vacation Crew. Projects can include installing wildlife viewing platforms, pulling tree stumps, and reconstructing drainages. 800-972-8606, www. americanhiking.org/events/vv

Wildlife refuges are always in need of a helping hand. More often than not, you just need to put on a pair of boots and start working. For example, the **Big Branch Marsh National Wildlife Refuge** in Louisiana has more than 10,000 acres of land, where volunteers can assist with cleaning, trail maintenance, and rebuilding facilities destroyed by Hurricane Katrina. 985-882-2000, www.fws.gov/bigbranchmarsh

Also in Louisiana, the 36,000-acre **Bogue Chitto National Wildlife Refuge** welcomes volunteers of all ages and skill levels to help clean heavily touristed areas. 985-882-2000, www.fws.gov/boguechitto

Vacations with a . . . Porpoise

Volunteering with animals can be a great way to get to know the native wild and marine life while helping to conserve, protect, and monitor endangered and threatened species.

AVIVA is a South Africa–based volunteer organization that provides experiences with protecting and preserving native animals. On the Tamboti Conservation Project, volunteers participate in workshops, biological research, and reserve management dealing with antelopes, mongooses, baboons, zebras, and warthogs. Placements run from 2 to 8 weeks, starting at $1,540. 27-0-21-557-4312, www.aviva-sa.com

Oceanic Society offers research expeditions, conservation efforts, and educational workshops for students in regions such as Costa Rica, Belize, and the Bahamas to study marine life. There are family-specific expeditions, such as Belize Family Week in which parents and children ages 10 and older can work with biologists to study dolphins and manatees and explore the coral reefs by snorkel. In Brazil, volunteers can collect data on the habitats of the endangered giant otters. Program prices range from $1,850 to $3,840. 800-326-7491, www.oceanic-society.org

Cosmic Volunteers has a variety of animal-related programs, including a wildlife hospital in Kenya, animal rescue centers in Ecuador, veterinary clinics in Ghana, and tortoise monitoring projects in the Galapagos Islands. 610-279-2052, www.cosmicvolunteers.org

Centre for Education, Research and Conservation of Primates and Nature operates a Nigerian sanctuary that has rescued more than 120 primates, mostly through donations to an adoption program. Short-term volunteers, who work for 3 months or less, are welcome if they can manage their own accommodations and meals. Skilled longer-term volunteers of 6 months to a year are offered room and board by the organization. 234-0-87-234670, www.cercopan.org

Best Friends Animal Society is a 33,000-acre ranch in the red-rock region of southern Utah. The sanctuary, which is funded entirely by donations, is home to about 1,500 homeless dogs, cats, horses, rabbits, birds, and other animals. The society works with humane groups and individuals to set up neutering programs, foster care, and adoptions. Volunteers are welcome to visit the animals, take them hiking, and even borrow a dog for a sleepover. You can also sponsor an animal for $25 a year or donate necessary equipment. 435-644-2001, www.bestfriends.org

In the Bahamas, **Project Potcake** has become quite a hit. The island's stray dogs, affectionately called "potcakes," are rescued for neutering before being released. Since 1999, the project has managed to reduce the population of strays by 75 percent. Volunteers can come in to walk the dogs, and if you fall in love, you can adopt a potcake to take home with you. www.potcakefoundation.com

Skilled Volunteer Vacations

The beauty of so many volunteer vacations is that they are open and accessible to all types of travelers who are willing to donate their time to help others. But if you've spent years developing your skills in the workplace, chances are there's a place for them as well. Skilled volunteer vacations are a way to utilize your expertise while helping those who are less privileged and really making an impact on the region that you're visiting. Many of the volunteer vacations that involve special skills tend to be longer in minimum length—usually requiring a commitment of at least 4 to 6 weeks. Volunteers who can make the time commitment can also make a lasting impression.

International Executive Service Corps (IESC) works with volunteers who have some sort of professional expertise to lend to developing nations. For example,

IESC was widely credited with creating or saving almost 10,000 jobs in Jordan, in addition to helping improve the business climate. Positions tend to be longer term than other volunteer vacations and cover more than 130 countries. IESC works with a "skill bank" of more than 8,500 volunteer experts and professional consultants, helping developing nations to grow through local technical and managerial assistance, training programs, workshops, seminars, and grants. There is no cost to volunteer through IESC, but you must apply to join the skill bank. 202-589-2600, www.iesc.org

Medical professionals of all types are especially welcome on **Mercy Ships,** though nonmedical professionals can help, too. Mercy Ships are essentially what they sound like—floating social services. While they began as ship hospitals traveling from port to war-torn port, this innovative program is presently expanding. For example, one of the Mercy Ships recently docked in the war-torn African nation of Liberia. The medical staff immediately began treating the many victims of the long civil wars (and general lack of medical care) in the capital city port of Monrovia. This ship, however, provides not only doctors but also engineers, technicians, and deck hands, who are helping European Union aid workers train and assist the understaffed workers at the White Plains water treatment plant. New pumps have been installed and existing ones upgraded to ensure a steadier flow of water to the capital. So whether your skills include helping build a water grid or saving lives, Mercy Ships could use your help. 903-939-7000, www.mercyships.org

Medical professionals might also try **Health Volunteers Overseas,** which focuses exclusively on putting these sorts of skills to use. Most HVO programs involve training local medical technicians, pharmacists, nurses, and even doctors in new techniques, but a variety of opportunities are available. 202-296-0928, www.hvousa.org

United Nations Volunteers, works with more than 7,000 volunteers each year, both domestically and internationally. Volunteers come from a database of more than 50,000 skilled professionals, primarily working to assist with businesses. Volunteers work through funded UN agencies worldwide in developing countries within Asia, Central Europe, Eastern Europe, the Middle East, and the Americas. 49-228-815-2000, www.unv.org

Do you dream in C++? Haunt Wikipedia? The tech-savvy can put their skills to use at **Geekcorps.** Harnessing the power of the nerd, high-tech workers geeking-out together can do things like wiring remote broadcast outlets in the Sahara to give them Internet access. Dozens of volunteers have descended on Mali to put the country's 14 radio stations online. For IT workers used to water-cooler chitchat, stringing cable up makeshift radio towers on the sands of Timbuktu could be the adventure of a lifetime. An outgrowth of the IESC, Geekcorps can help make it happen. 202-326-0280, www.geekcorps.org

South African White Shark Research Institute focuses on doing scientific research on the shark. Some duties include tissue sampling for genetic analysis, observing individual behavior, and interacting with tourists. This opportunity is located in Gansbaai, South Africa, which is near Dyer Island. This 14-day vacation accepts all applicants but is preferential to marine biology students and those who are interested in careers having to do with marine biology. The cost is $1,500 and includes room and board, all lectures, and transportation to and from the Cape Town airport. 27-21-552-9794, www.whiteshark.co.za

Disaster Relief

The aftermath of Hurricane Katrina showed many travelers a new way to spend their vacation, and made "voluntourism" a household term. Lending a hand after a major disaster brings people together in a way that no traditional sightseeing or adventure vacation does and can make a tangible difference to a struggling community. While Hurricane Katrina may have inspired Americans to donate their time to help others, disaster relief is sadly needed all too frequently in countries worldwide. Here are some resources to help you get started.

American Red Cross has at least 30 types of volunteer opportunities that help the organization respond to crisis and disaster relief in various parts of the world. Clerical work can include placing volunteers, organizing orientation courses, and distributing safety materials. Field work can include working in homeless shelters, interacting with youth groups, and leading blood drives. 800-733-2767, www.redcross.org

Hands On USA is the US-based affiliate of Hands On Worldwide, a nonprofit organization that is dedicated to providing disaster response and relief. Projects may include distributing supplies to a community in need, providing support in overcrowded medical clinics, removing debris, and finding shelters for displaced animals. Hands On volunteers played a huge role in post-Katrina relief. 228-257-6094, www.handsonusa.org

Salvation Army leads disaster-relief programs worldwide—in 2006, the organizations served more than 20,000 meals after the hurricanes that devastated the town of Greensburg, Kansas, and more than 2,000 meals after wildfires raged in Florida. Internationally, the Salvation Army World Services Organization aided with tsunami reconstruction as well as several other community and human rights projects. 703-684-5500, www.salvationarmyusa.org

CHAPTER 31

❝ You must learn day by day, year by year, to broaden your horizon. The more things you love, the more you are interested in, the more you enjoy, the more you are indignant about, the more you have left when anything happens. ❞

—ETHEL BARRYMORE

If you're a traveler with a special interest (and when you think about it, who doesn't have at least one special interest or fantasy when it comes to travel?), welcome to the brave new world of niche travel. In theory, something for everyone. Okay, that's the good news. Now, a caution: Niche, or affinity, travel terms are everywhere and often confusing or misleading. Ecotourism, multigenerational travel, gay and lesbian tourism, women's travel, agritourism, one-armed-fugitive-tourism . . .

So while there seems to be something for just about everyone these days, you still need to figure out a mutually agreeable definition of terms before booking your "affinity" trip or you'll run the very real risk of being sadly disappointed. Also remember that many of these categories are too broad. What does "adventure travel" mean? If you're looking to drive a racecar at

150 miles an hour around a track, should that fit into the same "adventure travel" category as hiking and white-water rafting?

Where does physically active travel cross the line to become thrill-seeking-behavior travel?

So, here's a sampler of available—and fast-evolving—affinity travel opportunities.

Thrill-Seeking Travel

From climbing mountains to jumping off them; from flying a plane to diving into the deep sea, some travelers crave that rush of adrenaline no matter where they go. While you can probably find your thrill-seeking adventure of choice, here are some unusual activities that you can try out during your next travels.

Adventure activity company **Covert Ops** lets you unleash your inner James Bond. During a 3-day program in Tucson, "trainees" take on a mission impossible: learn high-speed evasive driving (on and off the road) while crashing through barricades and running attack vehicles off the road. Green Berets teach you pistol marksmanship as you shoot (don't worry, it's paintball) while on the move. You'll master countersurveillance and espionage techniques as you learn how to communicate in secret and recognize types of explosives and traps. Program rates are $3,795. 800-644-7382, www.covertops.com

All your *Top Gun* fantasies can come true at **Air Combat USA**, one of the first civilian dogfighting schools in the world. Participants learn to fly aerobatic fighter aircraft and challenge one another through six "G-pulling" dogfights. Instructors come from both military and civilian backgrounds and sit alongside you in a SIAI Marchetti aircraft (you get control of the plane about 90 percent of the time). Multiple locations. 800-522-7590, www.aircombat.com

Cape Town, South Africa, helicopter and charter plane company **Civair** offers rides to both thrill seekers and more sedate travelers. You climb aboard a helicopter for an aerial tour of the city or the peninsula or—for a more blood-pumping activity—take an hourlong ride on a fighter jet, starting at $1,110. Want something a little more intense? Civair also has a jet fighter available for a real 1-hour thrill ride. Down to the Cape and back in . . . 8 minutes. And that's just for starters. 27-21-419-5182, www.civair.co.za

Thrill seekers who want to live in the fast lane can practice their turns at the **Mario Andretti Racing School.** Drive a full-sized, Indy-style race car for 3 to 66 laps on the same superspeedways the pros race on, reaching up to 180 miles per hour. True fans can take a ride with Mario Andretti himself in a fantasy package, which includes riding alongside the "driver of the century" around the Lowe's Motor Speedway, or drive 8 laps on your own and bond with Mario after the adrenaline subsides (starting at $1,000). 877-263-7384, www.andrettiracing.com

Bondurant Racing School in Chandler, Georgia, teaches aspiring racers to drive like the pros. Drivers jump into high-octane vehicles like a Corvette, Cadillac CTS, or Pontiac Grand Prix and learn the tricks of street driving or racing on a course. A 2-day high-performance driving course takes you through a slalom and accident-avoidance training and tests your track time on a 1.6-mile road course. A 1-day advanced teenage driving course teaches young students necessary skills like skid control, shifting, and braking techniques. A 3-day Grand Prix road-racing course tests your skills in a Corvette C5, where you'll learn maximum car control on a road course. Rates range from $1,175 to $5,475. 800-842-7223, www.bondurant.com

Dale Jarrett Racing School challenges you to live at full throttle, using Nextel/Busch series stock cars and race replicas that take you up to speeds of 165 miles per hour. Learn racing techniques like passing, drafting, and something called "dropping the hammer" (you'll have to do it to believe it), all on top NASCAR tracks like the Atlanta Motor Speedway, Kentucky Speedway, Lowe's Motor Speedway, and Talladega Superspeedway. Prices range from $150 for 3 laps to $3,495 for 60 laps. 888-467-1131, www.racingadventure.com

When in Rome . . . drive like the Romans. **Red Travel** has created a VIP Ferrari self-drive tour through Italy, where you can get behind the wheel of a Ferrari F430 Spider F1, Ferrari 612 Scaglietti F1, or Ferrari 599 GTB Fiorano F1. You can drive more than 600 miles through Lazio, Umbria, and Tuscany along the legendary Mille Miglia race route, with sightseeing stops in major cities and smaller towns along the way. Starting at $5,800 for a 4-day tour of Rome and Siena. www.finesthotels.net/ferrari/program2.php

Select Italy also arranges luxury Ferrari tours of Rome and the regions of Tuscany and Umbria—custom designed, of course. You can drive from one winery to the next in Montepulciano, tour the legendary Ferrari museum in Maranello, spend a few days in a 5-star hotel, or zip around Rome like a movie star. Your tour guide will lead the way in an Alfa GTV to help you navigate the secret routes in the Italian countryside. Since each tour is customized, prices vary, but keep in mind that the Ferrari deposit is $20,000! 800-877-1755, www.selectitaly.com

If you've got some money to spend, why not take it all the way to space? **Virgin Galactic**, the world's first spaceline, will shoot you into space on a specially designed spacecraft. From the countdown to release, you'll be pinned back into your seat as you accelerate to almost 2,500 miles per hour (that's three times the speed of sound!). As you reach the edges of the atmosphere, you'll experience ultimate quietness—and zero gravity. And below you is Earth like you've never seen it before. $200,000 starting in 2009. www.virgingalactic.com

Thrill-Seeking "Proposal" Travel

If you're an adrenaline junkie in your travels, you may have the same urges in all areas of life—even your marriage proposal! For those of you seeking more than just the thrill of the moment itself, consider popping the question in one of the following venues. Because whether she says yes or no, it's unlikely that she will ever forget the proposal—or you.

How many people do you know who got engaged while rolling around in a bubble sphere? Located at Mount Brighton in Brighton, Michigan, **Sphere USA** straps you inside a huge 12-foot inflatable ball. Two people can be strapped into the sphere, which has a 3-foot durable cushion of air between you and the ground. You are released to roll down a mountain, where you reach speeds of up to 30 mph as you pop the question (talk fast; it takes about 45 seconds to get down the hill!). Sphere USA also offers something called aqua sphereing: Wearing your bathing suits, you can both slip and slide inside the sphere (unharnessed) with 30 liters of water while rolling down a hill. 248-444-1486, www.sphereusa.com

Go face-to-face with your primal fears by diving alongside great white sharks—and proposing marriage at the same time! **Shark Diver** has packages in Mexico, the Bahamas, and Honduras, with varying levels of intensity, and they will help arrange underwater proposals right next to hungry sharks—with you and your sweetheart in a safety cage, of course. For $2,850, the Isla Guadalupe Shark Fleet Dive Package transports you from San Diego, California, to Isla Guadalupe for a 5-day cage-diving excursion with the great white sharks. Accommodations feature a range of rooms, including private staterooms, and onboard chefs will prepare almost any dish you like. Professional photography is also available for an extra fee. And for those concerned about the ecosystem, 10 percent of the proceeds go back to worldwide shark research. 888-405-3268, www.sharkdiver.com

Propose in outer space, or at least get the sensation that you are doing so. **Incredible Adventures** organizes the intergalactic adventure Zero Gravity and will even help you with proposal arrangements. Begin by boarding a plane at Florida's Kennedy Space Center, which is similar to the center where astronauts prepare for space travel. Fly, float, and flip through the cabin during your "weightless" proposal. For just over $3,000, the first stop is "Mars" for a taste of one-third gravity. Next, travel to the "moon" and experience lunar gravity parabolas. In lunar gravity, you weigh one-sixth of what you weigh on Earth. Finally, you arrive in "outer space." Nothing can prepare you for your first encounter with zero gravity—where you'll be bouncing about the cabin like human popcorn. 941-346-2603, www.incredible-adventures.com

If you want to add more of an "edge" to your proposal, perhaps jumping off a cliff with your heartthrob is the answer. **Over the Edge** offers bungee jumping at different locations in Idaho, which is considered a bungee mecca due to its tall scenic bridges with light traffic. Each bridge is a different height, ranging from 90 to nearly 500 feet. The 90-foot jump costs $30 per person, and the 500-foot costs $100. 208-731-1648, www.overtheedgebungee.com

Ravenchase can customize a treasure hunt through any city's landmarks, countryside, or institutions worldwide, so why not have your future fiancée unknowingly search for her engagement ring using handmade maps, codes, riddles, anagrams, puzzles, actors, gadgets, and more? Whether you are looking for a breathtaking jaunt through the back alleys of Paris or would prefer a hunt in your local neighborhood, Ravenchase can help you create a memorable proposal. Prices for a private proposal hunt begin at $2,000 in the United States and $4,000 internationally. If you'd rather spend your money on the wedding itself, though, you can sign up for a group hunt at just $25 per person. The company will arrange for you and your loved one to have the last three or four clues specially tailored to your secret proposal (sending you away from the group for some privacy)—at no additional cost. 888-588-8862, www.ravenchase.com

If you've ever fantasized about cornering your lover in a cramped airplane bathroom, why not make it a reality? **Mile High Atlanta** takes you and your bride-to-be up to over 5,280 feet above the earth's surface so you have the rare but legal opportunity to join the, uh, "club." The company is located at West Georgia Regional Airport near Carrollton, just a short drive from the Metro Atlanta area. For $299, you can have an hour flight in a Piper Cherokee Six designed exclusively for a romantic experience for you and your lover. For Valentine's Day, the company offers a "romance" flight that includes a bottle of champagne and flowers during a sunset flight. 770-301-9339, www.milehighatlanta.com

Nudist Travel

Hey, there *is* something for everyone, so if you prefer to frolic in your birthday suit, why not seek out destinations that cater to nudist (aka naturalist) travel? The American Association for Nude Recreation reports that nude recreation and travel has grown into a $400 million industry, up from about $120 million in 1992. The association itself grew by 75 percent during the 1990s; today the association has nearly 50,000 individual members and nearly 270 affiliated clubs, resorts, B and Bs, and RV campgrounds. And we're not talking about hidden little pockets of the world—clothing-optional resorts can be found all throughout the Caribbean, Mexico, South America, and other hot destinations, and nudist tour companies frequently charter mainstream cruise lines and resorts for their group trips. For a list of member companies, visit www.aanr.com.

The Austin-based **Bare Necessities** has been arranging nudist tours since 1991, starting with a 36-passenger dive boat and working its way up to a Carnival cruise in 2005 that attracted more than 2,000 passengers (and a whole lot of sunscreen!). The company has also coordinated nude trips aboard the *Star Clipper* on a cruise of the Mediterranean and a Holland America tour of Alaska (winter coats optional), starting at $999. Bare Necessities also works in conjunction with several nudist resorts worldwide, including the all-inclusive SuperClubs in Jamaica and Sorobon Beach Resort in Bonaire. 800-743-0405, www.bare-necessities.com

This one is for the record books: In 2003, the Houston-based **Castaways Travel** organized the first-ever Naked-Air, an all-nude flight from Miami to Cancun heading to Nude Week at the El Dorado and Hidden Beach resorts. The flight was considered a rousing success—fortunately, no hot drinks were served, and the all-important towels were put to use. Castaways also offers an all-nude cruise of the Danube River, on board a luxury Viking River Cruise ship, from $2,200 to $3,000. 800-470-2020, www.castawaystravel.com

All-inclusive resort brand **SuperClubs** runs the popular Hedonism II and Hedonism III resorts in Jamaica, which have nude areas. Even without the nudity, the name says it all. Hedonism resorts are the quintessential "couples" vacations, complete with toga parties, group hot tubs, and all the drinks you can handle. Prices start at $1,750. 877-467-8737, www. superclubs.com

Club Orient has its own property on the island of St. Martin in the Caribbean, where you can choose to drop your top (and everything else). If you haven't played volleyball in the nude, this is the place to start. 800-690-0199, www.cluborient.com

Berkshire Vista in Hancock, Massachusetts, offers naturalists the opportunity to go . . . nude camping. You can strip off your clothes to go hiking or biking, and best of all, no bathing suits are allowed in the pool, hot tubs, and sauna. Starting at $20 a night and up to $650 for full membership. www.berkshirevista.com

If you're planning to vacation in the Midwest, **Turtle Lake Resort** in Michigan is a family-oriented nudist colony, located on a lagoon with its own private beach. Guests can lounge in the nude for swimming, boating, hiking, and even shuffleboard! Starting at $10 a day for "rustic" accommodations and $30 for full-service sites. 866-321-4710, www.turtle-lake.com

Treasure Hunting

One thing I've learned about immersing yourself in a new city is that it doesn't have to involve tour buses or fancy hotels. Sometimes you can travel off the beaten path, right in the heart of the city. In many major urban centers, you can get to know the most unusual parts of town through a citywide treasure hunt. Think of it as your own personal *Amazing Race*: The idea is that you compete against other teams to answer questions, discover landmarks, and navigate the city, making you feel like a local in no time.

San Francisco Treasure Hunts takes place in the unofficial capital of the urban treasure hunt, partly inspired by offbeat Silicon Valley executives who created team-building for their employees. These races are often individually designed; they can be tailored for your family, company, or even your honeymoon. 415-664-3900, www.sftreasurehunt.com

Mr. Treasure Hunt arranges "urban sleuthing" throughout the Bay Area, usually focusing on a particular neighborhood. A San Francisco adventure can cover the neighborhoods of Haight-Ashbury, the Financial District, and Fisherman's Wharf, among others. Or try a Sonoma or Napa "road rally" drive around the area, following a special map that leads you to some interesting locations—including lots of wineries, of course. 415-412-8376, www.mrtreasurehunt.com

Dr. Clue coordinates treasure hunts worldwide. The New York hunts are particularly inventive, taking you through Greenwich Village, Wall Street, and even the Museum of Natural History. If you'd rather travel a little farther, try a treasure hunt in Dubai! You'll have to cover the city by car, but you'll find yourself navigating through everything from an Irish pub to an Egyptian pyramid. 415-861-1314, www.drclue.com

Urban Challenge organizes corporate and private treasure hunts in multiple cities, including New York, Atlanta, Boston, Miami, Cleveland, and Washington, DC. Two-person teams set off on foot or via public transit, finding 12 hidden checkpoints where you take a photograph of yourselves for evidence. 602-308-4868, www.urbanchallenge.com

It's elementary. **Watson Adventures** creates public and private hunts throughout the country. In New York, public hunts include the Grand Central Scramble for Families, where grown-ups and kids can find secret spots and clues throughout the great old station; a Boston-based Murder at the MFA hunt lets participants figure out who murdered a museum curator through a trail of clues connected with works of art; and a Halloween hunt invites families to solve questions while learning the history and legends of old buildings, statues, and graveyards. 877-946-4868, www.watsonadventures.com

For a more DIY option, try something called **geocaching**. This new sport started back in 2000 and combines the traditional treasure hunt with technology—participants hide a "cache," and hunters use online coordinates and GPS trackers to uncover the treasure. A cache can come in many forms, but the first item should always be a logbook, which contains information from the founder of the cache and notes from the cache's visitors. The logbook can contain much valuable, rewarding, and entertaining information. Larger caches may consist of a waterproof bucket containing the logbook and valuable items such as money, jewelry, maps, and books (it's only fair that you leave something behind in return). 206-302-7721, www.geocaching.com

Letterboxing is a lower-tech, less-precise version of geocaching. Using online clues, you find the location, leave your personalized stamp as a mark, and use the cache's stamp to mark your own letterboxing book to prove you've been there. Caches of letterboxing almost always consist of just a book and a personalized rubber stamp, making an affordable and family-friendly adventure. www.letterboxing.org

Genealogy Travel

Those with a bit of Irish in them can discover their roots through Genealogy Tours, where genealogists and historians take you through Ireland. Created by **Time Travel**, the trip includes traditional sightseeing, like a walking tour of Waterford City and visits to abbeys and ancient ruins, accompanied by expert historians to give you the personal details of the region's history and anecdotes. Most importantly, visits to libraries and archives, such as the Ulster American Folk Park and Research Library, give travelers the opportunity to research their heritage firsthand. Prices start at $3,798. 877-787-7807, www.timetraveltours.com/genealogy.html

Select Travel Service creates customized tours for guests to visit their ancestral roots in Europe—from seeking your Scottish clan to discovering your Jewish heritage in Russia. A recent heritage trip to England included a visit to the Office of Public Records in Kew, a lecture at the Society of Genealogists, and a visit to the Family Records Centre in Farrington, which records the births, marriages, and deaths in Britain since 1933. Additional research opportunities are available based on your historical interests. Prices vary, as each trip is customized per person or group. 800-752-6787, www.selecttravel.com

Bridge to Sweden can arrange private tours for Swedish-Americans, focusing on the villages, farms, and homesteads from whence your family hails. This can include general sightseeing tours or be as involved as getting in touch with your Swedish relatives to have dinner in their home, as well as meeting members of the local genealogical and historical societies. 011-46-176-10992, www.bridgetosweden.com

Routes to Roots caters to travelers looking to learn about their Jewish heritage. Miriam Weiner, known as the "first certified Jewish genealogist," has several connections in Eastern Europe to do genealogical research on your behalf, or she can arrange for a customized tour for you to do your own research in Poland, the Ukraine, Moldova, and Belarus—research tools include property and notary records, business directories, and Jewish community records. www.routestoroots.com

What If You Don't . . .

Even adrenaline junkies get bored sometimes. If you're someone who would rather skip the well-worn slopes and avoid the crowded beaches, you can still find your own experience by straying off the beaten path. I look to Las

Vegas as one of the best examples of a destination that has made its living off just one activity but also caters to visitors who just aren't into gambling. Gambling is the city's largest-grossing industry by far (the Strip alone took in $6,031,251,000 in 2005), but Las Vegas is a buzzing hub with hundreds of other activities, reaching out to theater lovers, high-class shoppers, spa addicts, and thrill seekers. So how do some other destinations measure up?

What If You Don't Ski?

Traditionalists might think, Why the heck would I go to a ski resort if I don't ski? There's only so long that you can sit around drinking hot chocolate while your friends are hitting the slopes. Here are some alternative outdoor adventures that let you skip the skis and still hit the mountains.

They say if you build it, they will come. Well, one thing is guaranteed—if you host the Olympics, you'll have to build it. **Salt Lake City** was home to the 2002 Winter Olympic Games, and with it came the construction of Olympic Park. Start with a tour of the facilities, to watch athletes train and test out some of the rides yourself. The Xtreme Zipline is the steepest zipline in the world—it starts you off at 1,100 feet above the ski runs and shoots you down a ski jump hill at up to 60 miles per hour. Little ones who are too small for the Xtreme (under 100 pounds but more than 50 pounds) can try out the Ultra Zipline, which slides you down a winter freestyle hill. Zipline rates are $15 to $22. The Alpine Slide is one of the longest in the world, with more than 3,000 feet of tracks that drop you down 550 vertical feet. And if you're feeling particularly adventurous, take a ride down the Comet, the 80-mile-an-hour bobsled that is the equivalent of a 40-story drop in just under a minute. We're talking 5 Gs of force here. And you thought *skiers* were thrill seekers? Bobsled rides are $200 a person. 435-658-4200, www.olyparks.com

 More Unusual Do Not Disturb Signs

"Shhhh, I am becoming one with my minibar."—*Shutters on the Beach, Santa Monica, California*

"Don't do it." Alternately, housekeepers put up the "Doing it" sign when they're in your room.—*Hotel Gansvoort, New York City*

"Tied up" when you want privacy; "Tidy up" when you don't.—*The Borgata, Atlantic City*

In **Telluride, Colorado,** you can try out something called snow biking. It's almost exactly what it sounds like—except that this bike requires no pedaling. Instead, it sits on two skis, and riders strap snow blades on their feet. You'll start off by riding on green trails and learn how to ride a quad ski lift with the bike. Telluride's Snowbike Adventures offers 2½-hour lessons for $65, and rentals are $30 for the bike and boots. 888-353-5473, www.telluride.com

Also in Telluride are the high-energy **Snowmobile Adventures.** You'll cruise through the snow-covered fields and forests on these self-drive vehicles and get a glimpse of Telluride's mining legacy as you travel the region's old ghost towns. No snow on the ground? No problem. In the summertime, you can hop on a four-wheel-drive vehicle to explore the mountainside. Dave's Mountain Tours snowmobile rates start at $150 per driver for 2 hours. 970-728-9749, www.telluridetours.com

Getting airborne is a no-brainer when you're snowboarding, but you can also fly hundreds of feet in the air in a glider plane. **Telluride Soaring** takes you in a sailplane from the Telluride Airport—at 9,080 feet above sea level, it's already the second-highest commercial airport in the United States and the highest commercial glider operation in the world! These 30- to 60-minute rides take you high over the San Juan Mountains, over the 14,000-foot peaks . . . without an engine so you're in perfect silence. Rates are $110 and $160. 970-209-3497

In **Deer Valley, Utah,** families pretend they're exploring the Yukon with a dogsled ride. This no-age-limit experience takes you through the Wasatch Mountain Range, pulled by a team of Siberian huskies, and starts at $350 per sled for a 35-minute ride. And if the jingling of sleigh bells captures your imagination, Deer Valley also offers real "one horse open sleigh" rides for couples and families starting at $100 for five people. 866-783-5819, www.bouldermountainranch.com

Forget rock climbing as you know it. **Snowbird Ski Resort** in Utah offers half- and full-day ice-climbing tours, in which you'll make your way up a sheet of ice-covered, vertical cliffs using nothing more than ice picks and your toes. It's not a sport for the fainthearted, but once you make it to the top, the spectacular scenery will make it all worthwhile. A half-day course starts at $171. 800-232-9542, www.snowbird.com

Don't forget about ski resorts in the summertime. They are mountains, after all, and with that comes a plethora of outdoor activities that mean you never have to strap on a pair of ski boots. Take a look at **Vail**—sure, it was opened in 1962 with the sole purpose of being a ski destination, with 193 runs on 5,929 acres of skiable terrain. But summertime is the perfect season to find discount hotels (they're about half off winter rates), hiking, mountain biking, and gondola rides. The Adventure Ridge Action Pass is $39 and lets you spend a day on top of the mountain; includes a lift ticket, lunch, three games of laser tag, hiking, and disc golf. Festivals and adventure sports competitions take place all summer long to keep the mountain scene thriving. 888-605-7573, vail.snow.com/summerhome.asp

It's the same deal in **Aspen** and **Snowmass**. The two Colorado towns have four mountains, and the resorts are known for having great family-friendly programming. In the summertime, you can jump into a game of family paintball, stop by Free Movie Night on Fridays, or send the kids off to the Silver Nugget Dig that hails back to Aspen's history as a silver-mining town. More adventurous types can take to the skies on a hot air balloon ride over the Rocky Mountains ($225), take the summer zipline that traverses over 1,000 feet, or ride the Silver Queen Gondola up to the 11,212-foot summit of Aspen Mountain and hike or bike down. 800-308-6935, www. aspensnowmass.com/summer_rec

What If You Don't Hula (or Surf)?

So you're in Hawaii and you'd rather skip the hula lessons. That's not such an unusual problem, but what about those of you who aren't even into lying on the beach? What if you were dragged along by your sun-worshipping significant other or rowdy bachelor friends? Well, as it turns out, beach destinations like Hawaii have plenty of other activities that make it your own trip to paradise.

On Oahu, you can get close to the islanders (not the ones in grass skirts and loincloths) at the weekly **Farmers' Market** at Kapiolani Community College. Hawaiian farmers and ranchers come together to sell fresh produce and flowers; local coffees; plenty of cakes and cookies; lunch plates like stir-fried vegetables, sushi, and grilled sausages; and locally made goods like honeys and jams. 808-848-2074, www.hfbf.org/FarmersMarket.html

If the farmers' market inspires you, go really native and head to **Honolulu Fish Auction** at the United Fishing Agency. While the rest of your group rises early to catch the waves, you can be at the auction by 5:30 a.m. (Monday through Saturday) to see buyers bidding on hundreds of thousands of fish— you'll quickly become familiar with all the local names like mahimahi and opakapaka. 808-536-2148

Also on Oahu, you can join a walking and driving tour of some of the most **haunted places** on the island. According to tour guides, the development of Oahu has desecrated ancient sacred grounds and burial grounds—tours take you through spots of reported supernatural activity, as well as visits to existing sacred areas such as the dwelling places of Hawaiian gods and sites thought to have been built by the island's legendary "little people," the Mehehune. $24. 877-597-7325, www.oahughosttours.com

Agritourism in Hawaii doesn't mean just walking through coffee plantations. On the island of Maui, the **Surfing Goat Dairy** is a 42-acre farm that produces goat cheeses—in fact, it's one of only two goat cheese farms in Hawaii. The Evening Chores and Grand Tour allow guests to feed and milk a goat themselves, see the cheese-making process, and try out some of the 25 different cheeses produced on the farm. $10 to $25. 808-878-2870, www.surfinggoatdairy.com

Forget getting lei'd in the airport. Hawaii is one of the ultimate destinations to catch spectacular natural scenery. To see all the natural beauty of the islands in one place, visit the little-known **Hawaii Tropical Botanical Garden** on the Big Island, a 40-acre valley filled with more than 2,000 species. You've never seen fruit trees, flowers, and tropical plants like these—they can grow to gigantic proportions, with giant bamboo, banana leaves, orchids, jackfruit trees, and huge clusters of flowering palm trees. A three-tiered waterfall is considered one of the most beautiful in the entire state, which is saying quite a lot. 808-964-5233, www.htbg.com

CHAPTER 32

Participatory/ Educational Travel

❝ I didn't really begin to learn anything until after I had finished my studies. ❞

—ANATOLE FRANCE

A recent study by the Travel Industry Association showed that in the past 3 years, more than 30 million adults took a dedicated trip where they learned or improved a skill, sport, or hobby.

The bottom line? More and more Americans are looking toward deeper, more-enriching experiences when they travel. The days of passive travel are over. These days, travelers want to get off the tour bus and get down and dirty when it comes to really exploring a region—whether that means joining an archaeological dig, learning native art, or figuring out how to milk a cow without getting kicked in the head.

Career Vacations
If you've ever had the urge to drop out, move to a remote island, and open your own coconut stand, you may want to try it out—perhaps with just a

little more structure and planning, perhaps even franchising that coconut stand—with something called a "vocation vacation." These experiential holidays allow you to try out a career or learn a skilled craft without having to make that ultimate commitment.

There are literally dozens of career opportunities that you can test-drive on your vacation, thanks to **VocationVacations.** That includes everything from alpaca farming in New York State or being a spa owner in Texas to restoring clocks in Laguna Beach. In Washington State, you can learn how to be a dude rancher at the K-Diamond-K Ranch. At the family-owned and -operated working ranch, you learn how to prepare meals with the chef, organize activities such as hayrides and barbecues, work with the cattle, and assist with sales and marketing. If your interests lean toward the finer things in life, you can study one-on-one with a wine sommelier in Boulder, Colorado, tasting and analyzing wine, pairing wine with meals, and learning the intricacies of wine retail. Programs range from $600 to $900 for 2 to 3 days. 866-888-6329, www.vocationvacations.com

After spending a weekend in a quaint bed-and-breakfast, you may have returned home with dreams and aspirations of running your own little inn. So now you can try . . . B and B boot camp! At the 25-room **Elizabeth Pointe Lodge** on Amelia Island in northeast Florida, you can learn the real "inns and outs" of running a B and B. Of course, no job is as easy as it looks: Boot camp starts you out at 6 a.m. in the kitchen with the baker, then to breakfast service and on to housekeeping. And it's not over at nighttime—that's when you learn all about lodging revenue reporting and operating report processes. A 3-day program is $1,050 (naturally including meals and lodging). 800-500-9625, www.lodgingresources.com

At the **Wedgwood Inn** in New Hope, Pennsylvania, owners Carl and Nadine invite visitors to a learning program to experience all the day-to-day operations of an inn. Each program is tailored to individuals but usually runs between 5 and 10 days. By the last day, you'll be running the inn by yourself. 215-862-2570, www.wedgwoodinn.com

If you're interested in the life of a lighthouse keeper, visit the **Rose Island Lighthouse,** in Newport, Rhode Island. Guests can participate in a week-long training program in which you spend a few hours a day learning how to raise and lower the flag at sunrise and sunset, take weather readings, do seasonal maintenance chores, and do light cleaning. Rates range from $700 to $1,800 a week, depending on the season. 401-847-4242, www. roseislandlighthouse.org

New Dungeness Lighthouse is located in the Dungeness National Wildlife Refuge in Washington State. The lighthouse has been continuously staffed by the 1,400 volunteer members of the lighthouse's association, and weekly guests are invited to stay in the Keeper's Quarters, which can sleep up to seven people (kids over 6 are welcome). Your working vacation will include giving tours to visitors and maintaining the lighthouse, with the rest of your days free for hiking, boating, and fishing in the Refuge. Association membership is $30 a year per family. 360-683-9166, www.newdungenesslighthouse.com

Fantasy Camps

If you've ever had dreams of stardom, fantasy camp can make it all come true . . . well, for a week anyway. The real purpose of fantasy camps is to let average people pay exorbitant fees to get up close and personal with their childhood (or adulthood) heroes. Celebrity instructors can teach you some tricks of the trade, and you may just walk away from the experience feeling like the star you've always dreamt of being.

Baseball fantasy camp started back in the '80s with the Cubs and the Cardinals, and now you can probably find a clinic from your own favorite team. If you're a Giants fan, the **San Francisco Giants Fantasy Camp** will train you how to be the baseball star you always wanted to be. Batter up and get hands-on instruction from sports legends; you'll eat, sleep, and breathe baseball for 6 days. You'll get full use of batting cages and pitching mounds and a final game of the Pros versus the Campers. $4,475 (air inclusive). 866-800-1275, www.mlb.com/mlb/fantasy/index.jsp

Hockey lovers get the chance to "skate with the Great One" at **Wayne Gretzky Fantasy Camp,** where you'll get 4 days of intensive practice followed by games with Wayne himself on your team. Evening events let you mingle with Gretzky and other celebrity guests, and you get to come home with your own set of hockey equipment. $9,999. 866-648-4996, www.waynegretzky.com

Attention, Steelers fans: The gold and black team's **Men's Fantasy Camp** takes place in Latrobe, Pennsylvania, each summer. Start your weekend with a tour of Heinz Field, plus on-field practices with players and coaches, a skills competition, and an evening banquet with head coach Mike Tomlin as guest speaker. A weekend course is $499. 412-697-7713, news.steelers.com/article/74117

If you're still having trouble perfecting that swing, try getting tips from the experts. **Jim Dent and Rick Bradshaw Schools of Golf** are located in Tampa and North Palm Beach, Florida, between late November and early January, when the pros are on hand to help you score that hole in one. Train with PGA professionals, with one pro per foursome. Plus you get to experience the entire golfing lifestyle, including cocktail parties and luxury accommodations. Rates start at $5,500. 800-790-2227, www.tourexperience.com

Don't worry if sports aren't your thing; those who harbor ambitions of being a rock star can head to New York City, Hollywood, or London for **Rock 'n' Roll Fantasy Camp**. It's the ultimate musical experience, whether you've jammed with the best or never picked up a guitar before. At the 5-day program, you'll learn under rock-and-roll legends like Roger Daltrey and Ted Nugent, write your own original song, have daily jam sessions with your bandmates, and get rehearsal time in a professional studio. The last night of camp culminates in a rocking Battle of the Bands where you live out all your celebrity fantasies. Starting at $9,499. 888-762-2263, www.rockandrollfantasycamp.com

Archaeology Expeditions

If you want to explore your inner Indiana Jones, try an archaeological dig on your next vacation. **Earthwatch Institute** invites guests to try their hand at excavating sites throughout the world, led by trained experts. In Peru, you can uncover ancient pieces from the Wari empire high up in the Andes (this involves working in high elevations, so make sure you're physically prepared). A teen program in England teaches the younger set to uncover and archive ruins from the Roman Empire. Expeditions are about $3,000 for 2 weeks. 800-776-0188, www.earthwatch.org

Archaeological Institute of America (AIA), the largest archaeological association in the United States, leads luxury tours through heritage areas to explore historical sites with expert leaders. Destinations include Croatia's Dalmatian Coast and ancient cities in Tunisia and Libya, plus small-ship tours around the Aegean Sea. AIA also has an extensive database of hands-on digs (not sponsored by the association) of varying levels of experience. Digs that require no experience include Betty's Hope Field School in Antigua ($2,900) and the Belize Valley Archaeological Reconnaissance ($1,950). 617-353-9361, www.archaeological.org

Take a step back in time on an archaeological dig with the **Biblical**

Archaeological Society's online database. Expeditions are in Israel, Spain, Italy, and Eastern Europe. In Paspardo, Lombardy, you'll survey rock carvings dating back to the Neolithic period, and you'll excavate, clean, and archive the ancient art. A 3-week dig in Tel Rehov, Israel, lets you explore sites dating back to the Bronze and Iron ages. Rates are about $300 to $500 a week but vary since the expeditions are individually operated by dig leaders. 202-364-3300, www.findadig.com

Crow Canyon Archaeological Center in southwestern Colorado is dedicated to preserving the history of the ancestral Pueblo Indians who inhabited this region more than 700 years ago. Programs for adults, teens, and families let you work alongside professional archaeologists on the excavation site and in the laboratory. The 170-acre campus is also a prime location for hiking and biking, and guests can take part in organized activities like creating their own rock art and storytelling. Rates start at $1,050 for adults and $950 for kids ages 12 to 17. 800-422-8975, www.crowcanyon.org

Conservation Expeditions

Travelers who have a passion for conservationism but can't dedicate their career to the field can take advantage of short-term expedition vacations. These trips combine the best of both worlds, as you can explore a new environment while dedicating your time and energies to making it a better place. (See Volunteer Vacations on page 527 for more opportunities.)

UK-based **Biosphere Expeditions** arranges conservation vacations worldwide, inviting participants of all levels of experience. A trip to Honduras includes surveying the Caribbean coral reef and marine protected areas. You'll be trained in coral reef survey techniques (PADI Open Water or equivalent qualification is required) and work alongside trained scientists to assess the reef's health. An expedition to the Azores Archipelago in the middle of the Atlantic Ocean brings you close to the whales, dolphins, and loggerhead turtles for photographing and recording for international monitoring databases. No previous experience is required, but you will be required to snorkel to collect whale skin samples. Rates are about $2,500 for 2 weeks. 800-407-5761, www.biosphere-expeditions.org

Global Vision USA offers a marine conservation expedition in the world's second-largest barrier reef, located in the Caribbean. Activities include monitoring the coral reef and fish, taking turtle nesting and crocodile surveys, and increasing educational awareness in local schools. No previous diving experience is required, but there is a diving test upon arrival, and scuba diving training is provided. This particular tour runs 5 to 15 weeks and starts at $3,070. 888-653-6028, www.gviusa.com

I-to-I offers several conservation opportunities worldwide, from rain-forest preservation to rehabilitating wallabies in Australia. A 2-week trip to Ecuador's Amazon teaches volunteers techniques in rain-forest conservation, with activities like reforestation, research, and community outreach to help locals protect more than 2,000 hectares of tropical wet forest. At a monkey sanctuary near Johannesburg, visitors assist in the Vervet Rehabilitation Centre and may help care for injured or orphaned monkeys as well as do general work around the center. Expeditions range from $895 to $1,795. 800-985-4852, www.i-to-i.com

The **Sierra Club** has expeditions in your own backyard, or at least within the United States. A weeklong trip to Canyonlands National Park in Utah invites volunteers to remove tamarisk, an invasive species that chokes out the regional trees and creates a fire hazard in the canyon. A trip to New York City combines a city tour with conservation efforts in Riverside Park, next to the Hudson River—working in association with the Riverside Park Conservancy, volunteers plant shrubs and flowers, prune existing foliage, and help with ongoing cleanup efforts. Prices start at $395. 415-977-5500, www.sierraclub.org

Agricultural Tours

Petting zoos may be fun for the little ones, but if you're desperate to show off your old 4-H skills, try lending a helping hand on a working farm, ranch, or factory. In most cases, agricultural tours are purely demonstrative—often they're little more than watching a cow being milked in a barn that conveniently leads you to a gift shop. But if you can find a participatory vacation, you can quickly become expert at picking your own tomatoes, pressing your own olives, collecting eggs from the coop, and sniffing out the finest truffles in the land.

Did you know that it takes 630 grapes to make one bottle of wine? You'll learn all that and more at the Sonoma Wine Country **Grape Camp** in September, where you'll get to immerse yourself completely in the wine experience, led by renowned local wine and food experts. At the 3-day camp, you'll start with a gourmet dinner followed by grape picking in the morning. You'll get the experience of tasting crushed grape juice, a wine-and-food-pairing workshop, wine blending, and a cheese-making tour followed by wine and cheese tasting. Sure, you'll have to roll yourself home, but you'll leave with a lifetime of knowledge. Starting at $1,500. 707-522-5860, www.sonomagrapecamp.com

The Schoolhouse Market in Warren, Vermont, is a family farm owned and operated by all five members of the Faillace family. At the market, you can find seasonal and organic Vermont produce, and locally baked pies and breads arrive on Thursday and Friday. Visitors can participate in a 3-day cheese-making workshop, starting with the four basic ingredients (starter, milk, salt, and rennet) that you combine, process, and age to make various types of Vermont cheeses: Aurora, a semihard, raw cow's-milk cheese; Vermont Brabander, a natural-rind, raw cow's-milk cheese; Cosmos, an aged, soft-ripened, raw sheep's-milk cheese; and Montagne, a peasant cheese of pressed, raw sheep's milk. $500. 802-496-4559 or 802-496-3998 (evenings), www.rootswork.org/three_shepherds.htm

Families with a taste for the great outdoors can come together at **Bar 717 Ranch** in Shasta-Trinity National Forest, California. You can learn the basics of ranch work by feeding the animals and milking the cows, step into the kitchen to make a mean blackberry pie, and learn the meaning of true humiliation at a family talent show. From $300 to $500 for kids and $700 for adults. 530-628-5992, www.bar717.com

If you've got a taste for goat cheese, why not learn how to make it yourself? At **Harley Farms** in Pescadero, California, guests go behind the scenes to learn how milk gets from the goat to your next dinner party. It's a truly hands-on experience . . . with the goat. Afterward, a cheese tasting teaches you how goat cheese can be used in an entire meal, from appetizers to dessert. $20. 650-879-0480, www.harleyfarms.com

There's no better way to cool off in the summertime than to make your own ice cream! At **Hilmar Cheese Company** in California, families are invited to "shake, rattle, and roll" their own individual ice cream. The big cheese tour also includes learning how cheese is made, packaged, and shipped off to the stores. $3 per person—can't get more reasonable than that. 800-577-5772, www.hilmarcheese.com

Shelburne Farms in Vermont knows that both kids and grown-ups like to get in on the fun. For the kids, sheep-shearing season in April is always an experience, as farmers demonstrate the process and then teach them how to spin, card, and dye their own wool. $10. Adults can get even more hands-on in a daylong sheep-shearing clinic led by a professional . . . sheep barber. $100. 802-985-8696, www.shelburnefarms.org

Cooperative Cravirola is a cooperative dairy farm in the Southern Alps (between Montpellier and Toulouse) made up of a collective of farmers, artists, and conservationists. Holiday workcamps invite travelers to assist with farm duties, including building maintenance and construction, goat herding, and spending the afternoons making cheese. If you're concerned about donating all your time, don't worry—gourmet meals with wine and, of course, cheese are served daily, with evening gatherings around the campfire. Sessions range from 1 to 4 weeks, starting at $54. 33-0-4-67-23-94-77, cravirol.club.fr/cravirola/anglaisdynamo.html

The world's oldest flight attendant called it quits in April 2007. Iris Peterson, who got her start in 1946, retired at age 85. In 1953 she became the first official lobbyist for the flight attendant union and changed several of its policies, including one that required stewardesses to leave the job when they got married. She also lobbied for increased safety standards on airplanes.

Be kind to bees at the **Beekind Honey Shoppe and Apiary** in Sonoma County, California. At the tasting bar, you can sample a huge variety of honeys and honey-related products, including white truffle honey, creamed honey, honey chocolate truffles, and honey roasted nuts. For a hands-on experience, you take a class to learn how to "extract the goods"—while getting face-to-face with the bees and grabbing the honey to take home with you. $15. 707-824-2905, www.beekindbees.com

Tillers' Training Center in Scotts, Michigan, sits on about 450 acres of woods, pastures, and crops. Visitors can stay overnight in the guesthouse and take various craft and agricultural courses. One of the more popular events is beekeeping, in which you get close (some would say too close) to the Tillers' beehives: Learn about seasonal care, queen management, and the big reward—extracting honey. Go home with a pint of your own honey collected from the private beehive. 800-498-2700, www.tillersinternational.org

Sequim, Washington, refers to itself as the "lavender capital of North America," and with eight lavender farms in the area, it may well be true. July's **Lavender Festival** lets you travel from farm to farm by shuttle learning how the fragrant herb is cultivated and dried. Grab a pair of scissors and pick your own bunch and then learn how to make a lavender wreath, wrap your bouquet in lace, and even make your own lavender oil. 877-681-3035, www.lavenderfestival.com

World-famous Kona coffee can be yours when you take a Roastmaster Tour at **UCC's Espresso Bar and Roastery** on Hawaii's Big Island. At the roasting and packaging facility, you learn the history and cultivation of Kona beans, and a "roasting guide" walks you through the different methods of roasting to create your own private coffee label. 808-328-5662, www.ucc-hawaii.com

If your tastes tend to run a little higher end, you may want to spend your month's salary on truffles—those pungent mushrooms that can sell for up to $2,000 a pound! But before you get dressed for dinner, try getting down and dirty on a truffle-hunting expedition. In Italy, tour company **Tartufi Bianconi** will take you on a hunt through the woods with their trusty truffle-hunting dog and then bring you back to taste dishes made with the exotic ingredient. 39-075-851-1591, www.tartufibianconi.it

Based in Italy, **Tuscan Wine Tours** offers, well, wine tours. But you can also learn about Italy's other great agricultural product: olive oil. A participatory tour lets you become a part of the process during the November harvest season—from picking to crushing and pressing the olives, followed by a lunch drizzled with your very own oil. $200. 39-320-307-5574, www. tuscan-wine-tours.com

Crafts and Hobbies

Those famous (and cuddly) **Vermont Teddy Bears** are yours for the keeping when you learn how to make your own bear. The factory, located in Shelburne, Vermont, has an on-site Bear Crew to help kids with stuffing, sewing, fluffing, dressing, and naming their own teddy bears, which come complete with an official Bear Birth Certificate. 802-985-3001, www.vermontteddybear.com

If you're on the West Coast, you can also learn how to make your own bear, at the **Basic Brown Bear Factory** in San Francisco. The factory tour walks you through the process of designing, cutting, and sewing and then brings you to the stuffing machine where you can stuff a bear yourself. From princess bears to cowboy bears to bears in bikinis, you can probably find your next best friend and bring him (or her) home with you. $12. 866-522-2327, www.basicbrownbear.com

Don't be scared by the name. At **Babyland General Hospital** in Cleveland,

Georgia, your kids won't be learning about "birthing no babies." They will, however, learn all about the birthplace of Cabbage Patch Kids. The iconic dolls from the 1980s are hand-stitched, individually named and dressed, and come with a set of adoption papers. The factory is actually housed in a former clinic and is laid out like a maternity ward. Visitors can see the fathers' waiting room and the nursery (there's actually an ICU for the preemies) as well as see dolls being "delivered" at the Magic Crystal Tree, where something called a Bunnybee determines the sex of the baby. Okay, it's about as creepy as it sounds, but the kids will love it. And of course, this is where they can choose and adopt their own Cabbage Patch Kid. Free (although "adoption" fees are $175 to $345!). 706-865-2171, www.cabbagepatchkids.com

Mrs. Grossman's Sticker Factory in Petaluma, California, is the oldest sticker factory in the United States. With more than 700 different stickers created here, kids will be wide-eyed as they watch millions of stickers get printed, packaged, and shipped. But they'll be in heaven when they're whisked off to the sticker art room, where they can design their own sticker postcards. 707-763-1700, www.mrsgrossmans.com

The iconic **Louisville Slugger** bat can be yours when you travel to Kentucky to tour the museum and factory. While visitors aren't able to start carving the wood themselves, you can get the next-best thing with your own personalized bat made inside the factory. 877-775-8443, www.sluggermuseum.org

Take a step back in time at the **Touchstone Center for Crafts** in Farmington, Pennsylvania, where you can join in 2-day programs to learn old-school crafts. There are dozens of courses available, including blacksmithing, stained-glass making, creating your own cooking utensils, or learning how to forge steel knives. 800-721-0177, www.touchstonecrafts.com

For crafty types with a love for the water, the **Philadelphia Wooden Boat Factory** offers hands-on boat-making classes. A two-weekend course teaches you boat-making techniques like lofting, steam bending, planking, and spar making. A more intensive three-weekend course teaches you how to build a Chesapeake Light kayak from scratch—and at the end of the course, you'll go home with a mostly completed boat that you'll have the skills to finish off on your own. Rates range from $300 to $1,500. 215-755-2400, www.woodenboatfactory.org

Firehouse Glass in Vancouver, Washington, offers private lessons that teach you the delicate art of blowing glass, creating glass beads, and etching your own carvings. A 4-hour course can accommodate up to three people, starting at $280. 360-695-2660, www.firehouseglass.com

In New Orleans, the **GlassWorks & Printmaking Studio** allows guests to watch and participate with master European artists. A "weekend sampler" for beginners includes torch working, glass sculpturing, and casting. Day visitors can learn how to create glass beads and make casts of their hands. 504-529-7279, www.neworleansglassworks.com

In New Zealand, you can learn the ancient Maori art of bone carving. Stephen Gilberg, aka the **Nelson Bone Carver,** starts you with a slab of bone straight from the butcher (don't worry, it's cleaned off first) and walks you through the process of carving, sanding, and polishing your own bone pendant in a 1-day workshop. $65. 0064-3-5464275, www.carvingbone.co.nz

Belgium continues to be the lace-making capital of the world, where hundreds of craftswomen create intricate designs by hand. In Bruges, lace maker Caroline Flokman offers a private lesson to teach you the old tradition (while feeding you plenty of Belgian chocolate—just make sure to wash your hands!). $81. 212-758-4275, www.visitbelgium.com/lace.htm

Japan has long been known for its fine pottery and ceramics, and the town of Mashiko boasts more than 400 pottery studios and kilns. **Tsukamoto** is perhaps the largest pottery facility in town, featuring an exhibition hall with a mind-boggling array of artwork and hands-on workshops to draw on unglazed pottery or even create your own vessels (it can take a few months to get them back home). 200 yen (about $2). 0285-72-5151

CHAPTER 33

Spiritual Travel

❝ **It's better to travel well than to arrive.** ❞

—BUDDHA

The concept of "spiritual travel" comes in all shapes and sizes. From a Muslim hadj to Mecca or a journey to the Holy Land in Israel to yoga retreats and New Age seminars, spiritual tourism is quietly growing throughout the world.

In the past, a faith-based trip usually referred to a church or temple that arranged a group tour for its members. But these days, travel companies are creating their own faith-based itineraries. These tours usually combine standard sightseeing with visits to churches, temples, monasteries, and other locations made famous by religious figures throughout history.

And if you had any doubts about the popularity of this market, consider this: The growth rate in spiritual travel has been nothing less than exponential. For example, **Globus Faith Vacations**, a leading tour company offering faith-based trips, is reporting a 650 percent increase in travelers since it opened its religious division in 2004.

With trips catering to Protestant, Catholic, and Jewish travelers (and those who are interested in these religious themes), Globus recently upped its number of religious tours due to the increased interest. Biblical-themed trips include a tour through Greece and Turkey to follow the footsteps of the Apostle Paul and a journey through Egypt and Jordan. Catholic-faith vacations include a visit to the shrines of Italy with stops in Rome, San Giovanni Rotondo, and Assisi. A 6-day trip to Mexico City takes you to the site of the Virgin Mary's appearance to San Juan Diego in 1531, as well as to Mexico's other famous shrines, including Blessed First Martyrs, San Miguel del Milagro, and Our Lady of Ocotlán. Protestant-themed tours include retracing the footsteps of Martin Luther and the European Reformation in cities such as Augsburg, Zurich, and Geneva, as well as cruising along the Rhine. Prices range from about $1,000 to $2,000. 866-755-8581, www.globusjourneys.com/faith

ARZA World leads Jewish heritage tours through Central Europe, Eastern Europe, and Israel. European stops may include the Warsaw Ghetto Memorial, the Jewish Museum in Prague, and memorial services in Auschwitz and Birkenau. Extensive tours through Israel bring passengers through Jerusalem, Tel Aviv, Eilat, and the Galilee region for 9- to 13-day excursions. 888-811-2812, www.arzaworld.com

Travelers can get away with **Journeys of Faith**, which operates small-group tours to explore Christian heritage. The 14-day Heart of France tour stops at traditional sightseeing spots, but guides include stories and history from a Christian perspective. You can learn about the early Protestant Reformers who taught at the Sorbonne and visit the Louvre to see how Christianity has been reflected in the arts throughout the ages. An 11-day heritage trip through Italy includes stops at the first Christian Church in Rome and a tour of Mamertine Prison, where many believe the Apostle Paul was imprisoned for preaching the gospel. Average prices range from $2,000 to $4,000. 816-261-0258, www.joftours.com

Christian Travel Finder offers cruises, tours, and retreats with a Christian focus. On board a Royal Caribbean ship, the Spirit West Coast cruise travels from Los Angeles to Puerto Vallerta, with Christian musicians and comedians performing throughout the 7-day trip, starting at $660. An 11-day Footsteps of Paul trip cruises the Mediterranean, through Greece and Turkey, with prices starting around $1,400. 888-518-7571, www.christiantravelfinder.com

Reformation Tours specializes in tours to Europe from a Christian perspective. The family-operated company has established relationships with regional officials and Christian groups, which means that passengers may meet local pastors and fellow churchgoers. Tours include 10 days following the footsteps of Martin Luther in Germany and traveling through Switzerland to better understand the formation of the Protestant church. 800-303-5534, www.reformationtours.com

The Israel Tour Connection offers several heritage tours, with discounts for bar mitzvah and bat mitzvah celebrations in Israel. The 12-night In Depth tour begins in Tel Aviv, with visits to cities like Caesarea, once the Roman capital of the region; Safed, the center of the Kabbalah movement; and Jerusalem. Some overnight accommodations are in kibbutz guesthouses. Rates range from $1,900 to $4,500. 800-247-7235, www.israeltour.com

206 Tours arranges pilgrimage tours throughout Europe, Russia, and Egypt. A trip through Eastern Europe visits the historical churches of Warsaw, the monasteries in Czestochowa, the convents of Krakow, and the chapels and abbeys of Budapest, Vienna, and Prague (starting at $2,199). A 10-night tour to Egypt starts in Cairo but skips the standard Nile cruise in favor of visiting the ancient cities of Tel Basta, Meniet Samannoud, Sahka, and Al Matariyah (starting at $1,599). 800-206-8687, www.206tours.com

Religious Service Vacations

(See also "Volunteer Vacations" on page 527)
Mercy Ships offers an innovative "floating charity" program that provides medical care and surgical procedures in poor and developing nations. Operating since 1978, Mercy Ships has performed more than 32,500 surgeries such as cleft lip and palate, cataract removal, straightening of crossed eyes, and orthopedic and facial reconstruction. Medical professionals are especially welcome, but nonmedical volunteers can assist with outreach opportunities such as renovating orphanages; building and maintaining clinics, schools, and homes; and assisting on board a Mercy Ship. 903-939-7000, www.mercyships.org

Habitat for Humanity International is a nonprofit, ecumenical Christian organization that builds and provides upkeep on housing for families in need. Since 1976, more than 200,000 homes have been built worldwide, from rural communities to inner cities—Habitat for Humanity was also instrumental in the rebuilding efforts after Hurricane Katrina. Volunteers get to slap on their hard hats and get involved with real hands-on construction, as well as community awareness and fund-raising efforts. 229-924-6935, www.habitat.org

American Jewish World Service is an international development organization motivated by Judaism's imperative to pursue justice. Jewish professionals can be placed with grassroots nongovernmental organizations worldwide, to act as consultants and provide training for local staff members. Summer volunteer vacations are open to students ages 16 to 24, who spend 7 weeks in rural regions of Africa, Asia, and Latin America to build and maintain homes and community resources. 800-889-7146, www.ajws.org

For some travelers, living and volunteering on a kibbutz is practically a rite of passage. In most cases, you can obtain information on traveling to Israel and institutions through the Israeli kibbutzim office, www.kibbutz. org.il/eng. You can also find first-hand experiences, facts, and links to kibbutzim Web sites at www.kibbutzvolunteer.com, which is operated by a British traveler who spent 2 years working on a kibbutz.

The Council of Religious Volunteer Agencies is an association of faith-based programs and is a good resource to find a variety of volunteer opportunities, including the American Baptist Churches USA—Volunteers in Mission, the Catholic Network of Volunteer Service, the Mennonite Voluntary Service, and the Presbyterian Church USA—International Volunteers. www.religiousvolunteers.org

Yoga and Meditation

Retreats that involve the yogic arts, meditation, and spirituality are becoming a popular choice among those who are hoping to explore ancient philosophies while attempting to reach a level of self-awareness and balance during their travels. There are literally thousands of yoga centers, meditation retreats, and spiritual centers located worldwide. Schools of thought can vary from Hinduism and Buddhism to Native American traditions, with everything in between, so it may take some research to find out which program works best for you. Do you prefer hot stone massages or a weeklong fast? Are you looking for a spectacular ocean-view room or camping out in the wilderness? Here are a few options to get you started.

 Spiritual Getaway

A 2006 study by the Travel Industry Association found that 35 percent of travelers said they were currently interested in taking a spiritual vacation. The appeal of a spiritual vacation seems to cross all age groups, with approximately one-third of each age group (18 to 34 years, 35 to 54 years, and 55-plus) expressing current interest in taking such a vacation.

Sedona Soul Adventures is a company that arranges retreats in Sedona, Arizona. You can go ultra-luxury with spa packages and couples' getaways or get spiritual with private meditation, yoga, breathwork, massage, and energy healing. Prices vary by package. Sedona Soul Adventures also coordinates spiritual journeys to sacred locations, including Egypt, Bali, and Machu Picchu. 877-204-3664, www.sedonasouladventures.com

> The Vatican is the world's smallest country, at 0.16 square mile. Monaco is next, at 0.7 square mile.

River Odysseys West frequently arranges a "river soul journey," which includes traditional outdoor activities like river rafting, hiking, and camping, as well as guided yoga, meditation, and relaxation sessions. There are programs available for women only, families, and couples as well as mixed groups. Prices range from $1,000 to $1,700 for 4-, 5-, and 6-day retreats. 800-451-6034, www.rowadventures.com

The Tree of Life Rejuvenation Center in Patagonia, Arizona, invites guests to stay as long as they wish, whether it's for a meal, overnight, or several weeks. Activities include chanting and meditation, a sweat lodge, fire ceremony, something called "spiritual gardening," and meals in an organic vegan live-food café. There are also detoxification sessions, healthy parent and baby programs, and holistic healing. Prices start at about $155 a night, including meals. 866-394-2520, www.treeoflife.nu

In the Berkshire Mountains of western Massachusetts is the **Kripalu Center for Yoga and Health,** which offers several courses in yoga, Reiki, and fitness. Their signature program, Kripalu R&R, allows you to determine the length of your stay and integrate the center's services with your own meditation and relaxation sessions. Program rates vary, but a yoga retreat ranges from $790 to $2,193. 866-200-5203, www.kripalu.org

The Feathered Pipe Ranch in Helena, Montana, is one of the oldest yoga retreats in the United States, hosting weekend and weeklong retreats and workshops. A "summer solstice" retreat includes various forms of yoga, chanting, meditation, and Thai yoga massage; starts at $1,400 for 7 days. A yoga and ceremony course is $1,495 and features yoga practices as well as writing, vision quests, and sweat lodge ceremonies. 406-442-8196, www.featheredpipe.com

The White Lotus Foundation, based in Santa Barbara, California, sponsors yoga, meditation, and breathwork retreats. The programs include gourmet vegetarian meals and opportunities for hikes, dance classes, arts and crafts, spiritual ceremonies, and discussion groups. Prices range from $500 to $650. 805-964-1944, www.whitelotus.org

Journeys for the Soul organizes retreats in Sedona, Mount Shasta, Hawaii, and Peru, among other places. A 4-day Sedona retreat, with yoga and meditation sessions and a Native American sweat lodge ceremony, provides a space for guests to experience physical and spiritual cleansing. A Peruvian retreat takes place at the Willka T'ika Retreat Centre with views of the Andes; the trip includes visits to Machu Picchu and other ancient sites, visits to the local mountain villages, and Andean spiritual ceremonies. Rates range from $1,195 to $3,795. 949-715-7902, www.journeysforthesoul.com

Spirit of Nature invites guests to sweat lodge retreats in Santa Fe, with sacred ceremonies, chanting and singing, and a vegetarian potluck. There is a suggested $20 donation for a daylong course, with private group and individual lodges available upon request. 505-913-0199, www.spiritofnature.org

The Bodhi Tree is a "forest monastery" located on 95 acres of land in Tullera, Australia. The monastery is nonsectarian, welcoming anyone who wishes to learn the practices of Theravada Buddhism. Retreats run from a weekend to 10 days, taught by resident monks and visiting spiritual leaders. www.buddhanet.net/bodhi-tree

Ananda Spa in the Himalayan foothills of India is considered one of the most exclusive spas in the world. Traditional spa treatments are available, as are yoga sessions and spa cuisine. There are also several wellness retreats with medical practitioners, spiritual healers, reflexologists, and yogis. Room rates range from $400 to $1,600. www.anandaspa.com

The Canadian company **Sacred Earth Journeys** arranges spiritual tours around the world, including healing in Bali, yoga in Havana, yoga and sea kayaking in Baja, an intensive yoga teacher training course in Thailand, and ayurvedic tours throughout India. Prices range from $1,000 to $3,000, depending on the length and location. 877-874-7922, www.sacredearthjourneys.ca

Ananda Meditation Retreat is located on 60 acres in Nevada City, California, with bungalows and cottages for guests. There are guided seclusions, personal meditation training, massage, and alternative healing programs available, with three vegetarian meals per day. Overnight accommodations range from $40 to $120. 530-292-3024, www.meditationretreat.org

Spirit Journeys offers spiritual retreats worldwide. A trip to Bali features daily classes in meditation and yoga, as well as tours of the island's temples and sacred lakes and visits to local priests and artisans. A 2-week journey to Thailand, Laos, and Cambodia includes visits to Buddhist temples, jungle and beach treks, and daily meditation and chanting. Specific gay and lesbian spiritual tours are also available. Rates start at about $3,000. 828-258-8880, www.spiritjourneys.com

Ganesh Yoga Retreats organizes 12-day retreats to India, in the foothills of the Himalayas. Retreats include intensive outdoor yoga sessions, plus tours to local temples, spiritual ceremonies at the holy Ganges River, white-water rafting, and various spa treatments. Rates are $1,775. 650-619-0408, www.ganeshyogaretreats.com

Silent Retreats

Silent retreats are great escapes for all different types, whether you are looking for some quiet time to reflect about your life, healing from an emotional or spiritual crisis, or going deeper into prayer or meditation. You definitely don't have to be a guru or mystic to reap the benefits of silent meditation, but you do need time and space to focus your thoughts. Keep in mind, if you can't imagine your day without cable, this may not be the place for you—these retreats usually reduce your life to the simplest form, with basic lodging in outdoorsy settings.

Santa Sabina Center in northern California's Marin County is located in a 100-acre Dominican University campus with woodsy surroundings, a courtyard, and mountain hiking trails that offer a bird's-eye view of the Bay Area. Guests can spend time lying in the sun, hiking, writing, or puttering in the garden. The center also offers several weekend programs exploring poetry and literature—these weekends are usually spent in silence with exceptions for discussion periods. The center can accommodate 58 overnight guests, and nearby residents often just show up for the day. 415-457-7727, www.retreatsonline.net/santasabina

Shambhala Mountain Center in northern Colorado, by Red Feather Lakes, is a 600-acre mountain valley retreat located at 8,000 feet. It was founded in 1971, inspired by Tibetan Buddhism, but incorporates various philosophies and practices like Jewish meditation and yoga. The center also coordinates weekend and weeklong meditation retreats, with prices ranging from $600 to $1,400. 888-788-7221, www.shambhalamountain.org

Rasayana Cove in Sarasota, Florida, is one of the more exclusive programs, hosting only one to three clients at a time. Guests receive specialized Kerala

Ayurvedic treatments, which are based on the ancient South Indian tradition of healing the body and mind with specific foods, massage, yoga, and oil treatments. In this private agricultural setting, there is no need to socialize with others, and guests frequently come with the purpose of spending time in silence. Costs range from about $330 to $400 per day, depending on the services that you receive. 863-494-7565, www.ayurvedicretreat.com

East Mountain Retreat Center in Massachusetts' Berkshire Mountains is an interfaith facility that offers arrangements for individual retreats without any prearranged activities or treatments. Private retreats are done mostly in silence, but arrangements can be made for activities like playing musical instruments or chanting, as well as consulting with a guide or teacher. Most guests prepare their own meals in the kitchen, but there is an option for a hot meal to be provided for dinner. The suggested donation is $30 per day. 413-528-6617, www.eastretreat.org

CHAPTER 34

❝ To travel is to discover that everyone is wrong about other countries. ❞

—ALDOUS HUXLEY

In my estimation, fear is the worst four-letter word starting with "F." And when it comes to travel, fear is a serial journey killer. It keeps us from exploring the world, from discovering new places and experiences.

Don't think you can—or should—travel to certain countries and regions? You will be pleasantly surprised—perhaps—to learn that you *can* get there from here, and in almost all cases, you can get there safely; you can immerse yourself in that culture, have a great experience, and make some new friends along the way.

And perhaps the overriding reason why you can—and perhaps should— get there from here: the power of travel and tourism. It is the largest industry in the world, employs the most people, and is singularly responsible for the gross domestic product of dozens of countries. In recent years, even rulers within the most difficult countries under the hardest dictatorships have had to come to grips with an economic reality: Forgetting the obvious benefits of building bridges and forging peace, travel and tourism was one salvation for their economy—and in many cases, the only one. And slowly, without hesitation, the doors opened. And those doors have been kept open by the flood of foreign exchange—these countries have been fueled by the currency provided by travel and tourism.

Here is just a small sampling of countries that are available to you.

Getting the Official Word . . .

Before traveling to any country where there may be risks to American travelers, many of you probably will check the US State Department Web site, www.travel.state.gov, which reports travel advisories for countries considered by the US government to be "high risk." If you feel you really must check the site, please do so with the understanding that these are "advisories," not official commands.

For example, a recent alert on the site pertaining to Indonesia warned Americans to stay away from large crowds and avoid buses. Think about it: I live in Los Angeles, and I stay away from large crowds and avoid buses. (In the case of LA, I have no idea where the buses go . . . that's scary enough!) But that advisory shouldn't keep you from going to Indonesia.

Another recent alert on the site warned against travel to Uzbekistan and was issued "to remind US citizens that the potential for a terrorist attack or civil disturbance still exists, despite the fact that there have been no violent incidents in Uzbekistan since May 2005." Translation: The potential for a terrorist attack or civil disturbance still exists . . . in Newark, and at least in my case, I'd head to Uzbekistan first!

If you still insist on getting official government opinions, remember that you always have options. Besides our own State Department, why not see what other governments are telling *their* citizens: Check the British government's Web site (www.fco.gov.uk) or the Australian site (www. smartraveller.gov.au).

Then there's a third option: local newspapers. You can find a list of hundreds of English-language newspapers and publications worldwide, from *Malta Today* to the *Turkish Daily News,* at these sites:

www.thebigproject.co.uk/news

www.kidon.com/media-link/english.php

And to learn details about a country's history, geography, government, and economy, visit the CIA's *The World Factbook* at www.cia.gov.

Afghanistan

202-483-6410, www.embassyofafghanistan.org

Despite the difficult years since September 11, there are no current restrictions on travel to Afghanistan—you can book a trip through a tour group or call the consulate to apply for a tourist visa. Since Kabul International Airport reopened, air travel to Afghanistan is the most convenient method of getting into the country. Airlines that fly into Afghanistan include KamAir, Pakistan International Airways, Indian Airlines, Air Arabia, and Qatar Airways.

As with any country, there are some regions safer than others. Most of the violence is localized south of Kabul, but it's relatively safe in Kabul and in the southwest and western regions. In the south, travel is difficult unless you have a lot of support on the ground, which is not easily available.

After the US invasion, it's estimated that about one-third of all public buildings and 40 percent of housing were totally destroyed. The remaining tourist attractions include the 6-hectare Babur's Garden (the tomb of the first emperor) and the Afghanistan National Museum, which reopened in 2004. You can also travel outside of Kabul to explore the country's mountainous regions and the Band-i-Amir lake regions. One of the main highlights of the trip is Bamiyan, where enormous Buddhas stood carved in the side of a cliff—the Taliban destroyed them in 2001, but you can still see the complete outline of the niche where the statues stood. Hotels are also starting to make their mark in the redeveloping city of Kabul. In April 2007, the government of Afghanistan and US-based General Systems International executed a 99-year lease agreement for the construction of a 209-room, five-star Marriott Hotel in Kabul. The five-star, 177-room Kabul Serena Hotel opened its doors in 2005.

Distant Horizons offers a 3-week tour called Crossing the Khyber Pass: Afghanistan and Pakistan. Begin by exploring the capital city of Kabul, which includes the Kabul Museum and Babur's Garden. Fly west to see the Musalla complex and on to Mazar-e Sharif, Afghanistan's second largest city. Then travel to Balkh, considered a "cradle of religion," and drive through green valleys to Bamiyan, once the center of the Kushan Empire. The tour will take you through the Khyber Pass into Pakistan's North-West Frontier Province, then north to Swat, where Buddhism flourished for centuries. $7,490. 800-333-1240, www.distant-horizons.com

Afghan Logistics & Tours provides both packaged and customized tours. Visitors are transported in all-new four-wheel-drive vehicles and stay in local guesthouses. The packaged tours run for 6, 10, and 15 days and can include a visit to Kabul, Babur's Garden, Television Mountain, and Chicken Street. Catch a Friday night buzkashi game (aka the goat-grabbing contest) and visit the Shomali Plain north of Kabul, the Shibar Pass, Bamiyan, the lakes of Band-i-Amir, Mazar-e Sharif, Balkh (a center of Buddhism), Ai Hafnium (the only Greek city in Central Asia, most likely founded by Alexander the Great), the Slang Tunnel, and the beautiful Punisher Valley. Tour rates vary due to the instability of fuel prices, but an individual traveler can expect to pay about $500 a day, and small groups of two or three people can spend $150 to $200. 646-382-5755, www.afghanlogisticstours.com

Hinterland Travel has several tours to Afghanistan, including a 21-day Road Tour that drives through Pakistan, Afghanistan, and Iran. A 24-day tour of Central and Northern Afghanistan starts in Islamabad, and takes you over the Khyber Pass to Allahabad and to Kabul for a city excursion. You'll spend about 4 days driving through the lakes of Band-i-Amir, Chak Charan, Minaret of Djam, Chist, and Obeh to Herat. Trips range from $3,458 to $3,756. 44-0-1883-743584, www.hinterlandtravel.com

Bhutan

212-826-1919, www.embassy.org/embassies/bt.html

For those Americans who have even heard of Bhutan, it is a country still enshrouded in mystery. The isolated country, located between China and India, is mostly free of tourists and still remains a rather poor, undeveloped nation. The first paved roads were completed in the 1960s, and televisions showed up only 8 years ago. You won't find any traffic lights, and until the 1970s, there was no national currency. My kind of place (seriously). Bhutan is an ancient culture with old-world village life, crumbling fortresses and monasteries, and plenty of nature for outdoor enthusiasts.

Of course, in a country that is so distant from mass tourism, getting there isn't always easy. While the US State Department says you can visit Bhutan only as part of an organized tour group with a recognized company, that's patently untrue. Contact your hotel ahead of time (yes, the Internet exists) and the hotel, such as Uma Paro, will make all the necessary visa arrangements for independent travelers or groups. The hotel will confirm the space, ask for a copy of the front page of your passport, and then make the arrangements for your visa and your Druk Air flights into and out of Bhutan. The only airport with regular commercial flights in Bhutan is located in the town of Paro and serves only the national carrier, Druk Air. The only cities Druk Air flies to are: Calcutta/Kolkatta, Delhi, Dhaka (Bangladesh), and Kathmandu (Nepal), as well as a weekly flight to Bangkok via Dhaka. It is impossible to just book a flight on your own to Bhutan (unless you're a resident of the country)—you'll need to be sponsored by a tour group or hotel.

Asia Transpacific Journeys, which was among the first US-based tour operators permitted to enter Bhutan, offers private custom trips as well as small-group trips. The small-group tour, Inside the Dragon Kingdom, includes a day hike to the Taktshang Monastery, a festival of pageantry and dance (at either Jakar or Ura), and tours throughout the cities of Paro, Thimphu, Trongsa, and Wangdu led by expert guides. A 14-day trip designed in conjunction with the World Wildlife Fund takes advantage of Bhutan's unspoiled beauty in the Himalayas and includes visits to monasteries and temples, day hikes through cloud forests and nature reserves to get up close and personal with local wildlife, and private folk dance performances. Rates range from $4,595 to $6,995. 800-642-2742, www.asiatranspacific.com

Wilderness Travel has several excursions, including a 16-day tour that takes you through the Himalayan mountain kingdoms of Nepal, Bhutan, and Tibet. The group also offers several treks through the Himalayas, including a 14-day Haa Trek that offers you views of Tibet and Chomolhari and a 9-day Chomolhari Trek that takes you to the remote and untouched Yanksa Valley ("Valley of Yaks"). Tours range from $3,395 to $4,595. 800-368-2794, www.wildernesstravel.com

Bosnia and Herzegovina
202-337-1500, www.bhembassy.org

Once war-torn nations divided by civil war, Bosnia and Herzegovina now boast the slogan "the heart-shaped land." The European Union (EU), under a United Nations mandate, is still in control of most parts of the Bosnian government, and in recent years, there have been significant strides in rebuilding the infrastructure to prepare the country for tourism.

That includes the city of Sarajevo, once home to the Winter Olympics and a rebounding destination for winter sports and skiing. It retains a significant café culture and several rebuilt landmarks, including the Sarajevo Cathedral and the Gazi Husrev-beg's Mosque. And under the EU's careful supervision, most cultural sites have been successfully restored.

The historic city of Mostar also offers visitors a number of interesting historical sites. Despite heavy damage during the war and continued divisions between the city's Croat and Bosnian residents, the city is aggressively courting tourists. The town's most famous landmark, though, is its bridge, Stari Most ("Old Bridge"). Destroyed during the war, the bridge was rebuilt using ancient methods and materials, reopening in 2004 and achieving UNESCO World Heritage status the following year.

> The United Nations' "Isolation Index" refers to the total sum of the square root of the distances to the nearest island, group of islands, and continent. Easter Island in the South Pacific is number one, located 2,000 miles from Chile and the nearest islands of Tahiti.

According to the State Department, US citizens are warned that "there are still risks from occasional localized political violence, landmines, and unexploded ordnance in Bosnia and Herzegovina. Criminal activity has also been on the rise, particularly in urban areas, with a marked increase in reports of residential break-ins and vehicle and petty theft. There exists a substantial organized crime presence throughout Bosnia and Herzegovina; however, violent confrontations between rival criminal elements usually occur in larger cities and pose little direct threat to Americans. In one suspected instance of a criminally related act, an explosive device was discovered on a public transit bus in Sarajevo in December 2005. Travelers are warned to exercise additional vigilance in urban areas to avoid being victimized during confrontational crime." Yes, I *always* exercise additional vigilance, especially during confrontational crime. (Don't you?)

Australian outfitter **Intrepid Travel** has two tours that include Bosnia and Herzegovina in their itineraries: A 14-day Balkan Adventure visits Bosnia and Herzegovina, Croatia, Hungary, Montenegro, and Serbia. A Central European adventure is 28 days and takes you to Austria, Bosnia and Herzegovina, Croatia, the Czech Republic, Hungary, Montenegro, Poland, Serbia, and Slovakia. Intrepid's tours tend to focus on cultural immersion, mixing traditional sightseeing with family homestays, eating in small local establishments, and visiting native artisans. Tours range from $1,150 to $2,300. 866-847-8192, www.intrepidtravel.com

Overseas Adventure Travel has a 16-day Crossroads of the Adriatic tour, which includes stops in Bosnia, Croatia, Montenegro, and Slovenia. Travel through the heart of the land, from Zagreb to Croatia and into Bosnia, where you dine with a local family and learn Sarajevo's war-torn history. The tour continues along the coastline, where you visit medieval villages, ancient monasteries, and palaces and take advantage of the waterfront activities. Rates start at $3,095, including airfare. 800-493-6824, www. oattravel.com

Colombia

571-315-0811, www.bogota.usembassy.gov/wwwsmane.shtml

In the imagination of most Americans, Colombia has long been synonymous with cocaine traffickers and drug violence—not exactly a hot holiday destination. And while local crime is still high, it's nowhere near the war-ravaged conditions of Colombia before 2002, when current President Alvaro Uribe took over.

These days, more and more visitors are ziplining through jungles in the shadow of snow-capped mountains or taking in the historic architecture and bustling nightlife of cities once better known for cartels—cities like Medellín, Cali, and Cartagena.

Airline transport into Colombia from Europe and the US is not generally difficult, because of its position in South America. Most major American airlines now offer nonstop flights to Bogotá from major US hubs, including Atlanta, Chicago, Houston, Miami, and Newark.

And even small low-cost carrier Spirit Airlines has applied to fly from its base at Fort Lauderdale–Hollywood International to Bogotá's El Dorado International. El Dorado, which has seen its traffic soar, is now beginning a massive overhaul due to be completed in 2011 that should greatly modernize the airport.

But Colombia still attracts relatively few tourists, meaning that low prices are much easier to find than in nearby countries like popular Costa Rica or even up-and-coming Panama.

De Una Colombia is one of the larger, and probably the most Colombia-centric, travel providers out there. Its prices are also indicative of how inexpensive the country can be. A 22-day small-group tour, for example, is just $1,300 and, other than international flights, covers just about everything you'll need. www.deunacolombia.com

Adventure Center, which operates in conjunction with existing tours from other companies, is working with two tour outfitters traveling to Colombia: First is a 22-night journey called Salsa and the Spanish Main that travels through Venezuela and Colombia (and ends in Quito, Ecuador). Optional excursions include scuba diving, snorkeling off the Caribbean coast, trekking, and an overnight visit to Maracaibo Lake to see the famous lightning phenomenon. The other, a 23-day trip from Caracas to Quito, includes several beach excursions, boating trips to nearby islands, and visits to ancient Indian villages. Rates start at $1,336. 800-228-8747, www.adventurecenter.com

Natura Vive focuses on "nature vacations" that, in Colombia, center around outdoor activities like white-water rafting and rock climbing. The company even operates a Rescue School for "river professionals" who seek to become rescue specialists for white-water rapids. 311-809-4207, www.naturavive.com

Cuba

www.cubatravel.cu

Most Americans assume that Cuba is off-limits—and technically, with the American embargo still in place, it almost is; emphasis on the word *almost*. Consider this: In 2006, for the second consecutive year, tourism in Cuba surpassed 2.3 million visitors, representing a 12 percent growth in the industry. And many of the visitors are your fellow US citizens. How did that happen?

The "trading with the enemies act," passed in 1963, specifically prohibits Americans from spending US dollars in Cuba. But it hasn't stopped Americans from visiting. Thousands go each year, through third countries—including Canada, Mexico, Jamaica, the Cayman Islands, the Bahamas, and places in Europe. They buy all-inclusive travel and tour packages from companies in those third countries—which include airfare, hotels, ground transportation, tips, and meals in Cuba. Technically, they're not spending any US dollars there, since they're going through third-party, third-country tour operators. The Cubans don't stamp US passports.

Has anyone been arrested or fined for doing this? In the 44 or so years the law has been on the books, the answer is . . . hardly. For the US government to crack down on this travel practice would require authorities to acknowledge how widespread it is. Unless you are a US business actively promoting and selling travel to Cuba—which would be a clear violation of the 1963 law—you have little to worry about. Of course, in the interests of full disclosure, if you choose to visit Cuba and omit that little fact when you fill out your blue-and-white US customs form to reenter the United States, you are in fact committing perjury.

Soon, perhaps, there will be even less to worry about. At this writing, a number of bills have been introduced in Congress (cosponsored by Democratic and Republican lawmakers) calling for an end to the ban on travel to Cuba. It is only a matter of time. (In fact, every single US cruise line has quietly charted eight viable harbors in Cuba, preparing to divert their ships to the island the minute the ban is lifted.)

If you want to go legally, know that permission for travel from the United States to Cuba is rarely granted and is generally restricted to journalists, researchers, and specialty groups. US citizens or those within the United States wanting to travel to Cuba need a specific license to enter the country. Visit www.travel.state.gov for more information on how to apply for and acquire the license.

For the government's official sanctions policy at this time, go to www.ustreas.gov/offices/enforcement/ofac/programs/cuba/cuba.shtml. The Cuban Portal of Tourism's Web site, www.cubatravel.cu, lists tourist offices worldwide, resources of travel to the country from almost everywhere but the United States, hotel accommodations, and other vacation resources and information.

RJ's Tours, Ltd. offers all-inclusive travel packages to Cuba. A 2-week escorted vacation package in February 2007 from Canada started at $2,999 and included airfare, tourist card, hotel accommodations, and all meals and activities. 780-415-5633, www.rjstours.shawbiz.ca/cuba.htm

Cubalinda.com is a travel agency that offers international and domestic flights to Cuba with hotel accommodations, tours, and activities. Packages of 2 to 8 days are also offered, from $164 to $824, and include hotel accommodations and tours. www.cubalinda.com

Haiti
202-332-4090, www.haiti.org

Long considered the "failed state" of the Americas, Haiti today still suffers from massive socioeconomic problems. However, thanks to the return of relative stability in 2006 under President René Préval, Haiti has begun to attract a small but growing number of visitors.

And with its central location in the Caribbean, Haiti is at least in the right neighborhood to develop into a well-traveled destination. Royal Caribbean ships, for example, make regular stops in Labadie, near Haiti's second-largest city, Cap-Haïtien, bringing almost 40,000 visitors ashore each month. Of course, Royal Caribbean marketed Labadie as being in "Hispaniola" for a while, until Haitian officials complained.

For now, enclaves like Labadie, which are essentially entirely operated by foreign travel companies, are all that most visitors see of the country. After all, even the Tourism Minister urged visitors to avoid the squalid capital, Port-au-Prince, and seek out the quieter corners of the island.

One of the longest-running and most respected travel providers in Haiti is called **Agence Citadelle,** which is now associated with American Express Travel Services. Established in 1946, Agence Citadelle's goal is to bring travelers to Haiti and can provide customized tours as well as arrange travel programs for businesses. 509-223-5900, www.agencecitadelle.com

The citadelle, by the way, is a relatively well-kept old fortress located not too far from Labadie. If Haiti is ever able to develop into a tourism hot spot, La Citadelle should be one of its prime attractions.

Iraq

202-483-7500, www.iraqiembassy.org

Daily bombings, sectarian violence, rampant corruption, spotty services, frequent kidnappings, and rising anti-Western sentiment make Iraq one of the least hospitable countries in the world at the moment. But, apparently, it all depends on where you go.

There's at least one part of Iraq that comprises a notable exception to the don't-go-to-Iraq rule. The northern third of the country, popularly called Kurdistan, is comparatively peaceful. Bombings and violence are relatively rare in cities like Sulaymaniyah and Erbil, which are controlled by an autonomous Kurdish government. Erbil, in fact, receives regularly scheduled flights from a number of Middle Eastern and European cities.

And here's the fun part: Check out the Web site www.theotheriraq.com to see its tourism commercials, encouraging Americans to visit. In at least one commercial, the Iraqis claim that one of the reasons to visit the region is that there are "less than 200" coalition troops based there. Now, that's a reason.

Austrian Airlines became the first European airline to fly to Iraq, going to Erbil (or Arbil or even Urbil) in 2006. Erbil is one of Iraq's largest cities (it's the largest in Kurdistan) and provides safe access to Mosul and Sulaymaniyah. Austrian Airlines now operates four times weekly, using Airbus 319 aircraft. 800-843-0002, www.austrianair.com

Hinterland Travel operates tours in Kurdistan year-round. Generally, everything but flights to and from the country is included, such as insurance and visas. Their tours have been on hold now for some time as they cannot guarantee travel around Iraq and access to the sites; however, they are optimistic that they will resume tours in 2007. In the meantime, they operate their exploratory tour, a North Iraq Kurdistan and Kurdistan Iran tour beginning in Turkey. www.hinterlandtravel.com

The Kurdistan Development Corporation offers travel packages to press and business travelers. Additionally, they provide services on airline travel, security advice, visa requirements, and activities in the region. www.kurdistancorporation.com

Iran

202-965-4990, www.daftar.org/eng

Iranian-American relations have been notoriously difficult since the Iranian revolution in 1979. Despite this, a few Americans do travel to Iran each year, and most find the country to be surprisingly safe. That reputation for safety was dented in March 2007 by the disappearance of an American businessman from Kish Island, a popular spot off Iran's coast.

Still, most tourists, even American ones, report feeling fairly welcome in Iran. Unlike many other "tough travel" destinations, Iran has not suffered from internal fighting in recent years, and its travel infrastructure is consequently in better shape.

The country also boasts a number of impressive UNESCO sites, including the ancient city of Persepolis, the intricate Dome of Soltaniyah, and Naqsh-I Jahan Square, as well as various monuments and art dating back hundreds and thousands of years to the Persian Empire.

Once again, the State Department urges Americans "to carefully consider the risks of traveling to Iran." And since the United States doesn't have formal relations with Iran, there is no embassy or consulate in the country to help in case of trouble. Travelers should apply 2 to 3 months ahead to the Embassy of the Islamic Republic of Iran for visas. www.irantravelingcenter.com/visa_iran.htm

Jerry Dekker, a professor of humanities at the New College of California, San Francisco, offers unique study tours to Iran that are open to nonstudents. Dekker lived in Iran for 10 years and speaks Farsi; he has high-level contacts within the country and operates what are perhaps the most unusual and immersive tours in Iran. A 2-week tour called the Silk Tour of Iran visits the centers of Shiraz and Isfahan, as well as pilgrimage sites like the desert town of Yazd and the holy city of Qom. $2,500. 415-437-3460, www.newcollege.edu

Geographic Expeditions has been traveling to Iran since 1993 and continues to include Iran in its ongoing itineraries. A 22-day Treasures of Persia tour begins in Tehran and travels southwest to Hamadan and into the bazaar city of Tabriz. You'll fly across northern Iran to Mashhad, deep into the interior into the desert region of Yazd. Rates start at $5,425. 800-777-8183, www. geoex.com

Iran Doostan Tours is an Iran-based travel company that offers adventure and custom tours specializing in interests such as skiing, trekking, camel riding, desert safaris, hiking, and diving. Iran the Ancient tours go through Shiraz and into the Narenjestan Gardens, visit various tombs and mosques throughout the countryside, and offer city tours of Isfahan and Tehran. www.irandoostan.com

Liberia

202-723-0437, www.embassyofliberia.org

Not everyone realizes that Liberia is the only country in Africa that was once an American colony. In 1821, the first ship of free African Americans landed in Liberia. But two brutal, devastating civil wars (1989–1996 and 1999–2003) nearly obliterated whatever progress Liberia had made up to then. And as you can imagine, not a lot of tourists have been stopping in either.

Today, Liberia's president is a Harvard-educated, democratically elected, former director of African Development for the United Nations named Ellen Johnson-Sirleaf. Africa's first elected female head of state, she is beginning to make tangible progress in the efforts to rebuild Liberia, despite having been in office only since January 2006. Refugee camps in neighboring nations are beginning to empty as Liberians return home. Relatively clean running water has been restored to more than a third of Monrovia, and the first post–civil war electric streetlights in the capital were turned on in July 2006.

Liberia still has enormous problems, though, and its tourism infrastructure was essentially shattered. Outside Monrovia, there are pretty much no hotels or infrastructure approaching Western standards. In Monrovia, a few hotels like the Mamba Point Hotel and the Royal Hotel (with the city's only sushi restaurant, the Living Room) are suitable for Western tourists. Just don't expect luxury—and be thankful if the generators can give you electricity to power the air conditioner.

Because the tourism infrastructure is in such bad shape, most visitors to Liberia are volunteers assisting with the recovery efforts. A vast array of nongovernmental organizations and volunteer programs have been welcomed into the country by President Johnson-Sirleaf.

UN Volunteers has created several opportunities for volunteers to travel to Liberia, including inviting professionals to teach at the University of Liberia—bringing together more than 1,000 United Nations volunteers and locals for a cleanup campaign in the city of Zwedru and raising awareness of domestic violence. 49-228-815-2000, www.unv.org

Mercy Ships is an organization that recently docked its ship *Africa Mercy,* the world's largest charity hospital ship, in Monrovia. After serving more than 275 ports, the ship *Anastasis* was retired, and the ship's surgical and health-care projects are now being carried out by the *Africa Mercy,* with a crew of more than 400 medical and development volunteers. The ship is expected to perform more than 7,000 operations a year, including cataract removal, cleft lip and palate reconstruction, and orthopedics. 800-772-7547, www.mercyships.com

Visions in Action is a grassroots organization that has traveled to Liberia to run education and training programs as well as assist 2,000 farmers in 40 communities to develop rice production. It produces a weekly radio show designed to inform the public of the efforts of humanitarian and development organizations. 202-625-7402, www.visionsinaction.org

Libya

202-944-9601, www.libyanbureau-dc.org

In 2004, the United States lifted the travel ban to Libya. Nowadays, travel to Libya is less risky and complex than reputed to be. In fact, airlines such as British Airways, Royal Jordanian, Lufthansa, and others have increased flights to the perceived off-limits country. In 2006, there were a reported 125,480 foreign visitors to Libya, more than 1,500 of which were Americans.

Still, Libya is very much in the grip of its mercurial leader, Muammar al-Gaddafi, whose foreign policy seems to veer between rapprochement with the United States and old-fashioned wall building. For visitors, this can mean that Libya sometimes solicits American visitors and other times spurns them, denying visas to Americans. Cruise traffic, in particular, is on the rise, but at this writing, while foreign cruise ships are openly encouraged to dock in Tripoli and Benghazi, passengers with US passports are not allowed off the ships. Why? When the US government recently denied a visa application to visit America by Gaddafi's son, the colonel reciprocated by closing the door on American visitors to Libya. But this could easily be lifted soon.

Visitors are attracted to a number of well-preserved Roman ruins, especially Leptis Magna. Libya's largely undeveloped beaches are also a draw for both foreign and domestic tourists.

Abercrombie and Kent offers a 15-day luxury Desert Road tour that travels to Egypt and Libya. Tours go through the major destinations of Tripoli, Leptis Magna, and Sabratha and include a private dinner with a Libyan family, a visit to an arts and crafts school, and 3 nights in the Adrere Amellal Ecolodge located in the oasis of Siwa, where it seems that time is standing still. Your final night will include a dinner cruise on the Nile, featuring local cuisine and cultural performances. Rates start at $7,470. 888-554-7016, www.abercrombiekent.com

Arkno Tours is a Libyan tour company with various customizable tour options. Services include assistance with entry formalities, customs, and passports; transportation; and tours. A 14-day tour of the classical cities starts off in Tripoli and travels to Libya's Roman and Greek cities—including the site of Leptis Magna, the World Heritage Site of Ghadames, the ancient Roman ruins in Ras al-Ghoul, and the sand dunes of the Grand Erg Oriental. An 8-day diving and cultural tour meets in Tripoli and takes you to the beach village of Janzour and on to several other beaches along the coast for day and night diving and sightseeing. www.arkno.com

The **Libyan Travel & Tourism Company** assists travelers with airport, hotel, and transportation booking as well as tours and activities. Tours can take you through the city of Tripoli and along the Mediterranean coast, as well as through the western part of the country to Sabratha and Leptis Magna. www.libyatravels.com

Myanmar (Burma)

202-332-3344, www.mewashingtondc.com

Traveling to and from Myanmar is no easy task, and it may take some serious thought and planning to accomplish. But once again, you can get there. The Burmese government, an authoritarian military junta, usually requires that a traveler be part of a packaged tour group that has received prior permission to enter the country. The country has been the site of great political unrest for some time, and two areas suffered major bombing attacks in 2005. Americans are cautioned (by the US State Department, of course) to avoid crowded public places such as shopping malls, markets, and demonstrations. Many parts of Myanmar continue to be off-limits to travelers due to drug trafficking and military operations, and travelers should know that many tourism-related projects were accomplished with the use of forced labor. That said, tourism is now starting to be actively encouraged in Myanmar, and in the long term, this may help the isolate country to open its borders to outsiders more readily. (Until a few years ago, the government would grant only a 7-day visa. That has now been extended to 14 days.) Though you can expect, as Americans, to pay higher prices than other travelers, it may just be worth the experience. There are some spectacular sights to be found throughout the insular country, like the beaches of the Bay of Bengal, the golden Temples at Bagan, and the floating gardens of Inle Lake, among many other memorable locations. A popular (and recommended . . . by me) cruise is down the Irrawaddy River.

Geographic Expeditions offers four trips to Myanmar. An 18-day Burmese Land of Gold tour includes land excursions and a river cruise. The Lost Kingdom of Arakan is a 10-day journey that takes you over the Bay of Bengal and then up the Kaladan River to 15th-century Mrauk-U and to temples in the more northerly regions; end your trip on the sandy beaches of Sandoway. Trip rates range from $2,859 to $6,585. 800-777-8183, www.geoex.com

Northern Ireland
202-462-3939, www.irelandemb.org

Northern Ireland has long been the site of violent conflicts between Protestant and Catholic campaigns, which has scared off tourists for some time. Here's a world record the folks in Northern Ireland were embarrassed about—which has now become quite the tourist attraction: The Hotel Europa in Belfast still takes the prize as the most bombed hotel in the world! And yes, it's still operating—bomb free for many years now.

Sadly, between 1966 and 1999 in Northern Ireland, 3,636 people were killed and 36,000 wounded due to the conflict, and visions of IRA bombings and gun violence still linger. Over the years, tourism increased after the cease-fire of 1994 but was quickly followed by a drop in travel after IRA violence returned. A tentative peace has prompted tourism officials to tout Northern Ireland as a destination for travelers. Certainly, Belfast is a thriving city with cultural sites, museums, galleries, and pubs to attract visitors, and the Irish countryside is teeming with ancient castles and rolling golf courses and is a haven for outdoor enthusiasts. Traveling to Northern Ireland independently is as easy as booking a flight to Belfast—the city has two airports of its own, and Dublin airport is a 2-hour drive.

Bike Tours Direct has a 7-night self-guided hiking trip to the county of Antrim, inviting guests to explore the countryside on foot. The nine Glens of Antrim are a major draw, as is a visit to the unspoiled Rathlin Island, the largest island in Northern Ireland. Travelers walk along the Causeway Coast and take in the cliffs of Torr Head, lakes, and fishing villages. Prices start at $1,000. 877-462-2423, www.biketoursdirect.com

Brendan Tours has a 10-day Best of Ireland North trip that takes you from Dublin to Belfast, with visits to the Glens of Antrim and the city of Derry, with an excursion to Connemara, where you can visit a lakeside abbey and an Irish Benedictine community of nuns. Your trip continues to the Cliffs of Moher and onto Bunratty, before you depart for Shannon, with the option to spend a night in Dromoland Castle. Tours start at $1,600. 800-421-8446, www.brendanvacations.com

Tauck Tours has a 12-day itinerary of the Best of Ireland, which includes Northern Ireland. Your introduction starts at the Cliffs of Moher and continues to the famous Ashford Castle. You'll travel to Connemara, visit Kylemore Abbey, head to Derry, and enjoy a private tour of the Old Bushmills Distiller, where real Irish whiskey is made. A city tour of Belfast is your final stop in Northern Ireland before heading down to Dublin for the remainder of the trip. And yes, you can even stop by the Hotel Europa for a drink. Just pick a seat away from the window! 800-788-7885, www.tauck.com

North Korea

kp.embassyinformation.com/?einfo (find North Korean embassies around the world, excluding the United States)

They don't call North Korea the Hermit Kingdom for nothing. This tightly controlled Communist country has largely been closed off to the rest of the world, and anti-American propaganda abounds. But don't let the rhetoric scare you. The North Korean economy is in shambles, and pressures within the country are mounting to open the door slowly to travel and tourism. On five occasions so far, North Korea has extended an invitation to travelers with US visas to enter the country for a very limited period of time, through a very select group of tour operators that have already established relationships with country officials.

In 2007, North Korea opened its border to travelers in honor of its annual Arirang Festival (aka the Grand Mass Gymnastics and Artistic Performance, or the Mass Games) in Pyongyang. Although invitations were offered to Americans in 1995, 2002, and 2005, the invitations came so close to the allotted window that most travelers couldn't go. In 2006, organized tour groups did book tours to North Korea, but the Arirang Festival was cancelled due to flooding that killed more than 150 people.

The festival is a massive, weeks-long performance involving more than 100,000 men, women, and children performing highly choreographed dance, martial arts, and gymnastic routines that can't be compared with any other type of performance. The athletes and artists perform in a stadium that seats 150,000, executing a series of precise calisthenics, including a complex routine of children flipping giant colored cards that display propaganda images.

All of this may seem overly extravagant for an impoverished country that relies on international aid to feed its population—more than half of which is suffering from malnutrition. The children who have been chosen for the games train year-round and then perform twice a day for several weeks in a row, with no break. Despite reservations that travelers may have over supporting this kind of event, the intent of producing this festival and inviting foreigners is clear. It's about the money and about building tourism as a viable source of income for the secluded country.

It takes about 4 hours from Seoul to get into North Korea. Tourists first need to visit Beijing to obtain the necessary visa—a procedure that rarely takes more than a day.

Keep in mind that, like a lot of tough travel, it won't be a very relaxing or cheap trip. You can pretty much forget about shopping or exciting nightlife. And at about $500 a day, amenities like clean water, medicine, and even electricity are often in short supply. Visitors are expected to abide by all local customs and laws, which include bowing to the statue of Kim Il Sung in Pyongyang. Interaction with the locals will be limited, at best. This is one of the most tightly controlled societies in the world, so you won't be mingling freely with the masses—in fact, you'll get severe warnings before your trip about talking to locals. Just don't do it. In addition, all tour operators work very closely with the North Korean government, so each itinerary will be strictly adhered to. Every group will have two English-speaking tour guides, partly to watch you and partly to watch each other. Thus, a trip to North Korea is—quite literally—at the top of my list for . . . people *watching*!

Asia Pacific sponsored a 12-day trip in 2006 that was $4,199, including airfare. In 2007, it led tours to North Korea during two separate windows, between April 15 and May 15 and between August 15 and October 15, timed with the Arirang Festival. 800-262-6420, www.northkorea1on1.com

Poe Travel works with a Beijing-based tour company and arranged a very quick tour from April 28 to May 1, 2007, for the Arirang Festival. There are plans to return to North Korea upon invitation in 2008, as well as offer tours to other "tough travel" countries. 501-376-4171, www.poetravel.com

San Francisco's **Geographic Expeditions** arranges trips in conjunction with British tour company Koryo Tours, traveling to both North Korea and South Korea. The 10-day trip starts at $6,595. 415-922-0448, www.geoex.com, www.koryogroup.com

Sri Lanka

202-483-4025, www.slembassyusa.org

A former jewel of the British Empire, Sri Lanka seemed to have high prospects for stability and prosperity when it gained independence in 1948. At first, Sri Lanka (formerly Ceylon) did seem headed for a very bright future—it elected one of the world's first female heads of state, Sirimavo Bandaranaike, in 1960.

But by the 1970s, the Tamil minority, which makes up about one-fifth of the island's population, was growing increasingly restless at what it saw as discrimination by the Sinhalese majority. A rebel group, known as the Liberation Tigers of Tamil Eelam, or more commonly the Tamil Tigers, formed in the 1970s and in the 1980s carried out a violent campaign to secure a homeland for the Tamils in the northern and eastern parts of the island.

The Tamil Tigers were also one of the first groups to use suicide bombers, with the first attack in 1987. Later Tamil suicide bombers killed Indian Prime Minister Rajiv Gandhi as well as a number of Sri Lankan leaders. Indeed, more than one analyst has pointed out that many of Al Qaeda's terror techniques were taken directly from the Tamil Tigers.

A cease-fire largely held from 2002 to 2006 and the country saw a resurgence in visitors, but an increasingly intense civil war between Sri Lankan and

Tamil Tiger forces has sent numbers plummeting. In fact, arrivals have been dropping even faster lately as the Tamil Tigers have grown bolder—using ships and even planes to attack government positions.

So while a few parts of Sri Lanka are relatively stable, the violence does affect Colombo—the capital and main entry point for visitors—in addition to many of the island's provinces.

Having said that, organized tour groups report few troubles.

Distant Horizons offers a Sri Lanka: Island of Serendipity tour that visits the city of Kandy, a UNESCO World Heritage site, and features the intricate Temple of the Tooth—believed to hold the only surviving relic of Buddha. Bombings and suicide attacks have plagued the Temple, with one in 1998 resulting in heavy damage (since repaired), as well as many deaths. The trip also hits other interesting sites, such as the ruins of Polonnaruwa, another UNESCO site. This trip usually occurs in March and in the past has started at about $5,475. 800-333-1240, www.distant-horizons.com

Asia Transpacific also offers Sri Lankan itineraries. Its main Sri Lankan tour, however, is timed to coincide with the Kandy Esala Perahera festival. Though this medieval pageant lasts 10 days, much of the 16-day tour is spent elsewhere in Sri Lanka. Prices start around $5,000. 800-642-2742, www.southeastasia.com

Turkmenistan

202-588-1500, www.turkmenistanembassy.org

Kazakhstan may get all the press, thanks to the international success of Sacha Baron Cohen's character Borat. But Kazakhstan is a relatively normal country compared with its bizarre Central Asian neighbor Turkmenistan.

Turkmenistan has only recently begun to become less isolated, following the death of the man who called himself Father of the Turkmen, Saparmurat Niyazov. Previously, most Western analysts considered Turkmenistan to be the most isolated, and one of the most bizarre, dictatorships in the world, second only to North Korea.

So how bizarre was Niyazov's Turkmenistan? He established an incredible personality cult, going so far as to rename the months after members of his family and declaring one of his books to be the centerpiece of all school curricula, not to mention that all newscasts, school days, and public functions feature the book. He also built a giant golden statue atop the tallest building in the capital, Ashgabat, that constantly rotates to face the sun, and he erected a massive complex in his hometown to honor his mother.

Despite, or perhaps because of, Niyazov's massive repression, Turkmenistan is considered to be a very safe country (assuming you're not a dissident). However, the country's isolation took a toll on its infrastructure, which is poor outside the major cities.

Still, what better time to go than now, before a Starbucks invasion happens in Ashgabat . . .

Adventure Center offers something called the Samarkand & Tamerlane's Testament tour. This 14-day tour includes time in the modern Turkmen capital, Ashgabat. After a day of sightseeing and shopping, you'll cross the Turkmen Karakum Desert to a remote desert community and to the ancient ruins of Kunye Urgench. Visitors will also have the opportunity to stay in a yurt with Uzbek families in the Kyzylkhum Desert. The trip costs between $1,140 and $1,270, though a local fee of between $350 and $380 will also be assessed. 800-228-8747, www.adventurecenter.com

CHAPTER 35

Medical Tourism

❝ Fortunately, we Americans live in a nation where the medical-care system is second to none in the world, unless you count maybe 25 or 30 little scuzzball countries like Scotland that we could vaporize in seconds if we felt like it. ❞

—DAVE BARRY

Talk about outsourcing. It's estimated that in 2006 about half a million Americans traveled out of the country to get medical procedures at a fraction of what they'd cost at home. It's called medical tourism, and it's here to . . . go abroad.

Since most cosmetic treatments aren't covered by insurance, more and more people are heading to countries like Brazil, Argentina, Thailand, South Africa, and Costa Rica for procedures like tummy tucks and face-lifts, all costing far less than you would find in the United States.

As people are becoming more aware of medical tourism, travelers are getting even bolder: With more than 46 million uninsured Americans and 250 million with restricted coverage, going abroad for even more serious procedures is becoming a major trend. Travelers are heading to countries like India and Malaysia for more invasive procedures like heart surgery, hip replacements, and cataract surgery—for as much as one-fifth or even one-tenth of the price in the United States.

Even more recently, medical tourism is actually becoming an employee benefit at some US companies. One employer, Blue Ridge Paper Products of Canton, North Carolina, offered one of its technicians a cut of the insurance savings to travel to India for gallbladder and shoulder surgery. Patrick Marsek, general manager of MedRetreat, a Maryland-based medical tourism operator, projects that the company will soon be working with insurance companies, corporations, and institutions. A hip replacement, for example, can cost about $50,000 in the United States. But your insurance company can realize significant savings if they waive your deductible and co-payment, send you and your significant other to Thailand or India for treatment, and put you up in a four- or five-star hotel after a lengthy hospital stay—for a total of about $20,000.

At this point, your instincts are probably kicking in—is medical tourism safe? Not surprisingly, the American Medical Association will not comment on medical tourism. And while I can't recommend any one medical tourism operator over another—or, for that matter, any one in particular—this is a

Botox, Lipo, and Everything in Between

In the United States, cosmetic procedures are on an upward trend: According to the American Society for Aesthetic Plastic Surgery, there were nearly 11.5 million surgical and nonsurgical procedures performed here in 2005 (81 percent were nonsurgical, such as Botox injections and laser hair removal, and 19 percent were surgical procedures like liposuction and breast augmentation). Since 1997, there has been an increase of 444 percent in the total number of cosmetic procedures.

PROCEDURE	1997	2005
Botox	65,157	3,294,782
Breast augmentation	101,176	364,610
Chemical peel	481,227	56,172
Eyelid surgery	101,176	364,610
Laser skin resurfacing	154,153	475,690
Liposuction	176,863	455,489

Source: *American Society for Aesthetic Plasic Surgery, www.surgery.org/download/20059yearcomparison.pdf*

situation in which doing your research ahead of time is absolutely mandatory. It's definitely not a good idea to travel to South America and then schedule a cosmetic or medical procedure; all of this should be done well in advance through a reputable resource. A reputable medical tourism company should take care of many details that can be overwhelming or confusing—companies often have developed relationships with particular hospitals, provide a list of doctors to choose from, book your airline tickets, and work out the details of your accommodations.

While it's not necessarily a better option to choose a US-based company, an American operation may work with a larger number of hospitals in a wider variety of countries and may be easier to maintain contact with than a foreign company. When it comes to liability, however, it probably won't matter where the tour operator is based—the hospital is liable for any wrongdoing, so you may want to brush up on malpractice laws in your country of destination. Few countries are as litigious as the United States, so while you may have a difficult time pursuing legal matters if something goes wrong, remember that lower malpractice rates are partially the reason that medical costs abroad are so much cheaper.

It's important not to think of surgical vacations as quickie drive-through procedures followed by a relaxing vacation. In fact, be wary of packages that tout the tourism aspect over the medical procedure—you probably won't be in the mood to go golfing or take a dance lesson after you leave the hospital. One of the major concerns about medical tourism is recuperation: the follow-up care that is usually mandatory after a significant procedure. This can mean a lengthy stay in the country in order to recover, whether it's in the hospital or in a clean, safe hotel where you have access to emergency care. In some situations, follow-up care may not even come as part of your package. It's important to determine whether this is the case, as some program operators may expect you to deal with side effects and post-op care once you've returned home. And when you're taking such a long trip to get treatment, you'll have an equally long flight home that could pose risks to your recovery.

When doing your research on a medical tourism operator, keep in mind some of the following issues. There are some referral companies that simply negotiate a discounted rate with a hospital and send you there for treatment, with little or no postoperative care. Look for a company that has actually visited the facilities and uses some criteria to choose which hospitals to develop a relationship with. One good reference is if a hospital has been accredited by the Joint Commission International (JCI), which is affiliated with the Joint Commission on Accreditation of Healthcare Organizations. JCI has international standards with which hospitals and clinics must comply. Criteria include: The organization has a process for admitting patients; patients with emergency or immediate needs are given priority for assessment and treatment; and during all phases of care, there is a qualified individual identified as responsible for the patient's care.

Bangkok's Bumrungrad International and India's Apollo Hospitals in Chennai, Hyderabad, and Delhi are among the recent JCI-accredited institutions. You can find a complete list of JCI-accredited hospitals at www.jointcommissioninternational.org/10241. However, keep in mind that hospitals that don't get these credentials might be accredited by different organizations in their own countries.

Medical Tourism Agents

MedRetreat is a US-based medical tourism company that has been in business since 2003. The company sent surveyors to hospitals abroad to determine whether the facilities meet its standards, and it currently works with hospitals in eight different countries (Argentina, Brazil, Costa Rica, India, Malaysia, South Africa, Thailand, and Turkey). MedRetreat can put together packages for cosmetic, dental, and medical procedures. This includes almost any procedure you can think of: butt lifts, Botox, dental bridges, teeth whitening, mastectomy, cardiology, and fertility treatments. The company works with you for up to a month in advance to coordinate with your doctor, determining whether medical tourism is a good option for you, and arranges almost all the details of your trip. Prices include an airport pickup, accommodation at a four- or five-star hotel, transportation to and from your appointments and procedures, and an interpreter if necessary. 877-876-3373, www.medretreat.com

Surgical Attractions, based in South Africa, arranges cosmetic surgery and procedures at five hospitals around Cape Town and Johannesburg. Although the company promises that it works with first-rate surgeons in world-class facilities, this is one of those companies that tend to emphasize the vacation part of the trip (called a "rejuvenation holiday") as much as the surgery. You can choose from bush safaris and wine-tasting tours; you'll probably be fine to go sightseeing after a round of Botox, but if you're opting for a more-invasive procedure, it's wisest to get your travels done before the surgery.

Each procedure includes an estimated length of stay, including your preoperative consultation, actual procedure, and recuperation days: a breast augmentation is about 9 days, a full face and neck lift is 12 days, and a lip augmentation is about 5 days. As for accommodations, you can choose from an apartment, guest lodge, or hotel—from standard luxury to ultra luxury. www.surgicalattractions.com

Healthbase Online works with 15 hospitals in Thailand, Singapore, India, and Mexico that have been internationally accredited (JCI or the International Organization for Standardization). There are plans to expand its services to Argentina, Brazil, Costa Rica, Malaysia, and Panama. You can register online for a free quote for a variety of cosmetic, dental, and even surgical procedures in cardiac health, oncology, and orthopedics. The company can also arrange for a local translator or guide, although it promises that all physicians and nurses speak fluent English. 888-691-4584, www.healthbase.com

Cosmetic Vacations plans surgery and vacation packages to Brazil, "the plastic surgery capital of the world," and currently arranges an average of 20 surgeries a month for Americans. The company works with just a handful of surgeons who are members of the Brazilian Society of Plastic Surgery and have been accredited by the Brazilian Ministry of Health. Plastic surgery in Brazil is about 40 to 50 percent cheaper than it would be in the United States: A breast augmentation package runs about $5,000 and includes airfare, accommodations, and sightseeing excursions along with the surgery (in the United States, the procedure alone would cost anywhere from $3,000 to $10,000). 877-627-2556, www.cosmeticvacations.com

With medical tourism growing increasingly popular, some companies are taking advantage of the surgery/vacation combination with some offbeat marketing schemes. In Argentina, a company called **Plenitas.com** is offering a breast enlargement and tango package. Fortunately, the tango lessons come *before* your surgery. Plenitas can also arrange treatments like hair transplants, gastric bands, dental implants, and even assisted fertilization. 877-639-0703, www.plenitas.com

Dental Tourism

There are more than a few reasons for citizens of Los Algodones, Mexico, to smile. Start with the fact that this tiny town, located just 7 miles from Yuma, Arizona, went from a sleepy agricultural hamlet to a thriving medical tourism destination. The town, which boasts a population of only 15,000, now has more than 350 dentists and 50 pharmacies. On an average day, up to 33,000 Americans cross the border to get lower-cost dental care—and by lower-cost, I'm talking about savings of up to 75 percent! Now add in the fun, if ironic, fact that *los algodones* literally means "the cotton plants" and is circus slang for cotton candy.

Dentists in Los Algodones generally don't accept insurance or even credit cards; the cash-only business is part of how they keep their costs down. For example, one patient was quoted $1,800 for a root canal in the United States, whereas it cost only $250 in Los Algodones. Even a basic teeth cleaning can cost upward of $200 here; in Mexico, you may pay about $30. Pharmaceuticals such as penicillin can go as cheap as $2.50 a pop.

The warm, dry climate in this desert area has long attracted retirees and older travelers to spend the winters in Arizona border towns. These senior citizens figured out that inexpensive prescription drugs and lower-cost medical care were available right over the border, leading to an enormous burst of dental offices and pharmacies that cater to Americans and even Canadians. Dentists usually hail from the city of Mexicali, about 40 miles away, and spend the fall and winter setting up office in Los Algodones, where they can earn thousands in US dollars over a few months.

To reach Los Algodones, you don't even have to drive across the border. Just park your car on the Arizona side of the border at a secured border parking lot run by the Quechan Indian Nation. Then, it's just a 10-minute walk to cross the border (remember, as of January 2009, you'll need a passport in hand). Although many clinics have walk-in services, it's recommended that you book an appointment in advance; the town has a carnival-like atmosphere with promoters standing on the streets shilling root canals and crowns instead of cheap tequila shots.

While you're probably wondering how safe these dental offices are, rest assured—dental schools in Mexico have extremely high standards that rival those in the United States. (And on a trip I did there to report on the town for the *Today* show, I met dozens of dentists who went to medical or dental school . . . in the United States.) And yes, the town even has a Web site: www.dentistsofalgodones.com

Tips on Medical Tourism

! Educate yourself on what kind of postoperative care you'll be receiving. After an invasive procedure, you may not be able to travel for several days or weeks. Make sure your tour company doesn't leave you stuck without accommodations after you're discharged from the hospital and that you have access to medical care for the duration of your trip.

❗ Remember that sunbathing can be a big no-no after many procedures, which can put a damper on the "sun, sea, and surgery" marketing efforts.

❗ Find out if your hospital has been certified by either the Joint Commission International or the International Organization for Standardization.

❗ There is no international certification board for physicians, so your doctor's training and credentials may not meet North American standards.

❗ If something goes wrong after your procedure, pursuing legal action can be difficult, if not impossible.

Postoperative Hotels

If you're planning on staying local for your cosmetic procedures, there are even hotels that will extend postoperative care to you—or maybe even perform the surgery.

The recovery facility can be as advanced as a special nursing floor in a long-term care facility, as simple as a private room in someone's house, or somewhere in between, such as a set of rooms with nursing care in the hotel. The level of staffing can range from registered nurses (RNs) or medical assistants (MAs) to unlicensed attendants providing a spare room and making a business out of changing bandages and catering to your needs after surgery. Fees can vary between $300 and $800 or more per night and may include transportation, food, hydraulic beds, medical supplies (but not medications), telephone use, and cable TV. Usually, the higher the level of care, the more costly but safer your stay will be. It's the world of beauty and post-op at hotels such as the Four Seasons Hotel in Chicago, Beverly Hills' Le Méridien Hotel, the Woodmark in Washington State, Miami's Mandarin Hotel, and the Stanhope Park Hyatt in New York—just to name a few.

Serenity Aftercare Facility in Santa Monica, California, is the very first cosmetic surgery aftercare facility in the United States that is located in a hospital. Serenity has been noted to be the postoperative care facility of choice for plastic surgeons located throughout Los Angeles and Beverly Hills. Suites are located on the second floor for privacy and discretion. Serenity is directly across the street from Dr. Steven Teitelbaum's office and surgery center, which makes it very convenient for Dr. Teitelbaum to drop in and mark your progress. Patients may choose to recover here after plastic surgery—in luxury suites as you'd find in an upscale hotel. This means that patients not only will be settled into their rooms about 5 minutes after leaving the operating facility but will have peace of mind knowing that Dr. Teitelbaum and his staff are right across the street throughout their recovery. The doctor usually makes rounds at Serenity at least twice a day, which saves patients from a long car ride to make postoperative visits to their plastic surgeon.

The amount of time one stays at Serenity varies with the surgical procedure and personal preferences. But for all guests, comfort, safety, and security are "must" factors here. Guests are pampered with discreet Lincoln and Mercedes chauffeured transportation with garage entrance, personal chef, private suites with waterfalls, remote-control sound systems, cable TV and VCR with many movies to choose from, fully adjustable electric beds, and individual climate controls in the suite. Privacy and discretion away from the press and public is also very important, and patients can simply enjoy a mini-vacation following procedures. Serenity has registered nursing staff available, and the nurse-to-patient ratio is one RN to every three guests. A rooftop rose garden is also available, offering city views to the east and sunset and ocean views to the west. Optional healing therapies include seven different massage techniques, manicures, pedicures, acupuncture, and aromatherapy. 310-315-1121, www.drteitelbaum.com/serenity.html

> JetBlue gave away T-shirts that stated "It was never meant to fly" over a picture of a chicken to promote its no-meals, no-frills policy.

Where else would Maggie Lockridge, owner of Le Méridien Hotel's **Shanteque**, find a unique profession and could probably only succeed? Nowhere but Beverly Hills. The cosmetic-recovery retreat is all about comfort and relaxation for those in post-op. An aromatherapy candle is lit on your table, soft classical music plays on the room's private entertainment center, the temperature is set at just the right degree, the bed is turned down with a pillow set aside for under your knees, the lighting is dimmed, and fresh lemon water and juices await you. Your assigned suite attendant has your ice mask ready to apply if applicable, and your comfort is their first priority. Instructions are given as to how to call your attendant, and you are requested not to get out of bed without her at your side. The drapes are then drawn, your clothes hung in the closet, and a final inspection of your comfort is made.

Of course, with comfort comes a price. At Shanteque, a queen suite postoperative night runs about $775, which includes preoperative dinner and transportation to surgery. A king suite with a large garden patio costs $875; a pre-op queen suite alone is $550. Package rates are also available, and an additional surgical guest in rooms costs $595 compared with a nonsurgical guest at $100.

The price includes all meals, 24-hour suite attendants, and transportation to Shanteque after surgery and to all scheduled doctor appointments. Additional services include: automatically controlled beds, individual climate control, full cable television and in-house, first-run movies, private marble baths with deep-soaking tubs, laundry and dry cleaning, masseuse/masseur, manicurist, cosmetologist specializing in cosmetic camouflage, and your own individual personal shopper. 310-284-6546, www.shantequeweb.com

At the **Four Seasons Hotel** in Chicago, a surgery center is located directly inside the hotel, and nurses can wheel you directly to the California queen waiting in your suite (translation: no one has to see you, and then . . . it's room service for the next few weeks!). For those patients who are recovering from surgery, the hotel has specific arrangements with several doctors' offices in the downtown area. Result: Doctors make "hotel calls." The hotel can cater to the specific needs of the guests, which can include designated housekeeping times, room service with items recommended and approved by the doctor's office, and even nail technicians available on call. And yes, there are special rates for patients who are having surgery either at the surgery center located in the building or from nearby doctors. The rates start at $300 for a standard room or $400 for an executive suite. 312-280-8800, www.fourseasons.com

Lake Washington's **Woodmark Hotel** is located east of Seattle and minutes from doctors' offices. It became a post-op recovery center for those experiencing cosmetic surgery when patients began flocking to the quiet site on their own. Guests are greeted by hotel management at a private back entrance of the hotel and are escorted by wheelchair, if needed, to their guest room via the back-of-house elevator. A welcome recovery amenity is sent to guests upon arrival—including chicken broth, tea, crackers, and juice. Food and beverage requests are tailored to each guest's dietary needs. Aveda Spa services are offered to guests, depending on the type of surgery, and nursing services are arranged by request by a local nursing agency. 800-822-3700, www.thewoodmark.com

Luxe Hotel Sunset Boulevard in Bel-Air is a boutique hotel situated on 7 acres of gardens. The hotel remains a tranquil setting surrounded by the ritzy area. With facilities on Rodeo Drive and Bel-Air, the Luxe offers those in recovery a quiet place to recuperate with 24-hour room services. Special rates for those in recovery start at about $149. 866-589-3411, www.luxehotelsunsetblvd.com

The Residence by Marriott offers accommodations in Beverly Hills for patients recovering from cosmetic surgery—the 186-suite hotel offers separate living and sleeping areas and plenty of space for relaxing. Guests have a fully equipped kitchen, a complimentary hot breakfast, and an evening social hour. The hotel has one-bedroom suites for patients who require extra rooms for visiting nurses or overnight care. Complimentary transportation within 5 miles of the hotel to local doctors and spa services in Beverly Hills is also offered, as are private entrances and exits. 310-228-4100, www.marriott.com/residence-inn/travel.mi

The Martino Resort and Spa in Costa Rica is a 34-suite five-star hotel. It offers everything from face-lift packages to tummy tuck packages. Price includes up to 14 days' assisted recovery, anesthesiologist, transfers to and from the clinic, all meals, medical assistance before and during the postoperative period, and handling all postoperative details such as cleaning, bandaging, and removing stitches. 888-886-5042, www.hotelmartino.com

Index

Boldface page references indicate illustrations.
Underscored references indicate boxed text or tables.